I0214075

Heaven and Hell in the Philippines: Journal of a Peace Corps Volunteer

Daniel H. Wieczorek

Other Books by Daniel H. Wieczorek

"English - Ilokano and Ilokano - English Dictionary"; 100 Pages; March 2011; Paperback and Kindle Editions

"English - Ilokano and Ilokano - English Dictionary - With Some Notes on Ilokano Culture"; 150 Pages; May 2012; Paperback and Kindle Editions

"A Book of Anagrams - An Ancient Word Game"; 116 Pages; January 2012; Paperback and Kindle Editions

"A Book of Anagrams - An Ancient Word Game - Volume #2"; 152 Pages; February 2012; Paperback and Kindle Editions

"Forest Resource & Allowable Cut - Fairbanks Working Circle (Alaska)"; 122 Pages; March 2012; Paperback and Kindle Editions

Some Books by Daniel H. Wieczorek & Kazuya Numazawa

"Climbing a Few of Japan's 100 Famous Mountains - Volume 1: Mt. Daisetsu (Mt. Asahidake)"; 66 Pages; December 2013; Paperback, Hardcover and Kindle Editions

"Climbing a Few of Japan's 100 Famous Mountains - Volume 2: Mt. Chokai (Choukai)"; 72 Pages; December 2013; Paperback, Hardcover and Kindle Editions

"Climbing a Few of Japan's 100 Famous Mountains - Volume 3: Mt. Gassan"; 70 Pages; January 2014; Paperback, Hardcover and Kindle Editions

"Climbing a Few of Japan's 100 Famous Mountains - Volume 4: Mt. Hakkoda & Mt. Zao"; 88 Pages; January 2014; Paperback, Hardcover and Kindle Editions

"Climbing a Few of Japan's 100 Famous Mountains - Volume 5: Mt. Kumotori"; 84 Pages; February 2014; Paperback, Hardcover and Kindle Editions

"A Pocket-Size Version of Climbing a Few of Japan's 100 Famous Mountains - Volume 5: Mt. Kumotori"; 90 Pages; March 2014; Paperback Edition

"Climbing a Few of Japan's 100 Famous Mountains - Volume 6: Mt. Shirane (Kusatsu)"; 80 Pages; March 2014; Paperback, Hardcover and Kindle Editions

"Climbing a Few of Japan's 100 Famous Mountains - Volume 7: Mt. Shibutsu"; 80 Pages; April 2014; Paperback, Hardcover and Kindle Editions

"Climbing a Few of Japan's 100 Famous Mountains - Volume 8: Mt. Kiso-Komagatake"; 72 Pages; April 2014; Paperback, Hardcover and Kindle Editions

"Climbing a Few of Japan's 100 Famous Mountains - Volume 9: Mt. Kitadake"; 62 Pages; June 2014; Paperback, Hardcover and Kindle Editions

"Climbing a Few of Japan's 100 Famous Mountains - Volume 10: Mt. Mizugaki"; 70 Pages; June 2014; Paperback, Hardcover and Kindle Editions

"Climbing a Few of Japan's 100 Famous Mountains - Volume 11: Mt. Shiroumadake (includes Mt. Shakushidake & Mt. Yarigatake)"; 178 Pages; July 2014; Paperback, Hardcover and Kindle Editions

"Climbing a Few of Japan's 100 Famous Mountains - Volume 12: Mt. Tate (Tateyama)"; 176 Pages; August 2014; Paperback, Hardcover and Kindle Editions

"Climbing a Few of Japan's 100 Famous Mountains - Volume 13: Mt. Yatsugatake (Mt. Akadake)"; 208 Pages; October 2014; Paperback, Hardcover and Kindle Editions

"Outdoor Photography of Japan: Through the Seasons"; 362 Pages; June 2011

"Japan Outdoors"; 78 Pages; October 2015; Paperback, Hardcover and Kindle Editions

Heaven and Hell in the Philippines: Journal of a Peace Corps Volunteer

ISBN-10: 0-9963626-9-X
ISBN-13: 978-0-9963626-9-6

Dedication & Acknowledgements

This work is dedicated, first, to my mother and father. They always encouraged me to be adventurous and live life to the fullest possible extent.

Of course I must also thank the Peace Corps itself for selecting me to serve my country in the capacity of a Peace Corps Volunteer.

I could never have made it through the first year, the culture shock, the problems which you'll read about, living with three different host families in my first 6 months and so on without the help and understanding of people you'll read about here – Ronald; my host brother, Nestor; my good friend, George; my sleeping companion for 446 nights; JB and Katie F.; fellow PCV's who helped me out immensely and of course all of the people who maintained contact with me through an abundance of letters and CARE packages for my 27 months of service. Thank you all. Thank you so very much.

Table of Contents

Foreword

Always try to keep in mind that this book was originally handwritten as a Journal. That means that parts may be extremely boring and mundane to you, the reader, but that those things were significant in the specific day of life for the author. Furthermore, due to it being written as a Journal, some tenses within sentences and paragraphs may not agree. As this was being transcribed from handwritten notebooks to this manuscript the author made an attempt to fix most of those problems, but surely some of them have been missed. For that reason we ask your patience and understanding while reading. An example of this might be *"Get up at 6:00 AM today and ate breakfast"* instead of *"Got up at 6:00 AM today and ate breakfast."* Another important thing to note is that most thoughts are a single sentence and due to that, each day/date is generally entered as a single paragraph. This may make it difficult for you to read at the beginning, but hopefully, you can become accustomed to it.

The author was assigned, as a Peace Corps Volunteer (PCV), to live and work in an upland farming community as an agro-forestry specialist. His previous receipt of a Bachelor of Science degree in Forestry and 15 years experience in Forest Management made him well qualified for the position. As the only American living there, and the first American most of the younger people had ever seen, there were many stereotypical ideas about what an American "should" be like. The people expected the volunteer to be different, but the volunteer's **GOALS** were just to be a respected, active, productive member of the community. He had to be a full time student of culture as well as language to eventually be accepted into the community, as shall be seen. Just these two aspects of the job made it the challenge of a lifetime – let alone trying to accomplish anything in the field of agro-forestry.

The author was and is gay. The Peace Corps had materials available for gay people to pick up and read at the training center and the author DID pick up those materials and read them before ever going out into the "field". There are a few places where gay encounters are mentioned, but not many. Why didn't the author make more complete entries for his sexual adventures? The answer is simple – in the Philippines people often read over your shoulder when you are writing something, same when you receive a letter and are reading it. This same thing happens with every piece of written material that a Filipino finds. Therefore the author did not comment about many encounters due to the fact that if a Filipino found this Journal in the author's hut, he or she would not hesitate at all to pick up and start reading it. The author felt that his and his friends' sex lives were not something that he wanted just anybody to read about. While transcribing this material the author has made a few comments concerning sexual encounters, but only where they can be remembered. Now, 30 years after the fact, they surely will not harm the people involved.

Another thing to be aware of is that the formats change slightly over time as the author experimented and learned how to make economical use of space in his Journal and attempted to carry some of that formatting over to this printed manuscript. The author also made notes of his daily expenses, you may find that very interesting. Keep in mind, however, that at the time the author was living in the Philippines the exchange rate was approximately ₱20 = US$1 and now (March 2016) it is more like ₱47 = US$1, so prices are probably quite different now, as well as the subsistence allowance. Note that most item expenditures are rounded to the nearest peso.

There are some culture notes scattered about through the book at places where it seemed appropriate to enter them.

Note that when you see something entered in brackets [---] it is something which was added as the author transcribed this material from his original handwritten Journal. It did not appear in the original handwritten Journal. In some cases this was done to clarify a point and in some cases it was done as something about an experience was remembered while transcribing the handwritten Journal.

In most cases Ilokano words are *italicized*, but surely there are a few places where the beta-readers and author missed one.

Keep in mind that research has shown that "culture shock" is something which can continue for nearly two years. There are many places where it may be evident to you that the author's reaction to something was probably due to culture shock.

When you get to the first page of the body of this Journal you will see how the author starts a new day. The following image is an example of how to interpret the information given at the beginning of each day.

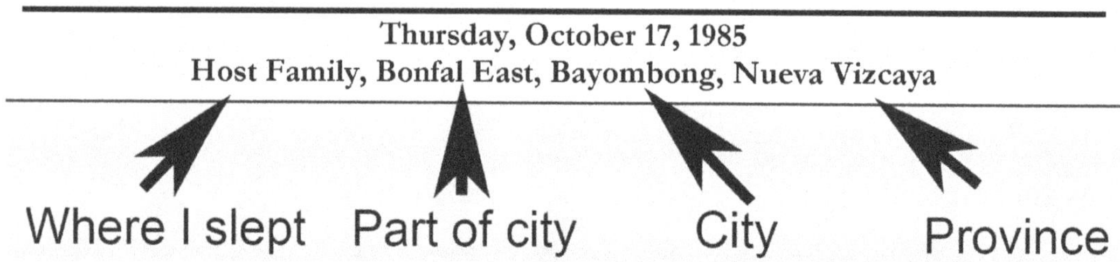

"Where I slept" indicates the home or other lodging where the author slept during the night of that day. "Part of city" indicates a named subdivision or section of the city. "City" of course is the major city. "Province" indicates the province where this city (or other lodging place) is located.

By the way, the Peace Corps gives volunteers what is considered a subsistence allowance when they are in country. In the author's case this amounted to about $100 per month during his two years in the Philippines. He later discovered that this was nearly equivalent to what the District Forester of his local Bureau of Forest Development Office was making, so the volunteer was in a pretty good place as far as money was concerned.

Peace Corps – The toughest job you'll ever love. This is the slogan of the U.S. Peace Corps and the author found it to be VERY true.

Peace Corps:

The Toughest Job You'll Ever Love.

Chapter 1
Fairbanks, Alaska to Durham, Oregon
August 23 – 27, 1985

Friday, August 23, 1985
Tent in Gravel Pit, Yukon Territory, Canada

Leave the house for the last time at 11:30 AM. Lunch and last minute things with Dave and then we say goodbye. Stop at Tok, Alaska for a bowl of soup and mail postcards to Dave, Dad, Chris and Mary. Animals seen today – one moose. First tank of gas = 271 miles per 21.5 gallons equals 12.6 MPG. Started trip at 131,000 miles on rig. First day 131,338 miles = 338 miles. Stop for night at gravel pit in Yukon Territory. Made it through customs, no problem.

$2,623.00 – $130.40 = $2,492.60							
Postage	71.40	Gasoline	36.50	Lunch	12.00	Coffee	1.50
Postcards	1.85	Supper	5.50	Toilet Paper	1.65	TOTAL	$130.40

* Forgot to tell Chris to forward HP stuff and that Dave has a shed key.

What a truly incredible day – moving out of my house and all, saying goodbye to my closest friend in the world. I'm too emotional of a being. I get way to upset by that kind of stuff, especially when leaving for two years!

* Tell Dave thanks for the little white pad.

I'm on the first day of an incredible new adventure. I can now begin to come down off the adrenaline rush of the last week. That adrenaline is a very potent drug that has some weird effects – if that's even what I've been running on, or does your brain produce something else under such stressful times?

Saturday, August 24, 1985
Tent in Gravel Pit, 15 Miles Southeast of Watson Lake, Y.T., Canada

$2,492.60 – 250.00 – 9.85 = $2,232.75							
USD $250 > $317.50 CAD $317.50 – 273.22 = $44.28 (Canadian)							
Breakfast	8.00	Coke	1.85			USD =	$9.85
Stamps	3.00	Bug Dope	6.50	Jacket	100.00	Toiletries	32.37
Beer	10.60	Gasoline	109.75	Supper	11.00	CAD =	$273.22

Up at 7:00 AM and hit the road. Stop for breakfast. Stop at Whitehorse, Y.T. for about 1.5 hours for buying of gas, beer, 222's, jacket and etc. Back on the road with a 12 pack of real Canadian Molson beer! Saw a bear this morning. Rain showers for the entire 600 miles traveled today. Stop at Watson Lake for supper and mail postcards to Dave, Tony and Dave #2. Got 11.43 MPG on one tank of gas today and 12.79 MPG on another tank, hmmm?!

Tonight the odometer reads 131,907 = 569 miles covered today.

Stop for the night at a gravel pit 15 miles SE of Watson Lake.

My watch is now 1 hour slow from local time.

Stopped and made it a point to pee in the Yukon River today and again at the Yukon/McKenzie Great Divide.

Remind Dave he's traveling with me.

Saw Northern Lights tonight.

Sunday, August 25, 1985
Tent – Somewhere in British Columbia, Canada

$2,232.75 – $100.00 = $2,132.75							
USD $100 > $130.00 CAD $44.28 + 130.00 – 120.60 = $53.68 (Canadian)							
Change	100.00					USD	$100.00
Coke	2.00	Lunch	4.60	Gasoline	107.00	Food	7.00
						CAD =	$120.60

Get up at 6:40 A.M and hit the road. First stop was Liard Hot Springs Park and about 1 hour messing around there. Had a nice soak and even a bus load of tourists took the quarter mile walk to the hot springs, but luckily they just watched. The water was quite hot. On the road again about 10:00 AM and then not stop for lunch until 2:00 PM or so – just a bowl of good soup. Then cross the summit of the Rocky Mountains – where it had snowed about six inches last night. The road was plowed but still lots of snow beside the road. Saw three Woodland Caribou or some kind of deer today – they were pretty strange looking animals to my eyes. Played with my altimeter today. This is the day I wanted and planned to stop before dark, but somehow it didn't happen. For 50 miles I looked for a place to stop. All roads advised me "Poison Gas Area – No Stopping, No Camping!" Finally I pulled off the road at a litter barrel and called it good enough for the night and here I am. I cooked Mountain House spaghetti and corn tonight and I'm drinking a beer.

Tonight the odometer says 132,425 miles which means I drove 518 miles today. One tank of gas at 210 miles on 17.5 gallons equals 12 MPG.

Got a photo of Folded Mountain – 2,060 meters.

$100 US dollars equals $130 Canadian today.

Postcard written to Dave today but not mailed.

Today feels like it's been an extremely long day!

Monday, August 26, 1985
Tent – Somewhere South of Quesnel, British Columbia, Canada

$2,132.75 – $32.00 = $2,100.75							
USD $100 > $130.00 CAD $53.68 – 53.68 = $0.00 (Canadian)							
Gasoline	25.00	Food	7.00			USD	$32.00
Coffee	2.00	Food	6.50	Gasoline	45.18	CAD =	$53.68

Stopped in enough daylight tonight to <u>nearly</u> get my supper fixed without a headlamp. I traveled 480 miles today for 132,905 miles on the odometer. So 1,903 miles into the trip. I've stopped at a litter barrel very close to a litter barrel which I've stopped at once before. I've probably still got a good strong 600 miles to go tomorrow, but I'm traveling off my map and don't know precisely where I am. Nothing really impressively amazing happened today other than that I hit Prince George and civilization. Somehow I only went 480 miles; just because that's the way it happened I guess. Stopped in Prince George to wash the rig, but that's really the only stop of the day. Used two tanks of gas; 233 miles with 21.5 gallons equals 10.84 MPG and 213 miles with 17.5 gallons equals 12.17 MPG.

Postcards to Chad and Dad and I'm going to write a letter to Dave upon completion of this. Boy I **<u>REALLY DID</u>** hit civilization today! Cars go by this spot so often it's hard to even get in a toke while sitting here in the cab with the light on – incredible! I really had to study how to park tonight so as to be visible from the least amount of highway as is possible.

Well, wrap it up here and start on letter to Dave.

Tuesday, August 27, 1985
Tony & Janet's House – Durham, Oregon

$2,100.75 – 38.75 = $2,062.00							
Coke/Beer	10.95	Gasoline	19.50	Supper	8.30	TOTAL	$38.75

Total trip cost was $561.

A very long day! Started today with the odometer at 132,905 miles and arrived at Tony and Janet's house at 133,478 miles for 573 miles today. Arrived at 9:45 PM local time, so total trip was 2,478 miles and took 103 total hours from the time I left Fairbanks. So, I averaged 24.06 miles per hour for the entire trip. No problems with snow goose [my pickup truck]. I had to add one quart of oil and replace the right front headlight. Dave, my brother, I call out to you and say "I made it." It was really a trip arriving in Durham. The freeway tried to freak me out and lose me and even tried to wreck me, probably, but I endured and made it through to the end. Today I used two tanks of gas – 204 miles on 17.5 gallons equals 11.66 MPG and 211 miles on 17.5 gallons equals 12.06 MPG. Guess I probably averaged 12 MPG for this trip.

Chapter 2
Durham, Oregon to Berkeley, California
August 28 – September 1, 1985

Wednesday, August 28, 1985 – My 38th Birthday
Tony & Janet's House – Durham, Oregon

A quiet day of getting my rig ready to take to the restoration shop (getting tarp off, stuff from under the seats, etc., etc.), unpacking things from all my boxes and trying to consolidate into a more compact package to take with me for the two year duration. Tony came home from work early and he helped me pack a while. We went over to Jim's place, whom I haven't seen in years.

Thursday, August 29, 1985
Tony & Janet's House – Durham, Oregon

$2,062.00 – 711.20 = $1,350.80							
Batteries	24.00	Binoculars	80.00	Camera	145.00	Tape Player	100.00
SW Radio	142.00	Film	124.20	Shoes	20.00	Shirts	28.00
Supper	33.00	Book	15.00			TOTAL =	$711.20

Today Tony and Janet both stayed home from work and they took me out to buy all the last minute things I needed (see Tony's addendum below). We took my rig to Truman Bell's shop today for restoration and I said my goodbye to my 14 year old rig for two years. I hope I still recognize it when I get back. Spent $711.20 today, which is detailed above, plus Truman wants $2,500 down payment on the rig restoration, so it was an awfully expensive day. Somehow, my accounts reconcile. My money dwindled significantly today! Hopefully I'll arrive in Manila with some semblance of $1,200 left. It's sure good to see Tony and Janet again. It's pretty amazing how things can remain so much the same over the course of years.

Tony's Addendum: My entry in Daniel's Journal here at our place in Durham on his way to the Peace Corps. It's been a day of running around – delivered Dan's rig to Truman Bell east of Gresham, running around downtown Portland buying last minute things for Dan, $715 spent at one store for camera, radio, tape player, binoculars and etc. Had a great dinner at Lee's Kitchen and topped off the evening with talk at home.

Friday, August 30, 1985
Tony & Janet's House – Durham, Oregon

WOW! Well, let's see – today my Indiana Jones hat and cabin pictures came from Mary. The hat is too big but I called San Francisco and they will exchange it for me upon arrival there. About 2:00 PM Steve & Deb arrived. It was pretty amazing seeing Steve again – and Deb, and their kid, Anna. Then Bob D. called and he'll get here at around midday tomorrow. Then later in the evening Tim C. even came over! Haven't seen Tim C. in years and years – not since Ann Arbor. It was practically too freaky. With all of these people around some strange memories of events, happenings, emotions and so on pop up in my mind. It's for sure, strange.

Good Night!

Saturday, August 31, 1985
Tony & Janet's House – Durham, Oregon

$1,350.80 – 88.68 = $1,262.12							
At REI	50.33	Pizza	16.35	Food	20.00	Radio Shack	2.00
						TOTAL =	$88.68

San and Jack arrived shortly after we went to bed last night and slept in the driveway in their camper shell. So, they were here for breakfast! Steve, Deb, San and I went to REI in Steve's rig and Tony & Janet met us there and we had a good time. I bought quite a bunch of stuff. Tim and Peg showed up soon after our return from REI. Bob D. came along in mid-afternoon. Around 6:00 PM Tim C. and Kathryn came over. That means for supper we had 14 folks – Kevin, Anna, Tony & Janet, Steve & Deb, San & Jack, Bob D., Tim C. & Kathryn, Tim & Peg and me!

Sunday, September 1, 1985
Tony & Janet's House – Durham, Oregon

Today I got up pretty early and Steve and I took a pretty good walk. By the time everybody had gotten ready to leave in the early afternoon it had been one hell of a weekend with 14 people in the house. Ardis even called last night and we talked for around ½ hour or so. Steve & Deb sewed the "pile" and zipper I bought at REI yesterday into a "sleeping bag" and really did a fine job on it. Tonight Tony and I got everything into my duffle bag and backpack and I'm ready to be off tomorrow. Tonight I want to write a short & sweet letter to Dave so that he'll know what's going on. It sure does my soul good to think of him and his dog Abe and my house.

Chapter 3
Berkeley, California to Manila, Philippines
September 2 – 6, 1985

Monday, September 2, 1985
Some Hotel – Berkeley, California

$1,262.12 – 80.00 = $1,182.12							
Lunch	3.00	Misc.*	7.00	Postage	40.00	Supper	18.00
Airport Limo	12.00					TOTAL =	$80.00

* Hereinafter you should think of Misc. as miscellaneous items purchased which could not specifically be recalled at the end of the day when I did my Journal. I generally made notes in a small pocket notebook of items purchased, but I did not always remember to do so.

Mailed letter to Dave and postcard to Dad.

This morning Tony & Janet took me to the airport and saw me off. What an experience the last week has been, hanging around and talking with my old friends. I arrived in San Francisco at 11:00 AM and started making new friends before we were hardly even in the Hotel Limousine. At 1:00 PM our first orientation/training session started and we went pretty strong until 9:30 PM. Then I called Mark W. and he was pretty freaked out to hear from me. We plan to go out and do something after training finishes tomorrow. Met lots of new people and did lots of new things today – too many people to even begin to try and keep names straight yet. These are the people that I am going to the Philippines with for the next two years though, so even though we will be scattered around all over the country I should try and learn all of the names. They are going to be my "family" I guess.

Tuesday, September 3, 1985
Some Hotel – Berkeley, California

$1,182.12 + 80 (pay) – 33.08 = $1,229.04							
Meals	21.70	Globe	6.38	Beer	5.00	TOTAL	$33.08

Today was a pretty intense day! What DID we do today? Practically too much to even begin to talk about. Went out and had a gyro for lunch and had excellent Thai food for supper at a nice Thai Restaurant just down the street from the hotel. They showed us a couple of films today and we had several types of indoctrination and training programs. We learned about the various reasons we might end up with the "Pan-Am Award" [basically this means you are sent home – kicked out of the Peace Corps – for some reason after entering your host country]. We also learned about malaria and the pills we have to take to prevent getting it and a lot of other "Health & Wellness" type of stuff. Went to Mark W's. house this evening.

Wednesday, September 4, 1985
Some Hotel – Berkeley, California

$1,229.04 – 57.60 = $1,171.44							
Meals	45.60	Coffee	3.00	Beer/Tip	9.00	TOTAL	$57.60

WOW! Today we got immunization shots, eyes checked and so on. Exchange my hat at TSI and then back to orientation classes at 2:00 PM. We had the "last night in the USA" dinner and party – just a few of us who have kind of become friends. It was kind of an expensive day.

Thursday, September 5, 1985
Some Hotel – Berkeley, California

Called Mark W. and I wrote a short letter to Dave G.

Today we got our passports. We all said "Goodbye!!" to the USA as we left the ground, and we were on our way to Manila, Philippines. At this point we've been air-borne for about 6.5 hours. We departed at about 12:00 N. This is the 3rd leg of this adventure for me. I left home two weeks ago tomorrow, driving from Fairbanks to Durham – that was the first leg. Then there was the week in Durham with Tony & Janet and all of my friends who came to see me off on this grand adventure. Then the 2nd leg was going from Durham to Berkeley and the three or four days in Berkeley. Now I am on the 3rd leg of this new adventure in my life. Well, time for an airplane snack – I'll see if I feel like writing more later on. These three days of comprehensive training have been really intense!

Later.

There are 85 of us for Regions 1, 2, 3 and 4 of the Philippines. We've all asked each other our names at least 85 times each too. For that same unexplainable reason as always – which I will never know or understand – I seem to have my gift of a smile, friendliness, warmth, whatever – and I am already getting to be fairly well known by most folks. I'm not afraid to stand up and make a fool of myself in front of a group by asking what may seem to be a dumb question – people appreciate that because they had the same question, but lacked the courage to ask it. So, I'm just being my same old Dan'l as I always am and I'm having fun with this entirely new series of adventures.

Friday, September 6, 1985
Missed Day – Due to Crossing International Dateline

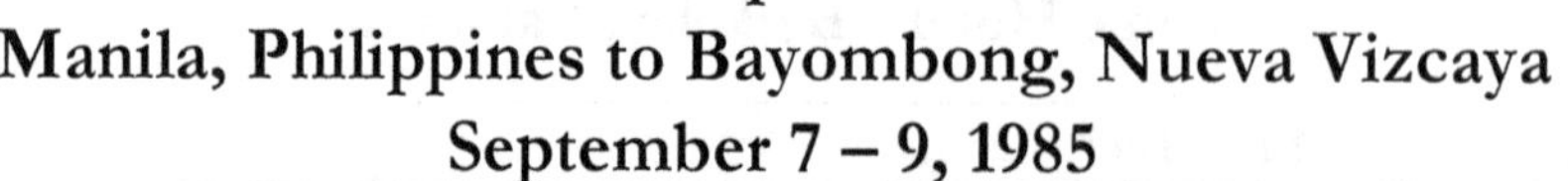

Chapter 4
Manila, Philippines to Bayombong, Nueva Vizcaya
September 7 – 9, 1985

Saturday, September 7, 1985
DATELINE MANILA, PHILIPPINES

$1,171.44 – 36.00 = $1,135.44 (Final Accounting of US Dollars)							
Meals	7.20	Bus Tip	3.00	Gifts	10.00	Headphones	3.00
Beer	9.00	Snacks	3.80			TOTAL	$36.00

₱955 – 50 = ₱905 (Begin Accounting in Philippine Pesos)							
Beer	50					TOTAL	₱50

It's 16 hours earlier in Alaska.

We are here! We were going for 26 hours from San Francisco to Manila – I don't even know the actual number of flight hours, I think about 13.5 hours is what it ended up at when we arrived in Manila and got our lai's [flowers around our necks]. Then we were off to the Manila Midtown Hotel, where we got checked in pretty quickly. Then a few of us that wanted to, went down to drink a couple beers – our first San Miguel's in country. We had already been going for 26+ hours and we still had the inertia to go get a beer! When we got to the room we found our Peace Corps Volunteer Medical Kit, a health handbook and a bunch of papers. They also paid us ₱905 so the final U.S. dollars can now be accounted for.

Additional entry for Saturday, September 7 [I can't remember why].

Slept in late and woke up at 9:00 AM. Then at 11:00 AM we had a meeting and then at about 12:00 N we were off to the welcome luncheon with the U.S. Ambassador and the Ministers of the various Ministries. At about 2:00 PM they let us go off on our own and some of us went down Mabini Street and finally to Rizal Park. After a few hours walking around the park we hired a jeepney to bring us back to this end of town – the Manila Midtown Hotel. Then after a break we went out to a supper we could barely eat because it was so much food and then we returned to the hotel. After a short swim here at the hotel we went (Mike S. and I) across the street for a couple of beers. Money is locked in the hotel lockbox, so no expense accounting tonight, I'm falling asleep anyway so, goodnight.

Sunday, September 8, 1985
Midtown Hotel, Manila, Philippines

We had a couple of meetings today, a good breakfast at Bumblebee Fast Foods and an excellent lunch there too. This afternoon they separated us into our Region

Groups and it seems that most of "the gang" that I hang out with is going to Regions 3 and 4. Unpacked my duffle bag again and it's beginning to seem that I brought lots of useless things. Went over to Smokey's hot dog stand for a cheap supper that ended up being more expensive than anything else all day – at ₱49.50! Jet lag is still being felt. I hope it's gone tomorrow. I'm going to try for a long sleep tonight. We started taking Fansidar malaria pills today.

Monday, September 9, 1985
Midtown Hotel, Manila, Philippines

Financial accounting – 9/7 – through today

₱905 – 643 = ₱262 + 552.30 = ₱814.30 ($30 converted to ₱552.30)							
Postcards	15	Coke	20	Rides	5	Meals	165.50
Postage	80	Tapes	80	Misc.	50	Lock	24
Lens Paper	35	Listerine	25	Unknown	138.50	Beer	5
						TOTAL	₱643

Ouch! Too much money already spent!

Letter & postcard to Dave; postcards to Chad, Dad, Chris & Mary.

What happened today? Well, I got my money out of the hotel lockbox and did a financial accounting through the present. I had some kind of placement interview with Clarita at 9:45 AM and then at 10:00 AM we got rabies shots and a TINE test for TB. Tomorrow we have to be ready to go at 5:30 AM and then we have a seven hour bus ride to Bayombong, Nueva Vizcaya via Tarlac Bus Company. I think I'm going to go to bed now, good night. Oh – it feels like I'm getting adjusted to the time difference now, but not to the heat. I'll be so happy to leave Manila.

Chapter 5
Bayombong, Nueva Vizcaya to Burgos, Cabarroguis, Quirino
September 10 – November 24, 1985

Tuesday, September 10, 1985
Host Family, Bonfal East, Bayombong, Nueva Vizcaya

₱814.30 – 109.40 = ₱704.90							
Meals	76.20	Coke	16.70	Beer	6.50	Fruit	10
						TOTAL	₱109.40

Today we were up at 4:15 AM and then on a bus at 5:30 AM and we traveled to Bayombong, Nueva Vizcaya. They gave us lunch and more talk and then they took us to meet our host families. My whole family seems like very nice people and they seem to think I'm nice too. It seems that they had not finished making my room yet, so I watched and helped a little. Then we ate supper – rice, chicken and beans. My host brother did not come home tonight – the family said that he is afraid to meet a foreigner and that he'll come back in a couple of days. Interesting.

Wednesday, September 11, 1985
Host Family, Bonfal East, Bayombong, Nueva Vizcaya

₱704.90 – 45 = ₱659.90							
Rides	8	Sandals	15	Beer	22	TOTAL	₱45

Well today was our first agro-forestry session, given by Clarita. It was disappointing actually; I don't feel that we learned much. Then we had our first language lesson with Kathy – it was not too bad actually. Today they also gave us the first clues about the areas we may be sent to and how we may be selected for the sites. Tomorrow at 5:00 PM I have my interview about the type of site I prefer. I'm really looking forward to getting used to this heat.

Thursday, September 12, 1985
Host Family, Bonfal East, Bayombong, Nueva Vizcaya

₱659.90 – 8 = ₱651.90							
Beer	5	Coke	3			TOTAL	₱8

Today was less than a 50 US cents in expenses day! Amazing!

Today we had four hours of technical training and four hours of intensive language training followed by my placement interview. I think I'll probably end up in a pretty remote place, probably most anywhere. Don told me we'll know where by the

24th, only 12 days away. My body is not used to the heat yet, although I am beginning to feel a little bit better about both the heat and the new culture, but God it's HOT.

Friday, September 13, 1985
Host Family, Bonfal East, Bayombong, Nueva Vizcaya

₱651.90 – 28 = ₱623.90							
Beer	5	Toiletry	20	Ride	3	TOTAL	₱28

Yikes, today was Friday the 13th. Nothing bad happened though. I feel like I lived 1.5 days today. We went on a field trip to the Santa Fe District Forestry Office in the rain, then we returned for four hours of language instruction and then home. In the evening there was a welcoming party. All in all it was an incredible day. At the welcoming party I joined in a Tinikling Dance – a kind of folk dance with bamboo sticks. I was the first male to volunteer, but after I broke the ice (I volunteered as quick as I could get my shoes off once they asked for volunteers) a few more males also volunteered. I guess we've been here a week now and it's been a truly incredible week.

Saturday, September 14, 1985
Host Family, Bonfal East, Bayombong, Nueva Vizcaya

₱623.90 – 17 = ₱606.90							
Beer	13	Ride	4			TOTAL	₱17

Today we had school for half a day and then we were on our own. It rained very hard for a while in the afternoon, but then cleared up and got nice again. Mother took me to the farm, where Ronald was spraying some leafy vegetable for some kind of rot. I saw and learned how people climb the coconut trees and knock down the coconuts. Then I watched how they break open the husk and make a carrying handle on it. Chester met us in the field and mother told him that I climbed the coconut tree and knocked down the coconuts, but actually a small boy did it. I saw and studied a nipa hut and also saw where a large spring comes from the ground. Also saw a very big tamarind tree. I saw and learned about the tamarind, papaya, mango, coconut and other trees today. I learned that both the banana and the papaya will have fruit in one year after planting. Had a difficult day in language. My teacher at NVSIT [Nueva Vizcaya State Institute of Technology] was very upset because I had not learned the new vocabulary words for today. Tonight Ronald, my host brother, helped me study (with much patience) and that really helped out. I was able to teach him some English vocabulary too.

Sunday, September 15, 1985
Host Family, Bonfal East, Bayombong, Nueva Vizcaya

₱606.90 – 10 = ₱596.90					
Beer	10			TOTAL	₱10

This morning we bought, or bargained for, a six month supply of rice. We had to sack it at the house next door then take it to the schoolyard and spread it out to dry. Then, however, it threatened to rain and we had to hurry and get all the rice sacked up again, but then no rain came. In the afternoon David and Mark stopped by and we walked to the river and then stopped at the corner store for a single bottle of beer, but some stranger bought us two more bottles each. Finally we got away and went back to our homes. After dark we went fishing with electricity! I guess I got in the way because father took me to an aunt's house, but Ronald and Herbert continued fishing.

Monday, September 16, 1985
Host Family, Bonfal East, Bayombong, Nueva Vizcaya

₱596.90 – 5 = ₱591.90					
Beer	4	Ride	1	TOTAL	₱5

Today we had four hours of language study and four hours of cultural indoctrination. We received rabies and typhoid shots. Rebecca helped me with translation today and Ronald and Herbert went fishing with electricity. It was hot today.

Tuesday, September 17, 1985
Host Family, Bonfal East, Bayombong, Nueva Vizcaya

₱591.90 – 0 = ₱591.90

Letter to Dad, postcards to Ardis B., Dave G., Jim W., Chris & Mary and Tony & Janet. I have not yet received any mail.

Not a lot happened today. We got out of classes early but did not have the opportunity to do much of anything with the extra time except drink a couple of beers! We had a briefing on our upcoming host volunteer visit and also the upcoming language test and another informational session about health and that's about all for today. OH – no language study at home tonight so the family and I just sat around and had a good time with each other rather than spending most of the evening doing the usual language study. Ronald and I are becoming good friends, it's good.

Wednesday, September 18, 1985
Host Volunteer Home, Villa Miemban, Cordon, Isabela

₱591.90 – 100 = ₱491.90

Rides	18	Coke	3	Lunch	42.50	Slippers	14
Juice	5	Misc.	17.50			TOTAL	₱100

Today we were off on our Host Volunteer Visit [sent out to an actual Peace Corps Volunteer's site to see what life is truly like as a volunteer]. Her name is Teresa L., in Cordon, Isabela – only about an hour from Bayombong, but it was difficult to get there. A bus went by the bus stop at 7:20 AM. but my Host Volunteer Visit [HVV] companions, Katie and JB, had not arrived yet, so we had to end up taking jeepneys to Solano and then to Santiago. We arrived 1.5 hours late but luckily Theresa was very patient and was still waiting at Letty's Canteen for us. We did some shopping in Santiago then off we went to our Barrio – Villa Miemban. The walk in from the place where the road ends was four or five kilometers. We were accompanied by some really fine people, one of them, Nestor is a person whom I already consider a friend [he was so very handsome]. Teresa's hut is really fine – I hope I can have an equally nice hut in the place where I end up. Katie and JB – husband and wife – will be replacing Teresa here in Villa Miemban when she ends her two years of service in November.

Thursday, September 19, 1985
Host Volunteer Home, Villa Miemban, Cordon, Isabela

Kololanti = firefly; *Lumabas ak laeng* = I am only passing.

WOW! What a day! Slept in until 6:00 AM and then off we went to look at some of the local "farms" and other things around Villa Miemban. Met the Barangay Captain and gave him my old flip-flops and then walked around all day in my new flip-flops and basically had very few problems with it, although I did fill a couple of toes with thorns. We returned to Teresa's house around noon and took a break for lunch and then *madam dama* (=after a while) we went out again and headed up the hill. Less than half way up, it started raining HARD on us, so we again came back to Teresa's house. By the time we got back we had all fallen down in the mud and were filthy so we showered by standing under the roof overhang. We did it naked and the neighbors got a good kick out of that. At the same time, we washed our muddy clothes. About suppertime Celia, Teresa's co-worker from the Division of Forestry, came and we made supper. I talked Teresa into letting me "wok" some vegetables for supper and she made mung bean soup. We had a fine meal and all present were satisfied. Later in the evening Nestor and Rufino – two Igorots – came over and after a game of Scrabble we all had a good time talking. For a while Nestor, Rufino Celia and Teresa talked 100% Ilokano and everything went over JB, Katie and my heads. Then I got Nestor alone and we had a half hour or so to talk and then they left. Everybody went to bed but I'm still up for a little while writing in my journal. I'm thinking of starting a letter to Dave G., but just looked at my watch and noted that it's 10:00 PM, so I guess I also should sleep. No money spent today.

Friday, September 20, 1985
Host Volunteer Home, Villa Miemban, Cordon, Isabela

Although this is being written on Saturday, what I want to say about Friday is that it was a very interesting day. *Agang angaw-ak* means "I am joking", but I'm NOT joking – it WAS a very interesting day. We prepared a row for planting ipil-ipil trees – we were Celia, Teresa, JB and I and my friends Nestor and Rufino. In the afternoon we went up on the hill and looked down on all of Villa Miemban – then finally we came down and ate supper. After supper was the best part of the day. My friends (*gayyem-ko*) Nestor and Rufino, the Barangay Captain and many other people came over. Katie and Teresa dressed in the Igorot skirts and JB and I, with the help of the Captain, dressed in a g-string and participated in: 1. an Igorot Dance, 2. Bontoc War Dance and 3. A Kankaney Dance. At that point we were pretty pooped out from being in the g-strings and we went to guitar music and singing. By the time all of this activity was done Nestor and I had exchanged addresses and I promised to write to him and also told him *"agsubli-ak"* (= I will return). Everybody left at midnight and we crashed then.

Saturday, September 21, 1985
Celia's House, Sinamar Norte, San Mateo, Isabela

We got up at 5:00 AM and started walking to the jeepney place at 6:00 AM. It was a long walk to the jeepney in the mud. Finally we got to Santiago and then from there we went to Teresa's already planned baptismal dinner in Oscariz, Ramon, Isabela. We ate lots of good food including *ASO*, or dog meat. Then we went to Magat Dam, the largest dam in Southeast Asia and then back to the dinner and then finally, back to Celia's house for a good evening of congeniality.

Sunday, September 22, 1985
Host Family, Bonfal East, Bayombong, Nueva Vizcaya

₱491.90 – 203 = ₱288.90							
Rides	90	Drinks	24	Lunches	48	Flip-Flops	14
Cheese	22	Toilet Paper	5			TOTAL	₱203

It was a long day. From Celia's house to Santiago to Letty's hut, to the hills and lots of sweating and HOT! Then return to Santiago, eat lunch at the Bureau of Forest Development Office and then to the Pantranco Bus Terminal for the ride back to Bayombong. I was the last one in Bonfal East to return (the last Americano) and my mother and father were very concerned.

To summarize the Host Volunteer Visit [HVV] – it was a very fine experience, something I would be very happy to do again. I made some permanent friends, not only in the Barrio, but also I believe Teresa L. to be a fine person. This experience was as good as any experience I had when I visited the Philippines as a traveler back in 1984. I finally got home at 8:00 PM and the family was preparing for Market Day.

Monday, September 23, 1985
Host Family, Bonfal East, Bayombong, Nueva Vizcaya

₱288.90 – 19 + 30 = ₱299.90							
Haircut	5	Beer	12	Ride	2	TOTAL	₱19

Today I had four hours of language study, two hours of HVV debriefing and then we had a 1 hour talk by Ed Slevin [Peace Corps Director for the Philippines at the time]. I met Ronald, my brother (*kabsat-ko*) at the bridge and he took me to the barber for a haircut. Mike S. and his host family came over in the evening and we sorted and bundled vegetables and drank beer all evening. It was a good evening, but I didn't get any studying done, that's for sure. Tomorrow we have to be at NVSIT [Nueva Vizcaya State Institute of Technology] at 7:00 AM for site placement. My stomach is not quite right these days, not sick, but not quite right either.

Tuesday, September 24, 1985
Host Family, Bonfal East, Bayombong, Nueva Vizcaya

Letter to Chris & Mary.

₱299.90 – 55 + 400 = ₱644.90							
Aerogrammes	48	Ride	2	Beer	5	TOTAL	₱55

Today we got our sites assigned to us. Mine is Burgos, Cabarroguis, Quirino. At first I was disappointed, but the more I read and hear about it, the happier I become. We had the site placement party from 4:00 to 7:30 PM. I went home fairly drunk I guess, it was fun anyway and that's what counts in life. These days life is quite fun for me. Janice, one of the older ladies, called it quits yesterday and went home. I guess she has really had some weird things come down around here. Wonder if there will be anybody else who calls it quits?

Wednesday, September 25, 1985
Host Family, Bonfal East, Bayombong, Nueva Vizcaya

₱644.90 – 30 = ₱614.90							
Stamps	5	Notebook	14	Ride	1	Beer	10
						TOTAL	₱30

We had four hours of language study in the morning and then a 1 hour BS meeting in the afternoon. Then come home and work on transferring language to new notebook until nearly dark. Then Ronald and I took the *"gasolino nuang"* (rototiller

= gasoline water buffalo), via the road, to the field and picked up mother and the pechoy and radishes. The sunset was very intensely beautiful as we went to the field and with my brother Ronald it ended up being the high point of the day. The language is really getting me down, that and the total lack of any mail yet

---

Thursday, September 26, 1985
Host Family, Bonfal East, Bayombong, Nueva Vizcaya

Letter to Nestor & Teresa L. in Villa Miemban.

₱614.90 – 21 = ₱593.90					
Beer	15	Rides	6		TOTAL ₱21

We had four hours of technical training and three hours of language study. Went out for a couple beers at the Greenfield Inn. That's all there is to say for today.

Friday, September 27, 1985
Host Family, Bonfal East, Bayombong, Nueva Vizcaya

Aerogramme to Dave M.

₱593.90 – 32 = ₱561.90					
Beer	22	Photos	10		TOTAL ₱32

We had seven hours of language study today – too intense!! There was a small party in the evening and my host brother Ronald joined me for a couple beers and then he and I came home.

Saturday, September 28, 1985
Host Family, Bonfal East, Bayombong, Nueva Vizcaya

₱561.90 – 12 = ₱549.90					
Beer	10	Rides	2		TOTAL ₱12

Today we had a field trip to District Forester Sarapi's tree nursery and learned how to plant citrus and narra trees. I talked with my language instructor, Abe, and had a good discussion about how the language study is going. I am really enjoying talking to the language instructors and other Filipinos and beginning to feel like I'm the wrong color. This afternoon I brought home orange and cacao trees to plant on the farm. In the late afternoon we went to the Barangay Captain's home and ate *pulutan aso* (*pulutan* = drinking snack and *aso* = dog meat) and drank beer. Then we had a hard time escaping. Tonight Coronado and his wife stayed here so Ronald & I had to share a bed. It was a pretty good day.

Sunday, September 29, 1985
Host Family, Bonfal East, Bayombong, Nueva Vizcaya

₱549.90 – 135 = ₱414.90							
Beer	60	Rides	75			TOTAL	₱135

Today Tom & Barbara, David F., Mike S and I took our families to Salinas Salt Spring in a jeepney. The families prepared a picnic lunch and the Salt Spring was incredible. Then we went to a picnic spot and ate the picnic lunch. Upon returning to Bonfal East, the family let me help with planting the rice and I planted about half of a row (5 plants wide). Hope that I didn't mess it up to badly. I'll take a look in a few days and see what it looks like. In the late afternoon I was tired, but still managed to do a bit of studying. My brother Ronald and I are becoming best friends, it will be hard to leave here in November.

Monday, September 30, 1985
Host Family, Bonfal East, Bayombong, Nueva Vizcaya

Aerogrammes to Tom L & Tim in New Zealand.
Letter from Dave G.

₱414.90 – 8 = ₱406.90							
Ride	1	Beer	4	Coke	3	TOTAL	₱8

Today I went to NVSIT visit and they changed my language instructor on me. Surprise! Even after the long discussion I had with Abe on Saturday. I have the teacher that nobody else will put up with. Hmmm?! Why me? Plus, I'm all by myself with her. I'm confused. Today I got my first letter and of course it was from David G. my *"napintas nga gayyem"* (best friend) in America it's really a beautifully written letter and I'm very happy. We had gamma globulin and rabies shots this afternoon. Meet Ronald at the guardhouse and we come home together. Study a lot in the evening.

Tuesday, October 1, 1985
Host Family, Bonfal East, Bayombong, Nueva Vizcaya

₱406.90 – 112 = ₱294.90							
Coffee	40	Toothpaste	30	Soap	11	Toothbrush	25
Beer	6					TOTAL	₱112

It was a very bad day in language class. It was a good thing it was only two hours long today! I practically ended up hollering at Fe, the new teacher. I guess I'm not in trouble but I had to tell Abe and also the language coordinator, Myra. It was a very bad experience. Ronald and I went to school together. I like to be with him, it's always a good time when we're together. Our small group had to do a schistosomiasis skit today and our group won first prize, a box of cookies – I got one of them. I played the part of the victim. We had a four hour field trip to NVSIT College of Forestry and planted some ipil-ipil seeds. Had a relaxing evening at home. Everything is okay.

Wednesday, October 2, 1985
Host Family, Bonfal East, Bayombong, Nueva Vizcaya

Postcard from Ardis B. – 2nd piece of mail!

₱294.90 – 15 = ₱279.90							
Beer	9	Ride	6			TOTAL	₱15

Today I had four hours of language training with Fe again, my 3rd day with her and it's really apparent, at least in my mind, that my learning curve has dropped to "NOTHING". I took the case of beer bottles from James Garden (Sunday) back today to get my deposit returned – that's ₱40! They told me to come back Sunday so I will – maybe. This afternoon I studied at NVSIT until 5:00 PM and then met Ronald and my old language instructor, Abe, and we went out for a beer. Got home a bit after 6:00 PM. It was a pretty nothing day other than being frustrated with my language teacher, Fe.

Thursday, October 3, 1985
Host Family, Bonfal East, Bayombong, Nueva Vizcaya

₱279.90 – 43 = ₱236.90							
Beer	4	Ride	2	Rice Cake	37	TOTAL	₱43

(Rice Cake was for mother)

I had four hours of language study with Fe again – BAD NEWS, MAN! After that we had the first part of a SALT Practicum [Sloping Agricultural Land Technology]. We made A-Frames and laid out contour lines for each crew x three crews. It was an okay session. In the evening I spent a couple of hours working on a letter to Dave G – my best friend in the USA. It was not a very exciting day in the life of Dan'l I guess.

Friday, October 4, 1985
Host Family, Bonfal East, Bayombong, Nueva Vizcaya

Mail letter to Dave G.

₱236.90 + 20 = ₱256.90

We went up on Bangan Hill today and worked on the SALT project some more. I got Abe back for my language instructor – *naimbag* (= good). I am feeling better again. Mother, Ronald and I worked on making the rice cake for the Barrio Fiesta tomorrow.

My Host Family. From left to right: Mother, Grandmother, Father, Robelyn (youngest sister), Rebecca (oldest sister) & her baby, Herbert (Rebecca's husband), me and Ronald.

Saturday, October 5, 1985
Host Family, Bonfal East, Bayombong, Nueva Vizcaya

₱256.90 – 15 = ₱241.90					
Beer	11	Boat	4		TOTAL ₱15

Well, today we went up on Bangan Hill again and helped the forestry students build the Kiosky. At noon was the Barrio Fiesta at NVSIT – all of the students and families gathered together again for an ample supply of food and drink! Mother and Ronald were my guests. It broke up at 4:00 PM or so and then we returned to the house, took a siesta and then it was suppertime. I'm always feeling like I'm doing something wrong, but I talked with Ronald about this and he says no – I'm not doing anything wrong. I don't know. We had a brownout in the evening.

Sunday, October 6, 1985
Host Family, Bonfal East, Bayombong, Nueva Vizcaya

WOW! We did a day and a half today. I slept in until 6:00 AM. Father, Ronald Herbert and I went over across the river to the farm, where father has some cows. We rounded up the cattle and then after that we went fishing with electricity. We stopped for lunch at some relative of my family and it was *"naimas"* (= delicious). In the afternoon we did more fishing and we were walking in a narrow stream with water up to our chests – like they do in the jungle adventure movies. Later on we eventually made it back to the family rest hut and Ronald climbed a coconut tree and knocked down five coconuts and we ate three of them. Then we returned home and ate supper and crashed. Ronald and I shared a bed again due to there being visitors.

Monday, October 7, 1985
Host Family, Bonfal East, Bayombong, Nueva Vizcaya

₱241.90 – 60 = ₱181.90					
Robelyn	20	Beer	40		TOTAL ₱60

Had language study all day! Started a letter to Dave M. at state forestry. After school several of us went for a couple beers and then returned to James Garden for trying to get back my bottle deposit again – they say return tomorrow. Herbert and Rebecca were there at James Garden and we had a couple more beers with them. *Bassit laeng nabartek-tayo* (= we were a little drunk). Nita is still here so Ronald and I sleep together again. *Sige – awan to problema* (= it's okay – no problem.)

Tuesday, October 8, 1985
Host Family, Bonfal East, Bayombong, Nueva Vizcaya

Letter from Nestor in Villa Miemban. Mailed film (12 rolls) for developing, letter to Dave M.

₱181.90 – 40 = ₱141.90							
Postage	18	Toiletries	22			TOTAL	₱40

Today we had four hours of language study, two hours of tech and 1 hour of First Aid training. It was a long hot day. I studied for several hours this evening.

Wednesday, October 9, 1985
Host Family, Bonfal East, Bayombong, Nueva Vizcaya

₱141.90 – 20 = ₱121.90							
Beer	15	Rides	5			TOTAL	₱20

Today we had language study for four hours, and then at 11:00 AM I had my language assessment. I guess it went pretty well, but I am weak on my linkers and markers. In the afternoon we had another tech session, four hours on Bangan Hill again working with the *buneng* (= machete). After class Abe and I went to the corner Sari-Sari store and had two beers each while working on my speech for my site visit. I got home at about 6:00 PM and Ronald has pinkeye! Nita, our visitor for the last two days had it when she arrived, so she probably gave it to all of us, great! I hope that I don't get it, but unfortunately chances are real good that I will. I'll try to get some medicine tomorrow.

Thursday, October 10, 1985
Host Family, Bonfal East, Bayombong, Nueva Vizcaya

₱121.90 – 21 = ₱100.90							
Beer	13	Rides	5	Coke	3	TOTAL	₱21

Today was such a drag. We had a culture session in the morning, which was pretty much a waste of time. In the afternoon we met our supervisors and talked about mutual expectations. After classes finished we took our supervisors home with us for supper. I discovered that he does not drink beer – at all! He's also a vegetarian – Hmmm! Oh well – *kasta laeng ti biag* (= such is life). We'll see what happens later on when I am working with him. The Peace Corps said that they'd send a van to Bonfal East at 8:30 PM to take our supervisors to the hotel, but they did not, so we all walked them to the highway and got a jeepney for them to take to the hotel. Such is life – again!

Friday, October 11, 1985
Host Family, Bonfal East, Bayombong, Nueva Vizcaya

₱100.90 + 40 – 40 = ₱100.90							
Beer	22	Toilet Paper	6	unknown	12	TOTAL	₱40

Today was some kind of supervisors conference and in the evening a supper at the Sabre Inn. Enough said.

Saturday, October 12, 1985
Francisco's House, Santiago, Isabela

₱100.90 + 1,300 – 43.50 = ₱1,357.40 (₱1,300 from PC for expenses over next few days)							
Dictionary	22.75	Rides	3	Tools	8.25	Beer	4.50
Misc.	5					TOTAL	₱43.50

Slept with Ronald last night, as it was my last night with the family. After a painful goodbye with the family this morning I went to the Sabre Inn to meet my supervisor, Francisco, for the trip to Santiago. It was pretty uneventful. We got to his house in Santiago and after spending some time there we went back into Santiago to get some stuff from market and learn where the offices are. We went to a movie – it was in Tagalog – lots of killing! After the movie we then returned to Francisco's house for supper and the night. All in all it was a good experience.

Sunday, October 13, 1985
Francisco's House, Santiago, Isabela

₱1,357.40 – 133.65 = ₱1,223.75							
Toothpaste	7.65	Beer	22	Fruit	30	Restaurant	34
Movie	18	Ice Cream	10	Rides	12	TOTAL	₱133.65

Today was quite a day in the life of Dan'l! Slept in until 6:00 AM, got up and ate breakfast, did toilet stuff and showered and then Francisco went to the field and I went and found Nestor from Villa Miemban, who is going to university here in Santiago. It was amazing that I actually found him. He was so very surprised to see me. It was quite an experience, as I didn't even expect to be able to find him, so it was even more amazing. He familiarized me with the public market in the morning and we had two beers together. Then he returned to Francisco's house for lunch with me. It turned out Francisco and Nestor knew each other from a training session that Teresa arranged last April! Then after lunch and socializing for a while Nestor and I went back into Santiago and went to another movie. We saw "I Have Three Hands", which was a Tagalog comedy and quite a bit better than the bloody movie we saw yesterday, "Junior Buang" – an action picture depicting a battle shocked soldier and the consequences to all involved. After the movie Nestor and I really realized how close we have become in such a very short time. It still blows me away how close people can become in such a short time when they both work at it. We went back to market and had Halo-Halo together and then we went to the park for our last few moments together before I had to catch the jeepney to return to Francisco's house. Nestor and I arranged it so that I will be able to stay at his boarding house when I come to Santiago. He sure is a nice person. We are *kabsat ken gayyem* (= brothers and friends).

Monday, October 14, 1985
Bunkhouse, Diffuncian, Burgos, Cabarroguis, Quirino

₱1,223.75 – 76.75 = ₱1,147							
Food	27	Rice	27	Beer	6.75	Rides	10
Misc.	6					TOTAL	₱76.75

Today, what a day! We went from Francisco's house to Santiago at 7:00 AM and then from Santiago to Diffun and the District Forester's Office. At the District Office I met several people who work for Francisco – all of them are nice people, of course. We waited for Jose Romero, the District Forester, to return in the afternoon. In the meantime, I met the mayor of Diffun. The mayor was a pretty cool guy. Then we went to lunch and finally after lunch the District Forester came into the office. They do "Management by Objectives" here and they really mean that. The whole office plays Scrabble, or reads books, or plays cards, or sleeps, or draws when they get tired of working. It's the most laid back office I've ever seen, that's for sure. At about 2:30 PM we made it out of the office and headed for Diffuncian, Burgos, Cabarroguis, Quirino. The pavement stops at Cabarroguis, the Provincial Capital. The District Forester wanted us to stop and meet the governor, but we did not do so. Francisco, like me, is kind of shy and, also like me, he does not enjoy talking to the higher up people. We got to Diffuncian at about 4:30 PM and met the caretakers of the project – they are nice people – David, Rose and their two children. Their home is very nice. The bunkhouse of the ISF is where I sleep. *Natalna ditoy* (= it's peaceful here.)

Tuesday, October 15, 1985
Bunkhouse, Diffuncian, Burgos, Cabarroguis, Quirino

₱1,147 – 26 = ₱1,121							
Beer	26					TOTAL	₱26

Today we waited for Rod, who is supposed to be my project companion, until noon then we went off – David and I – on our own, to meet several people in the project. They all seem like nice people, but very reserved and quiet. They were pleased to see and meet an American. I found out that David is Iglesia ni Cristo [Church of Christ], which throws a deep fear into me. YIKES! Anyway, after we got back from walking around Rod was finally there at the bunkhouse and I was very happy to see him. David is a really nice person, but I have some doubts about him as a competent worker. It was really good that Rod arrived so that there was another person there tonight. That broke things up nicely, as after I let David know – without a chance for any doubt left in his mind – that I did not want to become Iglesia ni Cristo he started acting a bit weird towards me.

Wednesday, October 16, 1985
Nestor's Boarding House, Santiago, Isabela

₱1,121 – 115 = ₱1,006							
Lunch	46	Asucena	60	Rides	9	TOTAL	₱115

Today Rod, David and I went to the Barangay Captain's House. He was not there again. We then proceeded to the mayor's office of the Municipio of Cabarroguis and spent a while there. His name is Mr. Herminiano S. Barcela and he was a nice guy, but we all ran out of small talk after a while. Then we went to the provincial capital but the governor was not there, so we talked to the provincial secretary until lunch-time and then ate lunch at the Capitol Cantina. Then we went to the Provincial Hospital at Cabarroguis. They have 11 doctors and I met two of them. After that we went to the Diffun Office and I left a note for District Forester Romero. Rod and I then went to his house in Sinsayon and then after a while we went to Nestor's boarding house in Calao West. I left my pack at Nestor's and then Rod and I went to a movie – "Bed Sins". After the movie we returned to Nestor's and went to an *Asucena* (= dog meat restaurant) for Aso (dog meat) and beer. Now I'm at Nestor's and Pastor Artemio Villacruz just wrote a beautiful blank verse poem of my name (see below). After a while Nestor and I went out for a walk and a talk and then back to his place and went to bed.

Your name, a poem – Daniel Hugh Wieczorek
D – Daniel, a name derived from God
A – An adventurous spirit – to serve mankind
N – Never unswerving in duty to love
I – Inspired of peace, the strong faith pursue
E – Ever to land to a distant land
L – Lovely in nature, near to the Creator.

H – Heavenly place you abandon for service
U – Under your commitment you serve
G – God gives life, you master to do good
H – High heaven's truly blessed you.

W – Winsome life, you give to others
I – Inspired for Humanity
E – Engrave our faith in your heart
C – Concern with our development
Z – Zeal with all your life to let us live

O – Onward you go with the Filipinos
R – Remember, we love you Daniel.
E – Exalting your desire to work with us
K – Kin in blood, brother through humanity.

Thursday, October 17, 1985
Host Family, Bonfal East, Bayombong, Nueva Vizcaya

₱1,006 – 392 = ₱614							
Bank	200	Meals	51	Rides	13	T-Shirts	90
Fruit	25	Misc.	13			TOTAL	₱392

Got up at 5:30 AM and then after breakfast we went out to Francisco's house [my supervisor]. I told him about the problem with David & Rose being Iglesia ni Cristo and that Rod and I get along better than David and I. I told him that I will try to get the day off on the 25th and attend the meeting for awarding of stewardship certificates at Gomez. I also told him that it appears that I will want to change my site from Diffuncian to Gomez – or somewhere! I told him that I left a note for District Forester Jose Romero. All in all I was quite frank and truthful with him and it seems like *"Awan ti problema"* (= no problem.) Nestor accompanied me to Francisco's house and then Nestor and I went back to his house, where I finished filling out Peace Corps forms. Then at 8:45 AM we went to the bank and I opened an account. By and by we went to the Public Market and I bought some T-shirts and some Lanzones to give my host family in Bayombong as a *pasalubong* (= present for giving upon return from travelling.) We went to lunch and after lunch, back to his boarding house for my pack. Then we went to the Vizcaya Liner bus place for a bus to Bayombong. I arrived home at 3:00 PM and was/am very happy to be back home, in a place where I can be straightforward, where they have come to know me and my ways and my limited knowledge of Ilokano language, my shortcomings, and I'm just accepted for whatever I am, whatever that is. The family says they missed me as much as I missed them and I believe them. Darn, I'm happy to arrive home. *Naragsak-ak ti isasangpet-ko dita balay* (= I am happy to arrive at this house.)

Friday, October 18, 1985
Host Family, Bonfal East, Bayombong, Nueva Vizcaya

Letter to Steve A.

₱614 – 286 = ₱328 (₱244 return to Peace Corps (see October 12))							
To PC	244	Present	20	Beer	21	Ride	1
						TOTAL	₱286

A typhoon is coming in today. There are #2 typhoon warnings! It rained all day, but we had classes as usual. I had four hours of language training and two hours of technical training. It was Robelyn's birthday. I really love my family. We have a really fine thing going between us. I am really happy here. The typhoon is really raining up a storm. Now we're going to a wedding dance at the Captain's house. My first dance and it was fun. The typhoon is coming in and because of it we had a brownout. Return home at 10:30 PM or so and the typhoon is really blowing now so I have to sleep in Ronald's room because the winds are coming from the direction of my room and the family is worried that they may blow my window in. Coconut leaves are falling tonight and those leaves ARE BIG! *Napigsa agtud-tudo* (= it's raining hard.)

Saturday, October 19, 1985
Host Family, Bonfal East, Bayombong, Nueva Vizcaya

Letter to Dad and Chris M.

₱328 – 22 = ₱306							
Movie	15	Ride	2	Dance	5	TOTAL	₱22

Today the typhoon raged until mid-afternoon. Last night the wind was so strong the house was shaking and Ronald and I slept in his room. I said that last night didn't I?! Today the river was over its bank's and the road is flowing! Water is flowing through the house maybe 4-6 inches deep on the floor. In the afternoon when it slowed down, Ronald and I took a walk to the river and the vegetable farm. Many banana trees are wiped out and many rice fields are wiped out. Bummer! It was my first typhoon and I'm surprised – they are pretty incredible, or at least this one was. Ronald said this was the second-worst one he has ever seen here. In late afternoon mother Ronald and I went to Solano for firewood and then Ronald and I went to a movie. We didn't return home until 7:30 PM. The whole family slept upstairs tonight, Ronald and I in my room, Rebecca in Ronald's and mother and father on the floor.

Sunday, October 20, 1985
Host Family, Bonfal East, Bayombong, Nueva Vizcaya

Letter to Ardis B.

₱306 – 23 = ₱283							
Beer	23					TOTAL	₱23

Today what did we do? Well, we *caras-caras* (= bail out) the house this morning and then bailed some more. We checked the rice field (*taltalon*), studied for a while and wrote a letter to Ardis. Then Ronald, mother and I went to the *bankag* (= vegetable farm) and picked – or rescued – the tomatoes that were mostly destroyed in yesterday's typhoon. It was a pretty dull day today, all and all, but at least I got to do some work bailing the house out and picking tomatoes. We were out until dark.

There's still no electricity. Ronald will not sleep with me tonight, things are back to normal. Rebecca is gone to Herbert's mother's house.

Monday, October 21, 1985
Host Family, Bonfal East, Bayombong, Nueva Vizcaya

₱283 – 70 = ₱213							
Postage	28	Beer	42			TOTAL	₱70

Today I had four hours of language study and four hours of technical training. No rain today. Oh, the typhoon's name was Saling and 30 people were killed. Ronald and I went out after school for a couple of beers. Mailed the letters to Chris M., Dad and Ardis that were written over the weekend. The electricity is back on tonight.

Natokol or *naguted* = cut, cut your hand.

Aglinong-ka = take shelter!

Tuesday, October 22, 1985
Host Family, Bonfal East, Bayombong, Nueva Vizcaya

Letters from Ardis B. & Chad D.

₱213 – 2 = ₱211							
Ride	2					TOTAL	₱2

Today we had technical training all day. We finished the SALT project on Bangan Hill. We were supposed to finish at 3:00 PM, but we ended up finishing at 11:00 AM. That surely surprised Clarita. The family got the letter today that I sent from Diffun last Monday the 14th. They seemed quite impressed by it. Even I must say that it sounds pretty nice. Now that I got a letter from Chad, I have his new address. Good night. Ronald and I sleep together tonight.

Wednesday, October 23, 1985
Host Family, Bonfal East, Bayombong, Nueva Vizcaya

Letter to Nestor. Package from Chris & Mary.

₱211 – 70 = ₱141							
Soap	7	Coffee	48	Beer	10	Coke	3
Ride	2					TOTAL	₱70

Today was four hours of language only. After that I did some translations and came home early, at about 3:00 PM. The package from Chris & Mary contained some *Alaska Geographic* & *Playboy* Magazines. YIKES! It feels like I absorbed lot of Ilokano today, but it's getting really hard to tell. For ten minutes I feel really good and then I seem to feel really down. Something strange, probably culture shock. I have to tell myself to "keep a positive mental attitude."

Thursday, October 24, 1985
Host Family, Bonfal East, Bayombong, Nueva Vizcaya

Letter to Chad.

₱141 – 0 = ₱141

It rained all day today. Went to school in the rain then school all day in the rain. We had four hours of technical training in the morning and four hours of language training in the afternoon. Then come home in the rain. House is not flooded, thank heavens. I did lots of translations in the evening. Ronald and I sleep together tonight.

Friday, October 25, 1985
Host Family, Bonfal East, Bayombong, Nueva Vizcaya

₱141 – 15 = ₱126							
Beer	13	Ride	2			TOTAL	₱15

Today we had four hours of language training in the morning and then four hours of tree identification in the afternoon. For language class we went to the Public Market and talked to some of the vendors, learned how to haggle over prices too. It was fun and interesting. Patricia was not at school today, *apay ngata* (= I wonder why?). Ronald helped me make a list of trees tonight. I went out for a couple of beers with the guys at Greenfield's. Chester and Ador came over later in the evening. We had *aso* (= dog) for supper.

Saturday, October 26, 1985
Host Family, Bonfal East, Bayombong, Nueva Vizcaya

₱126 – 48 = ₱78							
Movie	16	Beer	10	Rides	10	Coke	6
Misc.	6					TOTAL	₱48

Today it rained all morning. In our morning session we think of some men's and women's issues and discuss them. I had a talk with Teresa Lewis about Iglesia ni Cristo and also talked with Brooke about a site change. She says no problem. I escaped from school at 2:30 PM and came home. Ronald and I went to Solano to the movie *"I Have Three Hands"* and also part of *"Time Warrior"*. *"I Have Three Hands"* was very funny, but *"Time Warrior"* was not so good. After that we went to a place and had one beer only and then came home. It was a happy day.

Sunday, October 27, 1985
Host Family, Bonfal East, Bayombong, Nueva Vizcaya

₱78 + 50 – 93 = ₱35

Beer	50	Aso	33	Ambaling	10	TOTAL	₱93

Went to the farm with Ronald and mother and harvested *kamote* (= sweet potato vine) for the pig. Then we returned home, had a beer, cleaned the floor and other miscellaneous things. Eventually, after completion of homework, Ronald and I went to Solano, where we had a beer at SM and then three more at a beer garden where we also had some dog meat. It was a fun evening all in all. Oh, in the afternoon I bought ₱10 worth of *ambaling* (= big white grubs) and we had some of those for supper. Ronald is a fine brother. I wish I could have him as my *kadwa* (= companion) in Burgos. Such is life that I cannot though. Good night.

Monday, October 28, 1985
Host Family, Bonfal East, Bayombong, Nueva Vizcaya

₱35 – 25 = ₱10						
Beer	23	Ride	2		TOTAL	₱25

Today we had four hours of language training and four hours of technical training. We planted a FAITH [**F**ood **A**lways **I**n **T**he **H**ome] Garden at Chris's house. We planted patani, okra, munggo beans, ampalya, squash and maybe more. It is unfortunate that we'll only be here for two more weeks and therefore we will not get to see the results of all this work. I wish we could have done the FAITH Garden during our first week. We finished up eating the ambaling, which I bought yesterday, for breakfast. This evening mother went visiting somewhere and brought home some *aso* as a surprise. It was a gift from some auntie. Mark F. stopped by for a while after the FAITH Garden exercise. Tonight we borrowed a *carabao* (= water buffalo) and I rode it around the back yard for a while. It was more concerned about eating though, and didn't want to walk around. Ronald and I were riding tandem.

Tuesday, October 29, 1985
Host Family, Bonfal East, Bayombong, Nueva Vizcaya

Letter to Yip Chee Hong

₱10 – 10 = ₱0						
Beer	8	Ride	2		TOTAL	₱10

Today was only two hours of language study. Abe broke the news to us that he will no longer be our language teacher because he is needed to teach Bontoc language. Then we had two hours of Health Policies talks and then two hours of Ed Slevin speaking and then two hours of Nancy and pre-service training comments and questions. I returned home and we went to the *bankag* (= vegetable farm) and rode the *carabao* (= water buffalo) about halfway home. Ronald and I study until bedtime.

Wednesday, October 30, 1985
Host Family, Bonfal East, Bayombong, Nueva Vizcaya

₱00 + 100 – 23 = ₱77							
Beer	20	Ride	3			TOTAL	₱23

Today we took a field trip to Villa Verde and talked to some farmers about SALT and also about mushroom culture. It was a pretty dull day. Ronald had a KBL meeting and dance tonight. He said he would be home by 10:30 PM and I told him that if he was not then I would go looking for him. Well, he was not home at 10:30 PM, so I went and found him and we came home at 11:00 PM. Ronald has slept with me every night lately. We're definitely *napintas nga gayyem ken kabsat* (= best friends and brothers). There is no doubt in my mind that we are closer than my real brother in America and I are. I really deeply love and respect this family and brother of mine.

Thursday, October 31, 1985
Host Family, Bonfal East, Bayombong, Nueva Vizcaya

₱77 + 530 – 25 = ₱582							
Aso	10	Soap	10	Toilet Paper	3	Ride	2
						TOTAL	₱25

Today we had two hours of technical training and then four more hours of technical training. It was a very tiring day. That's all for today.

Friday, November 1, 1985
St. Mary's Pension, Baguio City, Benguet

₱582 – 370 = ₱212							
Rides	131	Supper	165	Chelako	30	Beer	18
Misc.	26					TOTAL	₱370

We left the house at 7:00 AM for the waiting shed. From there we took a bus to Carmen and then changed buses for one to Baguio City. We stayed at Saint Mary's Pension. We went to the public market to wander around and see things and then we went to supper and so on. I bought a chelako [a type of sweater] for Ronald and he is happy. It was an expensive day and you'll surely notice that the most expensive thing was the supper – nearly half the day's expense was supper! [At this point I cannot remember what we had or why it was so expensive, but for that price is must have been quite an amazing meal.]

Saturday, November 2, 1985
St. Mary's Pension, Baguio City, Benguet

₱212 + 350 – 190 = ₱372							
Meals	88	Rides	72.50	Beer	20	Candles	2
Misc.	7.50					TOTAL	₱190

WOW! *Mapantayo igid ti baybay!* (= We went to the seashore!) It was very beautiful at the seashore. Ronald and I escaped from the rest of the Americanos after breakfast, which was ₱50, and we managed to get to the ocean and have a day to ourselves until about 2:30 PM, at which time we had agreed to meet the other Americanos at California Beach. Unfortunately we did find and meet back up with them. When we got back to Baguio City, Ronald and I escaped again and went to Lourdes Grotto, where we said a prayer and lit a candle each. It is the day after All Saints Day so he said a prayer for his brother and sister who died and I said a prayer for my Bayombong family and for Ronald, my friend and brother. Then we returned to the pension and got ready and went to supper. Supper was only ₱38, the first reasonably priced meal that we have eaten on this trip. The day at the ocean was really incredible with Ronald and I being able to just be by ourselves. It's funny how much I wish there was or is a way for me to become a Filipino and to be able to shuck all I know about America and the American lifestyle. Of course I guess I'm rich, at least compared to most people here. It makes me so happy to see Ronald smile and be happy. He is certainly closer than my real brother. I cannot believe it. I hope that when I am finally able to communicate better in Ilokano I can find a way to express it to him somehow.

An amazing thing about today was to find out that Ronald had never been to the ocean before. This, despite the fact, that one side of his family comes from just a few miles from where we were today. I guess that a lack of money, or disposable income, prohibits your average Filipino from being to take little pleasure trips like this.

Sunday, November 3, 1985
Host Family, Bonfal East, Bayombong, Nueva Vizcaya

₱372 – 365 = ₱7							
Lodging	140	Meals	45	Rides	133	Coke	7
Presents	40					TOTAL	₱365

WOW! What a day. We got up at 6:00 AM and Ronald and I went for breakfast at Dangwa Tranco. Then we went to the Bishop's house to search for a dictionary which I had heard was published by the church. There was nobody there who could give me one so I left ₱5 and my name and address. Then we went to Burnham Park for a walk and met our Americano companions but we (both groups) stayed separate and we met at the Philippine Rabbit Bus Terminal at 11:00 AM and then went to the Pantranco Bus Terminal and took a bus bound for home. We got home quite late. I was so very glad that my brother Ronald was with me so that he could reinforce what I told my mother and father as our excuse for getting home so late. [The bus had a flat tire and had no spare tire, so they had to send a substitute bus to take us the remainder of the way home, and that's the whole truth.]

Ronald at the sea-shore near San Fernando City. Note that he is holding a Sea Urchin. Also note his smile. This was his first time (17 years old) to ever see the ocean or seashore.

Monday, November 4, 1985
Host Family, Bonfal East, Bayombong, Nueva Vizcaya

₱7 – 0 = ₱7

Today we had three hours of language study and then a two hour administrative meeting. Then we finished with two hours of technical training. What else can I say? Rogel is my new language teacher and I don't learn much new language anymore. Technical training is also getting to be pretty much of a bummer as it seems that they have run of stuff that they really want to teach us and it seems like they are just basically killing time nowadays. Oh well, things are very close to the end now and soon we will be off to our sites.

Tuesday, November 5, 1985
Host Family, Bonfal East, Bayombong, Nueva Vizcaya

I have no money (well, only ₱7)! Today we had language study all day and part of that was giving a speech. I think I did okay, though it was difficult. I think I did better than most people. I have not had any mail in quite a while and in addition to that there is lots of frustration around the place lately. Let me be clear that I am only frustrated with school, not the family or Ronald. We still have still lots of love for each other and it gets stronger every day! Ronald and I sleep together [and more] every night now and we are really close brothers. I believe it is really good for me. I think that it's quite possible that I would be really homesick if I did not have a close friend like Ronald. I think my language abilities are only as good as they are because of my private language tutor, Ronald.

Wednesday, November 6, 1985
Manila, Final Training Stuff

₱7 + 1,290 – 27 = ₱1,270							
Beer	18	Juice	4	Rides	4	Misc.	1
						TOTAL	₱27

Today I have no voice! I don't know where it went, maybe the tape recorder stole it during my speech yesterday, anyway no voice. Our host family payment and Walk Around Allowance arrived today. I took the host family payment home at noon and said goodbye to the family once again. They were happy that the money finally arrived and they said that their hearts hurt because I have to go to Manila with no money. I told them that my money arrived too and they were pleased. It's sure tough to leave this family with all of the love between us. At 1:00 PM we left for Manila. Patricia and I rode in the rig with Dave and Beth and we arrived in Manila at 7:00 PM or thereabouts. We went out for two beers and that's all. I miss the family already.

Thursday, November 7, 1985
Manila, Final Training Stuff

₱1,270 – 568 = ₱702							
T-Shirts	200	Deodorant	61.50	Tape	45	Stationery	40
Dictionary	50	Cookies	58	Supper	82	Coke	6.50
Breakfast	25					TOTAL	₱568

Got up at 5:15 AM. Shower and eat breakfast and then we leave for Mountain Lupa. It was a very educational day with Calvin Fox and we saw some more SALT projects. We also saw soap making. Upon our return to Manila, some of us went to Robinson's Department Store for some shopping for various things. I found a pretty good 2-volume Ilokano dictionary. After that we all went to supper at Pearl Garden and had good Chinese food – Michael P., Chester, Sue T. and Pat B. They were good company.

Friday, November 8, 1985
Manila, Final Training Stuff

Letter to the family in Bayombong.

₱702 – 225 = ₱477							
Breakfast	18	Maps	43	T-Shirts	52	Beer	5.25
Supper	86	Chocolate	16.50	Misc.	4.25	TOTAL	₱225

We returned to Mountain Lupa this morning and stayed there until noon. Then we returned to Manila and we all went to the Bureau of Maps and most people bought maps of the area they are going to be working and living in. Then we went to the Bureau of Soils and looked at Legume inoculants. Then we went to Robinson's Department Store again and I found a small *pasalubong* (= present from a journey) for Ronald and a San Miguel T-Shirt which says *"Ito Ang Beer"* (= This is Beer) for me. Then five or six of us went to the Seafront Restaurant for supper and a couple of bottles of beer each. Michael P. and I split a pizza. Michael and I are becoming good friends [I think he's gay too]. We all went to bed at 9:00 PM.

Saturday, November 9, 1985
Host Family, Bonfal East, Bayombong, Nueva Vizcaya

₱477 – 127 = ₱350							
Lodging	75	Meals	42	Market	3	Snack	7
						TOTAL	₱127

We got up at 4:00 AM so everybody could return to Bayombong today. We stopped at CLSU [Central Luzon State University] to see some fish ponds. Then we continued on and finally got home at about 2:00 PM. It was a pretty uneventful ride, what can I say about a long drive? I was happy to get home to Bayombong and see the family of mine! It's the best thing that can be said of the day. I was happy to see them and they were happy to see me. I bought the biggest size box of cookies or biscuits that I could find! The dictionary from the Bishop's House in Baguio City was brought by the Bishop. There was a phone call to the Training Center in late afternoon and I had to go to somebody's home and meet the Bishop and pick up the dictionary (see November 3.) That was kind of cool that the Bishop himself brought it!

Sunday, November 10, 1985
Host Family, Bonfal East, Bayombong, Nueva Vizcaya

₱350 – 20 = ₱330							
Beer	20					TOTAL	₱20

Today Ronald weeded the rice paddy, but I could not help in the morning. In the afternoon we had a Java stove building special session at Chester's house and when finished I went to the *bankag* (= vegetable farm) to help with the planting of pechoy until dark, then we returned home for supper, study and then sleep.

Monday, November 11, 1985
Host Family, Bonfal East, Bayombong, Nueva Vizcaya

Letter to Ardis B.

₱330 – 71 = ₱259							
Beer	20	T-Shirts	50	Ride	1	TOTAL	₱71

Today we studied language all day! Ronald and I went out for a couple of beers after school, which ended at 2:15 PM, and then we came home. I got a haircut today.

Tuesday, November 12, 1985
Host Family, Bonfal East, Bayombong, Nueva Vizcaya

Postcards to John D., Rolando T., Dad, Tim S., Tony S., Dave M., Chris & Mary, Vicki K., San & Jack, Tim C. and Steve A.

₱259 – 129 = ₱130							
Beans	18	Peppers	5	Knives	57	Beer	12
Ride	2	Raffle Tckt	15	Loan (Pat)	20	TOTAL	₱129

For language class Chester Nancy, Rogel and I went to market in Solano. I bought some things for the family and learned a few new language things and then we returned to NVSIT at 9:30 AM. In the afternoon we studied superstitions and folk beliefs and etc. After that we had an awards ceremony for trainees, Language Instructors and staff. Ronald and father are angry with each other tonight. It's really a bad scene and I feel bad about it, but what can I say, what can I do? Nothing, that's what.

Wednesday, November 13, 1985
Host Family, Bonfal East, Bayombong, Nueva Vizcaya

Postcards to Terry & Juana, Tom L., Bob S. and Dan T.

₱130 + 10 – 55 = ₱75							
Beer/Snack	52	T-Shirts	12	Ride	1	Pat Return	+10
						TOTAL	₱55

Today we had our final language interviews. It seems like it went okay or even good. Rogel, my teacher, has no interest in teaching anymore. Ronald and I met at 4:00 PM and went to Roberto's and had beer and *pulutan* (= drinking snack). We drank four beers each. It was raining heavily at bedtime.

Thursday, November 14, 1985
Host Family, Bonfal East, Bayombong, Nueva Vizcaya

₱75 + 4,039 – 698 = ₱3,416							
Rides	10	T-Shirts	75	Beth	30	Ron/Mindy	550
Beer	12	Misc.	21			TOTAL	₱698

Today was the final day of classes, so not much happened. We practiced songs for the swearing-in and graduation ceremony tomorrow, had a final administrative briefing and so on and got paid. I'm feeling really low these days; I just can't believe that I have to be leaving in two days. The family gave me my advance graduation gift this evening – a beautiful rattan pack and a straw hat. I'm really impressed. Ronald gave me a special remembrance this morning. I gave the family their remembrances this evening too. I gave Ronald two T-shirts. To mother I gave a nice kitchen knife and to father I gave one of the Peace Corps Agro-forestry group T-shirts. God knows I sure don't want to leave here on Saturday morning, but I must proceed onward to the next stage of life and of this adventure.

Friday, November 15, 1985
Host Family, Bonfal East, Bayombong, Nueva Vizcaya

GRADUATION and SWEARING IN CEREMONY!

₱3,416 – 325.25 = ₱3,090.75 – 2,899.75 (to savings envelope) = ₱191							
Dental Floss	28.80	Beer	21.25	Mosquito Net	95	Coffee	50
Ball Pens	10	Toilet Paper	8	Toothpaste	35	Soap	32
Nails	1	Mail	31.20	Ride	5	Misc.	8
						TOTAL	₱325.25

We went to Solano this morning and returned home in time for lunch. I bought a bunch of additional things, as can be seen by looking at today's expenses. Ronald and I walked to the road together for the last time – maybe. I went to NVSIT with him, my brother. I mailed all of the postcards which I have written over the last two days. Tonight mother, father, Ronald and I went to the graduation ceremony. It was quite an affair. I'm very happy that Ronald could come too. After it finished we returned home and I give Ronald the knife, dental floss and playing cards which I bought for him. He is a happy brother.

Saturday, November 16, 1985
Nestor's House, Villa Miemban, Cordon, Isabela

Letter to family in Bayombong

₱191 – 147 = ₱44							
Rides	8	Lunch	23	Food	36	Eggs	9
Meat	20	Fish	10	Beer	30	Coke	2
Misc.	9					TOTAL	₱147

Today I left the family in Bayombong. It was very difficult, possibly one of the most difficult goodbyes I have ever had to do in my life. My Bayombong Host Family got really close to me – and I to them, especially my brother Ronald. As I was leaving father told me "don't look back" – I guess that would have been bad luck or something. By 10:30 AM I was in Santiago thinking about the next stage of life, as this is only the next step, moving off from one present to a new future. I wrote a letter to the Bayombong family from the 456 restaurant and mailed it. At 2:00 PM I met up with Teresa L. and we left for Villa Miemban. I took two large bottles of San Miguel beer with me. We got there at about dark and I stayed Nestor's house. Rufino and a new friend, Danny, were here. Nestor's family is very warm and jolly, it's really pleasant here. We drank the two large bottles of beer and talked until bedtime. I feel really welcome and happy here and maybe I'm a bit jealous of JB and Katie because they get to come here and stay for two years. By the way, my brother Ronald and I slept together every night, at least since October 24th, or so. We have become very close brothers and I do mean brothers! He really enjoys receiving fellatio and then masturbating me.

Sunday, November 17, 1985
Nestor's House, Villa Miemban, Cordon, Isabela

₱44 – 0 = ₱44

Nestor and I got up late, 6:30 AM! We dug cassava for Teresa's *despedida* [going away party]. Then, by and by, we washed my pack and my shoes and bathed ourselves and then we went to Teresa's house to help with the party preparations. I learned how to butcher the chickens and ducks and cook both of them. It was fun and not really very much work. I learn and help out with what I can. Nestor and I stayed there all day and then we returned to his house to change our clothes. Then we returned to Teresa's house and the party began at 7:00 PM. There were lots of people for Teresa's party and it was a beautiful party and lots of fun. We stayed up the whole night and danced and sang and talked and made friends. I've got a lot of mental energy invested in Villa Miemban. There were games and a good time was had by all. I am a better friend to these people of Villa Miemban after this party. Nestor and I sang "Banbantay" [a folk song] alone and then a lot of people sang it as a group. Because JB and Katie were so late to arrive and because I was here helping all day, a lot of the people thought that I was to be the replacement Peace Corps Volunteer for them! We did native dances again with the g-strings and gongs and so on. There were only two g-strings so JB and I wore them again. Villa Miemban is a beautiful place and I am happy here – wish I could stay!

Monday, November 18, 1985
Nestor's House, Villa Miemban, Cordon, Isabela

₱44 – 0 = ₱44

At daylight today Nestor and I returned to his house from Teresa's party. I slipped in the mud and got my pants all dirty so when we got to Nestor's house, and after I took remembrance pictures of Nestor and some of the girls dancing, we laundered my pants and T-shirts and then we slept for three hours. When we got up, we went fishing with electricity with Nestor's brother. The electricity was weak so we didn't get many fish. When we returned to the house we pounded the rice for rice cake and then JB and Katie came by and stayed for a few hours, until it got dark. We butchered a chicken for them. After supper they left and we went to bed. JB was saying some insulting things about me and my ability speaking Ilokano that I didn't like very much. In my opinion he was being quite culturally insensitive. It seemed like it was talk that the native Ilokano peoples did not like either. It was a bad scene. I think he was just a bit angry because I got there before he and Katie did and because so many people thought that I would be the person to replace Teresa. Oh well, such is life. Anyway, I love Nestor and he loves me and we had a good time [no sex though].

Tuesday, November 19, 1985
Diffun, District Forestry Office, Cabarroguis, Quirino

₱44 + 900 – 41 = ₱903							
Beer	14	Rides	9	Lunch	18	TOTAL	₱41

Got up this morning at Nestor's house and give each other a big hug as we both know it's the last day for us here. We had breakfast and then bathed in the stream and then we left Villa Miemban – the 2nd time I've left Villa Miemban with a really good feeling about the place. Nestor and his family are really great folks. We left at 8:00 AM or so and got to the river pretty quickly. I think my feet are tougher than they were in September when I walked that trail barefoot. It's been a very gradual change, I can't really feel a difference when I rub my hand on the sole of my foot, but they sure feel tougher when walking barefoot. It's sad to say goodbye to Nestor and we made a plan for him to come to Burgos on December 2nd. I hope it works out. Then we went to Santiago and the 456 restaurant again and I think about the future again. Go to Nestor's boarding house and get my stuff and then stop at the bank and make a deposit. Then take the jeepney to Diffun. Everybody had already left the office, but at least I got to Diffun today. I'm at the beginning of another new experience, another new family to figure out. I'm staying at the office tonight. Nestor mentioned the word "lonely" to me last night. With the extended family style of living that they have here, is that possible? I guess it must be, but I cannot say that I understand it.

Wednesday, November 20, 1985
Francisco's House, Santiago, Isabela

Letter to Nestor.

₱903 – 4 = ₱899							
Beer	4					TOTAL	₱4

Today I was at the District Office in Diffun all day. Francisco showed up at 8:10 AM and we talked for a little while. I thought I would go to Burgos today, but as it turned out, my big event of the day was to go to the post office and meet the post office workers and talk with them for a while. I did get to make a couple of friends in the office at Diffun, namely Beethoven, Edgar, Ramelo and Yoyoi. At quitting time we went to Francisco's house for the night. A Regional Office Bureau of Forest Development person, Artemio Antolin was also here for the day and came along to Francisco's house for the night. So – for the day – I accomplished meeting five new people and talking to the post office people. While at the post office I mailed a letter to Nestor thanking him for the weekend and reconfirming our December 2nd meeting at Santiago. Life is okay. The postmaster of Diffun is Jamie Saluesta.

Thursday, November 21, 1985
Edgar's House, Diffun, Cabarroguis, Quirino

₱899 – 49 = ₱850							
Beer	17	Coffee	16.50	Food	15.50	TOTAL	₱49

Today was quite a day, I guess. We got up at 6:00 AM at Francisco's house, got ready and finally left at 7:20 AM or so. We did not arrive at Diffun until after 8:00

AM. Artemio, the Regional Office fellow, kept looking at his watch the whole way there and I didn't know what to make of that. Anyway, shortly after arriving at the Diffun Office we left for Diffuncian. The Regional Office guy wanted to see the IAP project [I can't recall what that acronym stands for] – so we got to Diffuncian at about 11:00 AM or so and then David had to cook lunch for us all. I don't understand this culture and its sometimes bizarre customs. It seemed like we went there for lunch for the Regional Office guy. He did not look at the project or anything, just lots of talk between him and Francisco. We stopped at Mendoza's store [the place where I am to stay] for a while and explained to them why I was not there yet and finalized that I would be there – that I will return on Sunday. We did not finalize the rent or anything like that. The trail into the IAP project was a muddy mess and I got my shoes all muddy again. So when we returned to Diffun I had to wash my shoes and my dirty clothes again. Of course it rained some more today. I went to market and practiced my Ilokano a bit and also bargaining. I bought some stuff for the Diffun family and had a beer and after the end of the work day I went to the house of Edgar and found out where he lives. We stopped at Garana's store and drank a beer and talked with Edgar for a while. Then we returned to Edgar's house and had supper and then after a while we went to sleep. That Regional Office guy is always testing me it seems like. I got tired of him and his constant testing and testing and that's why I went to bed quickly after supper. I can't take that kind of crap! Oh, I forgot, Ramel accompanied Edgar and me to Garana's store for drinking beer.

Friday, November 22, 1985
Edgar's House, Diffun, Cabarroguis, Quirino

₱850 – 40 = ₱810					
Beer/Coke	21	Lunch	19		TOTAL ₱40

Today what did I do? Well, there was a district meeting this morning, at which I had to say a bit in Ilokano. They talked about the upcoming Christmas party and decided to collect ₱40 from each person and that chicken and pork will be the food which will be served. I got to meet many new people today and I have already forgotten the names of ½ of them. We went to lunch with Hoven. Romero arrived at 6:00 AM or so and he chaired the meeting. Before lunch he preached to me for an hour or so and then after lunch everybody made a game of testing my Ilokano and I got super frustrated. Grrr! Study for a while in the afternoon and David came to the office [from Diffuncian] and informed me that I have to attend a meeting at Diffuncian on Monday morning and give a speech in Ilokano. I'll worry about that tomorrow I guess. What a week it has been! I went to Edgars for supper tonight with Ramel. These people are so nice I just can't believe it.

Saturday, November 23, 1985
Host Family, Bonfal East, Bayombong, Nueva Vizcaya

₱810 – 75 = ₱735							
Rides	7	Lunch	13	Toiletries	15	Fruit	17
Beer	23					TOTAL	₱75

Agawid-ak Bonfal East (= I went to my Bonfal East home) today. I left Diffun at about 8:00 AM and arrived at Bonfal East at about 11:45 AM. I waited at the waiting shed for Ronald until 12:15 PM or so. It was so very good to see him. Then we came to the house and it was good to see mother and father and good to be "home". I can't even explain how good it is to be home. It feels like such a good and happy day that even I cannot understand it. In the afternoon we went to the *bankag* (= vegetable farm) and Ronald climbed a coconut tree, harvested some coconuts and we ate coconuts! I'm happy; it's so good to be home. The entire family has colds – they say it's because of their sadness over my leaving.

Sunday, November 24, 1985
Mendoza's Store, Diffuncian, Burgos, Cabarroguis, Quirino

₱735 – 85 = ₱650							
Rides	27	Ronald	50	Beer	8	TOTAL	₱85

Slept in at Bayombong until 6:00 AM. Ronald and I got up and the day began with breakfast, of course. I woke up and the first thing I said was that I did not want to leave this house AGAIN! When we got ready and finally left at 8:30 AM or so Ronald accompanied me and we took a tricycle [a 3-wheeled motorcycle with a passenger compartment] to Solano and then the Vizcaya Liner bus to Cordon and then a jeepney to Diffun. We then changed to a jeepney to Diffuncian, but there was a truck stuck in the mud at the final bridge which we had to cross and the jeepney couldn't go any further, so Ronald and I carried some of my stuff to Mendoza's store and then we took the water buffalo and cart down the road for the rest of my stuff. When we took the water buffalo down for my stuff Ronald and I said our goodbyes and had a final beer and a tearful goodbye – again! It's so very sad to leave someone whom you love so much. Then I returned to Mendoza's store by myself – lots of new people to meet, new routines to learn, new language to learn, etc. It was difficult to say the least. There is very little English spoken here and then this evening, just to make things interesting, they spoke in Tagalog a good deal in their attempts to confuse me even more than I already am. Damn, I miss my Bayombong family and Ronald. They would never do that to me, it's just mean! Now it's 5:00 PM – Ronald, you should be home by now, I hope all is ok for you and you made it okay. If you're late then your family will be angry with me. Goodbye Ramos family, hello Mendoza family.

Chapter 6
Culture Notes #1

Alcohol in Community Culture

With all the money these people earned (or did not earn), an important factor of community culture was consumption of alcoholic beverages. I did not enjoy drinking to the point of losing control, but couldn't even walk down the road at 8:00 AM without having people holler from their porches; "Good morning, Americano come drink with us." This was frustrating to me and I wasn't quite sure how to say "no thanks" without possibly angering somebody. It is a part of Ilokano culture that anger cannot be shown, except when one has the alibi of inebriation. People would therefore, sometimes become belligerent and violent when drunk. This bottled up anger which they carried around with them would and could come to the surface when people were drinking. I was, for example, once struck by a drunken man merely for not knowing the name of the governor of a different province.

Religion – Iglesia ni Cristo

Another cultural aspect that came to my attention was religion. There is a religion in the Philippines called "Iglesia ni Cristo" which means "Church of Christ". My co-worker in Burgos, an employee of the Bureau of Forest Development (BFD), was a member of this religion (as mentioned previously). One of the precepts of this religion is the fact that a person can and does buy his or her way into heaven. I was asked by this co-worker to join his church, being told that if I did join, then the co-worker would receive ₱3,000 credit towards heaven. I politely refused, stating that I was Roman Catholic, but from that point onward there was a barrier to cooperative efforts between us. I was then sure that I was not going to be able to stay in Burgos for the entire two years, I already had two strikes against me in only one month (#1 did not enjoy drinking to the point of falling down drunk and #2, did not want to become Iglesia ni Cristo.)

Chapter 7
Burgos, Cabarroguis, Quirino to Gomez, Cabarroguis, Quirino
November 25, 1985 – January 19, 1986

Monday, November 25, 1985
Mendoza's Store, Diffuncian, Burgos, Cabarroguis, Quirino

₱650 – 18 = ₱632							
Rides	4	Vegetables	10	Misc.	4	TOTAL	₱18

What a day! I got up early – at 4:30 AM. Just couldn't sleep any longer. Nervous about the speech I was supposed to give I guess. I went to the nursery at 7:00 AM to bathe in the river there. The meeting was supposed to begin at 8:00 AM but it was raining so hard that only a few people showed up. They needed about 60 or so people for a quorum, so the meeting was postponed until Friday, when hopefully, the weather will be better. Therefore, I didn't have to give my speech but I did meet a dozen or so new people. I don't feel like I have any friends here yet though. Dado was here for the meeting and after we finished the non-meeting, he, David and I went with some of the other men and they drink a bottle of *Ginebra* [a cheap and foul-tasting alcoholic drink] while I attempted to convince them that I would not drink it and tried to explain life in Alaska and why I didn't want to be married and forty thousand other answers to their strange questions. After we left there, we returned to Mendoza's store and then went to the sawmill looking for the Barangay Captain – he was not there – but met other people and finally we went directly to the house of the Barangay Captain and he was not there either. I wonder why it is so difficult to find the Barangay Captain? Then Dado and I went to his house near Gundaway – I forgot the name of the village where he lives I'm sure it will stick in my memory by and by. I found myself smiling a lot today, I don't know why, I don't feel very happy – really there's nobody here to talk with or to, nobody to drink a friendly beer with. I feel tired because of all the concentration I needed for meeting new people today and trying to pay close attention to the Ilokano and understand as much as possible.

Tuesday, November 26, 1985
Mendoza's Store, Diffuncian, Burgos, Cabarroguis, Quirino

Letter to Bayombong family.

₱632 – 25 = ₱607							
Coke/Bread	7.50	Beer	13.50	Misc.	4	TOTAL	₱25

Today I got up rather late, at 6:00 AM. I went to the bathing place in the creek, but I think there must be a better place somewhere. I'll ask Lito tomorrow. After bathing, I went to the sawmill and found the Barangay Captain today and met a friend, but I forgot his name already. He works at the sawmill, as a timber scaler I think. We drank a bottle of beer and strolled to market; it's a tiny market in Burgos, not much there, that's for sure. I returned to Mendoza's store in the afternoon and looked at all my stuff and actually found the "lost" pictures of Nestor and me and the other pictures that Teresa L. gave me. I was happy to find them. I also found a nice lady who offered to do laundry for me. While I was writing the letter to the Bayombong family tonight I couldn't get away from people and even now as I get ready for bed my new host father is watching me – why?

Wednesday, November 27, 1985
Mendoza's Store, Diffuncian, Burgos, Cabarroguis, Quirino

Letter from Bayombong family, Bill N., and a *Newsweek*.

₱607 – 62 = ₱545							
Meat	33	Coffee	18	Veggies	11	TOTAL	₱62

The post office is in Gundaway. I didn't know that and found out by accident because David, Jesus, Ben and I were drinking beer at Gundaway and it just so happens that the brother of Ben was going to the Municipio and told me that's where the post office is. Surprise! This pen is going bad already, pens aren't worth much here. So, like I said, David, Ben, Jesus and I went to Gundaway and drank beer and ate and generally had a good time until 1:00 PM. Then I went to the post office and the public market and returned home. This afternoon I went and found Lito at his house and we went to Gilacio's house and helped him with his well digging for a while and then I returned to Mendoza's and ate supper. By and by Lito, Vergilio and Gilacio came here and visited for the evening. It was nice to have somebody to talk with.

Thursday, November 28, 1985
Mendoza's Store, Diffuncian, Burgos, Cabarroguis, Quirino

₱545 – 10 = ₱535							
Beer	10					TOTAL	₱10

Well, today was quite a day. I've been trying to get a letter written to Steve A. for some 30 hours now, without success. Today I went to the tree nursery to help David pull some ipil-ipil seedlings at somebody's house. Then we mudded them, after trimming, of course. I went to a birthday party at somebody's too – with David. In the afternoon as soon as I got home, Lito, my friend, came over and bought me some bread and a Coke and introduced me to his friend Rogel. Then it was suppertime. After supper I tried to work on Steve's letter again and the family immediately thought I was lonely and began to question me about anything and everything. Finally I escaped upstairs, but then Lito and Rogel returned here for an evening of talk. It's getting so that I do have some friends here, I guess. At this point they won't leave me alone when I want to be alone though. I'm going to Nestor's house in Villa Miemban on Saturday and Sunday.

Friday, November 29, 1985
Mendoza's Store, Diffuncian, Burgos, Cabarroguis, Quirino

₱535 – 25 = ₱510						
Beer	15	Contribution	10		TOTAL	₱25

There was a meeting today. Many people were there at the nursery. I went with my host father and we took a shortcut. I had to give my speech today. I didn't understand much of what went on, but I do know that the Christmas program is set for December 18th, so now I'm committed for December 18th to the 25th. On the 18th there is the party here, on the 19th I have to get ready, on the 20th is the party in Diffun, on the 21st and 22nd I'll be in Villa Miemban and then on the 23rd, 24th and 25th I'll be in Bayombong. It's the busiest Christmas schedule I've ever had, for sure, and I don't even know anybody yet! This afternoon I hung out with Lito and Rogel and we generally did our best just to kill time. It rained a lot today. I got my first leech (*alinta*) on my foot today and I also learned that umbrella is *payong*. I took lots of pictures today. Dang slide film, it's sure difficult to tell people it will take two or three months to get there remembrance pictures back – this is ridiculous. After the rains kind of slowed down we (Rogel, Lito and I) went to Herrera's and drank a beer and I got accosted by a couple of people who were too drunk for their own good. I found out there's a word for a little bit drunk but I forgot it already, of course. There is a brownout tonight, so it's quiet here and I think I'll go to bed pretty early. It's only 7:00 PM but possibly I'll crash as soon as I get done with this journal entry. Well let's try and summarize this week. There was the meeting (non-meeting) on Monday and then I went to Dado's house. On Tuesday I met the Barangay Captain and Mario. On Wednesday I went to Gundaway with Ben, Jesus and David. On Thursday I worked with David all day. Today – Friday – we had the meeting and I got to know some of the neighborhood folks around here better – including, of course Lito and Rogel. It's been a busy week for sure, not a bit boring; didn't have time to play any games – it was difficult just to find time to play with myself (and a place to be able to do it too). I'm still planning to go to Santiago tomorrow and then Villa Miemban and Nestor's house.

Saturday, November 30, 1985
Nestor's House, Villa Miemban, Cordon, Isabela

Letter to Steve A. & Ardis B. Film to Chris M.

₱510 + 500 – 210 = ₱800							
Rides	17	Food	68	Meat	9	Stationery	16
Postage	22	Beer	30	Bag	3	Coke	3
Lunch	42					TOTAL	₱210

Got up late, at 6:00 AM or so, and it was cold this morning. Eat breakfast then go and bathe in the creek, get ready and wait for a jeepney to Santiago. Finally got to Santiago, ate lunch, went to market and strolled for a while then caught a jeepney bound for Kakandongan, which is the place where you start walking for Nestor's house. It was good to escape from Burgos for the weekend. The jeepney got to Kakandongan at about 3:15 PM or so and I walked to Nestor's house and got here by 4:00 PM or so. It really felt good to get to a place where they really like me. Paul and his wife were here and they gave me a very warm welcome. By and by father arrived from the field and I had another warm welcome from him. We all talked for a while because Nestor is still on the mountain getting bananas. Nestor finally arrived at 6:30 PM or so and I hid and surprised him when he got here. Another warm welcome! We had dog meat for supper. It was like Nestor knew that I was coming. We ate supper and then I got out the two large bottles of beer that I brought with me and we all drank beer and ate leftover dog meat for our drinking snack. We talked about life in Burgos and life in general until bedtime. Nestor played the guitar for a while and we fell asleep. I'm so happy here, Nestor is such a good friend – there aren't words for it.

Sunday, December 1, 1985
Nestor's House, Villa Miemban, Cordon, Isabela

₱800 – 30 = ₱770							
Beer	30					TOTAL	₱30

Got up late today, 6:30 AM. First we went to check on the charcoal pit up the hill and Nestor explained to me about how charcoal is made and told me some good stories. Then we rode the water buffalo half way back to the house, tied it for pasturing and walked the rest of the way. Then we started to dig up the charcoal pit here at the house but it was still burning inside so we had to stop and cover it back up. After that we went fishing with electricity and had pretty good luck it seems to me – we got around a kilogram of fish in about 1.5 hours; much better than the last time we tried. Then we came back to the house and ate lunch. Oh, I forgot, we harvested some bananas too, about 500 or so. After lunch we took the water buffalo to Kakandongan with the bananas. We left here at about 2:15 PM and arrived there at about 3:15 PM and we ended up staying until dark and drinking two large San Miguel's there at the river with the *maestro* (= teacher) and then the teacher and his two children and the Barangay Captain came back with us. Nestor and I rode the water buffalo and the other four people rode in the water buffalo cart. We got back to the house at 6:45 PM or so, we ate supper and then just as we finished supper, JB and Katie came by and stayed until nearly 9:30 PM. Now Nestor has to go to the mountain and check the charcoal pit. It was a good day – had some good talking with Nestor and found out these people here really like me and are worried and concerned that the people of Burgos are not treating me very good. If the people here are going to worry so much about me, maybe it's better if I don't visit so often. In addition, it also kind of brings me down to come here and see how good JB and Katie have it compared to what I have at my site. I talked to Nestor today about how Teresa found this site. I hope JB and Katie are treating these people right. I sure would like to be here myself, but such is life – I am not, what can I say. Nestor is still not back from the mountain and checking the charcoal – please hurry. (He returned soon after I finished and we slept.)

Monday, December 2, 1985
Mendoza's Store, Diffuncian, Burgos, Cabarroguis, Quirino

₱770 – 149 = ₱621							
Ice Cream	19	Lunch	32	Rides	13	Brush	5
Meat	38	Veggies	42			TOTAL	₱149

Today I got up at 6:00 AM or so at Nestor's house. After a leisurely breakfast and leisurely bathing in the stream we (JB, Katie, Nestor and I) left for town. We hiked to Kakandongan and there were no jeepneys, so we kept hiking all the way to the highway. The same as last time, when we woke up this morning Nestor and I gave each other a big hug because today is the day I leave, and again I told him it's difficult for me to leave here. It's true! It seems to me that JB and Katie really have it soft and very easy at Villa Miemban. I only wish I had it so good here at Burgos and wish I had such good friends here as I do there at Villa Miemban. Nestor and I are really brothers and it really feels like it. It's good! I wish I could do more for him and his family, but I don't know what else is possible. I help in whatever small ways that I can when I am there, but I don't feel like it's enough. Nestor accompanied us only to Cordon, and there we shook hands and parted once again. He said that he and Rufino will come to see me on December 14th and 15th. I hope! I shed a few tears as we said goodbye, but I didn't let him see – only Katie saw. It's really hard to say goodbye to Nestor. Why don't I have a friend like that here in Burgos yet? At noon JB, Katie and I arrived in Santiago for the meeting about the mail – we found out where the "pouch" is going to be kept. It's about 20 minutes out of Santiago – a ridiculous pain in the ass actually. It's out at kilometer post 341 in Echange or something like that. [The Peace Corps recommended to us that we have all of our mail sent to the Manila Office and they would forward all of the mail in a pouch to a "reliable person" near us and we would be able to pick it up there. They warned us not to trust our local post offices. As stated above, this location was a pain for me to get to, and I ultimately told all of my friends in the USA to use my local post office as my address and I never had any troubles with mail theft or opening or any other mail problems.] Finally we got done talking about mail stuff at 3:30 PM or so and I rushed to the public market to do some shopping for the family in Burgos. I managed to catch the last jeepney at 4:00 PM or so. Even though there isn't a whole lot for me, I'm happy to arrive at this simple home and see my family again. I bought two *lukbans* (= pomelo fruit) at market to remind me of Nestor, so tonight after supper I ate ½ of one of them and thought about Nestor – my good friend – the whole time I was eating it. There's STILL no electricity here at the house, I don't know why, but there isn't. It's been out since Friday evening. Now that I've started this page I have to fill it (unofficial policy) [this was for my handwritten journal]. I wonder how some people end up becoming such close friends to each other? I guess there has to be a need and a desire on both people's parts to become friends, first of all. I'm sure Nestor and I, just like my brother in Bayombong, will stay friends for a long time. Today we talked about HOW – IF – WHEN Nestor will come to visit me in Alaska. That would sure be nice, but probably not even possible – who knows? Only time will tell the whole story. We'll wait until November, 1987 [close of my Peace Corps service] and see what happens in life. The other night I had a vivid color dream about potato chips. Oh, the people at the mail meeting were Mike S., Darrek, Dave C., Linda, Tracy, Pam, JB & Katie, Julie, Ray & Lois W. and I – I think that's all.

Tuesday, December 3, 1985
Mendoza's Store, Diffuncian, Burgos, Cabarroguis, Quirino

Letters to Dad, Fred & Cynthia (Christmas letters begin today).
Letters from Ardis B and Catherine; postcard from Rolando.

₱621 – 25 = ₱596					
Laundry	25			TOTAL	₱25

Today I didn't do much except dwell on too many negative things. Somebody brought three pieces of mail for me – a letter from Ardis, a postcard from Rolando and a letter from Catherine in Bonfal East. I studied Ilokano for several hours, wrote two letters in the early afternoon and then trimmed my beard – that took an hour, just to trim my beard. After I finished that I went and drank a couple beers with four guys from the Quirino Defense Department, Nestor, June, Wilfredo and Rudy – they, of course, want me to come to Cabarroguis and see them one day soon – everybody always does. On the way home from the People's Restaurant Ben Agpalasin stopped me at somebody's house and I had to stop for a while and talk and sing! Lito, my friend, came here in the evening to talk and be friendly. It's getting more to feeling like home here. I guess it's okay.

Wednesday, December 4, 1985
Mendoza's Store, Diffuncian, Burgos, Cabarroguis, Quirino

Letter to Bob S.

₱596 – 0 = ₱596

Today I actually did some work! I went with Vergilio and his family to the banana plantation – a long ways away – and I helped harvest bananas and banana blossoms. It rained all morning and continued until at least noon. We ate rice and tilapia for lunch at their rest hut and harvested about 2,000 bananas. On the way home we took a short bath in a stream – got dirty harvesting bananas and also going to the plantation and returning because the road was so muddy it was not possible to ride the water buffalo, it was too hard on the animal. We got home at about 3:00 PM or so and I wrote a quick letter to Bob S. Then it was about suppertime. The loggers who have been staying here returned today, apparently for the last of their stuff. Lito and his friend came by tonight, I don't know the name of the friend, I forgot it. Maybe it was Fernando. I'm tired tonight because of the long walk barefoot and more work than usual for me. Tomorrow I'm going with Lito to his other house on the mountain. Lito showed me a beautiful place to bathe today.

Thursday, December 5, 1985
Mendoza's Store, Diffuncian, Burgos, Cabarroguis, Quirino

₱596 – 40 = ₱556						
Beer	20	Snacks	20		TOTAL	₱40

I got up at 6:00 AM and went to bathe with Lito and Fernando at the beautiful waterfall that he showed me yesterday. Then we strolled to the mountain and the other house of Lito. We harvested some extremely spicy chili peppers and ate some Cheysa – an orange chalky fruit that sticks to your teeth very badly. We also went to the house of Lito's father and stayed there for a while and then we returned to Mendoza's store. There was lots of rain today. The loggers finished loading their stuff today and left for good. In the late afternoon I cleaned my room good and got more unpacked than I have yet been. Essentially that means that I got all of my books unpacked. This afternoon Lito and I went down to the People's Restaurant and drank a large San Miguel Beer. Tonight a faith healer is here at the house to help father with his shoulders. We'll see what happens I guess. I didn't write any letters today. My feet are kind of destroyed from all of my barefoot walking recently. I guess they'll continue to toughen up as time progresses. I hope so anyway!

Friday, December 6, 1985
Mendoza's Store, Diffuncian, Burgos, Cabarroguis, Quirino

Mail letters written over the past few days. Write letters to Chris M. & Nestor, but not mailed.

Letters from Nestor, Rebecca & Herbert, Bob S. and San & Jack. Also a *Newsweek* Magazine.

₱556 – 152 = ₱404							
Meat	35	Veggies	19	Coffee	18	Stamps	18
Mirror	8	Clothes	30	Coke	9	Notebook	2
Rides	13					TOTAL	₱152

Today I got up at 6:00 AM and my friend Lito and I went to the waterfall for bathing. Surprisingly, there was no rain today. After a while Lito and I went to the public market at Gundaway and bought all the stuff listed above. The short pants I bought are too small, but I can give them to somebody for Christmas or give them to Lito as a remembrance. We returned home at about 11:30 AM or so. The ride was quite literally hanging off the back of the jeepney. Got mail at the post office today – a letter from Nestor was the most valued, a letter from Rebecca and Herbert and the pouch with the *Newsweek*, plus letters from Bob S., and San & Jack. Jack is his usual old rambling self – always writes a lot without saying very much. Last night and tonight there's a faith healer here giving father a workout – I hope he doesn't mess him up. This afternoon I went to the waterfall bathing place and did some laundry; washed my shoes for the umpteenth time and also washed jeans, T-shirts, underwear, handkerchiefs and etc. Nestor writes the most beautiful letters – he is really a fine friend – because he is an Igorot?? I don't know. The letter from Rebecca is nice too. My letters from my Filipino friends mean more to me than the ones from my American friends. I was waiting for the letter from Nestor; I knew it would be worth waiting for. Should I send some of my American friends some of the Peace Corps T-shirts for Christmas? It's possible, but who specifically?

Saturday, December 7, 1985
Lito's House, Diffuncian, Burgos, Cabarroguis, Quirino

Write letters to Bayombong Family, San & Jack.

₱404 – 20 = ₱384							
Beer	20					TOTAL	₱20

I got up at the usual 6:00 AM and bathed at the waterfall with Lito. It was a pretty boring day really. I sat around and wrote a couple letters and studied some language. Lito cut grass in Rogel's banana plantation today, so he wasn't around to stroll with or talk to. In the late afternoon I went down to Ventura's Store and drank two San Miguel beers – regular size – and brought one large bottle home with me for Lito and I to drink later. Then, at about dark Lito returned from his work and as we were drinking the beer, Fernando showed up, so Lito, Fernando, father and I had only one beer to share. I went to Lito's house to sleep with him and Fernando tonight. My family thinks that I'm drunk! Oh well, such is life. [I was hoping for a sexual encounter, but no such luck.]

Sunday, December 8, 1985
Mendoza's Store, Diffuncian, Burgos, Cabarroguis, Quirino

Write letters to Ardis B., Bill J. and Dave M.

₱384 – 0 = ₱384

Today was a pretty slow day. I stayed at Lito's last night so this morning the family thought I was drunk! Weird! Anyway we got up at 6:00 AM and all went to the waterfall to bathe (Lito, Fernando and I). It rained really hard last so the stream was very high and muddy, nearly dangerous I'd say. Then after I returned home and ate breakfast I started the rest of the day. I went to the house of one of the family's sons to harvest a few coconuts and to stroll. I fell on my butt with a really resounding thud and it really hurt. The path was super slippery. I studied language for a few hours and helped Vergilio and Bicol at the fish pond a little bit. Then I searched for Lito to help him cut grass but I couldn't find him. I wrote a couple of letters this afternoon and also helped unload some bananas from the cart. It rained in the late afternoon and again in the evening. Lito has a headache tonight so I have no companion for sleeping. Maybe I'll write another letter.

Monday, December 9, 1985
Mendoza's Store, Diffuncian, Burgos, Cabarroguis, Quirino

Letters to Teresa L & Barb W.

₱384 + 300 – 53 = ₱631							
Post Office	26	Toiletries	19	Ride	5	Misc.	3
						TOTAL	₱53

I got up at the usual 6:00 AM and Lito and I went to the waterfall place to bathe. Then I went to Diffun and to the office. I mailed letters written over the past few days and mailed film to Chris M. for processing. There were Regional Office people at the office again today. Those Regional Office people are really a pain in the butt, if

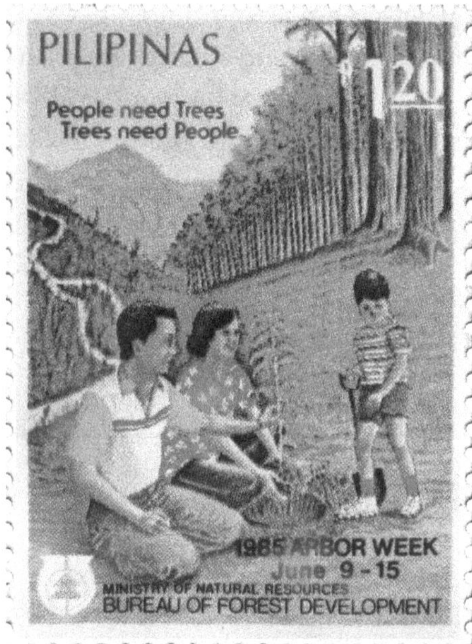

you ask me. Artemio was there again, as well as Francisco, Hoven, Edgar, Dado and Felix – everyone except Rody. So I left a note for Rody telling him that I want to see him again and to please come here soon. I actually kind of enjoyed the office a bit – but I enjoyed getting back home too. I got home at about 5:00 PM or so. Lito's girlfriend is at his house so no companion for me again tonight, that's why I wrote two letters.

I bought some of this stamp at the Post Office today, as you can see, it is a commemorative for Arbor Week and mentions the Ministry of Natural Resources Bureau of Forest Development. It was glued into my Journal notebook.

Tuesday, December 10, 1985
Host Family, Bonfal East, Bayombong, Nueva Vizcaya

Letters from Ronald & Peace Corps.

₱631 – 82 = ₱549							
Rides	12	Food	37	Coffee	16	Beer	17
						TOTAL	₱82

Today I went to the office in Diffun again. I was supposed to go to Magsaysay [I cannot recall why], but the river was so high that it was impossible to go there. Such is life! So I decided to go to Bayombong. I left the office about 1:30 PM and arrived in Bayombong at about 4:30 PM. I walked to the highway at 5:00 PM to meet Ronald – I met him when I was about halfway there. It is so good to see the family and good to see Ronald. Rebecca and Herbert are here today, it's good to see them all, but I wish I could see Ronald alone somehow to talk about how my life has been going. It's great to see the family anyway.

Wednesday, December 11, 1985
Host Family, Bonfal East, Bayombong, Nueva Vizcaya

₱549 – 24 = ₱525							
Beer	24					TOTAL	₱24

Today I got up late – at 6:30 AM. Ronald went to school and Herbert, father and I went fishing with electricity ALL DAY! I got a bit bored with the whole thing. Got home and the host mothers of both Mark and Chris were here and wanted to talk for too long! Ronald got home and it seems like he was trying to avoid me, I don't know. I don't understand, not a bit! He showed me two card tricks tonight. I have to leave early tomorrow so we went to bed early, at 9:00 PM. I'm only sorry that I cannot spend more time here. Maybe it's possible that I love my brother Ronald too much and I'm jealous – if so that's bad! I'm happy to be here anyway, this family loves me so much.

Thursday, December 12, 1985
David's House, Cordon, Isabela

₱525 – 33 = ₱492						
Beer	22	Rides	11		TOTAL	₱33

I got up at 5:00 AM today and left Bonfal East at 7:00 AM. Took a tricycle to Solano and then changed to the Vizcaya Liner to Cordon. I met David in Cordon at 9:30 AM for the Christmas party at the Magat Reforestation Project, which I found out did not start until 2:00 PM, so I left Bonfal East much earlier than I needed to. That made me angry is I really had to rush to get out of there early. Of course it was painful to leave again. When we got to Magat we found out that the Christmas party has been cancelled – such is life I guess! So, we strolled around Magat for a while. In the evening I went to David's house and it seemed like 50,000 people came by to ask me questions and accuse me of being rich. I got seriously frustrated with that. Again, such is life I guess, try to keep smiling. I stayed at David's house tonight.

Friday, December 13, 1985
Mendoza's Store, Diffuncian, Burgos, Cabarroguis, Quirino

Letter to Tony & Janet.
Letters from Steve A. & Chris M.

₱492 – 275 = ₱217							
Rides	20	Clothes	50	Food	47	Beer	8
Blanket	60	Lunch	26	Coffee	55	Misc.	9
						TOTAL	₱275

Today I got up at 5:30 AM at David's house in Cordon. I killed time until breakfast and bathed at the creek. After David's brothers went to the field, I went to Santiago and shopped and then went to Echange to get my mail. There was a package from Steve A., in fact two packages. There was a box of Bic pens and another box with only a 1986 calendar in it. Then I returned to Santiago and shopped for too many things, as can be seen above. I wrote a letter to Tony & Janet and mailed it from the Gundaway Post Office. At the post office there was a package from Chris M., the photos from the first two rolls of film, at least some of them. There are obviously some missing. I don't know what to do about this photo situation – it's frustrating to me. Diling's husband arrived tonight and spent the evening quizzing me. That gets me down.

Saturday, December 14, 1985
Mendoza's Store, Diffuncian, Burgos, Cabarroguis, Quirino

Letter to Chris M.

₱217 – 8 = ₱209							
Beer	5	Candy	3			TOTAL	₱8

Get up at 6:00 AM, bathe and do laundry in the stream and return for breakfast. Diling's husband spent the day quizzing me and I spent the day waiting for Nestor. He did not arrive until about 7:00 PM, but he did finally arrive and it's good to see him. Abe (Diling's husband) and I went to Dibibi at 4:30 PM and returned at about 6:30 PM., first time I've been to Dibibi. The people there seemed quite friendly. I got the words to the song "We Are the World" copied down today, by careful study of the tape. I don't believe how good I feel now that Nestor is here. He brought me three lukbans (pomelo) and some very spicy chili peppers!

Sunday, December 15, 1985
Mendoza's Store, Diffuncian, Burgos, Cabarroguis, Quirino

Letter to Steve A.

₱209 – 90 = ₱119							
Rides	30	Dog Meat	38	Food	22	TOTAL	₱90

It rained most of the night and most of the day. Got up kind of late at 6:30 AM or so and after a leisurely breakfast and waiting for the rain to stop, Nestor, Abe and I went to the beautiful bathing place at the waterfall. Then Nestor and I strolled to the nursery. There was nobody there, so I was able to show Nestor around in relative peace and quiet, as Abe did not insist on accompanying us. When we returned from there we got ready to go to Santiago and waited nearly 1.5 hours for a jeepney to come along. I got sick of Abe telling me how much he loves Chuck Norris movies and how great Rambo is and finally Nestor and I got to leave. Abe takes his gun everywhere he goes; he even took it to the bathing place this morning. Nestor and I arrived at Santiago at about 2:30 PM and went to the *Asucena* [dog meat restaurant] and had two bottles of beer each and some dog meat. We ate and we had some good talking time and firmed up our plan for me to go there for December 21st and 22nd and leave on the morning of the 23rd and then return there and stay from the 26th to January 1st. Today I told Nestor "I want you to come with me to America when I go home in 1987". He truly wants to and I'd like him to, but is it really possible, probably not, but if God permits, well we will see what happens! Who knows? We can only wish and hope.

Tonight Abe is gone to Manila, I'm happy he's gone! He drives me nuts with his habit of grinding his teeth and his two track mind – women and American movies. I wonder how long he will stay here. I've been writing in this notebook for two months now and it looks like it's about half full.

Monday, December 16, 1985
Mendoza's Store, Diffuncian, Burgos, Cabarroguis, Quirino

Letters to Bob S. and Tim & Peg S.

₱119 +5 = ₱124

I slept in until 6:30 this morning. It's REALLY COLD, it's 68°F (20°C). In addition to that, it's raining. I went to the stream and bathed despite the weather, it was nice because the water was warmer than the air. I didn't do much all morning, wrote a letter to Bob S. before lunch and studied and figured out what to give people for Christmas. At around 1:00 PM I went to Vergilio's house and after eating some rice cake, Bicol and I went to the special meeting to discuss the Christmas Party. That went on for three hours before it was finally over and we got to go home. Bicol is getting to be a pretty good friend now too; it's too bad he can't speak Ilokano [he was from somewhere else where they spoke a different dialect]. I'd really like to become his good friend. It seems that he's not ashamed to be seen with me, unlike Lito. I wore my blue Patagonia jacket all day today – that's how cold it was! It's still raining this evening. Before bed I'll write a letter to Tim and Peg S.

Tuesday, December 17, 1985
Mendoza's Store, Diffuncian, Burgos, Cabarroguis, Quirino

Letters to Nestor, Ronald and Dave G.

Got up late today – at 6:30 AM or so. It was cold again, same as yesterday – 68°F, but I bathed at the waterfall – alone – and got warmed up a little. I wrote the letters to Ronald and Nestor after breakfast and then I went to the nursery to have David tell me what's happening tomorrow and what the party will be like. I found out that I have to give an inspirational talk, so David helped me write it. Finally got done at about 4:30 PM and left the nursery for home. It was a pretty frustrating day – all I accomplished all day to better my future here was the speech for tomorrow. Lito and I talked for a bit in the evening. Our friendship does not seem like it's going anywhere. I wrote a letter to Dave G. before bed. I guess it was actually a pretty down letter. I sure wish I could make a good friend here.

Wednesday, December 18, 1985
Mendoza's Store, Diffuncian, Burgos, Cabarroguis, Quirino

₱124 – 25 = ₱99				
Beer	25			TOTAL ₱25

Today was the Christmas party at the nursery. Dado was supposed to be here at 7:30 AM, but of course he wasn't – so at about 8:00 AM father, Abe and I went (Abe returned at about 11:00 PM last night) – and I forgot, there were Christmas Carolers here at 2:30 this morning! I had to give my speech, of course, and sing Banbantay again. Some girl and I won one of the dance contests – a 7 in 1 – because they said I was best at the Ifugao dance. I also tried the sack race – very tiring! Met lots of new people, some good folks, some drunks. At around 3:00 PM we called it finished & I returned home. Then Lito, Rogel and I went to Ventura's Store for a couple of beers and then we managed to get trapped at the Peoples Restaurant by some drunks and they even came here to the house and continued to drink beer and *Ginebra* and due to that, I was forced to go to Lito's house to sleep. Those drinking people managed to piss me off really bad – they were really too drunk. I met a new friend today – Robert.

Thursday, December 19, 1985
Mendoza's Store, Diffuncian, Burgos, Cabarroguis, Quirino

Letters to Health Unit & Brooke F. Letters from Bob S., three from Ardis B., Terry S., Vicki K., Dave & Vicki, Linda S., and San & Jack. Also got two *Newsweek* Magazines.

₱99 – 0 = ₱99

Today I was up at the usual 6:00 AM and I returned home from Lito's. Lito has had a bad cold all week so there has been no companion for me to bathe with at the waterfall. The drunks from last night left this morning. I got all kinds of mail today and spent half the morning reading it and trying to keep it away from Abe and the others here. Both *Newsweek* Magazines have cover stories about the Philippines and the problems that are happening here right now. Dad is probably worried sick. [People Power Revolution, the downfall of President Ferdinand E. Marcos, and the accession of Corazon C. Aquino as President.] It was difficult to escape from Abe today, to say the least. This evening I went to the house of Lito for talking and gave him a deck of cards for Christmas. He was happy. Then he cooked a chicken for supper. Maybe Lito is a better friend than I have previously thought. Tomorrow I leave until January 2nd!

Friday, December 20, 1985
Nestor's House, Villa Miemban, Cordon, Isabela

₱99 + 600 – 87 = ₱612

Rides	37	Beer	25	Coffee	25	TOTAL	₱87

Today David was supposed to come to the house at 7:00 AM, but as he was still not there at 8:00 AM I left, walking to Ventura's Store for a ride, Of course Abe had to tag along, so he went on to Santiago. Today was the Christmas Party at the Diffun Office and I got there at about 9:15 AM. Of course people tried to get me to drink *Ginebra* – I refused of course. I had Ramel go and get two large bottles of San Miguel beer instead. There was lots of food and it was delicious; noodles, chicken, pork and more – too much, too delicious. I escaped the party at about 2:30 PM and got to Cordon at about 3:00 PM and headed for Nestor's house. I took a jeepney to the Vulcan turnoff, then finally, at around 4:00 PM a tricycle came along and I got a ride to Vulcan. I had to walk from Vulcan and it was 5:15 PM and nearly dark when I got to the mountain top. It was pretty crazy to be walking in the dark, but dark it was so I had no choice. So, I was stumbling along the path to Villa Miemban in the dark, of course it was raining and that meant that the path was slippery. Surprisingly I only fell down one time. I feel lucky about that, I could have fallen and broken my leg if I was unlucky. I had to walk very slowly and carefully. I got to Nestor's house at about 6:40 PM, and they fed me, of course. We talked for a while and soon the Barangay Captain came along and we talked with him for an hour or so. We didn't get to bed until 9:00 PM or thereabouts. It feels so good to be here at Nestor's again I. I gave him the letter that I wrote a couple of days ago but had not yet mailed.

Saturday, December 21, 1985
Nestor's House, Villa Miemban, Cordon, Isabela

₱612 – 0 = ₱612

Got up at 6:00 AM or so. Ate breakfast and did yesterday's journal entry and then Nestor and I went to the stream and bathed, washed dishes and took the water buffalos to pasture. It's really cold and windy today. I didn't bring a jacket with me and I'm sorry! After a while we went to fetch some water, but the spring fed water getting place was quite dirty, so we cleaned it out. Then while waiting for it to refill with water we strolled for a while and Nestor showed me more of their land and their fishpond. Conrado came by in the early afternoon and we played the guitar for a while and talked. Then Rufino came by in the late afternoon and we talked with him for a while. We didn't do a whole lot today except talk with people and stroll around and build our friendship even more. It makes my heart feel good to be with Nestor. When I am with him I want to stay here forever. When I'm at Burgos I just want to go home. We talked for the first time about both going to America in 1987 and making charcoal and getting rich and then returning here in 1990 or so and going into farming as partners. Could it be a possibility? Maybe!

Sunday, December 22, 1985
Nestor's House, Villa Miemban, Cordon, Isabela

Letter to Steve A. asking for chain saw information.

₱612 – 0 = ₱612

Got up this morning and after a while Nestor and his brother and I went fishing with the electricity to a beautiful place that I hadn't been to before. We got lots and lots of fish – filled up the basket with fish. We also got some big frogs. We returned to the house at 2:00 PM or so and ate lunch. By and by we did some laundry and bathed. In the evening Nestor cooked supper. I feel like I sure don't do much to help out here. I wrote a letter to Steve A. asking for chainsaw information for Nestor; he wants to know if they are significantly cheaper in the USA. I have to leave tomorrow. There's some doubt in my mind as to whether I should stay here for a whole week – that's an awful lot to ask of Nestor it seems. I guess I will return here on the 26th because I've already said that I will, I certainly can't go back on my word.

Monday, December 23, 1985
Host Family, Bonfal East, Bayombong, Nueva Vizcaya

₱612 + 1,119 – 602 = ₱1,129							
Rides	10	Postage	13	Aerogrammes	42	Calculator	256
Food	101	Beer	15	Coffee	56	Calendar	22
Short Pants	35	Lunch	32	Misc.	20	TOTAL	₱602

Today I got up kind of late and after making my journal entry for yesterday and eating breakfast, Rufino returned Nestor's guitar. Then after a while, one of Nestor's older brothers returned home. He checked the price of chainsaws in Manila to see how they compared to the prices in Santiago. The price is the same in Manila, that's hard to believe! At 8:40 AM I started walking for the river. I got there at about 9:15 AM and the Omega Lumber Truck was unloading bags of cement, so I helped with that and they gave me a ride to Cordon. I got to Santiago about 10:30 AM, not bad. I shopped for Christmas presents and went to the bank. I left Santiago at about 1:30 PM and arrived at Bonfal East at 3:30 PM. It was good to see the family again. Herbert is here too. Rebecca had her baby!

Tuesday, December 24, 1985
Host Family, Bonfal East, Bayombong, Nueva Vizcaya

₱1,129 – 7 = ₱1,122							
Coke	7					TOTAL	₱7

Today we all got up at 5:00 AM and we butchered a pig. Then we ate cooked pork and drank beer until noon. By that time we were all pretty drunk! Herbert left and I crashed out until 4:00 PM. Then I had nothing to do; I'm kind of homesick and I feel like Ronald is ashamed to be seen with me. Right now I can't see any reason to come here again for a long time. I'm really disappointed in the way today went. At 8:00 PM we went to the Bonfal East Christmas Party and stayed there until about midnight. Then we returned home and I gave my gifts to everybody and then to bed. I've got a headache and a sore foot and feel like shit on a stick right now.

Wednesday, December 25, 1985
Host Family, Bonfal East, Bayombong, Nueva Vizcaya

₱1,122 – 15 = ₱1,107							
Beer	15					TOTAL	₱15

We got up late because we went to bed late. At 9:00 or 10:00 AM Ronald and I went to Herbert's house and we saw Rebecca and the new baby. It was good to see Rebecca again. I gave them my Christmas presents. This afternoon we went to the vegetable farm and worked a little bit. Ronald talked to me about all of the different types of bananas that they have and we harvested some beans. We returned to the house at dark. Herbert and Rebecca came and Rebecca cried hard all during supper – WHY? I have no idea. I spent my evening outdoors to get away from it. At this point I don't really care very much if I'm culturally insensitive or culturally sensitive. I thought this would be a really happy Christmas Season but, to the contrary, the three days I've been here have been rather disappointing. The family has done an awful lot for me, but I feel alienated, out of place, like a man without a home or friends. It's been quite a bummer all in all, but it shouldn't be. Maybe it's just that time of the year to feel lonely – Christmas away from the people, places and things we know.

Thursday, December 26, 1985
Nestor's House, Villa Miemban, Cordon, Isabela

₱1,107 – 197 = ₱910							
Rides	11	Lunch	31	Food	65	Beer	30
Coffee, etc.	60					TOTAL	₱197

Today it was really, really cold when we got up late at 6:30 AM. We ate breakfast and after it warmed up a bit I bathed. Then I left Bonfal East at 8:40 AM. There were few jeepneys, but many people so I had to hang on the back of one all the way from Solano to Santiago. I spent an hour or so in Santiago buying the above and then took a jeepney to Kakilingan. Begin to walk to Vulcan and a tricycle came by, so I took a ride. Then walk from Vulcan to Kakandongan and just before I arrived there, Donny came by, so I rode the rest of the way with him. Then hike to Villa Miemban and made it on only 40 minutes today (from the river to Nestor's house). It was good to arrive here again. Nestor, JB and Katie were at the deer man's house [a man who had a deer as a pet] and I did not know where that was, so I took a stroll to the place where I knew Nestor was making charcoal. He had another batch going. After supper and talking, Nestor and I strolled to JB & Katie's house and Katie made some Christmas fudge and eggnog. It was good to talk with JB and Katie. Again, I say that I like it here and that I often end up writing more than a single journal page when I am here because we do so much.

Friday, December 27, 1985
Nestor's House, Villa Miemban, Cordon, Isabela

₱910 – 0 = ₱910

We got up late, about 6:30 AM. We ate breakfast and then we went out and hunted birds for a while and then we went to Nestor's brother's place and his rice field, where we harvested some rice with a small knife. It was hot! I found that the easiest way was to remove my glasses, because sweat was running down my face so bad that I couldn't see through them. At about 10:30 AM or so it got too hot to work even for them and we returned to the house to relax until later in the day when it cooled off. After lunch we slept for an hour or so to – a short rest. Then we got up and went back to the rice field to finish the rice harvest. When finished, we removed the rice from the stalks and after that, we went to a beautiful bathing place. When we returned from bathing JB met us and we went and looked at his little garden. We got back to Nestor's house at dark. Nestor is cooking supper now and I am doing this early because tomorrow morning we're heading to Santiago rather early.

Saturday, December 28, 1985
Nestor's House, Villa Miemban, Cordon, Isabela

₱910 – 55 = ₱855							
Rides	10	Beer	10	Food	15	Misc.	20
						TOTAL	₱55

We got up at 5:20 AM and got ready to go to Santiago. We left the house at 6:20 AM and got to Kakandongan at about 7:00 AM. There was no ride until about 7:30 AM so we got to Santiago about 8:30 or 9:00 AM. It was Nestor, 1 brother and I. We sold some narra wood and then we went to purchase some tin roofing for Nestor's house. We ended up going to two other lumber yards before we found the right price, but after waiting until noon we found that they would not deliver. We went to yet another lumber yard that they thought sure would deliver it, but they also would not agree to do so. We bought it there anyway and put it on Donnie's jeepney to bring to Kakandongan. Donnie charged us ₱100 to put it on the jeepney. We finally got to Kakandongan at 4:00 PM or so and loaded the tin roofing on the water buffalo cart and headed off into the sunset. After having to retie the ropes about four times we finally got it figured out – how to tie it so that we did not have to do it again. We got to Nestor's house about 5:30 PM, about dark. We were very tired and hungry. We walked a lot today and worked little – only mental work with the Ilokano and Igorot languages. I don't know why, but the family is speaking primarily Igorot today. At around 8:00 PM everybody except father went off to a wedding. I am just too tired and it rained a good deal today, so I know that the trail is pretty muddy, slippery and miserable. I feel a little bad about not going, after all this is one of the reasons I came here – but I am just TOO TIRED! Everybody else is too, but they are sacrificing anyway. I am so tired that at this point things are starting to spin in front of my eyes, and it's only 8:05 PM. Can you believe it? Such is life I guess.

Sunday, December 29, 1985
Nestor's House, Villa Miemban, Cordon, Isabela

₱855 – 0 = ₱855

As I said yesterday, everybody went to the wedding last night. Nestor did not return until nearly 10:00 AM this morning or so. The rest of us slept in until 7:00 AM this morning. I attempted to go and fetch water, but father would not let me and he went to do it himself. I did some laundry and bathed in the stream while waiting for Nestor to get home today. JB, Katie, Clarita and Celia stopped by for a while and I got to speak with Clarita about some of the problems at Burgos and told her that Francisco is not much help to me. We took a rest in the afternoon because everybody was up all night at the wedding. We got up and went and harvested bitwela's [a kind of fruit] and then Nestor and I prepared them and cooked some *pancit* [a kind of noodles] and had *pancit* and bitwela's for a snack. I'm beginning to feel like I make things difficult for the family here – maybe staying for a whole week is not the best thing I have ever done. I know it would be easier for them if I was not here. I'm happy here, but I'm a burden on the family too. I ate *langka* and *guyabano* fruit for the first time today.

Monday, December 30, 1985
Nestor's House, Villa Miemban, Cordon, Isabela

₱855 – 20 = ₱835							
Ginebra	10	Coke	5	Bread	5	TOTAL	₱20

Today we got up and the first thing we did was butcher the dog. They stuck the jugular vein and bled it out, trying to keep the dog calm while it was bleeding to death [a dog that dies calmly is supposedly tastier than one that dies in a panic]. I led the black and white dog to the butcher block and helped tie its legs and then helped hold it while Nestor stuck its throat. After bleeding it out, we built a fire and burned the hair off. I was surprised how difficult it was to burn off the fur or hair of the dog; it took a long time and a great deal of brushing off of the hair that was already burned.

After the hair was adequately burned off, we went to the stream and thoroughly washed the skin and then Nestor and Diego peeled off the skin. The skin is one of the dishes which is eaten as *kilowen ti aso* [skin of dog]. After the skin was peeled off we butchered the rest of the animal, including ALL parts! Then we brought the cleaned meat to the house and started cutting it up. I helped cut up the skin, intestines, liver and etc. By 1:00 PM we had it all cut up and we were eating an advance New Year's meal. The reason we did that was because Nestor's sister, Shelia, had to leave this afternoon. After eating and relaxing for a while Nestor and I accompanied Shelia to Vulcan and said our goodbyes to her. Then we immediately turned around and returned here to the house. By the time we got to the house it was pretty much dark. We bathed and then we ate some more dog meat for dinner, including *dinar daraan* [dog meat cooked in the dog blood]. We also ate the head. Nestor and I talked for a while before bed and I thanked him for letting me accompany him and his sister to Vulcan, and he thanked me for going along with them, saying that it meant a lot to his sister, and therefore to him. There are still times when I don't know if I do the right thing or the wrong thing, I try my best! I'm tired; I'll be able to sleep easily.

Tuesday, December 31, 1985
Nestor's House, Villa Miemban, Cordon, Isabela

The last day of 1985! Rufino came by at about 10:00 AM and stayed until 2:00 or 3:00 PM. We listened to tapes and I found out that we're supposed to party all night again tonight. Too much time to think again today. We rested only about 15 minutes and nobody could sleep so we got up again. We washed lots of dishes, got all of the ash off the bottom of all of the cauldrons, took a bath, polished the floor and then cooked again. Then after a short time, we went off to the party at the barrio hall. It wasn't too exciting – had to do the Ifugao dance again but there was only one g-string so JB and I didn't have to get dressed up, only dance. At midnight we did a countdown and said "Happy New Year." At around 1:00 AM we returned home and Nestor immediately disappeared, back to the party I guess. After two hours he came back home with four or five girls and I told him that this is an example of when a guy tells you "fuck you, man!" He only said that he was going to go to the toilet and then he ran away back to the party – I really don't understand why he could not have just told me that he was going to do so – afraid that I would want to tag along with him maybe? He asked me if there were any bad feelings and I said "yes, there are" and I went back to bed. He lied to me and I feel bad about. So, I crashed feeling bad and with bad feelings between us. I didn't sleep much as Nestor and the girls cooked all night and played the tape deck, making lots of noise. Such is life I guess.

Wednesday, January 1, 1986
Nestor's House, Villa Miemban, Cordon, Isabela

HAPPY NEW YEAR!

[NARAGSAK NGA BARU NGA TAWEN!]

Well, I left off yesterday with lots of cooking. We got up this morning and there were lots of people here, lots of rice cake, macaroni and fruit salads, noodles and etc. Rufino came over early and the four girls who helped Nestor cook all night were here. I escaped and took a walk to the top of the trail and when I was about half way back, father was there searching for me. I don't really know why. I didn't say where I was going, I just escaped. We returned and ate breakfast then we all went to the house of Diego's father-in-law where we talked a while, slept a while, ate a big lunch of dog meat and chicken and drank a bottle of *Ginebra.* Then we slept again. After a while we got up and returned home, where we ate again and slept again. Then we got up again and JB and Katie came here and after some more talking and drinking of rice wine JB and Katie left. It was good to have JB and Katie visit for a while. Rufino stayed the night. We all went to bed after JB and Katie left. I get this feeling of coldness from Nestor this evening, maybe because of my cultural faux-pas of not saying where I was going before I went on my hike, but I'm not sure. Maybe a week was (is) too long to stay and I have killed a part of something that was between us. I don't know; I just know that something between us is not the same.

Thursday, January 2, 1986
Mendoza's Store, Diffuncian, Burgos, Cabarroguis, Quirino

Letters from Vicki S., Ardis B., Family in Bonfal East, Tom H. and Tom L.
Postcards from Dave G., Ardis B. and Brooke F.

₱835 – 226 = ₱609							
Rides	20	Lunch	51	Coffee	35	Toilet Paper	20
Food	55	Fruit	30	Slippers	15	TOTAL	₱226

Today I got up at 6:00 AM at Nestor's. Rufino was here too. After a while Rufino went home and we got ready to go to town. At about 7:30 AM we were ready and Rufino and JB had returned so we all walked to the river together. JB and Rufino were going to work on the bridge. We got to Kakandongan and people said that the jeepney would return immediately. Nestor and I agreed to wait until 10:00 AM. The jeepney was not back at 10:00 AM so we started to walk. We made it halfway to Vulcan and the jeepney passed us going to the river so we finished walking to Vulcan and waited for it there. Nestor and I had a good long talk at Vulcan – it was good. Then we rode to Santiago and ate lunch and drank too large San Miguel beers and talked some more – a real good talk. We talked for two hours! Then at 2:00 PM we headed off to market, did some shopping, as shown above, and at 3:00 PM or so Nestor put me on the jeepney for home with two beautiful lukbans – one of which is the absolute biggest I've ever seen. I got home at about 4:00 PM or so and it was good to be home.

Abe is not here, thankfully! I talked with Diling for a while and I got mail. In the evening Lito and his friend Bicol came over to talk. It was good to see them all again and talk about Christmas, New Years and etc. I need to write a letter to Ardis B. tomorrow – her letter says she will visit here – arriving on February 4th or 5th.

Friday, January 3, 1986
Mendoza's Store, Diffuncian, Burgos, Cabarroguis, Quirino

Letter to Ardis B. explaining how to get here.

₱609 – 55 = ₱554							
Rides	10	Rope	1	Toiletries	14	Stamps	12
Food	2	Beer	16			TOTAL	₱55

Got up late, at 6:30 AM. Bathe in the stream, eat breakfast and write the letter to Ardis. Then go to the office in Diffun. Oh, I stopped at the post office and market in Gundaway first, and then continued on to the office. Francisco was not there, nor was Mr. Romero. Such is life. I strolled in Diffun and drank beer with Dado, Boy and one more person. Then we went Boy's brother-in-laws house for lunch and also the post office there to buy some stamps. Then we went back to the office and I wrote a note for Francisco then returned home. Abe is here again – SHIT! And, he's following me everywhere again! Damn it! So, I ate supper at Lito's house and spent the evening there and, believe it or not, Abe even showed up there after a while. So, at around 8:30 PM I returned home, did this journal entry and slept.

Saturday, January 4, 1986
Mendoza's Store, Diffuncian, Burgos, Cabarroguis, Quirino

Letters to Terry S., Tom L., Vicki K. & Bill N.

I got up at 6:30 AM or so and then bathed and ate breakfast and studied for a while. I made a battery holder for four batteries for the tape recorder/player and it also works for the radio. I made it out of bamboo. Then I washed some clothes in the stream and then returned home to eat lunch. In the afternoon I wrote the letters shown above and after a while my brother and best friend Ronald came for a visit – surprise. We strolled to the nursery – David and Rose were not there so we returned here. It rained today for the first time in several days. After a while the rain stopped and we strolled to the rice paddy and the fish pond. It was the first time I'd been to the rice paddy – Ronald inspired me to go I guess. I'm really surprised and I'm also very happy that he came to visit, even if maybe it's mostly just for a blow job. It's really good to see him. Mother sent a letter with him too! I'm very happy today – primarily because Ronald came here to visit.

Sunday, January 5, 1986
Mendoza's Store, Diffuncian, Burgos, Cabarroguis, Quirino

Letters to Tom H., Dave M. and start letter to Ardis B.

₱554 – 166 = ₱388							
Ronald	50	Ride	6	Food	64	Laundry	35
Misc.	11					TOTAL	₱166

Today Ronald and I got up late – at 6:30 AM or so and after doing toilet stuff and so on I took him to the beautiful bathing place – he was impressed! We returned here and ate breakfast and got ready to go. At about 8:30 AM we left and went to Gundaway, where I bought the above and Ronald took a jeepney headed towards Bayombong. His midterm exams are next week and he has some serious studying to do. I returned home after a while and wrote a couple of letters and then strolled to Lito's house, talked for a while, and somehow it got to be suppertime and I returned home. After supper it was rainy and cold so I retired upstairs to study the dictionary for a while, write this journal and listen to a couple of tapes. I got my homemade battery pack all rigged up and it works very well. It sure was nice that Ronald came yesterday. What a pleasant surprise.

Monday, January 6, 1986
Mendoza's Store, Diffuncian, Burgos, Cabarroguis, Quirino

Letters to Nestor and Bayombong Family.

Today I slept in until 6:30 AM. It was so cool today that I waited until after breakfast to bathe. Time passed slowly until 10:30 AM or so when I went to the Barangay Captain's house for lunch because today is Three Kings Day. His 21 year old son and I really took to each other. He is a student of Animal Science at NVSIT in Bayombong and his name is Jody. We all drank together and they wanted me to stay and sleep with Jody for the night but I could not [I cannot remember why]. He said that he'll come to my house on Saturday. I got a haircut today too so when I returned home I bathed again because of the short hairs on my neck. I spent some time at Lito's house and then returned home at dark. Abe returned tonight too – SHIT! Well, I feel like sleeping now

Tuesday, January 7, 1986
Mendoza's Store, Diffuncian, Burgos, Cabarroguis, Quirino

Letters to Health Unit, Bob S. & Chris M.
Letters from Yip Chee Hong, Bob S., Rolando Treejano and a note from JB.

₱388 + 373 – 235 = ₱526

Rides	30	Blanket	150	Postage	4	Toilet Paper	30
Candy	16	Beer	5			TOTAL	₱235

I got up at 6:30 AM. Rody is not here so I went to Santiago, got the pouch and then went to Echange to take the mail there and also to check my mail – there was none. I ate lunch there – rabbit meat and so on. After that I went to market and then finally I went to the office in Diffun. I don't know why, but I'm not feeling very good today. Rody and I will go to Gomez and stay there Thursday and Friday. I had hoped to be there all week but, such is life, two days is better than no days at all. I saw Bill S. at Echange.

Wednesday, January 8, 1986
Rody's House, Sinsayon, Isabela

₱526 – 74 = ₱452							
Rides	10	Lunch	25	Coffee	24	Cigarettes	10
Misc.	5					TOTAL	₱74

I got up at 6:30 AM, ate breakfast, bathed and then took a jeepney into Santiago. I cashed a check and got a present and went to Rody Cabayan's. He celebrated his son's birthday with dog meat and we drank beer all day with many people. Francisco stopped by at around 5:00 PM for a few minutes. I'm pretty darn drunk, so I'm doing this in a stupor and sleeping at 7:30 PM. If I'm lucky maybe one of the cute guest guys will come and sleep beside me and want to play around [did not happen].

Thursday, January 9, 1986
Barangay Captain's House, Gomez, Cabarroguis, Quirino

₱452 – 15 = ₱437							
Sardines	15					TOTAL	₱15

I got up at 6:00 AM, ate breakfast, met several of Rody's cousins, bathed and then at about 9:00 AM we left for Gomez. When we got to Diffun, Cory Aquino was giving a speech there. We didn't stop but there was a big crowd gathered at the municipal hall area. We finally got to the Gomez Junction at about 10:15 AM or so and walked to the house of the vice president of GUFA (Gomez Upland Farmers Association) – Dominador Deguzman. We got there at about 11:15 AM so we stayed there for lunch. We then went to the house of the Barangay Captain, Steven Natividad for coffee. From there we went to several houses and talked for a while at each house. Just before dark we returned to the house of the Barangay Captain to eat and sleep here for the night. It's cold here!

Friday, January 10, 1986
Mendoza's Store, Diffuncian, Burgos, Cabarroguis, Quirino

Letter to Nestor.

₱437 – 3 = ₱434							
Rides	3					TOTAL	₱3

We got up at 6:00 AM and ate breakfast. It was very cold so I didn't bathe today. We talked at the Barangay Captain's house until 9:30 AM and finally got going. We got as far as the Barangay Secretary's house and had to drink coffee again, then he went with us and we made it as far as the canteen – where they butchered a dog for me – I helped a little bit. Many people were there and we ate dog meat and drank *Ginebra* until 2:30 PM when we left. I got Rody to show me the nursery site [for agricultural type trees] and by then it was raining so we headed for home. I went as far as Gundaway with Rody to check the mail – no mail today. Then I returned home to Burgos. Gomez is a really friendly place. It's pleasant there. I suppose I'll most likely be transferring there, hopefully soon.

Saturday, January 11, 1986
Mendoza's Store, Diffuncian, Burgos, Cabarroguis, Quirino

Letters to Rolando and San & Jack G.

₱434 – 55 = ₱379							
Loan	25	Beer	21	Cigarettes	5	Snacks	4
						TOTAL	₱55

I got up late again, at 6:30 AM or so. It was cold today so I waited until after breakfast and a while longer before going to the creek to bathe. I also washed a bunch of clothes and that's about all I did all day. Oh, I got out my American Express pocket diary for 1985 and brought up to date. I also bought my first pack of cigarettes – bad news – have to quit before I get started! I hope it's not too late. In the late afternoon I went to Ventura's Store and had a beer. I also bought a Grande home with me, but didn't drink it.

Sunday, January 12, 1986
Mendoza's Store, Diffuncian, Burgos, Cabarroguis, Quirino

Letters to Herbert & Rebecca, Linda S. and JB & Katie F.

₱379 + 25 – 30 = ₱374							
Beer	20	Cigarettes	10			TOTAL	₱30

I got up very late today and it was so cold that I did not bathe. Eat breakfast and drink coffee. I did very little today. I wrote the letters to Rebecca and Herbert and Linda and in the afternoon I went to Vergilio's house and by and by Bicol (Esagani) and I went to Ventura's Store and bought the beer accounted for above. We took it back to Vergilio's house and drank it and then after a while a bunch of people collected there – one of them drunk, which made things difficult because he wanted to talk to me exclusively. Finally he left and Esagani and I picked a couple of lukbans and we ate them and then I came home. It's only 6:30 PM now so I'll probably write one more letter. Esagani says he will sleep here tonight – we'll see if he returns. I actually don't know whether to expect to him or not. It rained all day today. Esagani DID return and sleep here.

Monday, January 13, 1986
Mendoza's Store, Diffuncian, Burgos, Cabarroguis, Quirino

Letter to Ronald.

₱374 – 44 = ₱330							
Beer	11	Rides	10	Stamps	12	Misc.	11
						TOTAL	₱44

I got up at 6:30 AM, bathed and ate breakfast and then got ready to go to the office in Diffun. There were no jeepneys so I had to walk to the sawmill at 9:30 AM and then I finally arrived at the office at 11:00 AM or so. Talk with Francisco about Gomez and then eat lunch and go to the post office to mail letters from the last few days. In the afternoon I talk to Mr. Romero about transferring to Gomez. Rody and I will go to Gomez again Wednesday Thursday and Friday and try to find a host family and I'll probably move to Gomez next Monday. I stopped at the post office in Gundaway on the way home and learned that the truck that delivers the mail is broke down and no mail has been delivered in a week now. Then I returned home. Esagani is here tonight – study and talk together and now we're going to sleep together.

Tuesday, January 14, 1986
Mendoza's Store, Diffuncian, Burgos, Cabarroguis, Quirino

Letters to Brooke F., Nido and Ardis B.

₱330 – 5 = ₱325							
Cigarettes	5					TOTAL	₱5

I got up very late, at 7:00 AM. It was cold! I ate breakfast and socialized until 10:00 AM and then went to the waterfall and bathed. Upon returning I wrote a letter to Brooke F. about the impending transfer to Gomez and to Nido to inform him of the upcoming address change. I took a three hour siesta in the afternoon and probably won't be able to sleep tonight. When I woke up Lito had returned so we went to his place and talked for a while and then I returned to the house to eat supper. After a while Lito and Dominador came here and we drank the beer I bought the other day. That about wraps up this uneventful day. For the first time in several days there was some sun this afternoon, but by late afternoon it had clouded up again. Many people were here today and therefore I had to do lots of socializing.

Wednesday, January 15, 1986
Lito's House, Gomez, Cabarroguis, Quirino

₱325 – 20 = ₱305							
Cigarettes	5	Ginebra	15			TOTAL	₱20

I got up at 6:30 AM and it was cold again so I waited until after breakfast to bathe. Then I got ready to go to Gomez again. I met Rody at the road junction to Gomez at 10:40 AM and we walked to Gomez. We arrived there at lunchtime and ate at the house of the Barangay Secretary. Lito Mercado was there and we arranged that I will probably live at his house until completion of the bunkhouse. After lunch we strolled to Lito's house and spent a while there. After that, we went to the house of the teacher, the Barangay Treasurer and a few other places until we ended up at a place drinking *Ginebra* and smoking cigarettes. After a while we returned to Lito's house where they butchered another dog for me. Lots of people came there, including some nice people whom I want for brothers. Went to bed late, after eating much dog and drinking lots of *Ginebra* – about 10:00 or 10:30 PM probably. I decided that I will live at Lito's house when I move here.

Thursday, January 16, 1986
Mendoza's Store, Diffuncian, Burgos, Cabarroguis, Quirino

Letters to Dave G. and Yip Chee Hong.

₱305 – 15 = ₱290							
Cigarettes	10	Beer	5			TOTAL	₱15

Get up at 6:30 AM at Lito's house with Rody. After a while, four of us went for a stroll to lots of different places. We ended up at a place for lunch that I don't remember the name of the guy, but anyway we all ate there. Over the course of the day it was decided that Rody will come here to Mendoza's on Monday at about 10:00 AM or so and we'll take all my stuff to the junction where Rufo Tobias – the Barangay Secretary – will meet us at about noon and I'll make my move to Gomez. Now the hard part is tell the people here that I'll be moving on to Gomez. Mr. Romero said to just tell the people here that I'll be going there to help for a couple of months. Of course he is correct. I don't have any really close friends here so I won't be shedding any tears over leaving; that's one good thing. The people of Gomez seem to be very happy to have me coming to live and work there. I hope I'll be happier and more industrious there than I have ever been here.

Friday, January 17, 1986
Mendoza's Store, Diffuncian, Burgos, Cabarroguis, Quirino

I received 17 letters today. Bob S. – 2, Ardis B – 2, Chris M – 2, Cynthia B. – 2, Terry S., Steve A., Barb W., Bill N., Brooke F., Roselynn, San & Jack G., Nido, Les F. and a package from the Health Unit.

₱290 + 375 – 328 = ₱337							
Rides	26	Cigarettes	16	Toiletries	28	Lunch	30
Food	150	Veggies	20	Aerogrammes	58	TOTAL	₱328

I got up late today – at 6:30 AM. Ate breakfast and bathed and then got ready to go to Santiago. I mailed letters from the last few days there, ate lunch and then went to Echange. I had no mail there. Then I went to Gundaway and had several pieces of mail and finally a package from the health unit. Then I returned home and read my mail, at this point I know that there is mail missing – I know for certain. Maybe it is down below at the same place as it was once before, I'll check tomorrow or Sunday. It is frustrating to know that there's mail missing. Esagani is here again tonight to sleep with me.

Saturday, January 18, 1986
Mendoza's Store, Diffuncian, Burgos, Cabarroguis, Quirino

Letters to Chris M. and Bob S.

₱337 – 12 = ₱325							
Beer	5	Cigarettes	7			TOTAL	₱12

I got up at 6:30 AM and it was only 66°F this morning. Therefore I waited until later to bathe. Then before lunch I also washed clothes from the last week. I ate lunch and after lunch I went to the place where I thought my mail might be, but there was none – or so they say anyway. I don't know, there might or might not be! I stopped at Ventura's Store for a beer and there were a bunch of people there, so they were happy that I drank with them for a while, but I only drank one beer and then returned home. I strolled around to various places in the afternoon. Dominador went to Diffun to harvest rice. Esagani has gone to the place where they're making charcoal for the night. There were lots of people around here today. I also packed for the move to Gomez – and I'm nearly done except for the stuff which I will need for tomorrow. There are a bunch of aspirin moochers here today it seems, why, I wonder?

Sunday, January 19, 1986
Mendoza's Store, Diffuncian, Burgos, Cabarroguis, Quirino

Letters to Ardis B., Fred & Cynthia B. and Barb W.

₱325 – 10 = ₱315			
Cigarettes 10			TOTAL ₱10

I got up at 6:00 AM and it was 62°F this morning – the coldest I've seen yet. I wrote the first two letters above before I bathed. The old man went with me and insisted, of course, that we go to another place and not the waterfall. He took me to the muddy place where I went the first couple days I was here. Tomorrow I guess I'll have to go early again if I want to go to the waterfall. I finished packing my things today – at least everything that can be packed now. After lunch Esagani and I went to the place where they are making charcoal. It is close to a creek. I spent most of the afternoon there with Esagani, Gilacio and his wife and Danny Boy. I returned here at 5:00 PM or so and ate supper and then everybody except the old man and I went to Vergilio's. I think his wife is in labor. I guess I'll know for sure tomorrow if there's a new baby there, otherwise I'll never know. There is no doctor, only a midwife. Now I guess I'll write a letter or two, it's my last night here and I have nobody to sleep with tonight. Oh well, I have not had a sex partner other than my hand since I've been here. Hopefully things will be better at Gomez.

Chapter 8
Culture Notes #2

Site Transfer

I approached my BFD supervisor, a Filipino, with thoughts about a site change. My supervisor understood perfectly, and being a Seventh Day Adventist himself, he referred to the Church of Christ as "Iglesia ni tokak" or "Church of frogs" (see Culture Notes #1.) He encouraged a site change if that was what it would take for me to be able to be effective. He assigned a different BFD technician to accompany me to another village for purposes of evaluating it as a possible new work site. My new co-worker took me to the village of Gomez. Gomez is two miles off the road, behind the mountain from Burgos. On the first visit the community members of Gomez received me with open arms and enthusiasm. Gomez was (probably still is) a subsistence farming community of about 80 families spread out over 600 hectares (about 1,500 acres). At a later time I noted that "there are only two paying jobs in Gomez, the school teacher and the Peace Corps Volunteer." These people were just barely members of the cash society. They sold their excess fruit and vegetable crops at the bottom of the mountain for cash, and then immediately "traded" the cash for rice, clothing, or other necessities. On my first visit to Gomez the people butchered a dog for me and made me feel welcome and wanted. They made me feel warmer and more welcome than I had felt in my two months at Burgos, where the people had never even butchered a chicken for me. The average family in Gomez earned $500 or less per year from the sale of their farm products, so I anticipated no problems with alcoholics. There were, likewise no churches in the village so no problems could be foreseen in the area of religion either. My co-worker and I stayed there for two days strolling around, meeting people, and visiting their farms. After a second two day visit a week later, and the butchering of another dog, I decided to move there. My co-worker and I found a host family who would temporarily house me, and the next week I moved. Upon the recommendation of my BFD supervisor, I did not tell the people of Burgos that I was leaving for good. I merely told them that I was being assigned to Gomez for a couple of months.

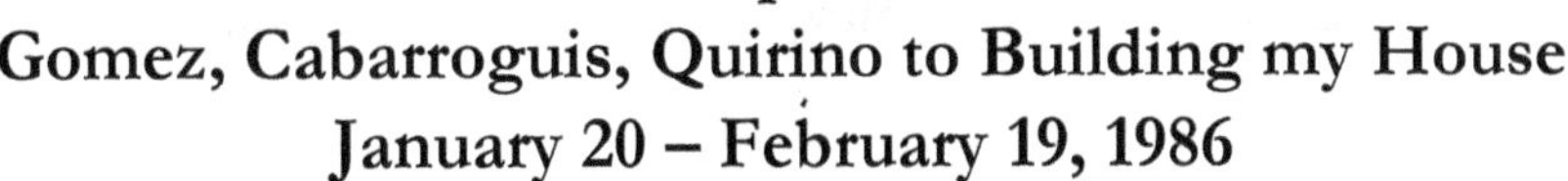

Chapter 9
Gomez, Cabarroguis, Quirino to Building my House
January 20 – February 19, 1986

Monday, January 20, 1986
Lito's House, Gomez, Cabarroguis, Quirino

₱315 – 15 = ₱300							
Cigarettes	5	Beer	7	Rides	3	TOTAL	₱15

I got up at 6:30 AM and found out that Vergilio's wife did have her baby last night. After eating breakfast and bathing, they requested that I pick the name for the new baby. I argued that I should not be the one, especially as I was leaving today and did not know when I would be back, but they insisted and therefore I named him Derek. Then I finished packing, took a few pictures of the house and so on and then waited for Rody until noon – then I decided not to wait any longer and got my things out to the road to go to Gomez. By and by a jeepney came along and I got my stuff to the Gomez Junction. I drank a Coca-Cola and ate some candy for lunch. My sendoff from Diffuncian was certainly nothing special, not even Lito was there, only the old man [my host father] and his only concern was that I should eat lunch before I leave. It was really strange, the whole scene really. At the Gomez Junction I found out after a while that the water buffalo cart (*cariton*) parked there was for me and that I should wait for the return of Daniel, the son of the Barangay Secretary. By and by Daniel returned and we loaded my stuff into the cart and headed for Gomez with the Americano Water Buffalo [they referred to light colored water buffalos as Americano Water Buffalos]. At about 4:00 PM or so we arrived at Rufo's (the Barangay Secretary) house and before long a small crowd gathered and there was some minor *Ginebra* drinking. Daniel prepared a delicious drinking snack of banana blossoms and everybody ate that. A little while before dark we headed for Lito's house [not the same Lito as I often referred to in Diffuncian] – oh, I forgot to say that Lito was also at Rufo's house. Lito and Daniel and a couple of other people accompanied me. I rode (*nagsakay-ak*) the water buffalo the whole way from Rufo's to Lito's; I'm getting pretty good at it, if I do say so myself. We arrived at Lito's house right at dark so Daniel returned home immediately and we prepared supper here and ate. After that, we all talked together for a while and finally, it's now bedtime. It seems real good for me here. I'm happy here, happier than I was at Mendoza's – at least so far. Tomorrow I'm supposed to help build a new house for Daniel. Okay, I will, it might be fun. [I built my own house in Alaska, so I was already an experienced house builder.]

Tuesday, January 21, 1986
Lito's House, Gomez, Cabarroguis, Quirino

Letter to Steve A.

I got up at 6:30 AM today. I didn't bathe today. It took a while to figure things out here at Lito's house. At 8:00 AM we went up the trail to the place where we were to meet Daniel and chainsaw some lumber from a tree. He was a few minutes late, but not much – that was a surprise to me. So we fell this big tree and turned it into 1 x 8's on the spot. I didn't do a whole lot other than the watch. I quit smoking cigarettes today – I had only two in the evening today. I have some kind of problem with my left foot, there's some kind of pimple or boil or something that hurts like hell. Now I've got jock itch, ringworm, something wrong with my right ear and now with my left foot – BUMMER! Is my mental attitude so bad that it's affecting my physical health? After we returned to Lito's house we went for a short stroll to the canteen area and I met some good people – some for the second time – and even now I have forgotten their names. I can't remember names. I also learned some new Ilokano words today. That's good, first new words in several days.

Wednesday, January 22, 1986
Lito's House, Gomez, Cabarroguis, Quirino

Letters from Chris M., Ardis B., Bob S. and Steve A. (chainsaw prices).

₱300 – 115 = ₱185							
Rides	10	Rice	29	Food	64	Kerosene	9
Cigarettes	3					TOTAL	₱115

I got up at 6:30 AM, ate breakfast and bathed in the rain shower. At 8:00 AM I headed down the hill to go to the Gundaway market and the office in Diffun. My host mother is sick – I don't know what the problem is, but it looks pretty bad to me. I hope that I don't get it. I got to the road at 9:30 AM or so. I went to Gundaway and the post office and there were the four letters listed above plus another package from the health unit. I did shopping as listed above and then went to the hospital for a gamma globulin injection – I got it at noon and then headed to the office. I talked with Mr. Romero about my house building and funds for the house – there are of course, no funds, so I told him we'll build a small house seeing as I'm only one who will be living there. Jamie drew up a plan – that was nice. Rody will come for the meeting tomorrow. Francisco helped me with my speech and then at 3:30 PM I headed for Gomez. I got to the junction at 4:30 PM and Lito was waiting for me. We headed up the mountain and got home right at dark.

Thursday, January 23, 1986
Lito's House, Gomez, Cabarroguis, Quirino

Letter to Nestor & form to health unit telling them I got the gamma globulin shot.

I got up at 6:30 AM and it was raining and COLD! A quack doctor was here for the morning. It was so cold I didn't bathe today. At 1:00 PM some people started showing up for the planned KBL meeting [I can't remember what that acronym means]. Because of the rain there were only a few people in attendance – a total of 31 people, including all of the speakers and myself were here. I gave my short speech. Rody came, as we planned yesterday, and the municipal secretary too. It finally stopped raining in the late afternoon. The speech by the municipal secretary was very long. The meeting was really about all that happened today. Rody had wanted to go home tonight, but the meeting didn't end until after 5:00 PM, so therefore he is staying here at Lito's house for the night. AWANEN! [This means "there is no more, already", I started using it at the end of every Journal entry going forward from here and I use it to this very day.]

Friday, January 24, 1986
Lito's House, Gomez, Cabarroguis, Quirino

Letter to Les F.

₱185 – 55 = ₱130						
Rody Loan	50	Cigarettes	5		TOTAL	₱55

I got up at 7:00 AM with Rody. We ate breakfast and bathed and then at about 8:30 AM or so Rody and I went to look at the site of the nursery [tree nursery] and my eventual house. We got very little sleep last night because the baby cried most all night. Rody left a bit before noon and I went and found Lito and Daniel and helped them make boards again. Daniel's wife brought us lunch there at the tree and we ate and talked. Then we cut more boards until 4:00 PM when Lito and I came home. We drank coffee and ate supper. I have a bad headache and hope that I'm not coming down with something. Maybe I've just been thinking too hard today. I'm having really serious thoughts today about calling it quits and going home. One-half of me says to quit and the other half says that I have to stick it out for the two years. Maybe my biorhythms are really down and bad today, but for certain whatever it is, it's a very low point. Tomorrow has to be better I think. I'll go to Bayombong tomorrow if I'm not sick, or else Villa Miemban – I'll sleep on my decision. AWANEN!

Saturday, January 25, 1986
Host Family, Bonfal East, Bayombong, Nueva Vizcaya

₱130 – 50 = ₱80							
Rides	18	Cigarettes	10	Beer	16	Toilet Paper	6
						TOTAL	₱50

Today I got up at 6:30 AM and after breakfast I bathed and walked down the mountain and headed for Bayombong. I arrived there at 12:30 PM. Ronald, Rebecca and Robelyn were home. Ronald and I looked at the rice field that I helped plant and it's already nearly ready to harvest. It feels so good to be here in Bayombong. After Ronald went to CMT [I don't remember what that means other than C?? Military Training] at 2:00 PM I strolled to the mushroom growing place and there is now a rice seedling field there! I talked with mother and Rebecca for a while about my recent thoughts about quitting. After a while I went to the Bayombong market and bought toilet paper and one beer and then I went to the waiting shed at Bonfal East and waited for Ronald. On the way home I talked with Ronald about my thoughts about quitting. If he's concerned, he doesn't show it. I don't know. When we returned home an uncle was here and then by and by father and Herbert arrived. Before supper we drank a small bottle of *Ginebra* and Herbert played the guitar with uncle playing along on the violin. It was good. I feel very happy here. Then we ate supper and after that they played guitar and violin again, and again it felt good. A couple of times I came close to crying I feel so good here. How can I feel so happy and welcome here and feel so bad at my site? [The obvious answer, looking back upon it all, is culture shock, which the experts say can last for up to two years.] At 9:00 PM I came upstairs to write and reflect on the day. It does my heart good to come here. I feel so happy and cheerful when I come here and that makes me feel so bad that I cannot be so happy at my site. Maybe after a while of adjusting, I will feel better at Gomez – I hope. If I don't start feeling better at Gomez after Ardis comes and goes, I will very likely call it quits. Ronald says "such is life" and I guess that's true, but I will feel very bad if I quit. I wonder if it's possible to change countries and would that make any difference? AWANEN!

Sunday, January 26, 1986
Host Family, Bonfal East, Bayombong, Nueva Vizcaya

₱80 – 20 = ₱60							
Ginebra	8	Cigarettes	12			TOTAL	₱20

We got up at 6:30 AM and went to the rice field and the place where we used electricity to catch fish. We did that for a while and then we returned home for a while and then we went to the river again to get more fish with the electricity, until around noon. We got maybe about a half a kilogram of fish and then we ate a picnic lunch and I had a chance to tell Ronald of my tentative decision to go home after Ardis leaves. I made that tentative decision at about 1:30 this morning as I lay awake in bed. I spend lots of time lately lying awake in bed thinking of going home. I guess I'm really homesick. But you've got to admit that three different host families to adjust to in less than five months is difficult for a person like myself, who has lived alone for lots of years! Anyway, after eating lunch we continued to fish for a while and then at 4:30 PM we built a fish trap where we will go when Ardis is here and get some fish for us to eat when she is here. Then we went to the nipa hut and gathered some bamboo to be able to burn some rice to make iniruban in the evening. Upon return to the house I bought a small bottle of *Ginebra* and by and by we all drank it – Herbert, Ronald, father and I – and then we ate supper. I was pretty fucked up, I admit, from the *Ginebra*, and after supper I had a long talk with the family about my tentative decision to return to Alaska. They took it in stride, as expected, after all – such is life! Then we made the iniruban – it's made by burning some red rice with the bamboo which we collected and then pounding it into a sticky mass and it's ready to eat – and delicious! It's very oily and rich. I finally retired upstairs to write this at 9:30 PM. The family is downstairs laughing while watching TV. I'm going to crash now. Tomorrow I'll go home to Gomez. AWANEN!

Monday, January 27, 1986
Lito's House, Gomez, Cabarroguis, Quirino

Letters from Dad (2), Bill N., Mark G., Ardis B. (2), State Forestry, Dave and Vicki M. (2), Tim S., Tim C. (2), Chad D. and Pauline M.

Letters to Dave and Vicki M., Bill N. and Tim C.

₱60 + 20 – 15 = ₱65							
Rides	10	Cigarettes	2	Beer	3	TOTAL	₱15

I got up at 6:30 AM in Bonfal East and ate breakfast and bathed. Mother went to the vegetable farm to get some veggies for me to take home with me, Ronald went to his university class and Herbert went to the office. Eventually mother returned home with the vegetables and after squeezing them into my pack and talking for a while, I left. It was a pretty good experience in Bonfal East; it saved me from deciding for sure to go home. I took a jeepney to Solano and the Vizcaya Liner to Cordon, where I drank a bottle of beer and ate some food and candy. Then I caught a jeepney for Gundaway, where I got all of the mail listed above – mostly Christmas cards, a month late. Then I caught a jeepney headed for Burgos and got off at the Gomez Junction. I walked up the mountain headed for home, but I stopped along the trail to read my mail – where I knew I could have some privacy. Then I continued on to Rufo's house and stopped there for coffee. Then I continued on home. Lito caught a good bunch of fish for supper and with the vegetables I brought home we had a really nice supper. After supper I retired to my room to read and write. AWANEN!

Tuesday, January 28, 1986
Lito's House, Gomez, Cabarroguis, Quirino

Letters to Dad and Mark G.

₱65 – 15 = ₱50							
Candy	5	Cigarettes	10			TOTAL	₱15

As I read back a couple of days in this Journal I see that on Sunday I was ready to go home, but on Monday I had more mental energy and today I'm even better and I'm ready to stay again. Maybe my biorhythms were only at an all time low, or maybe I needed some mental energy from the host family in Bayombong – or something. Anyway, I must remember them for the source of strength that they are and go there next time BEFORE I get to the point where I'm ready to go home. Today I got up late – at 7:00 AM. After breakfast I went to the store for cigarettes and then I went to Rufo's house, where Lito gets paid for his work lately. Then at lunchtime we returned home and after lunch I trimmed my beard and bathed. Then Lito and I strolled to his old vacant house, which is not finished, but it needs only to be completed to be livable. And the good thing is that all I'll have to buy are nails and some cogon grass for the roof. After that, Arsenio, Lito and I strolled to the rice field, the only one here in Gomez, and then to another house where I hadn't been before. We stayed there until suppertime and then returned home. After supper I retired to my room and wrote letters and this Journal. AWANEN!

Wednesday, January 29, 1986
Nestor's House, Villa Miemban, Cordon, Isabela

₱50 + 373 + 50 – 91 = ₱382 (Rody paid back ₱50 which he borrowed on 1/24)							
Cigarettes	13	Rides	17	Lunch	26	Coffee	15
Sardines	10	Ginebra	10			TOTAL	₱91

I got up at 7:00 AM and then at 8:00 AM I headed for the road. I'm going to Nestor's house in Villa Miemban! I got to the road at 9:30 AM and then to the office in Diffun at 10:30 AM or so. There was a telegram for me there – the Peace Corps in Manila is searching for Michael S. So I went to Santiago to send a telegram saying maybe he's in Bonfal East at his host family's place. Then I ate lunch at the 456 Restaurant and then I went to the jeepney place for Villa Miemban. I mailed letters which I'd written during the past few days and I finally got to Kakandongan at 3:45 PM or so and headed for Nestor's with an old man. We talked as we hiked along the trail and I got to Nestor's at 4:30 PM. He was there and happy to see me. He said he sent me a letter a few days ago. We talked until suppertime and then after supper we all drank the bottle of *Ginebra* which I brought with me. It's really good to see Nestor. It makes me happy to see him! After supper Nestor, father and I talked until bedtime and finished the bottle of *Ginebra*. AWANEN!

Thursday, January 30, 1986
Nestor's House, Villa Miemban, Cordon, Isabela

I got up the latest ever, at 7:30 AM. After breakfast we bathed and it rained HARD all morning. Due to the weather, we did not do any work today. Rufino came over and we ate a couple of lukbans. Before lunch we went and picked some *utong* beans [English is yard-long beans] and we had *utong* and sardines for lunch. In the afternoon Nestor, Rufino and I went to a valley where they have never logged yet. It was beautiful there. We were doing a search for fallen trees to make into charcoal. It looked like there's a lot of charcoal resource there. We returned down a different creek and then went to JB and Katie's for a while to talk. Before dark we returned to Nestor's house and ate supper. Diego came over in the evening and we all talked and talked. Now it's 8:30 PM and I'm tired. I walked a lot today. It feels good to be here and of course I don't want to leave tomorrow. AWANEN!

Friday, January 31, 1986
Lito's House, Gomez, Cabarroguis, Quirino

Letters from Nestor, Rolando, Bob G., Dave M., Steve A., San and Jack G. Dave and Steve both sent Smokey the Bear Calendars.

₱382 – 152 = ₱230							
Cigarettes	13	Lunch	37	Rice	27	Rides	10
Food	65					TOTAL	₱152

I got up at 6:00 AM and Nestor and I went out and got a papaya and picked some hot peppers. Then we returned to the house and went to the creek to bathe. At 7:30 AM JB and Katie showed up, as agreed upon yesterday, and after breakfast Nestor picked two beautiful red lukbans for me to take with me. It was 8:30 AM before we finally left Nestor's house. It was REALLY GOOD to see Nestor again. We mean an awful lot to each other – that is obvious. Our friendship and relationship is something real special. Anyway, JB, Katie and I had to walk to Vulcan and from there we took a tricycle to Cordon, where JB and Katie changed their clothes. We finally got to Santiago at 11:30 AM and we went to the 456 Restaurant and ate lunch. After lunch we ran into Ralph P. and Linda S. and after some talk I went to market and bought the food listed above. Then I went to the office in Diffun for only a short visit and then I continued on to Gundaway and the post office, where I got the letters listed above. It was real good to get Nestor's letter. I've been waiting for it for a long time – nearly a month now. As usual, his one page letter is more meaningful than six or seven pages that other people might send. It was a surprise to get a letter from Dave M., but I saved Nestor's letter for last because of the old saying "save the best for last". I finally got to the Gomez Junction and started the walk up the mountain at 4:45 PM. My companion was Fred – he walked fast and I was carrying lots, so I had a very big sweat and I'm very tired. I got home right at dark, after stopping at Rufo's house for a couple glasses of water. The family was happy to see me. It's now 8:27 PM and I'm a tired dog so I'm going to take my malaria pills and go to bed without writing any letters tonight. Good-night Nestor in Villa Miemban. AWANEN!

Saturday, February 1, 1986
Lito's House, Gomez, Cabarroguis, Quirino

Letters to Tim S. and Chad D.

₱230 – 5 = ₱225						
Cigarettes	5				TOTAL	₱5

I got up at 6:00 AM. After breakfast and toilet I bathed in the stream and then Lito and I started making the rounds distributing the notices of a meeting next Tuesday. We visited several places with notices and today I probably met a lot of new people. At lunchtime we returned home and that was when I noticed that I have some kind of crud growing between my toes. It's "*tarindanum*" in Ilokano, some kind of athlete's foot I suppose. It means my feet have been too wet for too long. I put some Whitfield's Ointment on it, I hope it helps. After lunch, Lito and I and a couple of other people went to a fishpond to get snails for Lito's fishpond. I took a one hour siesta and then we went to Rufo's house and helped with the building of that for a while. We made a couple of narra wood cants [a cant is a squared timber, roughly 10 inches x 10 inches] which he will take to the city and sell. At 5:30 PM we returned home for supper and now it's 6:45 PM and I'm going to write a couple letters, at least I hope so. AWANEN!

Sunday, February 2, 1986
Lito's House, Gomez, Cabarroguis, Quirino

Letters to Roselynn and Jim, San and Jack G., Bob G., Bob S., Terry S. and Chris and Mary M.

₱225 – 5 = ₱220						
Cigarettes	3	Vinegar	2		TOTAL	₱5

Today I got up at 6:30 AM. I ate breakfast and then bathed. Lito went to Gundaway for the day so I eventually went to the Barangay Hall and wrote letters until lunchtime. Arsenio came over this morning and his pregnant wife has malaria so I gave him some Tylenol – that's all I can do. After lunch and one more letter I strolled to the canteen for cigarettes and vinegar for making hot pepper sauce. Then I went to my future house. I looked at the creek near the house and looked around the house site real good. Then I talked with Amor and Bubot for a while and ate some coffee beans. I returned home before dark and Lito returned and he and several other people went out to get some eels. After a bit it REALLY RAINED HARD for an hour or so – so I wrote two more letters and then we ate a late supper and even now, at 8:15 PM, Lito has not returned home. Maybe he is staying wherever he ended up after the heavy rain. The creek is still really roaring now and it just right now is starting to rain again. Shit, I wish the rain would stop. I wonder if it ever really stops. I'm out of things to write about for today. Good night! AWANEN!

Monday, February 3, 1986
Lito's House, Gomez, Cabarroguis, Quirino

Letters to Steve A. and Pauline M.

₱220 – 10 = ₱210							
Cigarettes	5	Coke	3	Snack	2	TOTAL	₱10

I got up at 6:45 AM. Lito got home at midnight last night and was very noisy so I got woke up. It was raining lightly this morning so that we waited until 8:45 AM to go to Rufo's house. Then, after a bit we went to a fallen old tree and worked on making a couple of cants until noon. Then I ate lunch at Rufo's house and Lito returned home because his wife has a slight case of malaria. After lunch I slept for a while at Rufo's house and then when Lito had not returned by 2:00 PM I went to the store for cigarettes and a Coke. While I was there, it began to rain hard again, so I stayed there for a while. Then I returned home. Lito was at the Barangay Hall and Junior and Boy came by after a bit and Dominador too, and we all talked for a while. Then it was suppertime so Lito and I returned home. After supper I retired to my room to write the above letters. Rody did not come today as he was supposed to, I hope he comes tomorrow. AWANEN!

Tuesday, February 4, 1986
Lito's House, Gomez, Cabarroguis, Quirino

Letters to Gregorio R., Nestor, Rolando T. and Brooke F.

₱220 – 10 = ₱200							
Cigarettes	10					TOTAL	₱10

Today I got up at 6:30 AM. After eating breakfast I bathed and then it was time to go to the Barangay Hall for the meeting. Rody DID show up and he holds a pretty good meeting! He scheduled work days for the tree nursery and for fixing up my house. We're planning to fix up my house on February 18th. I hope everything comes together and that it really happens. Once I get my own house I'll really be much happier I believe.

The meeting ended at noon and several people ate lunch here at Lito's house. After lunch we went to my future house to show Rody and for Rufo to be able to prepare a materials estimate. Then we went to the canteen to talk with a bunch of people until 3:00 PM. Rody left and Lito and I came home and I went to the Barangay Hall to write some letters, as shown above. It's so easy to write to both the Bayombong family and to Nestor – they give me much happiness and good feelings. It's nice. At this point I have 14 letters to mail when I go to town on Thursday. AWANEN!

Wednesday, February 5, 1986
Lito's House, Gomez, Cabarroguis, Quirino

₱200 + 1,492 – 516 = ₱1,176							
Rides	20	Boots	120	Cigarettes	9	Flashlight	8
Lunch	28	Nails	150	Lamp	5	Toiletries	28
Postage	68	Food	80			TOTAL	₱516

I got up at 6:30 AM and after breakfast I decided to go to Santiago today because I think the banks are closed tomorrow. So, after bathing I left for Burgos. I got to Rufo's house at 9:15 AM and after he told me I need ten kilograms of nails I headed her Burgos. I got to the road at 10:00 AM and got a jeepney that was slower than molasses, so that I didn't finally get to Santiago until 12:00 N. Therefore both the bank and the post office were closed. I bought boots first and then ate lunch. Then I went to the bank, got nails and then went to market, where I bought a bunch of stuff for both me, my new house and also for Lito's house. I got done at 2:00 PM and headed for home. The jeepney I was in had two flat tires, so we had to stop in Cordon and get one fixed. I didn't even have time to stop at the post office in Gundaway. I arrived at the Gomez Junction at 4:15 PM and Daniel was waiting for me there with the cart and water buffalo to carry the nails and so on. We got to Rufo's house at 5:30 PM or so and Daniel, Lito, Rufo, Romeo and I drank *Ginebra* and beer until 7:30 PM or so when Lito and I headed for home. We got home at 8:00 PM and ate supper and now it's already 8:45 PM and past bedtime. I got and kept receipts for the boots and nails and I'm hoping I can get reimbursement for both the boots – from the health unit – as well as the nails for my house. Lito and I ate supper here alone as everybody else was already sleeping. We ate *bisocols* [big snails] and rice – it was delicious. Well that's all for tonight. AWANEN!

Thursday, February 6, 1986
Lito's House, Gomez, Cabarroguis, Quirino

Mail receipts for boots and nails to Peace Corps.

₱1,176 – 15 = ₱1,161							
Cigarettes	10	Coke	5			TOTAL	₱15

I got up at 6:30 AM. After eating breakfast and loafing around for a while, Lito and I headed for Rufo's but we met Rufo about halfway there. We then all went to the school and prepared it for voting tomorrow. We got halfway finished by lunch-time and I went to Lito's for lunch. After lunch I took a short siesta and when I woke up Lito was gone, so I wrote short letters to go with the above receipts for the Peace Corps. I strolled to Boy's house and stayed there for a while. George and Junior came there too and after conversing for a while I went to the store for cigarettes and while there I talked with Francisco, Amor and Lakey Espinoza for a while and then I went back to Boy's for more talk. After a while it was 5:30 PM and I went home. Lito was already here and his first cousin is also here visiting. After supper and talking for a while I retired to my room at 7:00 PM to write this. My spirits are really high today! I'm sure it's because Ardis B. is coming tomorrow. I had a headache all afternoon, but I don't know why. AWANEN!

Friday, February 7, 1986
Host Family, Bonfal East, Bayombong, Nueva Vizcaya
ELECTION DAY!!

₱1,161 – 137 = ₱1,024							
Rides	28	Coke	3	Cigarettes	16	Haircut	5
Toiletries	13	Lunch	18	Beer/Snack	12	Coffee	8
Meat	34					TOTAL	₱137

Got up at 6:15 AM and after breakfast I went to the school to watch a couple of people vote, and then I returned home and bathed and left for Burgos. I got to Burgos about 9:30 AM and caught a jeepney for Santiago. I got to Santiago at 11:00 AM and went to Letty's Restaurant to look for Ardis. At 2:00 PM, finally she telephoned and told me she was at one of the other Letty's Restaurants – I didn't even know there was more than one! So we finally were able to meet. We talked for a while and decided to go to Bayombong today, so I left my extra things at Nestor's boarding house and we caught a jeepney to Bayombong. We got to Bonfal East at about 5:45 PM. The family was happy to see us and it's really good to see them too. Ronald is really friendly and the whole family is really jolly tonight, so we went to bed late – it's now 9:30 PM and time to go to bed. AWANEN!

Saturday, February 8, 1986
Host Family, Bonfal East, Bayombong, Nueva Vizcaya

₱1,024 – 51 = ₱973							
Cigarettes	16	Beer	25	Whiskey	10	TOTAL	₱51

We got up at 6:00 AM. We ate breakfast and I dyed my pants with the dye that Ardis brought me, and while they were boiling I bathed. Ardis and Mother went to market to buy things for a picnic and when they got back we headed for the river. We (Herbert, Ronald and I) went to the fish trap that we built last time I was here and there were only a couple of fish there because it filled up with mud. Then Ronald, Johnny and I went to another two fish traps that they had built and there was nothing there either – so finally at 2:00 PM we ate lunch, with very few fish. After lunch and a swim we went to the vegetable farm and harvested some coconuts and drank coconut water and ate coconuts and papayas. Then we returned home and ate and drank some more alcohol and sang songs. I'm not feeling well so I took a short rest before supper. After supper I headed upstairs to bed. It's good we came here. AWANEN!

Sunday, February 9, 1986
Nestor's House, Villa Miemban, Cordon, Isabela

₱973 – 69 = ₱904							
Cigarettes	8	Rides	19	Food/Drink	42	TOTAL	₱69

We got up at 6:00 AM, ate breakfast and slowly got ready to leave. Mother sent some big papayas and some tamarind fruits with us and we finally left at about 9:00 AM. We stopped in Solano for a while to get some meat, peanuts and vegetables and we drank a beer there and then we caught a jeepney to Vulcan. At Vulcan we caught a tricycle to the junction and they charged us ₱10. Later on, both JB and Nestor told us that it should have only been ₱5. We got to Nestor's house at 1:30 PM or so and Nestor and Rufino were both in Santiago. After a while JB and Katie stopped by for a while and we ate some guyabano. Then JB and Katie left and Ardis and I strolled to the Barangay Captain's rice field, Melchor's big tree and then to the Barangay Hall and finally, to the hill where we went with Teresa the very first time I was here. We sat on the hill and talked for a while and then returned home. We took off to fetch some water and we met Nestor on the way to fetch the water, so he didn't let us go and fetch water. We returned to the house and talked for a while and then we strolled to the fishpond until dark. We returned home again and while cooking supper Rufino came by. We ate supper and after a while we went to the Barrio Hall to see if the pre-Valentine's Day dance was happening or not – it wasn't, but we hung out at the Barrio Hall until 9:00 PM playing guitars and so on. Then we came home and slept. Oh, Ardis brought me two "Made in America" flashlights and I gave one to Nestor. He is very impressed at how bright it is and he is happy for it. As usual it feels really good to be here at Nestor's house. He got my last letter today and I made him read it and it seems that he is agreeable to come to Gomez on the 17th, I hope so. AWANEN!

Monday, February 10, 1986
New Look Bakery – Lagawe, Ifugao

₱904 – 47 = ₱857							
Rides	38	Coke	5	Bread	4	TOTAL	₱47

We got up at 6:00 AM at Nestor's house because some cats were going crazy. We cooked breakfast and I wrote my journal from yesterday. By and by we ate breakfast and then Nestor cooked some peanuts and I bathed. Nestor picked five lukbans and after eating one of them we left at 10:00 AM headed up the trail. We stopped at the top to eat one more lukban, now we are down to three remaining. We got to Kakandongan at 11:30 AM or so and we drank a beer there. Mr. Viernes came and we helped him drink half of his beer and then we escaped at 12:30 PM. We walked to Vulcan and caught a tricycle and it took us to the highway. Then we continued on to Cordon and then to Diffun. We got to the office at 2:00 PM and escaped at 2:40 PM. We took another jeepney to Cordon drank a Coca-Cola and then we caught a jeepney to Bagabag. We waited there for a while for a jeepney to Banaue, but none came by nearly dark so I started asking questions of people. The Barangay Captain happened by and recommended that we go to the New Look Bakery and he told someone to show us where it was. So, here we are now, at the New Look Bakery. We don't yet know the price, but I'm sure it will be reasonable. They showed us a restaurant where we could eat supper, but it was closed. Three people accompanied us to another restaurant that was also closed, but they opened up for us after telling us they had only eggs and rice and us telling them that was fine. It ended up being the place where the Lagawe pouch is dropped off so they knew John D. They asked several questions and talked a while, we ate and then returned to the New Look Bakery and talked for a while and I did my journal. Now it's 9:00 PM and we're tired – time to sleep. AWANEN!

Tuesday, February 11, 1986
Stairway Lodge – Banaue, Ifugao

Postcard to Steve A.

₱857 – 307 = ₱550							
Postcards	28	Coffee	10	Lodging	50	Lunch	63
Sweater	85	G-String	60	Cigarettes	11	TOTAL	₱307

We got up at 6:00 AM and went to the same place for breakfast that we ate supper at last night. I left a note for John D. and then we returned to the room, packed, paid for the room and found a jeepney to Banaue at about 10:30 AM. Three girls at the jeepney stopping place in Banaue recommended that we go to the Stairway Lodge, the same place where I stayed in 1984, so we went there and rented a room. Then we strolled around until lunchtime and then returned to the Stairway Lodge for lunch.

Frederick and John [whom I met when I vacationed here in 1984] returned home from school for lunch and it was a surprise to see how much they'd grown in two years. In the afternoon we strolled some more and Ardis bought a bunch of baskets and we mailed them to the USA. We got back to the Stairway Lodge at 5:00 PM or so and I reintroduced myself to the owner [Frederick's father and John's uncle] and talked with Fred and John for an hour or so. Then we ate supper and after supper John, Fred Ardis and I went to the Folkhouse – there wasn't much there. We returned at 9:00 PM and John showed me how to tie the g-string. We talked for another hour or so and then went to bed. It was (is) really amazing to return here again after two years, really amazing! AWANEN!

Wednesday, February 12, 1986
Happy Home Inn – Bontoc, Mountain

₱550 – 120 = ₱430							
Rides	100	Cigarettes	16	Coke	4	TOTAL	₱120

We got up at 6:00 AM at the Stairway Lodge and ate breakfast. The weather was still rainy and miserable and therefore we decided to head for Bontoc and return here to Banaue on Saturday. We caught a jeepney to Bontoc after Ardis bought a necklace. We got to Bontoc at about 11:00 AM or so. Along the way we saw an amazing rainbow (photo below) and asked the jeepney driver to stop so that we could photograph it. At the time we arrived in Bontoc there were no more buses bound for Baguio City, so we decided to stay at the Happy Home Inn and go to Maligcong. We went to the local museum and after that we WALKED to Maligcong – without a guide. We successfully found it and we saw everything that I saw in 1984 plus, the church! Then we returned to the Happy Home Inn for a good supper and three or four beers each, and we met Elmer, a new brother for me. It was, when all is said and done, a good day. Ardis was a bit disappointed that we did not make it to Baguio City, but such is life, it's okay. There was no problem and a good time was had by all. AWANEN!

Thursday, February 13, 1986
St. Mary's Pension – Baguio City, Benguet

₱430 – 173 = ₱257							
Rides	140	Cigarettes	8	Postcards	8	Soft Drinks	17
						TOTAL	₱173

We got up at 6:00 AM, ate breakfast, paid the bill and caught a bus bound for Baguio City. It was a slow bus and it was a long, slow day. We spent eight hours on the bus, and finally after a couple of pee stops and a lunch stop we arrived in Baguio City at 4:00 PM. We drank a beer at the Dangwa Tranco Bus Terminal canteen and then went to St. Mary's Pension. We checked in and then went to search for supper place. Ardis wanted Mandarin food so we walked up and down Session Road and finally found a place that called itself "The Mandarin", so we ate supper there and watched the news and Ardis was going on and on about the crooked elections. [This was the election in which Marcos won by a landslide, but not really – Marcos was forced to flee the country and Corazon Aquino became the new president.] Finally she tired herself out and we finished our supper and left. On the way back to St. Mary's Pension we stopped at the Mountaineer Hotel, my old haunt of 1984 when I was here, for coffee and then we returned to St Mary's. Now it's 9:15 PM and we're both ready to crash – it was a long day! AWANEN!

The rainbow which we saw over the rice terraces during the jeepney ride from Banaue to Bontoc. I really wish you could see this photo in color, but it would quadruple the price of the book to have it printed in color.

Friday, February 14, 1986
St. Mary's Pension – Baguio City, Benguet

₱257 – 130 = ₱127							
Meals	110	Cigarettes	8	Rides	12	TOTAL	₱130

We got up at 6:00 AM. Tom H. [another Peace Corps Volunteer] came to visit last night at 9:30 PM and we talked to him for a while. We also ate breakfast with him and then he went his way and we went to the market, where Ardis took some pictures, and then we headed for San Fernando. We arrived in San Fernando about 10:30 AM and Ardis bought some seashell stuff. Then we strolled up the beach until about 2:00 PM, returned to California Beach ate a late lunch, killed some time and then headed back to Baguio City. We ate supper at Shakey's, strolled around for a while, drank coffee at a different place – where a drunken man came over to our table and was in tears over the cheating in the elections. He said that his country "is dying" and it was very sad – really kind of the most moving part of the day. Now it's 9:15 PM and we're going to sleep! Good night! AWANEN!

Saturday, February 15, 1986
Stairway Lodge – Banaue, Ifugao

₱127 + 300 (loan from Ardis) – 270 = ₱157							
Lodging	70	Rides	162	Cigarettes	12	Soft Drinks	7
Bronze	19					TOTAL	₱270

We got up at 5:30 AM, got ready, checked out and left for the Dangwa Tranco Bus Terminal. We ate breakfast there and then headed for Banaue via Bayombong. It was a long and hot trip. We met Robert on the bus, he got off at Aritao and then I sat with Hokay the remainder of the way to Banaue. We arrived in Banaue, checked in at the Stairway Lodge and then we went to the waterfall and to three different bronze smiths and I bought Fred and John each a bronze medallion. We returned to the Stairway Lodge for supper and then after supper we all – Fred, John, Ardis and I – went to a cultural show. It was interesting. Again, as in 1984, we were asked to dance the last dance. After that we returned here and now it's 10:30 PM and bedtime. Supposedly tomorrow we're going to go to Bataad. AWANEN!

Sunday, February 16, 1986
Stairway Lodge – Banaue, Ifugao

₱157 – 97 = ₱60							
Rice Bowl	25	Lunch	32	Cigarettes	16	Soft Drinks	24
						TOTAL	₱97

We got up at 6:00 AM, got dressed and ordered breakfast, but by the time they brought me the wrong breakfast, it was already too late to reorder because at 7:30 we all – John, Fred, Ardis and I – left for Bataad. The weather was good and it was beautiful until we started to walk out and then it rained a little. We got back to the jeepney at 1:30 PM and it was not going to leave until 3:00 PM, so Ardis and I started to walk back to Banaue. We walked about five kilometers before the jeepney came. In addition, we walked a lot going to Bataad and back to the jeepney place and therefore we were very tired. We got back to Banaue and the Stairway Lodge at about 4:00 PM and Ardis and I strolled a bit and we had a beer before we returned to the Stairway Lodge.

Then we returned to the Stairway Lodge for supper and Ardis gave John and Fred her remembrances and I apologized because I only gave them the small brass medallions. Oh well, such is life I guess. Tomorrow we go home to Gomez. AWANEN!

Some of the famous Bataad rice terraces. For scale note the man with the water buffalo at about the center of the photo.

Monday, February 17, 1986
Lito's House, Gomez, Cabarroguis, Quirino

Nestor and Ardis here!

₱60 + 1,800 – 915 = ₱945							
Ardis	300	Kitchen	325	Rides	44	Padlock	35
Food	124	Rice	33	Household	54	TOTAL	₱915

We got up at 6:00 AM, ate breakfast and caught a bus from Banaue to Bagabag and then a jeepney to Santiago. We arrived at Santiago at 10:15 AM and went to Lina's Restaurant and waited for Nestor until 11:00 AM. Then I went to the bank and after that I bought a bunch of stuff for my future kitchen. We also ate lunch at Lina's Restaurant and then we went to Nestor's boarding house, where we found him. Then Nestor, Ardis and I went and bought the rest of the needs for my house, as shown above. After that we caught a jeepney headed for Burgos and arrived there at 4:15 PM.

We drank a beer, bought some vegetables and started up the mountain to Gomez. Two people whom I know came by with a water buffalo and a cart and they carried all of our stuff up to Gomez. We stopped at Rufo's house for a snack and water and then continued on to Lito's house. We arrived at dark. I am so happy to see Nestor again, my good friend. AWANEN!

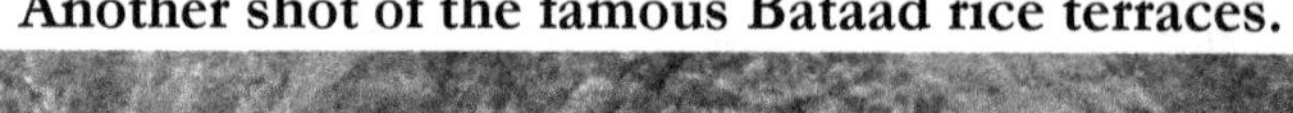

Another shot of the famous Bataad rice terraces.

Tuesday, February 18, 1986
Lito's House, Gomez, Cabarroguis, Quirino

Nestor, Ardis and Rody all here!

₱945 – 65 = ₱880						
Cigarettes	15	Ginebra	50		TOTAL	₱65

We got up at 6:30 AM, ate breakfast and bathed. Then people started showing up to help repair my house, so we went to my house site and slowly by slowly lots of people showed up with roofing grass, tools and etc. We started to work and it went really well; we removed all the boards from the inside of the house, removed the old roof and started making the new roof and putting it on. We also put up one new wall. About then it was lunchtime and everybody went to their homes for lunch, so I didn't have to furnish lunch. After lunch we all returned to the house site and worked on another wall and the roof. At 4:00 PM we went to the store and bought three bottles of *Ginebra* and everybody started to drink, so after that not much more work was accomplished, but this evening the roof is nearly complete and three walls are up. Rody is here tonight too so it's difficult at my house for mother – there are four staying here who she has to cook for. Sorry. We went to bed early. AWANEN!

Wednesday, February 19, 1986
Lito's House, Gomez, Cabarroguis, Quirino

Nestor and Ardis leave Gomez.

Postcards to Dave G., Dave M. and State Forestry

₱880 – 105 = ₱775							
Cigarettes	15	Beer	65	Rides	18	Bread	7
						TOTAL	₱105

We all got up at 6:30 AM and after breakfast, bathing and so on, Nestor, Ardis and I headed down the mountain. It rained last night so Ardis and Nestor got a taste of what my trail is like in the mud. They both removed their shoes about 100 feet from the house! We got to Burgos and I showed Ardis the sawmill, the place where they make charcoal and we went to Ventura's Store and Nestor and I split a large bottle of beer and Ardis drank a Coke. Then we caught a jeepney and Ardis and Nestor went to Santiago and I gave the money in advance to the driver. Then I went back up the mountain to Gomez and the people worked on my house some more and I helped out until lunchtime. After lunch I took a short siesta and then returned to my house site and helped out some more. Today we finished the walls, the cooking place and the floor. At about 4:30 PM I bought three bottles of *Ginebra* and some bottles of Coke for chaser and work stopped. A lot of work was accomplished today. Maybe we will finish tomorrow. I was sad to see Nestor go but I was a bit burned out on Ardis, so it was okay that she left. AWANEN!

Chapter 10
Culture Notes #3

Stereotypes

As the only American living in Gomez, and the first American most of the younger people had ever seen, there were many stereotypical ideas about what an American "should" be like. The people expected me to be different, but my GOALS were just to be a respected, active, productive member of the community. I had to be a full time student of culture as well as language to eventually be accepted into the community. Just these two aspects of the job made it the challenge of a lifetime – let alone trying to accomplish anything in the field of agro-forestry.

The people "knew", from their stereotypical ideas of an American, that I should be outgoing, friendly, informal, loud, rude, extravagant, wasteful, disrespectful of elders and authority, ignorant about farming, wealthy, generous, always in a hurry, that Americans live on bread and meat and don't eat rice or vegetables, and much, much more. Of course some of these ideas are often-times true. I had, however, already gone through ten weeks of culture and language training in addition to training in tropical agro-forestry techniques. I'd lived for a while in Burgos and had already lived with Lito's family in Gomez. I'd been in the Philippines, at this point, for about 5.5 months. I had already become extremely interested and immersed in the culture while living with three different Filipino host families and quite literally being accepted as a grandson, son, brother, and uncle in various families. I had already become a bit acculturated, so some of the stereotypical views that abounded had already been noticed and plans made to compensate for them; set answers to certain questions had already been thought through.

Acceptance Into Gomez

The people of Gomez very quickly noticed that I was immersed in learning the culture and language, that I was respectful of my elders, culturally sensitive, patient, and more. I had been working with my host father, Lito, a very small time logger, and my host father was impressed that I knew how to operate a chainsaw, and could even make a tree fall where I wanted it to. My host father, Lito, had spread the word that I appeared to be a good hard worker, and that I was smart too – even if I wasn't very good at speaking Ilokano. After only one month, approximately 60 community members turned out to help build a small, but adequate house for me. It was at this point that the real work began. I was a single male living alone in my own house. My friends and neighbors asked me if I wanted a living companion. I stated that I did not.

The people accepted this, but insisted that I at least take a sleeping companion. I refused this offer also, but then my neighbor and good friends informed me that the people were concerned that a ghost might enter my house at night and take possession of me. I was also informed that the people wondered what I was trying to hide at night. Did I spend the evening counting my money or masturbating, and was that why I was getting skinnier.

Having already accepted the fact that I had to be culturally sensitive, I decided that I had best do what the culture expected me to do if I was to have any luck in accomplishing my aforementioned goals. I realized that I WAS in Asia, where nobody but nobody sleeps alone, and as I had nothing to hide, I told my neighbor that I would accept a sleeping companion. The neighbor said that he would talk to the other neighbors and that night they would send over two or three bachelor sons to be my companions and that I could make a decision about which one of them I wanted for my permanent sleeping companion.

Sleeping Companion

As there is no electricity in Gomez, people more or less live by the sun. They eat at dusk, do the dishes, sit and talk, plan for tomorrow's work, listen to the radio (when they have money for batteries), and go to sleep between 8:00 and 9:00 PM. They then get up at 4:00 to 5:00 AM and start the process again. The first night in my new house, shortly after supper George, Bubot, and Junior, three bachelor sons of the various neighbors, showed up at my house. I was uneasy, but the boys tried to make me feel at ease. They rolled their sleeping mats out on the floor and lay down. I did the same and we were all asleep shortly. Junior woke everybody up about an hour later and said; *"makibirokak ti balbalasang" or "I'm* going to search for some girls." The other three people (George, Bubot and I) declined and sent Junior to satisfy his needs. He came back and woke us all up again later on, trying to convince us to go with him. We declined the invitation again and Junior left. The next morning George and Bubot stayed long enough to be sure that I knew how to get my charcoal lit, use my charcoal stove, and cook my rice, then they left. That day I told my neighbor that I didn't want Junior to come again, but that George and Bubot were welcome to return.

That night, and for the next several nights, George and Bubot returned to my house to sleep. I began to feel more at ease with them, but noticed that Bubot would ask questions every night about how much my radio and other belongings had cost in America, and if he could have them when I returned to the USA. By the end of a week Bubot had asked me the cost of everything that I owned, and he also wanted it all when I left to return to America. George, on the other hand, was more shy and reserved. He never asked if he could have anything, was mannerly, polite, never laughed at my fledgling Ilokano, and respected me as an elder is supposed to be respected. Only five or six people in the entire village had ever been beyond 4th grade in school, and for this reason there was absolutely no English spoken at all, other than numbers. I had to become proficient at Ilokano to be able to converse and understand what was going on around me. George was very helpful in this respect, while Bubot would spend half of the evening laughing at my efforts.

After about two weeks the novelty apparently wore off for Bubot, or maybe George said something to him, regardless he stopped coming to my house to sleep. George and I however, became the best of faithful friends, and George slept at my house virtually every night for the remaining 21 months that I lived in Gomez.

Sleeping Culture

The sleeping practices of the people were also noted to be different than in the United States. More cultural baggage that I had to stow away until my return home. In America people who aren't married, be they brothers or friends, will generally feel funny sleeping together, especially two males. Children in America are generally given their own bedrooms when they become old enough so that they may feel a need or want for privacy. When they are forced to sleep together later in life two males will spend the entire night making sure that they have several inches of space between them. Ilokano, and Philippine culture in general, has mats spread out on the floor of the largest room of the house and everybody sleeps shoulder to shoulder, hip to hip. What your older brother next to you, or your father and mother are doing is none of your concern. It can be said however, that this, plus watching the chickens, dogs, pigs, and water buffaloes made a youngster cognizant of the facts of life at a very young age. Young people were wise and mature in this respect and in many other respects, when compared to American youngsters. American youngsters will generally be found snickering about sexual connotations even when they are 16 years old, while the Filipino youngster will stop this immature action when he or she is about ten years old.

I had learned of this sleeping practice while living with my various host families, so I wasn't surprised, didn't think it out of the ordinary when Junior, Bubot, and George sandwiched me between them that very first night that we all slept together. As George and I became closer friends I came to like sleeping in contact with my friend. It gave me a sense of security, and seemed to make life in a strange land just a little bit less difficult.

The Village Grapevine

I quickly noticed that the village grapevine worked very effectively and that the stories which I told George were quickly known around the village. It also quickly became apparent that George was selective in what he passed on to the grapevine. He respected my personal life and did not pass on things that might hurt my credibility – for instance, George never passed on the fact that I knew virtually nothing about growing corn. As these stories passed through the grapevine people began to have more respect for me, and I gave George the primary credit for my eventual acceptance into the community. My credibility grew and grew as time progressed, as shall be seen.

On Being Gay

I had read some Peace Corps provided materials while in training which informed me that although gayness is generally accepted by Filipino people, that one should not make a big point of the fact that "I am gay," at least not at the start. I did (and do) happen to be gay and although I never came right out and told anybody, they eventually deduced it from the way I lived, acted, carried myself and even sat while relaxing. Of course after a very short time George knew of my desires and tendencies, but this is one of the personal things which he never spread through the grapevine. The materials which I had read in training indicated that one should do everything possible to establish the fact that one was a hard-worker, responsible, culturally sensitive and so on before allowing anybody to know that one is gay. Eventually I heard people talking about my gayness, but they never looked down upon me or made any comments or criticisms about it. I learned that one young male who was very obviously gay and knew of my gayness (Bubot) had spread the word about it. For a few days it was the talk of the village, but nobody ever made any derogatory comments to me and I also never noticed any difference in the way people treated me after they all learned of my being gay.

A Filipino male child who is too interested in cleaning the house, making flower bouquets, washing the dishes or generally hanging around mother's apron strings is assumed to have gay tendencies and will be treated as such. It is no problem. They accept the boy without question (I have no experience or knowledge with/of female gayness in Philippine culture.) It should also be noted that if a male sits with his legs crossed that people may assume that he is gay. A child once asked me if I was *"bakla"* (gay) just because I was sitting with my legs crossed.

There are also gay barbers. You can identify a gay barber because he has a nicer barber shop than the straight barber and while he is giving you a haircut he will tend to rub against you more than is called for. If a person doesn't like gay people then it's best to be culturally sensitive and just keep quiet and not go to that barber again in the future.

Chapter 11
Building My House through August 2, 1986

Thursday, February 20, 1986
Lito's House, Gomez, Cabarroguis, Quirino

Letters from Peace Corps (6), Ardis B. (2), Chris & Mary M., Vicki S., Jim & Roselynn, Bill J., Barb W., Abe F., San & Jack G., Tony S., Bob S., Liz and Dave G.

₱775 – 203 = ₱572							
Rides	8	Beer	10	Cigarettes	8	Coke	11
Lunch	13	Rice	15	Lock/Hasp	32	Notebook	3
Food	36	Brooms	32	Meat	35	TOTAL	₱203

I got up at 6:30 AM and got ready to go to the office as there's a Monthly District Meeting today. There was not much excitement there! Rody and I went to the meeting, stopping at the post office on the way. I got the above letters – twenty of them! WOW! After the meeting and lunch I went to market in Diffun and bought the above. In the afternoon the meeting continued, but I was able to escape at about 3:00 PM and head back to Gomez. My house is now close enough to completion so that I can surely move in tomorrow, so tomorrow will be a very happy day for me. All that remains to do is one door, some metal sheeting above the cooking place and digging the hole for the toilet. I also need a table and chairs but I'd say that's a relatively minor thing. Rody came back with me too; he's been here three nights, including tonight. It's okay, but after two weeks with people around all the time, I'm ready to be alone tomorrow night. AWANEN!

Friday, February 21, 1986
My House, Gomez, Cabarroguis, Quirino

₱572 – 32 = ₱540							
Charcoal	12	Cigarettes	20			TOTAL	₱32

We got up at 6:30 AM and after breakfast I went to my house and Rody left. There were only five or six helpers today. We built shelves and Lito went to make boards for the door and for patching some cracks. Before lunch I went to Rufo's house to borrow some nails. Julie cooked for me at my new house. We moved all of my belongings here first thing this morning. After lunch we finished the kitchen and everything else. In the late afternoon we drank one bottle of *Ginebra* before everybody went home. Junior came and cooked supper for me and Alfredo and Pedring came over in the evening for a while. Junior, George and Bubot slept here tonight. I'm very happy that my house is finished and I'm living in it now! People have some doubts as to whether I can cook for myself and do my own laundry. Such is life I guess. I hope that tomorrow night I can sleep alone here. Maybe I'll have to tell them, I don't know. Anyway, I'm happy my house is done. [While we were falling asleep I put my hand on Junior's tool and he then encouraged me to play with it some more. Well, after 20 minutes or so, it was in my mouth and we were both enjoying it. Bubot and George then asked Junior if he was masturbating when they heard the sucking noises. Junior told them that he was not, but that I was sucking his thing. At that point, the mood was lost and I went to sleep. Junior woke everybody up about an hour later and said; *"makibirokak ti balbalasang,"* or "I'm going to search for some girls." The other three people (George, Bubot and I) declined and sent Junior to satisfy his needs. He came back and woke everybody up again later on trying to convince us once again to go with him. We declined the invitation again and Junior left. I woke up a few hours later on, needing to go out to pee. When I returned Bubot was now beside me and he took my hand and placed it inside of his sleeping pants on his thing, using my hand to stroke himself. I obliged him, gladly. Bubot and I continued this sexual relationship from time to time, as will be seen.] AWANEN!

Saturday, February 22, 1986
My House, Gomez, Cabarroguis, Quirino

Letters to Ardis B., Chris & Mary M. and Dave & Vicki M.

₱540 – 15 = ₱525					
Cigarettes	15			TOTAL	₱15

We all got up at 6:30 AM. George and Bubot cooked breakfast for me and then they left. After bathing and eating breakfast all of Lito's kids came here; Julie polished my floor with a coconut husk and waxed it with the wax of a candle. All five of them spent the morning here making lots of noise. At noon they left and I told them I wanted to be alone in the afternoon so that I could do some writing, so they didn't return. But, in the afternoon there were people here too, so I went to Rufo's house for a couple hours! When I returned, of course people immediately showed up again. Alfredo started my supper for me and I told Junior that I wanted to sleep alone tonight so he and George didn't come to sleep here and I got to spend the evening alone and write the above letters and do some sorting that I needed to do. Lito stopped by just now and informed me that Junior is not trustworthy and to watch him like a hawk. Okay, thank you Lito, that's the impression I got to. AWANEN!

Sunday, February 23, 1986
My House, Gomez, Cabarroguis, Quirino

Letters to Tony S. & Peace Corps Language Trainer.

₱525 – 235 = ₱290							
Cigarettes	15	Coke	9	Rides	4	Nails	10
Teapot	35	Kerosene	3	Food	137	Household	22
						TOTAL	₱235

I got up at 6:00 AM and after cooking and eating breakfast I went to Gundaway to market. I bought the above and returned to Gomez. I arrived at Rufo's house at noon and ate lunch there. They showed me how to prepare pork with cabbage. Daniel slept at his new house for the first time last night. I moved into my house on the 21st and the other Daniel moved into his new house on the 22nd – amazing! I got home about 1:30 PM or so and did laundry in the stream and bathed in the stream and by then it was 4:00 PM, so I got ready to cook supper. I had rice and leftovers from last night and then sat down to write the above two letters. Now it's 9:00 PM and I'm tired, so a short entry tonight and I'm calling it quits. Good night. AWANEN!

Monday, February 24, 1986
My House, Gomez, Cabarroguis, Quirino

₱290 – 15 = ₱275							
Cigarettes	10	Coke	5			TOTAL	₱15

I got up at 6:00 AM and Alfredo came here and cooked breakfast for me – cabbage, dried fish and of course rice. After that I went to Lito's house and borrowed the coconut husk and returned home and waxed the floor again. Lito's wife came here to borrow some sugar and check up on me. After that I took a walk up the creek to the canteen and drank a bottle of Coca-Cola and ate some sugar cane candy for lunch. Then I strolled around the tree nursery area for a while and then I came back home and took a siesta for a while. When I woke up I bathed and after a while I started supper – long beans, pork and rice. In the evening Arsenio, Lito, Alfredo, Junior, another Lito and Tehring came here for a while. Then Bubot and George came here to sleep and I sent Junior away. Several people have now told me not to trust him so I guess I'll take their advice and try not to become too friendly with him. Now it's 8:00 PM and although I am not very tired, I guess I'll try to sleep, seeing as George and Bubot are already under their blankets. AWANEN!

Tuesday, February 25, 1986
My House, Gomez, Cabarroguis, Quirino

Letter to Bob S.

₱275 – 50 = ₱225							
Ginebra	35	Cigarettes	15			TOTAL	₱50

I got up at 6:00 AM and George and Bubot both went home. I prepared breakfast and ate – without any help – and then after breakfast I started to read a bit. Then a work party of eleven people showed up to dig my toilet pit. That was a surprise to me! They finished at about noon or 12:30 PM and they let me know they wanted three bottles of *Ginebra* – so I obliged them! Oh, I forgot they also helped clean up the yard. After that, we all went to the canteen and I bought three more bottles of *Ginebra.* After a while everybody was drunk and a fight came close to breaking out. I went inside and they put all machetes and knives inside. Tempers were really hot for a while – they wanted to kill each. After a while mother came to the store and accompanied me home; she brought me half a watermelon and it was delicious. I bathed and ate watermelon and then after writing a letter to Bob S., Lito and Rufo stopped by for a while. I ate supper of beans, pork and rice again and I'm now ready to write a letter to Dave G. I wonder who – if anybody – will show up to sleep with me tonight? Ah, George just arrived to sleep here. I am going to show him photos. Guess that I won't write the letter to Dave G. AWANEN!

Wednesday, February 26, 1986
My House, Gomez, Cabarroguis, Quirino

Letter to Dave G.

₱225 – 20 = ₱205							
Coke	10	Cigarettes	10			TOTAL	₱20

We got up at 6:00 AM and George went home. I cooked breakfast of cabbage and fish and then I saw Boy walk by and I ended up going with him to Calaocan. The road was slippery and Calaocan is far away, I had no idea. We searched for the bulldozer, but we didn't find it. We stopped at the Calaocan Barangay Hall for a while and I headed for home. Boy, however, continued to search for the bulldozer. I got back to the canteen at 12:30 PM and drank two bottles of Coca-Cola and ate coconut candy and then I returned home and cleaned up the yard a bit more. Then I studied Ilokano for a while and read my *Newsweek* Magazine. After that, I bathed in the creek and after a while Alfredo came by to check up on me. I cooked supper – long beans, pork and sweet potato. After supper Bubot and George came by to sleep and I showed them all my photos and the Philippines book, which they are looking at now. George is more impressed by it than Bubot. They are both getting to be a little less shy now than they were. AWANEN!

Thursday, February 27, 1986
My House, Gomez, Cabarroguis, Quirino

Letters from Dad, San & Jack G., John D. & Peace Corps.

₱205 – 43 = ₱162							
Nails	10	Candy	10	Cigarettes	15	Coke	5
Tomatoes	3					TOTAL	₱43

We got up at 6:00 AM and George and Bubot left. I cooked breakfast of cabbage and dried fish and then I washed dishes and headed down the mountain. I went to Gundaway and the post office and got the four letters shown above. Then I went to Agpalasin's Store and bought nails for my table and then I headed for Diffuncian for Esagani's birthday, but when I arrived Esagani was not there. He and Vergilio are in Santiago harvesting rice, so I ate lunch at Mendoza's Store and talked for three hours. Then it was 3:00 PM and they sent some fruits and vegetables home with me. I started walking up the mountain at 4:00 PM and arrived home a bit after 5:00 PM. Alfredo stopped by for a while and I cooked supper of squash, pork and rice, it was quite delicious, I'm a pretty good cook if I do say so myself. After that I washed dishes and then I went to the canteen and got Bubot to come sleep with me. When we got home George was waiting for us, so Bubot and George are here to sleep again. AWANEN!

Friday, February 28, 1986
My House, Gomez, Cabarroguis, Quirino

Letter to Barb W.

₱162 – 5 = ₱157							
Coke	5					TOTAL	₱5

We got up at 6:00 AM and George and Bubot left. I cooked breakfast and after eating and washing dishes, I went to Juanito Sebastian's house to remind him of the meeting next Tuesday, after all he is the President of the Farmers Association. He gave me some chili peppers and I came home and put them in the bottle of vinegar. Alfredo came by for a while and after that I strolled to the canteen and Bubot and I strolled to the place where they were making machetes. Then I returned home and did laundry, cleaned up the yard a bit and planted five banana trees in my yard. Then I started the letter to Barbara W., but too many people came by and I was unable to continue. After all of the people left I cooked supper of squash, pork, corn and rice and after supper more people came by. George came and showed me how to cook the corn on charcoal and also to sleep here. Bubot is going to Calaocan tomorrow so he is not here tonight because they have to leave early. AWANEN!

Saturday, March 1, 1986
My House, Gomez, Cabarroguis, Quirino

JB and Katie are here.

Packages from Tony & Janet S., Chris & Mary M., Dad and Dave M.

₱157 + 373 – 153 = ₱377							
Soap	10	Coffee	40	Sardines	15	Batteries	12
Rides	40	Ice Cream	15	Kerosene	3	Cigarettes	18
						TOTAL	₱153

We got up at 6:00 AM and George went home. I cooked breakfast, ate and headed down the mountain. I arrived at Burgos at 10:00 AM and left there at 10:45 AM. I arrived in Santiago at 11:45 AM and went to the Magnolia Restaurant to meet Katie and JB. There was a note there from Brooke F. saying to wait there for her. We therefore, ate lunch and waited. Brooke showed up at 1:15 PM or so and talked to us for a while and then we went to market and bought the above. I cashed a check, got packages from Brooke and we headed out at 3:00 PM. We arrived at Burgos at 5:00 PM and by the time we climbed the mountain and arrived at my house it was 6:30 PM and already dark. We cooked supper and talked and didn't go to bed until 10:00 PM. We found out from Brooke that Michael S., Ray and Lois W., Peg H., Helen M., Pat B. and Barb/John A. have all given up and gone home – that makes eight people from our group who have either been kicked out or left of their own accord. AWANEN!

Sunday, March 2, 1986
My House, Gomez, Cabarroguis, Quirino

JB and Katie are here. Ronald come from Bayombong.

₱377 – 0 = ₱377

We got up at 6:00 AM and I cooked breakfast for us. Then we strolled with Alfredo and Junior to the tree nursery, the canteen, the waterfall and then Rufo's house. At about noon Ronald showed up at Rufo's house – that was a surprise! We all returned home and ate lunch and by the time lunch was finally done Ronald had to leave – bummer – he was only here for three hours. Such is life I guess. After that JB and I built steps [dug steps in the soft soil] in the hill here below my house on the way to the stream. By the time that was done it was 5:00 PM. We fetched water, bathed and got ready to cook again. While eating supper Alfredo came by again and talked until 9:15 PM or so and then he left and I wrote yesterday's and today's journal entries. Now it's 9:45 PM and everybody is quite tired, so we're going to crash immediately. Good night. AWANEN!

Monday, March 3, 1986
My House, Gomez, Cabarroguis, Quirino

JB and Katie leave. Letter from Mark W.

₱377 – 80 = ₱297							
Rice	30	Coke	3	Cigarettes	21	Lunch	8
Rides	9	Candy	4	Veggies	5	TOTAL	₱80

We all got up at 6:00 AM, cooked, ate breakfast and got ready to leave. JB, Katie and I left here about 7:30 AM and we arrived at Burgos at 8:30 AM. We took a jeepney and arrived at the office at 9:30 AM. JB and Katie continued on. I worked on my speech until about noon and then went and bought five kilograms of rice and drank a bottle of Coke and returned to the office. Then I went out and ate lunch and after that I again returned to the office and worked on my speech until it was finished. Then I went to the post office in Gundaway. Few jeepneys were passing Gundaway so I had to make small talk with people for about an hour or so while I was waiting. I finally got to Burgos at 3:00 PM and started up the mountain at 3:15 PM. I got home at 4:00 PM and fetched water. Then I went to the canteen to ask Bubot to come and sleep here tonight. Then I bathed and started supper, which is cooking now. George and Bubot should both be coming here to sleep tonight. AWANEN!

Tuesday, March 4, 1986
My House, Gomez, Cabarroguis, Quirino

₱297 + 20 – 17 = ₱300							
Cigarettes	15	Candy	2			TOTAL	₱17

We got up at 6:00 AM and George and Bubot both went home. I cooked breakfast and then at 8:45 AM I went to the Barangay Hall for the meeting. At 10:00 AM Rody and two companions showed up. Then the meeting started and it continued until noon. We returned to my house for lunch. We cooked lunch and loitered around for a while and Rody arranged to buy a dog. Then we all went to the Barangay Captain's house because the forest guard or Montero wants to talk to him about narra smuggling in this area. That was totally boring. When we returned home the dog was already butchered and Lito, Alfredo, Kadog, Boy and more people were already cooking it. By and by we ate the dog and then Bubot came here to sleep. I'm happy he did because George is too shy to come when there are other people here (Rody and his companions from the office.) Bubot and I crashed early, because that's what we're accustomed too. I don't even know what time everybody else crashed, I suppose 10:00 PM to midnight or so. AWANEN!

Wednesday, March 5, 1986
My House, Gomez, Cabarroguis, Quirino

Letter to Dad.

₱300 – 10 = ₱290							
Cigarettes	10					TOTAL	₱10

We all got up at 6:00 AM, Bubot went home and we cooked breakfast. We finished the dog meat and rice and then we did dishes again. After that we surveyed the site for the tree nursery and when finished with that, we returned home and cooked lunch. After lunch Rody and his two companions left and I did dishes, laundry and bathed and then I went to the canteen, drank a Coke and returned home. After that I cooked supper and did dishes again and then George and Bubot came here to sleep. We studied Ilokano for a while and then at 8:00 PM we slept. AWANEN!

Thursday, March 6, 1986
My House, Gomez, Cabarroguis, Quirino

Postcards to Chris & Mary M., Dave M., Tony & Janet S. Letters to San & Jack G. and Mark W.

₱290 – 15 = ₱275							
Cigarettes	10	Coke	5			TOTAL	₱15

We got up at 6:00 AM and George and Bubot left. I cooked breakfast and ate and then Boy came and played with the radio for a while. I went and borrowed Alfredo's coconut husk and cleaned the house and porch really good. After that I strolled to the canteen and Bubot and I strolled to the charcoal pit of Amor for a while and then we went to their banana plantation. After that I returned home and ate lunch and the candy that Chris and Mary sent to me and some apricots. After that I wrote the above letters and cleaned around the yard. Then Alfredo came and watched me write one more letter. After that I bathed and did one day's worth of laundry. Alfredo returned until suppertime when he finally left – he is hard to get rid of! I ate corn, cabbage and chayote with rice for supper. I don't know who will come here to sleep tonight; surely George will come and maybe Bubot but we'll see who shows up. Now it's 6:11 PM and although my supper is cooked, I haven't yet eaten it. Ah, George and Bubot both came to sleep. AWANEN!

Friday, March 7, 1986
Nestor's House, Villa Miemban, Cordon, Isabela

Postcards from San & Jack G. (2) and Tony S. Letters from Chad D. and Teresa L.

₱275 + 1,492 – 170 = ₱1,597							
Cigarettes	25	Rides	14	Postage	7	Lunch	28
Food	33	Notebook	6	Meat	37	Veggies	15
Coke	5					TOTAL	₱170

We got up at 6:00 AM and George and Bubot left. I washed dishes from last night, cooked breakfast and ate it and then washed the dishes again. It's raining and miserable. I left my valuables at Alfredo's house, ate the papaya that Ronald brought with him last Sunday and then I headed down the mountain. I went to the post office and got the above mail and then I continued on to Santiago and bought the above. Then I caught a jeepney headed to Diadi and then I took a tricycle to Vulcan and walked from there to Nestor's house. Nestor was working at their rice field and I saw him from the trail and stopped there. It's so nice to see his smiling face again! We strolled and got food for supper and then JB came by and we all ate supper. Then father returned home and he ate. JB stayed until 8:30 or 9:00 PM before he left – rather late! We all slept immediately. I'm feeling good to be here at Nestor's house. It's always a good feeling to come here. I like it here. But, now I am happier at Gomez too, now that I have my own house. AWANEN!

Saturday, March 8, 1986
Nestor's House, Villa Miemban, Cordon, Isabela

We got up at 6:00 AM at Nestor's house and cooked, ate, washed dishes and so on. After all of that, JB came by and Nestor, JB and I went to build a new rice field near the fishpond. Then at 10:30 AM or so we returned to the house of Nestor and ate cherries and lukban. Then we strolled to the rice field near the house and checked up on the beans and hot peppers. After that we strolled to a tamarind tree while eating sugar cane. Nestor climbed the tamarind tree and knocked down a bunch of them and then JB, Nestor and I ate a bunch of tamarinds. After that we returned to the house and ate lunch. JB started walking to his tree nursery and Katie came by. Nestor and I went to the new rice field and burned the dry grass and dug around in the ground a little. Then we went up the hill and we harvested a lot of chili peppers and took them all back to Nestor's house. Then we bathed in the stream and went to the Barrio Hall to visit JB and Katie. JB and Katie cooked supper of macaroni and cheese and it was not enough so Katie made donuts too, but even that was not enough. At 8:30 PM Nestor and I returned home and ate some more because there was no rice at JB and Katie's. Now it's 9:30 PM and late! We spent many hours with JB this visit. He was around last night, this morning and then we went there this evening too. But, Nestor and I also had some good hours to talk together – at the new rice field and also at his house when we had alone time. Oh, I stubbed my toe and it hurts like the devil. AWANEN!

Sunday, March 9, 1986
My House, Gomez, Cabarroguis, Quirino

₱1,597 – 290 = ₱1,307							
Rides	20	Lunch	55	Food	98	Household	117
						TOTAL	₱290

We got up at 6:00 AM, ate a pretty quick breakfast and then got ready to go. Nestor gave me lots of chili peppers, a bottle of real coffee, three lukbans and an Ilokano/English Bible! What a friend, I can't believe it. Then we walked to Vulcan together and got a tricycle to the highway and then a jeepney to Santiago. Once there, we went to Lina's Restaurant and drank a couple of beers each and ate lunch. Then we did our "joint venture" marketing – ha. After that it was only 1:00 PM, so we had another beer and then Nestor put me on a jeepney for home. I arrived at Burgos at 3:30 PM and

Lito was there to be my companion hiking up the mountain. After many stops, we finally got home at 5:30 PM and now I'm cooking the pork and preparing it so that it's possible to keep it for a week. George is already here to sleep and Alfredo came by and he removed the husk from my coconut shell so that I can use it to polish my floors. Now I don't need to borrow one when I want to polish my floors. AWANEN!

Monday, March 10, 1986
My House, Gomez, Cabarroguis, Quirino

Letter to Bill J.

We got up at 6:00 AM and George went home. I washed the dishes from last night and cooked breakfast. Lito came by at 8:00 AM and we went to make boards for my table. We finished that at 11:00 AM and we made a new path behind my house to the creek – along the top of the old log which was lying there. It was hot today. I bathed at about 2:30 PM and then took a siesta for about ½ hour. In the evening I wrote a letter to Bill J. At 7:10 PM George had not come yet so I went and searched for him at his house and he said that he is dirty, so he is shy to come tonight. But, I told him I was not concerned about that and asked him to come, so he did. I studied Ilokano with George for a while and now it's 8:12 PM and we are listening to the radio drama and ready to sleep as soon as it finishes. AWANEN!

Tuesday, March 11, 1986
My House, Gomez, Cabarroguis, Quirino

Letters to Health Unit, Teresa L., Chad D. and Chris & Mary M.

₱1,307 – 30 = ₱1,277							
Charcoal	20	Cigarettes	10			TOTAL	₱30

We got up at 5:45 AM, George left and I cooked breakfast, ate and started a letter to Chad, but then Lito came and we planed boards for my table until 12:00 N. At noon he went home and I cleaned up the yard some more – mostly pushed stuff down the hill some more. I then gathered sticks to make a small fence to plant some chili pepper seeds. After that I took a break and then I finished planing the boards for my table – alone. I cleaned up all the planer chips and eventually bathed in the creek. Then I took a break again and eventually cooked supper of beans, pork and rice. It was delicious! I wrote letters in the evening and George came to sleep. Now it's 7:40 PM and time to sleep I guess. I'm tired, I did a good days work. AWANEN!

[End of handwritten notebook #1 of 5]

Wednesday, March 12, 1986
My House, Gomez, Cabarroguis, Quirino

₱1,277 – 13 = ₱1,264							
Coke	3	Cigarettes	10			TOTAL	₱13

We got up at 6:08 AM and George left. I cooked and ate breakfast and washed dishes and then Rufo came by to check up on my table and bench planing work and, of course he had to show me how to do it better. Then we went to the Barangay Hall for the meeting and election of officers. We went at 8:30 AM and Rody and his companions didn't show up until after 10:00 AM. Despite the lack of a quorum, they elected new officers. The meeting lasted until 12:15 PM and then Rody and his two companions, along with Rufo, came here to eat lunch. After lunch, at around 2:00 PM they left to survey somebody's land and I planed the porch and waxed it. Then I did laundry and cleaned up planer chips again and it was time to cook supper. Alfredo and Junior's father came by and stayed until 7:30 PM. Now it's 8:15 PM and George and I are now the only ones here and it's about time to sleep. I'm glad Rody and his companions are not sleeping here tonight – they're staying at the place they went to survey. Good night. AWANEN!

Thursday, March 13, 1986
My House, Gomez, Cabarroguis, Quirino

Letters to Abe F. and Jim & Roselynn S.

₱1,264 – 20 = ₱1,244							
Coke	3	Cigarettes	10	Candy	7	TOTAL	₱20

We got up at 6:00 AM and cooked breakfast. George ate here and then he left and went home. After breakfast I relaxed for a while and then I went to Alfredo's and borrowed his gardening tools and prepared a small seedbed for chili peppers. I cut a bunch of sticks for a small fence and finally I planted the chili pepper seeds. I didn't bother eating lunch because it was very hot today – the temperature was about 85°F or so by noon. In the afternoon I went to the canteen and bought cigarettes, drank a Coke and talked for a while and then returned home and ate coconut candy. Then I took a siesta for around an hour, got up and bathed in the stream and wrote the above letters. It's now 6:40 PM and George is not here yet. Now it's 7:00 PM and George has arrived. We studied a bit of Ilokano and I finished writing this. AWANEN!

Friday, March 14, 1986
My House, Gomez, Cabarroguis, Quirino

Letters from Nestor, Bill N., Mark G., Steve A., Mike Mc., Bob S., Vicki S. and Peace Corps.

₱1,244 – 15 = ₱1,229							
Ride	5	Cigarettes	10			TOTAL	₱15

We got up at 5:00 AM and George left. I cooked breakfast of cabbage and dry fish for breakfast again. Then I washed dishes, bathed and left for the office in Diffun. I arrived there at about 8:30 AM waited for Jacob Fillian to arrive [I don't remember who this was – no idea at all!] until 10:30 AM. We talked for a little while and then we all ate lunch and came to Gomez. This was the first time I got a ride all the way up the mountain – good deal. Jacob and all of us went to the tree nursery site and then we returned here. He asked me all kinds of questions about training in May and I gave him straightforward answers. After they left I fetched water and bathed. Now I'm cooking supper. At 7:20 PM I went to get George and he came to sleep at my house. Oh, I also went to the post office in Gundaway today. AWANEN!

Saturday, March 15, 1986
My House, Gomez, Cabarroguis, Quirino

Letter to Steve A.

₱1,229 – 15 = ₱1,214							
Coke	5	Cigarettes	10			TOTAL	₱15

We got up at 5:45 AM, George left and I cooked and ate breakfast. After breakfast I washed the dishes and relaxed for a while and then I went to Arsenio's house to help him do some building. I mostly made crosspieces for the roof and carried grass and passed it up to the roof when they called for it. It got hot again today, 85°F or more at noon. I came home, despite their protests to eat at Arsenio's house. I tried to explain that I can't eat when it's too hot, but I don't think they understood. I wrote the above letter, took a siesta for an hour and then returned to do more of the same work at Arsenio's house. I came home at 4:45 PM, bathed and started cooking – mungo beans and pork is all I have left. It's now 6:20 PM. [later] Now it's 8:00 PM and I went to get George. He is looking at the new *Salaysayan* Magazine [a Peace Corps magazine which was published and distributed monthly.] AWANEN!

Sunday, March 16, 1986
My House, Gomez, Cabarroguis, Quirino

Letters to Bill N. and Bob S.

₱1,214 – 204 = ₱1,010							
Food	116	Cigarettes	26	Rides	4	Drinks	19
Soaps/TP	24	Batteries	9	Misc.	6	TOTAL	₱204

We got up at 5:45 AM and George left. I washed last night's dishes and cooked breakfast – there is nothing left but dried fish! At 7:30 AM I left for Burgos and arrived there with Junior at 8:30 AM or so. Then I took a jeepney to Gundaway to get food. I spent lots of money there today and even drank a beer. Then I had lunch there too. Then I returned to Burgos, where George, Lito, Rufo and several other people were hanging out for some reason. They didn't want to head up the mountain until the weather cooled, off but I came up the mountain alone, unpacked and prepared the pork for keeping. Then I wrote the letter to Bob S. and cooked supper of squash, bagoong, tomatoes and pork and ate it with rice. It was delicious. At 7:30 PM George came and now it's 8:10 PM and about time to go to sleep. I wrote the letter to Bill N. after supper, but before George came. Damn, it was hot today. AWANEN!

Monday, March 17, 1986
My House, Gomez, Cabarroguis, Quirino

We got up at 5:15 AM and George left. I cooked breakfast of repolyo and dried fish. I barely finished breakfast and dish washing and then Rufo came to build my table. We worked on that until noon and then I cooked lunch for us – repolyo and pork. Rufo approves of my cooking; it's the second time he has eaten here. After lunch we both took a short siesta and then we got up and continued work on the table again. Later on he made the benches and I planed them and then we finished the table, but only at about dark. I spent an hour cleaning up the yard and Arsenio dropped by for a while. I bathed and then finally at about 7:00 PM I started cooking supper. It's now 7:30 PM and the rice is cooking. I'm drinking coffee and writing this while sitting at my new table – it's really nice. I also have to cook the beans and pork and George should be here in a while. I guess that's all for tonight. The moon is first quarter tonight, but it's very bright. AWANEN!

Tuesday, March 18, 1986
My House, Gomez, Cabarroguis, Quirino

Letter to Mike Mc.

₱1,010 – 15 = ₱995						
Cigarettes	10	Coke	5		TOTAL	₱15

We got up at 5:30 AM and George left. I washed dishes from last night and Arsenio came to cut grass. After breakfast we cut grass until noon and Arsenio went home for lunch. I went to the canteen to buy cigarettes, coconut candy and Coke and talk for a while. I returned home at 1:15 PM and took a short siesta and then Alfredo came for a while and Arsenio returned to cut more grass. We all cut grass until 4:30 PM and then we stopped and drank coffee and talked until about 6:00 PM. Arsenio left and I bathed in the creek [I'm going to stop referring to bathing in the creek – if I am in Gomez and this Journal says that I bathed then you can assume that it was in the creek, there was no other place to bathe. The nice stream flowed just to the side of my house and there was a nice hole there for bathing and doing laundry.] Oh, I forgot, I did laundry today too – at lunchtime and I bathed then too. After bathing for the second time I started cooking supper, which is now nearly finished. It's 7:10 PM now and supper is ready to eat as soon as I stop writing this. Arsenio returned at 2:30 PM to cut more grass. Bubot came home today, but he brought visitors so he won't be sleeping here. AWANEN!

Wednesday, March 19, 1986
My House, Gomez, Cabarroguis, Quirino

Letter to Mark G.

₱995 – 60 = ₱935							
Arsenio	40	Coke	3	Cigarettes	17	TOTAL	₱60

We got up at 5:20 AM and George left. I washed dishes from last night and then I cooked breakfast, ate and did dishes again. Arsenio came to cut grass some more. We both cut grass until noon and then Alfredo and Junior came here to talk for a while. I made coffee and cleaned around the yard with the small knife and then I went to Arsenio's house for a bit. Then I went to the canteen and I also fetched water at about 2:00 PM. Arsenio returned to cut grass again and we both cut grass until 4:30 PM, when we finally finished. We drank coffee again and I started to cook supper of long beans and pork and Alfredo came **again** – he is always here. Bubot stopped by to say goodbye [I cannot recall where he went, or why]. Despite the fact that I asked Alfredo to leave, he is still here – even now! He doesn't know when to leave. Oh, I paid Arsenio for all of the grass cutting that he has accomplished. AWANEN!

Thursday, March 20, 1986
Forgotten Lodging, Banaue, Ifugao

Letters from John D., Tom & Barb H. and Rolando. Postcards from Dad and San & Jack G.

₱935 – 75 = ₱860							
Rides	12	Lunch	10	Food	12	Beer	25
Coke	8	Misc.	8			TOTAL	₱75

We got up at 5:20 AM and George left. I did the dishes from last night, cooked breakfast, ate and did dishes again. I gave my leftover foodstuff to Alfredo and left my valuables at his house and then I headed for Burgos. I arrived at Burgos at 8:30 AM and continued on to Gundaway and picked up my mail. Then I went to the office in Diffun for the monthly meeting, ate lunch there and then I headed for Banaue for training [I cannot recall what this training was for and my Journal does not say]. At Bagabag I ran into JB and Katie and we caught a jeepney to Lagawe and from there a jeepney to Banaue. We arrived in Banaue at 5:00 PM and JB, Shannon and I went for a beer. Then at 6:30 PM we had supper and then we all went to the Folkden and drank a beer or two. Now it's 9:50 PM, past bedtime! Some people are still out drinking and carousing, but it's time for this kid to call it a night and go to bed. AWANEN!

Friday, March 21, 1986
John's House, Cababuyan, Ifugao

₱860 + 64 – 72 = ₱852							
Rides	10	Cigarettes	15	Postcards	17	Basket	30
						TOTAL	₱72

I got up at 5:30 AM and ate breakfast early, bathed and then went down to Central Banaue. I ran into John D. first thing in the morning and then Katie and I returned and we spent the day in class. We broke for lunch and then we returned to class again until 2:00 PM and then JB, Katie and I went back down to Central Banaue. I bought a small shoulder type rattan basket to carry eggs in and then we ran into John and Fred at their auntie's shop. On the spur of the moment we decided to go to Cababuyan for the night, so we left at 4:30 PM and got to Cababuyan at 5:30 PM or so. After a while we butchered a chicken and ate supper. Several people came by to talk and then at 8:30 PM everybody left and we went to bed. John, Fred and I slept together in a real bad tonight. AWANEN!

Saturday, March 22, 1986
Forgotten Lodging, Banaue, Ifugao

₱852 – 50 = ₱802							
Rides	3	Cigarettes	10	Beer	20	Coke	15
Candy	2					TOTAL	₱50

We got up at 5:20 AM at Cababuyan. John cooked breakfast and it was super delicious maybe because we ate it with native rice. At 6:34 AM we left Cababuyan and at 7:09 AM we arrived at Oong – it only took us 35 minutes to climb up the trail. John's father is Gabriel and his mother is Casilda. From Oong we caught a jeepney to Banaue at 8:00 AM. We arrived in Banaue and had to attend classes all day, right up to suppertime. After supper I walked down to the Stairway Lodge and found John and Fred and we talked on the porch for a while. Then John and I went to his house and he gave me about two kilograms of that delicious native rice and we arranged that I will come to Cababuyan on April 30th and that he will come back to Gomez with me on May 1st. At 8:10 PM I came back to the hostel, as there is supposed to be a party tonight, but it's now 9:30 PM and it hasn't yet started. Hopefully it will start soon; if not then I'll have a beer and go to bed. AWANEN!

Sunday, March 23, 1986
Nestor's House, Villa Miemban, Cordon, Isabela

₱802 – 52 = ₱750							
Rides	20	Cigarettes	10	Watermelon	15	Coke	4
Candy	3					TOTAL	₱50

We got up at 6:00 AM, ate breakfast and got ready to leave. We caught a jeepney to Bagabag and we got there at 9:15 AM or so. We waited until 10:30 AM for a jeepney to Santiago. JB, Katie and I got off at the stop before Vulcan and after a few moments we caught a tricycle to Vulcan. We walked from Vulcan and got to Villa Miemban at 1:00 PM. Nestor was sleeping because he was up all night, so I slept for an hour and then we strolled to the tree nursery. After that we planted some hot pepper seeds in Nestor's garden and then it was suppertime. After supper we planned a trip to Bontoc and we decided to meet in Vulcan on April 5th in the afternoon. Nestor also says he will come out to Gomez on the 30th of March. AWANEN!

Monday, March 24, 1986
My House, Gomez, Cabarroguis, Quirino

Postcard to Ronald R. Letter to San & Jack G.

₱750 – 316 = ₱434							
Rides	15	Food	79	Postage	57	Lunch	26
Coke	6	Groceries	114	Household	19	TOTAL	₱316

We got up late at Nestor's house – at about 6:20 AM. Then we slowly got ready to leave. Nestor picked three lukbans for me and also gave me seeds of two kinds of beans and some mahogany seeds. Finally, at about 8:00 AM I left. I got to Santiago, after walking to Vulcan, taking a tricycle to Cordon and then a jeepney to Santiago, at around lunchtime. I ate lunch and went to do shopping and I managed to get out of Santiago at 1:00 PM or so. I stopped at Gundaway but there was no mail for me. So, I got a ride to Burgos, headed up the mountain at 3:00 PM and got home at about 4:00 PM. I unpacked, bathed, prepared the pork for keeping, using the no cook method and then did dishes before dark. As I was leaving Villa Miemban Nestor actually said "thanks for coming." It seems that we continue to become closer friends. We'll meet in Gundaway on Sunday. I miss him always. Now it's 7:00 PM and I'm waiting for George to come. Maybe I'll write a letter. AWANEN!

Tuesday, March 25, 1986
My House, Gomez, Cabarroguis, Quirino

Letters to Nestor, John D, Tom & Barb H. and Rolando T.

We got up at 5:20 AM and George left. I cooked breakfast and ate and then washed dishes. It rained for the rest of the morning and one-half of the afternoon. Alfredo came by this morning and stayed until noon. Junior came at around noon and Lito's kids came shortly after that I was sanding and finishing my table. Of course they had their hands in everything. After they left Boy came and I after he left I went to fetch water and then I trimmed my beard and bathed. Then I started cooking supper of pork, beans and the long semi-hot chili peppers. I wrote the above letters to John and Tom/Barbara this morning and the letter to Nestor this evening. It's now 7:45 PM and I'm about ready to go searching for George so I can go to sleep. AWANEN!

Wednesday, March 26, 1986
My House, Gomez, Cabarroguis, Quirino

Letter to Gregorio R.

₱434 – 10 = ₱424							
Cigarettes	10					TOTAL	₱10

We got up at 5:30 AM and George left. It was raining. I cooked breakfast of beans, dried fish and rice, ate and then washed dishes. Alfredo, Pedring and Boy came by to talk for a while. Then after a while we went to Alfredo's house and got some water buffalo manure and chicken manure and some good soil from near the creek and mixed it all together and I planted some lukban seeds. I got 25 planted before I gave up because of the rain and the soil being too wet and practically flowing! I cooked lunch of beans and the long green chili peppers while Alfredo and his wife looked at the "Philippines" book. After lunch I locked the door and played with my HP-71 calculator for a while. I set the time and date and wrote a clock program and then I took a half hour siesta. I got up and bathed and then went to the store and bought cigarettes. I cooked supper and George came early – good I'm happy with George, he never laughs at me when I speak Ilokano. AWANEN!

Thursday, March 27, 1986
My House, Gomez, Cabarroguis, Quirino

Letters from Jim W., Fred & Cynthia B., Tim N.K. Postcard from Vicki S.

₱424 – 212 = ₱212							
Cigarettes	44	Food	44	Rides	16	Gabion	35
Misc.	17	Kerosene	7	Haircut	5	Lunch	29
Drinks	15					TOTAL	₱212

We got up at 5:30 AM and George left. I cooked breakfast, ate, washed dishes and headed down the mountain for Burgos. I got to Burgos at 8:30 AM or so and then to Gundaway at 9:00 AM. I picked up my mail from the post office, as shown above, and then I continued on to Santiago and mailed letters from the last few days. The bank was closed for this Holy Thursday Holiday so I couldn't get any money – bad news! I ate lunch, shopped and caught a ride back out this way. I started walking up the mountain at 2:37 PM at arrived at my house at 3:30 PM or so. Alfredo came by and lots of other people too and they all worked on making the handle for my gabion [a tool kind of like a hoe and a pick-axe combined]. I gave all of them marienda and coffee and then they all left and I cooked and ate supper. Now it's 7:10 PM and I'm waiting for George to come. AWANEN!

Friday, March 28, 1986
My House, Gomez, Cabarroguis, Quirino

Letter to JB & Katie F.

We got up at 5:30 AM, George left and I cooked breakfast, ate and washed dishes. Then Lito's wife came by and got some garlic from me and took my sleeping bag and thick blanket to wash them for me. I started to do my laundry and Lando came by – drunk – and insisted that I come to Lito's fish pond NOW – so I did. They were draining it. I had an idea to start their siphon, which they couldn't get working, but my idea didn't work either. They were using bamboo hollowed out and fitted together and it was not air tight at all. So, we made the drainage ditch deeper and then we managed to start the siphon by using Francisco's idea. I finally escaped at 1:00 PM and came home and did my laundry – I had lots of dirty clothes. It was 4:00 PM by the time I finished laundry. Then I bathed and after that a bunch of people came by and I gave them all coffee. Then I cooked supper of clams from Lito's fishpond with onions, garlic and ginger and ate it with rice. I gave the remainder of the clams and some fish to Alfredo. Now it's 7:00 PM and I'm waiting for George. I have a backache. Maybe I'll write a letter to JB and Katie tonight. AWANEN!

Saturday, March 29, 1986
My House, Gomez, Cabarroguis, Quirino

₱212 – 35 = ₱177					
Pork	35			TOTAL	₱35

We got up at 5:20 AM and George left. I cooked breakfast, ate, washed dishes and then I cut grass in the yard behind the house until noon. I took a break and ate some bananas. After my lunch of bananas, George brought me some pork – they butchered a pig today. Then I cut some grass in the front yard and that's really all I did today, but I cleaned for several hours. Lito's wife came by twice today. After I finished cleaning and cooking the pork, Alfredo and I bathed at the bathing spot together – did he just want to see my naked body or what, why did he want to bathe together anyway? Then all of Lito's kids came by for an hour while I cooked supper.

After eating a big supper and washing dishes George and Alfredo came by and we tried to burn some brush, but it was too wet to burn. Now it's 8:10 PM and George is playing with the radio. AWANEN!

Sunday, March 30, 1986
My House, Gomez, Cabarroguis, Quirino

Nestor is here!

₱177 – 73 = ₱104							
Food	23	Drinks	26	Misc.	4	Rides	6
Watermelon	6	Soap	8			TOTAL	₱35

We got up at 5:20 AM and George left. I cooked breakfast, ate and washed dishes and then at 7:30 AM I left for Burgos. From Burgos I took a jeepney to Gundaway and bought the above. Nestor found me at 9:45 AM or so. We finished shopping and walked to the junction to catch a ride. There were few rides and few people at market today, maybe because it's Easter. The weather is hot and we sweated a lot. We finally got to Burgos and walked up the mountain to Gomez, arriving at my house at 12:25 PM. We relaxed for a while and then we ate the lukban that Nestor brought. Oh, I forgot we cooked and ate lunch here too. After a while we bathed and cooked supper. We ate and it's now 9:30 PM and we're both very tired. We will sleep quite soon. AWANEN!

Monday, March 31, 1986
My House, Gomez, Cabarroguis, Quirino

Nestor is here!

We got up at 5:40 AM and the first thing we did was to wash the dishes from last night. Then we cooked breakfast, ate and did dishes again. Nestor showed me how to prepare my garden the best way. We dug with the gabion and made three flats and we planted yard-long beans. We also planted several other things and then on the side of the hill we made individual holes and planted okra and squash. After we were finished with all of that we ate watermelon and then rested for a while. When we woke up I had a bad headache. After a while we went to the site of the tree nursery and we fetched water. Nestor showed me how to sharpen my machete and then after a while we bathed and cooked supper of winged beans, yard-long beans, pork and rice. After that we talked a bunch and studied a bit of Ilokano. Now it's 10:15 PM and as soon as I finish this we're going to sleep. AWANEN!

Tuesday, April 1, 1986
My House, Gomez, Cabarroguis, Quirino

Nestor leave.

₱104 – 14 = ₱90					
Cigarettes	10	Coke	4		TOTAL	₱14

We got up late – at 5:40 AM, cooked and ate breakfast. After doing dishes Nestor and I talked for a while and then he left at about 8:10 AM. I returned Alfredo's gardening tools and talked with him for a while and then got ready to go to the meeting. Alfredo, Mateo and I went but we were the only ones to show up. We waited until 9:30 AM and gave up. Rody finally showed up at my house at 10:30 AM and visited for a while and then slept while I prepared my quarterly report. While writing that I also cooked lunch. We finished lunch at 1:00 PM and Rody left at 2:00 PM. I took a short siesta and then watered the garden, fetched water and went to the store for cigarettes. Then I returned home and cooked supper, did dishes and now I'm writing this and waiting for George to come. Maybe I'll write a letter while I am waiting for him to arrive. AWANEN!

Wednesday, April 2, 1986
My House, Gomez, Cabarroguis, Quirino

Letters to Chris & Mary M., Fred & Cynthia B., Jim W. and Quarterly Report to Peace Corps.

₱90 – 10 = ₱80				
Cigarettes	10			TOTAL	₱10

We got up at 5:40 AM and George left. I cooked breakfast, washed dishes and relaxed for a while and then I waxed the floor, the table, the benches and everything else I could think of. I wrote letters to Fred and Cynthia B. and Chris and Mary M. and then my brother Jim. I drank some hot chocolate for lunch and then Amor came by. We began to take a short siesta and then Alfredo came by too, so we all took a siesta for about two hours. We got up, ate lunch, washed dishes and then I went to the canteen for cigarettes and a Coke. Then I returned home and explored a bit around the back "jungle" of my yard. I discovered some good size gabi [taro] so I dug one up for supper. Then I bathed and cleaned the gabi, started supper and read *Newsweek*. I ate supper and did dishes and now it's 6:45 PM and I'm waiting for George to come. Maybe I'll write another letter, I don't know yet. AWANEN!

Thursday, April 3, 1986
My House, Gomez, Cabarroguis, Quirino

Letter to Tim N. K. Letters from P.C. Health Unit, Brooke F. & Vicki S.

₱80 + 1,865 – 278 = ₱1,667

Cigarettes	40	Food	8	Rice	29	Rides	16
Carborundum	32	Stationery	14	Lunch	28	Kitchen	31
Marilens	74	Drinks	6			TOTAL	₱278

We got up at 5:40 AM and George left. I cooked breakfast and did dishes and at 8:00 AM I headed for Burgos. From there I caught a ride to Gundaway and went to the post office and then I continued on to the office. Francisco was not there, nor was Mr. Romero, the District Forester, so I signed my quarterly report and continued on to Santiago. I cashed checks, ate lunch, mailed my quarterly report to the Peace Corps and bought the above – the carborundum stone for sharpening my machete and knives. Then I caught a jeepney to Burgos. It was very hot in Santiago and lots of drunks were hanging out at Rogel's canteen. I got home about 5:00 PM, fetched water, bathed, put things away and started supper. Now it's 7:00 PM. I haven't eaten yet and George is not yet here. I have a headache, probably because it was too hot in Santiago. I had a nice companion to climb the mountain with, but I don't know his name. He was 17 years old – too young for me, but a cutie! AWANEN!

Friday, April 4, 1986
My House, Gomez, Cabarroguis, Quirino

Letter to Dave M. Postcards to Tony & Janet S. and Dad.

We got up at 5:10 AM, I did dishes from last night and George left, did he stick around just to see if I would wash the dishes before starting to cook with them again? Anyway, I cooked breakfast, ate and did dishes again and then wrote the above letters. WOW – the *utong* [yard-long beans] that I planted just four days ago are already up and around 2 – 3 inches tall overnight! Seeds sure germinate quickly in this heat. At 11:00 AM I went to Rufo's house to let him know there's no seminar tomorrow. He wasn't there but Daniel was, so I told him and he will tell his father. On my way back home I removed the bushes which block the view of my house from the road. At 1:00 PM I took a short siesta and then got up watered the garden and fetched water. Then I trimmed my beard and bathed. I didn't do a hell of a lot today! I cooked supper and ate too late to do dishes. Now it's 7:15 PM and I'm waiting for George to come. This is my last night here for ten days. I guess I'll miss the place, the people and my house. AWANEN!

Saturday, April 5, 1986
Stairway Lodge – Banaue, Ifugao

₱1,667 – 200 (leave at home) – 170 = ₱797							
Rides	39	Postage	24	Meals	89	Misc.	18
						TOTAL	₱170

We got up at 5:30 AM and George left. I cooked breakfast and then left for Burgos at about 8:40 AM. I stopped at Gundaway and checked the post office and then continued on to the office in Diffun to leave a note for Francisco saying that I'm taking vacation. I then I continued on to Santiago and ate lunch with Julie and strolled with her for an hour. Then I caught a jeepney to Vulcan and waited for Nestor for about forty minutes. We decided to go as far as we can today, so we caught a jeepney to Bagabag and then to Lagawe. Then, with some difficulty, we got a jeepney from Lagawe to Banaue at 7:00 PM. We arrived in Banaue at about 8:00 PM and there were no rooms at the Stairway Lodge, but they put together a bed for us and of course they are their usual very friendly and pleasant selves. It's good to be here with Nestor. AWANEN!

Sunday, April 6, 1986
Nestor's Aunt's Home, Tadian, Mountain

₱797 – 141 = ₱656							
Meals	36	Bread	5	Rides	100	TOTAL	₱141

We got up at 5:40 AM and waited around while drinking coffee. Then we ate breakfast and got ready to leave. We caught a jeepney for Bontoc at 7:25 AM and arrived in Bontoc at 10:30 AM and then, practically immediately, we caught a jeepney for Tadian. We arrived at Tadian at 1:00 PM and immediately found Nestor's aunt. After a bit of talking we went to their house and then everybody talked in both Igarot and Ilokano languages, it seemed all mixed up to me, I was confused. By and by we ate lunch – they served a red rice – it was the first time I'd ever seen red rice and it was so delicious that I could have eaten it all, but I didn't. After lunch we talked and then after a while we strolled to several houses where nobody was home! We finally found one of Nestor's uncles at home and talked there for a while and then returned to the aunt's house. We talked and goofed off and talked and then ate supper – with that delicious red rice once again. Now we're listening to the radio and it's time for bed. We had a good day – I'm always happy when I'm with Nestor. AWANEN!

Monday, April 7, 1986
Nestor's Aunt's Home, Tadian, Mountain

₱656 – 10 = ₱646							
Cigarettes	10					TOTAL	₱10

We got up late at 5:40 AM. We ate breakfast and then got ready to go to the school. They want to know what I can suggest for them to do – after just a few hours here! Then we ate marienda with the school principal and after that we strolled to a trade school on the mountain. After that we went to the mountaintop, but we didn't even stop on the mountaintop. Then we returned here by a roundabout way and ate lunch. After lunch we went to a house where we had to drink a bottle of *Ginebra.*

Then we went to a different house for supper – and another bottle of *Ginebra.* Then we continued on to yet another house, where there were lots of people. While there we had to drink some rice wine. After that we went to another house and then another house where they even had a TV, so we had to watch TV until 9:30 PM then we finally got to come home. I cried on Nestor's shoulder until about 10:30 PM about the difficulties I had this day. It really was a difficult day, too many different languages and too much alcohol. AWANEN!

Tuesday, April 8, 1986
Nestor's Aunt's Home, Tadian, Mountain

₱646 – 20 = ₱626						
Cigarettes	10	Snacks	10		TOTAL	₱20

We got up relatively late, at 6:00 AM, ate breakfast and got ready to stroll. Somebody decided that today we would go to Cagabutan, over on another mountain. It was a three hour hike over there and of course we walked fast so there wasn't much time to observe the beauty, but that's life in the Philippines I guess. We got there and saw the enchanted eel and fed it in its pool and then we ate lunch there and got ready to return home. Oh, of course we had to see the school first and take some photos. Then we started home. We had a record time going until we stopped at some other barrio to talk and then we lost all of our time. We finally got home at somewhat after 5:00 PM. They butchered a chicken and we ate. Some other cousin also came here to eat. Now Nestor and his cousin are out strolling; I remained behind. I want to go home I don't know what Nestor will say if I tell him. I'm having trouble adjusting here – it's a new dialect for me and I'm tired of continuous talking and a million hours of sitting around on "standby". I'm tired of meeting people who don't even introduce themselves and nobody bothers to introduce me other than to say that this is another cousin or another relative. How long have we been here now? I don't see how I can possibly last nine or ten days like our plan calls for. I think I must tell Nestor that I'll stick it out for one more day and if I don't start feeling better in my mind then I want to go home. I know he will be disappointed, maybe even a little angry, but I hope he doesn't feel obligated to leave just because I want to – that is my only big worry – that he will insist on leaving too, if I do. Now it's 8:00 PM and I think I'll try to crash, even though Nestor has not yet returned. AWANEN!

Wednesday, April 9, 1986
Nestor's Uncle's Home, Gayang, Mountain

₱626 – 15 = ₱611						
Cigarettes	10	Bread	5		TOTAL	₱15

We got up at 5:00 AM and got ready to leave. When Nestor returned last night at 10:00 PM I woke up and told him I wanted to go and he told me that he already planned to leave today. At first I didn't believe him, I even thought I had just talked him into leaving and felt very bad and somewhat angry about it, but finally he convinced me and it was obvious this morning that the family was expecting us to leave. So, we caught a jeepney to Supang and after a couple of hours there and some food we left for here – Gayang. We walked here from Supang. It was a really beautiful walk of about two hours. We arrived here at about 1:30 PM and after a while of talking we bathed and then returned and talked some more. Then we ate supper and now it's 9:15 PM and time for bed. AWANEN!

Gayang, at the base of that small mountain there, and it's terraced rice fields, in the early morning sun.

Thursday, April 10, 1986
Small Inn, Sagada, Mountain

₱611 – 114 = ₱497							
Cigarettes	10	Bread	10	Rides	38	Lunch	25
Supper	31					TOTAL	₱114

We got up at 6:00 AM, ate breakfast and got ready to leave. We left at about 8:00 AM and got to the road about 9:00 AM. We couldn't get a ride to Bontoc until nearly noon. Nestor and I had a good long talk while we waited. A friendly man on a bus made it stop for us while we were waiting and we got a ride as far as Sagada. We arrived in Sagada at about 1:30 PM. We ate lunch, found a small inn to stay at and took a siesta for a while. We woke up kind of late, at about 5:00 PM, and strolled around until dark. Then we found a place to eat supper, ate and then returned to the inn and talked until now. It's 9:45 PM and we're getting ready to sleep. It was a really good day and I had a really good talk with Nestor. I feel really good about today. Good night. AWANEN!

Friday, April 11, 1986
Nestor's Cousin's Home, Bontoc, Mountain

₱497 – 120 = ₱377							
Breakfast	18	Lodging	50	Cigarettes	15	Souvenirs	11
Snacks	11	Rides	5	Misc.	10	TOTAL	₱120

We got up at 6:00 AM and prepared to go for a stroll. We went to Latipan Cave before breakfast, just Nestor and I, and it was a really beautiful place to see. Then we searched for and found a place to eat breakfast. After breakfast we returned to the inn and prepared to leave. We left at 11:30 AM but there were jeepneys until 12:30 PM, so we arrived in Bontoc at about 1:30 PM, and as luck would have it, there were no more rides to Banaue. So we walked around a bit and Nestor found a lost cousin – Antony S. – and we strolled around with him for a while, visited his home and talked. After a while we strolled again and Nestor and I went for a swim. Then the three of us ate supper and then we went to a place called "The Family Club" and drank beer and listened to slow music until after 10:00 PM. Then we returned to Antony's house and it's now 10:45 PM and time to sleep. AWANEN!

Saturday, April 12, 1986
Nestor's Friend's Home, Lawig, Ifugao

₱377 – 153 = ₱224							
Rides	136	Drinks	9	Cigarettes	8	TOTAL	₱153

We got up late, at 6:00 AM, and got ready to leave Bontoc after breakfast. We went to the bus stop at 7:30 AM or so and left at about 8:00 AM, going straight to Lamut. We arrived in Lamut at about noon and then after waiting a while, we caught a tricycle to Lawig, where Nestor went to high school. I asked him why he ended up here for high school but he wouldn't tell me. Anyway, we arrived here at 1:30 or 2:00 PM, ate lunch and killed time until 4:00 PM and then we took a twenty minute stroll. Then we returned to Nestor's friend's house, where Nestor and his friend butchered a duck for supper. I escaped by myself for a while – today and here I really feel like I don't belong. The expression "three's a crowd" keeps hitting me in the head and I'm the third one. Today Nestor won't even answer half of my questions. Is he embarrassed because of my understanding only a little of what's being said, or what? I don't know. I'm really feeling low tonight at 8:30 PM. AWANEN!

Sunday, April 13, 1986
My House, Gomez, Cabarroguis, Quirino

₱224 – 205 = ₱19							
Rides	20	Drinks	15	Cigarettes	45	Batteries	43
Lunch	20	Food	62			TOTAL	₱205

We got up at 5:30 AM, drank coffee, bathed and then ate breakfast and got ready to leave Lawig. We took a tricycle to Lamut, where Nestor bought me a beautiful machete, then we continued on to Bagabag and then to Santiago. We arrived in Santiago at about 10:30 AM and after Nestor helped me at market, we ate lunch and drank a Hallo-Hallo. Then he put me on a jeepney for home after we said goodbye until next time. It was difficult say goodbye. I can't believe that Nestor gave me the machete, and all I gave him was a coin purse from Sagada and a set of Energizer batteries. I arrived in Burgos at about 2:00 PM and started up the mountain about 3:00 PM I guess. I got home and fetched water, bathed, cooked some pork which I bought in Santiago, cooked the rest of supper and then ate. As I was finishing supper Alfredo came by with my bag of valuables and after eating supper and washing dishes we talked for a while. I told him my stories and then his wife hollered that his supper was ready, so he left. Now it's 7:30 PM and I'm waiting for George to come so we can sleep. While I'm waiting I'll fill this page with reflections on the past week. Sometimes it was very difficult for me and sometimes quite easy. I guess nobody ever said that the Peace Corps would be easy! Nestor and I are really fine friends and I certainly hope that it's possible for him to come to Alaska with me in 1987. All in all, our stroll for the last nine days was really fine. We really did stroll quite far and wide. I hope it strengthened our friendship and I hope Nestor is not sorry that he took me along. We don't really understand what makes each other tick, but that's the result of two different cultural upbringing. Thank you Nestor. AWANEN!

Monday, April 14, 1986
My House, Gomez, Cabarroguis, Quirino

Letter to Dad.

We got up at 5:15 AM and George left. I started cooking breakfast of dried fish and vegetables and after eating, I did dishes, took a break and then I did laundry from the last week, which took until 10:30 AM. Then I relaxed for a while and then I cooked lunch of mungo beans. After lunch I wrote a letter to Dad. I haven't gone to get my mail in close two weeks so there is probably lots of it for me at the post office.

I finished the letter to Dad at 2:30 PM and then took a siesta until 3:30 PM, when Lito's kids came and woke me up. As usual, they were asking for everything in the house. I watered the garden, fetched water and then bathed. After that I started cooking supper and they left. My supper is beans, pork and rice. George came at 7:00 PM. Now it's 7:20 and AWANEN!

Tuesday, April 15, 1986
My House, Gomez, Cabarroguis, Quirino

We got up at 5:15 AM and George left, but before he left I asked him to tell his father that I want to go and see their vegetable farm. I cooked breakfast, did dishes and got ready for the day and at 7:15 AM Alfredo came to take me to their vegetable farm. We had to climb the mountain to get there, although it's probably only about 20 minutes away. We arrived and Alfredo showed me what's going on there and then we went and found George and I helped him remove all the banana trees which didn't have fruit. We only removed one kind of banana trees. We cut down banana trees until 10:30 AM and then we ate lunch and rested until 12:30 PM. Then we went to work again cutting down more banana trees until we were done, at about 3:00 PM. Then Alfredo and I returned home and George stayed there to pasture his water buffalo. We arrived home at about 3:30 PM, talked for a while and then I bathed and cooked supper. Alfredo showed me how to cook *sabunganay* [banana blossom] for supper. Now it's 7:00 PM and George is here. AWANEN!

Wednesday, April 16, 1986
My House, Gomez, Cabarroguis, Quirino

Letter to Nestor. Film to Chris M.

₱19 – 5 = ₱14				
Coke	5			TOTAL ₱5

We got up at 5:20 AM and George left. I cooked breakfast, ate, washed dishes and then cleaned the house really good. After that I cleaned up the ground and then I did two days worth of laundry. Junior came by at about noon and slept while I cooked lunch. I ate lunch and then Junior invited me to play with his thing. I jacked him off and he helped me do the same and then we both slept for a while. When we woke up, Junior left and I wrote the letter to Nestor and then I returned the charcoal sacks to Mr. Espinosa and drank a Coke and ate some bananas at the canteen. After that I fetched water and Alfredo came by to talk for a while. I bathed while he read a magazine and then I started cooking supper and Alfredo left. After eating supper and doing dishes I wrote to Chris M. and asked him to have prints made of all of the photos on this roll of film which I'll mail soon. Now it's 7:40 PM and George is not here yet, wonder why? I'll smoke a cigarette and then holler for him to come. AWANEN!

Thursday, April 17, 1986
My House, Gomez, Cabarroguis, Quirino

Mail tax stuff to Chris M. Letters from Barb W., Bob S. (2), San & Jack G., Katie F., Gregorio R. (2), Ronald R., Chris & Mary M. Postcards from Dad, Vicki S., Ann T., Liz R. and Bill J. Package from P.C. Health Unit

Brooke F. is here.

₱14 + 300 – 275 = ₱39							
Rides	4	Postage	75	Rice	83	Kitchen	40
Cigarettes	40	Sack	5	Batteries	12	Food	16
						TOTAL	₱275

We got up at 5:15 AM and George left. I cooked breakfast, washed dishes and got ready to leave. I left at 7:30 AM. I stopped at the post office in Gundaway and got the above letters and then I went to the office in Diffun. I talked with the District Forester for a while because Francisco was not there again. Brooke showed up at the office at 11:00 AM and we all talked for a while and then we went to the Diffun post office to mail letters. After eating lunch at the office we headed for Gomez and arrive here about 2:30 PM or so. After a while of talking we strolled to the tree nursery, Francis' rice field, Anaceta's citrus farm and then we returned home. I cooked supper, bathed and we ate and talked some more. Now it's 8:20 PM and George is not here yet. I wonder if he will come or not; if he doesn't Alfredo said that he will. The community wants to be sure that I am not having sex with my P.C. boss! AWANEN!

Friday, April 18, 1986
My House, Gomez, Cabarroguis, Quirino

Letter to Bob S.

Brooke F. leave.

We got up at 5:30 AM, George came – despite his shyness – last night, but he left immediately when we got up this morning. Brooke and I cooked and ate breakfast and talked for a while and then Brooke and I went to Rufo's house, but he was not there. I hung out at Rufo's for a while and Brooke headed down the mountain. After I got tired of waiting for Rufo I returned home and wrote the above letter to Bob S. After that I took a siesta in preparation for tonight's wedding. Junior came here to sleep again, but he did not invite me to masturbate him this time and I did not offer to do so. [As a matter of fact, Wednesday was the final time that Junior and I ever engaged in any kind of sexual play. I don't know what it was about him, but I just did not enjoy doing anything with him.] After I woke up I watered the garden and then Junior woke up and left. I fetched water and a bunch of kids and Amor came by. The kids were okay, but I can't stand Amor so I locked the door and went to Alfredo's house. After a while I returned home, bathed, cooked supper, ate and washed dishes and then Alfredo, Junior and somebody else came by and after that we all, including George, went to the wedding. I left by myself at 11:00 PM. George says he will wake me up when he comes home – we'll see. It's now midnight, good night. AWANEN!

Saturday, April 19, 1986
My House, Gomez, Cabarroguis, Quirino

Letter to Ardis B.

I got up at 5:30 AM. George did not come last night, he stayed at the wedding all night. I cooked breakfast, ate and did dishes and then I did laundry and then wrote the above letter. After that I read the rest of my mail from the other day and then I cleaned up the area below the house that has the banana trees growing on it. I didn't eat lunch today but I took a long siesta because I only slept a little last night. When I woke up I watered the garden and then Arsenio and his wife came by and we talked for a while. After they left I fetched water, trimmed my beard, shaved and then cooked supper. Then at just 6:30 PM I went to get George. It's now only 7:00 PM but he's ready to sleep and I'm also about ready. I have to get up and leave early tomorrow. AWANEN!

Sunday, April 20, 1986
Forgotten Resort, Caba, La Union

₱39 + 400 – 119 = ₱320							
Rides	88	Lunch	15	Ice Cream	8	Coke	3
Cigarettes	5					TOTAL	₱119

We got up at 4:10 AM and I gave George my leftover food. I showed him where to water the garden and he left. I cooked breakfast and was ready to leave by 6:30 AM. I arrived at Cordon at 8:10 AM and left there at 9:00 AM. I arrived in Rosario at 3:30 PM and Caba by about 4:30 PM. It was strange to see all the old faces again, interesting to see how people have developed and what they've developed into. Actually there were not too many surprises. Amazingly, I don't seem to have any more to write tonight. It seems to always be like this when I'm in training mode. Now it's 9:35 PM and I guess time to say good night. AWANEN!

Monday, April 21, 1986
Forgotten Resort, Caba, La Union

I got up at 5:40 AM, showered and took an early walk on the beach and watched the sunrise. At 6:30 AM we ate breakfast and then at 7:30 AM classes began. I had a language session with Mark F. and Chris E. and then we took a break for lunch at noon. We had classes again in the afternoon and we finished at 4:30 PM. I went for a swim and after a while I watched the sunset [*lumnek ti innit*] with a Filipino brother. After that I ate supper and then went for another walk up the beach. I met a couple of Filipino brothers and talked with them for a while and then returned to the resort, drank a Coke and came to the room. Now it's 9:10 PM. AWANEN!

Tuesday, April 22, 1986
Forgotten Resort, Caba, La Union

₱320 – 20 = ₱300							
Cigarettes	5	Candy	6	Soap	3	Beer	6
						TOTAL	₱20

I got up at 5:00 AM and took a beach walk searching for shells. I walked quite a ways up the beach and returned just in time for breakfast. I talked with some interesting people along the way and in general I had a good walk, but I didn't find any shells to speak of. I expected to at least find a few! We had language classes all day – yesterday went fast but today went very slowly. We even translated a folktale, which was really boring. After classes were finished I went for a swim and talked with my same friend from yesterday; his name is Nelson. I found out that Ilokano for sunrise is *rumuar ti innit*. Maritess, our supposed language instructor didn't know that! Now it's 7:50 PM, too early to sleep. I guess that I'll take a short walk. I don't feel like writing a letter. AWANEN!

Wednesday, April 23, 1986
Forgotten Resort, Caba, La Union

₱300 + 222 – 10 = ₱512					
Cigarettes	5	Beer	5		TOTAL ₱10

I got up at 5:30 AM and strolled up the beach for a while again and talked to some people about Bangos or milkfish. Then I returned for breakfast and then went to class once again. We spent the entire day studying language. After class I went for a swim. My friend Nelson did not come by today I wonder why. My language interview is at 8:00 AM tomorrow. It's now 8:15 PM and I guess I don't have anything more to say. Maybe by and by Jerry and I will take a stroll – he's one of the people who works here and is quite obviously gay. Now it's 9:06 PM. Jerry and I took a walk up the beach and returned, he got dizzy and extremely tired. [WOW! We walked up the beach hand in hand and then after a while we found an isolated rest house near the beach and played around for a while. He assumed that I wanted to have anal sex with him and explained that he did not want to do that because he has already had surgery two times due to anal tears. Apparently he'd been with some what I would call sexual predators who did not care about anything except their own pleasures. I, on the other hand, am kind of the opposite – my pleasure comes from seeing and being a part of my partner's pleasure. I did not want to have anal intercourse with Jerry. I wanted to give him a blow job, which he permitted. Apparently it was the first time he had ever experienced such pleasure in his life. He came and came and came. It was so exciting for him that it took all of the energy out of him and he was so dizzy and smiling so hard that he could hardly walk back to the resort. WOW!] AWANEN!

Thursday, April 24 1986
Forgotten Resort, Caba, La Union

Letter to Liz & Randy.

₱512 – 32 = ₱480							
Dog Meat	20	Cigarettes	12			TOTAL	₱32

I didn't sleep good last night because it was extremely hot. I got up at 5:40 AM and took a very short walk before breakfast. I had my language interview at 8:00 AM and got a rating of 3+ but what does really mean? Barb, Maritess, I and a couple of other people went to see a fish pond in the area at 10:30 AM – way down the beach. We returned at 12:45 PM and ate lunch. We didn't have classes this afternoon so I wrote the above letter. I slept for 25 minutes before afternoon marienda and then we had a 4:30 PM meeting about the next two days happenings. This evening there's a total lunar eclipse – cool! Jerry has no time to stroll tonight, he says tomorrow night will be good for him. At this point after seven months I'd like to give a special mention to seven special people, Ronald in Bayombong, Bubot, George and Junior in Gomez, John and Frederick in Banaue and Jerry – here in Caba. All of them have been special friends in a special way, if you know what I mean. AWANEN!

Friday, April 25 1986
Forgotten Resort, Caba, La Union

Letter to Barb W.

₱480 – 10 = ₱470							
Cigarettes	10					TOTAL	₱10

I got up at 5:45 AM and didn't even take a beach walk. I ate breakfast and then went to class at 7:30 AM. Today we had a general tech session and it was generally pretty boring. We had a lunch break and then had to return to class again until 4:00 PM. After that I went for a short swim and then took some sunset pictures and after that I ate supper. After supper lots of people went to Wallace to listen to some band which is playing there tonight. Around 8:00 PM I went for a short walk and now it's only 8:20 but I think I'm going to crash. There is nothing more to say about today. AWANEN!

Saturday, April 26 1986
Forgotten Resort, Caba, La Union

Letter to Chris & Mary M.

₱470 – 180 = ₱290							
Cigarettes	15	Bar Bill	126	Jerry	35	Coke	4
						TOTAL	₱180

I got up at 5:20 AM, showered and went out on the beach and talked to a fisherman about the Bangos (milkfish) again. After a while it was time to return for breakfast. After breakfast we had classes again. Today we had a session on dealing with the Philippine bureaucracy, which was really good. Other than that, today was kind of boring once again. The session as a whole – looking at the entire week – was really good; it was an educational week. After classes were finished I took a swim and watched the last ocean sunset and then we ate supper. After supper Jerry and I took one last stroll up the beach – we make good companions. Everybody is now partying and several people have already left to return to their sites. It's now 9:06 PM, time to say good night I guess. AWANEN!

Sunday, April 27 1986
Nestor's House, Villa Miemban, Cordon, Isabela

₱290 – 110 = ₱180							
Cigarettes	10	Rides	71	Coke	6	Food	11
Lunch	12					TOTAL	₱110

I got up at 5:10 AM, strolled on the beach for the last time and then waited for breakfast. Breakfast was late, not served until 7:00 AM. I ate and got ready to leave. I left at about 8:30 AM and took a mini-bus to Carmen and then a Pantranco Bus to Kakilingan. I was lucky and wasn't at Kakilingan for five minutes and a jeepney came by, despite the fact that it was already 4:00 PM. I got to Kakandongan at about 4:30 PM and walked to Nestor's house, getting there at about 5:10 PM. He was home and has a new haircut! We were happy, as usual, to see each other. After a while we strolled and watered his garden and talked for a bit. Supper was kind of late and it's now 9:20 PM, really late for all of us. I hope we go to bed soon. AWANEN!

Monday, April 28, 1986
My House, Gomez, Cabarroguis, Quirino

Letters from Steve A., Ardis B., Yip C.H., postcards from Teresa L., Ardis B., San & Jack, G. and Rolando T. Photos from Ardis B.

₱180 + 300 – 365 = ₱115

Cigarettes	39	Food	216	Rides	14	Lunch	29
Drinks	12	Stamps	12	T-Shirt	35	Misc.	8
						TOTAL	₱365

We got up at 5:40 AM, ate breakfast and I left Villa Miemban at 8:00 AM. I had to walk all the way to Vulcan. From there I got a ride via tricycle and then took a jeepney to Santiago. I arrived in Santiago at 10:30 AM or so, went to the bank, ate lunch, did my shopping and headed for home. I stopped at the post office in Gundaway and got the above mail and then continued on to Burgos. I started climbing the mountain at 3:00 PM and got here at 3:45 PM. I fetched water and bathed then I cooked my pork and my supper. I finished supper late and I'm going to do dishes in the morning. George went to a wedding tonight so Alfredo came to sleep here. It's hot today! AWANEN!

Tuesday, April 29, 1986
My House, Gomez, Cabarroguis, Quirino

Letters to Gregorio R. & family; Biographical information to Fritz G.

We got up at 5:00 AM and Alfredo left. I washed dishes from last night and then cooked breakfast. After eating breakfast and doing dishes again I loafed for a while and then did laundry from the past several days. After finishing laundry I went through tons of Peace Corps papers and rearranged them all and threw away a stack of papers an inch thick. Rufo and the teacher's husband stopped by and said they need to talk to Rody and/or Francisco regarding taxes. After that I wrote the above letters, drank a cup of coffee and took a short siesta from 2:00 to 3:00 PM. Upon waking I cleaned the garden and then watered it. Then I fetched water, bathed and cooked supper. Lito's kids stopped by for an hour or so. George said that he will come as soon as they finish supper, I hope so because I'm anxious to tell him some stories. Now it's 6:51 PM, maybe he'll be here by 7:00 PM or shortly thereafter. AWANEN!

Wednesday, April 30, 1986
John's House, Cababuyan, Ifugao

₱115 + 300 – 70 = ₱345							
Rides	25	Lunch	13	Gifts	16	Coke	2
Ice Cream	2	Misc.	12			TOTAL	₱70

We got up at 5:15 AM and George left. I cooked breakfast, washed dishes and left Gomez at 7:00 AM with Arsenio and his wife. We arrived in Burgos at 8:00 AM and waited for a ride. I stopped at the office for a while and then waited for a ride again. I arrived in Cordon at 11:00 AM and once again waited for a ride. I arrived in Bagabag at noon and waited once more for a ride. I arrived in Lagawe at 2:00 PM and waited for a ride. I arrived at Oong at 3:45 PM John was waiting for me, good. We walked to Cababuyan and after a while we bathed, ate supper, talked and now it's 8:00 PM and it's time to sleep. AWANEN!

Thursday, May 1, 1986
My House, Gomez, Cabarroguis, Quirino

John D. staying here.

₱345 – 100 = ₱245							
Rides	32	Food	14	Marienda	14	Cigarettes	40
						TOTAL	₱100

We got up at 5:00 AM and prepared to leave Cababuyan. We ate breakfast and then left at 7:30 AM. We were lucky with rides and arrived at Burgos at 12:00 N. We climbed the mountain to Gomez and arrived at 1:00 PM. I showed John around the yard, showed him the bathing place and so on and then we took a short siesta. We woke up and watered the garden and then a bunch of people came by to see the new pictures which I received from Ardis B. a few days ago. After they left we fetched water and bathed and then cooked supper. John brought about ten kilograms of native rice with him, nice. George came early and Junior also came. Everybody is really shy and I can't seem to figure out a way to break the ice, so it's really quiet. AWANEN!

Friday, May 2, 1986
My House, Gomez, Cabarroguis, Quirino

John D. staying here.
Letters to Ardis B., Steve A. and Ann T.

₱245 – 10 = ₱235							
Coke	6	Cigarettes	4			TOTAL	₱10

We got up at 5:00 AM and George left. We did the dishes from last night and then cooked breakfast, ate and washed dishes again. In the morning we cleaned the garden and lawn and put the runo [a type of woody stemmed grass, used for "stick" supports for vine plants] in the garden for the *utong* beans to climb up. Lito's kids came here and they went in the house despite the fact that I was not there – little bastards! When they left it was time to cook lunch so we cooked lunch, ate and then I wrote the above letters while John listened to the radio drama. Then I tried to take a siesta, but John didn't want to so we strolled to the tree nursery, to the canteen and to one rice field and then the waterfall. Then we returned home, cooked supper, ate and washed dishes. Alfredo is here and John and he have been bullshitting for an hour. Now it's 6:45 PM. I hope George comes early, I'm tired tonight. AWANEN!

Saturday, May 3, 1986
My House, Gomez, Cabarroguis, Quirino

John D. staying here.
Letter to San & Jack G.

We got up at 5:00 AM, George left and we cooked breakfast. John was outside cutting grass even before breakfast. After eating breakfast and doing dishes we cleaned some more of the lawn and swept the usual part of the yard. We quit early and strolled around past Lito's fishpond and up to some house on that trail and then to the other road that goes to Burgos. After that I went to Juanito's house and talked with him for a while and then we returned home and cooked lunch. After lunch we rested for a while but didn't sleep. I sharpened all of my machetes, wrote the above letter, watered the garden, fetched water and cooked supper. After eating supper and washing dishes, Juanito came to get his photo and after a while I went to get George to come here as a hint for Juanito to leave. Now 8:50 PM, Juanito is gone and John and George are reading the BFD comics while I do this. AWANEN!

Sunday, May 4, 1986
My House, Gomez, Cabarroguis, Quirino

John D. staying here.
Letter to Dad.

₱235 + 65 – 181 = ₱119							
Food	81	T-Shirt	30	Drinks	22	Ride	5
Cigarettes	30	Kerosene	8	Toilet Paper	5	TOTAL	₱181

FIRST RAIN! We got up at 5:00 AM and George left. We did dishes from last night and then cooked breakfast and then John and I went to market in Gundaway. After drinking a Coke and strolling through the whole market once we bought our food and we were done at 9:30 AM. We got back to Burgos at 10:00 AM and talked with people at Rogel's store until 11:00 AM and then walked up the mountain and arrived home at 11:43 AM, it took 40 minutes to go down and only 43 minutes to climb back up the mountain! Why? We didn't do much else today. I read my *Newsweek* Magazine, did laundry and listened to the thunder just before the rain. Today was the first thunder and lightning storm of the season, the first rain in well over a month. It was a really heavy rain – with lots of thunder and lightning. Now it's 7:20 PM and George is here so I guess it's time to sleep. AWANEN!

Monday, May 5, 1986
My House, Gomez, Cabarroguis, Quirino

John D. staying here.

₱119 – 5 = ₱114				
Coke	5			TOTAL ₱5

[If you are wondering who John D is, he is a Filipino male whom I met when I vacationed/traveled here in the Philippines in 1984. The first reference to him that is here is back on February 11 – at the Stairway Lodge in Banaue.]

We got up at 5:00 AM, George left and we cooked breakfast. After eating breakfast, doing dishes, brushing our teeth and so on we went to Alfredo's, where they had been butchering a water buffalo since 2:00 AM. I got more than a kilogram of meat for only ₱20, to be paid in September [I can't remember why this was the case]. Then I returned home to cook it. After cooking it and preserving it, John and I cooked lunch, ate and then went in search of a cave that people have been telling me about. We could not find any cave on the first mountain we went to so we went to Jody's house and by and by he took us to two different caves in a totally different mountain than the one we first went to. The second cave was filled with bats. Rather interesting. Then we returned to Jody's house for a while and then we went to Rogel's store and drank a Coca-Cola. At 3:00 PM we started back up the mountain. We walked slowly because we were tired of walking and it was hot. Then we bathed, cooked supper, and now 6:45 PM and already I feel like sleeping. AWANEN!

Tuesday, May 6, 1986
My House, Gomez, Cabarroguis, Quirino

John D. staying here.
Letter to Teresa L.

₱114 – 10 = ₱104				
Coke	10			TOTAL ₱10

We got up at 5:00 AM and George left. John and I cooked breakfast and then John did the dishes and then we sat around until 8:00 AM. Somebody came to get me for the Forestry meeting at 9:00 AM. Rody had still not arrived at 10:00 AM. In fact, he didn't come at all. We talked about the problem of the land taxes and also I informed them that one of my house posts has been destroyed by ants. A bunch of people came to the house after the meeting to get the group photos that Ardis took when she was here and to study the situation of my house post. Then they all left and John and I cooked and ate lunch. I wrote the letter to Teresa and then we took a siesta for an hour. When we woke up we went to the canteen and I asked Bubot to come here and sleep tonight – but it's dark now and he isn't here so he's probably not coming. It's now 7:00 PM and we're waiting for George. There was another thunder and lightning storm tonight but not as hard as the one on Sunday. AWANEN!

Wednesday, May 7, 1986
My House, Gomez, Cabarroguis, Quirino

John D. staying here.
Letters to Bill J. and JB & Katie F.

We got up at 5:00 AM and George left. John and I cooked breakfast and did dishes and got ready for the day. Mateo came and wanted to buy my calculator and he was actually angry because I wouldn't sell it to him! After he left we got some bamboo from Alfredo for the squash trellis but John didn't know how to put it up, so we gave up on that project. We started to do some garden work but the handle on the gabion broke so we didn't get far. Then we got the old panaw grass from the building up the hill from me for garden mulch and then we had lunch. After lunch I wrote the letter to Bill J. then we took a siesta and when we woke up we went to the canteen for a Coke. Upon returning I trimmed my beard, bathed and then started supper. There was another thunder and lightning storm this evening. After supper I wrote the letter to JB and Katie and went and got George at around 7:15 PM. He didn't want to come but I talked him into it. AWANEN!

Thursday, May 8, 1986
My House, Gomez, Cabarroguis, Quirino

John D. staying here.
Letter from Dave G. and photos from Ardis B.

₱104 – 64 = ₱40							
Rides	10	Charcoal	7	Drinks	21	Misc.	8
Food	10	Lunch	8			TOTAL	₱10

We got up at 5:00 AM and George left. We cooked breakfast, ate, washed dishes and then got ready to go to the office. We arrived at the Barangay Captain's house at about 7:15 AM. He was supposedly sick, but he was out planting his rice field anyway, so John and I went on without him. We stopped in Gundaway at the post office and got the above mail then continued on to the office. Mr. Romero, Francisco and Rody were not there so I talked with Dado. After that, John and I strolled to the Diffun Market and then returned to the office. I left a note for Mr. Romero and we headed home. We arrived at Burgos at about 1:30 PM or so, talked for a while with the people at the intersection and then headed up the mountain. We stopped at the Barangay Captain's house, told him about the land taxes and then came home. After relaxing for a few minutes we went to the canteen to get a new bag of charcoal, fetched water, cooked, ate and washed the dishes. It rained again but only a little. Now it's 6:30 PM and we're waiting for George already. AWANEN!

Friday, May 9, 1986
My House, Gomez, Cabarroguis, Quirino

John D. staying here.

₱40 + 400 – 368 = ₱72							
Gabion	35	Food	126	Lunch	31	Rides	17
Postage	62	Drinks	12	Ice Cream	10	Cigarettes	39
Misc.	36					TOTAL	₱368

We got up at 5:00 AM and George left. We cooked breakfast and washed dishes and then at 7:00 AM Daniel Tobias stopped by to get us for his house blessing. We stayed there until nearly 9:00 AM and then went to Santiago. John didn't have much to say about the big town, maybe he was too shy or something, I don't know. I got a haircut and mailed all of the recent letters I've written and bought the above in preparation for Ronald coming tomorrow. At 1:15 PM we caught a jeepney and arrived at Burgos at 3:00 PM and then climbed the mountain and got to the house at about 3:50 PM. John fetched water and I put away food and then bathed and cooked supper. It started to rain again at about 5:15 PM and now, at 6:15 PM, it has slowed down considerably. I hope George will come early, maybe at 6:30 PM or thereabouts I'll go and get him. AWANEN!

Saturday, May 10, 1986
My House, Gomez, Cabarroguis, Quirino

John D. staying here.

We got up at 5:00 AM and George left. We did the dishes from last night, cooked breakfast and ate, and then Daniel C. came here and we waited until 9:00 AM for more help to replace the house post that has been destroyed by ants. In the meantime, Daniel made a handle for the new gabion. At 9:00 AM Dominador came and Daniel left. John and I talked with Dominador for a while and then he left. John used the gabion and I removed some of the low-hanging bamboo from the garden and we pulled weeds. Oh, forgot to mention that I did laundry this morning before gardening. At noon we quit work and cooked lunch and then we rested and listened to the radio drama. At about 3:00 PM John fetched water and then we gardened again until the rain came at about 4:00 PM. After that we read for a while and at 5:00 PM we started cooking supper. We finished cooking and ate and then John did the dishes. Ronald was supposed to come today but he did not show up and I wonder why. Now it's 6:40 PM and at 7:00 PM I'll go get George – if possible – lately he is very stubborn about not wanting to come, maybe because John is here? AWANEN!

Sunday, May 11, 1986
My House, Gomez, Cabarroguis, Quirino

Letter to Dave G.

John D. staying here.

₱72 – 30 = ₱42							
Coke	10	Marienda	12	Rides	8	TOTAL	₱30

We got up at 5:00 AM and George left. We cooked breakfast, ate, did the dishes and then Alfredo came by for a while. Then John and I strolled to Burgos and went to Mendoza's store at about 10:00 AM or so, and ended up eating lunch there. Then we caught a ride and went to Dibibi. At Dibibi we walked up the river a little ways and went for a swim and then we returned to the road and after drinking a Coke and talking with a drunk for a while, we caught a ride to Glory's Store. We got to Glory's at about 3:00 PM or so and then headed up the mountain. We arrived home at about 4:00 PM and I went to fetch water but the spring was super dirty so we bailed it out and then fetched water at Alfredo's spring. We cooked and ate supper and then George, Junior and Alfredo visited and when Junior and Alfredo left, George stayed. Now it's 7:00 PM and everybody is tired. AWANEN!

Monday, May 12, 1986
My House, Gomez, Cabarroguis, Quirino

John D. staying here. Rody stay too.

We got up at 5:00 AM and George left. We cooked breakfast, ate and did dishes and then we started making a trellis for the squash to climb up. At about 9:30 AM Rody came. Oh, I forgot, we went to Francisco's, Lakey Espinosa's and Pedring's places in search of bamboo but they all said no to us, in so many words. When Rody came we stopped work and took a break and then we cooked lunch, ate and did dishes and John and Rody built the trellis for the squash while I cleaned around the yard. I'm severely frustrated this afternoon – John I tried to build the trellis for two days and then Rody came and did it in three hours! What can I show these people that they don't already know? They can already do everything better than I can! Now it's 6:40 PM and my stomach is hurting, I hope I'm not getting sick, I hope it's just frustration getting to me! AWANEN!

Tuesday, May 13, 1986
My House, Gomez, Cabarroguis, Quirino

John D. staying here.

₱42 – 10 = ₱32							
Coke	10					TOTAL	₱10

We got up at 5:00 AM. George didn't come last night! We did dishes from last night, cooked breakfast and ate, washed dishes and bathed and strolled to several houses. Rody asked each of them how many seedlings (tree seedlings) they planted this month and so on; then he doubled all the numbers for his report. We returned home for lunch and at 1:30 PM Rody left. He was going to stay another night, but I talked him out of it. After he left John and I went to Pedring's and got the bamboo which he had cut for me and then we returned home and built the extension for the squash trellis. I'm equally as frustrated today as I was yesterday; I'm tired of visitors maybe. I don't know what to think. Now it's 6:00 PM and I'm cooking supper. I hope George comes early. I have to pull myself out of this rut of frustration that I'm in. So far it hasn't rained today I hope it doesn't let loose before George arrives. AWANEN!

Wednesday, May 14, 1986
My House, Gomez, Cabarroguis, Quirino

Postcard to Ronald R.

John D. staying here.

₱32 – 10 = ₱22					
Coke	10			TOTAL	₱10

We got up at 5:15 AM. George didn't come last night and there was a hatch of *simut-simut* – some kind of flying insect, possibly a kind of termite? There were literally millions of flying, crawling, irritating insects – the air was filled with them and they got into everything. Eventually – maybe about midnight – they all disappeared but before that it was impossible to sleep. Anyway, today we finished the trellis for the squash and planted four ginger plants and that's really all we did. In mid-afternoon John decided that he will go home tomorrow, so I'll go as far as Gundaway with him to get mail. He's been a big help to me while he's been here. Oh, we also improved my mini tree nursery today. The rains came at about 5:00 PM, but they weren't too strong. We cooked and ate supper early so that if the insects come again we are done before they come. Last night George said he would come early tonight. I'll go in search of him at 7:00 PM if he isn't here by then. AWANEN!

Thursday, May 15, 1986
My House, Gomez, Cabarroguis, Quirino

Letter to Chris & Mary M.

Letters/packages from Chris & Mary M., Gregorio R., Seeds from Mike Mc., Gamma Globulin from Health Unit.

John D. leave.

₱22 + 100 – 36 = ₱86							
Coke	12	Rides	10	Food	4	Cigarettes	10
						TOTAL	₱36

We got up at 5:00 AM and George left. We cooked breakfast, ate, washed dishes and then got ready to leave. We left at 7:00 AM for John to go home and for me to go to Gundaway to get mail. We drank our last Cokes together at Rogel's store and continued on. I got off at Gundaway and John continued on. I went to the post office and got the above mail and ended up being trapped by the mayor for an hour, trying to talk me into marrying a Filipina, but I managed to escape and I got back home at around 11:00 AM. I cooked lunch read mail and wrote a letter to Chris M, fetched water and not much else. I expected an *Alaska Geographic* Magazine from Chris but instead I got a *Newsweek*, a *US News and World Report* and a newspaper – bummer! Now it's 5:25 PM and I'm cooking supper of squash. I hope George comes early tonight. I'll holler for him at 6:30 or 7:00 PM. It rained early today and only a little bit, thank God for small favors. AWANEN!

Friday, May 16, 1986
My House, Gomez, Cabarroguis, Quirino

Postcards to Gregorio R., Bell's Auto & Rolando T.
Letter to Ted Stevens (Alaska Senator).

₱86 + 300 = ₱386

We got up at 5:00 AM and George left. I cooked breakfast, ate, washed dishes, waxed the floor, did the laundry and weeded the garden. Then I transplanted some tomato plants and watered them and then it was lunchtime. I cooked lunch, ate, did the dishes and then wrote the above letters. I wrote to Senator Ted Stevens to ask about how to take Nestor to America. Then I packed for my trip tomorrow. It seemed like it took a long time to pack but it probably didn't really. The rain came early today, about 3:00 PM or so and it was a really hard rain, but not too much thunder and lightning. I cooked supper of squash for the third day in a row. George and Alfredo came after supper and Alfredo got some of the seeds that I received from Mike Mc. And then he left. Now it's 8:06 PM and time to sleep. AWANEN!

Saturday, May 17, 1986
Malate Pension, Manila

₱386 – 223 = ₱163							
Rides	90	Postage	3	Food	78	Cigarettes	44
Misc.	8					TOTAL	₱223

We got up at 5:00 AM and George left. I cooked breakfast, ate, did dishes, bathed and then left Gomez at about 8:00 AM. I arrived at Burgos at 9:00 AM and waited for an hour for a ride. I got to Santiago at 11:00 AM, ate lunch and then got out of Santiago at 1:00 PM on a bus. It was a long bus ride and it rained most of the way from Bayombong to Manila. I arrived in Manila at about 8:30 PM and made it to Malate Pension at about 9:45 PM. I had a beer and ran into a bunch of the usual people, ate a second supper and now it's 11:00 PM, about three hours past my normal bedtime. I wonder what time I'll wake up tomorrow morning, probably not at my usual 5:00 AM I suppose. AWANEN!

Sunday, May 18, 1986
Forgotten Inn, Cebu City, Cebu

₱163 + 400 – 179 = ₱384							
Rides	23	Lodging	25	Meals	125	Coke	6
Misc.	8					TOTAL	₱179

I got up at 5:30 AM, showered and ate breakfast. Some of us went to Malacanang Palace but we couldn't get in because of a recent burglary, so we went back to Malate Pension and then we strolled to Robinson's Department Store. After that we returned to the pension and checked out and then went to the Seafront Restaurant and ate a brunch that set me back ₱90 – WOW – it was wonderfully delicious though and we just ate and ate and ate. From there we went to the airport and checked in and I found Rody and Francisco and we all took a plane to Cebu. We arrived here at about 5:00 PM and we found the place where we are supposed to stay and so on. At 6:30 PM we ate supper, drank beer and etc. and now it's very close to 10:00 PM. I'm up late again tonight! As soon as I finish this I look forward to hitting the hay. Lots of money was spent in the last two days. I wonder what George did today maybe he sold bananas. AWANEN!

Monday, May 19, 1986
Forgotten Inn, Cebu City, Cebu

₱384 + 566 = ₱950

I got up at 5:15 AM, showered and took a short walk and then waited around for breakfast until 6:45 AM. After breakfast classes began promptly at 8:00 AM. We stopped for marienda at 10:00 AM and I met a new brother Rafael Aviles, a cooperator of Tom. We stopped for lunch from 12:00 N to 1:30 PM and then had classes again in the afternoon from 1:30 to 5:30 PM. Then we had supper and after supper we had more classes from 7:30 to 9:00 PM. Finally, at 9:00 PM our free time began. Now it's 9:30 PM and bedtime. AWANEN!

Tuesday, May 20, 1986
Forgotten Inn, Cebu City, Cebu

₱950 – 28 = ₱922							
Beer	20	Cigarettes	8			TOTAL	₱28

I got up at 5:00 AM, showered and got ready for the day. Again today it was not possible to get coffee until 6:30 AM. I ate breakfast and got ready for classes. We asked for earlier coffee and more food, we'll see if it does any good. Ambassador Bosworth stopped by to talk to us at 11:00 AM for 45 minutes and then we had lunch. After that we went to Naalad, where they are farming on 70° slopes; it was impressive but I didn't really learn anything from it. Then we returned here. Rafael and I are becoming good friends and Francisco is frustrating me because he wants me to try EVERYTHING we see when I get back to Gomez. We ate supper and then had a session from the NFTA (Nitrogen Fixing Tree Association). They gave us a lot of information. Now it's 9:30 PM and I'm tired. AWANEN!

Wednesday, May 21, 1986
Forgotten Inn, Cebu City, Cebu

₱922 – 55 = ₱867							
Peppers	3	Cigarettes	39	Mango	5	Laundry	8
						TOTAL	₱55

I got up at 5:00 AM, bathed and got ready for breakfast and then once again had to wait for coffee until 6:30 AM. We are all getting tired of that bullshit, but nothing can be done about it. At 10:00 AM we went to the Bureau of Forest Development tree nursery and they weren't ready for us at all so that was a worthless session. Then we returned for lunch. At 1:30 PM we went to a BPI nursery [sorry but I don't remember what that stands for] and we got hands-on experience budding and grafting. They did a good job with us. After that we returned here for supper and the 7:30 to 9:30 PM session. Now it's past 9:30 and I'm tired. Rafael's and my friendship is growing, it's nice to have a friend here. AWANEN!

Thursday, May 22, 1986
Guba, Accommodation at World Neighbors Site

I got up at 5:00 AM, bathed and waited for breakfast until 6:30 AM again. We drank coffee and ate and so on and then we had class starting at 7:30 AM, which lasted until nearly noon. Then we had lunch and at 1:30 PM we left for the World Neighbors site. We arrived there and took a tour of a couple of farms and then we returned to the house for supper, which was not until 7:00 PM. We were supposed to start class again at 7:30 PM, but it didn't start until about 8:30 PM so after a bit, some of us skipped out before it was finished and went to sleep. At 11:00 PM a bunch of girls came to the house and gossiped about ½ of the night, probably about which one of us they wanted to marry so that they could have a free ride to the USA, so we got very little sleep tonight. This is being written on May 23rd, so I can say that I only got about four or five hours of sleep last night. AWANEN!

Friday, May 23, 1986
Forgotten Inn, Cebu City, Cebu

₱867 – 22 = ₱845							
Candy	3	Cigarettes	2	Coke	11	Laundry	6
						TOTAL	₱22

I got up at 4:30 AM at Guba because those girls in our room were up and talking. We had to wait for breakfast until 6:30 AM here too, and of course it wasn't enough. We went to the field to work at 7:30 AM and only after designing our own plan did they bother to tell us what the property owner actually wanted to do, so of course we had to ditch our plan and do as the property owner wanted. Why didn't they start off by telling us what the property owner wanted, did they want to see if any of our groups would come up with the same thing or what? So, we made five canals – lots of work and lots of sweat for sure. We stopped for lunch from 11:30 AM to 1:30 PM and then went back to work. Then they had a demonstration of planting Napier Grass and Madre de Cacao and they finally let us stop at 4:00 PM. They talked for an hour and then we returned to the house and waited until a jeepney came, at 5:00 PM. We arrived back at ECOTECH at 6:30 PM, showered and ate. I'm going to crash early tonight – very tired! Now it's 8:50 PM and I want to sleep. Today was Clarita's birthday so I drank two beers with her. AWANEN!

Saturday, May 24, 1986
Malate Pension, Manila

₱845 – 125 = ₱720							
Shells	24	Postcard	5	Mango	10	Beer	14
Rides	15	Supper	57			TOTAL	₱125

I got up at 5:40 AM, bathed and got ready for breakfast and waited until 6:15 AM before it was possible to get coffee. After coffee and breakfast we had classes again this morning, which actually seemed to go pretty fast, and before we knew it, it was time to do the evaluations. Ed Slevin [Peace Corps Director – Philippines] came to do the presentation of certificates and then after lunch we were finished. We waited until 2:45 PM and then we went to the Cebu Airport and took a flight to Manila. Most of us are again staying at Malate Pension. Tom & Barb H., Chester, Dave C. and I went to supper and now it's 9:30 PM and we are back at the pension and it's time to wrap this up and crash I guess. AWANEN!

Sunday, May 25, 1986
Malate Pension, Manila

Postcard to George.

₱720 – 308 = ₱412							
Rides	7	Meals	95	Groceries	31	Notebook	15
Desserts	53	T-Shirts	35	Photos	35	Postcards	24
Shells	10	Seeds	3			TOTAL	₱308

I slept late and didn't got up at 5:40 AM. Then I showered and got ready for the day, ate breakfast and so on and then said goodbye to Rafael, my new brother. After that, Sue T., Mike and I went over to Chinatown to look around. We stayed there until 2:00 PM or so and then we returned to the pension and ate lunch on Del Pilar Street. After that we strolled around a bit more and then came back to the pension. I wrote a postcard to George and then we went out to supper at the Aristocrat Restaurant. After supper we went to Dunkin' Donuts and ate donuts. I ate lots and lots of sweets today. We also literally ate our way across Chinatown this afternoon. Now it's 9:45 PM and I'm sleepy. Rafael is gone – I have to write him a letter soon. [No, we never had sex, but if my gaydar was working, well, you know what I mean.] It was an expensive day! AWANEN!

Monday, May 26, 1986
Malate Pension, Manila

Postcard to Ronald R.

₱412 – 262 = ₱150							
Rides	12	Seeds	2	Meals	163	Marienda	19
Pizza	7	Stamps	24	Book	27	Coke	8
						TOTAL	₱262

I got up late, at 5:45 AM, showered and got ready for the day and went down to breakfast at 6:20 AM or so. After breakfast we went to the BPI and the Peace Corps Office. I got seeds at BPI and three packages from Alaska were waiting for me at the Peace Corps Office. Of the three packages, I sent one box back to America, I gave one box away and one box goes with me back to my site – it's heavy – such is life I guess. In the afternoon I ate lunch and then Mike P. and I went off to the book stores in search of Forestry books. There were none. At 4:30 PM a bunch of us went to the Seafront Restaurant for happy hour and then we ate Mongolian Barbeque for supper. Now it's 10:40 PM, the latest I've been up in a while. AWANEN!

Tuesday, May 27, 1986
Malate Pension, Manila

Letter to Mike Mc.

₱150 + 1,315 – 1,288 = ₱177							
Postage	833	Seeds	60	Laundry	15	Meals	145
Lodging	100	Marienda	37	Masking Tape	44	Washcloth	21
Cigarettes	23	Coke	10			TOTAL	₱1,288

I got up at 5:45 AM, showered and got ready for breakfast. After breakfast Mike P., Sue T. and I went to the Peace Corps Office. We got an MIF kit [I don't remember what that means], supplies, reimbursement for ten photos, travel reimbursement from Alaska to Durham – finally – and reimbursement for two days of travel. Then we went to BPI to got Calla Mandarin and Guava Apple seeds. After that, we went to the post office and got some "People Power" commemorative stamps and aerogrammes. Then Sue T. and I went to the embassy to cash our travel reimbursement checks. We ate marienda there and then returned to the pension for lunch. After that we went back to the Peace Corps Office to get our MIF results, which were negative – no parasites in my stool – I was surprised. Then we returned to the pension again and I wrote the above letter, took a siesta for an hour and then JB, Katie and I went to the India House Restaurant for supper. After that we once again returned to the pension, checked out and said goodbye. It's now 10:00 PM and it's time to sleep. I'll get up early tomorrow, get ready and leave. AWANEN!

Wednesday, May 28, 1986
Nestor's House, Villa Miemban, Cordon, Isabela

₱177 – 90 = ₱87							
Rides	80	Marienda	5	Coke	5	TOTAL	₱90

I got up at 5:00 AM, showered and got ready for the day, drank coffee and then found a jeepney to the Pantranco Bus Terminal. I got to Pantranco at 7:00 AM, bought a ticket and left Manila at 7:30 AM. I met a new friend, Willie Rivera, on the bus; he bought me lunch and we talked all the way to Solano, where he got off. I got to Cordon at 2:30 PM and there were no tricycles, so at 3:00 PM I started walking. I got to Villa Miemban at about 4:45 PM and saw Nestor working on the hill, so I whistled and he came running down. Like usual, it's good to see Nestor and it's real good to get out of Manila and back to the provinces, where people are honest and friendly. Now it's 8:00 PM and we're tired, so it must be time to sleep. AWANEN!

Thursday, May 29, 1986
My House, Gomez, Cabarroguis, Quirino

Letters from San & Jack G. (+ two postcards), Ardis B., Dave G., Vicki K., Bill N., three from Peace Corps. Package from Dave M.

₱87 + 300 – 204 = ₱183							
Rides	15	Drinks	26	Food	98	Cigarettes	39
Postage	1	Scrubbers	9	Lunch	16	TOTAL	₱204

We got up at 5:20 AM, ate breakfast and I got ready to leave Nestor's house. I left at 8:00 AM and got to Kakandongan and there was actually a jeepney there – surprise! I went to Santiago and bought food and then to the post office and got the above letters. Then I headed for home. I arrived at Burgos at 4:00 PM, climbed the mountain and got home at about 5:00 PM. I cooked the pork which I bought and then cooked supper and ate. I finished supper at about 7:00 PM and went to Alfredo's to get George at 7:30 PM. He said he will come in a little while. If he's not here at 8:30 PM I'll go search for him again. I hope he comes so I don't have to search for him again. I'll look at my mail while I wait for him. AWANEN!

Friday, May 30, 1986
My House, Gomez, Cabarroguis, Quirino

Letter to Dave G.

We got up at 5:00 AM and George left. He came at 10:00 PM last night, so we only had a short sleep. After George left I did last night's dishes and then cooked breakfast of cabbage and dry fish. After eating breakfast I washed dishes and then did laundry, lots of it, I even washed my blanket. After that I cleaned the garden and they're already fruits on the wild *parya* [*parya* is known as bitter melon in English, it is *Momordica charantia*], there are small beans on the *utong* bean plants and the squash are close to blossoming. At noon I stopped, made coffee only for lunch and wrote the letter to Dave G. Then I sorted and reshuffled all of the stuff I brought home from Cebu and Manila. I slept for an hour and then it rained. After the rain stopped Alfredo, Junior and a bunch of other people visited – even George. When they left I fetched water and then showed Alfredo the garden. After he left again I cooked supper and I even had time to wash dishes. Now it's 7:00 PM and George said he'd come early tonight. We'll see – what he says and what he does are often not the same, as is the habit of Filipinos. Oh, I also filed away the stamps which I bought in Manila the other day and glued several of them in my journal. AWANEN!

Here is a photo of my Journal which shows the stamps which were referred to just above. The four stamps in the upper left are the "People Power" Commemorative Stamps referred to on May 27th.

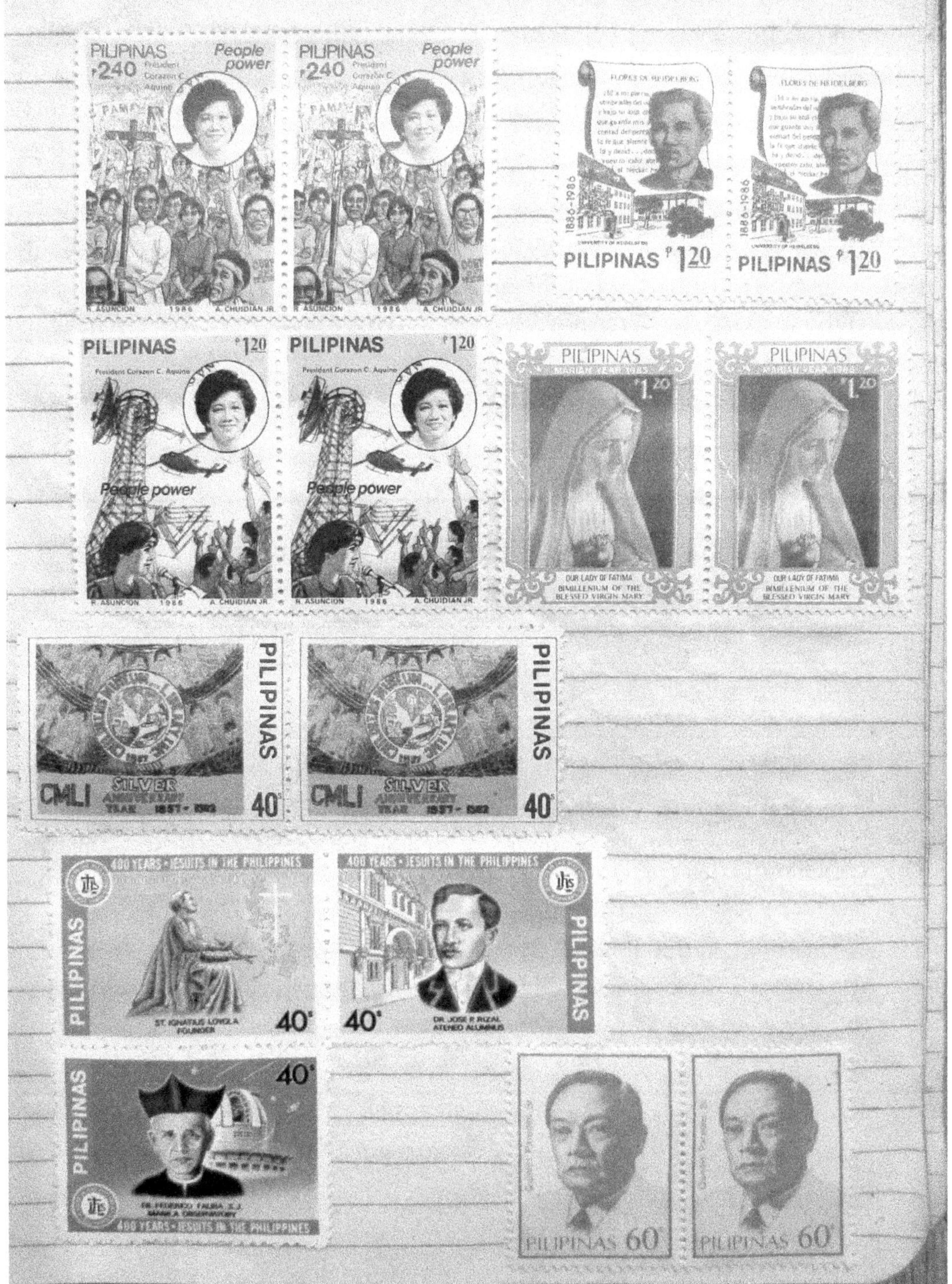

Saturday, May 31, 1986
My House, Gomez, Cabarroguis, Quirino

Letter to Bob S.

We got up at 5:00 AM and George left. I cooked breakfast, ate and did the dishes and then this morning I cleaned more of the yard while Lito's kids were messing around here. After they left I worked in the garden for the remainder of the morning. I had coffee only for lunch and then wrote the letter to Bob S. After that I made a garden notebook. Lito's kids came again and I worked in the garden some more. I pulled weeds in one corner and planted the ampalaya in that spot. Then I also planted bush sitao, contender beans, winged beans, sweet corn, white radish and sweet bell peppers. There are *utong* beans that are ready to be harvested as soon as the ones I bought are eaten up. About the time I was done, the clouds moved in and so I bathed and started recopying my notebook dictionary. After that I cooked supper and washed dishes. Oh, I forgot to say that it only rained a little bit. After supper I continued to recopy my dictionary and now it's 7:15 PM and I'm waiting for George to come, hopefully any minute now. I can hear lots of people passing on the road up above, wonder what's happening, maybe there's a party? AWANEN!

Sunday, June 1, 1986
My House, Gomez, Cabarroguis, Quirino

₱183 + 300 – 298 = ₱185							
Rides	16	Lunch	23	Marienda	12	Food	120
Kerosene	8	Soap	10	Flashlight	38	Insecticide	35
Sprayer	25	Cigarettes	5	Toilet Paper	6	TOTAL	₱298

We got up at 5:00 AM and George left. I cooked breakfast and got ready to leave for Santiago. I headed down the mountain at 7:30 AM and finally get to Santiago about 10:00 AM. I finished my shopping by noon, ate lunch at the Magnolia Restaurant and then headed for home. I ended up on a really slow jeepney and didn't get to Burgos until 2:30 PM. I finally got home at about 4:00 PM, fetched water, went to the canteen to tell Bubot that I'm home and then I came home and cooked pork and ate supper. Bubot stopped by for a while during the time I was cooking supper. There was only a minor hatch of *simut-simut* tonight because there was no rain today. Now it's 7:05 PM and I'm waiting for George. He said he'd come early tonight. Really? AWANEN!

Monday, June 2, 1986
My House, Gomez, Cabarroguis, Quirino

Letter to San & Jack G.

We got up at 5:30 AM, late because George didn't come until 2:00 AM this morning and I didn't sleep well until after he came. I seem to be really accustomed to sleeping with a companion. He said he won lots of marbles (that's why he was late – there was a marble playing marathon I guess). He left immediately and I did dishes from last night and then cooked breakfast. After eating and washing dishes I cleaned house again and then worked in the yard and garden again. Alfredo came and read *Newsweek* for a while and I worked. I gave him a bunch of the seeds that Mike Mc. sent. At noon I stopped and cooked lunch and wrote the letter to San and Jack and then took a two hour siesta. Surprisingly, nobody came by and woke me up! Upon waking I fetched water, bathed and started cooking supper. Alfredo and Pedring came by to talk and drink coffee. They left and I ate supper and did dishes. Now it's 6:50 PM and I'm already waiting for George. I hope to heck he comes early tonight, really! I have lots of questions for him. At 7:00 PM I'll holler for him – ten minutes more. Oh, there was no hatch of *simut-simut* tonight and no rain today either. AWANEN!

Tuesday, June 3, 1986
My House, Gomez, Cabarroguis, Quirino

Letters to Bill N., ICE (request catalog) and National Research Council (request pamphlets).

We got up at 5:00 AM and George left. I cooked breakfast, ate, washed dishes and got ready for the day. At 7:45 AM I went to Alfredo's to ask about the monthly meeting and he said everybody had gone to the funeral of a child who died a couple days ago and that there was no meeting. I came home and started digging up more space for additional garden area. At about 10:00 AM Rody and Rogel came and shortly after that, Alfredo and another person who I don't know came by. We talked about making the nursery [tree nursery] and decided to aim for June 17th by calling a special meeting. I wrote a letter to Dominador Deguzman, the President of GUFA [Gomez Upland Farmer's Association], to be delivered by Rogel, asking him to call a special meeting. I'll see what happens. After lunch Rody and Rogel left at about 2:00 PM and then I fetched water, bathed and wrote the above letters to ICE and NRC. Then I cooked supper early, washed dishes and wrote the letter to Bill N. Now it's 6:55 PM and I'm waiting for George. AWANEN!

Wednesday, June 4, 1986
My House, Gomez, Cabarroguis, Quirino

Letters to Vicki K. and Ardis B.

We didn't get up until 5:25 AM today because George didn't come until about 11:30 last night as he and Junior went fishing. George left and I cooked breakfast, ate and did the dishes and so on and then sprayed the squash vines for squash beetles with Folidol and that seems to have solved the problem. Then I worked up the rest of the small garden plot to the north of the house, which I had originally planned for sweet potatoes, oh well, now it's sweet corn and beans. Then I made lunch – just coffee – and wrote the above letters. I slept for an hour and upon waking I started working up the ground under the squash trellis for more squash and cucumbers. After that I bathed and went to the canteen for a Coke. Then I fetched water. While cooking supper I went and asked George to come right after supper and he said yes. Really? We'll see. Now it's 6:55 PM we had no rain again today – three days with no rain – wonderful. AWANEN!

Thursday, June 5, 1986
My House, Gomez, Cabarroguis, Quirino

Letters to Yip Chee Hong, Brooke F. and VAC.

₱185 – 5 = ₱180							
Coke	3	Cigarettes	2			TOTAL	₱5

We got up at 5:00 AM. George came at 7:30 PM last night and he left right away this morning. Alfredo came and got the mungo bean seeds that I showed him yesterday and then I worked in the garden some more. I dug up the rest of the area under the squash trellis this morning and then at around noon I took a break and wrote to Brooke F. [my Peace Corps Associate Director] about my current disappointments and so on. Then, in the afternoon, I cleaned up the yard some more on the southeast side of the house. Also in the afternoon Boy came by and he fell most of the trees below my house on the southeast side; he's going to make charcoal with the wood. At 3:30 PM or so I fetched water and went to the canteen for a Coke and a cigarette. Upon returning home I harvested some of my *utong* beans for supper – I had to supplement it with some squash, as there were not enough beans for a good meal. After supper I wrote the letter to Yip. George came at about 7:15 PM and now it's 8:10 PM so we're going to sleep. AWANEN!

Friday, June 6, 1986
My House, Gomez, Cabarroguis, Quirino

Letters from Chad D., Barb W., San & Jack G. & postcard arrive for George.

₱180 + 200 – 225 = ₱155							
Rides	16	Drinks	18	Lunch	24	Cigarettes	1
Nails	27	Flip-Flops	15	Postage	20	Fertilizer	10
Tongs	9	Food	69	Notebook	16	TOTAL	₱225

We got up at 5:00 AM, I showed George the trees that Boy fell yesterday and then he left. I cooked breakfast, ate, washed dishes and got ready to go to town. At 7:35 AM I left for Burgos and then went to Gundaway to get mail. The postcard to George, which I mailed in Manila, arrived today and I'm anxious to give it to him.

After that I continued on to Santiago for shopping. I finished before noon and ate lunch at the Magnolia Restaurant and then headed for home. All of my eggs broke as I ran for the jeepney so I tossed them. The plastic bag the eggs were in broke too so there was a mess in my shoulder bag. I arrived home at about 4:00 PM, fetched water, bathed and cooked supper. I ate and washed dishes and now it's 6:30 PM. I'll try to wait until 7:30 PM before I holler for George tonight. I'll see if he comes before that. I'll study Ilokano for a while before he comes. AWANEN!

Saturday, June 7, 1986
My House, Gomez, Cabarroguis, Quirino

Ronald come and spend the night.

₱155 – 8 = ₱147					
Coke	8			TOTAL	₱8

We got up at 4:55 AM and George left. I cooked breakfast, ate, did dishes and then spent about 1.5 hours doing laundry. After doing laundry I looked at the garden and then I updated my address file in my HP 41 calculator so is that it is presently complete and correct. After that I made coffee for lunch and then at about 1:00 or 1:30 PM Ronald came – surprise! It was good to see him here again. It's been four months since we last saw each other. We exchanged stories for a while and a guy from Calaocan, stopped by to talk. Oh, I forgot – two Jehovah's Witnesses stopped by this morning for a while too. I also created a detailed expense report today for the time since December 1st – I'm getting ready for the annual cost-of-living survey. Ronald and I fetched water and drank a Coke at the canteen and then returned to the house. I bathed and started supper – Ronald brought lots of food with him. Now it's 8:00 PM and raining a hard rain. It's the first time in five days or more – great for the garden. AWANEN! [Of course Ronald wanted a blow job tonight, and I gladly obliged him.]

Sunday, June 8, 1986
My House, Gomez, Cabarroguis, Quirino

Ronald spend another night here.

We got up at 5:25 AM, late today but I don't know why, maybe because it's Sunday. We cooked breakfast, ate, did the dishes and Ronald bathed and wash his clothes while I looked at the garden. Only some of the things which I just planted are germinating. The Philippine radish is, but not the American radish. Some beans are up, but not the American beans, and some corn is up too. After that, at about 9:00 AM or so we strolled to the canteen and the nursery and got an unripe *langka* to cook for lunch. We returned via the high road and stopped at Alfredo's house for a while to talk with George and by then it was too hot to stroll any more so we returned home and played dama [a card game], and cooked the *langka* and some pork for lunch. In the afternoon we didn't do much. We sorted some seeds, read the Sumaka Guide, fetched water, bathed and that's about all. At about 4:30 PM it rained again. We started cooking supper late and ate late so there was no time to do dishes. Now, at 7:06 PM, Ronald's listening to tapes. Surely George won't come, such is life and it's probably for the better so that I can give Ronald what he really wants badly – another blow job. I was surprised at Ronald's shyness with people when we were strolling around to various places today. AWANEN!

Monday, June 9, 1986
My House, Gomez, Cabarroguis, Quirino

Ronald leave.

Letters to Tom & Barb H., Rafael Aviles, Dave & Vicki M.

We got up at 5:00 AM, washed dishes from last night and then I cooked breakfast. We ate and then Ronald and I did dishes. After that he bathed and got ready to leave. I gave him a bunch of seeds for their farm and I guess he probably left at about 8:30 or 9:00 AM. Then I fertilized each individual plant in the garden, I harvested some *utong* beans, a nice bunch like you would buy in the market, and then I waxed the porch floor and gave the house a good cleaning. I three-hole punched all the papers from Cebu and put them in a notebook and then I cooked coffee only for lunch and wrote some of the above letters. By the time I finished with that it was 2:20 PM so I napped for an hour. At 3:30 PM it rained, just a little bit today though. After the rain stopped I fetched water and bathed, boy was it humid, and it still is. At 4:45 PM I started cooking supper and now it's 6:25 PM and I'm finished with supper and dishes are washed. I'm waiting for George. I'm sure I'll have to holler for him. I think I'll write a letter to Dave and Vicki now. I still have 45 minutes before I can holler for George. AWANEN!

Tuesday, June 10, 1986
My House, Gomez, Cabarroguis, Quirino

Letter to Barb W.

We got up at 5:30 AM, George left and I cooked breakfast, washed dishes and then cleaned the west and south side yard up some. I sharpened my machete and that was it for the morning. I had coffee only for lunch and wrote the letter to Barbara W., she is now in West Germany – that's a surprise. I took a nap in the early afternoon and then went to the canteen and drank a Coke and smoked a couple of cigarettes. After returning home I fetched water and then bathed. I cooked supper, ate and washed dishes and shortly after that Bubot came to sleep here tonight – first time in a long time. There was no rain today, just thunder and lightning and threatening, but no rain at all. Now it's 7:10 PM and I'm waiting for George to come. At 7:30 PM I'll holler for him. What else happened today? Well, nearly everything in the garden is now germinating and everything looks good. AWANEN! [After we were asleep, Bubot woke me up, took my hand and put it on his thing and of course I ended up giving him a blow job.]

Wednesday, June 11, 1986
My House, Gomez, Cabarroguis, Quirino

Letters from Jim & Roselynn, Vicki S. and John D., quarterly report form from Peace Corps.

₱147 + 100 – 120 = ₱127							
Food	92	Rides	4	Coke	12	Cigarettes	2
Kerosene	8	Household	2			TOTAL	₱120

We got up at 5:00 AM and George and Bubot left. I cooked breakfast, ate, washed dishes and got ready to leave. I left for Gundaway at 7:15 AM and arrived at Burgos at 8:00 AM and Rogel and I went to Gundaway. I went to the post office and got the above letters and mailed the letters that I wrote over the last few days. After that I went to market and bought food and headed for home. I arrived at Burgos at 10:45 AM, climbed the mountain and got home at 11:35 AM or so. I had coffee only for lunch and read mail that I received today and then took a rest for an hour. Upon waking I pulled weeds in the garden and then it rained, but only a little. After the rain ended Alfredo and Pedring came for a while. I was cooking supper when they came so they only stayed for a brief time. Now it's 5:45 PM and I'm still cooking. It will be *langka* and rice for supper. I hope Bubot does not come tonight, but I hope that George comes early, about 7:00 PM or so. If not maybe then maybe I'll write a letter. AWANEN!

Thursday, June 12, 1986
My House, Gomez, Cabarroguis, Quirino

Make an order to Patagonia Gear for some clothing items. Letters to Chad D. and Roselynn S.

We got up at 4:58 AM. Bubot came last night but I told him I wanted to be alone. George came real early – I was still eating supper. Before George left this morning we harvested some *utong* beans for them and then I cooked breakfast, ate and did dishes. Lito came by and he returned my calculator that he had borrowed. Then I started clearing the weeds from the site of the tree nursery to be. I didn't get too far on that project before I got burned out and then I built a barricade on the path that people have been coming up the hill through my yard on. Yesterday they destroyed one of my banana trees. I had only coffee for lunch and then made a Patagonia order and wrote the letter to Chad. After that I took a rest for an hour, fetched water, trimmed my beard and bathed. Then the rain started. There was only a little bit again today but lots of thunder. Now it's 6:30 PM and I'm waiting for George. It's nearly dark so maybe he'll be here soon. It was a pretty lazy day, actually. AWANEN!

Friday, June 13, 1986
My House, Gomez, Cabarroguis, Quirino

Letter to Mary H.

₱127 – 5 = ₱122			
Coke 3	Cigarettes 2		TOTAL ₱5

We got up at 4:55 AM and George left. I cooked breakfast, ate and did the dishes. Then I relaxed for a while and then played with my HP-71 calculator. I wrote some programs for Peso value to Dollar value conversion and for Dollars to Pesos. Then I reentered the timber cruise program and tested it out. I realize now that I don't have documentation for the BASIC timber cruise program with me. By the time I got it entered into the calculator it was lunchtime so I cooked coffee for lunch and wrote the letter to Mary H. thanking her for the razors she sent me and asked her if she'd like to continue corresponding; it's up to her now. Then I took a one hour siesta and after that I fetched water and went to the canteen for marienda and then I cleaned the tree nursery site for an hour. Then I bathed and started supper. I'm having beans *tabungaw* [a type of bottle gourd] for supper, along with rice – of course. There's been no rain yet today but there has been lots of thunder and lightning. At 7:15 PM I'll holler for George. Now it's 6:40 PM, so I'll holler for him in about 35 minutes. Oh, the rain just started, wonder how long it will continue? AWANEN!

Saturday, June 14, 1986
My House, Gomez, Cabarroguis, Quirino

Letter to Chris & Mary M. Postcards to Dad, Jerry J. and Willy R.

₱122 + 200 – 5 = ₱317			
Coke 3	Cigarettes 2		TOTAL ₱5

I got up at 5:00 AM. George didn't come last night because his parents went to Escoting and he had to be the companion for his younger brothers and sisters so, upon waking, I cooked breakfast, ate and did the dishes. I then did some laundry and harvested *utong* beans – lots of them! After that I relaxed and wrote letters. For lunch I had only coffee again. At 1:15 PM I finished writing letters and napped for 20 minutes and then I fertilized the squash and the Baguio beans to the southeast of the house. I went to the canteen and fetched water. Before I bathed George came by to talk and said they had no food for supper so I gave him a chayote and then bathed. He said he will come tonight, at least I think I understood correctly, we'll see. Now it's 6:00 PM and I'm cooking supper, *tabungaw* again, *utong* beans and *bagaoong*. I also cleaned weeds/grass in the nursery site area for an hour this afternoon. Nestor is supposedly coming today or tomorrow, so at this point I assume tomorrow. AWANEN!

Sunday, June 15, 1986
My House, Gomez, Cabarroguis, Quirino

Nestor come today and spend the night.

₱317 – 155 = ₱162							
Rides	4	Food	115	Coke	10	Cigarettes	2
Household	24					TOTAL	₱155

We got up at 5:00 AM and George left. He did come early last night. I cooked breakfast, ate, washed dishes and got ready to go to market. I left the house at 7:20 AM. My companions were using water buffalo carts so it was slow going down the mountain. I got to Gundaway at about 8:30 AM and finished shopping at about 10:00 AM and then arrived back in Burgos at 10:40 AM. I climbed the mountain and got home at 11:30 AM. Nestor arrived at just about exactly noon. Of course it was good to see him again. We cooked lunch, ate, did dishes and by then it was already 2:00 PM or so. We looked at the garden vegetables, fetched water and bathed and by then it was 5:00 PM so we cooked supper. Now it's 8:10 PM and we're pretty tired. I had no siesta today. It's nice that Nestor is here. Of course George will not come tonight, he's too shy. It was a rather expensive day. AWANEN! [Does it amaze you when I tell you that Nestor and I never once had sex? I had the opportunity once, and if I can remember, I'll mention it when we get to that point in the story.]

Monday, June 16, 1986
My House, Gomez, Cabarroguis, Quirino

Nestor leave today.
Continue on letter to Chris & Mary M., letter to Brett B.

We got up at 5:00 AM, washed dishes from last night and then cooked breakfast, ate and did dishes again. After that we got ready to stroll but Alfredo and Mateo came by to talk and hung out until about 9:30 AM. They left and Nestor and I strolled up the alternate trail, the one which comes out at the Gomez sign, and then we returned via the normal trail. We arrived back home at 11:30 AM, ate the pineapple that Nestor brought and cooked lunch. After eating, Nestor got ready to leave and left at 2:30 PM – bummer! He was only here for one day, such is life I guess. I napped from 2:30 to 3:30 PM and then went to the canteen, fetched water and upon returning home I bathed, looked at the garden and then it rained a little bit. I didn't cook supper because I was still pretty full from our rather big lunch, so I continued the letter to Chris and Mary for two more pages. Now it's 6:51 PM and I'm waiting for George. At my usual 7:15 PM I'll holler for him. Maybe I'll write a letter to Brett B. and ask about visiting Batanes. AWANEN!

Tuesday, June 17, 1986
My House, Gomez, Cabarroguis, Quirino

Letter to John D.
Built tree nursery today.

We got up at 5:00 AM and before George left he showed me the rambutan tree which he had told me about previously. Then I cooked breakfast, ate and hurriedly washed dishes, hurriedly because I thought some people would come early to start working on the tree nursery. However, nobody showed up until nearly 8:00 AM, Lito first and then Alfredo. Next was Anaceta and slowly by slowly other people arrived and we got started. I ended up cutting nearly all of the parts for it with my machete that Nestor gave me – it's a great tool. Everybody went home for lunch except Rody and Rogel so I cooked, we ate and I did dishes. About then people returned for the afternoon session. We finished at about 4:00 PM and I gave everybody a cup of coffee and then they all left. Somehow, despite our original plan for an 8 foot by 20 foot or 160 square foot nursery, it ended up being 14 feet by 24 feet or 336 square feet, more than double the original plan. The plan called for eight posts and we ended up with 15 posts. Now it's 6:45 PM, I'm waiting for George and I'm tired. I'll holler for him at my usual 7:15 PM if he isn't here by then. I got a new blister today. AWANEN!

Wednesday, June 18, 1986
My House, Gomez, Cabarroguis, Quirino

Letters to San & Jack G. and Vicki S.

₱162 – 55 = ₱107							
Loan Alfredo	50	Coke	3	Cigarettes	2	TOTAL	₱55

We got up at 5:00 AM and George left. I went to get him at 7:00 PM last night because it rained hard starting at about 6:45 PM. After a while this morning he came back and we harvested my *utong* beans for them – even the little ones. Then after cooking and eating breakfast and doing the dishes I sprayed the *utong* beans and squash – the insects were really over taking the *utong* beans in the lower garden. After spraying, oh, I also sprayed the house posts, I bathed and did laundry and then it was time to start lunch. I actually cooked a small lunch today. After lunch I wrote the letter to San and Jack and then napped from 1:30 to 2:00 PM. When I woke up I went to the canteen and drank a Coke and then I fetched water and picked up scraps around the tree nursery. Then I started working on supper. Now it's only 5:30 PM and I'm writing this while supper cooks. Oh, I forgot to say that I waxed the house floor again today. AWANEN!

Thursday, June 19, 1986
My House, Gomez, Cabarroguis, Quirino

Letters to San & Jack G. & Vicki S.

₱107 – 5 = ₱102							
Coke	3	Cigarettes	2			TOTAL	₱5

We got up at 5:00 AM and George left – he came early last night and I didn't even have to holler for him. I cooked breakfast, ate, washed the dishes and got ready for the day. This morning I played with the HP-71 calculator trying to figure out file operations, specifically for an address file. I worked on that until noon and then I cooked coffee for lunch. I finished playing with the HP-71 at 1:40 PM and napped until 2:30 PM. Then I went to the canteen to talk and drink a Coke. After that I returned home and weeded the garden for a while and removed a couple branches from the big tree that is laying in the garden and then I bathed. The sky was really threatening today but it only rained lightly for a couple of minutes. I cooked supper, ate and did dishes and now it's 6:45 PM and I'm more or less waiting for George. I wonder what time he will come tonight? I'm not enthused enough to write a letter tonight, but you never know, I might. AWANEN!

Friday, June 20, 1986
My House, Gomez, Cabarroguis, Quirino

Letters from San & Jack G. (including Kool-Aid) and Jerry J.

₱102 + 300 – 312 = ₱90							
Food	188	Rides	16	Coke	14	Household	30
Ice Cream	16	Kerosene	7	Lunch	30	Magazine	4
Candy	5	Cigarettes	2			TOTAL	₱312

We got up at 5:00 AM and George left. He came without my having to holler for him again last night. I cooked breakfast, ate, did dishes and by 7:10 AM I was ready to leave. I arrived at the post office in Gundaway at about 8:20 AM and got the above letters. After that I went to the office in Diffun – there was no monthly meeting today because Mr. Romero is leaving his position today, to be replaced by a new District Forester, so at about 10:15 AM I headed for Santiago and spent the above money. I arrived back in Burgos at 3:30 PM and started climbing the mountain at 3:55 PM. I arrived home at 4:43 PM, fetched water and started cooking. George came to tell me that he and Junior are going to a wedding in Calaocan tonight, so he will not be coming to sleep. I thanked him for telling me and he left. I finished cooking supper, ate and did dishes. Now it's 7:15 PM and I have no companion to sleep with me tonight so I'll read or write or something. Oh, I mailed 12 letters today, written over the last ten days or so. AWANEN!

Saturday, June 21, 1986
My House, Gomez, Cabarroguis, Quirino

₱90 – 5 = ₱85							
Coke	3	Cigarettes	2			TOTAL	₱5

We got up at 5:00 AM. At 7:30 PM last night I went to get Bubot so he came to sleep and he left as soon as we got up this morning. I cooked breakfast, ate and washed the dishes and then got ready for the day. I did laundry this morning, even my blanket and sleeping bag. That took quite a while. For the rest of the morning I cut grass around the house – it looks pretty good again – but there's still lots more to cut. I made coffee for lunch and read *Newsweek*. After that I took a half-hour siesta and then I got up and cut more grass. The rain came early, at about 1:00 PM, but only a little today. After finishing cutting grass, at 3:00 PM, I went to the canteen for Coke and cigarettes and then returned home and bathed and started supper at 4:45 PM. Now it's 5:20 PM, so in about two hours I'll holler for George if he isn't here before that but I hope he'll be here by 7:00 PM. I didn't write any letters today, maybe later on, but I don't know to whom I want to write anything. AWANEN!

Sunday, June 22, 1986
My House, Gomez, Cabarroguis, Quirino

Letter to Steve A.

₱85 – 10 = ₱75							
Charcoal	7	Coke	2	Cigarettes	1	TOTAL	₱10

We got up at 5:00 AM, George left and I started cooking breakfast. While coffee water was heating I started to pick beans and then I ate breakfast, washed dishes and got ready for the day. I went to Alfredo's for a while to talk and then returned home and cleaned the yard on the north side of the house. After that I picked the rest of the *utong* beans and by then it was 10:30 AM and I played with the HP-71 for three hours. I figured out how to make an address file and by then it was 2:00 PM and I cut grass around the house and around my bathing hole until 3:00 PM. Then I went to the canteen for a Coke and cigarettes. I returned home and cooked supper, ate and now it's 6:47 PM. George will be late because they haven't eaten yet, so maybe I'll write a letter if I can figure out who I want to write to. AWANEN!

Monday, June 23, 1986
My House, Gomez, Cabarroguis, Quirino

Letter to Abe F.

We got we got up at 4:55 AM and George left; he came a little late last night, about 7:45 PM, because their supper was late. I cooked breakfast, ate and did the dishes and then got ready for the day. I cut grass in the lawn until 10:00 AM or so and then it rained. I wrote a letter to Abe and then continued to work until 11:00 AM or so, when it rained again. I worked on my quarterly Peace Corps report and then cooked lunch of rice and sardines. I finished up the quarterly report at 1:00 PM and napped until 2:00 PM. Then I cut more weeds – I accomplished quite a bit today in the weed cutting department. I stopped at 3:15 PM and went to the canteen and drank a Coke. Then I fetched water and returned home. It rained again so I bathed in the rain. By then it was 4:30 PM so I started cooking supper. I'm now done with supper and dishes are washed. It's 6:45 PM and I'm waiting for George. I hope their supper is earlier tonight and hope he comes earlier. Maybe I'll write a letter, but I can't figure out who to write to. AWANEN!

Tuesday, June 24, 1986
My House, Gomez, Cabarroguis, Quirino

₱75 – 5 = ₱70							
Coke	3	Cigarettes	2			TOTAL	₱5

We got up at 4:50 AM, George left and I started cooking breakfast. Then I harvested some *utong* beans. George was going to return and help because I gave them all to his family, but he didn't, so I went there to give them to his mother. After I finished breakfast I got ready for the day and I took two boxes of books to the school. The school children came to my house and carried the other three boxes. There ended up being enough books so that each student was able to have five or eight books. After that I returned home and cleaned the yard until about noon. I cooked lunch of mungo beans and rice and finished my quarterly report at about 2:00 PM and then I slept from 2:30 to 3:30 PM. I went to the canteen for my daily Coke and cigarettes, fetched water and returned home. Then I bathed and now it's 5:45 PM and I'm cooking supper. George has been late every night lately because their supper is late, I wonder why and I also hope they eat earlier tonight and I hope he comes earlier. It's typhoon season now and the weather is overcast and cool with rain on and off, but so far no big winds or heavy rains here. AWANEN!

Wednesday, June 25, 1986
My House, Gomez, Cabarroguis, Quirino

Letter to Tony & Janet S.

₱70 – 5 = ₱65						
Coke	3	Cigarettes	2		TOTAL	₱5

We got up at 5:00 AM, George left and I started cooking breakfast. I had *tuyo* [dried fish], an egg and squash blossoms. After eating and washing dishes I got ready for the day and went to Alfredo's for a few minutes to talk. Then I returned home and started the day's work. I cleaned more of the south yard. I cleaned quite a bit today. I worked until 11:30 AM at it and then I started lunch – coffee only today. I wrote a letter to Tony and Janet and then got inspired to rewrite the HP-71 address program to also store the last date I wrote that person a letter. I got done with that at about 3:15 PM or so and went to the canteen for my daily Coke and cigarettes. Then I fetched water, returned home and bathed. After bathing it rained a little bit, but only a little. Then I started cooking supper, ate and washed dishes. Now it's 6:33 PM and I'm hoping George will come early, as he did last night, before I get started on writing a letter. AWANEN!

Thursday, June 26, 1986
My House, Gomez, Cabarroguis, Quirino

Letter to Tom L.

₱65 – 5 = ₱60						
Coke	3	Cigarettes	2		TOTAL	₱5

We got up at 4:50 AM, George left and I cooked breakfast of tuna, an egg and some squash blossoms. After eating breakfast and doing the dishes I got ready for the day and went to Alfredo's to talk for a while again. Then George and I went to their vegetable farm. I asked to go up the mountain with him to see it and to get some native mangoes. So we went together to their *bankag* [vegetable farm] and I must say that I am impressed. They've really got a lot of things growing on their farm. George gave me some okra and some mangoes and we harvested two *langka's* and after about two hours or so I came home. Then George came here for a while and after he left Alfredo came for a while. I started lunch of rice and sardines and then after eating and doing dishes I worked some more on the HP-71 address program. I quit at 2:50 PM and napped for half an hour then I went to the canteen for a Coke and cigarettes. Then I fetched water and started cooking supper. Now it's 5:45 PM and supper is cooking. Maybe I'll write a letter tonight, but I don't know to whom. I hope George comes early. AWANEN!

Friday, June 27, 1986
My House, Gomez, Cabarroguis, Quirino

Letters from Mark W., Brooke F., Ardis B., package from San & Jack G.

₱60 + 300 – 75 = ₱285							
Food	41	Rides	11	Coke	3	Cigarettes	4
Envelopes	3	Marienda	13			TOTAL	₱75

We got up at 4:50 AM, George left and I started cooking breakfast. George returned to harvest some *utong* beans for them and then I finished cooking breakfast, ate, washed dishes and got ready for the day. At around 8:00 AM George and I left for Burgos. From Burgos we went to Gundaway, went to the post office and I received the above mail. After that we went to market and bought the above food then we went to Barcela's store, where we got nuts and bolts for their water buffalo cart. After that we returned to Burgos and climbed the mountain. We got home about 12:15 PM and I put things away and played with the HP-71 again. It seems like I have finished the address program so that it now also will keep a record of the last letter received date and also the last letter sent date. Then I went to the canteen for a Coke and cigarettes, fetched water, bathed and cooked supper – *utong* beans again tonight. Now it's 6:53 PM and I'll study Ilokano and wait for George. AWANEN!

Saturday, June 28, 1986
My House, Gomez, Cabarroguis, Quirino

We got up at 4:55 AM and George left. I started cooking breakfast. It rained really hard during the night and two runo supports for *utong* beans got knocked over by it. So after breakfast I got ready for the day and played with the HP-71 again. I got all the addresses, letter write dates and received dates entered into it and it seems like it's free of any programming bugs. Then I weeded the southeast garden until noon. Lito's wife came and borrowed the solar calculator again. I started coffee water and got some runo for the Baguio beans while the water was heating. Then I rewrote the address program so that it can handle foreign addresses. Then at 3:40 PM I went to the canteen for cigarettes. They had no Coke today. Then I returned home, fetched water and put up the runo which I got earlier. I bathed, cooked supper, ate and washed dishes. Alfredo came by while I was eating supper and talked for a while. Now it's 6:50 PM and I'm waiting for George. Maybe I'll write a letter to somebody and maybe I won't. AWANEN!

Sunday, June 29, 1986
My House, Gomez, Cabarroguis, Quirino

Aerogrammes (2 of them) to San & Jack G.

We got up at 4:55 AM, George left and I started cooking breakfast – a tuyo and squash blossom omelet and *utong* beans. I ate and washed dishes and after breakfast I harvested more *utong* beans and then I got ready for the day. I sorted the beans out so as to eat the buggy ones first, and then I did laundry. That took one and a half hours or so. After that I entered my foreign addresses into the HP-71 program for foreign correspondents, along with the write and received dates of letters. By then it was 12:30 PM and I made coffee for lunch and wrote the above two aerogrammes to San and Jack thanking them for the package and answering their questions. By the time I finished it was 3:00 PM, so I fetched water and returned home. I out-planted my hot pepper plants then I bathed and started supper. Now I'm done with supper and dishes are washed. It's 6:55 PM and I'm waiting for George. Alfredo came for a little while before supper but tonight he stayed to watch me eat and then he left while I was eating. It's hot and humid today. I guess I'll study Ilokano for a while. AWANEN!

Monday, June 30, 1986
My House, Gomez, Cabarroguis, Quirino

Letter to Mark W.

We got up at 4:55 AM and George left. Last night in his sleep he said very plainly *"Nasapa ti baboy ti agsubsub."* or "Early the pig will root." He was right. When I went to get squash blossoms for breakfast Pedring's pig was there digging up my squash vines – it destroyed five of them! I hollered *"Igalut yo ti baboy, okinana."* or "Tie up your pig goddamn it!" Of course they didn't but it made me feel better anyway. So, I cleared grass again today and at noon I sharpened my machete. I cooked lunch and wrote the letter to Mark and then I slept from about 2:00 to 2:40 PM. Then I got up and went to the canteen for a Coke and cigarettes, fetched water, trimmed my beard and bathed. Then I cooked supper of *utong* beans, *parya*, *bagaoong* and, of course rice. After eating and doing dishes I studied for a while. Tomorrow I have to go to Diffun and visit the office. Now it's 7:05 PM and I'm waiting for George. I'll continue writing on the letter to Mark for a while and hope that George comes soon. AWANEN!

Tuesday, July 1, 1986
My House, Gomez, Cabarroguis, Quirino

Letter from NRC (National Research Council).

₱285 – 105 = ₱180

Rice	50	Kerosene	6	Coke	6	Cigarettes	3
Lunch	14	Batteries	10	Food	10	Rides	6
						TOTAL	₱105

We got up a little late, at 5:13 AM, so it was light enough to harvest beans and therefore George and I harvested *utong* beans for his family and then he went home and I cooked breakfast, ate and washed dishes. Then I got ready to go to Diffun for the meeting with the new District Forester. I didn't get out of here until late due to getting up late and also harvesting the beans and then I also stopped at the Gundaway Post Office on the way. I didn't get to the Diffun office until after 10:00 AM. The meeting went until 11:45 AM and then we went to eat lunch. After lunch I went to market and bought the above. I also bought some rice. I returned to the office and after a while I left for home. I got to Burgos at 2:50 PM and headed up the mountain. I arrived at the house just before 4:00 PM. I bathed and cooked supper, ate and washed dishes and now it's 7:04 PM. I succeeded in getting the new ten kilograms of rice hung up from the ceiling rafters [so that mice cannot get into it] and I'm waiting for George. I hope he's a little early tonight, I'm tired. AWANEN!

Wednesday, July 2, 1986
My House, Gomez, Cabarroguis, Quirino

Letters to Alaska State Div. of Forestry and National Bookstore (request BOSTID pamphlets).

₱180 – 5 = ₱175							
Coke	3	Cigarettes	2			TOTAL	₱5

We got up at 5:00 AM and George left. I cooked breakfast, ate, did dishes and got ready for the day and then I did the little bit of laundry that I had to do. I weeded in the garden and then started to clean the grass out of the tree nursery. I worked in the nursery until 11:30 AM and then made coffee for lunch and wrote the above letters. From 1:30 to 2:00 PM I napped and when I got up I went to fetch water. After that I went to the canteen for the daily Coke and cigarettes and then I returned home and cleaned weeds in the nursery some more until 4:15 PM. Then I stopped to bathe and also started cooking supper. This morning Lito stopped by to borrow my calculator and he stopped by again while I was cooking supper to return it. For supper I had the usual *utong* beans and *parya* and now it's 7:00 PM and I'm finished with supper and dishes are washed. When finished with this I'll study Ilokano for a while and wait for George to come. WOW – it's July already I can't believe it. In just four more days it'll be ten months in country and in 13 more days and it'll be eight months as a Peace Corps Volunteer. AWANEN!

Thursday, July 3, 1986
My House, Gomez, Cabarroguis, Quirino

Letter to Bob S.

₱175 + 602 – 5 = ₱772							
Coke	3	Cigarettes	1	Candy	1	TOTAL	₱5

We got up at 5:00 AM and George and I harvested beans for them and then he left and I cooked breakfast, ate, washed dishes and got ready for the day. Mateo stopped by to get some aspirin – he said he has had a headache for two days. Then I cleaned grass in the nursery area some more until 11:30 AM and made coffee for lunch. After lunch I wrote the letter above to Bob, I haven't heard from him in a long time. I napped from 1:30 to 2:00 PM, got up and went to the canteen for a Coke and cigarettes. I didn't fetch water today because tomorrow morning I'm going to Bayombong. I returned home at 3:00 PM and cleaned in the nursery area some more until 4:15 PM. Then quit, bathed and started cooking supper – *utong* beans and *parya* again. After eating, I did dishes and packed my bag. Now it's 7:12 PM so I'll study a bit and wait for George. I think he'll be late tonight because I heard them splitting wood for their cooking fire at 6:30 PM. Well that's it for today I guess. AWANEN!

Friday, July 4, 1986
Host Family, Bonfal East, Bayombong, Nueva Vizcaya

₱772 – 95 = ₱677							
Rides	14	Marienda	13	Cigarettes	4	Lunch	36
Toilet Paper	6	Coke	2	Gifts	20	TOTAL	₱95

We got up at 5:00 AM and George left. I started cooking breakfast and noticed that the big pig had dug in the squash patch again so I went to look and the fucking thing destroyed all the varieties of squash from America. I called George to come back and look at it – just to have a friend to complain to – and then I continued cooking breakfast, ate, washed dishes and got ready. I took my bag of valuables to Alfredo's house and talked for a while. Then I left for Burgos at 8:15 AM, arrived in Santiago shortly after 10:00 AM and finally got out of Santiago at 11:30 AM by Vizcaya Liner bus. I got to Solano and ate lunch and then continued on to Bonfal East from there. I arrived at 2:00 PM and Herbert and Rebecca were here. It was good to see the family again. After a while Ronald and Herbert went fishing with the electricity and I stayed at the house because I have a headache. Eventually at around 7:00 PM they returned. We ate supper at 8:00 PM and it's now 9:20 PM and everybody is watching TV – the Mrs. World Pageant. I'm tired. AWANEN!

Saturday, July 5, 1986
Host Family, Bonfal East, Bayombong, Nueva Vizcaya

We got up at 5:35 AM and slowly got ready to eat breakfast. I think I even bathed before breakfast. Then maybe at 9:00 AM or so Ronald and I went to their vegetable farm, where we looked at the holes some "treasure hunters" have been digging [there were stories that somebody had buried chests of gold there long ago]. We ate a couple of coconuts and that's really about all we did today. I'm disappointed that the red *kamote* that I gave them is about all gone and Ronald didn't bother to tell me when he came to Gomez. I've been talked into staying until Monday morning it seems. We returned to the house for lunch and in the afternoon we didn't do much either. We took rice seedlings to the rice field for father to plant and looked at the treasure hunters holes again. Boy, the hours pass slowly here – there's nothing for me to do and Ronald sometimes acts like he doesn't want to be around with me. The family is now 100% faithful TV addicts. It's now 8:50 PM and Ronald won't even come upstairs to help me with the new Ilokano I learned today. AWANEN!

Sunday, July 6, 1986
Host Family, Bonfal East, Bayombong, Nueva Vizcaya

We got up the latest (for me anyway) that we have in a long time – 5:40 AM. We got ready for breakfast and we finally ate at 7:30 AM or so. Then I thought we were going to the farm today but Herbert went and got his battery recharged and we went fishing with the electricity. Ronald and I got to put out four fish nets, which didn't catch any fish, and we prepared lunch for the five of us. We ended up fishing until 4:00 PM or so and then we returned to the vegetable farm and got the *kamote* for clay soils and ate a couple of coconuts. Essentially it was a day of sitting around and doing nothing – going for a swim whenever the body got too hot due to sitting in the sun at the river and that was about it. It will be good to go back to Gomez tomorrow. Actually, when I come here I end up not doing much of anything but sitting around. It's now 9:00 PM and Ronald just came upstairs. I guess he wants a final blowjob before I leave in the morning. AWANEN!

Monday, July 7, 1986
Nestor's House, Villa Miemban, Cordon, Isabela

₱677 – 38 = ₱639							
Rides	14	Marienda	5	Gifts	17	Cigarettes	2
						TOTAL	₱38

We got up at 5:35 AM and got ready for breakfast. Ronald got ready for school and the two of us ate first and then both of us got ready to leave. Ronald had a class at 7:00 AM so he left first. I left with Herbert at about 8:00 AM and caught a Pantranco Bus for Kakilingan. I arrived there at about 9:30 AM, bought a pasalubong for Nestor's family and ate marienda. I waited for a tricycle and I got to Vulcan at about 10:00 AM. I walked to Villa Miemban and got there about 11:30 AM. Nestor was planting rice and father was plowing in the rice field and therefore there was nobody home when I arrived. At about noon father arrived at the house and cooked lunch and after that I took a siesta. I woke up at 3:00 PM, fetched water and took a stroll while waiting for Nestor. I saw him from the hill above the place where the corn is growing at about 4:00 PM or so and I went down the hill to meet him. It's good to be here, it's peaceful. Now it's 8:10 PM and supper is cooking. I have some problem with my foot, not sure what is wrong, but it hurts. AWANEN!

Tuesday, July 8, 1986
Nestor's House, Villa Miemban, Cordon, Isabela

We got up at 5:40 AM, cooked and ate breakfast and got ready for the day. After that we planted about 50 papaya seedlings. There's a number 3 Typhoon Warning today – Gading is the typhoon's name – so we bet on when the rain would start and then we headed off to Rufino's tree nursery to get some coffee seedlings. We got there at about 9:30 AM or so and it was already raining. After a while we managed to dig 30 coffee tree seedlings and we headed back to Nestor's house. We got here at about 11:30 AM or so and cooked lunch and ate it. Then, due to the rain, we took a siesta – a pretty long one. When we got up, we went to get beans, peppers and *kangkong* for supper. We ate bananas all day today and we're really farting up a storm. We prepared the food for supper and Nestor cooked it. We ate and now it's 8:47 PM and I'm listening to tapes and writing this journal entry and that's about all. It's been a good day, a close day for Nestor and I and I feel good about today. I guess it's time to close and talk ourselves to sleep. AWANEN!

Wednesday, July 9, 1986
My House, Gomez, Cabarroguis, Quirino

Nestor spend the night here.

₱639 – 176 = ₱463							
Rides	23	Food	96	Toilet Paper	4	Lunch	25
Cigarettes	3	Coke	5	Sardines	10	Crackers	5
Haircut	5					TOTAL	₱176

Typhoon Gading!

We got up at 6:15 AM and the wind was blowing very hard due to Typhoon Gading. All of Nestor's corn is destroyed. There is lots of damage here at Villa Miemban. It was a very silent house this morning with everybody wondering and worrying about the effects of this storm on their food/cash crops. By and by we got ready to leave – I didn't know for sure if I would leave today or not until kind of the last minute, but Nestor and I went to Santiago. We had to walk all the way to Kakilingan and we picked up the Baguio Banana suckers which I left there on Monday. Then we took a jeepney to Santiago – there were very few people in Santiago. We drank a beer, ate lunch and I got a haircut. Then we went to the bank, but it was closed, so we went to Marilen's Store/Restaurant for lunch and Katie was there. We talked with her for a while and then went outside and JB came along. Katie asked Nestor if he was coming here and at that point I decided to try and talk him into it, so I did convince him to come here to Gomez. Then we went to market and got a bit of food and at 3:00 PM we caught a jeepney headed for Burgos. We arrived at Burgos at 4:00 PM or so and shortly after that we headed up the mountain. We arrived here at the house at 5:15 PM or so. The trail was muddy and slippery. There's lots of damage here too. My garden is destroyed, everybody's corn and bananas are destroyed, things really look bad here. I can even see Alfredo's house now from my porch because so many trees blew down. One of my coffee trees broke off, most all of the avocados fell off the tree – the only thing left is the squash. The wind was really strong here. We went to Alfredo's for a while to get my valuables and then we cooked supper. Now it's 8:57 PM and we're listening to the radio drama and talking and we're about ready to sleep. There's lots of work ahead – the typhoon did lots of damage! AWANEN!

Thursday, July 10, 1986
My House, Gomez, Cabarroguis, Quirino

Nestor spend the night here.

We got up at 5:30 AM and washed the dishes from last night. Then we picked a few beans for breakfast, cooked breakfast, ate it and did the dishes again. We then got ready for the day. It was rainy and windy off and on all day as the typhoon slowly passed by. We planted the Baguio banana suckers which I brought home from Bayombong and also the *kamote* and built a fence around the *kamote* from the branches of the *kahoy* tree that fell in the typhoon – the one to the north of the house. By then it was time to start cooking lunch. After lunch we took a siesta while the rain continued. When we woke up Nestor built a fence around the squash and I cleaned up the mess from the fallen trees and branches in the creek and also the south yard. By the both finished our projects it was 4:00 PM so we fetched water and then thought about bathing, but the stream was super muddy so we didn't bother. We started cooking supper at about 5:00 PM, ate, and now it's 7:40 PM and Nestor is studying the dictionary. There is lots of news about the typhoon on the radio tonight. It sounds like it's pretty bad from Manila northward, including Baguio City. AWANEN!

Friday, July 11, 1986
My House, Gomez, Cabarroguis, Quirino

Nestor leave today.

Letters from Nestor, Bill J. Postcards from Ardis B. (2) and San & Jack G.

₱463 + 1,865 – 350 – 1,500 – 365 = ₱113							
Food	160	Rides	26	Lunch	55	Batteries	24
Coke	10	Cigarettes	5	Thermos	75	Misc.	10
						TOTAL	₱365

[I don't remember what all of those pluses and minuses are in the expenses.]

We got up at 5:20 AM and did the dishes from last night. Then we cooked breakfast, ate and did the dishes again. We got ready to leave for Santiago and left here at about 8:30 AM. We stopped at Gundaway and I got the above mail. We finally got to Santiago at 11:30 AM and went to the bank and I got money. Then we ate at the 456 Restaurant, went to market and then we drank a Halo-Halo [Google it]. After that, Nestor put me on a jeepney headed for home. I left Santiago at 3:00 PM and arrived at Burgos at 4:15 PM, climbed the mountain and got home at 5:10 PM. I started cooking supper immediately and now it's 6:25 PM and I'm still cooking supper. I hope George will come relatively early tonight. I'll probably holler for him as soon as I'm done with supper. It was a good time with Nestor but I'm happy to be alone again. I've been with other people for the past seven days. AWANEN!

Saturday, July 12, 1986
My House, Gomez, Cabarroguis, Quirino

We got up at 5:00 AM and George left. I did dishes from last night, cooked breakfast, ate, washed dishes, re-hung the clothesline (it got blown down in the typhoon) and then did laundry from 8:00 to 10:30 AM. Then I cleaned the little patch of lawn to the north of the house until 12:15 PM and stopped for coffee. I worked on the Peace Corps living expenses questionnaire until 2:00 PM and then Alfredo came to talk for a while. At 2:30 PM the sky got black and there was lots of thunder so I went to fetch water and went to the canteen. Oh I forgot, this morning I cleaned out the spring and cut grass on the path to the spring, so the water looked pretty good and clean this afternoon. After I returned from fetching water I cleaned up the fallen *utong* beans in the southeast garden – removed them and did some weeding there too. I quit at 4:15 PM, bathed and then cooked supper. Now I'm finished with supper and dishes are washed. It's 6:50 PM and I'm waiting for George. I think I'll read my *Reader's Digest* until he comes. Last night I had to holler for him. AWANEN!

Sunday, July 13, 1986
My House, Gomez, Cabarroguis, Quirino

Complete Peace Corps expenditures questionnaire and write a detailed letter to go with it.

We got up at 4:50 AM and George left. I started cooking breakfast, ate and did dishes and then after that I got ready for the day. Alfredo came and we stood the *utong* beans in the lower garden back up. He planted okra, Kentucky beans and kabatitti for me. He left at 11:00 AM and I removed the broken coffee tree that was beside the porch and then Junior came. I stopped working at 12:30 PM when Junior left. I worked on the Peace Corps expenditure questionnaire until 3:00 PM. Alfredo returned at 2:00 PM and some person from Calaocan stopped by for an hour or so to talk. Finally at 3:30 PM I told Alfredo I was going to fetch water and when I returned three more people were here from Calaocan! At 4:00 PM I bathed and then started supper. I think I was visitor free from 12:30 to 1:00 PM or so and then again after 4:15 PM. Holy shit, I hope nobody else comes today. Now it's 6:45 PM, I'm done with supper and I'm waiting for George to come. Oh, I also planted more squash and cucumbers in the place where I previously had only squash. AWANEN!

Monday, July 14, 1986
My House, Gomez, Cabarroguis, Quirino

Letter to San & Jack G. and begin letter to Sue T.

₱113 – 5 = ₱108							
Cigarettes	3	Coke	2			TOTAL	₱5

We got up at 5:25 AM. I don't know why we slept late. George left and I cooked breakfast, ate and washed the dishes. After that I picked beans and then sprayed the remaining ones for insects. I took a half bath to remove the insect spray from my body and then I sharpened my machete and stopped for coffee for lunch. I wrote a letter to San and Jack. The sun refused to shine today; I guess there's another typhoon coming. After lunch I collected *kahoy* for a fence for the southeast garden area and built that fence until 3:15 PM or so when I went to fetch water. I also went to the canteen. When I returned Alfredo came, but I bathed anyway and he waited for me. I cooked supper and while I was eating it started raining lightly. I did dishes and after that it rained really hard for 20 minutes or so. Now it's letting up, I hope it stops so that George will come. Now it's 6:50 PM and of course I'm waiting for him. The main garden area just got really flooded – and I mean FLOODED! Maybe I'll write another letter before George arrives. AWANEN!

Tuesday, July 15, 1986
My House, Gomez, Cabarroguis, Quirino

Finish letter to Sue T.

₱108 – 10 = ₱98						
Cigarettes	2	Charcoal	8		TOTAL	₱10

We got up at 5:00 AM and George left. He was really down [depressed] last night, but I don't know why, I couldn't drag it out of him. I suspect it's because of all the damage to their farm due to Typhoon Gading. I cooked breakfast, ate, did dishes and got ready for the day. First I went off in search of charcoal, which I found, but it was pretty far away. The important thing is that I found some to buy. I returned home and cut more *kahoy* to finish the fence in the southeast garden area. Then I finished building that fence and weeded the whole area really well. I stopped for lunch of just coffee and I wrote more on the letter to Sue T. After that I napped for a half hour and then I got up, fetched water and went to the canteen. Upon returning home I trimmed my beard, bathed and started supper of *utong* beans, *parya* and squash. Now I'm done with supper and dishes are washed. It's 6:43 PM and naturally I'm waiting for George. I hope he's back to his good natured self tonight. While waiting for him I'll attempt to finish the letter to Sue. AWANEN

Wednesday, July 16, 1986
My House, Gomez, Cabarroguis, Quirino

Letter to Bill & Andi J.

₱98 – 6 = ₱92						
Cigarettes	2	Coke	4		TOTAL	₱6

We got up at 5:00 AM and George left. I cooked breakfast of squash and rice, ate, did dishes and got ready for the day. I cut more *kahoy* and enlarged the fence in the southeast garden area because I caught a pig inside of it. Then I planted corn there, along with muskmelon and some of those funny black seeds that nobody knows what they are. After that I sharpened my other machete and then it was lunchtime. I drank coffee and wrote a letter to Bill and Andi J. After that I took a siesta for an hour and then I went to the canteen for a Coke and cigarettes. I returned home and trimmed grass and then swept part of the southeast yard. Then I bathed and cooked supper of *utong* beans and pork, and then did dishes. I read my *Newsweek* for a while and now it's 7:00 PM and I'm waiting for George. I hear dishes rattling at their house so maybe he'll be here in a while, I hope. Last night it was 7:45 PM before he came. I guess I'll study Ilokano until George comes. AWANEN!

Thursday, July 17, 1986
My House, Gomez, Cabarroguis, Quirino

Letter to Brooke F. and to Health Unit about my ear problem and my foot, which seems to be permanently asleep.

₱92 – 5 = ₱87							
Cigarettes	2	Coke	3			TOTAL	₱5

We got up at 5:10 AM and George left. I started cooking breakfast of eggs, tuyo and squash blossoms. I harvested beans while the coffee water was heating. After breakfast I did dishes and got ready for the day. Pedring came and wanted some malaria medicine for his child, but I only have exactly enough for myself so I gave him several herbal cures and told him that's all I can do for him. Then Alfredo came and I gave him some ideas about food that is good for his ulcer. After that I cleaned grass on the little hill directly to the north of the house and then I had coffee for lunch and wrote to Brooke about the passing of my depressed state. I napped for a short time and went to the canteen for a Coke and upon returning home I fetched water. Then I trimmed grass directly to the south of the house and the rain started – not hard – just a nice steady rain. I bathed at 4:15 PM and then started cooking supper – *utong* beans of course! Now it's 6:45 PM and it's raining lightly again. I'm waiting for George to come and I hope he comes before it starts raining hard. I'll study Ilokano while waiting for him. AWANEN!

Friday, July 18, 1986
My House, Gomez, Cabarroguis, Quirino

Letters from Jerry J., San & Jack G., Steve A., Tony S., Brett B., Brooke F. Package from Patagonia Gear. Tree book from JB and postcard from Ardis B.

₱87 + 300 – 127 = ₱260							
Cigarettes	2	Food	73	Rides	4	Coke	3
Kerosene	8	Oil	28	Soap	9	TOTAL	₱127

We got up at 5:00 AM and George left. I cooked breakfast, ate, did the dishes and got ready for the day. I headed down the mountain – it was muddy the whole way. I went to Gundaway to the post office and mailed letters from the last week and got the above mail. WOW – with all the mail I got today it felt like Christmas. Then I went to market and bought the above. It was a pretty cheap shopping trip actually. I returned to Burgos, headed up the mountain at 10:55 AM and got home shortly before noon. I read mail and drank coffee for lunch and then I took a 15 minute nap and George came to give me some bananas – a nice surprise. The rains started about 3:30 PM, fortunately I bathed just before they came. It was a very hard rain for 40 minutes or so. I cooked supper, ate and did dishes. The stream where I bathe and wash dishes is really large tonight. Now it's 6:56 PM and I'm waiting for George. I'll study Ilokano for a while. I got a new cut on the bottom of my right foot, it's small but it hurts like hell, hope it doesn't get infected. AWANEN!

Saturday, July 19, 1986
My House, Gomez, Cabarroguis, Quirino

Letter to Ardis B.

₱260 – 5 = ₱255						
Cigarettes	2	Coke	3		TOTAL	₱5

We got up at 5:00 AM and George left. I cooked breakfast – a squash blossom omelet and tuyo again. After eating, I did the dishes and got ready for the day and then I polished the floor, cleaned the bookshelf, the bedding shelf and everything in the house. Then I relaxed for a while and after that I cleaned the part of the yard to the northwest of the house – between the house and the nursery. By then it was time for noon coffee and I wrote the letter to Ardis B. A guy from Calaocan stopped by for a while and by then a storm was threatening, so at about 2:30 PM I fetched water and went to the canteen for my daily Coke and cigarettes. Then I returned home and went to talk with George for a while and he came here and showed me where their old house used to be. They moved because of ghosts. He left and I picked dead leaves off the *utong* beans, bathed and cooked supper. Now it's 7:03 PM and I'm done eating and dishes are washed. There's been no rain yet today despite the early threats of it. I'm waiting for George. I'll study Ilokano and read my *Newsweek* while waiting for him. AWANEN!

Sunday, July 20, 1986
My House, Gomez, Cabarroguis, Quirino

Letter to Tony & Janet S.

George and I woke up at 4:15 AM to pee and he left to pasture his water buffalo [also known as nuang and also as carabao] and I went back to sleep until 5:00 AM. Then I got up and cooked breakfast – a squash blossom and one egg omelet again with tuyo and rice. I ate, did dishes and got ready for the day. First I harvested beans and then Alfredo stopped by for a few minutes. After that I did laundry and some girl came to watch me. After that she wanted to "hang out" so I spread out the new charcoal to dry and then she left. Weird! I trimmed grass in the rest of the area between the house and the nursery and then it was lunchtime. I wrote the above letter until 1:30 PM and then napped until 2:00 PM and then I got up and rain was threatening, so I took the clothes off the line and collected the charcoal and then the rain started. It rained pretty hard for a while. I made a hurricane cover for my kerosene lantern and crushed up the dried hot peppers. Then I started supper and now it's 6:47 PM and I'm done eating and dishes are washed. The corn that I planted on Wednesday is up one to two inches tall already – only four days! It was peeking above the ground yesterday, just a tiny bit. All of the stuff that Alfredo and I planted last Sunday is up too. The *kamote* is looking real nice. Now I'm waiting for George. AWANEN!

Monday, July 21, 1986
My House, Gomez, Cabarroguis, Quirino

Letter to Brett B., Brooke F. and Nestor.

₱255 – 5 = ₱250						
Cigarettes	2	Coke	3		TOTAL	₱5

We got up at 4:50 AM and George left. He came at about 7:00 PM last night. I started breakfast – another squash blossom omelet and tuyo! I'm supposed to go to the office today for our monthly meeting but my foot is too sore because of the new puncture wound (see last Friday) so I didn't go. I cut the last two branches of the tree which is laying in the garden and that's really about all I did today – my foot is too sore to do much else. I wrote the above letter to Brett this morning I told him Nestor and I will come on August 27th and then I wrote Nestor to tell him that we should meet at Lina's Restaurant in the afternoon of August 26th. By then it was noon and I wrote the letter to Brooke F. and answered her letter that I received last Friday. After that I napped for a while, woke up and chased the pigs away from the garden and went to the canteen for a Coke and cigarettes, my daily ritual. After that I returned home, bathed and cooked supper. I ate and finished washing dishes at about 6:15 PM and the rain started immediately after that. Now it's 6:55 PM and it's still raining pretty hard, I hope it stops soon so that George can come. I'll wait as long as my patience holds out before hollering for him. I'll study Ilokano for a while. AWANEN!

Tuesday, July 22, 1986
My House, Gomez, Cabarroguis, Quirino

Letter to Steve A.

We got up at 4:50 AM and George left. I started cooking breakfast, but before I could finish it I had to pick some squash blossoms. I ate, did dishes and got ready for the day and then Rufo stopped by and invited me to eat corn-on-the-cob at 1:00 PM, so I said "yes" and then I harvested *utong* beans, looked at the garden, transplanted a couple of sunflowers and killed time until 10:30 AM. Then I stopped and wrote the letter to Steve. I finished that at noon and swept part of the south lawn and then at 12:45 PM I went to Rufo's house. I ate lots of corn-on-the-cob and had a relaxed couple of hours, it was actually quite nice. I returned home at 3:00 PM, fetched water, went to the canteen for cigarettes and then the rain started, but despite the blackness of the clouds it only rained a little bit today so I bathed and then cooked supper, ate and did dishes. After supper and dishes I swept more of the south lawn. I quit when it got too dark to see. Oh, I put nylon twine on my pot handles this morning to keep from burning my hands. Now it's 7:00 PM and I'm waiting for George. Last night he didn't come until nearly 8:00 PM, after hollering for him. I hope he comes earlier tonight. Now I'll study Ilokano for a while. AWANEN!

Wednesday, July 23, 1986
My House, Gomez, Cabarroguis, Quirino

My Peace Corps Service is 40% complete today!

We got up at 5:00 AM and George left, he came relatively early last night. I started cooking breakfast immediately, ate, did dishes and got ready for the day. I planted some five month old papaya seeds which I had soaked in water for about 18 hours before planting. I put five seeds per hole all over the place. When that project was completed I cleaned the nursery area some more until 11:30 AM. George's younger brother brought me a big bunch of *utong* beans and I started work on writing up the tree information for our tree notebook [a project which some of us Peace Corps Volunteers undertook to possibly help out future volunteers.] I worked on that until 2:00 or 2:30 PM and four people came from the office – the District Forester, Edgar and two people who I don't know their names. They stayed until 3:30 PM and then left. Then I wandered around the yard for a bit just looking at what I have done so far. I bathed and started supper. My supper was *utong* beans and a couple of *parya.* After eating I washed dishes and now it's 7:00 PM and I'm waiting for George. I saw their cooking smoke start at 6:30 PM so he'll probably be late tonight. I'll study Ilokano and read my *Reader's Digest* until he gets here. I hope he comes by 7:30 PM. There was no rain today, not even a drop. AWANEN!

Thursday, July 24, 1986
My House, Gomez, Cabarroguis, Quirino

₱250 – 5 = ₱245							
Cigarettes	2	Coke	3			TOTAL	₱5

We got up at 5:00 AM and George left. He didn't come until 8:00 PM last night, after I hollered for him several times. I cooked breakfast, ate, did the dishes and got ready for the day. George said I could come with him to their vegetable farm today but when I went there he had already left. I felt bad about that so I finished cleaning grass around the tree nursery area. Alfredo stopped by for a while and brought more beans to give me. He left after a bit and I finished cleaning the nursery area at 12:30

PM. George then came by for a short while and I showed him all of the new questions that I have for him [I can't recall what this was about.] He left and I worked on Gmelina for the tree book some more. I finished that at 3:10 PM and went to the canteen and then fetched water and before I bathed Arsenio came to talk, so I didn't bathe until 4:30 PM. Now it's 6:30 PM and I haven't yet eaten; I'm trying to use charcoal dust again to make my fire. I should have learned from the last time I tried to do that, but guess I didn't. I'll probably finish supper too late to do dishes tonight. I hope George comes early. AWANEN!

Friday, July 25, 1986
My House, Gomez, Cabarroguis, Quirino

Letters from Steve A., Mary H., Ardis B., John D., ICE, Ted Stevens and a package from Mark W.

₱245 + 200 – 98 = ₱347							
Food	74	Rides	2	Kerosene	8	Coke	11
Cigarettes	3					TOTAL	₱98

We got up at 5:00 AM and George left. I cooked breakfast, ate, washed the dishes and got ready and then left for Burgos at about 7:10 AM. I got there and waited a long time for a jeepney to Gundaway. I finally got to the post office and got the above mail and then I went to market and got the above items. I finished at market and returned to the post office for stamps but they didn't have any. I caught a jeepney headed back to Burgos, arrived there, drank a quick Coke and headed up the mountain at 11:02 AM and arrived at home at 11:51 AM – 49 minutes to climb the mountain. I had coffee and kankanen for lunch, read my mail and then I took a siesta from 1:30 to 2:30 PM. When I got up I pulled weeds in the yard area south of the house and then Alfredo, his wife, Boy and his wife came and talked until 4:40 PM. When they left I bathed and then cooked supper. Now it's 7:09 PM and I'm finished with supper and dishes are washed so I guess I'll reread my mail while waiting for George and maybe I'll study a little. AWANEN

Saturday, July 26, 1986
My House, Gomez, Cabarroguis, Quirino

Postcards to Steve A. and Mark W.

We got up at 5:00 AM and George left. I started cooking breakfast, ate, did dishes and got ready for the day. After that I harvested *utong* beans and then did laundry – it took me until 10:00 AM to finish the laundry even though there wasn't much today. It rained a little bit last night but not even enough to wet the ground good, therefore there's been no rain to speak of for five days. I watered the new squash that is coming up and then Alfredo came and talked for a while. He left at 11:00 AM and I sprayed the squash for squash beetles – they are really doing a job on all of the new leaves. After that I took half of a bath to remove the insecticide from my body and then I drank coffee for lunch and worked on the information for the tree book again. I'm finished now with Gmelina and avocado and I'm about half done with cacao. I took a 40 minute siesta and then fetched water, bathed and started working on supper. Now it's 6:55 PM and I'm done eating and washing dishes and waiting for George. Maybe I'll write a post card to Steve A. and Mark W. Well that's about all I guess. Oh, my watch band broke today. AWANEN!

Sunday, July 27, 1986
My House, Gomez, Cabarroguis, Quirino

₱347 + 200 – 265 = ₱282							
Food	55	Rides	15	Coffee	52	Candy	19
Coke	9	Cigarettes	2	Envelopes	18	Household	30
Bread	35	Ice Cream	30			TOTAL	₱265

We woke up at 4:30 AM and George left to take his water buffalo to pasture. I went back to sleep until 5:05 AM and then cooked breakfast, ate, washed dishes and got ready to go to Santiago. I left here at 7:20 AM and arrived in Santiago at 9:20 AM. I bought the above and then met Brooke F. [my Associate PC Director] at 11:00 AM at the Magnolia Restaurant and from there we went to the Friendship Restaurant and Ed Slevin's wife, Pam L., Brooke and I were talking. After a while JB & Katie, and Linda S. showed up and we talked until 2:30 PM. I left Santiago at 3:00 PM, arrived at Burgos at 4:20 PM and managed to catch a 6x truck up the mountain. I arrived home at 5:00 PM and I was too tired or lazy to cook supper. I looked at the garden and around 94% of the corn that I planted on July 16th has germinated and it looks real nice. We need some rain. Right now there's thunder and lightning so maybe it will rain after a while. Brooke confirmed that Stacy Mc. and James P. have early terminated – that's 16 people out of 58 or 28% of our group who have quit and headed for home already. Now it's 7:02 PM and I'm waiting for George, hope he comes before the rain begins. AWANEN!

Monday, July 28, 1986
My House, Gomez, Cabarroguis, Quirino

We got up at 5:10 AM and George left. I cooked breakfast, ate, did dishes and got ready for the day and then I went to Alfredo's to talk for a bit and George had already gone to the vegetable farm, so I decided to go too. I walked up the mountain to their farm and we got some galeon for pig food and Boy and his wife got a bunch of *utong* beans and then we returned. It was only 9:30 or 10:00 AM when we got back and I thought maybe we could stroll a bit, but no, we couldn't, so I relaxed for a while and then worked on cacao for the tree notebook. That's really all I did for the rest of the day until 3:30 PM when I quit and went to fetch water. After that I returned home and started cooking supper and Alfredo, Pedring, Boy and all their wives and kids came by and watched me peel garlic and onion. Then Alfredo helped me break up the *utong* beans and I cooked and ate. After supper Alfredo and Pedring left. I washed dishes and at 6:45 PM it started raining. Now it's 6:55 PM and it's already letting up so maybe it will stop soon, we'll see. AWANEN!

Tuesday, July 29, 1986
My House, Gomez, Cabarroguis, Quirino

Letter to San & Jack G. Tree Notebook to Tom & Barb H.

₱282 – 2 = ₱280					
Cigarettes	2			TOTAL	₱2

We got up at 5:00 AM and George left. I cooked breakfast, ate, washed dishes and got ready for the day and then I went to Alfredo's house and told him I was going to their vegetable farm to help George. He told me that George had left. George's mother was crying I couldn't figure it all out but I did understand that George and his father had a fight and George took off, left home, whatever. So I went and found Boy and asked him about it and he said that George went to Escoting. At that point I decided to go look for him. I told Boy and he told me to take the high road to possibly catch the jeepney that George might be on, so I ran up to the top of the mountain and down the high road and walked halfway to Gundaway and then a jeepney passed and George was in it. I stopped the jeepney and asked George to get out and talk to me for a little bit, so he did. I tried to talk him into not going but he told me he was just strolling for two or three days to Escoting. I couldn't talk him out of going despite anything I said and despite the fact I was crying, so he caught the next jeepney and I came home. After crying for a while I went and told Alfredo about our encounter, trying my hardest not to cry. Then I returned home and worked on the tree notebook, continuing on cacao. Just before I finished that, this guy who I don't know stopped by and he hung out here for a couple hours. Then I finished writing about cacao and tried to siesta, but I couldn't sleep thinking about George. After that I went and fetched water and saw Bubot and asked him to come tonight but I don't know if he will. I returned home and started the letter to San and Jack and then Alfredo came and we cried on each others shoulders for a good hour. Then he went home and I cooked supper. The rain started at about 4:30 PM and now, at 6:45 PM, it's still continuing. I finished cooking, eating and doing dishes in the rain and now I'm waiting for Bubot, but I don't really think he'll come – he would have been here before now if he was going to come. I'm really sad and down that George left. He told me he will return in two or three days, so if he isn't back on Friday I'll go to Escoting on Saturday and search for him. Bubot did not come to sleep. George has slept here exactly 100 nights – I just counted in my journal. AWANEN!

Wednesday, July 30, 1986
My House, Gomez, Cabarroguis, Quirino

Letter to Ardis B.

₱280 – 1 = ₱279				
Cigarettes	1			TOTAL ₱1

I got up at 5:00 AM and of course there was no George. I had a terrible night's sleep. I cooked breakfast, ate half heartedly and did dishes. I was even crying before breakfast. I got ready for the day. There were thick clouds all day today – even the weather is sad because George is gone. I went to Alfredo's house for an hour or more this morning. I returned and picked beans and thought of all the times that George has helped me pick beans. Then I removed the old dead *parya* from the trellis. Boy came for a while and tried to console me. After he left I dug a drainage ditch for the water so it can cross the garden more easily. I drank coffee for lunch and wrote the above letter to Ardis then I wrote some in Ilokano to George. I swept the lawn and a bunch of wives came to try to console me. Then I went to Alfredo's for another hour and then I returned home and bathed and cooked supper. I ate and washed the dishes and went to Alfredo's to get George's blanket so at least I have his smell to remind me of him. I talked there for another 45 minutes and now it's 7:30 PM. Please return tomorrow George. AWANEN!

[I wrote some on a letter to George in Ilokano every day that he was gone and I will insert that letter at the end of this saga.]

Thursday, July 31, 1986
My House, Gomez, Cabarroguis, Quirino

Letter to Chris & Mary M.

₱279 – 2 = ₱277				
Cigarettes	2			TOTAL ₱2

I got up at 5:20 AM – no George, no companion to sleep. I cooked a small breakfast, ate, washed the dishes and got ready for the day. I went to Alfredo's to talk for an hour or so and then returned home. Some pigs destroyed my corn while I was at Alfredo's house – I hollered for George and cried some and then I started reading *"Friday"* a book by Robert A. Heinlein. Junior came by to beg some rope for a belt for his new machete. Alfredo came to talk for a while at about 11:00 AM. They both left and I continued reading for a while. I stopped at noon, drank coffee and wrote the above letter to Chris and Mary. After that I wrote more on the letter to George and then I read until 3:30 PM. I fetched water, bathed and cooked supper. Pedring came by to talk for a while and when I washed dishes he left. Now it's 7:00 PM and of course there is no George and no sleeping companion. I'm about as down as down can be. I already put the mats on the floor. It was a typhoon type rain today for a while. Please return tomorrow George. AWANEN!

Friday, August 1, 1986
My House, Gomez, Cabarroguis, Quirino

Letters from Vicki S., Bill N., two postcards from Chad D. Letter from the Peace Corps telling me to come to Manila about my foot problem.

₱277 – 66 = ₱211							
Cigarettes	4	Coffee	20	Food	35	Coke	3
Rides	4					TOTAL	₱66

I got up at 5:15 AM and of course there was no George again. I cooked breakfast, ate, did dishes and went and talked with Alfredo. Then I got ready to go to Gundaway. I left here at 7:20 AM and it was raining hard all day and chilly. I went to the post office and got the above letters and then to market. There wasn't much activity at market today. I got done marketing and waited as several jeepneys passed. I searched in each one for George. I arrived back in Burgos at 11:20 AM and saw footprints of shoes on the trail, so I thought – George! I ran up the mountain and eventually I caught up to Lito, not George. I arrived home at 12:00 N, read my mail and then went to Alfredo's – there was no George, only rain. At 4:30 PM I started cooking supper, ate, washed dishes and went to get Bubot to come here and sleep. I'm lonely, it's the fourth night of no companion to sleep with tonight. It's nice to talk with Bubot. [We talked about whether I should go to Escoting tomorrow and try to convince George to return home. We had a long discussion about whether that was the right thing for me to do or not and Bubot convinced me that I should do it. After that Bubot and I were playing around and I ended up sitting on his thing and moving up and down. After a few minutes we realized that was not working for either of us and I lifted off him and laid down on my stomach and told him *"ikabil mo"* or "you put". He immediately understood what I meant and he stuck his thing in my anus. He didn't have to do much pumping before he was cumming. And, it was amazing. I had never cum so hard or so long in my life, and have never done so again. I am not a fan of anal sex, but this one time exception was extraordinary. After we were both breathing normally again Bubot said "that was wonderful".] AWANEN!

Saturday, August 2, 1986
My House, Gomez, Cabarroguis, Quirino

₱211 – 60 = ₱151							
Cigarettes	5	Rides	16	Bread	3	Coke	6
Eggs	10	George	20			TOTAL	₱60

We got up at 5:15 AM and Bubot left. I had coffee only for breakfast, bathed and got ready for the day. I took my bag of valuables to Alfredo's and left at 6:30 AM for Escoting. I arrived at Diadi at 9:00 AM and started walking the five kilometers to Escoting at 9:10 AM. I arrived there at about 10:15 AM and found Alfredo's sister's house and found George. I also saw Tracy C. and she asked me what I was doing in her village. [Tracy was the Peace Corps Volunteer who was working in Escoting.] George and I managed to find a place where just the two of us could talk and after about a half hour or so of talking through my tears, I talked him into returning home tomorrow, or at least he said he would come home tomorrow and he told me I can believe him. At first he said he was going to stay there for a long time. I cried on his shoulder – literally – and told him about how bad his father's ulcer is, that his father is no longer angry, that we all miss him, that if he didn't return I would probably go home to Alaska and that I haven't been able to eat or sleep for four days. I also told him he should return. I told him he had lied to me on Tuesday when he told me that he would return home in two or three days and asked him how I knew if I could believe him when he says he will return tomorrow. He admitted that he had lied on Tuesday but said he wasn't lying about returning tomorrow and that I could believe him, so we went back to Ligaya's house, I ate an early lunch there and then left at about 11:30 AM. I had to walk to Diadi again and then I caught a ride to Cordon. I managed to finally find a jeepney headed for Burgos, despite the heavy rain. I finally got to Burgos at 3:30 PM, headed up the mountain and got home at 4:20 PM. I went straight to Alfredo's house and told my story for half an hour and then came home and cooked supper. Now it's 8:00 PM and I'm very tired. I walked some 15 kilometers today. George didn't want me to sleep there – he said he wanted to return home alone tomorrow, otherwise I would have slept there tonight. It rained all day today. The pigs dug up my whole garden today while I was gone. This typhoon is very slow in leaving. Hopefully I'll have a sleeping companion again tomorrow night. AWANEN!

Ilokano letter to George mentioned on July 30th follows for next seven pages. Scanned directly from Journal. English translation will follow.

Apo ni George - agsuratak kenka met.
Mailiw ak kenka unay, unay. Naliday
ak unay, unay! Naikapis ak ngamin haan
mo nga naibagam kaniak pumanaw ka.
Naragsak ak nagbirok ka taytay bigat.
Agyamanak ti nagtungtong tay, ngem
pasinsiya ngamin nasapul ka ti pumanaw.
Nagaddu nga sangit idiay balay yo
ken ditoy balay ko tatta nga aldaw.
Na padasek ti naginana ak taytay malem-
ngem nasakit ti ulok ngamin ti
nagsangit isunga haan nga makatin
ti maturog ak. Sapay la koma agsublieka
intono Huebes wenno intono Viernes.
No haan mo nga agsublieka intono
Viernes umay ak idiay Escoteng intono
Sabado, ken agbirok ak para kenka
manen, kasla taytay bigat. Tatta
Alas siete kinse - napigsa ti tudo!
Agsangit ti riknak manen. Awan ka
kadikket nga gayyem ken kabsat.
Ayayatenka, unay kasla ti agpayso nga
kabsat ko. Agsangsangitak manen - masapul
ti agsardeng ak ~~to~~ daytoy nga surat.
Agsublie kan to man kabsat!! Inkabil ak ti
ikammen mo ditoy ti datar ken ti pungan
mo - uray no awan ka. Nagangot ak ti

2 L.G.

July 29 (continued)

pungon mo - nabanglo ka! Agpanpan-unotak kenka. Sapay la koma adda ka. Sapay la koma mailiw ka koniak kas la mailiw ak kenka. Toy ray malem umay na ni tatang mo ditoy ken nagsangit kami. Agdanag ak para kenka nadikket nga kabsat. Kuna na ni tatang mo no agsublieka ditoy haan na naunget.

July 30. Alas dos.
Kadikket nga kabsat ko ni George. Agsuratak kenka ti riknak manen. Castoy latta ak - nalidday ken maka cangsangit ak. Basit ti ~~m~~ naturog ak idi rabii ken madi ti taga inep ko. Nagriingak alas dos, alas tres, alas quatre ken nagbirok ak para ti imam ngem siempre awan! Nagdingngeg ak ti timek mo uneg ti naturog, nakitak ti rupam ken ti isem mo. Nagdingngegak ti naibagam ti nangan ko. "Daniel." bimmangon ak alas cingo - kas la kanayon ken nagsangit-ak - manen. Nagluto ak ti pangbigat ko ken madi ti raman. Nalpas ak ti pangbigat ken ti aginnaw ken napan ak

3 L.G.

July 30 - Letter to George (continued)
idiay balay yo. Naturog na ni ~~na~~ tatong mo - awan ni nanang mo - napan na idiay borkag yo ken nagburas na. Nag idda-ak ti datar yo ken nagsangitak manen. Nag riing na ni tatong mo ken nagtong tong kami panggep sika ken nagsangit kami manen. Nagsublie ak ditoy balay ko. Nagikat ak ti parya naguapo ti paguliom. Haan ko nga nangan ti pang-aldaw. Madi mabalin - nasakit ti ulok ken ti buksit ko. Agsublie kan to man, kabsat. Dandanni ak ti mapan idiay Escolang tatta nga aldaw. Segoro haan nga mabalin ti aguray ak intono Sabado. No haan nga mabalin ti maturog ak manen intono rabii segoro mapanak intono kigat agsapa. Agdanag ak panggep sika. Naliday ak unay, talipungawen ak unay. Awan kadwak! Ag sab sabong da dua nga karabasa ken awan ka ti ipakitam kasano ti ikabil ti sabali nga sabong. Diak ammo ania ti agaramidek. Intono agsublie ka - mabalin ti tumulong ka man ti agalad ti daga ko. Idi kalman kaano nagbirokak kenka nag subsub ti baboy ti utong manen! Ag tinnulong ta man!!! Agpasyar ta man!!! Awanen tatta kabsat.

4-L.G.

July 30 - letter to George (continued)
Kabsat ko - nadikket nga gayyem ko.
alas siete majortatta. Haan nga mabalin
ti agpuh'aw ak para kenka. Napanak
taytay idiay balay yo ken bimmulodek
ti ules mo. Awan sabali ti kaduwak ti
usaren ngem mabiit laeng ken agwalis.
ak ken ikabil ti ikammen, pungan ken
ules mo idiay ti datar - sapay la koma
ammomen nakasagana-ak ti agsublieka.
Awan ti agadal idi rabii - segoro
awan ti agadal ak tatta nga rabii
met. Haan ko nga mangan ti kendi ngamin
awan ka. Nagburas ak taytay bigat ken
nagpanunot ak panggep amin ti daras
nagburas ta idi napinpintas ti utong ko.
Agsublie ka man intono bigat! Awanen tatta.

July 31 - alas dos.
Nabanogannak unay idi rabii - naturogak
ken nagkapet ak ti ules mo ken nagangot ak
ti baggim. Awan ti agadal.
Nagriingak alas cingo biunte ti bigat -
naladaw! Awan ka. Nagsangit ak. Naglutoak
ti pangbigat ngem nangan ak bassit.
Kumutkutong ak ngamin awan ka, ken ngamin
naliday ak kabsat ko, nadikket nga gayyem
ko. Napanak ~~idid~~ idiay balay yo ken

5-L.G.

July 31- letter to George (continued)
nangan da ti baboy ti mais ko.
Nagpukaw ak para kenka- "Agsublie ka man, ni George," ken nagsangit ak manen. Haan nga mabalin ti malypatak panggep sika. Ag pos opis ak intono bigat- sapay la koma makita ka idiay ti jeepney, wenno sapay la koma adda kan kaano summangpet ak ditoy intono bigat. No awan ka intono bigat mapan ak idiay intono Sabado- agpaysa, sigurado. Sapay la koma mamati man amin naibagak ditoy ngamin ~~pp~~ papan ko amin. Kayat ko ti matay, ngamin awan gayyem ko. No awan ka haan ko nga kayat ti sabali nga gayyem. Kanayon agbubuya ak ti dalan- sapay la koma makita ti rupam, ngem awan ken awan. Awan ti aramidek- aramidek ti danum ti matak laeng (Nalypatakon ti Ilokano) Masapul ti ag tong tong ta- addu. Awanen tatta. Uray naliday ti ulep. Agsangsangit da uray ~~napp~~ napigpigsa ngem siak! Agdadanag ak para kenka nadikket nga kabsat.
Alas siete ti rabii. Haan mo agsublie tatta nga aldaw kabsat. Maymaysak ti maturog manen. Inkabilakan ti ikkamu

6 - L.G.

July 31 - letter to George (continued)
pungon ka iles mo ditoy ti
datar. Uray tatta aggiggigamak ti
ules mo nga naimbag kasla kanayon
aggigaimak ti imam. Segaro naaasdaw
mo kaano nakitamo siak idiay
ti dalan idi martes. Sapay la koma
mabalin ti mimatiak ti naibagam
abay ti dalan idi martes. Sapay
la koma daytoy nga rabii ti maoudi
ti maturog maymaysak. Sapay la
koma, unay, adda ka manen intono
bigat ti rabii. Masapul ti makitaka
manen sakbay agbagtit akon!
makasangsangitak manen. itwonn-
Aug 1. Alas tres majan.
Ayon ka? naibagam agsubliekan dua
wenno tallo nga aldaw? Limmagto da ti baboy
ti alad ken nagsubsubda ti karabasa manen.
nagsubsubda ti utong met. Tumuleng ka
man? Agalad ta!? Agbagbagio manen.
Agtudo amin ti oras tatta nga aldaw.
Segaro aguraykа ti agsardeng ti tudo.
Diak Ammo! Umay ak idiay intono
bigat nasapa. naawat ko ti surat
nagaupo ti Peace Corps, kuna da - "Daniel
umay ka ditoy ni Manila panggep ti
napipikil nga sakam." Umuna masapul ka

7 L.G.

Aug. 1 - letter to George (cont.)
ti agsublie umuna. Ag panpanunot ak
panggep agawid ak idiay Alaska. Nalidday
ak umay ngamin awan ka - ken uray
segoro haan mo nga kayat siak.
Diak ammo. Madi ti riknak ngamin
awan ka. Apay ngata naglastog ka
panggep agsublie ka dua wenno tallo
nga aldaw. Kunak mabalin ti
mamati mo. Uray nalidday ak ngamin
haan nga mabalin ti mamati ti
maibagam. Segoro uray tatta - agsublieka
sakbay ti rabii ngem awan sa
met. Apay ngata? Agsurat ak pay
madan dama. Napanak idiay Gundaway
taytay bigat. Nagbirok ak uneg amin
ti jeepney para Luna para kenka - ken
naguray ak lima nga logan sakbay
nagawid ak. Nakitak ti tugot nga
sappatos idiay dalan - sadiwa - isunga
nagtaray ak ngamin kunak ti tugot mo.
Ngem - nagtiliw ak ni manong Lito - haan
sika. Agsublieka man - kadikket nga
kabsat - sakbay ti rabii - Haan mo nga
ammo kasano kaliday ak! Umay ak idiay
nasapa inton bigat. Segoro pumanaw
ak alas sais ti bigat.

English translation of letter to George that you've seen for the preceding seven pages. At least, this is what I wanted it to say. I was not (and am not) a native speaker of Ilokano so there may be several errors in my Ilokano.

July 29th.

Dear George,

I will write to you also. I miss you very, very much. I'm very, very sad. I am disappointed because you didn't tell me that you will leave. I am happy that I searched for you this morning. Thank you for our talk, but I am sorry because you needed to leave. There was lots of crying both at your house and here at my house today. I tried to rest this afternoon but I had a headache because of all the crying and therefore it was not possible to sleep. I hope you will return on Thursday or Friday. If you don't return on Friday I will come there to Escoting on Saturday and search for you again, like this morning. Now it's 7:15 PM and raining hard. I am able to cry again because you are not here, my closest friend and brother. I love you very much, like a real brother. I'm crying again and I have to stop writing. Please return soon brother. I put your sleeping mat and pillow here on the floor, even if you are not here. I smelled your pillow – you have a good smell. I'm thinking about you and wish you were here. I hope you are missing me like I am missing you. This afternoon your father came here to my house and we cried together. I worry about you, my close brother. Your father said that if you return here he is not angry.

July 30th, 2:00 PM.

My closest brother George, I feel like writing to you again. I am like this – sad and able to cry. I slept only a little last night and my dreams were bad. I woke up at 2:00 AM, 3:00 AM, 4:00 AM and searched for your hand to hold, like we do, but of course there was no hand. I heard your voice in my sleep, I saw your face and your smile, I heard you say my name "Daniel". I got up at 5:00 AM like always, and cried again. I cooked my breakfast and it tasted bad. I finished breakfast, washed dishes and went to your house. Your father was sleeping and your mother had gone to the vegetable farm to harvest food. I laid down on your floor and cried again and your father woke up. We talked about you and cried again. I returned here to my house and I removed the *parya* from the trellis. I didn't eat lunch, it wasn't possible, I had a headache and a stomachache. Please return soon brother. I'm nearly ready to go to Escoting today, maybe it's not possible for me to wait until Saturday. If it's not possible for me to sleep again tonight maybe I'll go tomorrow morning. I am worrying about you. I'm very sad and very lonely. I have no companion. Two of my squash are blossoming and there is no you to show me how to harvest the blossoms. I don't know what to do. When you return is it possible, please, to help me fix my garden. Yesterday while I searched for you the pigs rooted up my beans again. Let's help each other please. Let's stroll together please. I have no more right now brother.

My brother and close friend, it's 7:30 PM now. It's not possible to holler for you. A while ago I went to your house and borrowed your blanket. There is no other companion to use it, but in a bit I'll sweep the floor and put our mats, pillows and blankets on the floor. I hope you already know that I'm ready for you to return. There was no studying last night, maybe none tonight either. I also will not eat candy because there is no you. I harvested beans this morning and thought of all the times we harvested beans together when they were more beautiful. Please come home tomorrow. I have no more now.

July 31st, 2:00 PM.

I was very tired last night. I slept and held on to your blanket and could smell your body. I didn't study. I woke up at 5:20 AM, late, and of course there was no you. I cried. I cooked breakfast, but ate only a little. I'm already getting thinner because there is no you and because I'm sad, my brother and close friend. I went to your house and the pigs ate my corn while I was there. I hollered for you "please return George" and I cried again. It's not possible to forget about you. I will go to the post office tomorrow. I hope I'll see you in the jeepney or I hope you will have arrived home by the time I return tomorrow. If there is no you tomorrow then I will come there on Saturday – really. I hope you believe all that I am staying here because I mean it all. I nearly want to die because I have no friend. If there is no you then I don't want another friend. I am always watching the trail, I hope I will see your face coming home, but no and no and no. I make tears only. We need to talk – LOTS! I have no more now. Even the clouds are sad, they are crying even harder than I am. I'm worrying about you my close brother.

7:00 PM. You did not return today brother. I'm alone to sleep again. I put your sleeping mat, pillow and blanket here on the floor. Even now I'm holding tightly to your blanket like I always hold your hand. Maybe you were surprised when you saw me there on the road on Tuesday. I hope this is the last night I sleep alone. I hope very much that you are here again tomorrow night. I need to see you again before I go crazy. I will cry again now. No more today.

August 1st, 3:30 PM.

Where are you? You said you would return in two or three days. The pigs jumped over the fence and rooted up my squash again. They also rooted up the beans. Please help me. Let's make a fence. It's a typhoon again – raining all day today. Maybe you are waiting for the rain to stop, I don't know. I will come there tomorrow morning. I received a letter from the Peace Corps and they said "Daniel come to Manila about your sore foot" but first you need to return. I'm thinking about going home to Alaska. I am too sad because there is no you and maybe you don't even like me, I don't know. I feel bad because there is no you. I wonder why you lied to me about returning in two or three days. I thought it was possible to believe you. I am even sad because it's not possible to believe what you say. Maybe even now you are returning, maybe before tonight, but probably not. I wonder why not. I'll write more after a while. (Later) I went to Gundaway this morning and searched for you on all of the jeepneys bound for Burgos. I waited for five rides to pass before I gave up on you and returned home. I saw a fresh shoe print on the trail and therefore I ran because I thought it was your shoe print, but I caught up with Lito not you. Please come home close brother, before tonight. Don't you know how sad I am? I will come there early tomorrow morning. Maybe I will leave here at 6:00 AM.

I wrote the complete story of what happened during the past week and submitted it to the Peace Corps, thinking that they might be able to use it for something. I was correct and they printed it in the monthly ***"Salaysayan"*** Magazine. The story is reproduced below. Line drawings were done by Sue T.

From Salaysayan Magazine
Peace Corps Philippines
October 1987

A RICH AND RARE EXPERIENCE

Story by Daniel Wieczorek

What is involvement? The dictionary gives several meanings, but I think my definition would be "to become a part of or to have something become a part of you."

A fellow PCV once commented to me, "I really feel that if you cling too tightly to other volunteers, you'll never have a really satisfying experience here…". I responded, "I feel that how close you get to your Filipino brothers and sisters will determine, in the long run, how good/satisfying/fulfilling your Peace Corps experience is." Once at my site, I developed some close personal friendships, one in particular – maybe because we both put so much mental energy into developing it.

Over the course of a week, I realized just how important and close that one friend is, and how deeply involved I am with his family. If I don't accomplish anything more than what I did that one week, I can still say that my Peace Corps experience has been richly rewarding and fulfilling – for I had the rare opportunity to bring a family back together.

As soon as I moved into my own house, friends and neighbors asked if I wanted a companion. I said no, as most volunteers do, but it quickly became obvious that the people felt I was trying to hide something. Plus, they were genuinely worried about me because of the ghosts in the area! I thought, "Well, this is Asia, where nobody but

nobody sleeps alone, and since I have nothing to hide, I could have somebody spend the nights with me." I chose my neighbor's 17-year-old son George as my permanent sleeping companion. He was mannerly, polite, laughed at my fledgling Ilocano the least and was the least concerned about how much my belongings cost and would I give them to him when I went home. I'm old enough to be George's father, but we've become closer than me and my real brother back in America.

I quickly came to enjoy and value George's presence every night. He never fails to call me Manong, or older brother. In this mountain barrio of Gomez, Cabarroguis, Quirino, there are no sari-sari stores, no place to go have a drink or eat ice cream; there isn't even electricity. Life virtually comes to a halt at dark. Without George, there would be nothing to do except read a book or write a letter by kerosene light, further destroying my eyes.

George, upon his arrival each evening, sweeps the floor, closes the windows, rolls out the sleeping mats, and we talk. In pure Ilocano, he tells me what he did that day. With a fourth grade education, George knows English colors and numbers and that's about the extent of it. We converse with lots of examples, drawings on the floor or in the air, and searching my Ilocano dictionary. George is highly motivated to have the most productive bankag, or vegetable farm, on the mountain so his daily stories are always interesting and informative. When he finishes, I tell him what I did during the day and ask him the Ilocano for some new weed, fruit tree or insect that I've dragged home that day. If it's still early, I'll tell stories about life in Alaska or life in America in general. No matter how twisted my Ilocano is, he never laughs at me; he only tries to understand, then tells me how to say it more beautifully. About 8:00 PM we go to sleep and like a clock, George always wakes up within teen minutes of 5:00 AM We roll up the sleeping mats, fold the blankets, put it all on the shelf and he leaves.

One Tuesday, I was to help George on his farm-weeding the area where he had planted 60 mandarin trees. But when I went to his house, his father looked angry and then his mother began crying. His father told me George had "left home." He explained what had happened, but all I really understood was that George and his father had argued and when his father told him to leave – meaning to go to the farm – George packed his bag and left. I ran down the mountain and caught George as he passed in a jeepney. We had a good talk but no matter what I said, he insisted there was no problem and he was only going to visit his aunt and uncle in Escoting for a few days. Then he was off on the next jeepney.

I slowly and sorrowfully climbed back up the mountain. I told his mother and father about our conversation, we all cried, and his father told me that his anger is very fast to disappear and that even now he was no longer angry. He said he didn't think

George would return in a few days because he would be afraid. I offered to go to Escoting if George didn't return on Friday, and his parents were quite happy that I would consider acting as the go-between. So, for three days we all cried and worried a lot, and I got to know that family in a much deeper way than I had previously known them.

Every night I put George's sleeping mat, pillow and blanket on the floor as if he was going to return moment. I believe in ESP and mind-to-mind communication, so I assumed George would know somewhere inside him that I was ready for his return and he'd also know I'd be coming to get him on Saturday.

George didn't return on Friday so I headed for Escoting in a downpour. After an hour's walk down our mountain, an hour's jeepney ride and another hour's walk into Escoting, I arrived. Upon finding George, I asked when he was returning, and he answered, "Not for a long time." We went where we were able to talk uninterrupted and I delivered messages from his father, mother and friends in Gomez, and told him of my own personal sadness. By the time I was done, we were both crying, and when I asked again when he was coming home, he said, "Tomorrow." Since he had left alone, he wanted to return alone, so I would go ahead and he'd be home about noon on Sunday.

I arrived back home in Gomez at dusk, sore-footed after walking barefoot in the mud for 15 kilometers. When I talked to George's parents, they were very happy and relieved.

Back at my house, I ate a good supper for the first time in four days and slept well for the first time in four nights, secure in the knowledge of what I had accomplished. Sunday morning, I cleaned house, did laundry then WAITED. At 11 :37 AM, George's father's neighbor hollered my name and said George had arrived. I ran to their house and saw the happiest group of faces I think I've ever seen in my life.

George and I shook hands and I thanked him, but then left so they could be alone as a family. By and by, George came to my house. I asked if he was happy to be home and even before he answered "Wen (yes), Manong," I knew by the smile that stretched from ear to ear that he was as happy as any 17-year-old could be. What an incredibly warm feeling for me!

When he came that night to sleep, we both had long stories to tell. One thing I asked him was if he knew somehow that I would be coming to Escoting for him. He answered, "Yes, I knew you would come."

This photo shows me with George shortly after he arrived home on August 3rd, 1986.

Chapter 12
Culture Notes #4

Anger

The situation discussed for the previous several pages was one of the most enlightening experiences I had with anger. I learned that if two people are angry with each other, it takes a go-between or intermediary to patch up the differences.

I saw this in action once while living with my host family, during training in Bayombong. My host father and 18 year old host brother exchanged words in anger, and for two days after that the father and son would not be seen in the same room together, while the mother acted as an intermediary to patch up their differences. I was even drawn into the problem when my host mother asked me to tell Ronald, my host brother, that he should respect his father and why. My host mother informed me that Ronald would surely listen to me.

As you read in the previous several pages, I was drawn into the very center of an argument by being expected to play the part of the intermediary after George and his father had an argument in Gomez and George left home for four days. George had gone 40 kilometers away, to the home of his Aunt and Uncle in another village. I had the opportunity to go and try to act as the intermediary between George and his father. I received specific instructions from George's parents about what to say when I found George, and off I went, to attempt to convince George that he should come home. I was extremely proud that I succeeded in this attempt, and to everybody's relief George did come home.

The Necessity of Demonstration

The peoples farms were, for the most part, a mile up the mountain from their houses for the reason that actual stewardship of the land was given to them after the fact. This shall not be gone into in greater detail. Because the farms were far away from the house, if the family did not go to the farm on a given day they had nothing to eat except rice and salt. The expense of meat forced the people to live nearly exclusively on fruits and vegetables and, of course rice. A meal that had meat in it was considered something special. The people raised chickens and about once a month they would butcher a chicken. Due to having these chickens, they often had eggs as a part of their meals, although possibly only two or three eggs for a family of six.

As you have seen, I started out by demonstrating how to grow a beautiful back yard garden. In training, you may remember that I learned of a gardening technique called F.A.I.T.H., an acronym for ***F**ood **A**lways **I**n **T**he **H**ome.* I had a great deal of enthusiasm for it and after two months of just telling people about it, I came to the conclusion that another aspect of **L**esser **D**eveloped **C**ountry (LDC) culture is that people have to be shown that something is truly better before they will be convinced to try it. They are not going to take anybody's word for anything – after all, this is the way their ancestors did it – so it must be right. I therefore obtained some help to clear approximately a 10 meter by 15 meter patch of abandoned, sterile ground near my house, and I planted a FAITH garden. Within two months I was harvesting more fresh vegetables than I could eat and was giving the excess to George's family. I was also being culturally sensitive in another respect, and had switched to a diet of fruits, vegetables and rice for all three meals a day, seven days a week. People came from far away and viewed my FAITH garden with amazement. With just this little piece of land I was getting all this food, and it seemed to be just because I had put all that old dead grass (mulch) on the ground. I explained to the people that when the old dead grass rotted it would make fertilizer. Before anybody else tried FAITH gardening the soil had improved enough so that it supported a good population of earthworms again and the neighbors pigs became a problem because of this. The favorite food of pigs is earthworms, I was told, and therefore the more earthworms there are, the more problems there would be with pigs. The people refused to tie up or pen their pigs, so I requested George and his father's help to fence my garden. We built a fence of split bamboo – which endured only about two months before the pigs broke it down. By the end of approximately six months I had given up in the battle against the pigs, and the FAITH garden was abandoned. This brings to light a strange cultural aspect. The people would rather let their pigs run loose and eat good than be able to eat good themselves. By tying or penning their pigs and bringing them food, they could have grown the most beautiful gardens imaginable, but they would rather let their pigs roam free. People who lived far from pigs had already begun FAITH gardening and all in all I could see no big advantage in attempting to continue to fight the pigs. It was extremely frustrating to see a beautiful garden destroyed as regular as clockwork by them. It didn't matter, as the seed was growing in my mind to demonstrate something larger, something that would have longer range effects, and truly be an accomplishment that I could be proud of.

The First Year Draws to a Close

At this point my first year was drawing to a close. I had learned a lot about culture, beliefs, customs, and folklore as well as the language of the Ilokano people. In addition to learning that people had to be shown that a new method of doing something made sense before they would try it, I had also learned the cultural aspects of birthdays, Christmas, weddings, anger between two people, and much more. Some of these cultural aspects shall now be addressed.

Birthdays

An Ilokano birthday celebration, unlike an American one, where the guests bring presents for the person who is celebrating, contrasts in the respect that the Ilokano birthday celebration sees the person who is having the birthday, if he or she invites friends for the birthday celebration, cooking a big meal of special foods and feeding all the guests. There will however, be no gift giving. People don't have money to be able to give presents, they never have had, and therefore a birthday isn't even considered a time to give gifts.

Christmas

Christmas, on the other hand, is considered a time to give gifts, but unlike the USA where many people seem to forget the true meaning of Christmas and see it as a time to clean up in the presents department, the Ilokano looks upon Christmas as a day to relax, eat special food, celebrate as and with the community and with the family, and have a happy time. Any presents exchanged are fairly inconsequential, but important and special to the person receiving them. A typical present may be a bar of soap, a pair of fingernail clippers, a small mirror, or a towel. Christmas was a very special time to me as it showed me how close George and I had actually become. For Christmas, George gave me a whole cooked chicken, and I gave George a T-shirt with a design on it. I was extremely moved by George's present to me. I knew that the family itself could only butcher about one chicken a month for its own use, so although small, I looked upon this gift as a gift of a month's supply of meat. I hugged George so tight that I practically broke his ribs. (Watch for this story coming up in just a few more months, at Christmastime.)

Opening Presents

Another Ilokano aspect of gift giving is that the receiver does not open a gift in the presence of the giver. The giver knows that whatever present he or she has given is small and inconsequential, so the receiver is not expected to open it in the presence of the giver and embarrass him or her. The receiver of the gift will only open it after the giver has left. I had, of course, learned this from George. Whenever I had to be gone from Gomez for a Peace Corps meeting, seminar, or training I would ask George to watch my house and guard my garden from the pigs, and upon my return I would always bring George some small present, usually a pair of short pants. Shorts, or short pants (similar to an American swimsuit) were the normal work garb and as such were a high demand item. The first time I brought George a "thank you for guarding the house present" and gave it to George that night when he came to my house to sleep, George politely thanked me and placed the newspaper wrapped package in the corner. I asked George why he didn't open it and he obligingly explained. I then explained the custom in America and asked George to please open the package because I wanted to see his smile. George obliged and opened the package, and he was thrilled. He told me that I didn't have to bring him anything just for guarding my house and garden, especially because the pigs had broken through the fence again and destroyed more of it. I made it a habit however, to bring back a pair of short pants or a T-shirt for George every time I had to be gone for a few days. After that first time George would always hold the package a minute and look at me with eyes that questioned "Should I open it now?" I would merely shake my head yes and George would open it. This was one area in which, because of our friendship, I did not have to strictly follow the cultural norm.

Cooking and Lighting

While you've been reading you have possibly noticed several references to the purchase of charcoal and even a reference to trying to cook with charcoal dust. You have probably therefore asked yourself why, and been longing for a further explanation about that.

Most people used an open fire in their homes, placed in a corner of the kitchen upon a metal backed shelf at a suitable height for comfortably cooking upon. I used a charcoal stove which I will insert some photos of at the close of this section. The charcoal is placed in the upper portion of the stove and easily lit with a small piece of newspaper placed under it. Air is drawn into the charcoal from underneath it and it acts rather like a chimney. The charcoal burns very hot and the ash falls through the holes between the upper and lower portions of the stove. If you are confused I suggest that you do an image search for "Philippine charcoal stove" (without the quotes) on the internet and you'll find an abundance of photos.

Maybe you have also noticed the purchase of kerosene under the listed expenses that you've been shown. You have probably also asked yourself what that is used for. Well, remember way back on page 93 when I mentioned that there is (or at least was) no electricity in Gomez? Therefore the kerosene is used for kerosene lamps. Now, at the mention of kerosene lamps you are probably imagining something relatively fancy that you have seen somewhere in the past. You should get those thoughts out of your head and try to visualize a small glass jar, like a jelly or jam jar, something with a metal lid which can be screwed on it. Okay so far? Now imagine using a large diameter nail and making a hole in the lid of that jar. Then take a small rag and twist it tightly and then insert it downward through the hole you have just made in the lid of the jar, leaving around ¼ inch of that "wick" sticking out of the top of the hole. Fill the jar with kerosene, let the wick soak up the kerosene and then light it and there is your kerosene lamp. That was what most people used for lighting when I was there.

Photos Courtesy: Red Clay Pottery Crafts

Chapter 13
August 3, 1986 through October 17, 1986

Sunday, August 3, 1986
My House, Gomez, Cabarroguis, Quirino

Letter to Tracy C.

I got up at 5:15 AM, no George. I cooked breakfast, ate, washed dishes and got ready for the day. I went to Alfredo's for a while to talk and the rain finally stopped, so I did laundry and finished with that at about 10:30 AM. There was lots of dirty laundry today. George returned at 11:37 AM and Boy hollered for me, so I went to their house for a little while to talk and then George came here for a little while and I showed him all of the pig digging that has occurred over the past few days. He returned home and I cleaned house for the first time since he left. Then I stopped for coffee and wrote to Tracy telling her in some detail what I was doing in Escoting yesterday. After that, with George's return, I'm motivated to do something again so I tried to repair pig damage. At 3:30 PM I went to Alfredo's found George and took some pictures of him and with him. Then I bathed, cooked supper, ate did dishes and even before 7:00 PM George came. Boy am I happy. Thank you God. AWANEN!

Monday, August 4, 1986
My House, Gomez, Cabarroguis, Quirino

Wrote up the story of the past week.

We got up at 5:25 AM, I don't know why we woke up late. George left and Bubot came to talk for a while. I cooked breakfast, ate, did dishes and got ready for the day. I went to Alfredo's to talk for a while and then returned home and spent the next four hours writing up the long story of the trials of the last week. Alfredo came for an hour or so and he left at lunchtime. I drank coffee for lunch and continued to write. I don't know what time I finished. I weeded the garden for a while and then it rained gently from about 3:15 to 4:00 PM. After that I fetched water, bathed and started cooking supper. I ate, did dishes and now it's only 6:25 PM. I'm hoping George will come early again tonight, maybe even earlier than last night. I'd like to show him that strange bamboo that I found down by the creek. He and Boy harvested bananas again today and again they wouldn't allow me to go with them, I don't understand why. Oh well. I'll read *Newsweek* for a while and study Ilokano. AWANEN!

Tuesday, August 5, 1986
My House, Gomez, Cabarroguis, Quirino

Rody is here and spend the night.

We got up at 5:00 AM, George left and I cooked breakfast, ate, did dishes and got ready for the day. There was a meeting today and Alfredo was the first one to arrive. The meeting was supposed to begin at 8:00 AM but Rody didn't show up until about 9:00 AM. There were about 40 people here at my house for the meeting, which wrapped up at about noon. Dominador Deguzman brought a bag of rice and a bunch of fish to the house for lunch and Alfredo cooked it all for us. It was really nice of him, good old Alfredo. I did dishes after lunch and then in the afternoon Lito and Anaceta brought a bunch of coconut fronds and we put those on the top of the tree nursery for shade for the seedlings. By 4:00 PM we had planted 500 or more seeds of lukban, guapple, guyabano, salamagi and mahogany. Everybody left and I cooked supper. We finished eating at about 7:00 PM or so but we couldn't do dishes, it was too dark to see. Rody is sleeping here so of course George won't come. I asked Bubot to come, but he didn't want to either. Such is life I guess. Rody told me he'll be staying until Thursday – it would be nice if he left tomorrow. AWANEN!

Wednesday, August 6, 1986
My House, Gomez, Cabarroguis, Quirino

Rody is here for the night again.

₱151 – 2 = ₱149					
Cigarettes	2			TOTAL	₱2

I got up at 5:00 AM, did dishes from last night, cooked breakfast, swept the yard and then at 6:20 AM Rody got up and we ate breakfast and did dishes again. Then we got ready for the day and we went and got some soil for the nursery – four big burlap bags full – and then we planted another 240 seeds of mahogany and fireball. With the 600 seeds that we all planted yesterday that makes 840 seeds planted in the nursery. We quit at 11:00 or 11:30 AM and I cooked lunch, we ate and I did dishes again. Then Rody slept and I cleaned up the nursery, watered everything and strolled to Alfredo's. I returned home at 4:00 PM, fetched water and then the rain started. I cooked supper and we ate early enough to do dishes, but the creek is the highest I've ever seen it so it wasn't possible to do dishes; I'll have to wait until tomorrow again. Now it's 6:45 PM and it's still raining really hard. Oh, Alfredo came by at about 5:15 PM and gave me a bunch of beans, okra and kabatitti, so we did manage to have enough food for a sufficient supper. He left when we ate. The papaya seeds which I planted two weeks ago (July 23rd) have mostly germinated, much to my surprise. AWANEN!

Thursday, August 7, 1986
My House, Gomez, Cabarroguis, Quirino

Rody left today. Letter to Bill J.

We got up at 5:00 AM, even Rody! I washed the dishes from last night, cooked breakfast, we ate and then I did the dishes again and got ready for the day. After that I strolled to Alfredo's to talk for a while and help George build his fish pond for a little while. Then I returned home and Rody and I filled 76 seedling bags with soil. He then headed down the mountain and I returned to help George until around noon. Then I returned home and wrote the above letter and it rained for an hour or two. I figured out how many letters I've written to people and how many they've written to me. Then George and Alfredo came to help me improve the fence around the squash area. George and I also planted 76 Madre de Cacao seeds in the dirt filled plastic bags – the sacks that Rody and I filled this morning. After finishing the fence George and Alfredo left, I fetched water and bathed, cooked supper, ate and washed dishes. It was nice to have dishes for only one person again. Now it's 7:21 PM and George should be here any minute. If he isn't then I'll holler for him at 7:30PM. AWANEN!

Friday, August 8, 1986
My House, Gomez, Cabarroguis, Quirino

Letters from San & Jack G., Chris & Mary M., two from Dad, Ted Stevens (map), Fred & Cynthia B., Barb W., IRS, package from Steve A.

₱149 + 300 – 307 = ₱142							
Cigarettes	5	Food	44	Rides	16	Lunch	50
Coke	4	Coffee	112	Household	14	Postage	26
Candy	16	Kerosene	8	Batteries	12	TOTAL	₱307

We got up at 5:00 AM and George left even before rolling up the sleeping mats, weird. I cooked breakfast, ate, did dishes, got ready for the day and left for Burgos. I stopped at Gundaway and got the above mail. The backpack arrived from Steve A. After that I continued on to Santiago to cash a check. I arrived at about noon, so I ate lunch before going to the bank. Then I went to Marilens and got some household things and toilet paper. Then I went and did my marketing and headed for home. I left Santiago at 2:25 PM, arrived at Burgos at 3:42 PM and got home at 4:30 PM. I fetched water and bathed. The pigs got inside the squash place again, despite the new fence, and did some more minor damage. I talked with Alfredo and Boy while I was cooking supper and then they left when I ate. I washed the dishes, figured out today's expenses and put letter received dates in the HP-71. Now it's 7:15 PM and I'm waiting for George to come. I have a headache. It rained this morning before I went to Burgos. AWANEN!

Saturday, August 9, 1986
My House, Gomez, Cabarroguis, Quirino

We got up at 5:00 AM, George left and I cooked breakfast, ate, did the dishes and got ready for the day. Then I did laundry and finished that at 8:30 AM. After that I went and talked with George for a while about planting seedlings. Then I tried my best to improve the fence around the *kamote* and George came. He helped me with the *kamote* fence and then we filled 81 bags with soil and planted 45 more Madre de Cacao seeds, 22 raintree seeds and 14 latokko seeds. I am now showing a total of 941 "baglings" in the nursery. After we finished that, George left. The first fireball tree (planted August 6) is already germinating. I stopped for lunchtime coffee and packed to go to Manila tomorrow and then I read *Newsweek*. I went to Alfredo's for a while to talk and upon returning home I trimmed my beard, bathed and cooked supper. Now I'm done eating and dishes are washed. It's 6:46 PM and I'm hoping George will come early. This is my last night here for a while. I'm going to Manila about my foot that has been half asleep for 1.5 or two months now and is also infected. There was only a little rain today, I hope no more comes tonight so that the trail is good tomorrow. Now I'll study Ilokano for a while. AWANEN!

[By the way, it has never been mentioned, but at this point my feet are tough enough so that I go everywhere barefooted. I wear flip-flops when I go to Gundaway or Santiago, to the city so to speak, but at all other times I am barefooted. It took about six months for my feet to get toughened enough to be able to do this painlessly at all times. Tomorrow, when I go to the big city of Manila, I will wear real shoes. And, that's the only time I wear shoes – when I go to some Peace Corps seminar or training session somewhere or when I go to the big city.]

Sunday, August 10, 1986
Malate Pension, Manila

₱142 + 200 – 160 = ₱182							
Rides	99	Toiletries	12	Cigarettes	4	Coke	8
Meals	26	Candy	8	Ice Cream	3	TOTAL	₱160

We got up at 5:00 AM, I gave George my leftover food and he left. I cooked breakfast, ate, did dishes, bathed and left at 7:20 AM. I arrived in Santiago at about 9:40 AM or so and ate marienda, got shampoo and toilet paper and caught a ride to the Pantranco Bus Terminal. I left Santiago at 10:40 AM and we stopped in Bayombong at the Sabre Inn for lunch. After several more stops along the way we arrived in Manila at about 6:20 PM or so. I caught a jeepney to Quiapo and then a jeepney to Mabini Street and walked to Malate Pension. I finally got to the pension at 7:20 PM. It took me exactly 12 hours from the time I left Gomez. Now it's 7:46 PM and I'm going to get supper ordered and eat. I'm thinking about George and wondering what he is doing about now. Usually he is at my house by now and we would be talking about the day's activities. Is he already asleep by now or are they all sitting and talking? Is he thinking of me also? AWANEN!

Monday, August 11, 1986
Malate Pension, Manila

Postcards to Ronald and George. Letter to Steve A.

₱182 + 700 – 745 = ₱137							
Meals	160	Cigarettes	8	Books	200	Medicine	157
Rides	6	Postage	144	Postcards	19	Candy	1
Seeds	32	Coffee	10	Misc.	8	TOTAL	₱745

I got up at 5:10 AM, showered and got ready for the day. I ate breakfast and wrote a postcard to Ronald and then I went to the Peace Corps Office and then to the doctor's office. They examined me and said to return at 4:30 PM. I went to BPI to got pallang seeds and then returned to Malate Pension, where I ate lunch. Then I went downtown and got a book, some postcards, stamps and aerogrammes. Then I continued on and went back to the doctor's office and they said that I have a pinched nerve because of squatting too much. Then I got a ride that ended up in Quiapo because the bus driver fucked me over. After that I took a jeepney to Mabini and stopped at Dunkin' Donuts for donuts and coffee. Then I continued on to Malate Pension. I ate supper and now it's 9:55 PM and time for bed. Oh, I wrote a postcard to George while I was relaxing at Dunkin' Donuts and a letter to Steve A. while eating supper. Hello George! AWANEN!

Tuesday, August 12, 1986
Malate Pension, Manila

Letter to San & Jack G.

₱137 + 400 – 438 = ₱99							
Meals	173	Lodging	75	Cigarettes	14	Candy	16
Rides	4	Toiletries	20	Coin	30	Marienda	20
Hat	18	Presents	25	Washcloth	10	Lazones	10
Ice Cream	16	Beer	7			TOTAL	₱438

I got up at 5:30 AM, ate breakfast and went to the Peace Corps Office to get released for going home tomorrow morning. Yea! Then I went to Robinson's Department store and got some stuff. I found a five peso coin, a rare thing, so I bought it. I ate lunch at Shakey's Pizza and went to the embassy to talk about taking Nestor to America, but I got no satisfaction there. I returned to Malate Pension and ate ice cream and then I went off to Baclaran market, where I got some short pants, a hat and washcloth for George. Then I returned to Malate Pension again. I talked with people for a while and then I went to the Lucky 77 Pension for supper. Now it's nearly 9:15 PM, already late. I'm going home early tomorrow morning. Oh, I wrote a letter to San and Jack G. while eating supper and I also met an Ilokano brother there at the Lucky 77. AWANEN!

Wednesday, August 13, 1986
My House, Gomez, Cabarroguis, Quirino

₱99 + 300 – 197 = ₱202							
Rides	86	Meals	14	Food	47	Cigarettes	11
Coke	10	Pasalubong	12	Marienda	17	TOTAL	₱197

I got up at 5:15 AM, showered, packed and left Malate Pension. I went to Dunkin' Donuts for breakfast and then to the Pantranco Bus Terminal and took the 7:00 AM bus. It was a pretty uneventful trip except for one flat tire along the way. I did some food shopping along the way at places where we stopped and picked up a bit more food in Cordon, where we arrived at about 3:00 PM. Then I caught a ride from there to Burgos, started walking up the mountain at 4:18 PM and arrived home at 5:02 PM. I fetched water, looked at the garden, bathed, had only coffee for supper and then spent an hour or so unpacking everything. I went to Alfredo's for a bit to give him the crackers I bought for them and they gave me some dried water buffalo meat. I returned home and it's now 7:00 PM. I'm waiting for George to come and if he's not here by 7:30 PM I'll holler for him. AWANEN!

Thursday, August 14, 1986
My House, Gomez, Cabarroguis, Quirino

Letter to BOSTID (about their high prices), San & Jack G. and start on one to Chris & Mary M.

We got up at 5:00 AM and George left. I cooked breakfast, ate, did dishes and got ready for the day. Then I went to Alfredo's and talked with George for a while, Alfredo had gone to their vegetable farm. I got more soil and after a while George came and we filled more bags with soil and then it rained and I started writing the letter to Chris and Mary M. Then it was lunchtime – I had coffee only for lunch – and after that George returned again to fill more bags. All in all today we filled 254 bags and planted Golden Shower and Katurai seeds. We also did a good count of all bags today and there is a grand total of 1,242 in all. After that I fetched water, bathed, cooked supper, ate, washed dishes and I just got started on my journal when George came. Now it's only 6:55 PM. Pedring stopped by and talked to me while I was eating supper and then he left. I want to talk with George about an idea that is growing in my mind. AWANEN!

Friday, August 15, 1986
My House, Gomez, Cabarroguis, Quirino

Letters from Sue T., Barb H., Nestor, Jerry J., Katie F., Tim C., Bill J. and Chris & Mary M.

₱202 – 52 = ₱150							
Cigarettes	4	Rides	4	Food	23	Postage	7
Marienda	5	Candy	5	Coke	4	TOTAL	₱52

We got up at 5:00 AM. George was bitten by something during the night and it looks pretty bad so I gave him some Caladryl Lotion for it and then he left. I cooked breakfast, ate, did dishes and got ready to go to Burgos. I left at 7:20 AM and went straight to Gundaway market, did my shopping and then went to the post office and got the above mail. I then returned to Burgos, climbed the mountain and got home at 11:55 AM. I drank coffee, ate kankanen and read my mail. Then I made guacamole and took it to Alfredo's. George wasn't there, he took bananas to town to sell for somebody. I stayed at Alfredo's until 3:30 PM and then went and fetched water, bathed and started cooking supper. There's another typhoon on it's way so it rained off and on all day today. Now it's only 5:10 PM and I'm still cooking supper. I hope George comes early tonight. It amazes me how good of friends we really are. AWANEN!

Saturday, August 16, 1986
My House, Gomez, Cabarroguis, Quirino

Finish letter to Chris & Mary M. Write letters to Ronald, Dad, Tim C. and Jerry J.

₱150 – 10 = ₱140							
Cigarettes	1	Charcoal	9			TOTAL	₱10

We got up at 5:15 AM and George left. I cooked breakfast, ate, did dishes and got ready for the day. I went to Alfredo's for a while to talk. It rained off and on again all day today. I returned home and finished the letter to Chris and Mary and then did a postcard to Ronald about why I'm not there for his birthday and then I had lunch of coffee only. Alfredo came, I removed the old *utong* beans and he put the runo around the Tobias beans. We also weeded the garden. Then I went to Anaceta's to buy charcoal, talked with him for a while, returned home and wrote the letter to Tim C. Alfredo came again to talk and help cut up things for supper. I started the charcoal and Alfredo left. I put on the rice to cook and then bathed while it was cooking. I ate supper, did dishes and now it's 6:46 PM and I'm waiting for George, of course. Last night he came at about 7:00 PM because I went and got him. I'll see what time he comes tonight, soon I hope. I'll study Ilokano while waiting for him. AWANEN!

Sunday, August 17, 1986
My House, Gomez, Cabarroguis, Quirino

Letters to Sue T., Chad D. and Dave & Vicki M.

We got up at 5:15 AM and George left. I cooked breakfast, ate, did dishes and got ready for the day. Then I went to Alfredo's a while to talk. He left for their vegetable farm so I returned home and wrote letters to Chad D. and Sue T. I told Sue that I'll try to come visit her on October 11th, at our 50% mark. I drank coffee for lunch. It rained off and on again all day today so I didn't do any laundry. In the afternoon I packed plastic seedling bags for a while and then I went and got George and we ended up planting another 132 Golden Shower seeds. Now we have 1,374 bags with seeds planted in them in the nursery. We finished at 4:20 PM and then I went and fetched water, bathed and started cooking supper. Alfredo came and we talked about me possibly buying a water buffalo. Why am I thinking of such foolishness, I don't know! Am I thinking of it as an investment, a return here someday, who really knows? Does God even know the answer to this one? One day I'm lonely and want to go home and the next day I'm talking about buying a nuang! Now it's 7:45 PM and I'm waiting for George. I guess I'll start a letter to Dave and Vicki M. I have a feeling George will be late tonight, although I don't know why. AWANEN!

Monday, August 18, 1986
My House, Gomez, Cabarroguis, Quirino

Letter to Fred & Cynthia B.

We got up at 5:15 AM and George left. The sky was actually clear, so after cooking, eating breakfast and doing dishes I got ready for the day and went to Alfredo's to talk for a while. I returned home at 8:00 AM and did laundry – lots of it! It took until nearly 11:00 AM to do it all. Then I relaxed for a while and at 12:00 N I went to ask George to come here for a while. He did and confirmed that my biggest papaya tree is a female. After that it rained for a little bit so I quickly removed the clothes from the clothesline and got them indoors. I drank a cup of coffee for lunch and finished the letter to Dave and Vicky that I started yesterday. Oh, I also weeded the southeast garden today. By the time I finished the letter it was 4:00 PM so I fetched water, bathed and started cooking supper. I finished eating, did dishes and now I'm writing a letter to Fred and Cynthia. It's 6:40 PM and I'm waiting for George. He's come before 7:00 PM the last two nights so he probably won't come until 8:00 PM tonight, we'll see what happens. AWANEN!

Tuesday, August 19, 1986
My House, Gomez, Cabarroguis, Quirino

Letter to JB & Katie F.

₱140 + 200 – 0 = ₱340

We got up at 5:15 AM and George left. I cooked breakfast, ate, washed dishes and got ready for the day and about then my stomach was suddenly very sore. I went to Alfredo's to talk for a little while and then returned home and lay down until 10:30 AM. Then I got up again and didn't feel quite as bad so I started making the second flat of trees in the nursery. I ran out of bamboo so I stopped and wrote the letter to JB and Katie and drank coffee for lunch. At 2:30 PM I went and got George and we got another piece of bamboo and finished putting together the second flat for the tree nursery. He then went home and Alfredo and his wife came to try to talk me into buying Boys dog for ₱200! I don't really need or want a dog so I told him money was short, but then he tried to borrow the money so he could buy it! I put the nix on that pretty fast and then at about 3:40 PM he left. I fetched water, bathed, cooked supper, ate and did dishes and now it's 6:40 PM and I'm waiting for George. He will probably be late tonight. He came at about 7:40 PM last night. I'll work on finishing the letter to JB and Katie, or at least work on it, until George comes. AWANEN!

Wednesday, August 20, 1986
My House, Gomez, Cabarroguis, Quirino

₱340 – 153 = ₱187							
Food	33	Rides	11	Rice	55	Contribution	30
Cigarettes	4	Postage	7	Coke	6	Candy	3
Household	4					TOTAL	₱153

We got up at 5:15 AM and George left, he came before 7:00 PM again last night. I cooked breakfast, ate, did the dishes and got ready for the day. I left for Burgos at 7:00 AM and I caught up with George on the high road. He was going to Burgos to sell bananas. I went to the post office and had no mail. I went to market and bought the above and then I continued on to the office in Diffun. The District Forester wasn't there but we had our monthly meeting without him so it was short and sweet. After the meeting finished we went to lunch and after that we returned to the office. At 1:00 PM I headed home. I bought rice and lots of food today as I thought Rody was coming to do some surveys but he's not. George carried my stuff up the mountain in the water buffalo cart and when Francisco Espinosa saw that he gave me some grief about why I wasn't carrying my own rice, so fuck him, I carried my own rice the rest of the way, despite having an empty nuang cart that could have carried it for me. I got home at 4:00 PM, fetched water, cooked supper and did dishes. Now it's 6:43 PM and I'm waiting for George. I think he'll be late tonight as they got home late. AWANEN!

Thursday, August 21, 1986
My House, Gomez, Cabarroguis, Quirino

Letter to Barb W.

We got up at 5:15 AM and George left. He came at 7:30 PM last night. I cooked breakfast, ate, did dishes and got ready for the day and then I went to Alfredo's for a minute but nobody was home so I returned home and put a wire around my cracked charcoal cook stove and cleaned up the grass in the north yard. By then it was lunchtime so I wrote the above letter and drank coffee. In the afternoon I cleaned grass in the south yard and swept the lawn then doctored my foot – I now have four infections on my right foot, what the hell is going on anyway? George hauled a cant for Lito today and they decided to take it all the way to Burgos. They left at 4:00 PM and he told me they might not get home until 1:00 AM or so. So I'm reading a book tonight and maybe by and by I'll write another letter. Now it's 6:30 PM, I think I'll go buy some cigarettes. There was a little rain this afternoon, but not much, not even enough to wet the ground. AWANEN!

Friday, August 22, 1986
My House, Gomez, Cabarroguis, Quirino

Letters from Ardis B., San & Jack G., Brett B., D. Wilder, Chad D. Package from Peace Corps Medical Office, ICE catalog.

Letter I mailed to George in Manila arrived.

Postcards to Chad D., Chris & Mary M.

₱187 – 75 = ₱112							
Medicine	5	Rides	5	Coke	9	Cigarettes	5
Food	6	Cooking Oil	27	Soap	10	Kerosene	7
Ice Cream	1					TOTAL	₱75

We got up at 4:40 AM and George left. He actually arrived at about 9:30 or 10:00 PM last night so I was surprised that we woke up a little early. I cooked breakfast, ate, did the dishes and then got ready for the day. I left for Burgos via the high road and got there even before 8:00 AM. I continued on to Gundaway and got there just a bit after 8:00 AM. I went to market and got the above and then went to the post office and got the above letters. I waited there for an extra hour for the Friday mail truck, which didn't come, and then I returned home before 12:00 N. I didn't do much in the afternoon; my right foot is swollen and sore. I went to Alfredo's and had a nice talk with George about chickens. Now it's 7:01 PM and George went to Calaocan to attend a wedding so he won't be coming tonight. I guess I'll read, maybe write a letter and maybe study. There was no rain again today. AWANEN!

Saturday, August 23, 1986
My House, Gomez, Cabarroguis, Quirino

Letter to Dave G.

I got up at 5:10 AM with no George. I cooked breakfast, ate, did the dishes and got ready for the day. George came for a few minutes this morning and looked at tree seedlings and then he left. He said they had arrived home from Calaocan at about 3:00 AM. I did laundry from 7:30 to 8:30 AM and darn little else today. I read more of the *"Hunt for Red October"* book and at noon I stopped reading and drank coffee while writing the letter to Dave G. In that letter I reflected upon the last year. I left Fairbanks a year ago today! Gosh it has been a long – but short time! In the afternoon I watered all the nursery seedlings – it was 92°F today and the hot wind blew again. In the late afternoon it clouded up and thundered for a while and then it ended up raining about 10 or 20 drops. It's the 5th day without rain now. I fetched water, cooked supper, ate, washed dishes and now it's 6:31 PM and I'm waiting for George. I sure hope he is early tonight – I haven't studied anything at all for the past two nights and need to do so. AWANEN!

Sunday, August 24, 1986
My House, Gomez, Cabarroguis, Quirino

Letters to Bill J. and John D.

We got up at 5:15 AM and George left. He came at about 7:00 PM last night. It was good to talk with him again. I cooked breakfast, ate, got ready for the day and then did dishes. I went to Alfredo's and talked until 8:30 AM and then returned home and filled some more plastic bags with soil. After a while George came and we filled another 116 plastic bags. Then it was lunchtime so George left. I drank coffee and wrote the above two letters then at 3:30 PM I went and helped Alfredo dig a post hole for a while. Then George and I came here and planted seeds in the 116 bags. We planted 19 Golden Shower, eight Narra, four Lanzones, 61 Gmelina, five Damortes, and 19 *Acacia auriculiformis*. After that it rained pretty hard for a little bit. I fetched water and bathed at 4:30 PM and started supper after that. Now it's 6:30 PM and I'm finished with supper and dishes and it's acting like it wants to rain again. I hope George comes before the rain does – if it comes at all. I'm already waiting for him so I guess I'll study for a while and read *Newsweek*. AWANEN!

Monday, August 25, 1986
My House, Gomez, Cabarroguis, Quirino

Letter to Mary H.

We got up at 5:20 AM and George left; he came at about 7:30 PM last night. I cooked breakfast, ate, washed the dishes and got ready for the day. Then I went to Alfredo's to talk for a while and then decided on the spur of the moment to follow George to the vegetable farm. I met him there and shortly after that we came home. I rode the water buffalo part way home, until I fell off and got two nice gashes in my forehead. After that I carried the vegetables and walked. We got home and I cleaned my wound and George put medicine on it for me. I drank coffee for lunch, wrote the above letter then laid down for an hour – my forehead hurts, but no big deal I guess. Then I went to Alfredo's and helped George and Alfredo work on the addition to their house that they are building. At 4:00 PM I returned home and fetched water, trimmed my beard, bathed and then started cooking supper. Just as supper was done Alfredo came here for just a little bit. His wife was cooking so I hope their supper is early and hope George comes early. Now it's 6:41 PM and I'm waiting for him. We had just a few drops of rain today. AWANEN!

[End of handwritten notebook #2 of 5]

Tuesday, August 26, 1986
Tuguegarao Airport, Cagayan

Letters from Ardis B., Chad D., Dad. Package from Chris & Mary M. (photos).

₱112 + 300 – 192 = ₱220							
Rides	96	Cigarettes	8	Toilet Paper	6	Candy	6
Beer	18	Marienda	6	Lunch	40	Postage	2
Misc.	10					TOTAL	₱192

We got up at 5:10 AM, I gave George my leftover food and he left. I cooked breakfast, ate, washed the dishes and got ready for the day. I went to Alfredo's to talk for a while and then returned home to pack. I finished packing, took my valuables to Alfredo's and left at about 8:00 AM. I stopped at Gundaway and got the above mail and then continued on to Santiago. I killed some time there, ate lunch, left my pack at Lina's Restaurant and headed to the bank. I happened to meet Nestor on the way to the bank at 1:00 PM so we went returned to Lina's Restaurant. We drank a couple of beers and then went to the bank and then to the Pantranco Bus Terminal. We left Santiago at about 3:40 PM. We had some minor bus problems, but arrived at Tuguegarao at about 7:00 PM. We ate supper at the Pantranco Bus Terminal and then we found a tricycle to the airport. The people there were really friendly and let us sleep at the airport. They even gave us cots to sleep on, so we went to sleep at around 7:30 PM. It's good to see Nestor again. AWANEN!

Wednesday, August 27, 1986
Brett's House, Ivana, Batanes

₱220 + 1,300 – 1,260 = ₱260							
Airplane	1,255	Vegetables	3	Cigarettes	2	TOTAL	₱1260.

We got up at 5:10 AM at the airport and went to a canteen, ate breakfast and then returned to the airport. We brushed our teeth changed our shirts and waited for the airplane. The plane left shortly after 8:00 AM and we arrived at Basco, Batanes at 9:15 AM or so. Brett met us at the airport, we went to a bunch of places and met people and talked with them and finally at 1:00 PM or so we got a jeepney. We went to Uyugan, where Brent gave a softball clinic, and we ended up drinking a bunch and eating supper there. Then we returned to Brett's house and he passed out on the grass in his backyard practically immediately. Now it's 9:10 PM, we're tired, burned out, frustrated with all the questions and silly comments from people and I'm ready to go to sleep beside Nestor. The school principal made the decision for us that we'll go somewhere tomorrow. There were strong winds today and also some good heavy rains. Is a typhoon coming? AWANEN!

Thursday, August 28, 1986 – My 39th Birthday
Brett's House, Ivana, Batanes

[I'm 39 years old today.]

₱260 – 51 = ₱209							
Rides	36	Bread	9	Cigarettes	6	TOTAL	₱51

Nestor and I got up at 5:15 AM and searched for a bathing place, found it, and were able to bathe. By and by Brett got up and after a while we ate breakfast. Then we took a beach stroll until 11:00 or 11:30 AM and found a bunch of seashells and other neat things. Then we returned to Brett's house and his roommate came along with some good size fish for lunch. Brett cooked that along with *parya* and eggs and we had a nice lunch. Then we had a plan from yesterday to go to Itbud with the teachers again, so we did that. I thought the plan was for a picnic, but they had a meeting so we strolled to the old abandoned LORAN Station and then we returned to the teacher's meeting place and had to get half drunk again. We finally got home just before 6:30 PM and then I felt really bad – a headache, stomachache and chills – so I slept until supper was ready. Now it's 9:27 PM and I'm feeling a bit better, but still not great. [I can't remember if I even told anybody that it was my birthday, my journal does not say anything about it at all, it's possible that I did not even remember that it was my special day.] AWANEN!

Friday, August 29, 1986
Brett's House, Ivana, Batanes

₱209 + 100 – 64 = ₱245							
Rides	42	Coffee	18	Cigarettes	4	TOTAL	₱64

Nestor and I slept late and got up at 5:45 AM or so. We bathed and then headed for Basco to eat breakfast. After breakfast we went to the BFD [Bureau of Forest Development] office and waited there until the rain stopped and then we ate marienda and walked up the mountain to a radar station where we could see both sides of the island from. It was pretty cool despite the fact that it rained on us off and on. At a break in the clouds we went down the mountain and got back to Basco and ate lunch there. We bought food for the next couple of meals and we caught the jeepney back to Brett's house. By the time we got home I was really feeling really bad again, with a sore throat, headache, stomachache and aching joints – it feels like good old American flu. We ate supper at about 5:00 PM and then relaxed a bit. Then we went down the road a little ways and ate supper again at a neighbor's house. Then we played cards – Fish and Crazy Eights – and at 9:00 PM we returned home. Now it's 9:17 PM and there is only ten more minutes of electricity so I'm going to lay down pretty quickly. AWANEN!

Saturday, August 30, 1986
Brett's House, Ivana, Batanes

₱245 – 25 = ₱220							
Food	20	Cigarettes	5			TOTAL	₱25

Nestor and I got up really late – at 6:45 AM. A typhoon came and it is continuing today. My sore throat and general malaise is also continuing so we spent lots of time today doing nothing, but I guess that's good. It was a good day to try and recover from whatever is wrong with me. Everybody is feeling rather poorly today – Nestor, Brett and also his roommate, was it something we ate? Brett has been a really good host while we've been here, we haven't really had to lift a finger to help him prepare meals or anything. I feel like he's been pretty patient with us. Tonight is the fourth night here. I hope to hell the weather gets at least marginally better tomorrow so we can at least take another stroll on the beach. AWANEN!

Sunday, August 31, 1986
Brett's House, Ivana, Batanes

₱220 – 115 = ₱105							
Garlic	60	Cigarettes	8	Coke	20	Bread	8
Rice	19					TOTAL	₱115

We got up late again – at 6:45 AM. The reason we slept so late is because the typhoon is continuing unabated. Brett went to church and when he returned we ate breakfast and then we talked and killed time until it was lunchtime. We were hoping the typhoon would stop today, but no such luck. In the afternoon Brett and I taught Nestor how to play cribbage and he won several games. We had a late marienda and then after a while we ate supper. After supper we filled out immigration forms. [I don't remember why that was necessary – maybe a necessity for the airport?] After that we went and searched for and found ₱60 worth of garlic [this area was famous for exceptionally large and delicious garlic], returned to Brett's house and cleaned it up a bit. Now it's only 9:00 PM and they have already turned the electricity off on us, so I guess it's time to end. [In this area they turned the generators which made electricity off at night.] AWANEN!

Monday, September 1, 1986
The Monsignor's House, Basco, Batanes

₱105 + 100 – 158 = ₱47							
Rides	20	Beef	35	Food	36	Cigarettes	10
Marienda	42	Coffee	15			TOTAL	₱158

We got up at 5:45 AM and got ready to leave Ivana to catch the plane. We got to Basco at about 7:30 AM, and at 8:00 AM they already told us the flight was cancelled because of the weather. We got our tickets changed to Wednesday and went to the canteen to eat breakfast. Then we bought some food, ate marienda and killed time at the canteen until lunchtime. Then we went to the Monsignor's birthday lunch party and saw a movie – *"King Solomon's Mines"* – and then we went to the jeepney place for a while and waited. A drunk ended up punching me because I didn't know the name of the governor of some other province (see page 42). After that the jeepney didn't come, so now it's 8:00 PM and we are at the Monsignor's house, where we'll spend the night. The typhoon is signal 3 today so the wind is REALLY blowing. We finished the immigration forms just now so we're going to sleep. AWANEN!

Tuesday, September 2, 1986
Brett's House, Ivana, Batanes

₱47 + 180 – 57 = ₱170							
Rides	21	Cigarettes	10	Marienda	26	TOTAL	₱57

Nestor and I got up at 5:40 AM at the Monsignor's house and then after a while we left and ate breakfast at the canteen. We killed some time there and then at about 9:30 or 10:00 AM we got a jeepney back to Ivana. Brett made lunch for us again, we drank some coconut milk and ate some coconut meat and then at about 1:00 PM Nestor and I took a stroll up the same beach we strolled on the other day. We returned to Brett's house at 3:00 PM or so and after a while we ate and drank some more coconut meat and milk. We played some "Lucky 9", some solitaire and killed time and now it's 7:50 PM. Darn, I'm really getting burned out on Batanes, I really hope our plane gets in and out of here tomorrow. [Tonight was the closest I ever came to having sex with Nestor. I was sleeping and he woke me up and told me that he couldn't sleep, did I have any ideas how to get to sleep? I suggested that he jack-off, telling him that he would surely be able to sleep after that. He said that he couldn't because he had no jack-off rag, so I told him to cum in his underwear. He woke me up again a little while later and told me that he had an idea for a rag "your hand, Daniel", but he quickly added that he was only joking. I am sure that I could have had some kind of sex with him at that point, but by that time in our relationship I guess that I had too much respect for him, because I refused and went back to sleep. He did not wake me up again and we did not talk about it on the following day, so I don't know what he did.] AWANEN!

Wednesday, September 3, 1986
My House, Gomez, Cabarroguis, Quirino

Finally back home!

₱170 + 100 – 190 = ₱80							
Rides	29	Cigarettes	10	Breakfast	30	Marienda	5
Food	63	Candy	14	Presents	39	TOTAL	₱190

We got up at 5:30 AM and got ready to go to Basco again. We ate breakfast and went to Basco. We drank coffee at the canteen and then at 8:00 AM we went to the airport. There was a plane today so we said our goodbyes and at 9:40 AM the plane left. We arrived it Tuguegarao at 10:40 AM or so, ate lunch went to the Pantranco Bus Terminal and got on a bus for Santiago. We arrived in Santiago at about 2:45 PM or so and Nestor and I'm hurried through marketing, drank a quick Halo-Halo together and then we both went our separate ways to get our jeepneys. My jeepney didn't leave Santiago until 4:47 PM and I didn't arrive at Burgos until 6:00 PM. When I got about to Rufo's house it was already dark and I had to use my little flashlight the rest of the way home. I arrived at about 6:40 PM or so and hollered for George. Immediately he and Alfredo came and then George fetched me some water to drink. I told stories for a while, Alfredo left, I unpacked for George and gave him his remembrances and we slept. It's certainly good to be home, for sure. I'm happy go strolling and also happy to return home. I must say that it was one heck of a vacation for Nestor and I. AWANEN!

Thursday, September 4, 1986
My House, Gomez, Cabarroguis, Quirino

Letter to Nestor.

We got up at 5:00 AM and George left. I cooked breakfast, ate, did dishes and got ready for the day. Then I went to Alfredo's to talk for a while and then I returned home and did laundry until 10:30 AM. After that Alfredo came here for a while and he left about 11:00 AM. George had returned from the vegetable farm by then so I went to see the water buffalo cart of corn that he harvested – lots of corn! We talked for a while and then I returned home and wrote the above letter to Nestor. I went to Alfredo's again and watched George repair the water buffalo harness [baticola] and then George came here for a while. I asked him some questions about happenings while I was gone and after a while he returned to their vegetable farm for another load of corn. I harvested three squash and cleaned up the garden a bit. I swept the south lawn area, then fetched water and then I looked at the tree nursery, bathed and started cooking supper. Alfredo give me a big chunk of *tabungaw* so I had it for supper. I ate, washed dishes, went to the canteen for cigarettes and stopped at Alfredo's momentarily, they were eating so I left. Now it's 6:45 PM and I'm waiting for George. I hope he comes soon – oh, he's here now. In the letter to Nestor I told him that I'll meet him early on October 10th at Lina's Restaurant. AWANEN!

Friday, September 5, 1986
My House, Gomez, Cabarroguis, Quirino

Letters from Brooke F., Jim & Roselynn S., San & Jack G. Postcards from Ardis B., Tony S. and Mark W.

₱80 + 300 – 95 = ₱285							
Food	71	Rides	2	Coke	9	Candy	2
Envelopes	3	Cigarettes	4	Marienda	4	TOTAL	₱95

George got up and left at 4:15 AM to pasture his water buffalo so he could haul a cant today. I got up at 5:15 AM, cooked breakfast, ate, did the dishes and got ready to leave for Burgos. From there I continued on to Gundaway, did my shopping and then went to the post office and got one and a half weeks worth of mail, as shown above. I returned home and got here at about 11:30 AM. I read mail until about 2:00 PM and then I rested a while. At 3:00 PM I went to Alfredo's to talk for a while. George returned at about 3:30 PM – his cant is 66 board feet. At 4:15 PM I returned home, bathed, fetched water and cooked supper. George went to Burgos with his cant and says he won't return tonight, but will sleep there. Now it's 6:10 PM so I think I'll go and see if Bubot wants to sleep here tonight, it's raining, but not too hard so maybe he'll want to come. Bubot didn't want to come. AWANEN!

Saturday, September 6, 1986
My House, Gomez, Cabarroguis, Quirino

Letters to Brett B., Jim & Roselynn S., Chris & Mary M. and Ardis B.

I got up at 5:15 AM with no companion, cooked breakfast, ate, did the dishes and got ready for the day. I went to George's – he got home about 6:00 AM. He came to the house for a while to talk about last night and then he returned home to sleep. It rained off and on all day today so I got on a letter writing spree. First I wrote to Ardis, then Chris and Mary, and then Roselynn. After that I worked in the garden for a while, until the rain forced me to stop. Then it was 12:30 PM so I napped until 2:00 PM. I woke up and after a bit Junior, George and Juanito Sebastian stopped by on their way to Burgos. George told me he and Junior are going to somebody's house that died to play games and therefore he won't be coming tonight either – two nights in a row of no George – bummer! At 3:15 PM I went to Alfredo's to talk for a while. I returned home at 4:15 PM, fetched water, bathed and went to Bubot's to ask him to come to sleep tonight. He can't come because his folks are in Burgos for the wake too, so he has to guard the house. I cooked supper, ate, did dishes and went to Alfredo's again for a while and now it's 6:50 PM. Maybe I'll write another letter or something. AWANEN!

Sunday, September 7, 1986
My House, Gomez, Cabarroguis, Quirino

Letters to Tony S. and Brooke F. Postcard to Dad.

I got up at 5:15 AM with no companion again. I cooked breakfast, ate, did dishes and got ready for the day. I went to Alfredo's to talk for a while and then returned home and did laundry; there was only a little bit today seeing as I did it on Thursday. After that I polished the floor of the house and also the porch, the table, the benches and everything. George got home from the wake at 10:30 AM so I went there to talk with him for a little while, but he was tired and didn't want to talk so I talked with Alfredo until lunchtime and then returned home. I wrote the letter to Brooke and then to Tony and then the postcard to Dad. Then I started entering the sunrise and sunset program into my HP-41 again, for some reason it suffered a memory lost error. I worked on that until 4:00 PM and then fetched water, trimmed my beard and bathed. Then I started supper and George came for a few minutes. I redug the *utong* patch yesterday and the pigs have already dug it all up so I'm scared to replant. I showed George and then he left. I cooked, ate supper, did dishes and now it's getting darker. It gets dark earlier these days. Now it's 6:35 PM and I'm waiting for George, he says he'll be coming early tonight, I hope so. AWANEN!

Monday, September 8, 1986
My House, Gomez, Cabarroguis, Quirino

Postcard to Chad D.

We got up at 5:10 AM and George left. I went to his house at 7:00 PM last night and helped them remove corn from the ears until 8:30 PM and then George and I came here. [After the corn harvest it is necessary to shell it and then take just the corn, without the ears to sell it.] I cooked breakfast, ate, did the dishes and got ready for the day and at 7:10 AM I was ready to go with George to the vegetable farm and help harvest corn. We harvested a lot, removed the skins [husks] from about half of it and then we returned to their house at about 11:15 AM. I stayed there and talked for a while until about noon and then I returned home and finished entering the sunrise and sunset program in the HP-41. I wrote the postcard to Chad and took a half-hour nap and then I got up and dug up some dirt in the southeast garden area, attempting some small scale contour farming there to avoid soil loss. I'm not yet sure what I'll plant there, probably beans. I worked on that until about 4:10 PM and then I fetched water, bathed and started cooking supper. Is that really all I did today? It was hot and hard work harvesting corn but I enjoy helping George. Now it's 6:30 PM, I'm done with supper, dishes are washed and after a while I'll go to Alfredo's house and help them *agpusi* [shell corn] again. Until then I'll study Ilokano. I guess I have no more to say today. AWANEN!

Tuesday, September 9, 1986
My House, Gomez, Cabarroguis, Quirino

Letters to San & Jack G. and Tom & Barb H.

We got up at 5:20 AM and George left. I helped shell corn last night until 8:45 PM and then we came here and quickly slept. I cooked breakfast, ate, washed the dishes and got ready for the day. Then I went to Alfredo's house and helped shell corn. When we finished that, at about 8:30 AM, we went to the vegetable farm and I helped harvest more corn. I helped with that until we quit and then we returned home shortly after 11:00 AM. Then I hung out at Alfredo's talking until 11:30 AM or so and came home. I don't really know if George likes me to help with the harvest or not, he doesn't say. Anyway, I wrote the above letter to San and Jack and then rested for a half hour or so. I got up and looked at the two books that Ardis sent me on village development and then I fetched water, looked at the tree nursery and garden, bathed and started cooking supper. Now it's 6:20 PM and I'm done eating, dishes are done and I'm already waiting for George. It will be another hour before I can holler for him. They said there will be no corn shelling tonight, I'll believe it when I see it. I guess if they do shell corn then I'll go and help for a while and see what happens. Maybe I'll write another letter. AWANEN!

Wednesday, September 10, 1986
My House, Gomez, Cabarroguis, Quirino

Letter to Bob S.

We got up at 5:10 AM and George left. I went and got him at 7:15 PM last night. I cooked breakfast, ate, did dishes and got ready for the day. Then I went to

Alfredo's and helped them shell the corn from yesterday afternoon's harvest. Then we put it in the sun to dry further. At that point George returned with this morning's load of corn. I talked with him for a while and then I returned home at about 11:00 AM and wrote the above letter. By the time I finished that it was 1:30 PM or so and after killing time for a while I returned to Alfredo's at about 2:15 PM to help shell this morning's load of corn. I returned home at 3:30 PM and started rereading the *"Survival Kit for Overseas Living"* book. I stopped at 4:10 PM, fetched water, bathed and started cooking supper. Then I continued reading long enough to discover that I'm in the second stage of culture shock. Then Lito brought a friend by with a badly cut finger. I doctored that and bandaged it up and they left. Then I ate and did dishes and now it's 6:40 PM. After a while I'll go to Alfredo's house to help shell corn again. It seems like it might rain. AWANEN!

Thursday, September 11, 1986
My House, Gomez, Cabarroguis, Quirino

Letters to ICE (request pamphlets) and Ronald. Postcard to Mark W.

We got up at 5:00 AM and George left. I went and helped them shell corn again last night and we came here at 8:45 PM and slept immediately. I cooked breakfast, ate, washed the dishes and got ready for the day. Then I went to Alfredo's to talk for a while and then returned home and watered the seedlings. Then I cleaned some grass from around the tree nursery. After that I worked on a letter to ICE and then went to Alfredo's and asked George to come for a while, which he did. He left after I showed him the garden and the nursery and then I did the postcard to Mark W. After that I rested for just a few moments and then went to Alfredo's again; oh, I swept the south yard first. I helped them shell corn again until 4:15 PM then returned home, fetched water, bathed and started cooking supper. Lito stopped by for a few minutes to use my calculator and then I finished cooking supper, ate, washed the dishes and now it's only 6:20 PM. I hope George comes early tonight. As there's no corn shelling tonight, it's possible. I'll have to wait and see what happens. Maybe I'll write another letter while waiting for him. AWANEN!

Friday, September 12, 1986
My House, Gomez, Cabarroguis, Quirino

Letter from Katie F.

₱285 + 1100 – 314 = ₱71							
Food	64	Coffee	93	Lunch	26	Candy	17
Kerosene	8	Marienda	24	Toilet Paper	12	Batteries	13
Rides	15	Household	10	Cigarettes	5	Haircut	5
Coke	6	Ice Cream	16			TOTAL	₱314

We got up at 5:00 AM and George left. I went to their house last night at 7:15 PM and we shelled a load of corn. We came here at about 8:45 PM and slept immediately again. I cooked breakfast, ate, did dishes and got ready for the day. Alfredo, his wife, Alfie and I went to Burgos. From there I continued on to Gundaway and the post office and then on to Santiago. I shopped for the above and then searched for another PCV at The Magnolia Restaurant and at the 456 Restaurant there was nobody whom I could find – I wanted to talk with another American for a while. Then I ate lunch at the 456 Restaurant and after that I got a haircut and headed home. I arrived at Burgos at about 2:30 PM and walked to the fishpond, where Alfredo's family was waiting for me. I put my pack on their cart and then after a while we headed up the mountain. I didn't wait at every rest stop, so I arrived home at about 3:50 PM, fetched water, bathed and then went to their house and talked with George until the family arrived at 4:30 PM. I brought my stuff home, cooked supper, ate and washed dishes. Lito stopped by to use the calculator again and now it's 6:35 PM. In a while I'll go to George's, there is corn to shell tonight. AWANEN!

Saturday, September 13, 1986
My House, Gomez, Cabarroguis, Quirino

Letter to John D.

We got up at 5:30 AM and George left. We got up late because I went and helped them shell corn last night and we didn't finish and come here until 9:40 PM and we probably didn't sleep until 10:00 PM or so. I cooked breakfast, ate, washed the dishes and got ready for the day and then I went and talked with Alfredo for a while. Then I went off in search of charcoal. I found only half a sack of charcoal, bought it and returned home at 9:00 AM. Then I slept until 11:00 AM, got up, drank some coffee and then wrote the above letter. Then I just killed time for a while and finally at about 2:00 PM I went to Alfredo's to talk with George for a while before he went out on the afternoon corn run. George left and I stayed there and helped shell corn until 4:00 PM and then I returned home, fetched water, bathed and started cooking supper. Alfredo's wife gave me some ground corn to try; it's pretty tasty. I cooked half rice and half ground corn and then I cooked the rest of my supper, ate did dishes and now it's 6:45 PM. We're supposed to shell corn again tonight so I'll return to Alfredo's when I see them starting to work. In the meantime maybe I'll start a letter to JB and Katie or else somebody else. AWANEN!

Sunday, September 14, 1986
My House, Gomez, Cabarroguis, Quirino

Letter to JB & Katie F.

We got up at 5:30 AM and George left. I went to help them with shell corn last night until nearly 10:00 PM and then George and I came here and slept immediately.

This morning I cooked breakfast, ate, did dishes and got ready for the day. Then I went to Alfredo's and helped shell corn again until 8:00 AM. After that I returned home and did laundry. That took me until 9:00 AM and then I worked on the above letter to JB and Katie until 11:00 AM and then I took a nap until 12:30 or 1:00 PM. I got up, drank some coffee and then at about 2:00 PM I went to Alfredo's house again for a while. We had just settled back and relaxed when the rain threatened, so we had to collect all of the corn that was drying in the sun and then we started shelling rejects. George went to the vegetable farm again and Alfredo and I continued to shell corn until 4:15 PM, when I returned home, fetched water, bathed and started cooking supper. I ate, did dishes and returned to Alfredo's and then I returned home again. Now it's 6:35 PM and after a while I'll return to help them shell corn yet again. Now we're doing rejects and there isn't too much left to do, so hopefully we'll finish up by 8:30 or 9:00 PM and be able to come here relatively early tonight. AWANEN!

Monday, September 15, 1986
My House, Gomez, Cabarroguis, Quirino

Letter to Dave M., birthday postcard to Jim W. (my brother).

We got up at 5:30 AM and George left. I went and helped with the corn shelling last night until 8:30 PM and then George and I came here and slept practically immediately. This morning I cooked breakfast, ate, did dishes and got ready for the day and then I went to Alfredo's to talk with him for a while. He also went to the farm to help carry corn so I returned home and napped from about 8:00 until 9:30 AM. I don't know how George keeps doing this day after day after day. He acts very tired. When I got up at 9:30 AM I did the postcard to brother Jim. I wonder if he even thought of me on my birthday? Then it was lunchtime. I ate leftover rice and drank coffee and after that I wrote the letter to Dave M. and asked him for another music tape. Then it was 1:00 PM and I went back to George's and watched them play marbles until 2:00 PM or so. We emptied the two carts of corn and George went to the vegetable farm again. Alfredo and I shelled corn until I left at 4:15 PM. I fetched water, bathed, cooked supper, ate, did dishes and now it's 6:45 PM. In another half hour or 45 minutes I'll go and help shell corn again. I can only hope we'll stop by 8:30 PM or so tonight. I have had no new Ilokano words in a week now. AWANEN!

Tuesday, September 16, 1986
My House, Gomez, Cabarroguis, Quirino

Letters from Dad & Ardis B. The PC Nurse stayed here tonight.

₱71 + 200 – 28 = ₱243							
Marienda	7	Cigarettes	5	Rides	5	Food	11
						TOTAL	₱28

We got up at 5:30 AM and George left. I went and helped them shell corn until 9:40 PM last night and then George and I came here and we slept immediately. This morning I cooked breakfast, ate, did the dishes and got ready for the day and then I went to Alfredo's for a bit. Then I headed down the mountain and went to Diffun to meet the Peace Corps nurse and her driver. I got to Diffun at about 9:00 AM and they arrived there at about 9:30 AM. We talked with Francisco for a short while and then we went to market and after that we drove to Burgos. We left their truck at Fred Dacanay's house and walked up the mountain. We arrived at my house at about 11:00 AM or so and I cooked lunch, we ate, washed dishes and then I went to Alfredo's to talk with George for a short time and then returned home. In the afternoon we didn't do much. I showed the nurse and her driver the local water source and the two of them immediately stopped drinking the water! I bathed and she cooked supper. I washed the dishes and then Amor came for a short time. Then I went to Alfredo's to talk for a while and now it's 7:40 PM and I'm about ready to sleep. AWANEN!

Wednesday, September 17, 1986
My House, Gomez, Cabarroguis, Quirino

Letter to Dad. The PC Nurse left.

We got up at 5:20 AM and I cooked breakfast for us. We ate, I washed the dishes and then at about 7:00 AM they left (the nurse and her driver). I went to Alfredo's at 7:30 AM and helped shell corn until George arrived at 11:00 AM and then George came here for a few minutes and when he returned home I drank coffee and wrote the above letter to Dad. From 12:40 until 1:00 PM I slept. As soon as I woke up, I returned to Alfredo's and helped to shell corn again until 4:40 PM. I spent lots of hours today shelling corn. I returned home, fetched water quickly, bathed quickly and then cooked supper of *utong* beans and *parya.* I ate and did dishes in the near darkness and went to the canteen and bought cigarettes. I returned home at 6:30 PM and George came just a bit after that, as we finished shelling all of the corn this afternoon. Ah, what a day! I feel good in my mind because of all the help I gave Alfredo and George this week. AWANEN!

Thursday, September 18, 1986
My House, Gomez, Cabarroguis, Quirino

We got up at 5:30 AM and George left. I cooked breakfast, ate, did dishes and got ready for the day. At 7:15 AM I went to George's vegetable farm and helped harvest corn. Alfredo went too and by 10:00 AM we had filled two carts with corn – we worked pretty fast I'd say; I don't know if George would agree, but it seemed so to me. We got back to George's house at 11:00 AM exactly and I drank a cup of their water and came home. I drank a cup of coffee and tried to figure out who to write to, but I couldn't pick a specific person so I didn't write to anybody. I took a half hour siesta and at 1:30 PM I returned to George's and we shelled the two carts of corn and finished at 4:10 PM. It seemed like that went pretty fast. Then I returned home, fetched water, bathed, cooked supper, ate and did dishes. I went to the canteen for a minute to get cigarettes and then to George's house to talk for another few minutes. They hadn't eaten their supper yet. Now it's 6:32 PM, I hope they eat soon and that George comes relatively early again tonight. I'll holler at 7:15 PM if he isn't here by then, but I think he'll be here before that tonight, I hope. AWANEN!

Friday, September 19, 1986
My House, Gomez, Cabarroguis, Quirino

Letter from Dave G., package from Chad D., postcard from San & Jack G., a *Reader's Digest* and quarterly report form from Peace Corps.

₱243 – 143 = ₱100							
Rides	4	Coke	6	Cigarettes	5	Cooking Oil	28
Soap	10	Envelopes	5	Food	55	Kerosene	8
Ice Cream	3	Coffee	19			TOTAL	₱143

We got up at 5:15 AM and George left. He came before 7:00 PM again last night. I cooked breakfast, ate, did dishes and got ready for the day and then I went to Alfredo's and helped put corn in the sun to dry. Then at 7:30 AM I headed down the mountain for Burgos. I went to Gundaway – the post office and market, did my shopping and then returned home, arriving here at 11:30 AM. I read mail and then at 1:00 PM I went to George's to ask him to help me water the tree seedlings. He said *"madam dama"* [by and by] so I came home and pulled weeds in the south lawn until 3:00 PM and then went to George's to help take in the dry corn. Then George and I came here to water the seedlings. He left immediately upon finishing and I fetched water, bathed and cooked supper. I ate and did dishes and then I went and helped shell corn until they ate supper at 7:00 PM. Now it's 7:10 PM and in a little while I'll go back to help shell corn more – IF they shell more corn tonight, we'll see what happens I guess. AWANEN!

Saturday, September 20, 1986
My House, Gomez, Cabarroguis, Quirino

I woke up at 5:40 AM and George had already left without me even hearing him leave. I went to their house last night and helped shell corn until 9:00 PM and then we came here and slept immediately. I cooked breakfast, ate, did dishes and got ready for the day and then at 7:30 AM I went to Alfredo's house and helped shell corn until 1:00 PM. George returned from harvesting bananas at about 11:00 AM and then he helped shell corn too. I returned home and ate my leftover rice and drank coffee for lunch while reading my *Reader's Digest.* Then at about 1:30 PM I returned to Alfredo's and helped shell corn some more until 3:00 PM or so, when we finished with all the current rejects. [Rejects, in this case, refers to misshapen ears of corn, ears that are not perfectly shaped and are therefore more difficult to shell.] Then I returned home and pulled weeds in the south lawn until 3:45 PM or so. Alfredo came and helped for a little while and then we both bathed at 4:20 PM or so. I fetched water and started cooking supper and Alfredo drank a cup of coffee. He left at about 5:00 PM and then I ate supper and did dishes. It's getting darker much earlier now and I have to do dishes by 6:00 PM or else it's too dark to see. I went to the canteen at 6:10 PM and then to George's. I returned home at 6:30 PM and George said he'll come soon. Now it's 6:37 PM and we'll see what happens. Tonight we start studying by listening to the Ilokano drama on the radio. AWANEN!

Sunday, September 21, 1986
My House, Gomez, Cabarroguis, Quirino

Letter to Chris & Mary M.

We got up at 5:20 AM and George left. He came a bit late last night, at about 7:00 PM. We listened to the Ilokano radio drama for study. I cooked breakfast, ate, did dishes, got ready for the day and then I went to Alfredo's and helped spread the shelled corn in the sun to dry. I returned home at 7:40 AM and did laundry until 8:30 AM and then I polished and waxed the floor, the table, the benches and even waxed the kitchen floor – for the first time. I finished at about 11:00 AM and then napped until noon. [When you read about waxing the floor you are surely picturing something very different than what I am talking about. The "tool" used for polishing and waxing floors, tables, benches and so on that I used is called a *lampaso*. It is the outer husk of a coconut (Google it and then look at the images) cut in half. To merely polish the floor you just put this under your foot and exert as much pressure on it as you can and push it back and forth across the floor, table or bench. To wax the floor, one rubs a candle on the polishing surface of the *lampaso* and then does the pushing of it back and forth across the floor. You would be surprised at how well it works.] I woke up when it started raining, grabbed the clothes off the line and then quickly went to Alfredo's to help get the corn in before it got wet, but he had already finished. I returned home and wrote the above letter. I asked for the status of my affairs [Chris was managing my financial and other affairs while I was gone] and I asked him to renew my *Alaska Magazine* subscription. Then I swept the yard, under the house and everywhere and after that I pulled weeds in the plastic bags of seedlings. Alfredo came and helped and then some ladies came by selling blankets. We went to Alfredo's because his wife would surely want some. I returned home at 4:00 PM, fetched water, bathed and started cooking supper. I washed the dishes and now it's 6:10 PM and raining pretty hard again. It'll probably be an hour before George comes. What will I do for an hour, I don't know, study and read maybe. AWANEN!

Monday, September 22, 1986
My House, Gomez, Cabarroguis, Quirino

₱100 + 100 – 80 = ₱120							
Rides	8	Cigarettes	5	Coke	3	Bread	2
Rice	58	Misc.	4			TOTAL	₱80

We got up at 5:30 AM and George left. He didn't come last night until about 7:45 PM because they had visitors. I cooked breakfast, ate, did dishes, got ready for the day and went to Alfredo's to talk for a while. Alfredo and George went to their vegetable farm to harvest corn and I headed down the mountain for the monthly meeting at the office in Diffun. I got there at about 9:00 AM and the meeting started at 10:00 AM. It ended at 12:00 N and we went out for lunch. After lunch I went to buy rice and then I got a jeepney back for Burgos. I arrived at Burgos at about 1:35 PM and headed up the mountain. I got home at about 2:20 PM, drank some coffee relaxed and cooled off for a while and then at about 3:00 PM I went to George's to help shell corn. I returned home at 4:15 PM, fetched water, bathed and started cooking supper. It started raining at about 3:30 PM and quit at about 5:30 PM. After eating supper and washing dishes I went back to George's and helped them finish shelling corn. We finished at 6:15 PM and they started eating immediately. Now it's 6:22 PM and I expect George by 6:45 PM tonight, I hope so anyway, but have to wait and see what happens. I have a headache. AWANEN!

Tuesday, September 23, 1986
My House, Gomez, Cabarroguis, Quirino

₱120 + 50 – 20 = ₱150				
Alfredo repay loan (see June 18)	+50	Pay Alfredo for use of nuang		20
			TOTAL	₱20

We got up at 5:30 AM and George left. He came at right about 7:00 PM last night. I cooked breakfast, ate, did dishes and got ready for the day and then I went to Alfredo's to talk for a while. Alfredo and Sip left for Diffun to sell corn. George remained home and I talked with him for a while longer and then returned home to go search for charcoal. I went to three places but could find no charcoal. I returned to Alfredo's and talked with George for a while and then came home and strengthened the fence around the *kamote*. After that I started working on my quarterly report for the Peace Corps for an hour or so. I took a 15 minute siesta, got up, went out and got three bags of dirt and then I went back to George's and rain was threatening so we brought in the corn that was drying in the sun. Then I returned home and packed 98 bags with dirt and planted *Acacia auriculiformis* seeds. I finished at 3:45 PM and rain was really threatening so I fetched water and bathed. Alfredo came for a while to talk and when we could hear the rain coming through the trees he left – at about 4:20 PM. After that I cooked supper and ate. It rained hard for an hour. When the rain stopped I did the dishes and then I went back to George's at 6:00 PM. They were eating supper and he said he'll come soon. Now it's 6:11 PM and I'm expecting him by about 6:30 PM. AWANEN!

Wednesday, September 24, 1986
My House, Gomez, Cabarroguis, Quirino

We got up at 5:15 AM and George left. He came at about 6:50 PM last night. I cooked breakfast, ate, did dishes, got ready for the day and then went to George's to talk for a while. He and Alfredo were just leaving for the vegetable farm so I put on my long pants and went with them. I left last but got there first. We harvested two carts of corn and I photographed the whole process. We finished packing the carts at 11:00 AM and headed home. We arrived at about 11:40 AM. It was a really hot day today. I rested at their house for a little while and then came home at about 12:30 PM and ate leftover rice and drank coffee for lunch. I worked on my Peace Corps quarterly report some more. At about 2:20 PM I went back to Alfredo's to help shell corn until 4:25 PM and then I came home, fetched water, bathed, cooked supper, ate and did the dishes. At 6:05 PM I went back to George's and helped shell corn until we finished it up at 6:45 PM. Then they ate supper. I harvested my first okra today. Now it's 6:58 PM and I'm expecting George by 7:15 PM if they don't have visitors tonight; I hope they don't. Now I'll study a little bit. To date we have hauled in 26 carts of corn. AWANEN!

Thursday, September 25, 1986
My House, Gomez, Cabarroguis, Quirino

We harvested the last of the corn today. We got up at 5:30 AM and George left. He didn't come until 11:40 PM last night because they went and helped Pedring shell corn. I cooked breakfast, ate, did dishes, got ready for the day and went to George's to talk for a while. Then I went to the farm and helped them harvest the last one and a half carts full of corn. We harvested corn for three weeks and it's now done. Somehow it's an anti-climax. Everybody was so tired today that we were all in a half bad mood. We got home at 11:15 AM and after resting at George's for a while I came home, drank a cup of coffee and napped for an hour. Then I pulled some weeds in the nursery and at 2:15 PM I returned to George's. We emptied the carts and shelled corn until I came home at 4:20 PM. I fetched water, bathed and then started cooking supper. I ate, did dishes, went to the canteen for cigarettes and then to George's to talk for a while, until their supper was ready at 6:20 PM. I'm really tired tonight, I hope George comes as soon as they're done with supper. I hope there is no corn shelling or anything else tonight! Now it's 6:31 PM and I'll study for a little bit and hope that George is here by 7:00 PM. We'll see what happens. AWANEN!

Friday, September 26, 1986
My House, Gomez, Cabarroguis, Quirino

Letters from Barb W., Fred & Cynthia B., JB & Katie F., Bob S. Postcards from San & Jack G., Mark W., Chad D. Socks from Anne S.

₱150 + 200 – 123 = ₱227							
Food	58	Rides	5	Coke	6	Cigarettes	5
Kerosene	8	Candy	11	Coffee	18	Toilet Paper	7
Sack	5					TOTAL	₱123

We got up at 5:30 AM and George left. I went and got him at 7:00 PM last night and we slept practically immediately. I cooked breakfast, ate, washed the dishes, got ready for the day and went to George's for a couple of minutes to talk. Then I headed for Burgos and Gundaway. I got the above mail and bought the above items at market and then returned home. I arrived back home at 11:20 AM, read mail, ate lunch, drank coffee and then I napped for about 20 minutes. At about 2:00 PM I went back to Alfredo's and when George returned from bathing at the fish pond we came here and weeded the nursery and its perimeter. Then I showed George the garden, asked him some questions and at 4:00 PM he went home. I fetched water, bathed and started cooking supper. Then I ate, did dishes, went to the canteen and then to George's house. At 6:15 PM they were eating supper. We're going to shell corn after a while so when I hear them start I'll return to help. Now it's 6:22 PM. AWANEN!

Saturday, September 27, 1986
My House, Gomez, Cabarroguis, Quirino

We got up at 5:40 AM and George left. I went and helped them shell corn last night until 9:45 PM and then George and I came here and slept immediately. I cooked breakfast, ate, did dishes, got ready for the day and then I went to George's and we sat around talking until 8:00 AM. Then we all shelled corn until 11:45 AM or so when they ate lunch and I came home. I ate my leftover rice, drank coffee and then I finished up my Peace Corps quarterly report. I napped for 20 minutes or so and when I got up I went to fetch water. Then I returned home, looked at the nursery and then at 1:45 PM I went back to George's and we all shelled corn again until I came home at 4:20 PM. I bathed and started cooking. When it was ready I ate, did dishes and finished up with that at 6:03 PM. I went to the canteen for my fix of cigarettes and then returned home. Now it's 6:17 PM and after a bit I'll go back to George's and help shell corn again. There isn't too much left – we ought to finish up all the rest of the last three carts by 8:00 or 8:30 PM – I hope. My hands are sore and I'm tired. I guess that's all there is for today. AWANEN!

Sunday, September 28, 1986
My House, Gomez, Cabarroguis, Quirino

Letters to Bob S. and Dave G.

We got up at 5:20 AM and George left. I helped them shell corn last night until 8:30 PM and then we came here and slept soon after. I cooked breakfast, ate, did dishes and got ready for the day. I went to Alfredo's but they had all gone to Gundaway to sell corn so I returned home and did laundry until 9:15 AM. Then I slept until 10:00 AM, got up and wrote the above two letters. I ate lunch and drank coffee then did some cleaning around the yard; I swept the south lawn again and trimmed the weeds in the north lawn. I also pulled weeds in the garden for an hour. Actually it was a pretty lazy day. I quit everything at about 4:00 PM, fetched water, trimmed my beard, bathed and then I started cooking supper of *utong* beans, okra and hot chili peppers. I ate, I did dishes and went to the canteen for my daily fix of cigarettes and then I stopped at George's. They were eating so I waited till they were done and it was dark and then I came home. George said that he would come soon. I don't know, there was lots of hollering there a little while ago. I don't know what the problem is, maybe George will tell me, but I doubt it. Now it's 6:35 PM and I'm waiting for George. AWANEN!

Monday, September 29, 1986
My House, Gomez, Cabarroguis, Quirino

Letter to Fred & Cynthia B.

We got up at 5:30 AM and George left. He came at 6:40 PM last night – early. I cooked breakfast, ate, did dishes and got ready for the day and then I went to George's to talk for a while and watched his mother give him a haircut. He left to cut grass around the school at about 8:00 AM and at about 8:30 AM I came home and worked in the south garden until 11:00 AM and then I stopped for lunch and also wrote the above letter. At 1:00 PM I went and got George to help me remove the one fairly large log that the squash were growing behind and then I continued picking up more soil. A martines bird came to eat insects for a couple hours and Arsenio came to talk for 30 or 45 minutes. Then I continued to prepare soil until about 4:00 PM. I accomplished preparation of four lines today, running north and south, in the south garden. It looks good. I fetched water, bathed and started cooking supper. After eating supper and doing dishes I went to the canteen to get cigarettes and then to George's to talk, but they were eating so I left. George said that he would come soon. Now it's 6:15 PM. I'll see if he makes it here before 7:00 PM, I don't really think he will, he sure is tired though so it's possible, we'll see what happens. AWANEN!

Tuesday, September 30, 1986
My House, Gomez, Cabarroguis, Quirino

Letter to Barb W.

We got up at 5:40 AM and George left. He didn't come until 7:40 PM last night because they had visitors. I cooked breakfast, ate, did dishes, got ready for the day and went to George's. We shelled corn until 10:30 AM and then we went to the vegetable farm, where George got vegetables for their days food and I got a nice bunch of hot peppers. We got back to their house at 12:30 PM and I came home, ate my leftover rice and wrote the above letter. Then at 2:00 PM I returned to George's house and helped to shell corn again until 4:20 PM. They gave me two pepino melons. I returned home, fetched water, bathed and started cooking supper. It was nice to go to the vegetable farm with George today, it was not really work, just a nice stroll and George showed me some growing things that I had not previously known. Now it's only 5:12 PM, but I have fetched water, bathed and am cooking supper. The reason I'm doing everything, including writing this, early is because the whole neighborhood is going to Alfredo's this evening to shell corn and I want to be the first one there. I wonder what time we'll finish shelling corn tonight, maybe 11:00 PM, or maybe not until 11:30 PM. I'll have to wait and see is all. I'll make a note in the entry for tomorrow, George has now slept here 141 nights. AWANEN!

Wednesday, October 1, 1986
My House, Gomez, Cabarroguis, Quirino

Letter to JB & Katie F. Postcard to Chad D.

₱227 – 27 = ₱200				
Charcoal	27			TOTAL ₱27

We got up at 6:30 AM and George left. We shelled corn last night, or this morning, until 2:00 AM and then we came here and slept immediately. As soon as we got up I went to Henry's to buy charcoal. I bought three sacks, carried it home and then finally at 7:45 or 8:00 AM I started cooking breakfast. I got that done, ate, did dishes and got ready for the day. After that, at 9:00 AM, I slept until noon and then I got up, ate lunch, drank coffee and wrote the letter to JB and Katie. I figured my expenses for September and after that I worked in the southeast garden for a while, but only for about 45 minutes. I quit at 4:00 PM, fetched water, bathed and then started cooking supper. I ate, did dishes, made my run to the canteen and then want to talk with George for ten minutes or so and ask him to please come as soon as they are done with supper. It's now 6:03 PM and if he isn't here by 7:00 PM I'll go and get him. It rained last night pretty long and hard and there is now a thunder and lightning storm threatening. I hope the rain holds off until after George arrives. There were 10 or 12 of us shelling corn last night. George told me that maybe we shelled 15 or 18 *kabans* in total [also *kavan* – a Philippine unit of measure, defined by the 19th century Spanish colonial government as being equal to 75 liters, but different for rice, cacao, corn, etc.] AWANEN!

Thursday, October 2, 1986
My House, Gomez, Cabarroguis, Quirino

Letters to San & Jack G. and Tom & Barb H.

We got up at 5:50 AM and George left. I went to get him at 6:30 PM last night but we got trapped there by the rain until 7:30 PM and then we came here. I cooked breakfast, ate, did dishes, got ready for the day and went to Alfredo's to talk for a while. After that, at 7:40 AM I went to the vegetable farm to help George cut down the corn stalks. We did that until 11:15 AM or so and then we came home for lunch. I drank some water at their place and then came home. I ate lunch and drank coffee and then from 12:20 to 1:20 PM I napped. Upon getting up I repaired the fence around the *kamote* again – the pigs broke it down **again** last night. Then I worked in the southeast garden until 4:00 PM, quit, fetched water and bathed. After that I started cooking supper. I ate, did dishes and then went to the canteen for cigarettes. Upon returning, I went to George's to talk for a few minutes. He was getting ready to catch a chicken for their supper. Now it's 6:20 PM and he's just catching the chicken, I can hear it squawking, so he'll undoubtedly be quite late tonight as their supper will be quite late. So, I guess I'll study for a while and then write a letter. AWANEN!

Friday, October 3, 1986
My House, Gomez, Cabarroguis, Quirino

Letters from Bob S. and Nestor. Medicine from Health Unit.

₱200 + 250 – 385 = ₱65							
Screen	30	Food	91	Lunch	25	Marienda	16
Cooking Oil	16	Rides	14	Cigarettes	11	Coke	3
Ice Cream	17	Coffee	84	Toilet Paper	5	Postage	10
Seeds	8	Candy	20	Household	35	TOTAL	₱385

We got up at 5:40 AM and George left, he came at about 8:30 PM last night. I cooked breakfast, ate, did dishes, got ready for the day and then went to Alfredo's to talk for a while and after that I headed down the mountain. I went to the post office in Gundaway and got the above mail and then I went to the office to have Francisco sign my quarterly report. After that I continued on to Santiago, where I mailed letters and the quarterly report. I cashed checks, shopped, ate lunch and ice cream and finished up at about 1:30 PM. The jeepney left at 1:52 PM and arrived at Burgos at 3:00 PM. I headed up the mountain at 3:15 PM, got home at 4:00 PM and unpacked. I fetched water, bathed, cooked supper, ate and did dishes all by 6:00 PM. Now it's 6:34

PM and everything is done. I'm waiting for George to come. I'm hoping to hell he comes earlier tonight than he has been coming lately. If I'm lucky he'll come before 7:00 PM tonight, we'll see what happens. AWANEN!

Saturday, October 4, 1986
My House, Gomez, Cabarroguis, Quirino

We got up at 5:30 AM and George left – after a bit – I heard a pig in the *kamote* and was first up to chase away the pig. I cooked breakfast, ate did dishes, got ready for the day and then I went to Alfredo's to talk for a while, but George and Alfredo had both gone to the vegetable farm, so I went too and helped them cut down the corn stalks and clean the field. It rained on and off all morning, all day in fact – I wonder if there is a typhoon coming, in probably yes. We returned from the farm at 11:30 AM and after a few minutes at George's I came home to find three pigs rooting in my garden. They had been in the *kamote* again too. I chased them away with my machete and then I napped from 1:00 to 2:00 PM, got up, drank a cup of coffee and worked in the southeast garden some more. I finished the "plowing" today and planted *utong*, pole beans from America and three kinds of squash from America, guess I'll see what happens this time, if the damn pigs don't destroy everything again. I stopped at 4:15 PM, fetched water, bathed, cooked supper, ate, did dishes, went to the canteen and then to George's house. They had finished eating but he still had to catch a chicken – why? Now it's 6:30 PM and I hope George comes early tonight; he came at 8:30 PM last night because Junior and Brando came to visit them. AWANEN!

Sunday, October 5, 1986
My House, Gomez, Cabarroguis, Quirino

Letter to Bob S.

We got up at 5:40 AM and George left. He came a bit before 7:00 PM last night. I cooked breakfast, ate, did dishes, got ready for the day and went to George's to talk for a while. Then I returned home. It rained off and on again all day today so it was not possible to do laundry and therefore I spent the morning cleaning house. I cleaned the bookshelf, the blanket and pillows shelf, the kitchen, the porch and everything. Then I looked at all of my stuff that's still in my duffle bag and laughed at what I brought with me from America! Alfredo came for a while, from about 10:30 to 11:15 AM or so, and when he left I ate lunch and drank coffee. Then I napped from noon to 1:00 PM, got up and started working on the above letter. I quit working on that at 2:00 PM or so and went to talk with George for a few minutes. I returned home and finished planting the southeast garden – squash and pallang. Then I weeded in the east garden and George came. We looked at everything, picked bugs off the tree seedlings and then he went home. I fetched water, bathed, cooked supper, ate, did dishes and went to the canteen. I returned home and now it's 6:16 PM. I'll finish the letter that I started earlier while I'm waiting for George. He'll probably be late tonight, we'll see. AWANEN!

Monday, October 6, 1986
My House, Gomez, Cabarroguis, Quirino

Letter to Mark W.

We got up at 5:40 AM and George left. He came before 7:00 PM again last night. I cooked breakfast, ate, did dishes and got ready for the day. It rained all day today. I went to the canteen to talk for a while and Alfredo was there too so I stayed for quite a while. Then I went to Alfredo's house to see if George had gone to the vegetable farm; he had so I went too and we pulled weeds above the trail in the rain until 11:15 AM or so. We accomplished quite a bit considering we didn't start until about 9:00 AM. We returned home and I hung out at George's for a while and then came home at about 12:30 PM or so. I ate lunch, drank coffee and then napped from 1:30 to 2:30 PM. When I got up, I sharpened my machete and killed time for a while. At 4:00 PM I fetched water, bathed despite the rain, cooked supper, ate and did dishes in the rain. Then I went to the canteen and then to George's. They were just cutting up a chicken. Now 6:18 PM and I don't expect George before 7:00 or 7:15 tonight so I'll try to write a letter to Mark W. I hope the rain stops tomorrow so that it's possible to do laundry. AWANEN!

Tuesday, October 7, 1986
My House, Gomez, Cabarroguis, Quirino

We got up at 5:55 AM and George left. He didn't come until 7:30 PM last night, when I hollered. The rains are continuing today, quite hard. I cooked breakfast, ate did dishes in the rain, got ready for the day and then I went to Alfredo's to talk for a while. There was supposed to be a forestry meeting today but Alfredo had gone to move the water buffalo, George had gone to the vegetable farm and his mother was doing laundry, so I returned home and waited until 9:00 AM to see if anybody would show up for the meeting. Not a single person came so I walked past the Barangay Hall to see if maybe the meeting was there, but nobody was there either. Then I went to the vegetable farm and helped George cut down grass in the rain it was my first day to actually use the *tabas* [the cutting tool – photo on page 229]. We quit at 11:00 AM and returned home. I talked there for a few minutes and then came home, ate lunch and napped from noon to 1:00 PM. The sun came out for a little while and I tried to reinforce the fence around the *kamote* but finally gave up. I put two *kamote* vines in the nursery and one in the southeast garden. I weeded the garden for a while and also planted some ginger and then the rain started hard again. At 4:00 PM I fetched water, bathed in the rain, cooked supper, ate, washed dishes and then went to the canteen.

At 6:00 PM I went to George's and they were already eating so I expect him to come before 7:00 PM tonight. Please stop raining tomorrow! AWANEN!

Wednesday, October 8, 1986
My House, Gomez, Cabarroguis, Quirino

Letter to Ardis B.

We got up at 6:00 AM and George left. He came just a bit before 7:00 PM last night, when I hollered for him. I cooked breakfast, ate, did dishes and got ready for the day. Today it only rained until noon. I went to George's and he had gone to the farm and Alfredo had gone to Burgos to sell bananas, so I went to the farm and helped George pull weeds. His forearm is sore from using the *tabas* so much yesterday so he didn't cut grass today. We pulled weeds until 10:40 AM and then he gathered vegetables and we came home. We arrived at about 11:40 AM and I came to my house shortly thereafter, ate lunch and drank coffee. At about 12:30 PM George came and we improved the fence around the *kamote* and then we replanted the *kamote* that the pigs had dug up yesterday. I showed George the rest of the garden and he left at 2:30 PM. I killed time until 4:00 PM, fetched water, bathed and then started cooking supper. I finished eating supper at 5:30 PM, did dishes and went to the canteen for cigarettes. Then I went to George's house and Junior was there running off at the mouth like Junior does, so I came home. Now it's 6:21 PM and certainly George won't come before Junior leaved, which will probably be late. I'll write a letter to Ardis. I hope the sun shines tomorrow, I have to do laundry. AWANEN!

Thursday, October 9, 1986
My House, Gomez, Cabarroguis, Quirino

We got up at 5:40 AM and George left. He came at about 8:45 PM last night – when Junior left. I cooked breakfast, ate, did dishes, got ready for the day and then I went to Alfredo's house and watched him build a pig pen for a bit. After that I came home and did laundry; I started before 8:00 AM and finished up at about 10:00 AM. I had one and a half weeks worth of laundry to do. After that I cleaned house; I removed all the things from the north. south and west walls and cleaned them all. I stopped at noon for lunch of leftover rice. Alfredo stopped by for a while – he wanted to borrow some burlap sacks but I only had one to loan him. I cleaned house some more and polished the floor with the *lampaso* and then at 3:00 PM it clouded up for the daily thunderstorm and then it rained until about 4:00 PM. After the rain stopped I fetched water, shaved above and below my beard, bathed and then started cooking supper of squash and beans. I ate, did dishes, went to the canteen for cigarettes and then to George's and he was ready to come here at about 6:15 PM, so now it's 6:43 PM and we're listening to the Ilokano radio drama. I hope that he will explain more of it to me when it's finished. AWANEN!

George at their farm holding the *tabas*, the tool used for cutting down dead corn stalks, grass and so on. This is a wicked tool and should be used with great care. Using it causes an abundance of blisters. Note the banana trees behind him, these were also a part of their farm. Note that he is barefooted.

Friday, October 10, 1986
St. Mary's Pension, Baguio City, Benguet

Letters from Bill N., Steve A., Dave G., Ronald, JB & Katie F. and Dave M. Packages from Dave G. (toys) and Chris & Mary M. (pants and book).

₱65 + 200 – 230 = ₱35							
Cigarettes	20	Rides	8	Postage	3	Candy	7
Toilet Paper	5	Supper	28	Bus	119	Marienda	17
Bread	9	Misc.	14			TOTAL	₱230

We got up at 5:30 AM and George left. I cooked breakfast, ate, did dishes, got ready for the day and then I went to Alfredo's to give him my valuables and say good-bye. Then the rain started. It rained for half of the walk down the mountain so the trail was very muddy. I got to Burgos at 8:30 AM and there were no rides. I had to walk past the Barangay Captain's house before a jeepney came along. I stopped at Gundaway and got the above mail and then continued on to Santiago. I didn't get to Lina's Restaurant until 11:45 AM and Nestor was waiting for me. We went to the Pantranco Bus Terminal and finally got out of Santiago at 1:30 PM. We arrived in Carmen at about 7:30 PM and then got a bus to Baguio City at 8:45 PM. We finally got to Baguio City at 11:20 PM, walked to St Mary's Pension, got checked in and ate supper at about midnight. We talked for a short while and then we went to sleep. It was a long day for sure! AWANEN!

Saturday, October 11, 1986
St. Mary's Pension, Baguio City, Benguet

My Peace Corps Service is 50% complete today!

₱35 + 800 – 459 = ₱376							
Meals	189	Shoes	130	Dictionary	50	Ice Cream	30
Cigarettes	39	Rides	6	Coke	15	TOTAL	₱459

We got up at 6:20 AM, bathed and headed out for breakfast at the Dangwa Tranco Bus Terminal. We ate breakfast and then we strolled through the public market and I bought new shoes. After that we strolled up Session Road and to the Bishop's house to buy a dictionary and grammar book. By the time we finished there it was nearly 10:30 AM so we bought ice cream and went to Burnham Park to eat it. We strolled around Burnham Park until lunchtime and then we went to the Dangwa Tranco Bus Terminal again for lunch. After lunch we returned to St. Mary's Pension from 1:00 to 2:30 PM and then we headed off to Camp John Hay. That ended up being a disappointment – we determined that supper there would be way too expensive for our budget so we returned to Baguio City and ate at the Mandarin Restaurant, where Ardis and I ate back in February. After that we finished our day's strolling by walking home. My new shoes gave me blisters so my feet are now sore. Nestor and I ended up trading shoes at Camp John Hay, but the damage was already done to my feet and it was too late so now I have to walk around with sore feet for a while. Now it's 7:51 PM and we're about ready to sleep. AWANEN!

Sunday, October 12, 1986
St. Mary's Pension, Baguio City, Benguet

₱376 – 179 = ₱197							
Meals	89	Brooms	36	Short Pants	33	Q-Tips	10
Fruit	1	Bread	4	Rides	6	TOTAL	₱179

We got up at 6:15 AM and got ready to go for breakfast at the Dangwa Tranco Bus Terminal again. After eating we searched for, and finally found, the people that Nestor knows here in Baguio City. We sat and waited for a while at their place and then we all left for Nestor's cousin's house. We spent the day there – it wasn't a very exciting day for me at all, I hope it was a good day for Nestor, but personally I sat there and counted each and every hour as it passed by from 10:30 AM, when we arrived there, until 3:30 PM, when we finally left and returned to central Baguio City. We strolled for a while and then we went to market and bought grass brooms. After that we ate supper at the Dangwa Tranco Bus Terminal once again and then returned to St Mary's Pension. We're heading for home tomorrow. This is certainly turning into an expensive trip for me – again. I'm getting weary of always paying for everything. Now it's 7:41 PM and Nestor is already under the covers and sleeping. AWANEN!

Monday, October 13, 1986
Nestor's Cousin's House, Vulcan, Cordon, Isabela

₱197 + 400 – 445 = ₱152							
Lodging	210	Meals	76	Rides	105	Bread	13
Misc.	7	Ice Cream	34			TOTAL	₱445

We get up at 5:30 AM packed and checked out of St. Mary's Pension. We headed for the Dangwa Tranco Bus Terminal once again, ate breakfast and then after eating and asking about buses to Isabela we went to the Pantranco Bus Terminal. They said there was a bus straight to Santiago, but of course it didn't show up and we had to take a bus to Carmen. Then we had a two hour wait for the next Santiago bus, so we went to market, ate ice cream and I was nearly out of money so I changed a $10 bill that I had for emergency use at the rate of ₱20.1 = $1. Then we took a jeepney from Carmen to Kakilingan and arrived right at dark. We walked to Vulcan in the mud and we made a new plan to sleep at Nestor's cousin's house there. He asked about water buffaloes for sale and it seems there are lots of them available for purchase there. We slept at about 8:00 PM and had a good night's sleep. AWANEN!

Tuesday, October 14, 1986
Nestor's House, Villa Miemban, Cordon, Isabela

We got up at 5:40 AM at Vulcan, ate breakfast and got ready to leave. I looked at one water buffalo for sale for ₱7,000 and we searched for another, but they ended up saying that it wasn't for sale. Then we headed for Villa Miemban and Nestor decided to take a "shortcut" that actually ended up being a very "longcut". It took us three hours to get to Villa Miemban. When we arrived at his house Nestor cooked lunch, we ate and then took a nap from 12 to 1:00 PM. We got up and I watched them while they worked on a new water buffalo cart. Then Melchor, Rufino and three or four other people came by with *"arak"* [a terribly strong, locally made alcoholic drink] so we drank for a while and then I retired to inside the house and laid down half drunk. Finally at about 7:00 PM they all left. Nestor cooked supper, we ate and now it's 7:57 PM and we're more or less ready to sleep. I wanted to see JB and Katie while I was here this time, but no such luck I guess. AWANEN!

Wednesday, October 15, 1986
My House, Gomez, Cabarroguis, Quirino

Letters from San & Jack G., Terry S., Bob S., Chris & Mary M. and John D. Package from Jim & Roselynn S.

₱152 – 83 = ₱69							
Food	36	Household	8	Rides	6	Postage	3
Coke	6	Marienda	6	Coffee	18	TOTAL	₱83

We got up at 5:40 AM and we took a stroll to the rice field before breakfast, then we cooked and ate breakfast and I got ready to leave Villa Miemban. We finally got it together and left at about 8:15 AM or so and arrived at Vulcan at about 10:00 AM or so. There were no tricycles there, but eventually a jeep (not a jeepney) came by and I begged a ride. I got to Cordon at about 11:30 AM, did my shopping there and then got a jeepney to Gundaway. I stopped at the post office at 12:30 PM and the postmaster was there, so I was able to get the above mail. Then I caught a jeepney to Burgos, arrived about 1:30 PM and started up the mountain at 1:40 PM. My pack was really heavy, so I didn't arrive home until nearly 3:00 PM. I fetched water, unpacked and then it was 4:00 PM or so. I bathed and started cooking supper and Alfredo and Boy came by to talk for a while, but when I started eating supper they left. Now it's 5:47 PM and I'm about ready to take the grass broom that I bought as a gift for Alfredo to their house. AWANEN!

Thursday, October 16, 1986
My House, Gomez, Cabarroguis, Quirino

Letter to Jim & Roselynn S.

We got up at 5:30 AM and George left; he came at about 7:00 PM last night – after I hollered for him. I gave him a bunch of the toys that Dave G. sent and I also gave him the short pants I bought for him in Baguio City. I cooked breakfast, ate, did the dishes, got ready for the day and went to Alfredo's for a short time to talk. Then I went to the farm with George and we pulled weeds, but only until 9:00 AM, because the sun came out, so we came home to put corn in the sun to dry. Two forest guards came while I was at George's and we talked with them for a while and then they went back to the office in Diffun. Then at about 11:00 AM, I came home, ate lunch, drank coffee and played with my HP-71 calculator until 2:00 PM. Then I took a nap until 3:00 PM. Amor stopped by for a short while on his way to Diffun and when he left I looked at the garden and cleaned house until 4:00 PM. Then I fetched water, bathed and started cooking supper. I ate, did dishes, went to the canteen for cigarettes and then to George's house. They were eating supper so I left immediately. Now it's 6:12 PM. I hope George comes soon. Maybe I'll start a letter to somebody. AWANEN!

Friday, October 17, 1986
My House, Gomez, Cabarroguis, Quirino

Letter to Chris & Mary M.

We got up at 5:15 AM and George left. He came at 6:30 PM last night – early – and I didn't even holler! I cooked breakfast, ate did dishes, got ready for the day and went to George's to talk for a few minutes. They were all getting ready to go to Diffun to sell corn so I came home at 7:30 AM and did laundry. I finished that before 10:00 AM – even my blanket. Then I finished the letter to Jim and Roselynn that I started yesterday and after that I weeded the garden for a while and removed about half of the okra plants that were growing way too thick and I can't even tell that any were removed because they were so thick. Then I ate lunch and took about a 20 minute nap, got up and cleaned the south lawn. I also swept the north lawn and by then it was 2:30 PM and I wrote the above letter to Chris and Mary. I finished that at 3:30 PM, fetched water and packed to go and search for a water buffalo tomorrow. Then I bathed and started supper. I ate, did dishes and went to George's for a few minutes. Now it's 6:25 PM and we're going to shell corn tonight. I hope we quit relatively early so that I can wake up early tomorrow morning and make it to Kakilingan by 9:00 or 10:00 AM. AWANEN!

Chapter 14
Culture Notes #5

An Overdue Note on Acculturation

It would be easy, when studying with a group of Americans all day, to find oneself wanting to go out and drink a few beers with those same people in the evening, especially when the alternative is to go home to a host family and be immersed in a language that is not understandable, and in a way of life and love that is foreign to the one that a person knows and understands. I, however, was 15 – 20 years older than the other PCV's in my training group and for this reason I did not really feel at ease with those "spoiled American kids." I would therefore, go home to the host family every afternoon immediately after classes, in fact I and my host brother, who was attending university near the site where our PCV training was being held, would often accompany each other home. Another aspect of being older than average was my ability to recognize that two years is an extremely short time, that it generally takes a year in a new job just to become productive, and therefore I had better get started on the road to understanding what makes a Filipino tick so as to be able to be effective in my work.

Going into the Second Year

As has been mentioned a couple of times above, a seed had been growing in my mind for a larger demonstration than just my FAITH garden. I had noticed and been frustrated ever since my arrival in Gomez, by the farmers' normal practice of plowing up and down the slopes versus across the slopes (contour farming). I had seen with my own eyes the deep erosion gullies that resulted from this practice as the rains were funneled straight down the mountainside. The people didn't like the fact that if it rained immediately after planting, half or more of their corn seed ended up in the stream at the base of the mountain, but they didn't seem to know what to do about it. I had stressed contour plowing in virtually every meeting of the farmers association that I had addressed. I had talked with George about the problem and George had explained that the reason the people plowed up and down the mountain was because that was the way it had been done forever, that the water buffalo did not like pulling the plow across the hillside, that no, he'd never tried plowing across the hillside; his father had told him how to plow, so he did it the way his father instructed. I wanted to change this practice before my time was up. I had established credibility for myself, was a respected member of the community, was considered an industrious person with a great deal of patience, and much more, and thought that I could accomplish this new task which I set for myself.

My thought was to purchase a water buffalo and do a full blown demonstration farm. I presented the idea to George, who thought it was a good idea and told his father about it. George's father talked with me, and offered to let me use a part of their farm for whatever I wanted to do. I was certainly somewhat apprehensive about the thoughts of purchasing a water buffalo as I didn't know the first thing about raising a large animal. I therefore discussed it at length with George. It was our main topic of conversation for several nights. I had to be sure that George would show me all that I had to know about the "care and feeding of a water buffalo", that he would show me how to farm, and that we could help each other on our farms. I wanted to be absolutely sure that George wasn't just saying what he knew that I wanted to hear. After about two weeks of talking and being reassured by George, I made the decision to go ahead. George's father offered to help me find and purchase a water buffalo. He told me that I could expect to pay about ₱5,000 to ₱8,000 ($250 – $400 at that time) for a water buffalo. We searched far and wide, and every place we went the sellers wanted ₱10,000 as soon as they discovered that it was me, the rich Americano, who was doing the buying. George's father came up with the plan of telling the next seller that we were buying the water buffalo for him, not for the Americano, and in that way we might be able to find one that I could afford. Using this trick, we found a 12 year old female (a strong, healthy animal in the prime of life) for the price of ₱6,000 ($300). I bought it, and George, true to his word, showed me how and where to pasture it, when, where and how to bathe it, when to make sure it was in the shade, and so on for the first several days. I had already ridden George's water buffalo enough so that I would no longer fall off and land on my head, so George just had to keep a loose eye on me to be sure that I didn't do something stupid. Water buffalo are extremely smart, and a well trained one will respond to several voice commands as well as rope (non-verbal) commands. I purchased my water buffalo in October, right at the start of the fall plowing/planting season. My plan was to plow my farm on the contour, thereby showing people that a water buffalo could walk and plow on the contour just as easily, in fact, as it could pull a plow up and down the mountain. With the help of several friends the eight foot tall cogon grass was removed from the area where I was to farm, I found a plow that the owner happily traded for a $5 solar powered calculator, and George taught me how to plow with a water buffalo. We plowed my farm on the contour, and immediately George requested and received his fathers permission to plow their farm on the contour also. There were a few other people who had not yet plowed their farms, and when these people saw that it was possible for the water buffalo to work on the contour they followed George's and my example. Over the course of the growing season everybody who had plowed on the contour noticed that their farms did not develop erosion gullies, and that none of their seed ended up in the stream at the bottom of the mountain.

I felt elated at this easy success. The next planting season only one die-hard farmer continued plowing/planting up and down the slope. The results of this ended up being a very dramatic demonstration of the benefits of contour plowing. About two days after the completion of planting there was a real gully-washer of a rain storm, and the one farmer who had plowed up and down the slope was wiped out, virtually all of his corn seed had ended up at the bottom of the mountain. The people who had plowed on the contour were very quick to note that they had lost none of their seed.

That next planting season I introduced hybrid corn to George. I bought one kilogram of this seed in town and gave it to George to plant on a corner of his farm. I traded George some of his home grown seed for the hybrid corn, pointing out to George that this was "special" corn seed, and that I wanted George to plant it on his farm and watch it in comparison to his other corn, as the soil on his farm was better than the soil on my farm. George, and for that matter most of the people were by now willing to place some little bit of faith and trust in what I was saying, so George did not hesitate to accept and plant the hybrid seed. I also informed George that he should not save the seed from this corn, that the next year it would be smaller and less healthy than this year. It was difficult to explain why this was so, that hybrid crop seeds tend to revert back to the characteristics of a single parent if saved and planted again. Maybe George didn't understand, but he was intelligent enough to realize that there was a good reason why he should not save and plant the seed obtained from the hybrid corn. He and his family were highly impressed by the results of the hybrid corn, and stated that it was worth the extra expense of purchasing this special seed over saving their own and that next planting season they would plant all hybrid corn seed. My credibility and spirits again soared with this latest success. My credibility had been rising rapidly ever since my first demonstration of FAITH gardening. It leveled off for a time period, and then when I bought my very own water buffalo my credibility again increased rapidly.

Owning a Water Buffalo (Nuang)

After I bought the water buffalo (**nuang**) the people of Gomez were rather amazed. They knew that I was industrious and more but they never expected to see me riding and using my own nuang! As I became proficient at riding the creature, using it to plow my farm, helping George by using it to pull carts of bananas down the mountain, and so on, the people actually became proud of "our Americano." I soon noticed that when I made my weekly trip to the public market, ten kilometers and two hours away, people that I didn't even know would make comments to me about my nuang. I knew that the only way these strangers could know was because the people of Gomez had told them. It was soon known far and wide that "the Peace Corps at Gomez owns a nuang."

After owning my nuang for about one month, there was a Sunday afternoon when it was grazing around George's yard, and George's bull nuang hopped on and mated with my nuang. George and his family were impressed, and told me that I was very lucky. I asked them how long it would be before she would calf. The people, no matter who I asked, said that it took the same nine months that it took for people. However, I had a book that said the gestation period for water buffalo is 320 days, or about ten and one-half months. The people insisted that the book was not correct, that it was nine months. After nine months came and went and there was no calf, but the nuang was obviously pregnant, the people said maybe it would be ten months. It ended up being 315 days. I had taught the people something else that they had never been sure of. At that point I only had one month remaining in my service after my nuang calved, but I noted that within that last month, two different families had come to me with the date their water buffalo was serviced, and they asked me when their water buffalo would calve.

After my nuang became pregnant my credibility seemed to go up even further. The people seemed to think that I had somehow planned for her to become pregnant so that I could see a new calf before I went home. Water buffalo do not become pregnant often, as the cow has a silent heat, and the only one who knows she is in heat is the bull. As people's nuangs are generally used on the farm all day and tied up when they aren't actually being used, there is little opportunity for a bull and cow to come together during the 18 – 24 hour estrous cycle. Even George, in his 18 years, had never seen a newborn nuang calf, and had no real idea how long the gestation period was. In my two years I only saw two calves – my own and one other. Then when my nuang actually calved the people were truly impressed. It was unfortunate that I only had one more month to go. The peoples respect for me was so great and my credibility was so high at that point that more people might have even been able to be talked into planting some citrus fruit trees, as George had already been convinced to do.

Chapter 15
October 18, 1986 through January 22, 1987

Saturday, October 18, 1986
My House, Gomez, Cabarroguis, Quirino

Letter to JB & Katie F. Letter from JB & Katie F.

₱69 + 400 – 222 = ₱247							
Rides	22	Cigarettes	11	Lunch	41	Marienda	9
Ice Cream	40	Household	6	Candy	7	Crackers	9
Coffee	26	Food	45	Misc.	6	TOTAL	₱222

We got up at 5:20 AM and George left. We shelled corn last night until midnight then came here and slept immediately. I woke up with a splitting headache, so I didn't even cook breakfast. At 7:00 AM I went to Alfredo's and talked with George for a while and then Alfredo and I left for Burgos. We got to Kakilingan at about 9:45 AM and met Nestor and his cousin to go searching for a water buffalo for me. We only found two for sale. One of them was ₱10,000 and the other one was ₱9,000. It's probably needless to say, but I didn't buy either one of them. That took until 1:00 PM and then Nestor went home and Alfredo and I went to Santiago, where I shopped for food. At 3:30 PM we caught a jeepney bound for Burgos. We arrived at 4:30 PM, headed up the mountain immediately and arrived home at about 5:15 PM. I fetched water, bathed and went to George's house to ask him to come early. That was 6:00 PM and they were just starting to cook so I can't expect him before 7:00 PM at the earliest. If he's not here by 7:15 PM I'll holler for him. In the meantime maybe I'll write a letter to JB and Katie. AWANEN!

Sunday, October 19, 1986
My House, Gomez, Cabarroguis, Quirino

We got up at 5:55 AM and George left. He came just before 7:30 PM last night, after I hollered. I cooked breakfast, ate, did the dishes and got ready for the day then went to Alfredo's to talk for a few minutes. After that I came home and did laundry; I even washed my sleeping bag today. Then I killed time for a while – pulled weeds in the lower garden, ate lunch, drank coffee and went to talk with George for a while. I returned home and after a bit it started raining – shit – it will take days for my sleeping bag to dry! Alfredo came and we napped for a while and then I went to their house again to ask George to come help me search for worms on the tree seedlings. After a while he came and we searched for and removed worms and then he left. I fetched water, bathed, cooked supper, did dishes and now it's 5:59 PM. We're going to shell corn again tonight so I'll go there as soon as I finish with this. I hope that we don't go until midnight again. AWANEN!

Monday, October 20, 1986
My House, Gomez, Cabarroguis, Quirino

Letter from Ardis B.

₱247 – 133 = ₱114							
Rice	55	Cigarettes	11	Rides	16	Lunch	29
Ice Cream	16	Food	6			TOTAL	₱133

We got up at 5:55 AM and George left. We shelled corn last night – 10 or 12 of us – until 11:30 PM and then we came here and slept after just a tiny bit of talking. I cooked breakfast, ate, did the dishes, got ready for the day and then I went to George's to talk for a few minutes. Then I headed down the mountain for Burgos in the rain. It rained all day today. I stopped at the post office and then I went to the office for the monthly meeting. It was very boring and I managed to escape at 11:30 AM. I bought rice at Unite's and then went on to Santiago where I got ₱7,000 from the bank, hopefully for my very own water buffalo. I got out of Santiago at 2:45 PM and got to Burgos at 3:50 PM. I headed up the mountain immediately and got home at 4:30 PM. I went to George's for a few minutes and told them that I got the money to buy a water buffalo and then I returned home, fetched water, bathed and began to cook supper. They finished shelling the last of the corn today and I didn't get to see the last ear of corn shelled. It's now 6:21 PM, I've eaten and dishes are washed. I'll holler for George at 6:45 PM if he isn't here before then, which I hope he is. It feels like it was a long day, I'm tired. AWANEN!

Tuesday, October 21, 1986
My House, Gomez, Cabarroguis, Quirino

Letters to Dave G and Dave & Vicki M.

We got up at 6:00 AM and George left. He came early last night, at about 6:30 PM. I cooked breakfast, ate, did dishes, got ready for the day and Alfredo came here and said let's stroll to Calaocan to search for a water buffalo, so we did. When we were about three-quarters of the way there we met the guy who we were going to see so we didn't go the rest of the way. Alfredo asked him how much for his water buffalo and he said ₱7,000 so Alfredo came back with a offer of ₱5,500. The guy came back with a counteroffer of "maybe ₱6,000", but that he'd have to think about it. Alfredo made sure that the guy understood that it was for himself and not for me, to keep the price down – smart thinking. So, we came home and after a while I went to Alfredo's to talk and ask him what he thought and then I came home and wrote the above letter to Dave G. I napped from noon to 1:00 PM and then George came for a while and explained to me what all had been decided and not decided about the water buffalo purchase [I cannot remember what this was all about]. After that I worked on the letter to Dave M. until 4:00 PM and then I fetched water, bathed and started cooking supper. It rained all morning and started again just as I was washing dishes this evening so I didn't go to George's this evening. Now it's 6:06 PM and I'm hoping George will come by about 6:30 PM and tell me the news about the water buffalo. In the meantime I'll finish the letter to Dave M. and study. AWANEN!

Wednesday, October 22, 1986
My House, Gomez, Cabarroguis, Quirino

Letter to Steve & Deb A.
Nuang Buying Day!

₱114 + 6,000 – 6,000 = ₱114			
Nuang 6,000			TOTAL ₱6,000

We got up at 5:40 AM and George left. He came just before 7:00 PM last night. I cooked breakfast, ate and Alfredo came. I did dishes, got ready for the day and then Alfredo and I headed off to Calaocan to buy a water buffalo for me. We got to Calaocan at about 8:40 AM and Alfredo had to convince the guy again that he wanted to sell his water buffalo, but then he decided that he wanted ₱7,000 and Alfredo had to convince him again that he only wanted ₱6,000 for it – after all, yesterday evening he had sent word that he agreed to ₱6000. He finally succeeded with his convincing, we paid for the water buffalo and started home. I rode the whole way. It rained all morning again so the trail was muddy and slippery, but no problem. We arrived home at 11:15 AM or so and I hung out at Alfredo and George's until noon and then came home. At 2:00 PM I went back to their house and at 2:30 PM George and I went to pasture my water buffalo. We returned home and I fetched water and wrote to Steve and Deb. Then at 4:15 PM or so we went and got all three water buffaloes from pasture. We returned and at 5:00 PM I came home with my water buffalo, fetched water and started supper. I didn't bathe today. Alfredo came to talk for a while. George's rooster is staked under my house but I don't understand why. My water buffalo is tied outback. Now it's 6:46 PM and I hope George comes soon. AWANEN!

[As a side note, you may recall that I mentioned previously (in the Foreword, on page viii) that as a PCV we were given a living allowance every month. This was given in the form of a book of checks, which were each dated so that we could not cash them all at once and then be flat out broke. I had been saving all of the money that I could, minus, of course, travel to Batanes, Baguio City and so on with Nestor. Note that on this date I wrote a letter to Steve A. He saved all of the letters which I wrote to him and recently gave them all to me. I just read the one which I wrote him today and it notes that I am very proud of my nuang, but that the ₱6,000 which I paid for it represented virtually my entire savings account here in the Philippines.]

Thursday, October 23, 1986
My House, Gomez, Cabarroguis, Quirino

Letters to Bill N. and Ronald.

₱114 + 315 = ₱429

We got up at 5:20 AM and George left. He came just before 7:00 PM last night. I started cooking breakfast. George showed me to release the nuang as soon as we woke up. Pedring came to get some medicine for his infected leg. Alfredo came to talk and then Junior, and then George came to get his rooster from under the house. They all left and then I ate, did the dishes and got ready for the day. I tied my nuang to the *kahoy* and went to George's to see if he would show me where to pasture it. After a while he came and showed me a place to put it on the other side of the creek. Then I worked on highlighting words that I don't know in the Ilokano Dictionary. After a while I ate lunch and drank coffee. George, Alfredo and one other person went down the mountain today to sell corn. I wrote the letter to Bill N. and at 2:00 PM I went to Alfredo's and Sip [Sip is George's younger brother] showed me where to pasture my water buffalo for the afternoon. Then at 4:00 PM I fetched water, bathed in the rain – it rained all day again today – and then I cut up vegetables for supper. At 4:30 PM I went to get my water buffalo and then I cooked supper, ate, washed dishes and went to the canteen. I went to George's a few moments ago and they are just cooking supper so he won't be here before 7:00 PM. Now it's 6:00 PM so I'll study for a while and maybe write another letter. AWANEN!

Friday, October 24, 1986
My House, Gomez, Cabarroguis, Quirino

Letters from Tom & Barb H., Mark W., San & Jack G. and Brooke F.

₱429 – 174 = ₱255							
Rope	48	Rides	4	Cigarettes	7	Misc.	15
Food	47	Household	15	Marienda	8	Candy	10
Coffee	20					TOTAL	₱174

We got up at 5:30 AM, I released my water buffalo and George left. I went to George's house and got him last night at 7:00 PM in the rain. I cooked breakfast and Alfredo and Boy Belasco came to talk for a few minutes and then I ate, washed dishes, got ready for the day and we all left to go and do the water buffalo transfer papers. Unfortunately, when we got to Burgos a guy told us that the bank manager wasn't there today to do it, so Alfredo and I continued on to market and then the post office. I got the above mail and then we returned home. We arrived at my house at just about exactly 1:00 PM and Alfredo helped me make the pasturing rope for my water buffalo. At about 4:30 PM George, Sip and I went to get the water buffaloes and bathe them, so I didn't get home until after 5:00 PM and then fetched water, bathed and started supper. Now it's 6:12 PM and supper is still cooking. I hope George comes relatively early tonight, maybe about 7:00 PM at the latest, we'll see what happens. Supper is ready to eat now. AWANEN!

Saturday, October 25, 1986
My House, Gomez, Cabarroguis, Quirino

We got up at 5:30 AM and George left. I went to get him at 7:15 PM last night. I cooked breakfast, ate, did dishes, got ready for the day and went to George's and he, Alfredo, Bubot and I went to the vegetable farm to work at clearing MY vegetable farm. We cut grass until lunch – it's damn hard work, believe me, swinging that *tabas.* We ate the lunches we brought with us and rested during the heat of the midday sun and then we harvested some bananas. After that we continued to cut grass on my farm until about 4:30 PM or so and then we quit, picked up the bananas, loaded them in the cart and finally, a bit after 5:00 PM we headed for home. We got home at 5:45 PM and I quickly fetched water and started cooking immediately. Now it's 6:24 PM and I just pulled the rice off the charcoal and now I'm cooking eggplant. Without a doubt, as soon as I finish supper and dishes and go to the canteen for cigarettes I'll go and get George, if he isn't here before that. I really hope he is here before that though. Today was a long day with lots of hard work, no doubt about it. AWANEN!

Sunday, October 26, 1986
My House, Gomez, Cabarroguis, Quirino

Letter to San & Jack G.

We got up at 5:20 AM and George left; he came just before 7:00 PM last night and so did Alfredo – to talk about the problem with my water buffalo's foot. I cooked breakfast, ate, did the dishes and got ready for the day. I pastured my water buffalo at 7:30 AM. I did laundry until nearly 10:00 AM and then Sip and I went to get my water buffalo. George and Alfredo went to Burgos to sell bananas. I returned home and cleaned around the house and by then it was lunchtime so I ate lunch, drank coffee and napped for a half hour. I got up and wrote the above letter to San and Jack and then it was 2:00 PM and Sip and I again went to pasture my water buffalo. I returned home and finished the letter and then cleaned under the house and flattened out the water buffalo tracks to the south of the house. I went to George's at 4:15 PM and talked for a few minutes and then at 4:30 PM Sip and I went to get my water buffalo. We arrived at Alfredo's and we put the pine tar on my water buffalo's sore foot. I returned home, fetched water, bathed and started cooking supper. Now it's 6:10 PM and I'm still cooking. I hope George comes relatively early tonight – about 7:00 PM or so. Maybe I'll start another letter after supper, I'll see what happens. AWANEN!

Monday, October 27, 1986
My House, Gomez, Cabarroguis, Quirino

Letter to Bob S.

₱255 – 163 = ₱92							
Medicine	60	Cigarettes	7	Sacks	14	Food	33
Coke	9	Ice Cream	17	Candy	7	Rides	16
						TOTAL	₱163

We get up at 5:30 AM and George left. He actually came before 6:30 PM last night. I cooked breakfast, ate, did dishes, got ready for the day and went to Alfredo's to talk for a minute, but he wasn't there and George had gone to the farm, so at 7:30 AM I headed down the mountain for Burgos. I talked with Rogel for a few minutes about the problem with my water buffalo's foot and then I headed for Santiago in search of the necessary medicine. The jeepney to Santiago took two hours – it was very slow. So, I got to Santiago at 11:00 AM and talked with the people at the veterinary supply place and they told me that Negasunt is the medicine I needed to buy – it's expensive. I searched for some other PCV's to talk with, but I couldn't find any so I ate ice cream, went to market, got some minor food items and headed home. The jeepney got stuck in the mud before the Burgos Barangay Captain's house so I walked from there. I stopped at Rogel's house for a while and got home at 3:40 PM. Alfredo brought my water buffalo home and we put the medicine on its foot and then I fetched water, cooked, ate and did dishes. My water buffalo is under the house so that its foot stays dry. Now it's 6:12 PM and I hope George comes before 7:00 PM, but probably not two nights in a row, we'll see what happens. AWANEN!

Tuesday, October 28, 1986
My House, Gomez, Cabarroguis, Quirino

We got up at 5:20 AM and George left; he came just before 7:00 PM last night. I cooked breakfast, ate, did dishes and got ready for the day. I was ready at 7:30 AM and went to the farm, but I couldn't find the *tabas* that Alfredo said he had hidden so I watched George *"agsagad"* [harrow the field] after pasturing my water buffalo. I pulled weeds for George for an hour or so and then at 10:30 AM we came home. We left our water buffaloes there to pasture (or graze). I ate lunch, drank coffee and then at 12:15 PM I went back to George's and at 1:00 PM we went back to the farm. We burned his wind rows of corn and then he started plowing. I tried to plow a little bit but I didn't do too good at it so he took back over and I went to my farm and pulled the dry grass back from the banana trees and the calamansi [a type of citrus] trees and then we burned the grass on my farm. I helped with the plowing process a little, not really plowing but removing the weed roots from the already plowed area. At about

4:30 PM we got our water buffaloes and came home, arriving at about 5:00 PM. Now it's 6:26 PM, water has been fetched, I've bathed, I'm done cooking and supper is cooling in front of me right now. Please George, come early tonight. Oh, I punctured a vein on the top of my foot today and it bled – a lot. AWANEN!

Wednesday, October 29, 1986
My House, Gomez, Cabarroguis, Quirino

Letter to Ardis B.

We got up at 5:25 AM and George left. He came just before 7:00 PM again last night – after I hollered. I started cooking breakfast, tied my water buffalo on the other side of the creek, finished cooking, ate, did dishes, got ready for the day and went to George's to see what the plan for the day was, only to discover that there was no plan. He was waiting for Kudog to do a temporary water buffalo swap, but I don't know why. I returned home and at 9:00 AM he showed me where to put my water buffalo until 10:30 AM. I did laundry – only four T-shirts and one pair of short pants – and then I got my water buffalo and put it in the shade by the house. I ate lunch and drank coffee and then George came for a little bit and we drank Kool-Aid and looked at the garden. He left and I slept from 12:30 to 1:30 PM and then at 2:00 PM I hollered to see about pasturing my water buffalo. George came and showed me where to pasture it for the afternoon and then I returned home and wrote the above letter to Ardis. At 4:00 PM I cut up things for supper. George came and got his rooster from under the house and then I went and got my water buffalo. I came home, tied it up, fetched water, bathed, cooked supper, ate, did dishes and now it's 6:35 PM and I'm waiting for George. I'll holler for him at 7:00 PM if he isn't here by then. Now I'll study a bit. My foot is sore and swollen so today I'm limping around and there's a big clot of blood just under the skin. AWANEN!

[Many times now you have read that "I'll holler for George" or "he came after I hollered" and you must wonder what that's all about, so let me explain. George, Alfredo's eldest son, lived at his father's house, which was just through a few banana trees about 100 meters from my house. So, if George had not arrived, generally by about 7:00 – 7:15 PM, I would holler through the trees *"George, umay-ka man ditoyen"* which translates as "George, please come here already". Then Alfredo would holler back something like *"Mangmangan"* ("we're eating") or George would holler back *"Wen, Manong"* ("yes, older person").]

Thursday, October 30, 1986
My House, Gomez, Cabarroguis, Quirino

Letter to Terry S.

We got up at 5:30 AM and George left. He didn't come until nearly 7:15 PM last night, after I hollered for him. I started breakfast, took my water buffalo to pasture and then I returned home and finished cooking. I ate, did dishes and got ready for the day. It rained off and on all day today. I went to Alfredo's to talk for a while and then returned home. After a while George came and we moved tree seedlings around in the nursery so as to put all of the empty bags together to be able to replant them. He left at about 11:00 AM to eat lunch, so I did the same. Then I figured October's expenses to date and did some other paperwork. After that I napped from about noon until 1:00 PM, got up and after a while I went and moved my water buffalo at 2:15 PM. [You ask why? Because we would pasture our water buffaloes by tying them to a short stake driven into the ground with a rope that was about ten meters in length. After a few hours the water buffalo would have eaten all of the grass within that ten meter radius and needed to be moved to a new spot to be able to find more grass.] I returned home and wrote the above letter and by then it was 4:00 PM so I fetched water, cut up vegetables for supper and then went to get my water buffalo at 4:20 PM. Then I returned home and started cooking supper. The rain continues now at 4:56 PM. After eating supper and doing dishes I'll go to the canteen and get cigarettes and then stop at George's to ask him to come early tonight. If they haven't eaten yet by then maybe I'll write another letter or else study for a while; I hope he comes early tonight though. AWANEN!

Friday, October 31, 1986
My House, Gomez, Cabarroguis, Quirino

Letter from Dad and seeds from San & Jack G.

₱92 + 200 – 220 = ₱72							
Rides	16	Kerosene	7	Cigarettes	7	Marienda	8
Lunch	30	Coffee	51	Rice	11	Coconut	4
Batteries	12	Curry	35	Food	24	Candy	15
						TOTAL	₱220

We got up at 5:45 AM and George left – he actually came at 6:15 PM last night. I started cooking breakfast and George came to get my water buffalo to take it to pasture. I ate, did, dishes got ready for the day and headed down the mountain for Burgos and eventually Santiago. It rained all day due to Typhoon Susan. I got to Santiago and the only things I really needed were coconut, diket and sugar for making rice cake tomorrow, so I shopped very quickly. I ate lunch at 11:15 AM and was ready to head for home. I stopped at Gundaway to get mail but there was nobody at the post office, so I let myself in with my house key – which happened to fit their door lock! So, I got my mail and headed home. I climbed via the high road – in the mud it's easier than the low road. I got home at about 3:30 PM, read my mail and George brought my water buffalo for me. Then Alfredo came, we talked for a while and he helped cut up things for supper. Now it's 6:15 PM and I'm going to finish this and go fetch water and go to the canteen for cigarettes and then take the rice cake ingredients to George's house and hope he's ready to come here already. AWANEN!

Saturday, November 1, 1986
My House, Gomez, Cabarroguis, Quirino

Postcard to Chris & Mary M.

We got up at 5:30 AM and George left; he came just before 7:15 PM last night, after I hollered. I started cooking breakfast, pastured my nuang, ate, did dishes and got ready for the day. I went to George's to talk for a while and then returned home and did laundry. It stopped raining after I finished doing laundry and it even got hot, that was nice. I did some straightening up of the house and then went to George's to see if he wanted to plant some trees seeds; he said by and by. I waited a while and then ate lunch and wrote a postcard to Chris asking about the film which I sent him in April. I started packing for Manila and George came. We replanted all the plastic bags that didn't have anything growing in them yet. Oh, I forgot, I went to get my nuang at 10:45 AM. We stopped planting at 2:30 PM and pastured our nuangs again. When we returned, we planted seeds until we were finished. Remi brought rice cake for me. I fetched water, trimmed my beard, bathed and then it rained hard for 45 minutes. Fortunately, my clothes were already dry. At 4:30 PM we went to get our nuangs and then we returned to our homes. I cooked supper, ate, did dishes and now it's 6:47 PM and I'm waiting for George. I'm packed and ready to go to Manila in the morning. Now I'll study for a few minutes. I hope George comes soon. AWANEN!

Sunday, November 2, 1986
Malate Pension, Manila

₱72 + 200 – 132 = ₱140							
Rides	86	Cigarettes	12	Coke	4	Marienda	9
Toilet Paper	6	Lunch	15			TOTAL	₱132

We got up at 5:30 AM, I gave George my nuang's pasturing rope and foot medicine and he left. He didn't come until 8:15 PM last night. I left Gomez at 6:15 AM, took a jeepney to Santiago and then left Santiago at 9:20 AM. Pantranco Buses are on strike so I had to take this old beat up Sarki Tours bus which had a weak engine and a flat tire, and then lots of traffic didn't put us in Manila until 6:00 PM. I found a Mabini Street jeepney and got to Malate Pension at about 7:00 PM. I saw JB right away and we talked for a bit. There were no dorm rooms available so I ended up in a private room at ₱80 per night – bummer! After a shower we all went over to Brook's house for a party. There wasn't much excitement, but lots of talking. Now it's 10:49 PM, very late for me to be going to bed tonight, so I'll call it good and end. AWANEN!

Monday, November 3, 1986
Malate Pension, Manila

₱140 + 400 – 405 = ₱135							
Meals	162	Postage	210	Postcards	3	Rides	4
Ice Cream	9	Marienda	5	Coke	4	Cigarettes	8
						TOTAL	₱405

I got up at 4:40 AM, showered and got ready to leave. At 5:30 AM the buses left for the special Mass by Cardinal Sin. Peace Corps Director Ruppe and Cory Aquino were there! It was quite nice. After that I went to the Peace Corps Office for medical stuff, got done with that and talked with Brooke for a while. They made a dentist appointment for me and then we had luncheon speeches and finally lunch at 1:00 PM or so. Then I waited around to get my travel reimbursement and Sue T. and I went to the dentist for my 3:00 PM appointment. I got my teeth cleaned and checked and they're all okay. Then I went to the post office to buy aerogrammes and then to Harrison Plaza looking for a book on water buffaloes. After that I returned to Malate Pension and some of us went to the Seafront Restaurant for Mongolian Barbeque – it was delicious. Now it's 9:48 PM and it's still very hot today. I'm going to finish this and crash. Tomorrow at 9:00 AM we leave for Tagaytay. AWANEN!

Tuesday, November 4, 1986
Forgotten Lodging House, Tagaytay City, Cavite

₱135 + 100 – 156 = ₱79							
Breakfast	30	Room	93	Cigarettes	15	Candy	5
Coke	3	Cookies	10			TOTAL	₱156

I got up at 5:30 AM, showered, got ready for the day, ate breakfast at Malate Pension and then headed over to the Peace Corps Office. I caught the bus to Tagaytay City from the Peace Corps Office at 9:00 AM and got here at about 11:00 AM. I checked into a room and then I ate lunch – food is short here – shades of the Cebu training – bummer! All afternoon we had training sessions and more training sessions. There was not a lot to get out of it all and not too interesting, but not too boring either. We stopped for supper, which was also short on food. We sat around for a while and talked after supper and then we went to the evening session from 7:30 to 9:15 PM. That entire session was spent on honesty, thievery and etcetera. I left before it was over. Now it's 9:49 PM and noisy in the hall but I'm going to try and sleep anyway. AWANEN!

Wednesday, November 5, 1986
Forgotten Lodging House, Tagaytay City, Cavite

Postcard to George.

₱79 – 22 = ₱57							
Cigarettes	18	Coke	4			TOTAL	₱22

I got up at 5:30 AM showered, got ready for the day and went upstairs for breakfast. After breakfast I wrote the postcard to George and dropped it off at the post office and then went to class. There was another planning session today, but first we had an address from Director Ruppe and then after the address we had marienda. Then we had the planning session and then lunch and then back to class again. They kept us busy until 7:00 PM and then we had a supper break. After that I found Sue T. and we talked for a while and took a walk out to the Taal Volcano Overlook. Now it's 9:50 PM and I think I'll shower before bed because Sue and I have a plan to walk back to the overlook in the morning for some pictures before breakfast. AWANEN!

Thursday, November 6, 1986
Malate Pension, Manila

₱57 + 300 – 178 = ₱179							
Marienda	16	Ash Tray	20	Household	15	Candy	5
Cigarettes	17	Supper	100	Rides	5	TOTAL	₱178

I got up at 5:30 AM and got ready to go upstairs for coffee and then breakfast. Then I got ready for the day and Sue T. and I went for a walk to the Taal Volcano Overlook place again. We took some pictures and talked for a while and then returned for class, which was really bullshit this morning. We finished at about 11:30 AM, ate lunch and then at 2:00 PM we headed back to Manila. We arrived in Manila at about 3:15 PM and I give the Peace Corps some more pee and blood samples and then went to Malate Pension to check in. They had a dorm type room this time. After a while several of us went to the Seafront Restaurant for supper. We returned from there and talked for a while and now it's 9:23 PM. I'm going to finish this and sleep. It was a pretty unexciting day. AWANEN!

Friday, November 7, 1986
Malate Pension, Manila

Received ₱918 per diem payment.

₱179 + 600 – 719 = ₱60							
Meals	200	Seeds	123	T-Shirts	105	Books	70
Ice Cream	30	Cigarettes	5	Rides	5	Presents	36
Lodging	50	Laundry	29	Candy	6	Food	24
Fruit	13	Coke	8	Misc.	15	TOTAL	₱178

I got up at 5:30 AM, showered, went downstairs, ate breakfast and talked with people for a while. Then I went over to the Peace Corps Office and got my per diem payment and after that Chester and I headed out for Rizal Avenue and some book stores. We finished that, returned to Malate Pension for lunch and after that Chester went to the dentist and I went to Robinson's Department Store in search of gifts. I returned to Malate Pension at about 4:00 PM and killed time until JB and Katie, Chester and I went out to supper at an expensive Japanese restaurant. After supper we returned to the pension to eat ice cream and then I came up to my room. Now it's 9:44 PM and I'm ready to sleep. AWANEN!

Saturday, November 8, 1986
Host Family, Bonfal East, Bayombong, Nueva Vizcaya

₱60 + 200 – 158 = ₱102							
Meals	24	Rides	72	Presents	37	Bread	5
Beer	20					TOTAL	₱158

I got up at 5:10 AM, bathed and went downstairs. I met JB and Katie and we took a taxi to the Dalin Liner Bus Terminal and right away there was a bus. There's a typhoon going on again so we had real strong rain most of the day. I got off at Bayombong at about 1:00 PM, bought a gift and headed for Bonfal East. I arrived here at about 1:30 PM or so and it felt good to come to this home again. My family is happy to see me! We sat and talked for quite a while. After dark Ronald and I went to Solano to get medicine for Barbara, Rebecca's baby, because she has diarrhea. In Solano we drank two beers each and then we returned home and ate supper. After that Herbert and three companions came here. Now it's 8:48 PM and I'm tired. AWANEN!

Sunday, November 9, 1986
Host Family, Bonfal East, Bayombong, Nueva Vizcaya

₱102 + 117 – 10 = ₱209					
Cigarettes	10			TOTAL	₱10

We got up at 6:00 AM and I got ready for the day. We finally ate breakfast at about 8:30 AM and it was raining hard so we sat around for a while doing nothing and then slept for a while. One of Herbert's companions bought a 4x4 and they woke me up to tell me that I have to drink to celebrate. After a while we went to the vegetable farm – about eight or nine of us – in the 4x4. We got a few coconuts, drank the coconut milk and ate the meat and then we went to a house where Herbert's sixty-year-old companion wants to BUY a 17 year old wife!! The father of the girl wasn't home so we waited and waited and waited. It rained more and finally at 3:00 PM we came home and ate lunch. After that I had a headache so I slept for an hour or so again. At 4:30 PM or so I went back downstairs and we ate some dog meat. Finally at about

7:40 PM or so we ate supper. Father, Herbert's companions and Herbert still had not returned at that time. They came home about 8:05 PM and the old man succeeded in making a deal with the girl's father to buy her for his wife, so he is happy (I wonder what the girl feels like though?) Now it's 8:47 PM and I'm bored out of my mind. Today has really dragged on forever – it feels like a week. I'll be happy to go home tomorrow. AWANEN!

Monday, November 10, 1986
My House, Gomez, Cabarroguis, Quirino

Letters from Ardis B., Chad D., San & Jack G. and Bob S. Package from Bob S. too – Kool-Aid & batteries.

₱209 – 84 = ₱125							
Cigarettes	10	Rides	9	Household	4	Marienda	5
Coke	4	Food	52			TOTAL	₱84

We got up at 5:45 AM, talked for a while, ate breakfast, bathed, got ready for the day and left Bonfal East at about 8:15 AM. Ronald and I walked to the waiting shed and Chester was right behind us. Then Ronald's uncle happened to come along and the three of us companioned to Solano. From there we got a Vizcaya Liner and continued on to Cordon. I got off at Cordon at about 10:30 AM and I went to market there. I did my shopping and then caught a jeepney to Gundaway, got to the post office at 12:01 PM and of course there was nobody there – gone to lunch. They came back at 12:30 PM, I got my mail and left. I got to Burgos at 1:10 PM, climbed the mountain via the high road and got home at about 2:10 PM. I fetched water and started to unpack and then Alfredo came to talk for a while. He left at about 3:45 PM and I bathed and then started cooking supper. At about 5:00 PM Alfredo brought my water buffalo back and talked for a while until 6:15 PM. He left, I ate, washed dishes and it started raining hard. Now it's 6:33 PM and I'm waiting for George to come – I hope the rain stops soon and I also hope George comes soon. AWANEN

Tuesday, November 11, 1986
My House, Gomez, Cabarroguis, Quirino

Letter to Bob S.

We got up at 5:30 AM and George left. I went to get him just after 7:00 PM last night. I started cooking breakfast and took my nuang to pasture but I forgot the rope and had to return for it. I returned to the place where I left her and she was gone so I hollered for George and he came and helped me find her and pasture her. I returned home again, finished cooking breakfast, ate, washed dishes and got ready for the day. Then I went to George's for a minute and he had gone to Burgos to sell mandarins so

I returned home, cleaned the floor, the table, the benches and etc. and then slept from 9:00 to 11:00 AM. Then I went and moved my water buffalo. It rained off and on all day so I didn't have to bring her home. I returned and wrote the letter to Bob S. and then Alfredo came by. We trimmed off the dead leaves on my banana trees and started pulling weeds in the lawn and then it rained hard so we quit and talked until 3:00 PM. Then he left and I pulled weeds until 4:00 PM and went to get my water buffalo. She ran and I fell off. I got back on and she ran again and I fell off again. I finally got home and hollered for George. After a while he came and I told him the story. He left again, after saying he will come early tonight. I fetched water, cooked supper, ate, washed dishes and now it's 6:16 PM and I'm waiting for George. I'll study and read my *Newsweek* until he comes or else holler for him at 7:00 PM. AWANEN!

Wednesday, November 12, 1986
My House, Gomez, Cabarroguis, Quirino

Letters to Dad and Nestor.

We got up at 5:30 AM and George left; he came just after 6:30 PM last night. I put my nuang on the other side of the creek, cooked breakfast, ate, washed dishes and got ready for the day. Alfredo came to borrow my pickaxe and then I went to his house and asked George if he wanted to go to the farm today, but he didn't so I pastured my nuang and then went and helped him repair their broken cart. It rained off and on all day again and at 10:00 AM it rained hard so I came home. I slept from 11:00 AM to noon, got up and went to move my water buffalo. After that I ate lunch and wrote the above letters to Nestor and Dad. At 4:00 PM I fetched water and bathed. At 4:30 PM I went to George's and we went to get our water buffaloes, he left his there so it was a new experience for me to be riding my nuang and see George walking. As we were coming down the hill I asked George to come early tonight; he said yes, but who knows? Now it's 5:47 PM and I'm only cooking supper. It's going to be a late supper for me tonight it looks like. I'll eat, do dishes and hope that George comes early. I'll holler for him at 7:00 PM if he isn't here yet by then. AWANEN!

Thursday, November 13, 1986
My House, Gomez, Cabarroguis, Quirino

We got up at 5:45 AM and George left; he came at 6:45 PM last night without hollering. I cooked breakfast, ate, did dishes, got ready for the day and then pastured my nuang. George didn't wait for me. After that I talked with George for a while and then came home and laid down but didn't sleep. I got up and went to move my nuang at 10:00 AM and George didn't wait for me again. After I moved her I returned home and waited for George until 11:30 AM and then went to the farm to search for him, but he wasn't there. I hollered and searched and then I returned home at lunchtime.

At 2:00 PM I went back to George's house, but he had not yet arrived so I went and moved my nuang again and returned home. At 3:30 PM I went to the farm again and hollered and searched some more and then searched all of the pasturing places for his nuangs but I couldn't find them or him. I got my nuang and came home, but George still hadn't arrived. By that time we were all getting worried about him. I waited at his house and he finally showed up at 5:10 PM and said that he had gone to a birthday party. Now it's 5:53 PM and I'm still cooking supper. I hope George comes early, I have lots of stories to tell him tonight about all my wanderings in search of him today. George has slept here 172 nights now. AWANEN!

Friday, November 14, 1986
My House, Gomez, Cabarroguis, Quirino

Letters from Bob S. Packages from Chris & Mary M. and Cynthia B. Postcard arrived that I sent George from Tagaytay.

₱125 + 100 – 138 = ₱87							
Coffee	27	Kerosene	7	Rides	6	Cookies	4
Candy	14	Coke	3	Postage	3	Cigarettes	9
Food	56	Misc.	9			TOTAL	₱138

We got up at 5:45 AM, I gave George my water buffalo pasturing rope and he left. I cooked breakfast, ate, did dishes and got ready to go to Burgos. I arrived there at about 8:30 AM and had to wait until 9:15 AM for a ride so I didn't arrive at Gundaway until about 9:45 AM. I got my mail, did my shopping and then I returned to the post office and waited for them to sort today's mail. Then I caught a jeepney for Burgos at about 11:15 AM. I climbed the mountain via the high road. I started up the mountain at 11:45 AM and got home at about 12:30 PM. I went to George's but he had gone to Burgos to play some numbers game because he had a dream last night. At about 2:00 PM Alfredo came and we went and searched for my nuang to move it to new pasture. We found it at about 3:00 PM, moved it and returned home. At about 3:30 PM George came home and shortly after that I came home. I fetched water, bathed and started cooking supper. My water buffalo is remaining at pasture tonight. Now it's 5:55 PM, I've eaten and dishes are washed. It rained all day again today. I'm waiting for George; he came at 6:15 PM last night so he'll probably be late tonight. AWANEN!

Saturday, November 15, 1986
My House, Gomez, Cabarroguis, Quirino

Letter to Chris & Mary M.

We got up at 5:45 AM and George left. He came at 6:30 PM last night. I started cooking rice, drank a quick cup of coffee and we went to move our nuangs.

Then I returned home, finished cooking breakfast, ate, did dishes and got ready for the day. I did laundry until 10:00 AM and then we went and got our nuangs. It was sunny all day today. After that I did very little. I pulled weeds in the north yard for a while and then at noon I ate lunch and drank coffee. George said he would come to help clean the nursery but he never did all day. At 1:30 PM we took the nuangs back to pasture and then I returned and talked with Alfredo until 2:30 PM. Then I came home and started the letter to Chris and Mary. At 3:30 PM I stopped, fetched water, bathed and cut up onions and garlic for supper. At 4:30 PM we went to get our nuangs and George broke the news that he's going to a wedding at Calaocan tonight and therefore he won't be coming – bummer! It wasn't really a very productive day but I enjoyed the sun. Things are starting to dry out. Now it's 6:30 PM so I guess I'll finish the letter to Chris and Mary and maybe do another letter too, seeing as I'll have no companion tonight. It's even clear tonight and there's nearly a full moon. AWANEN!

Sunday, November 16, 1986
My House, Gomez, Cabarroguis, Quirino

I got up at 5:30 AM with no companion. I drank a cup of coffee, started cooking breakfast and took my nuang to pasture. Then I returned home, ate, did dishes and got ready for the day. I went to George's house until 8:00 AM and listened to the story about the wedding. I returned home and did more laundry again today. I finished that and rested until it was time to go get our nuangs at 10:00 AM and then I returned home and finished the letter to Chris and Mary that I started writing yesterday. I took some pictures of my winged beans and then I ate lunch, drank coffee and pulled weeds in the south lawn. At 1:30 PM I took my nuang back to pasture and upon returning, I stopped at George's to see if he wants to pull some weeds in the nursery – he said no, so I came home and started to put runo in the southeast garden and George came to help with the nursery! We did that until 3:30 PM and then I fetched water, cut up vegetables for supper and went to get my nuang at 4:30 PM. I returned home, bathed and now it's 5:45 PM and I'm still cooking supper. I hope George comes early tonight. Last night he came at about 7:00 PM and then at 7:30 PM Alfredo came to tell him that Junior was waiting for him. George thought that they weren't going to the wedding after all, but they ended up going. Now supper is ready and I'm going to eat. AWANEN!

Monday, November 17, 1986
My House, Gomez, Cabarroguis, Quirino

We got up at 5:30 AM and George left; he came just after 6:00 PM last night. I started cooking breakfast, drank coffee and took my nuang across the creek only for temporary pasturing. I ate, did dishes, got ready for the day and then Alfredo, George, Sip and I went to the vegetable farm. We left at about 7:30 AM. Oh, I forgot, Junior came before we left and gave me some pork, I don't know why. George was harrowing when we got to the farm. Alfredo used my nuang to plow and I removed the weeds from the plowed area. After a while George planted corn, first the popcorn that I gave him and then the yellow corn. We stopped at 11:00 AM and ate the lunch we had taken with us, rested for a while and then we continued work again at about 1:30 PM or so. We worked until 4:30 PM and came home via a really steep path that I had never traveled before, I didn't fall off my nuang though. I got home, fetched water, took a quick dip in the creek, but not a full bath and started cooking supper. Now it's 6:06 PM and supper is still cooking. I hope George manages to time his coming with my completion of eating and washing dishes. We had no rain today and it wasn't too hot either, overall it was a pretty nice day. AWANEN!

Tuesday, November 18, 1986
My House, Gomez, Cabarroguis, Quirino

Postcard to San & Jack G.

We got up at 5:30 AM and George left; he came just after 6:00 PM again last night. I started cooking breakfast, drank coffee and put my nuang on the other side of the creek. Then I finished cooking, ate, got ready for the day and George, Alfredo and I went to the vegetable farm. Today we started plowing my farm. I removed runo by the roots with the pickaxe, Alfredo plowed and George planted vegetables on his farm. We worked at that until 11:30 AM and stopped for lunch. After we finished eating George went back to the house to get more seed. He returned immediately and starting at about 1:30 PM we continued working. Alfredo plowed more of my vegetable farm and I removed roots. What a long day – really! We worked until a bit past 4:30 PM and then Alfredo and I were waiting for George to come up the hill to meet us and head for home. By and by Alfredo hollered but George had apparently already left, so we came home and got here at about 5:15 PM. I fetched water and bathed but I didn't start cooking until 6:00 PM or so. Now it's 6:28 PM and I wasn't even going to cook tonight but I think George will be late because when I went there they weren't yet eating and there were a bunch of people visiting. The MAF technician returned today. I discovered that my HP-41 calculator was stolen today. Somebody broke into my house without making a mark on anything and stole it. They must have had quite a search because it was pretty well hidden in a box of clothes. That appears to be the only thing missing!! AWANEN!

Wednesday, November 19, 1986
My House, Gomez, Cabarroguis, Quirino

We got up at 5:00 AM and George left; he came right at 7:00 PM last night, just as I finished washing dishes – wonderful timing. I told him about the theft of my calculator and we talked about that for a while and then we slept. Seeing as we got up early, I cooked breakfast, ate did dishes, got ready for the day and I was ready to go to the farm at 7:00 AM, but Alfredo, his wife and I talked about the calculator theft until 7:30 AM and then we left for the farm. The plow broke yesterday so all I did today was remove roots from the area on my farm that Alfredo plowed yesterday. George loaned out the *sagad* (harrow) so I couldn't even try to *agsagad*, oh well. We stopped at 11:30 AM for lunch and then George and I started making a *calapaw* (a covered rest hut). We dug holes for the corner posts and then he continued to plow for a while and I continued to remove roots from my farm until 4:30 PM. Then we came home, I fetched water, started cooking supper, bathed and now it's 6:02 PM and I'm still cooking. I hope George comes early again tonight; he's been early every night this week, so tonight he'll probably be late, we'll see what happens. AWANEN!

Thursday, November 20, 1986
My House, Gomez, Cabarroguis, Quirino

Letters to Mark W. and Fred & Cynthia B.

We got up at 5:30 AM and George left. I went to get him at 7:00 PM last night. I started breakfast drank coffee and put my nuang on the other side of the creek to pasture. I finished cooking, ate breakfast, did dishes, got ready for the day and took my nuang to a better pasturing place. Alfredo went to town today and George went to the farm. I stayed home and put up runo for the beans in the southeast garden to climb on and then I wrote the above letter to Fred and Cynthia. I moved my nuang and then goofed off for a while. I ate lunch and slept for an hour and then when I woke up I started on the letter to Mark W. I went and moved my nuang again, returned and finished the letter to Mark. I tied the runo in the southeast garden and Pedring came and got another hundred bags of tree seedlings. Then at 4:15 PM I went to George's for a few minutes to talk and after that I went to get my water buffalo. Oh, I forgot, at 3:30 PM I fetched water, trimmed my beard and bathed. After I returned with my water buffalo I started cooking supper. Now it's 5:40 PM and I hope George comes early tonight, without hollering. Maybe after eating and doing dishes I'll start another letter, we'll see what happens as the evening progresses. Today marks the 55% mark in my 26.5 month stay here. It rained last night and showered off and on today. AWANEN!

Friday, November 21, 1986
My House, Gomez, Cabarroguis, Quirino

Letters from Bill & Andi J., JB & Katie F. and Brooke F.

₱87 + 300 – 232 = ₱155							
Rides	8	Cigarettes	13	Coke	3	Marienda	11
Household	15	Coffee	27	Food	59	Candy	17
Rice	53	Misc.	26			TOTAL	₱232

We got up at 5:45 AM and George left; he came at 6:45 PM last night. I gave him my nuang pasturing rope before he left and then I cooked breakfast, ate, did dishes, got ready for the day and headed down the mountain for Burgos at 7:20 AM. I got a ride to Gundaway pretty quickly, got the above mail, did my marketing and went to Diffun, where I found out the meeting day had been moved to Monday; so I'm not going to go. I puttered around the office for a while and ate lunch in Diffun. I left there at 1:20 PM or so, stopped at the post office again, but the truck didn't come today with mail, so on to Burgos. I climbed via the high road; it's in much better shape than the low road right now. I got home at about 3:30 PM, fetched water, bathed and started cooking supper. I ate, did dishes and went to George's for a few minutes to see why my nuang hasn't been returned – it's because Alfredo had arrived home late and tied her at his house. Okay, I don't know why, but no problem. Now it's 6:06 PM and when I was just at Alfredo's they had not eaten yet, but I hope George manages to come before 7:00 PM. AWANEN!

Saturday, November 22, 1986
My House, Gomez, Cabarroguis, Quirino

Letter to JB & Katie F.

We got up at 5:30 AM and George left; he came just before 7:00 PM last night – before I hollered. I cooked breakfast, did dishes, got ready for the day and then I went to George's, but Alfredo and George had gone to two different banana plantations to harvest bananas. Alfredo had taken my nuang (that must be why he put her at his house last night) and George had gone to the banana plantation near my farm, so I went there and helped harvest bananas. We filled up the big cart and came home by a different path than usual because the usual path presently has some huge holes. We got home at about 11:30 AM and I came home to eat lunch. Then I napped for 45 minutes, got up and wrote the above letter to JB and Katie. I returned to George's for a few minutes to talk, but he had gone to meet his father with the other cart so I came home and worked in the southeast garden for a while. I quit at 4:00 PM, fetched water and bathed. I kind of slacked off all day today so I wasn't hungry and didn't bother to cook supper. Alfredo came to get some medicine for his ulcer and we talked for an hour and then Sip came to get him for supper and brought me some chicken, so he left. Now it's 6:30 PM and I'm waiting for George. Maybe I'll start a letter to Ardis. AWANEN!

Sunday, November 23, 1986
My House, Gomez, Cabarroguis, Quirino

Nuang mating day.
Letter to Ardis B. and Bob S.

We got up at 5:30 AM and George left; he came at 6:40 PM last night. I cooked breakfast, ate, did dishes and got ready for the day. I went to George's to return the plate that Sip brought the chicken on last night. They had gone to Burgos to sell bananas today so I returned home and did laundry until 9:30 AM or so and then I took a short break and built tree protectors around the three small banana trees that the pigs keep eating and I planted one Madre de Cacao seedling near the toilet. Then I cleaned the area around the *kamote* patch, ate lunch, drank coffee and wrote the above letter to Ardis. I took a break and fetched water and then I started the letter to Bob S. At 4:00 PM I quit, bathed and started cooking supper. Then I happened to go to George's just in time to see their bull nuang mate with my cow nuang. So, it's now apparent that she's not yet pregnant (the person whom I bought her from thought she was already pregnant and that was why he wanted additional money at the last minute). I came home, finished cooking supper, ate, did dishes and now it's 6:14 PM. George has been here every night lately before 7:00 PM so we'll see if that same pattern continues tonight; in the meantime I'll try to finish the letter to Bob then I'll study if George isn't here yet by then. AWANEN!

Monday, November 24, 1986
My House, Gomez, Cabarroguis, Quirino

We got up at 5:30 AM and George left. I went to get him last night at 7:00 PM and we came here at 7:30 PM. I had an earache last night, very strange – I have not had an earache in years. I cooked breakfast, ate, did dishes, got ready for the day, went to Alfredo's and we went to get my nuang on the way to the farm. I harrowed for a little bit and then Alfredo finished the harrowing and he plowed my farm again. Then we planted. First was pallang then *utong*, lettuce, eggplant, watermelon, beets, peas, turnips, pechoy (Chinese cabbage) and radishes – plus a little sweet corn and *parya*. That took until noon and then we ate and rested for a while. In the afternoon I helped clean the *kasabaan* (banana plantation). My job was to remove the dead leaves from the banana trees. We stopped at 4:30 PM and came home. We bathed our nuangs and then continued on to the house. I cooked supper and ate a little but I couldn't finish it all because I have a splitting headache. I did dishes and now it's 6:47 PM and I'm waiting for George; he said he's going to listen to the Ilokano radio drama at their house tonight before he comes, if that's true it will be 8:30 PM before he comes, I hope he was only joking me – we'll see I guess. AWANEN!

Tuesday, November 25, 1986
My House, Gomez, Cabarroguis, Quirino

Letter to Brooke F.

We got up at 5:45 AM and George left; he didn't come until 8:30 PM last night, after the radio drama. I cooked breakfast, ate, did dishes, got ready for the day and pastured my nuang. Then I went to talk with Alfredo until he was ready to go to the farm. I remained home today to rest and recuperate. I sewed up my pants which had the gaping hole in the knee and re-sewed buttons on one of my shirts. I went and moved my nuang at 10:30 AM and then returned home and wrote the above letter to Brooke. I cooked mungo beans for lunch, finished all that at 1:00 PM and napped until 2:00 PM. Then I went to move my nuang again and when I returned I talked with Alfredo's wife for a while and then came home. I fetched water, bathed and killed time for a while and then at 4:30 PM I went and got my nuang and brought her home. Then I went to George's for a few minutes to talk, returned home, cooked supper, ate, did dishes and now it's 6:51 PM and George just came. Earlier he said he'd be late tonight but he's early anyway, so I'm happy. AWANEN!

Wednesday, November 26, 1986
My House, Gomez, Cabarroguis, Quirino

Letter to Bill & Andi J.

We got up at 5:45 AM and George left. I started cooking breakfast, drank coffee and then put my nuang on the other side of the creek to pasture. I finished eating, did the dishes, got ready for the day and talked with George for a while about chickens. After that I pastured my nuang and returned and talked with George for a while longer. It rained all day today so we didn't go to the farm. I returned home, cleaned house and rearranged my books. At 10:30 AM I went to move my nuang, returned home and killed time until lunch. I ate and then napped from 12:00 to 1:30 PM. I woke up and there was a guy taking shelter under the roof of my porch – he was a real asshole and just wanted to argue about anything and everything so at 2:00 PM I just told him that I had to move my water buffalo, locked the house and left. I moved my nuang and went to Alfredo's house where the MOS people had just sprayed DDT for mosquito/malaria control. I talked for a while, came home and the MOS people came and sprayed my house too. I wrote the above letter to Bill and Andi and highlighted more words in the Ilokano dictionary which I don't yet know. Alfredo came to talk and I started cooking supper. When it was finished Alfredo left and I ate and now it's 6:18 PM and dishes are done. I'm waiting for George; he says he'll come after the radio drama again tonight – bummer. AWANEN!

Thursday, November 27, 1986
My House, Gomez, Cabarroguis, Quirino

Letter to Chad D.

We got up at 6:00 AM and George left; he came at about 6:30 PM last night. I cooked breakfast, ate, did dishes, got ready for the day and went to move my water buffalo. Then I returned and Alfredo and I went to the place near the farm where a guy is making charcoal and I ordered five sacks and then we went to the farm. At 10:00 AM I came back to move my nuang, returned home and used the *lampaso* to clean the floor to remove the DDT residue. Then I ate lunch and read part of the book Chris and Mary sent me entitled *"America 2040"* – it's pretty good and also fast moving. I napped for an hour, got up and drank a cup of coffee and then went to Alfredo's house, talked with his wife for a while and then I went to move my nuang shortly after 2:00 PM. I returned home, fetched water, wrote the above letter and then bathed and started cooking supper. I went to George's for a while and they gave me some peanuts, which I came home and cooked. Now I'm finishing cooking supper at 5:52 PM. After eating and washing dishes I'll read more of the *"America 2040"* book until George comes. He says he'll come early tonight, whatever that means. AWANEN!

Friday, November 28, 1986
My House, Gomez, Cabarroguis, Quirino

Letters from San & Jack G., Tom & Barb H., Bob S., Barb W. and Health Unit.

₱155 + 300 – 173 = ₱282							
Cigarettes	10	Rides	4	Kerosene	7	Candy	14
Marienda	15	Food	80	Coffee	27	Household	6
Misc.	10					TOTAL	₱173

We got up at 5:40 AM and George left; he came about 6:45 PM last night. After drinking coffee and starting the rice we went and moved our nuangs and then I returned home, finished cooking breakfast, ate, did dishes, got ready for the day and at 7:40 AM I left for Burgos. I got a ride to Gundaway fairly quickly, but it was a slow one and it took 40 minutes to go ten kilometers, so I got to Gundaway at 9:30 AM, stopped at the post office and then continued on to market to do my week's shopping. Upon finishing with that I returned to the post office and waited while they sorted today's mail. Then I walked to the junction and waited for a ride. I headed up the mountain at 11:50 AM and arrived home at about 12:45 PM via the high road. I read my mail, ate lunch, drank coffee and took a 40 minute siesta. Then I woke up and went to George's to talk for a while. I returned home at 4:15 PM and finished reading the rest of the stuff that the Peace Corps sent and now it's 5:30 PM and I'm cooking supper. My nuang is remaining at pasture tonight. I hope George comes early tonight but I'll have to wait and see what happens. I had no visitors at all today. AWANEN!

Saturday, November 29, 1986
My House, Gomez, Cabarroguis, Quirino

We got up at 5:45 AM and George left; he came at about 6:40 PM last night. I cooked breakfast, ate, did dishes, got ready for the day and went to Alfredo's to find out what the plan of the day was. We went to the farm – George left first. We got there in the rain – it rained on and off all day again – I thought I would help cut grass in the banana plantation but Alfredo told me it would be better if I cut the grass on the remainder of my farm so that's what I worked on. I'm not a very efficient grass cutter, I'm very slow and I didn't even finish it over the course of the whole day. We stopped at about 11:00 AM for lunch, ate and then we set back to work practically immediately. I continued cutting the grass on my farm and they continued cutting grass in the banana plantation next to my farm. I was surprised when we quit early – at about 3:30 PM – and came home. When we got home I fetched water, bathed, went to George's for a couple of minutes and then returned home to start supper. Now it's 5:13 PM and the rice is cooking. After supper I'll do dishes and read my book *"America 2040"* while waiting for George. I hope he comes early tonight; he said he might listen to the radio drama at their house again, but we'll see what happens. AWANEN!

Sunday, November 30, 1986
My House, Gomez, Cabarroguis, Quirino

Letter to Bob S.

We got up at 5:45 AM and George left; he came just before 7:00 PM last night. I started cooking breakfast, drank coffee and then took my nuang to pasture. I returned home, finished cooking breakfast, ate, did dishes, got ready for the day and read the *"America 2040"* book for a while. I didn't do laundry today because it rained all day. After a while I finished reading the *"America 2040"* book. I hope Chris and Mary send me the second one in the series as it was a good book. At 10:15 AM I went and moved my nuang in the rain then I returned home after a brief stop at George's. Then I started calculating November's expenses. After that I figured averages for all items for the last 12 months using the good old HP-71 (at least the thieves left me one calculator). I ate lunch, drank coffee, napped from 1:40 to 2:10 PM and then I went and moved my nuang again and stopped briefly at George's again. I returned home and wrote the above letter. After that I prepared things for supper and at 4:50 PM I went and fetched water and started the charcoal fire. Then I went to the canteen for cigarettes and stopped at George's to ask him to come early tonight. He said he'd be a bit late tonight due to a singing contest on the radio which he wants to listen to. I returned home, finished cooking supper, ate, did dishes and now it's 6:34 PM and I'm waiting for George. I'll just have to wait and see what time he comes tonight. The rain has finally stopped. AWANEN!

Monday, December 1, 1986
My House, Gomez, Cabarroguis, Quirino

Letter to Barb W. and Health Unit.

We got up at 5:45 AM and George left – he didn't come until 8:15 PM last night because the singing contest ran late. I cooked breakfast, ate, did the dishes, got ready for the day and went to George's for a little bit. Then I went and moved my nuang and returned home. I wrote a program for the HP-71 for calculating averages for expenditures and after I was done with that and the testing of it I reentered the timber cruise program into the HP-71. By then it was past lunchtime so I ate, drank coffee and then took a siesta from 12:15 to 1:00 PM. When I got up I started the letter to Barbara and then I went and moved my nuang at 2:00 PM. I returned home and continued working on the letter to Barbara, went and fetched water, returned home and continued on the letter some more. I included the addresses of the refugee programs that she asked for and also gave her a list of what to bring with her and what not to bring. I finished that at 4:00 PM, bathed and prepared things for supper. At about 4:30 PM I went to George's for a few minutes and asked him to come early and then I went to the canteen for cigarettes. I returned home and started cooking supper. Now it's 5:43 PM and the vegetables are cooking. My nuang is staying at pasture tonight. I ate, did the dishes and now I'm waiting for George; I hope he comes early tonight; we'll see what happens. I'll holler for him at 7:00 PM if he isn't here yet by then. It rained most of the day today. AWANEN!

Tuesday, December 2, 1986
My House, Gomez, Cabarroguis, Quirino

We got up at 5:45 AM and George left; he came at about 6:05 PM last night, while I was still eating supper. We ran out of things to talk about and slept at about 7:15 PM. I cooked breakfast, ate, did dishes, got ready for the day and went to Alfredo's for a few minutes prior to moving my nuang. After I moved her I returned home and highlighted more words in the Ilokano Dictionary until Alfredo came here to talk. We talked until nearly 10:30 AM when I moved my nuang again and he left. I returned home and did laundry; the sun was shining weakly and it looked like it wouldn't rain. I finished the laundry, ate lunch, drank coffee, highlighted more words in the dictionary and at 2:00 PM I went to George's and talked for a few minutes and then I went to move my nuang. After that I returned to Alfredo's house and talked there until 3:00 PM. Then I returned home and pulled weeds in the southeast garden. There are several *utong* beans already fruiting and the pallang (winged beans) will be flowering in a couple days; I can't believe it, I only planted the *utong* beans on October 4th and the winged beans on October 5th, not even two months ago. I finished that at 4:30 PM took the clothes off the line – not yet dry – and then I fetched water and started cooking supper. I went to George's and then the canteen for cigarettes. George says he will be early tonight, but I can only wait and see if he really is. It's raining lightly now at 5:25 PM and I'm cooking my rice. AWANEN!

Wednesday, December 3, 1986
My House, Gomez, Cabarroguis, Quirino

Tom & Barb H. visit and stay here.

We got up at 5:45 AM and George left; he came at about 6:15 PM last night and we listened to the Ilokano radio drama. I cooked breakfast, ate, did dishes, got ready for the day and then I went and moved my nuang first thing. After that I went to George's to talk for a while and then Alfredo and I went off to Kudog's place to buy charcoal. We talked there until 10:00 AM and George and Junior came there after a while too. They had a cockfight – that was impressive! Then we returned home and I moved my nuang. After that I cleaned the *kamote* patch and then ate lunch, drank coffee and cleaned the yard more. At 2:20 PM I went to move my nuang again and then I went to get George to come here for a few minutes to show him some strange vine growing in the southeast garden. He came and looked at it, but he didn't know what it is. Then I continued cleaning the yard for a while. At 4:00 PM I fetched water, bathed and started cooking. Then at about 5:00 PM Tom and Barbara [fellow PCV's from I can't remember where] arrived, so I added more rice and cut up more vegetables and showed them around the place. We finished eating supper and Alfredo came by to talk. Tom did dishes and Alfredo stayed until 8:00 PM and then he went home. We were pretty tired so we retired to inside and after a while we slept. AWANEN!

Thursday, December 4, 1986
My House, Gomez, Cabarroguis, Quirino

Tom & Barb H. stay here.

₱282 – 10 = ₱272					
Cigarettes	10			TOTAL	₱10

We got up at 5:50 AM and I started the rice cooking. Then Tom and Barbara got up, we finished cooking, ate, Barbara did dishes and we got ready for the day. At about 9:00 AM we went and got my nuang and headed for the farm. We got there at about 10:00 AM and I showed Tom and Barbara all of George's farm and we looked at my farm too. The pallang is now coming up, the beets are up and also the *utong*, the pink and white beans from America (cranberry beans) and the Indian corn. Things are looking pretty good. I showed them George and Alfredo's banana plantation and then at about 11:00 AM we headed home. We pastured my nuang above the school and we got home at about noon. We washed up a bit and went to Boy's for the baptism lunch, but they weren't ready yet and Jose Garcia was already drunk so after a bit we went to George's house and met George and his mother and then returned home for coffee. At 2:15 PM Boy came and got us and we went there and ate, laughed and joked. Then at 3:45 PM I went and moved my nuang, but Tom and Barbara stayed there. When I returned home Tom and Barbara had escaped and were at the house. We went and fetched water, returned and started supper. Now it's 7:39 PM and supper is still cooking – I hope it hurries up, I'm hungry. It rained off and on all day today. AWANEN!

Friday, December 5, 1986
My House, Gomez, Cabarroguis, Quirino

Tom & Barb H. leave.

Letters from Sue T., Chad D. (and package too), Dad, John D., Brooke F., San & Jack G., JB & Katie F. and Ronald.

₱272 + 345 – 525 = ₱92							
Cigarettes	9	Rides	32	Coffee	52	Soap	20
Kerosene	7	Lunch	18	Coke	3	Batteries	12
Cooking Oil	22	Veggies	28	Candy	15	Treats	92
Household	22	Curry Powder	88	Postage	3	Food	90
Charcoal	12					TOTAL	₱525

We got up at 6:00 AM, started the rice cooking, drank a cup of coffee, I went to George's and told him where my nuang was pastured and then returned home. We finished cooking breakfast, ate, Barbara did dishes and we left the house at 8:50 AM. We arrived in Burgos at 10:15 AM, got a ride to Gundaway and I got my mail. Then we continued on to Santiago and arrived at 12:50 PM, ate lunch, had some ice cream and at 2:20 PM Tom and Barb left for Banaue and I rushed to do my shopping. I finished at 3:30 PM, left Santiago at 3:45 PM arrived at the bottom of the high road at 4:50 PM and headed up the mountain. I got home at 5:45 PM and I went to George's immediately to tell him that I'm home and asked him to please come early. I returned home, unpacked, put stuff away and at 6:15 PM George came. I calculated today's expenses and now it's 6:54 PM and time to end. AWANEN!

On December 3rd I mentioned that George and Junior had a cockfight.
On the following page is a photo of George with his fighting cock.
These were very impressive roosters, to say the least.

Just below is the very first photo that was taken of me on my very own nuang. This photo was taken by Tom, of Tom and Barbara H., who were guests at my humble abode for the previous couple of days.

Saturday, December 6, 1986
My House, Gomez, Cabarroguis, Quirino

We got up at 5:45 AM and George left; he came at 6:15 PM last night. I started cooking rice, drank coffee and then went to George's to pasture my nuang, which spent the night at their house, but he had already left to pasture both of them, so I waited for him to return and thanked him for pasturing my nuang. Then I returned home and finished cooking, ate, did dishes, got ready for the day and cleaned house until 10:00 AM. Then I went to George's and we went together to move our nuangs at 10:30 AM. After that I returned home and I cleaned house some more and read the mail that I got yesterday. At 12:30 PM I stopped for lunch, from 1:00 to 2:00 PM I napped and then I went to move my nuang. I returned home and highlighted more words in the Ilokano

Dictionary. Then I looked at my belongings and selected a bunch of things that I can give away for Christmas presents. At about 3:00 PM Alfredo came, I quickly went and fetched water so that I could make coffee for us and then we talked and drank coffee until 4:20 PM. He left and I bathed and started cooking supper. I went to get my nuang and now it's 5:46 PM and I'm still cooking – God damn wet charcoal! I hope George comes early, but we'll see what happens. AWANEN!

Sunday, December 7, 1986
My House, Gomez, Cabarroguis, Quirino

Letters to Brooke F. and John D.

We got up at 5:45 AM and George left; I went to get him at about 7:00 PM last night and then ended up staying there talking until nearly 8:00 PM. I started cooking breakfast, drank coffee and then went and pastured my nuang. I returned home and finished cooking, ate, did dishes and got ready for the day. I did laundry, as there was no rain today. I finished laundry at 10:00 AM, went and moved my nuang, returned home and then spread my charcoal out to dry. After that I wrote the letter to Brooke and then ate lunch and drank coffee. I laid down and rested from 1:00 to 1:30 PM and when I got up rain was threatening so I took the clothes off the line and picked up the charcoal. I moved my nuang at 2:00 PM, returned home and then went to George's to ask him to help me remove some of the shade from the tree nursery. He was reluctant to do so, but he came and we did that – plus – we also planted the remainder of the *Acacia auriculiformis* seeds and then I highlighted more words in the dictionary, went and got my nuang at 4:30 PM, fetched water, returned home and started cooking supper. Now it's 5:47 PM and the rice is nearly cooked. I hope George comes early tonight, but I don't know because there is another singing contest on the radio, just have to wait and see what happens. AWANEN!

Monday, December 8, 1986
My House, Gomez, Cabarroguis, Quirino

Letters to San & Jack G. and Dad.

We got up at 5:45 AM and George left; he didn't come until 9:00 PM last night because a bunch of them went for a stroll. I started cooking breakfast, drank coffee and put my nuang on the other side of the creek because I thought we were going to work at the farm today. After eating breakfast, doing dishes and getting ready for the day I went to George's and Alfredo told me that he had to help fix the road today. George and I pastured our nuangs and then we walked to the farm. George collected some food for their pig and I looked at my farm. The peas are now up, along with the *parya*, more pallang, the Indian corn, the cranberry beans from America and I don't know what else. We returned home at 9:00 AM and I talked with George until 10:00

AM and then returned home and weeded the lower garden for a while. At 11:00 AM I moved my nuang, returned home and ate lunch. After lunch I wrote the letter to Dad and then I moved my nuang again and talked with George some more. The weather was nice this morning, but it started raining at about 1:30 PM and it's been raining ever since. It was a chilly 66°F this morning with a high today of only 72°F. Now it's 5:49 PM and I'm still cooking supper. George told me that he'll come early tonight, I hope so, but we'll have to wait and see. I wrote the letter to San and Jack just before supper. AWANEN!

Tuesday, December 9, 1986
My House, Gomez, Cabarroguis, Quirino

Letter to Chad D.

We got up at 5:50 AM and George left; he came at 6:40 PM last night. I cooked breakfast, ate, did dishes, got ready for the day and went to talk with George for a minute and then I moved my nuang. I returned and talked with Alfredo for a while and came home and did not much at all. At 10:30 AM I went to move my nuang again and then I returned and talked with George for a half hour or so. I returned home, worked on weeding the lower garden until lunchtime, ate lunch, drank coffee and slept for an hour. I got up and wrote the letter to Chad, thanking him for the cookies that he sent and then at 3:00 PM I went and moved my nuang again. I returned and talked with George until 3:45 PM and then returned home, fetched water, bathed, prepared the vegetables for supper and started the charcoal fire. I put the rice on to cook at 4:30 PM, went and got my nuang, bathed her in the stream below the house and tied her for the night. I went to Alfredo's for a few minutes to talk, returned home and the rice was done so I started cooking the vegetables and then returned to George's to ask him to come early tonight. I returned home again and started this journal entry early. Now it's 5:34 PM and the vegetables are nearly cooked. I'll eat, wash dishes and hope that George comes early, we'll see. If he's not here at 7:00 PM I'll holler. At 7:00 AM this morning it was again only 66°F and the high today was again only 72°F. There was only a little bit of rain today. AWANEN!

Wednesday, December 10, 1986
My House, Gomez, Cabarroguis, Quirino

₱92 – 37 = ₱55						
Charcoal	35	Cigarettes	2		TOTAL	₱37

We got up at 5:35 AM and George left; he came at about 6:15 PM last night. I started cooking breakfast, drank coffee and went to pasture my nuang. Then I returned home and finished cooking breakfast, ate, did dishes got ready for the day and went to George's to talk for a while. He was splitting firewood so I returned home and weeded the lower garden and removed the okra that is finished fruiting. George came to tell me that he knows where there's some charcoal that I can buy. After a while Alfredo came to talk and he stayed until 11:30 AM when I said I had to go and move my nuang. I moved her, came home, ate lunch, drank coffee and then slept until 1:00 PM. After a little while George came and we went and I bought three sacks of charcoal. We returned home and I helped him pick up the firewood that he had split and we put it under shelter. At 2:15 PM I went and moved my nuang and it rained hard for 15 minutes. I returned home and started figuring out how many days I've had visitors here. Alfredo came again at 4:00 PM and talked for a while and then I went and fetched water and prepared things for supper. At 4:30 PM I went and got my nuang, bathed, cooked supper, ate, did dishes and now it's only 6:05 PM but everything is done and I'm waiting for George, oh he is here right now. AWANEN!

Thursday, December 11, 1986
My House, Gomez, Cabarroguis, Quirino

Letter to Tom & Barb H.

₱55 – 5 = ₱50					
Cigarettes	5			TOTAL	₱5

We got up at 5:40 AM and George left; he came at 6:05 PM last night. I started cooking breakfast, drank coffee, pastured my nuang, returned home, finished cooking, ate, did dishes, got ready for the day and went to George's to talk for a few minutes. I returned home and pulled some more weeds in the lower garden and then I stopped at 10:00 AM and went to move my nuang. I returned home, killed time for a while and a guy came who I don't know and we talked for a while. I pulled weeds some more and that guy left – he didn't want to help pull weeds. I stopped at noon for lunch and coffee and then took a nap from 1:20 to 2:00 PM. I went to George's and he showed me his chickens. I still don't know a Texas chicken from a regular chicken! Then I moved my nuang, returned home and wrote the letter to Tom and Barb. I finished weeding the lower garden and Alfredo came. We cut up food for supper and then he left and I went and fetched water and then bathed. At 4:30 PM I lit the charcoal fire, started cooking my rice and went to get my nuang. I returned home, went to George's for a minute to ask him to come early and he said yes. I came home and continued cooking. Now it's 5:36 PM, the vegetables are done and I'll eat as soon as I'm done with this. I'll do the dishes after a while, wait for George and I'll study until he comes. AWANEN!

Friday, December 12, 1986
My House, Gomez, Cabarroguis, Quirino

Postcard to Tony S. No mail received today!

₱50 + 320 – 166 = ₱204							
Cigarettes	5	Food	65	Rides	4	Candy	27
Coffee	27	Household	5	Marienda	8	Bread	5
Misc.	20					TOTAL	₱166

We got up at 5:45 AM and George left; he came at about 6:25 PM last night. I started cooking breakfast, drank coffee and put my nuang on the other side of the creek. I finished cooking, ate, did dishes, got ready for the day and went to Alfredo's for a moment on my way to Burgos. There was very little rain this week so the trail down the mountain was in pretty good condition, but it still took an hour to get to Burgos for some reason, guess I walked slowly. I went to Gundaway and had no mail today. I went to market and did my shopping and then went to the post office again but the truck hadn't come yet so I headed home. I got to Burgos at 10:50 AM, climbed the mountain and got home at 12:01 PM via the high road. I ate lunch and slept for a half hour. Mateo stopped by and got six seedlings and left. I went to George's to talk with him for a few minutes and then returned home. I fetched water, pulled weeds in the southeast yard until 4:00 PM and then Alfredo came to talk. I prepared stuff for supper, started cooking and Alfredo left. I cooked supper and Alfredo returned my nuang and he left. Now it's 6:11 PM and I'm waiting for George. I guess I'll study for a while. AWANEN!

Saturday, December 13, 1986
My House, Gomez, Cabarroguis, Quirino

Postcard to Nestor.

We got up at 5:40 AM and George left; he came about 6:25 PM last night. I started cooking breakfast, drank coffee, pastured my nuang, returned home and finished cooking, ate, did dishes, got ready for the day and went to George's to talk for a few minutes. Then I returned home and did laundry. There was no rain again today; there's been none for a week or so now and it's really nice to have things dried out really good. After finishing laundry, I cleaned the house and swept the yard, which took until 10:00 AM. George and I went and moved our nuangs and bathed them and then he came here for a minute to take my picture but the film messed up and I destroyed the 12 pictures on that roll of film. After all I played with my HP-71 for a while the – memory module is fucking up, probably too damp. I ate lunch, drank coffee and played with the HP-71 some more and then at about 2:00 PM, just as I was getting ready to take my nuang back to pasture, Alfredo came with his wife and kids. They brought some *kaboy* [a kind of cassava dessert] to eat. They left at about 2:45 PM and then I pastured my nuang and killed time until 3:45 PM. Then I fetched water, bathed and prepared the fixings for supper. At 4:15 PM I went and bathed my nuang and took her back to pasture for the night. Now it's 5:17 PM and Ronald was supposed to come today, but I'd be willing to bet he won't be coming now. I'm cooking supper and when it's done I'll eat, wash dishes and hope George comes early. AWANEN!

Sunday, December 14, 1986
My House, Gomez, Cabarroguis, Quirino

₱204 + 300 – 384 = ₱120							
Rice	250	Cigarettes	10	Food	22	Rides	6
Candy	12	Coffee	27	Marienda	10	Kerosene	7
Household	40					TOTAL	₱384

We got up at 5:40 AM and George left; he came at 6:30 PM last night – he was here when I finished washing dishes. I cooked breakfast, ate, did dishes and got ready for the day. It rained for a half hour. I went and got my nuang from pasture and George, his mother and I went down the mountain. I pulled a half cart of bananas using my nuang – it was my first time to pull a cart with my nuang – interesting! We didn't get to Burgos until about 9:40 AM and after that I continued on to Gundaway and shopped for the above. I bought a *kaban* of rice – a whole 50 kilograms – and then we caught a ride back to Burgos at about 12:30 PM. We ate lunch and waited for the heat of the day to pass and then we headed up the mountain at about 2:00 PM. The yoke broke on George's nuang and he hitched the two carts together until eventually it pulled the box of the front cart [if you do not understand what this means, well, now in 2016 I don't either]. We finally got home at about 4:30 PM and Alfredo came. We drank coffee and I bathed my nuang and took her to pasture. I returned home and now it's 6:06 PM and I haven't started cooking yet, but I'm just having Miki noodles so it will be quick to cook. I hope George comes about 7:00 PM. AWANEN!

Monday, December 15, 1986
My House, Gomez, Cabarroguis, Quirino

Start letter to Sue T.

We got up at 6:00 AM and George left; he didn't come until 7:40 PM last night. I cooked breakfast, ate, did dishes, got ready for the day and went to George's to find out what time the Christmas program starts at the school. They said it will start at 8:00 AM so I came home and got dressed and returned there. At 10:00 AM we still hadn't left so I returned home and hid until I was sure they had all left [I was totally frustrated by then and didn't feel like going to a party at the school anyway] and then I moved my water buffalo and went to the farm to kill time. I returned home at about 1:00 PM and Alfredo came immediately and said he had a gift from George. A whole cooked chicken is what it was! (See Culture Notes – page 192.) I was really sad and depressed before that, but George's present did wonders for my spirits – to know that he cares enough about me that he would give me a present of a whole cooked chicken!

Alfredo stayed until 2:20 PM when I went and moved my nuang again; that is George and I went together to move our nuangs. I returned to George's and we talked for a while. Then I fetched water and started the letter to Sue. I went to George's again and we talked until 4:10 PM when I came home to start cooking supper. I cooked, ate, did the dishes and now it's 6:08 PM. I hope George comes early tonight as I have a Christmas present for him too. In the meantime I'll study and continue writing on the letter to Sue. Thank you so much George, for the present, thank you more than you can ever know! AWANEN!

Tuesday, December 16, 1986
My House, Gomez, Cabarroguis, Quirino

Finish letter to Sue T. Christmas postcards to Bob D., Tim C., Ardis B. and Steve A.

We got up at 5:50 AM and George left; he came at 6:40 PM last night. I cooked breakfast, ate, did dishes, got ready for the day and went to Alfredo's to tell him I have a headache and can't go to the farm today. I don't really have a headache but I wanted to write some Christmas letters so I returned home and finished the letter to Sue and then I rested from 9:00 to 10:00 AM. I got up and wrote some more postcards and then I went and got my nuang and bathed her at 11:00 AM. I returned home and wrote more until 2:00 PM and when I finished I took my nuang back to pasture. I returned home and worked on postcards until 3:15 PM or so and then I trimmed my beard and hair and after a while I bathed, went and fetched water and then I got things ready for supper. I went and got my nuang and George still had not returned from the farm so I returned home and my charcoal had gone out, damn wet charcoal. I re-started it and went to George's to ask him to come early. He said maybe their supper will be late. So will mine, now it's 5:47 PM and the rice is just getting finished, so I'll probably finish eating and washing dishes at about 6:30 PM or a bit after that. I hope George arrives no later than 7:00 PM, but can only wait and see what happens. Maybe I'll do another postcard. AWANEN!

Wednesday, December 17, 1986
My House, Gomez, Cabarroguis, Quirino

Christmas postcards to Tom L., Chris & Mary M., Dave G., Vicki K., Dave & Vicki M., Dan & Chris T., Tim & Peg S., Bob S., Terry & Juana S., Mark W. and Jim W.

We got up at 5:50 AM and George left. He didn't come until 8:30 PM last night as Junior had some firecrackers and they shot them off. I put my nuang on the other side of the creek, cooked breakfast, ate, did dishes, got ready for the day and went to Alfredo's, but he had already left for the farm. I told his wife I still had a headache and would remain home so I came home and wrote some more Christmas postcards and reentered my foreign address file into the HP-71. I went and bathed and got my nuang at 11:00 AM, returned home, ate lunch, drank coffee and then I took a half hour nap. I got up and took my nuang back to pasture, returned home and did more Christmas postcards. I got tired of doing that so I planted *kangkong* in the southeast garden. I got things ready for supper and then at 4:30 PM I went and got and bathed my nuang. I got home and the rice was just starting to boil. I went and asked George to come as soon as they finish supper tonight and he said yes. Then I went to the canteen for cigarettes and saw Rufo there and wished him happy holidays. I returned home and now it's 5:36 PM and the vegetables are cooking. I hope George really does come early tonight, I'll study for a while with him and if he's late I'll do another Christmas postcard or two. We had no rain today. AWANEN!

Thursday, December 18, 1986
My House, Gomez, Cabarroguis, Quirino

Christmas postcards to Bill N., Mike Mc., Liz & Randy, Dave W., Phyllis R., Dick F. and a letter to JB & Katie F.

I got up at 6:10 AM. George got up and left at 4:00 AM to pasture his nuang. He came at 6:45 PM last night. Today George and Junior are pulling cants from Calaocan. I started cooking breakfast, drank coffee, pastured my nuang and then returned home and finished cooking, ate, did dishes and got ready for the day. Then I went to George's just as he was leaving for Calaocan, so I talked with Alfredo for a while and then returned home and wrote more Christmas postcards and cut grass in the area immediately south of the house so that the nuang doesn't get stick-tights in her coat. I worked on that until 10:30 AM, when I went to get my nuang. Then I returned home, did more postcards and then napped from 12 to 1:00 PM. Then George returned home and I went there at 2:00 PM to talk. Then they took their cants down the mountain at 2:30 PM. At 2:45 PM I pastured my nuang again, came home and did more postcards, fetched water at 4:00 PM and then bathed and prepared things for supper. At 4:45 PM I went to get my nuang. It was a beautiful sunny day today, no rain. Now it's 5:38 PM and the vegetables are nearly cooked. I hope George comes early tonight, he said he would. I want to write a letter to JB and Katie and invite them here for New Year's. I'll see what happens. AWANEN!

Friday, December 19, 1986
My House, Gomez, Cabarroguis, Quirino

Letter from JB & Katie F. and IRS – nothing from friends in the USA.

₱120 + 500 – 545 = ₱75							
Cigarettes	10	Lunch	40	Food	110	Rides	18
Candy	25	Coffee	80	Household	5	Ice Cream	15
Marienda	30	Postage	70	Kerosene	8	Christmas	30

Haircut	5	Pack	37	Treats	62	TOTAL	₱545

We got up at 6:00 AM and George left. I went to get him at his house last night at 9:20 PM and we came here and slept immediately. I put my nuang on the other side of the creek, cooked breakfast, ate, did dishes, got ready for the day and headed for Burgos at 7:40 AM. I went to Gundaway to get my mail, but it was the second week in a row with no letters from the USA. I continued on to Santiago, shopped, ate lunch, finished with everything at 1:15 PM and caught a jeepney headed for Burgos. I arrived at the bottom of the high road at about 2:40 PM, climbed the mountain and got home at about 3:40 PM. I unpacked and put everything away, fetched water, bathed and when I saw George I went to talk with him for a while. He said he'll come as soon as they're finished with supper tonight and he even said "really". Well, I hope that's true. Now it's 5:54 PM and Alfredo just returned my nuang. I'm not eating supper tonight, just drinking coffee and reading my new *Reader's Digest.* There was no rain again today. I have a headache and I hope George comes early. Maybe I'll go and get him at about 6:30 PM. AWANEN!

Saturday, December 20, 1986
My House, Gomez, Cabarroguis, Quirino

We got up at 6:00 AM and George left; he came at 6:20 PM last night. I started cooking breakfast, drank coffee, put my nuang on the other side of the creek, returned home, finished cooking, ate, did dishes and got ready for the day. Then I went to Alfredo's and he, I and Brando went to Brando's farm to *agtabas* – I returned the favor of him helping me out with the grass cutting on my farm. We finished that at 10:30 AM, picked a nice bunch of squash blossoms and returned home at 11:00 AM. I talked with George for a while, came home and ate lunch and was about ready to siesta, but remembered that I had left my machete at the banana plantation, so I returned there immediately to get it. I returned and talked for a while with Alfredo, Junior and George and then I returned home. Alfredo came and helped me to repair the ½ wall around my toilet hole and we cleaned up all of the weeds, up to the road on the west side of the house. Alfredo hung out here until 4:35 PM when I fetched water and then he left. At 5:00 PM I went to the canteen for cigarettes and I went to George's to ask him to come early. I came home to discover that somehow my rice had spilled off the fire. I started over; now it's 5:21 PM and my rice is cooking again. George said he'll come early tonight; I hope he'll be here just a bit after 6:00 PM. It's been raining all day today. My rice is now done, I'm going to end and eat. AWANEN!

Maybe you've been wondering what a water buffalo cart looks like? On the following page is a photo of George taking a cart load of charcoal to market to sell. Back on Sunday, December 14th you may remember that I said that the yoke broke on George's nuang. In this photo you can see a yoke, it's the thing that crosses the neck of the nuang and bears the weight of the cart.

Sunday, December 21, 1986
My House, Gomez, Cabarroguis, Quirino

Begin letter to Chris & Mary M.

We got up at 5:30 AM and George left; he came at 5:40 PM last night, while I was still eating supper. I started breakfast, drank coffee and took my nuang to pasture. I returned home and finished cooking, ate, did dishes, got ready for the day and went to George's for a few minutes. Then I returned home and he came here to borrow my nuang – okay – so I showed him where she was pastured and helped him bathe her and then I returned home and did laundry. That took until nearly 11:00 AM because I got a late start. After that I weeded in the southeast garden until noon, ate, drank coffee and laid down for a while. Then I got up and finished weeding the southeast garden. Then Bebot's kids came and hassled me for a while but when I started working on the letter to Chris and Mary they left. After a while Remi, her companion and 12 kids came. SHIT! Noisy and bothersome! After a while they left and I went to George's for a while he pulled two small cants down the mountain today. I returned home, fetched water, bathed, prepared things for supper and then Alfredo passed by and said that Boy Belasco was on his way so I went to his house to wait. We talked about transferring the nuang ownership papers on Tuesday or Wednesday of this coming week. Now it's 6:11 PM and I'm cooking my vegetables. I hope George comes at about 7:00 PM tonight, we'll see what happens. AWANEN!

Monday, December 22, 1986
My House, Gomez, Cabarroguis, Quirino

Letter (Christmas card) from Brooke F.

₱75 + 100 – 100 = ₱75							
Peanut Butter	40	Marienda	5	Rides	8	Lunch	12
Cigarettes	10	Cookies	25			TOTAL	₱100

We got up at 5:45 AM and George left. He came at 6:20 PM last night, while I was still eating supper. He had my nuang so I didn't have to pasture her this morning. I cooked breakfast, ate, did dishes, got ready for the day and left for Burgos at 7:40 AM. I went to the post office and got the above letter and then continued on to the office in Diffun. There was no meeting today, the fuckers had the meeting and party on Friday; oh well, such is life. I hung out at the office and ate lunch there and then at 1:00 PM I headed home. I got to Burgos at 1:40 PM and climbed the mountain via the high road. I got here at about 2:40 PM and Alfredo came immediately. At 4:00 PM I told him I was going to fetch water. He left, I fetched water and then returned and prepared things for supper. I bathed and then started cooking at 5:00 PM, late because George says that he will be coming late tonight, that he's going to stroll with the guys for a while. SHIT! Oh well, such is life. He said he'll be coming about 10:00 PM or so. I hope he comes before that, but if he doesn't, well what can I say – it's the Christmas season with nearly a full moon and everybody wants to stroll. Now it's 5:47 PM and the rice is nearly done. I still have to cook my vegetables, eat, wash dishes and so on. AWANEN!

Tuesday, December 23, 1986
My House, Gomez, Cabarroguis, Quirino

Ronald come for part of the day.

We got up at 5:45 AM and George left. He came at about 6:45 PM last night as he decided not to stroll. I started cooking breakfast and drinking coffee and just as I was sitting down to eat Ronald came. Surprise! We shared my small breakfast. He slept-over near the fish pond at Burgos last night. We finished eating, did dishes got ready for the day and then we went to George's and he showed me where my nuang was and Ronald and I continued on to the farm. I showed him the farm and then we returned home, cooked lunch, ate and then he left at 1:00 PM! Huh?? Why didn't he stay for the night, I don't understand. Alfredo came and put the notches in my nuang yoke then at 2:00 PM he left. George and I went to move our nuangs. I returned home and started working on my quarterly report for the Peace Corps; I worked on that until 4:00 PM, stopped, fetched water, bathed and went to get my nuang. Then I went to George's to ask him to come early and he said maybe he would stroll tonight. I hope he doesn't. Now it's 5:21 PM and I'm having leftover mungo beans and rice for supper tonight, nothing else. It rained most of the day today. AWANEN!

Wednesday, December 24, 1986
My House, Gomez, Cabarroguis, Quirino

₱75 – 5 = ₱70				
Cigarettes	5			TOTAL ₱5

We got up at 5:50 AM and George left. I went to get him last night and we came here at 7:10 PM. I started cooking breakfast, drank coffee and went to pasture my nuang. Then I returned home, finished cooking, ate, did dishes and got ready for the day. I went to George's for a short time but there were lots and lots of people there as they are butchering a pig today, so I returned home, killed time and slept for a while to drown my seasonal sorrows. I got up and worked more on my quarterly report and then went to get my nuang. I saw George at the nuang bathing place and told him I'll come to their house after some of the people leave. I returned home and worked more on the quarterly report and then at noon I ate lunch, drank coffee and then napped again. I got up and shortly after 2:00 PM I went to pasture my nuang. I returned home and Alfredo came here to talk and then Pedring too. They stayed until 4:00 PM when I went to fetch water. Then I bathed and at 4:30 PM I went to Alfredo's to talk for a bit. At 4:45 PM I went to get my nuang. I returned home, went to the canteen for cigarettes and then to George's for supper – Christmas supper! After supper I gave them their presents and they were very happy. At about 6:30 PM George and I came here and opened the big can of cookies that I had and we ate cookies and drank coffee until bedtime. Oh I gave George his present too and he was very happy. Everybody is happy, even me, by the end of the day. AWANEN!

Thursday, December 25, 1986
My House, Gomez, Cabarroguis, Quirino

CHRISTMAS DAY!

We got up at 5:30 AM and George left. I started cooking breakfast, drank coffee, went to pasture my nuang, returned home, finished cooking breakfast, ate, did dishes and got ready for the day. I went to George's to talk for a while and then returned home and worked on my quarterly report some more. After a while Alfredo came and we talked until about 10:45 AM, when I went to get my nuang. Oh, I forgot, I did laundry this morning too. There was no rain today so it even got dry! I returned home with my nuang, ate lunch, drank coffee and laid down from 1:00 to 1:45 PM and then I got up and killed time for a while. I took my nuang back to pasture and then returned home and asked George to come here, but Junior was there, so it was hopeless. By and by Alfredo, his wife and kids came here to talk for a while. Everybody left except Alfredo and at 4:00 PM we prepared things for supper and drank coffee. At 4:30 PM I went to get my nuang and when I returned I asked George to come here for a while to talk and he did. Now it's 5:45 PM and my rice is done, but I'm still cooking my vegetables. George said he's going to stroll tonight and may not be here until 10:00 PM or after. I hope he changes his mind again and comes early, we'll see what happens. AWANEN!

Friday, December 26, 1986
My House, Gomez, Cabarroguis, Quirino

Letter to Tony & Janet S.

We got up at 6:00 AM and George left; he came at 10:40 PM last night. I started cooking breakfast, drank coffee and took my nuang to pasture. I returned and finished cooking breakfast, ate, did dishes and got ready for the day. I went to George's to talk for nearly an hour and then I returned home and killed time. I started the letter to Tony and Janet and then at 10:30 AM I went and moved my nuang. Upon returning, I stopped at George's to talk some more, until noon. I returned home, ate lunch, drank coffee, finished the letter to Tony and Janet and laid down for a half hour. At 2:00 PM I went to move my nuang and she was not where I had left her so I searched for 1.5 hours. I was pretty pissed off by the time I returned. I asked George if he had moved my nuang and he said yes, so I hollered at him and asked why he hadn't told me. Then I cooled off and apologized all over myself and asked him when we should go and get our nuangs. He said 4:30 PM, so I came home and prepared food for supper. Alfredo came, at my request, and I asked him if I had done a bad thing by hollering at George. He said yes, but that even a Filipino would have done likewise and that George should have told me. At 4:30 PM we went to get our nuangs and George said he'd come early tonight. Now it's 5:40 PM and my rice is still cooking. I hope that George truly comes early. I'll holler for him at 7:00 PM if he isn't here yet by then. AWANEN!

Saturday, December 27, 1986
Host Family, Bonfal East, Bayombong, Nueva Vizcaya

₱70 + 500 – 86 = ₱484							
Cigarettes	10	Rides	13	Present	20	Marienda	15
Lunch	16	Household	7	Misc.	5	TOTAL	₱86

We got up at 5:40 AM and George left; he came at 6:00 PM last night, before I even ate supper. I started cooking breakfast, drank coffee and took my nuang to pasture, returned home, finished cooking, ate, did dishes and got ready for the day. I did laundry – only one shirt, bathed and then went to get my nuang. George went to get a cant today so I left my nuang for Alfredo to pasture. At 10:40 AM I left Gomez. I got to Burgos and had to wait until 1:10 PM for a ride to Cordon. Then I had to wait another hour for a ride to Solano and I didn't finally get to Bonfal East until 5:30 PM. It was good to see the family again and everybody is happy that I'm here. I'm even happy to be here. As I was leaving Burgos today I got the news that father Mendoza died yesterday [my host father from November 24, 1985 through January 19, 1986]. Now it's 8:55 PM, I'm tired and have a headache. I wonder what George is doing? AWANEN!

Sunday, December 28, 1986
Host Family, Bonfal East, Bayombong, Nueva Vizcaya

₱484 – 40 = ₱444							
Cigarettes	14	Priest	10	Barbara	10	Candy	6
						TOTAL	₱40

We got up late, 6:30 AM. After a while we ate breakfast, got ready for the day, bathed, I changed my clothes and at about 9:00 AM we left for Herbert and Rebecca's house. I thought the baptism was supposed to be at 9:00 AM, but it ended up being at 9:00 AM Filipino time [to be explained later], so there was eating and drinking before the baptism. There was one drunk old man really hassling me – damn old fart! At 11:30 AM we went to the church and little Barbara got baptized with me as a Godfather. Then we returned to Herbert and Rebecca's place and they sent the one old drunk home, so no more hassles from him! Then we had a big dinner and then, of course Ronald, father and Herbert wanted to drink some more. I drank very little and mostly tried to stay out of the way. At 3:00 PM or so some of us came home but father and Ronald remained there. Melchor, Ronald's cousin from Maddela, and I talked here at the house. At 5:30 PM mother returned from the farm and at 6:00 PM, father, Ronald and Herbert came home. Father was falling down drunk and Ronald and Herbert were also pretty drunk. All in all, what a fucked up day it was! It was not a lot of fun for me, to say the least. AWANEN!

Monday, December 29, 1986
My House, Gomez, Cabarroguis, Quirino

Letter from Steve A., postcards from Chad D. and Ardis B. Package and letter from Peace Corps Health Unit.

₱444 – 202 = ₱242							
Rides	21	Cigarettes	10	Food	30	Postage	3
Kerosene	8	Household	13	Candy	6	Ice Cream	20
Crackers	20	Coffee	26	Short Pants	45	TOTAL	₱40

We got up at 6:30 AM, late again. Herbert decided that he wanted to cook the dog's head so we didn't get around to eating breakfast until about 8:30 AM or so and then, just as I was leaving at 10:00 AM, Kris I. and his girlfriend, Marcia, walked by so I talked with them for a while and finally got to the bus stop at 10:30 AM. I continued on to Santiago and arrived there at 11:45 AM or so. I mailed all of the letters and postcards that I'd written over the past few days along with my quarterly report, ate lunch, shopped for the above and got out of Santiago at 1:40 PM. I got to Gundaway at 2:35 PM, stopped at the post office and got the above mail and then continued on to Burgos. I arrived at the bottom of the high road at 3:30 PM, climbed the mountain and got home at 4:30 PM. I unpacked, fetched water, started the fire and went to ask George to come early. He said yes. Now it's 5:42 PM and Alfredo is here looking at my *Newsweek* and we're drinking coffee. I haven't yet had time to read my mail. I hope George really does come early. Alfredo said that a bunch of the young bachelors are at his house, so maybe they'll go for a stroll and George will be quite late. AWANEN!

Tuesday, December 30, 1986
My House, Gomez, Cabarroguis, Quirino

I got up at 6:00 AM with no companion; George had visitors sleep at his place last night; they strolled until midnight and then Bubot and two or three others slept there. He came for a couple minutes at midnight to tell me and then he left. I cooked breakfast, ate, did dishes, got ready for the day and went to George's to talk for a while. He pulled a cant from Bikibik today – there were about eight people who were involved –so I put up some pieces of wood on the southeast corner of the southeast garden where pigs have been entering. There was rooting there yesterday afternoon and again early this morning. I rested from 11:00 AM until noon, got up, ate lunch and after a while Alfredo came to talk for a few minutes and then he left. I rested again from 2:30 to 3:00 PM, got up and killed time for a while. I fetched water, bathed and prepared things for supper. I cooked, ate, did dishes and went to Alfredo's to wait for George. He finally arrived home from hauling cants at about 6:00 PM and said he would come soon. Now it's 6:20 PM and I expect him by 7:00 PM – I hope. It was sunny all day today and I washed my two blue packs this morning. The oldest one is really mildewed, practically falling apart, I hope the new one doesn't get mildewed too. All in all I really didn't do much today. AWANEN!

Wednesday, December 31, 1986
My House, Gomez, Cabarroguis, Quirino

We got up at 5:50 AM and George left; he came just before 7:00 PM last night. I started breakfast, drank coffee and took my nuang to pasture. I returned home, finished cooking, ate, did dishes and got ready for the day. George pulled his cant to Burgos today. What did I do? Well, this morning I mostly worked on monthly expense summaries, yearly expense summaries, how many days I was gone from my site, how many days I've had visitors and so on. Then at 10:00 AM Sip and I went and got are nuangs and bathed them. I returned home and continued working on summaries of various things until lunchtime and then I ate. After lunch I continued working on summaries. I finally finished everything up at about 3:00 PM or so and Alfredo and his wife came and talked until 4:15 PM or so. I prepared things for supper, went to get my nuang, bathed her and then I fetched water, bathed and started cooking supper. Now it's 5:43 PM and there's been no rain today. I'm cooking rice – again – the first batch somehow spilled on the floor. I don't know what's going to happen tonight, I'll have to wait and see if George even comes or not. There might be a New Year's dance at the Barangay Hall, but nobody seems to know for sure. AWANEN!

Thursday, January 1, 1987
My House, Gomez, Cabarroguis, Quirino

Letter to Steve A.

We got up at 5:50 AM and George left; he came at 9:00 PM last night after saying that he might not even come. I was supposed to go there for a late New Year's supper last night but my stomach was really hurting so I didn't go. George came for a half hour or so at about 7:30 PM and I cried on his shoulder and told him how homesick I am. I've been really down lately, I hope it passes now that the holidays are over. I started cooking breakfast, pastured my nuang, returned home, finished cooking, ate, did dishes and got ready for the day. My stomach is still sore so I just killed time resting for a while and then I started the letter to Steve. I went and got my nuang at 10:30 AM and then continued on the letter to Steve. I ate lunch, laid down for a while, got up and continued the letter for a while and then I went and pastured my nuang again. I returned home and worked more on the letter; it's a letter about reflections on the past year. I finished the letter shortly after 3:00 PM, went and fetched water, returned home and killed time for a while. Then I prepared stuff for supper and Pedring came and talked until 4:30 PM when I went to get my nuang. After getting my nuang I went to the canteen and to George's for bit. He said he'll be early tonight, we'll see what happens. Now it's 5:43 PM and the vegetables are cooking. It rained off and on all day today, is that what January weather will be like? Have to wait and see I guess. Maybe I'll write another letter after supper. AWANEN!

Remember back on October 22nd when I told you that Steve A. saved all of the letters which I wrote to him and recently gave them all to me? I just read the one which I wrote him today and as I mentioned in my journal entry just above, it's a letter about reflections on the past year. For that reason I am going to include that letter here as a kind of summary of what I've done/accomplished in my year here.

Letter to Steve A. January 1, 1987.

Happy New Year to you Brother Steve. I'll be home this year. I've been here for 16 months now and there's 10.5 months to go. I feel like talking <u>with</u> you but the best I can do is talk <u>to</u> you, okay? I received your letter of December 7th on December 29th and you asked where I've been this year, so I marked up one of my maps showing all of the places I've been and I'm sending it back to you [included here after this letter]. As I sit here this New Year's Day it's raining and I'm in a pretty bad state of depression, homesickness, whatever. Last night I broke down and cried on George's shoulder saying *"Mailiwak nga perme"* or, "I'm very homesick" over and over. I didn't really realize what a sad state I was in, but the tears helped a bit to cleanse my soul.

So let's try and look back over the past year and see what I've done or accomplished to try and ease the pain a little bit, okay? Well a year ago I wasn't here (in Gomez) yet and 95% of all conversations went over my head. I moved here to Gomez on January 20, 1986, after two months of living in Burgos.

On January 25th 1986 I was so very down that I was ready to call it quits. My new host family in Gomez had five kids, five puppies and five piglets and I was awake half the night every night with one thing or the other crying squealing or barking.

On February 7th Ardis came and I strolled with her for ten days; that did wonders for my spirits, I came back to the world of the living so to speak. Ardis came here to Gomez on February 17th and on February 18th we all started fixing me a house of my very own. February 21st was the first night in my new house. If you remember back to then, I was on top of the world; who could be happier than a person in a new house, especially after having had to adjust to three host families in six months. The people sent three different companions to sleep with me. Several people told me not to trust one of them, Junior, so after just two nights of him sleeping here I asked him not to return. The second one of them, Bubot, was nosy and half the time too lazy to even come, and after a while he stopped coming at all. The third one, George was and is one of the most respected young men in Gomez; industrious, an honest guy, smart and reliable. He's the only person in the Philippines who gave me a Christmas present – a whole cooked chicken! That meant more to me than you can even begin to imagine. Over and over in the past year George has showed me that we really have become very close friends. A lot of people here want to be your friend only because they think maybe you'll take them to America when you go home – not George though – he doesn't even want to go to America; he's basically pretty happy with the cards that life has dealt him.

In March I cleaned a spot for my garden. I cut all the tall weeds down on my land, attended a conference in Manila and started my very first small tree nursery with 25 seedlings. Last but not least, I planted my first vegetable garden too.

In April I took a ten day stroll and went to Banaue, Bontoc and the Sagada areas with Nestor. I helped George at their vegetable farm for the first time; we removed an entire old banana plantation with our machetes and my Peace Corps supervisor came for a day, looked at my garden and we strolled around Gomez. I went to Caba in La Union Province (not on the map) for some follow-up language training.

May saw the end of our 1.5 month dry season. John, my friend from Banaue, came for 15 days. There was training in Cebu about nurseries and nursery management.

In June I harvested lots of beans from the garden, people saw my success and several people started backyard gardens. We built the big tree nursery. I started having problems with pigs rooting up my garden because the beans I planted are nitrogen fixing and therefore the soil is getting better and there are more earthworms, which is what the pigs are searching for.

In July, Typhoon Gading hit and destroyed half of everything and I spent most of July cleaning up the mess from the typhoon. I harvested more beans, researched three tree species for a tree book that I and a couple of my fellow PCV's are attempting to prepare. On July 29th George left home and I got to be the third person, the go-between, to go and talk him into returning home. He returned home on August 4th. I started planting seeds in the big tree nursery. I went to Manila about my half asleep foot and they determined that I had a pinched nerve and gave me some medicine to encourage nerve regeneration/healing.

In August I had lots of problems. Every little cut seemed to get infected. My neighbors told me that in August things get infected easily because everything is so dusty. I fell off the first nuang that I tried to ride and I have two nice scars on my forehead to tell stories about upon my return to the USA. Nestor and I went to Batanes for my birthday and I returned to Gomez on September 3rd.

In September I helped George and his family nearly every day – harvesting corn, husking corn and shelling corn. A Peace Corps nurse came here for one night to see what life in the provinces is really like. She has lived in the Philippines her whole life but was shocked to see people walking barefoot. She asked why and I told her, quite simply, that they don't have money for shoes.

It sure would be nice if you could come visit me. No matter how detailed I try to make my stories to you, you'll never understand what life is really like for me here. I talk about lighting with kerosene and you probably picture an Aladdin lamp, or at least the type of kerosene lamp with a globe, when in reality I have a medicine bottle with a rag sticking out of the top of it. I talk about cooking on charcoal and you probably picture me cooking on a charcoal grill. I wish I could draw! The Philippine charcoal stove I use is QUITE different than any charcoal grill that you've ever seen.

Rain was scarce in September and I had to water tree seedlings in the nursery several times during the month.

In October – are you completely bored yet – I replanted my garden, helped George cut down corn stalks at the farm, strolled to Baguio City for two days only and spent about one and a half weeks searching for a water buffalo to buy.

On October 23rd I bought one. Then we started cutting down the tall grass on what was to become my vegetable farm.

In November I had to go to Manila for a mid-service conference. I learned all about pasturing a water buffalo, where the various pasturing places are, how and when to bathe the water buffalo and why it is necessary and I became more adept at riding it. I helped George plow and harrow his vegetable farm and he helped me do the same with mine; in fact he did nearly all of my plowing and harrowing for me, using my water buffalo. I had an entry into my house and somebody stole my HP-41CX calculator – bastards. I helped George harvest bananas.

My nuang got mated on November 23rd so should calve in August. I planted my farm. The tree nursery was looking pretty nice and people saw it and several people started making backyard nurseries – my second accomplishment as far as improving people's actual lives. I also noticed that people's respect for me went up about a thousand percent when I bought my water buffalo. They're really proud of "our Americano" who is already skillful in riding a water buffalo, has a farm, eats the same food they do and so on.

In December I wrote lots of Christmas postcards and continued learning about water buffalo care and maintenance and garden and farm maintenance. I had to fight Christmas season depression and homesickness. I pulled my first cart of bananas down the mountain and I went to Bayombong for two days to be a godfather to my host sisters child. I watched it rain, fought with depression and homesickness some more.

December 30th marked 60% done in my 26.5 month stay here.

There have been several breaks since I started this at 8:46 AM and it's now 3:02 PM. I'm going to break again and go fetch water. When I return I'll answer your letter and wrap it up. Oh, I thought of more that I should mention – in the past year my feet have gotten incredibly tough; I don't even believe the things I am capable of doing barefoot. My body has also gotten tougher – climbing this mountain, pasturing my nuang – up the mountain, going to the farm – up the mountain; it seems that everything is "up the mountain". I've learned new meaning to the word patience. I've really gotten into watching things grow – the fruits and vegetables in the garden – and that's one thing I'm really going to miss a lot when I return to Alaska. Oh, Steve, I've learned a lot about myself and about life and about involvement with other people and about patience and and and and and …

My water buffalo wasn't really pregnant when I bought her, as I previously told you, otherwise she wouldn't have allowed herself to be mounted on November 23rd, so, like I said, the new date that I might be able to expect to see a water buffalo calf is sometime in August – if she is pregnant now. A bull tried to mate her again about a week ago and she wouldn't let him so I hope that means she is pregnant now.

I guess that takes care of everything that I'm going to say this time. I hope you write again soon. Take care.

Peace, Joy, Love

Dan'l

Here's the map – or a close approximation of it – that I included with this letter.

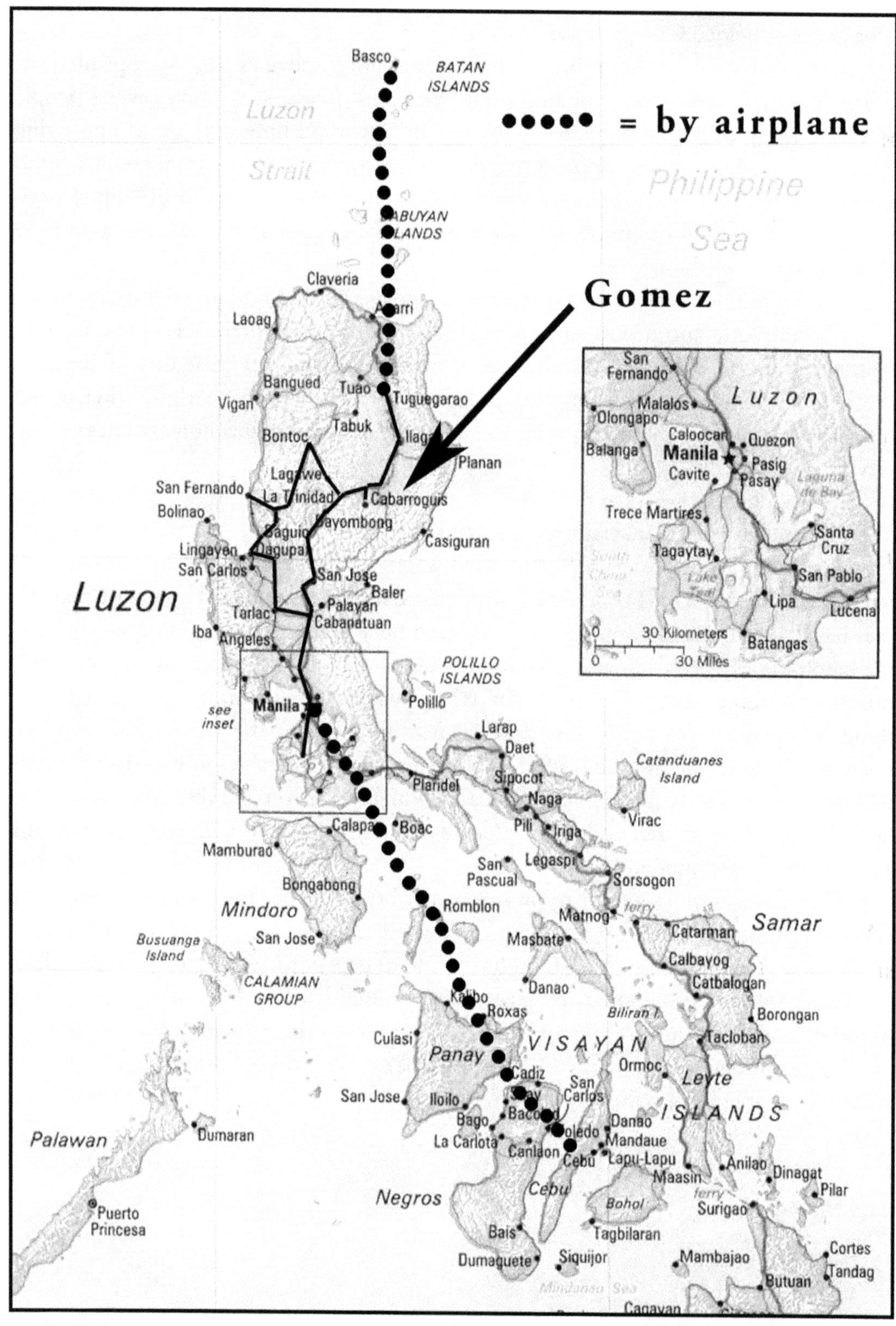

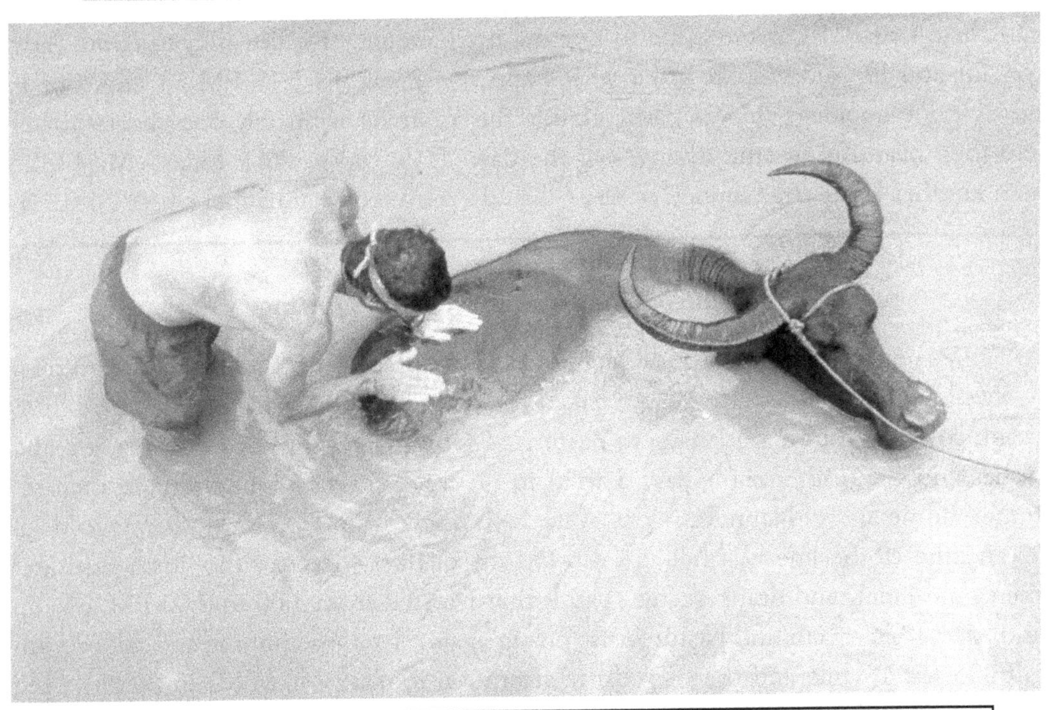

Just above is a photo of me bathing my water buffalo after bringing her back from pasture. These animals are prone to overheating and need to be cooled like this two or three times a day. When she was resting in the water like this I rubbed her down to get the stick-tights and other stuff our of her sparse hair and she really loved this. This is how I generally dressed when in the village, but sometimes I wore a T-shirt during the sunniest part of the day.

Friday, January 2, 1987
My House, Gomez, Cabarroguis, Quirino

Letter to Ardis B.

We got up at 5:45 AM and George left, he came at 6:30 PM last night. I started breakfast, drank coffee, pastured my nuang, returned home, finished breakfast, ate, did dishes and got ready for the day. I went to George's to talk for a while and he had gone to the farm to get some fuelwood so I worked on the above letter to Ardis. At 10:15 AM I went to George's and then went and got my nuang. Upon returning I rested for a half hour and then continued on the letter to Ardis. Then I ate lunch and finished the letter to Ardis. I went to get George to take my picture on my water buffalo – which he did – but the camera fucked up and by the time I was done messing around I had to throw away 13 rolls of film today – bummer! George left and I worked on searching for words from my small red dictionary which had not yet been put in a bigger one that I am making. I stopped working on that at 3:30 PM, bathed and then 4:00 PM George came to borrow my hammer. I asked him to come early tonight and he said yes, we'll see what happens. Now it's 5:19 PM and my rice is nearly done cooking. It was partly cloudy this morning with only one short shower and then beautiful weather the rest of the day. It got up to 80°F today. Maybe I'll start another letter after supper, or else I'll study, we'll see what happens. AWANEN!

Saturday, January 3, 1987
My House, Gomez, Cabarroguis, Quirino

We got up at 5:40 AM and George left. He came at 6:15 PM last night and then at about 6:30 PM Alfredo came and talked for a half hour. I started cooking breakfast, drank coffee and took my nuang to pasture. I returned and finished cooking, ate, did dishes and got ready for the day. I went to George's for a few minutes and then returned home and did laundry – lots of it. It took me from 8:00 to 11:00 AM to do it all and the clothesline was full. I even did my blanket. I swept the north yard and then I ate lunch and drank coffee. After that I rested from 1:00 to 2:00 PM, got up and after a bit I went and pastured my nuang again. I returned home and talked with Alfredo for a while and then killed the afternoon looking for words in my little red dictionary that have not been transferred to my bigger one yet. I worked on that until 3:30 PM, stopped and went and fetched water. Then I bathed, prepared the things for supper and started the rice cooking. Then I went and got my nuang and went to George's to talk for a few minutes and asked him to come early. He said yes, but we'll have to wait and see. Now it's 5:30 PM and my vegetables are cooking. It was hot today, above 80°F again, and there wasn't a drop of rain. AWANEN!

Sunday, January 4, 1987
My House, Gomez, Cabarroguis, Quirino

₱242 + 325 – 5 = ₱562					
Cigarettes	5			TOTAL	₱5

We got up at 5:45 AM and George left. He didn't come until 12:45 AM this morning because they strolled again. I started cooking breakfast, drank coffee and went and pastured my nuang. I returned home, finished cooking, ate, did dishes, got ready for the day and went to Alfredo's for a while. George pulled a cant to Burgos today. I returned home after a while and did a little bit of laundry. After that I tried to sleep a bit, but for some reason I couldn't, even though I only slept a little bit last night. I got up and read the book *"Contact"* by Carl Sagan. Alfredo came to talk and at 11:00 AM I went and got my nuang. I ate lunch and played with my HP-71 calculator for a while. The 4k memory module is messed up and caused a total memory loss. I reentered some programs and then took a nap for an hour. I got up at 2:15 PM and pastured my nuang again, returned home and read some more in the book.

At 3:45 PM I stopped, fetched water, bathed and prepared things for supper. I went and got my nuang and gave Alfredo some beans. Now it's 5:46 PM and supper is cooked but not eaten yet. George has not yet returned from Burgos. The weather today was above 80°F again and there was no rain. I hope George arrives from Burgos soon and hope he comes here relatively early. AWANEN!

Monday, January 5, 1987
My House, Gomez, Cabarroguis, Quirino

Letters from Terry S., Yip Chee H., Dave G. Package from San & Jack G. (trowel and candy).

₱562 – 520 = ₱42							
Cigarettes	10	Meals	50	Food	135	Rides	16
Candy	25	Coffee	55	Kerosene	7	Ice Cream	15
Marienda	10	Postage	10	Batteries	12	Film	120
Household	5	Coke	5	Short Pants	45	TOTAL	₱520

We got up at 5:40 AM and George left after I gave him my *wayway* (nuang pasturing rope); he came at 7:15 PM last night. I drank coffee, got ready for the day and headed down the mountain. I got to Burgos at about 7:30 AM, continued on to Gundaway, got mail and then continued on to Santiago. I did my shopping and finished at 11:30 AM. I bumped into JB and talked for a couple minutes and then went to the bank. After that I met JB and Katie at the 456 Restaurant, we talked and left there at 2:30 PM. I returned to the clothes store where I had taken George's short pants to be tailored but they still weren't ready so I had to wait until 3:00 PM for them to be finished. Then I went to the jeepney place. I left Santiago at 3:40 PM, arrived in Burgos at 4:40 PM and climbed the mountain via the high road and got home at 5:30 PM. There's been no rain in four or five days now so the trail is in pretty good condition. Now it's 6:18 PM and George is here so tonight's entry is a short one. It was hot and dry all day today. AWANEN!

Tuesday, January 6, 1987
My House, Gomez, Cabarroguis, Quirino

We got up at 6:10 AM and George left; he came at 6:15 PM last night. I started cooking breakfast, drank coffee and went to pasture my nuang. I returned home, finished cooking, ate, did dishes, got ready for the day and went to George's for a few minutes. Then I returned home and continued reading the *"Contact"* book. I laid down and rested from 9:30 to 10:30 AM and then I went to George's for a half hour. At 11:00 AM I went to move my nuang, returned home and read some more and then ate lunch and drank coffee. Then I read some more, napped again from 1:00 to 1:45 PM, got up and read some more and then at 2:30 PM I went to move my nuang again. I returned home and read some more. At 3:30 PM I went and fetched water, bathed and prepared things for supper. At 4:35 PM I started cooking and went to ask George if I need to get my nuang or if she can remain at pasture overnight. He asked me if she had drank water and I said yes, at 2:30 PM, so he said she could stay at pasture. I returned home again and George said he'd come as soon as they're done with supper, but they hadn't started cooking yet. Now it's 5:13 PM and my rice is nearly cooked. I'll read after eating supper and doing dishes. Today it rained all day and it was quite chilly. AWANEN!

Wednesday, January 7, 1987
My House, Gomez, Cabarroguis, Quirino

We got up at 6:00 AM and George left; he came at 6:45 PM last night. I cooked breakfast, ate, did dishes, got ready for the day and went to George's. He was preparing to go to the farm to harvest beans so I went and got my nuang and rode to the farm and by and by George showed up there. He and Sip harvested beans and I weeded some on my farm. When they finished harvesting beans they helped me for a half hour or 45 minutes and then they left. I came home at noon and stopped at George's to talk for a while and his mother gave me a bunch of beans, I didn't expect that. I came home and discovered that one wall of my outhouse had fallen down and that the chickens had made a couple of good sized holes in my porch roof. I hollered for George to come and see and he did. He helped to repair the wall on the outhouse and then he left. I ate lunch, slept from 1:30 to 2:15 PM, got up and drank coffee and then went to move my nuang. I finished reading the book *"Contact"* at 4:00 PM and I went and fetched water and prepared things for supper. I started cooking, went and got my nuang and returned home. I finished cooking, ate, did dishes and now it's 6:00 PM. George may be here any moment or it may be an hour. I'll study and read my newest *Newsweek*. It rained most of the morning and then on and off all afternoon. AWANEN!

Thursday, January 8, 1987
My House, Gomez, Cabarroguis, Quirino

Letter to Dave G.

We got up at 5:50 AM and George left; he came at 6:40 PM last night. I started cooking breakfast, drank coffee and put my nuang on the other side of the creek because I thought I might go to the farm today. I finished cooking breakfast, ate, did dishes, got ready for the day and went to George's for a few minutes. He went to Calaocan today to pull a cant. It was cold and rainy so I decided not to go to the farm. I went and pastured my nuang, talked with Alfredo for a while and then returned home and polished the floors with the *lampaso*. At 11:15 AM I went to move my nuang, returned home, ate lunch, drank coffee, reentered all of the addresses into the HP-71 and immediately I had another memory lost condition. That took until 2:15 PM and then I went to move my nuang again. I also took her to drink and bathe. I returned and talked with Alfredo until 3:30 PM and then came home, fetched water, bathed and prepared things for supper. I started cooking and then went to George's in time to see him head for Burgos with his cant at 5:00 PM, so he probably won't be here until 10:00 PM or so, SHIT! I'll probably write a letter or two after supper. Now it's 5:20 PM and my rice is nearly cooked. It rained most of the day today. AWANEN!

Friday, January 9, 1987
My House, Gomez, Cabarroguis, Quirino

Letter to Nestor.

I got up at 6:00 AM. George got up and left to release his nuang at 5:30 AM. He came at 8:20 PM last night. I cooked breakfast, ate, did dishes, got ready for the day, went to George's for a while and then went and moved my nuang. After that I returned to George's and helped him make a new harness for hauling cants. We finished that at 10:40 AM or so and then I went and got and bathed my nuang. I returned home, ate lunch and after that I napped from 12:30 to 1:30 PM. Then I killed time until 2:00 PM and took my nuang to pasture again. I returned home and looked up words from the red dictionary and transferred them to the other dictionary again. I worked on that until 4:00 PM, fetched water and prepared things for supper. At 4:30 PM I went to get my nuang from pasture and bathed her. I went to George's to talk for a few minutes and asked him to come early tonight. He said yes, but we'll have to wait and see what really happens. Now it's 5:21 PM, my rice is done and the vegetables are cooking. I didn't do a heck of a lot today. Oh. I harvested some *utong* beans in the southeast garden and gave them to George; not too many, but better than nothing. Maybe I'll start a letter after supper. It was cloudy this morning but sunny and nice all afternoon. AWANEN!

Saturday, January 10, 1987
My House, Gomez, Cabarroguis, Quirino

We got up at 6:00 AM and George left; he came at 6:40 PM last night. I started cooking breakfast, went to pasture my nuang, returned and finished cooking, ate, did dishes and got ready for the day. George went to Calaocan to pull a cant today and Alfredo went to harvest bananas so I returned home and did laundry until 10:00 AM or so. At 10:30 AM I went and got and bathed my nuang, returned home and laid down until 11:45 AM and then I got up, ate lunch and then actually napped from 12:30 to 1:30 PM. I got up, drank coffee and then took my nuang to pasture. I returned and helped George repair the one cart with the two broken bolts on the wheel and then we calculated the board footage of his cants. Lito told him that the total was

67 board feet but actually it's 76 board feet. We worked on that until 4:00 PM and then I came home, fetched water and prepared things for supper. At 4:30 PM I started cooking and went and got and bathed my nuang and then I returned home and finished cooking, ate and did dishes. I saw George at the creek bathing his nuang and asked him to come early; he said yes. Now it's 6:25 PM and maybe he'll be here soon. I'll sweep the floor now and put down the sleeping mats. There was no rain today and it was only 62°F this morning – the coldest so far this season. In the afternoon it was beautiful weather. AWANEN!

Sunday, January 11, 1987
My House, Gomez, Cabarroguis, Quirino

Letters to Terry S. and Ronald.

We got up at 6:00 AM and George left; he came at 6:50 PM last night. I started cooking breakfast, drank coffee, went and pastured my nuang, took some pictures of the sunrise and returned home. I finished cooking breakfast, ate, did dishes and got ready for the day. George and Alfredo both went to Burgos today. I went to my farm to get my pickaxe and I also finished weeding in some areas. I also harvested a nice bunch of bitwela's. I headed home at about 9:45 AM and got my nuang and bathed her on the way. Shortly after I got home I ate lunch. Boy came to talk for a while and when he left, I bathed and did a little bit of laundry. I laid down and rested for about 40 minutes and then at 2:15 PM I took my nuang back to pasture and returned home. I pulled some weeds in the north yard and not much else this afternoon. At 3:00 PM I went and fetched water and then Boy came again to get some aspirin. He left and at 4:00 PM I prepared things for supper. At 4:30 PM I went and got and bathed my nuang. Now it's 5:09 PM and George just arrived home from Burgos. I'm cooking rice now and when I finish this I'll go to George's and ask him to come early, but he'll probably be somewhat late, as they probably haven't started cooking yet. It was 76°F for the high temperature today, with no rain. This morning it was 64°F. AWANEN!

Monday, January 12, 1987
My House, Gomez, Cabarroguis, Quirino

Letters from Liz & Randy, San & Jack G., Chad D., Chris & Mary M., Dad and Fred & Cynthia B. Also received a *Reader's Digest.*

Letter to Chris & Mary M.

₱42 + 400 – 203 = ₱239							
Cigarettes	10	Lunch	9	Food	84	Rides	12
Candy	5	Coffee	36	Marienda	25	Postage	5
Misc.	17					TOTAL	₱203

We got up at 6:00 AM, I gave George my *wayway* and he left. He came at 8:00 PM last night, when I went to get him. I drank coffee, took my bag of valuables to George's and left at 6:45 AM. I arrived in Burgos at about 7:45 AM and caught a jeepney. I went to Gundaway, getting there at 8:15 AM. I got my mail and continued on to Cordon, bought the above, ate a late breakfast or early lunch and headed for home. I got back to Burgos at 12:45 PM, climbed the mountain via the high road and got home at 1:40 PM. I thought George and I might pull a cant today so I unpacked and went there, but there were no cants to pull so I came home and read mail. Then from 1:20 to 2:15 PM I napped. I got up and took my nuang to pasture, returned home, trimmed my beard and bathed, prepared things for supper, started cooking and went to George's to ask him to come early; he said maybe it will be a late supper for them again tonight – shit! Now it's 6:03 PM and maybe I'll write a letter. I probably can't expect George before 7:00 PM and I'll probably have to holler for him. The weather was hot and dry today. AWANEN!

Tuesday, January 13, 1987
My House, Gomez, Cabarroguis, Quirino

Letter to San & Jack G.

We got up at 6:10 AM and George left. He came about 6:40 PM last night. We got up late because it was cold and rainy today. I started cooking breakfast, drank coffee, took my nuang to pasture, returned and talked with George for a few minutes. Then I came home, finished cooking breakfast, ate, did dishes and got ready for the day. I returned to George's to talk for a few minutes and then I returned home and finished the letter to Chris and Mary that I started yesterday. Then I laid down and tried to sleep, but it was too cold to sleep. I drank coffee to get warm and then at about 10:30 AM I went to move my nuang and returned to George's once again and talked for a while. I came home and tried to sleep again and had no luck again. I read my new *Reader's Digest* and looked up words from the red dictionary for a while. Then I wrote the letter to San and Jack. After that I looked up more words to highlight and at 2:45 PM I went to move my nuang. I did not eat lunch today. I returned to George's once again for a few minutes and then came home and looked up more words. At 4:45 PM I went to George's to ask him to come early and then I returned home and ate breakfast leftovers for supper. I did dishes and now it's 6:04 PM. I hope George comes before 7:00 PM tonight. it's been 64°F all day today and I wore my Patagonia jacket all day. I hope it doesn't get much colder tonight. Maybe I'll work on another letter until George arrives. AWANEN!

Wednesday, January 14, 1987
My House, Gomez, Cabarroguis, Quirino

Letter to Fred & Cynthia B.

We got up at 5:50 AM and George left; he came at about 6:10 PM last night. I cooked breakfast, drank coffee, ate, did dishes, got ready for the day and then went to George's, but he had gone to the farm. I went to move my nuang and then returned and talked with Alfredo for a while. I returned home and didn't do much of anything. I laid down for a while but couldn't sleep so I got up and drank coffee. At 10:35 AM I went to move my nuang. I stopped at George's upon return to talk some more and then I came home, ate lunch, drank coffee and laid down again but couldn't sleep again. I started the above letter to Fred and Cynthia and then at 2:30 PM I went and took my nuang to drink, to bathe and then took her back to pasture. I returned home and finished the letter to Fred and Cynthia and then fetched water. I looked up words from the red dictionary again. I worked on that until 4:00 PM and then prepared things for supper. At 4:30 PM I started my fire, started the rice cooking and went to ask George if my nuang could remain at pasture tonight and he said yes. I talked with him for a while and returned home. I finished cooking, ate, did dishes and now it's 6:06 PM and I'm waiting for George, but I don't expect him to come too much before 7:00 PM tonight. There was no rain today, but it was cloudy and cold all day. AWANEN!

Thursday, January 15, 1987
My House, Gomez, Cabarroguis, Quirino

We got up at 6:15 AM and George left; he came at about 6:30 PM last night. I started cooking breakfast, drank coffee and went and moved my nuang. I returned home, finished cooking, ate, did dishes and got ready for the day. I went to George's but he had gone to the farm so I returned home and pulled weeds in the yard until 10:15 AM when I went to George's to talk for a few minutes. Then I went and moved my nuang, returned and talked with George for a few more minutes and returned home. I laid down for a bit, but couldn't sleep so I got up, ate lunch and then pulled more weeds in the yard. After that I started pulling the weeds in the tree nursery again. George said he'd come and help but he got busy with a different project at their house and didn't come. At 2:15 PM I went and moved my nuang again, returned and continued weeding in the nursery until 3:30 PM and then I bathed at 4:00 PM – Brrrr! The creek water was cold! I started preparing things for supper and at 4:30 PM I started the fire, went and got my nuang and returned home. I went to George's for a few minutes to ask him to come early and then I ate supper, did dishes and now it's 6:08 PM and I'm waiting for George; I hope he comes early again tonight. Now I'm reading the book *"Friday"* by Robert Heinlein for the second time. It didn't rain today, but it was cool and cloudy most of the day. AWANEN!

Friday, January 16, 1987
My House, Gomez, Cabarroguis, Quirino

Letter to Chad D.

We got up at 6:00 AM and George left; he came at 6:30 PM last night. I started cooking breakfast, drank coffee and took my nuang to pasture. I returned and talked with George for a minute and then came home and finished cooking, ate, did dishes and got ready for the day. George pulled two cants to Burgos today. I finished weeding and cleaning the nursery and by then it was 10:30 AM so I went and got my nuang. Oh, I forgot, first off today I did laundry and after that I cleaned the nursery. I laid down for a few minutes and then got up and ate lunch, drank coffee and then I laid down for a few minutes again. I got up and started cleaning the south lawn and Alfredo came to borrow some nuang medicine. I gave it to him and continued cleaning the south yard. Alfredo returned to help and then it was 2:00 PM so I pastured my nuang. I returned and Alfredo had practically finished the weeding. We finished that and he wanted to sweep the yard too, so I went and fetched water while he was sweeping. Then we drank coffee and he left at 4:00 PM. I prepared things for supper and at 4:30 PM I started cooking and then went to get and bathe my nuang. I came back home, finished cooking, ate, did dishes and now it's 6:02 PM and I'm waiting for George. Junior returned from wherever he had been strolling today so maybe George will be late if Junior goes there to tell stories. The weather today was cool but sunny. AWANEN!

Saturday, January 17, 1987
My House, Gomez, Cabarroguis, Quirino

We got up at 6:00 AM and George left; he came at 6:50 PM last night. I started cooking breakfast, drank coffee and took my nuang to pasture beside the school. I returned home, finished cooking breakfast, ate, did dishes and got ready for the day. Then I already knew that George had gone to the farm so I packed my lunch and headed there. I arrived sometime before 9:00 AM and pulled weeds on my farm until noon and then we all ate lunch – George, Alfredo, Sip, Bunag and I. We returned to work at 1:00 PM and continued weeding. At 3:00 PM George left to go home as he's going to a wedding tonight in Burgos. Alfredo, Sip and I continued to work. I worked alone all day today and the others worked on their farm. We quit at 3:30 PM, harvested some beans and then around 4:00 PM we all headed for home. We got home about 5:00 PM and I started cooking supper immediately after fetching water. I cooked, ate, did dishes and now it's 6:52 PM and George is going to the wedding, so he won't be coming tonight – bummer. I suppose I'll read for a little while and then sleep early. I'm pretty tired anyway after a full days work in the sun. The weather today was sunny and hot all day but it clouded up and rained lightly starting at about 5:15 PM. AWANEN!

Sunday, January 18, 1987
My House, Gomez, Cabarroguis, Quirino

Letter to Bob S.

I got up at 6:10 AM with no companion. I started cooking breakfast, drank coffee and then took my nuang to pasture. I returned, finished cooking, ate, did dishes and got ready for the day. I went to Alfredo's to talk for a while and then returned home and finished reading the book *"Friday"*. Then I laid down for a while, but I couldn't sleep. At 10:30 AM I went to move my nuang and by then George had returned, but was sleeping. I returned home and reentered the "AVERAGES" program into the HP-71. I tested it out and by then it was nearly 1:00 PM so I ate lunch and then laid down for a while again. At 2:15 PM I went to George's for a few minutes to talk and then when the rain slowed down I went to move my nuang. I returned home and started the letter to Bob. I quit working on that at 3:30 PM, harvested some pallang, *utong* and *tarong*, fetched water, bathed and prepared things for supper. At 4:30 PM I started my cooking fire and went to George's to ask him to come early. Then I went and got my nuang, returned home and went to George's again. They had no food so I gave them about half of my pallang. Now it's 5:22 PM and my rice is cooked and the vegetables are nearly done. After eating supper and doing dishes I'll finish the letter to Bob and wait for George. It rained off and on all day today. AWANEN!

Monday, January 19, 1987
My House, Gomez, Cabarroguis, Quirino

Letter to Health Unit.

Letters from Ardis B., Cory A., Tom & Barb H., Mike P., ICE and JB & Katie F.

₱239 – 74 = ₱165							
Cigarettes	10	Lunch	23	Food	11	Marienda	13
Rides	8	Misc.	9			TOTAL	₱74

We got up at 6:00 AM, I gave George my *wayway* and he left. He came at 6:30 PM last night. I drank coffee, got ready for the day and at 6:45 AM I headed for Burgos. I arrived there at 7:45 AM and continued on to Gundaway and the post office. After that I continued on to Diffun. There was no meeting again today. The other news is that Rody has transferred to Ilagan, is that good news or bad news? I talked with Francisco until noon about plans and problems and then we went and ate lunch. At 1:00 PM I headed for home. I stopped at the post office again and then continued on to Burgos. I got to Burgos at 2:15 PM and arrived at my house at about 3:05 PM. I read my mail and noticed that my GG (Gamma Globulin) shot was due on January 12th so I wrote a quick note to the Health Unit telling them that I haven't received my package yet and then I prepared things for supper. At 4:20 PM I fetched water and started cooking my rice. I went to George's and they were just arriving home from the farm and hadn't started cooking yet. Now it's 6:14 PM and I'm hoping that George makes it here by 7:00 PM tonight, but maybe he won't; we'll see what happens. There was no rain today. It was hot and dry; I went to Burgos via the low road and returned via the high road. AWANEN!

Tuesday, January 20, 1987
My House, Gomez, Cabarroguis, Quirino

We got up at 6:20 AM and George left; he came at 7:00 PM sharp last night. I started cooking breakfast, drank coffee and took my nuang to pasture beside the school. I returned home, finished cooking, ate, did dishes and got ready for the day. I went to George's and there wasn't a soul there, so off I went to the farm. I helped George pile wood for making charcoal for an hour and then I went and worked on weeding more on my farm. George left at about 11:00 AM or so, but I took my lunch with me, so I stayed and ate at noon, relaxed a while and then started weeding again at about 1:00 PM. I kept at it steadily until 3:30 PM and then stopped and picked a few cranberry pole beans, got my nuang and headed for home. I bathed my nuang and got home at about 4:15 PM. I fetched water, bathed, prepared things for supper and at 4:45 PM I started cooking. I went to George's for a while to talk and to ask him to come early, but even now at 5:30 PM I don't see any cooking smoke there yet, so I think he probably won't be here until after 7:00 PM. Anyway, now it is 5:35 PM, my supper is cooked and I'm going to finish this, eat and do dishes. We had no rain today, it was sunny off and on all day and I'm tired. George has slept here 233 nights now. AWANEN!

Wednesday, January 21, 1987
My House, Gomez, Cabarroguis, Quirino

Letter to Tom & Barb H.

₱165 – 5 = ₱160							
Cigarettes	3	Crackers	2			TOTAL	₱5

We got up at 6:00 AM and George left; he came at 6:30 PM last night. I started cooking breakfast, took my nuang to pasture and then I returned home, finished cooking, ate, washed dishes and got ready for the day. I swept the south yard again and then I went to George's to talk for a while. Alfredo and his wife went to town so George was there alone; it was nice to talk with him today. I moved my nuang and talked with George a while longer then returned home and started weeding the *kamote* patch. Then it was noon, so I ate lunch and after that I napped from 12:20 to 1:20 PM. I got up, weeded in the *kamote* patch some more and at 2:00 PM I went to move my nuang. I returned and talked with George some and he told me that he's going to a wedding in Burgos again tonight – shit! That makes two weddings this week. I returned home and finished weeding the *kamote* patch and planted pallang there with the *kamote*. Then I fetched water, returned and weeded around the outhouse until 4:00 PM. I prepared things for supper and then at 4:30 PM I lit the charcoal fire, went and got and bathed my nuang and then I returned home, ate, did dishes and now it's 6:50 PM and I still hear Junior and George talking at George's house, so maybe they won't go to the wedding, if I'm lucky. The weather today was cloudy most all day with a very few light showers. AWANEN!

Thursday, January 22, 1987
My House, Gomez, Cabarroguis, Quirino

Letter to Dad.

I got up at 6:10 AM with no companion because George did go to the wedding last night. I started cooking breakfast, drank coffee, took my nuang to pasture, returned and finished cooking, ate, did dishes and got ready for the day. I went to Alfredo's and George had not yet arrived home from the wedding. I returned home and finished the letter to Tom and Barb that I started yesterday and then I finished weeding the south yard and swept it again. At 10:00 AM I went and moved my nuang, returned home and started weeding the lower garden where nothing is currently planted. I worked on that until lunchtime and then ate lunch and drank coffee. I napped from 12:35 to 1:30 PM, got up, drank coffee and went to move my nuang again at 2:00 PM. I returned home and continued weeding the lower garden until 3:30 PM and then I stopped and dug up the pallang in that area which has finished fruiting. I read that the large tubers are edible so I cooked and ate them for supper and they're quite tasty. Then I fetched water, bathed and prepared things for supper. At 4:30 PM I went to George's to ask him to come early and also went to get and bathe my nuang. I returned home and finished cooking supper. Two guys whom I don't know stopped by to get some seedlings, only about a total of ten though. I started eating supper and Junior came to get more plastic bags for planting tree seeds and he also took six seedlings. I finished eating supper, did dishes and now it's 6:26 PM and I'm waiting for George. I hope he comes before 7:00 PM. It showered very lightly off and on today. AWANEN!

Chapter 16
Culture Notes #6

Weddings

Due to the fact that there have been two weddings mentioned in the past week, it must be time to include a culture note about weddings.

The wedding celebrations which I saw and took part in were substantially different from what we are familiar with in the United States. I personally only attended two weddings, and that was enough, I did not want to attend any more than that. To me they were long and boring. Everybody in the village is automatically invited, by word of mouth, to all weddings. I went to the first two that I was invited to, primarily out of a sense of obligation to the village. A wedding party starts about 8:00 PM, outdoors, after about 30 – 50 people have arrived. The village members will have rented a battery powered record player with HUGE speakers and about six to ten 45-RPM records. The single girls (*balasang*) sit on benches on one side of the dirt "dance floor" and the bachelors (*baru*) mill around in the crowd. This is where the young men generally meet the girl that they will eventually marry. If I may be allowed to leave the wedding party momentarily to present another point of interest that is appropriate at this time: there is no dating as such, no mixing of the sexes in normal day to day activities. The bachelors and *balasangs* never mix in other places. Aside from wedding parties the only way a bachelor can see a girl that he likes is to ask a minimum of two friends to go with him to her home. There they will sit in a group with the family of the girl and converse until maybe 9:00 or 10:00 PM, and then go home; a late night! The chances are slim that a bachelor has ever been alone with his bride until after the wedding.

For this reason wedding parties are important events where a bachelor and a *balasang* can actually be close and even touch! Despite the fact that a young man may be particularly attracted to a certain girl, he is expected to divide his dances between all of the girls. It would look very bad and be the talk of the village if a bachelor danced with the same *balasang* more than about five times during the night.

Back to the wedding party: The battery powered phonograph is playing the same six to ten 45-RPM records over and over at about 100 decibels, and the bachelors can pay "the master of the phonograph" to play a special request, from the very limited selection of records. This raises money for the bride and groom. The dancing goes on until dawn and then most people go home. The bride and groom go to a church, with a few INVITED people, and a priest joins the two together as husband and wife. The new husband and wife return home, and by then anybody who wants to, is waiting at their house to congratulate them. At about noon some pigs and/or goats and/or dogs will be butchered by the guests. These may be donated by other village members, but if not, then the groom is expected to furnish them. There must be enough food to satisfy the hunger of however many guests may show up. If there were to be a shortage of food on the wedding day, it would be a very bad omen, indicating that food would be in short supply during the couples entire married life. This day is merely for storytelling and such. The bachelors and *balasangs* have all gone home and this part of the wedding party is for the adults. About 4 – 5:00 PM the crowd eats and soon disperses, to be able to be home before dark. The bride and groom finally get to relax and be alone for the first time. All the cleaning up of the food and so on has been done by the guests. I could easily visualize the bride and groom breathing a sigh of relief and falling asleep in each other's arms immediately, that is, if they weren't too shy this first night.

The "Art" of Moonlight Strolling

You have seen some references to the people "strolling" around until late at night and George not coming to sleep at my house, or coming quite late. Back on page 93 it was mentioned that batteries were quite precious to these villagers and they had to be saved to be able to use for listening to the radio. Therefore, for the two or three days before and after a full moon, if the skies were clear, people would use the bright moonlight as an opportunity to walk around and do whatever they did. It seemed to me that it was generally the young bachelors who took these strolls, so I suspect that they would go the home of some *balasang* that one of the bachelors felt an attraction for. Remember just above I told you that "Aside from wedding parties the only way a bachelor can see a girl that he likes is to ask a minimum of two friends to go with him to her home. There they will sit in a group with the family of the girl and converse until maybe 9:00 or 10:00 PM, and then go home; a late night!" This is what these strolls around the full moon were.

There could also be other purposes, for example doing some illegal fishing with dynamite or electricity, stealing other people's crops of fruits and/or vegetables and so on. It is sad to say, but when various crops were ready to harvest (especially the precious corn) around the full moon that George sometimes had to spend the night guarding his corn field! Even that precaution did not always save the day, so to speak, due to the large size of the corn fields.

Chapter 17
January 23, 1987 through April 18, 1987

Friday, January 23, 1987
My House, Gomez, Cabarroguis, Quirino

Letters from Ronald, Sue T. and Vicki K.

₱160 + 300 – 230 = ₱230							
Cigarettes	10	Food	83	Rides	4	Candy	18
Coffee	27	Marienda	40	Kerosene	7	Soap	9
Household	6	Misc.	26			TOTAL	₱230

We got up at 6:15 AM and George left; he didn't come until 8:00 PM last night because their supper was late. I gave him my *wayway* before he left, drank a cup of coffee and headed for Burgos at 6:45 AM. I stopped at Rufo's to talk about trading a calculator for his plow and then proceeded on to Burgos. I continued on from there to Gundaway, stopped at the post office and got the above mail and then I went to market, did my shopping and headed for home. I got back to the house at about 11:15 AM and went to George's for a few minutes to get my valuables. Then I returned home, ate a small lunch and weeded the lower garden some more. Then I napped from 2:20 to 3:00 PM, got up and went to fetch water. I returned, bathed and prepared things for supper. At 5:00 PM I went to George's to get my nuang and to ask him to come early. Now it's 5:42 PM and supper is nearly finished cooking. I'm having *utong*, *parya*, *tarong* and Miki noodles for supper, no rice tonight. It was dry and sunny again today; even the lower trail is okay for wearing flip-flops all the way to Burgos, although I returned via the high road; it's still better than the low road. AWANEN!

Saturday, January 24, 1987
My House, Gomez, Cabarroguis, Quirino

Letter to Sue T.

I got up at 6:10 AM. George got up at 5:00 AM and left to release his nuang, as he was pulling a cant from Calaocan today. He came at about 7:00 PM last night. I started cooking breakfast, drank coffee and went and pastured my nuang and then I returned and finished cooking, ate and then Alfredo came and we went to Rufo's to inspect the plow that he might trade me for a calculator. Alfredo approved of the plow and so I traded my solar calculator for it and then returned home. I washed the breakfast dishes, got ready for the day and then cleaned rust off the plow and sanded it's tooth, took it to Alfredo's and we did some minor repairs on it. I went and got and bathed my nuang at 11:00 AM, returned home, ate lunch and started writing a letter to Sue T. Then I laid down to nap for a while, but I couldn't sleep, so I got up and weeded more of the lower garden area until 4:00 PM. Then I fetched water, bathed and at 4:30 PM I went to get and bathe my nuang. I went to George's to ask him to come early; I hope he does. Now it's 6:03 PM and while I'm waiting for him I'll work on the letter to Sue some more. I hear Junior at George's house so I can only hope that George will arrive early tonight. The weather today was cloudy and cool until 10:30 AM or so and then it was bright sun until 4:00 PM, when it clouded up again. It hasn't rained today, not yet anyway. AWANEN!

Sunday, January 25, 1987
My House, Gomez, Cabarroguis, Quirino
George's Birthday

Letter to Vicki K.

We got up at 6:10 AM and George left; he didn't come until 7:20 PM last night, after I went there at 7:00 PM and asked him to come soon. I started cooking breakfast, drank coffee and took my nuang to pasture. I returned home, finished cooking, ate, did dishes and got ready for the day. George pulled his cant to Burgos today. The first thing I did was finish the letter to Sue T. and by then it was 10:00 AM and time to move my nuang. I returned home and pulled weeds in the lower garden for a while but the sip-sips [a small biting fly] were really thick today so I didn't do that for very long, but it was lunchtime anyway, so I ate and then napped for a while. Then it was 2:00 PM so I went and moved my nuang, returned home and started writing the letter to Vicki. I fetched water, returned home and entered the "Happy Birthday" program into the HP-41 and rewrote it for the HP-71 and put it there too – cool. By then it was 4:00 PM so I fetched water, prepared things for supper, lit the fire and went to move my nuang. I returned home and stopped at George's to ask him to come early and he said yes, he will come as soon as they finish supper; I hope so. Now it's 5:54 PM, I'm done eating, dishes are done and I'm waiting for George already. The weather today was rainy, cool and windy. The high temperature was only about 70°F today. I think I'll look through my medical kit and check for expired drugs. AWANEN!

Monday, January 26, 1987
My House, Gomez, Cabarroguis, Quirino

Letter to Dave M.

We got up at 6:15 AM and George left; he came at 6:20 PM last night and I gave him his birthday present of really nice short pants, but they are way too big – shit! It was really cold this morning so I cooked breakfast, ate, did dishes and got ready for the day before I went to move my nuang. After I moved her I returned and talked with George for a while and then I returned home and wrote the letter to Dave. By then it was 11:00 AM so I went and moved my nuang again and helped George repair the one *dalayday* [the harness used for pulling cants with the nuang]. Tomorrow I get to pull my first cant using the *dalayday*. I returned home, ate lunch and then did laundry in the rain. Hopefully it will be dry by Wednesday afternoon when I have to go to the Diffun office. That took until nearly 3:00 PM and then I went and took my nuang to bathe and drink and then back to pasture. By then it was nearly 4:15 PM so I went home and prepared things for supper, fetched water and bathed. At 4:35 PM I started cooking supper and then went to ask George to come early. I returned home at 5:05 PM and the rice was done. I cooked the vegetables and ate. While I was eating Alfredo brought me some of their supper and it was delicious, although I don't know what it was. Now it's 6:13 PM and I'm waiting for George. I know they've eaten so he should be here soon. The weather today was cold and it rained off and on all day. AWANEN!

Tuesday, January 27, 1987
My House, Gomez, Cabarroguis, Quirino

We got up at 5:30 AM and George left; he came at 6:40 PM last night. We got up early because of our plan to pull cants today, so I started cooking breakfast, drank coffee and as soon as it was light enough to see I went to move my nuang. I returned home, finished cooking, ate, did dishes and got ready for the day. I packed my lunch and at 7:30 AM I went to George's. We waited until 9:40 AM and decided there would be no cants to be pulled today, so I returned home and Sip came practically immediately to tell me to get my nuang – there were cants to be pulled. So, George and I got our nuangs, ate lunch and at 11:10 AM we left – George, Junior, Brando's brother and I headed for the location of the cants. We got to the cants at 1:10 PM and after loading them on the *dalaydays* we headed for home. My cant was 55 board feet and George's was 73 board feet. We had a difficult trek home due to steep hills and the cants kept wanting to roll away, but we finally made it just before 6:00 PM. I unhooked and bathed my nuang and took her to pasture and now it's 6:42 PM. It was a long hard day and I'm tired; I'm not eating supper tonight either, I'm too tired and it's too late to cook. The weather today was rainy off and on all day. Tomorrow we're going to pull the cants to Burgos. Oh, I was riding my nuang for nearly seven hours today and my ass isn't even sore, I guess it has finally got calluses in the right spots. AWANEN!

Wednesday, January 28, 1987
BFD Office, Diffun, Quirino

Letters from Bill N., two from Chad D., Tim C., Dad, Barb W., Ardis B. – and two packages, San & Jack G. – plus a package, JB & Katie F, package from Bob S.

₱230 + 500 – 15 = ₱715							
Cigarettes	5	Marienda	4	Ride	4	Postage	2
						TOTAL	₱15

We got up at 5:30 AM and George left; he came at 7:15 PM last night. I started cooking breakfast, drank coffee and went and moved my nuang. I returned home, finished cooking, ate, did dishes and got ready for the day. At 7:40 AM I went to George's and immediately went to get my nuang. At about 8:15 AM George, Junior, Brando's brother and I headed for Burgos with our cants. George and I were last to arrive at Burgos by quite a few minutes because we had lots of problems with his *dalayday* and my cants. We got to Burgos and got rid of our cants at about 10:30 AM, took a short break and I headed home alone. George and Junior stayed behind trying to get paid, but I don't know if they succeeded or not. I got back home at about 12:20 PM, talked with Alfredo for a while and went home to eat and get ready. I was ready at 1:45 PM and went to Alfredo's to leave my bag of valuables and to see if George had arrived yet; no he hadn't. I left again at 2:00 PM, arrived at Burgos at 3:00 PM, Gundaway at 3:40 PM, got the above mail and continued on to Diffun and the office. I arrived at about 4:50 PM and now it's 5:19 PM and maybe this is my only chance for privacy tonight. I have to meet my new Peace Corps Associate Director, Cery Abad in Maddela tomorrow at 8:00 AM. I was told that several people will be sleeping here at the office tonight, which is why I said that maybe this is my only chance for privacy. It rained a little on and off today. AWANEN!

Thursday, January 29, 1987
Ralph P's House, Maddela, Quirino

₱715 – 58 = ₱657							
Cigarettes	9	Marienda	7	Ride	9	Food	24
Misc.	9					TOTAL	₱58

I got up at 5:15 AM, got ready for the day, drank coffee and I was ready to leave by 6:15 AM. I went out to the road to wait for a ride and a Basco Transportation Bus came along at 7:00 AM. I was less than half way to Maddela and Cery passed the bus. Fortunately, we saw each other, so he stopped and I rode with him the rest of the way to Maddela. We arrived at the MAF office at about 8:15 AM and then we went to the mayor's office and after a while Ralph P. came by and we talked a while longer. Then we went to the BFD office in Nagtipunan. We hung out there until around noon and then we went to eat lunch. After lunch we went to the proposed BFD site and it was very much like the Diffuncian Nursery and bunkhouse and etc. It sounded like they want a fish and animal production person more than they want an agro-forestry type person. We finally returned, went to market and bought things for supper. Then went to Ralph's house and cooked. We had a rather late supper, about 7:30 PM or so. Now it's 9:16 PM, the latest I've been up in quite some time, I'm tired. AWANEN!

Friday, January 30, 1987
Ralph P's House, Maddela, Quirino

₱657 – 35 = ₱622							
Food	13	Coke	6	Cigarettes	10	Misc.	6
						TOTAL	₱35

We got up at 5:45 AM and after a while we cooked and ate breakfast. We got ready for the day and at around 8:30 AM Cery and his driver left. Ralph and I goofed off for the rest of the morning, cooked an early lunch and ate about 11:45 AM. After lunch we hiked right behind Ralph's house up onto the mountain with his neighbor, who is also named Alfredo. We hiked up this pretty nice looking creek and to a waterfall, where we bathed. Then we headed back down. We picked some snow peas on the way home and talked with several different groups of people. We got back to Ralph's house at about 4:00 PM or so, killed time for a while and cooked a late supper. We didn't eat until practically 8:00 PM and then two people came over to talk and ended up staying here until a bit after 9:00 PM. They left and now it is 9:30 PM, Ralph just finished washing dishes and we're about ready to call it a day and crash. AWANEN!

Saturday, January 31, 1987
My House, Gomez, Cabarroguis, Quirino

₱622 – 180 = ₱442							
Nuang Meds	70	Food	32	Marienda	33	Rides	10
Cigarettes	10	Lunch	15	Misc.	10	TOTAL	₱180

We got up at 6:30 AM; late because we stayed up until 11:30 PM last night talking with people and smoking!! We got REALLY HIGH! Ralph cooked breakfast, we ate, got ready for the day and talked until 11:00 AM or so. Then we went to Maddela and I did shopping as shown above. We ate lunch, strolled for a while and then we went and had a beer and I went to the bus station at 1:45 PM. I left Maddela at around 2:20 PM and didn't arrive at Gundaway until 4:00 PM and then Burgos at 4:25 PM. I climbed the mountain via the high road and got home at about 5:20 PM. I fetched water, started cooking and Alfredo came to talk for a while; until his wife called him for supper. I went to ask George to come early and he said yes. Now it's 6:26 PM and my vegetables are nearly done cooking. I'll eat, do dishes, wait for George and hope that he comes early tonight. AWANEN!

Sunday, February 1, 1987
My House, Gomez, Cabarroguis, Quirino

We got up at 5:45 AM and George left; he came just before 7:00 PM last night. I started cooking breakfast, drank coffee and went and moved my nuang. I returned home, finished cooking, ate, did dishes, got ready for the day and went to Alfredo's. George pulled cants to Burgos today. I hung out at Alfredo's until 9:30 AM and then returned home and read all of the mail that I picked up last Wednesday. Then I used the *lampaso* to clean and wax the floor of the house. Alfredo came and we talked until 11:40 AM and then he left. I went to move my nuang and returned home, ate lunch and laid down for a half hour, but I couldn't sleep. Sip brought me some *aso* [dog meat] – Esco, Alfredo's dog, died while I was gone. Then I got out the HP-71 and played with the text editor. I recopied the foreign address file and figured out how to manipulate it using the EDTEXT program. I worked on that until 2:45 PM and then went and moved my nuang and took her to drink and bathe. I returned home and played with the HP-71 until 4:30 PM, fetched water, bathed and then started cooking supper. Tonight I had just a few vegetables and the dog meat. I ate, did dishes and now it's 6:19 PM and I'm waiting for George; hopefully he'll be here before 7:00 PM. It rained most of the day today. AWANEN!

Monday, February 2, 1987
My House, Gomez, Cabarroguis, Quirino
Voting Day for New Constitution

We got up at 5:45 AM and George left; he came at 7:40 PM last night, late due to another singing contest on the radio. I started cooking breakfast, drank coffee and went to move my nuang. I returned home, finished cooking, ate, did dishes and got ready for the day. I went to George's to talk for a while and then I returned home and played with the HP-71. I reentered all of my USA addresses as a text file and wrote the program to update the last wrote and last received dates for letters using the HP-41 translation pack. It took a great deal of the work out of it. I finished debugging the program at about 11:20 AM and went to move my nuang, returned home and ate lunch. Then I played with the HP-71 some more until about 3:00 PM and went to move my nuang again. I returned home got ½ ready to go to town tomorrow, fetched water and then swept the north yard. After that I bathed and prepared things for supper. At 4:30 PM I went and got and bathed my nuang, returned home, finished cooking, ate, did dishes and went to George's to talk for a while. It's going to be a late supper for them tonight I'm afraid. The votes on the new constitution in Gomez wear 90 "yes" and 65 "no". The weather today was rainy in the morning and then sunny and fairly nice in the afternoon. Maybe I'll write a letter until George comes. AWANEN!

Tuesday, February 3, 1987
My House, Gomez, Cabarroguis, Quirino

Postcard from San & Jack G.

₱442 + 145 – 424 = ₱163

Cigarettes	14	Rides	16	Food	162	Marienda	9
Household	26	Kerosene	7	Lunch	66	Coffee	54
Candy	13	Toy Jeep	40	Misc.	17	TOTAL	₱424

We got up at 5:45 AM, I gave George my *wayway*, and he left. He came at about 6:40 PM last night. I drank coffee and hit the road for Burgos at 6:30 AM, arriving there at 7:40 AM. I caught a jeepney, stopped at Gundaway and got my mail at the post office and then continued on to Santiago. I arrived there at 9:45 AM and went to Letty's Restaurant. I ran into JB and Katie there and we talked until 11:45 AM and then I went to the bank, where I happened to run into Willie S. and Ralph P. We did our banking and then we went to the 456 Restaurant for lunch and stayed there talking until 1:30 PM. Then I went to Marilen's to get some things and then to market. I finished everything at 3:00 PM and caught a jeepney. I arrived in Burgos at 4:40 PM and climbed the mountain via the high road, getting home at 5:35 PM. I started the rice cooking and went to Alfredo's to ask him how to cook *pusit* (squid) and I gave him half of the fresh *pusit* and returned home to cook. Now it's 6:34 PM and the *pusit* is cooking. I hope George comes early tonight, I'm tired and I want to sleep. It rained most of the day and both the high road and the low road were a mess. AWANEN!

Wednesday, February 4, 1987
My House, Gomez, Cabarroguis, Quirino

Letters to Jim & Roselynn, Bob S. and Ardis B.

We got up at 6:00 AM and George left; he came at 7:00 PM last night. I started cooking breakfast, drank coffee and took my nuang to pasture. Then I returned home, finished cooking, ate, did dishes and got ready for the day. Alfredo and his wife went down the mountain to sell bananas today and George went to the farm. I finished the letter to Jim in Roselynn that I started two days ago and by then it was 10:00 AM so I went and moved my nuang. I returned home and started the letter to Bob and then started to get an idea of how to write a program to add up all the letters I've written and received. At this point I've written 363 letters and received 380, an 82.6% response rate – pretty good. Then I finished the letter to Bob, ate lunch, took a break and by then it was 2:30 PM so I went and moved and bathed my nuang and stopped at Alfredo's on the way home to talk for a half hour. I came home at 4:00 PM and prepared things for supper. At 4:30 PM I started cooking and also started a letter to Ardis. At 5:20 PM supper was done, so I ate and did dishes. Now it's 6:19 PM and I'm already waiting for George, I hope he comes early tonight. I'll finish the letter to Ardis while waiting for him. The weather today was rainy most of the day and it never got above 64°F – Brrrr! One of these days it's got to start warming up again. AWANEN!

Thursday, February 5, 1987
My House, Gomez, Cabarroguis, Quirino

Letter to San & Jack G.

We got up at 6:00 AM and George left; he came at 6:50 PM last night. Upon getting up this morning it was the coldest I've yet seen here in Gomez, it was an even 60°F. It was SO cold and, raining too, that I cooked breakfast, drank coffee, ate and got ready for the day before I moved my nuang. George and Alfredo both went to the farm today to *agtabas*. After moving my nuang I returned home and wrote a letter to San and Jack. That took until 11:00 AM and then I rewrote the Happy Birthday program for my HP-71 so that it's even better than before! Then I ate lunch, drank coffee and about then the sun actually came out, so I weeded in the lower garden some more, just to be able to work in the sun. I quit at 2:00 PM, fetched water and then went to bathe and move my nuang. I got back home at about 3:15 PM and drank a cup of coffee and then got brave and bathed in the cold creek!!! Then it was 4:00 PM so I prepared things for supper and at 4:30 PM I started cooking. I went to Alfredo's to talk but he wasn't home, so I talked with his wife for a while and then returned home. I finished cooking, ate, did dishes and now it's 6:27 PM and I'm waiting for George, although I'll be surprised if he makes it before 7:00 PM tonight. It's going to be a late supper for them as they didn't get back from the farm until about 5:30 PM. The high temperature today was 66°F. AWANEN!

Friday, February 6, 1987
My House, Gomez, Cabarroguis, Quirino

We got up at 6:10 AM and George left; he didn't come until 7:30 PM last night because of their late supper. It was 60°F again this morning – two days in a row of this cold weather. I started cooking breakfast, drank coffee and went to move my nuang. I returned home, finished cooking, ate, did dishes, got ready for the day and then I got a late start on laundry, at about 9:00 AM. I worked on that until 11:10 AM. Alfredo and George both went to the farm today. After finishing laundry I took a break and then I went to move my nuang. I returned home, ate lunch and then napped from 12:40 to 1:40 PM. When I got up I cut the dead leaves off my banana trees and pulled weeds in the lower garden until 3:00 PM and then I went and bathed and moved my nuang, which took until 4:00 PM. I returned home and prepared things for supper at 4:30 PM and then I started cooking the rice. At 5:00 PM I saw George at their house so I went to talk with him for a few minutes and asked him to come early; he said yes, but undoubtedly their supper will be late again tonight, so we'll see if he gets here before 7:30 PM, I hope so. Now it's 6:29 PM and I'm done eating, done with dishes and waiting for George. I'll start a letter to JB and Katie while I'm waiting. The weather today – there was no rain but there was no bright and warm sun either, the high was 70°F. AWANEN!

Saturday, February 7, 1987
My House, Gomez, Cabarroguis, Quirino

Nestor come and spend the night.

We got up at 5:50 AM and George left; he came at 6:40 PM last night. I cooked breakfast, ate, did dishes, got ready for the day and then I took my valuables to Alfredo's, went and got my nuang and went to the farm for the day. I arrived there at about 8:30 AM and George was already plowing so I went to my farm and started pulling weeds. I pulled weeds until noon and then we all ate lunch and took a break. We went back to work at 1:00 PM. I pulled weeds again until 3:30 PM, harvested some mustard greens and headed for home first. I bathed my nuang and got home at about 4:30 PM and – surprise – Nestor was waiting here for me. He said he had arrived at about noon and he showed me how to break into my house very easily! I started the rice cooking and we prepared the vegetables, cooked supper, ate, did dishes and talked for a while. Now it's 7:20 PM and time to do some serious bullshitting! It's been a long time since Nestor and I last saw each other. AWANEN!

Sunday, February 8, 1987
My House, Gomez, Cabarroguis, Quirino

Finish letter to JB & Katie F.
Nestor leave.

I got up at 6:00 AM, started the rice, drank coffee and went to pasture my nuang. I also took a lukban to George's house. When I returned home Nestor was up and we finished cooking breakfast, ate, did dishes and got ready for the day. Then we went to Alfredo's on the way to the farm and he was repairing my plow, so we helped him with that for nearly an hour. Then we continued on to the farm. I showed Nestor my farm and how weed filled it is and then showed him George's farm and how beautiful the corn is. By then it was nearly 11:00 AM so we started back for home. We came home by the side path that leads to the nuang pasturing place above the house and we moved my nuang, returned home, cooked lunch, ate and did dishes again. Then we bathed and Alfredo came to talk for a bit. After a while Nestor left, he said he'd take the high road so I gave him directions and he left. I showed Alfredo pictures of my house in Alaska and then at 3:20 PM I went to water, bathe and move my nuang. I returned home, prepared food for supper, cooked, ate, did dishes and went to George's until 6:35 PM. I returned home and now it's 6:48 PM and I'm waiting for George to come. They haven't eaten yet so undoubtedly he'll be somewhat late. There was light rain on and off all day today and it wasn't very warm. I'm going to write some more on the letter to JB and Katie now. AWANEN!

Monday, February 9, 1987
My House, Gomez, Cabarroguis, Quirino

We got up at 6:00 AM and George left; he didn't come until 7:50 PM last night because of their late supper. I cooked breakfast, ate, did the dishes and got ready for the day. I went and got my nuang and George, Alfredo, Sip and I went to the farm. Alfredo took my plow on the cart. We got to the farm, I pastured my nuang and then used sandpaper on my plow tooth to polish and smooth it so that soil does not stick to it. Then I went and weeded my farm while George and Alfredo worked on plowing the newly cleared area on their farm. We stopped at 12:30 PM, ate lunch and rested until 1:15 PM and then we went back to work again. There are already a few small winged bean (pallang) fruits on the plants which I planted on November 24th – only two and a half months ago. I weeded until 3:30 PM, stopped and headed home. I arrived at about 4:40 PM, started the rice cooking and prepared the vegetables. When things were done cooking I took the Maalox liquid to Alfredo – his ulcer is acting up again – but he hadn't yet arrived so I returned home ate, did the dishes and went back to Alfredo's to tell him how much Maalox to take, we talked for a while and I asked George to come soon, but now it's 6:50 PM and they haven't eaten supper yet so I'll be lucky if he makes it before 7:30 PM tonight. It was rainy and sunny on and off all day today, crazy weather. Well, I'm now waiting for George, like every night for nearly a year now. AWANEN!

Tuesday, February 10, 1987
My House, Gomez, Cabarroguis, Quirino

Letter to Dad.

₱163 + 700 – 8 = ₱855						
Cigarettes	5	Soap	3		TOTAL	₱8

We got up at 6:00 AM and George left; he didn't come until 7:30 PM last night due to their late supper. I started cooking breakfast and took my nuang to pasture. I returned home, finished cooking, ate did dishes and got ready for the day. I went to George's for a couple of minutes but he had gone to the farm and Alfredo had gone to the Barangay Assembly Meeting so I returned home and did laundry – even my shoes, so that they are clean to go to Manila. I finished that at 10:00 AM, drank coffee and went and got my nuang at 10:30 AM. I returned home and started packing for Manila. At about 11:30 AM or so Francisco and my new coworker came. Francisco showed him the trail to Gomez. We talked together until they left at 1:40 PM and then I took my nuang back to pasture and it clouded up. I returned home and took a siesta from 2:20 to 3:20 PM, got up and more or less finished packing. Junior came to get some aspirin and he left at 4:00 PM. I fetched water, bathed and prepared things for supper. At 4:45 PM I lit my fire and went and got and bathed my nuang. Then I returned home, finished cooking, ate, did dishes and went to George's to talk for a while. Now it's 6:47 PM and they will be eating late again tonight because they were just butchering a chicken when I was there, so I'll finish packing and maybe write a letter while I'm waiting for George. AWANEN!

Wednesday, February 11, 1987
Malate Pension, Manila

Letter and film from Ardis B., letter and book from Chad D., letter from Dave G., books from BOSTID and ICE.

₱855 – 306 = ₱549							
Cigarettes	35	Rides	68	Food	44	Marienda	51
Household	25	Postage	4	Magazine	30	Supper	49
						TOTAL	₱306

We got up at 5:50 AM, I gave George my *wayway* and extra food and he left. He came at 8:05 PM last night due to their late supper. I drank coffee, took my valuables to George's house and left Gomez at 6:40 AM. I arrived in Burgos at 7:30 PM, caught a jeepney to Gundaway, got the above mail at the post office (a package of books from ICE arrived that I ordered on September 11, 1986 – four months ago). I continued on to Cordon and arrived there at 9:20 AM. Eventually I was able to get on a bus bound for Manila and had an uneventful trip, we had no flat tires and no breakdowns. I arrived in Manila at about 5:20 PM and caught a jeepney to Quiapo and then another one to Mabini Street and I got to Malate Pension at about 5:30 PM – 11 hours after I left Gomez! I took a shower and relaxed over a Coke and a milkshake and then I went to Robinson's Department Store where I found a pretty nice photo album for Alfredo, but I didn't buy it because I want to search at some other places tomorrow and see if I can find a nicer or better one. I returned to Malate Pension, sat down to eat and a couple nice ladies from Switzerland joined me for supper. Now it's 8:57 PM and we're eating ice cream. After this I'm going up to the room and sleep. I wonder if George is already asleep? AWANEN!

Thursday, February 12, 1987
Malate Pension, Manila

Postcard to George.

₱549 – 402 = ₱147							
Meals	62	Marienda	37	Postage	206	Rides	4
Food	93					TOTAL	₱402

I got up at 5:30 AM showered and got ready for the day. I went downstairs, drank coffee, ate breakfast and then at 8:00 AM I went over to the Peace Corps Office. They took some blood and made a dental appointment for me for 2:30 PM. I searched for Brooke, but she wasn't there, oh well. I finished my business there and then walked down Rizal Avenue and took a trip to the book stores, like I always do. Then I went to the post office to get aerogrammes and stamps. I returned to Malate Pension and ordered lunch at 1:15 PM. At 2:00 PM it still hadn't been served so I left and went to the dentist; my tooth has to be capped – shit! After I finished at the dentist I went to Dunkin' Donuts, drank coffee, ate a donut and wrote a postcard to George. I returned to Malate Pension and talked with people for a while and then I went to a grocery store looking for some peanut butter and bread. I returned to Malate Pension again and Egan, a fellow from Canada, and I went to supper at the Lucky Pension. It was expensive and they only gave us a little food – bummer! We returned to Malate Pension and now it's 9:39 PM and time to crash. AWANEN!

Friday, February 13, 1987
Malate Pension, Manila

Letter to Dave G.

₱147 + 200 – 135 = ₱212							
Meals	60	Marienda	47	Cigarettes	24	Coke	4
						TOTAL	₱135

I got up at 5:30 AM, showered and got ready for the day. I went to eat at a different place and then returned to Malate Pension for coffee only. After that I went to the Peace Corps Office and gave them a stool sample; they couldn't find any worms, despite the fact that my blood work shows that I probably do have some, oh well. I went and talked with Brooke for a while and she suggested that I write up something about winged beans for the newsletter, so I worked in the office there for about four hours and wrote an article about winged beans. I typed it and turned it in to Brooke at about 2:15 PM and returned to Malate Pension. After a while I ate ice cream, drank a Coke, ate some bread and peanut butter and talked with various people. I wrote a letter to Dave G. and then at 7:00 PM Egan and I went to the Aristocrat Restaurant for supper and then to Dunkin' Donuts for coffee and donuts. We returned to Malate Pension and now it's 10:21 PM, past bedtime. What shall I do tomorrow, who knows? AWANEN!

Saturday, February 14, 1987
Malate Pension, Manila

Letter to Chad D.

₱212 – 145 = ₱67							
Meals	107	Fruit	30	Coke	8	TOTAL	₱145

I got up relatively late, at 6:10 AM. I showered and went downstairs for breakfast today. Then I went over to the Peace Corps Office and into the Volunteer's work area to rewrite and type my story about when George ran away from home. The photocopy person even showed up about the time I finished, so I was able to photocopy it and leave a copy at the *Salaysayan* Office. I finished that up at about 12:30 PM and came back to Malate Pension. We (Egan and I) ate some Mangosteens and they were so delicious that Egan and I went back to the fruit market for more, they're really amazingly wonderful. We returned to Malate Pension again and ate a tuna sandwich and then talked for an hour or so. Then I wrote the letter to Chad and after that Egan and I went out to the Bungalow Restaurant for supper. We talked until 9:30 PM or so and then returned to Malate Pension. Now it's 10:25 PM and I'm tired, I'm going to drink a glass of water and crash. AWANEN!

Sunday, February 15, 1987
Malate Pension, Manila

Postcards to Ardis B. and George.

₱67 + 300 – 248 = ₱119							
Rides	5	Meals	95	Marienda	43	Household	21
Presents	84					TOTAL	₱248

I got up at 6:10 AM, showered, got ready for the day and went downstairs for coffee. Five of us went to Dunkin' Donuts for coffee and donuts and after that we went to the Seafront Restaurant and hung out there until noon eating brunch. We ate one hell of a lot of food. After that three of us went to Silahis – a native crafts place and spent until 3:30 PM looking around there. Then we returned to Malate Pension, drank a coke, a milkshake and a *buko* [iced coconut water]. After a while I went up to the room and took a half hour nap from 5:00 to 5:30 PM and then I went back downstairs to talk for a while. At about 8:00 PM I took off alone for Dunkin' Donuts again for another coffee and more donuts and I also wrote postcards to George and Ardis. Now it's 9:12 PM and I'm ready to sleep. Heck, I wish I was home in Gomez sleeping with George beside me right now. AWANEN!

Monday, February 16, 1987
Malate Pension, Manila

Receive per diem payment of ₱1,548.

₱119 + 200 – 224 = ₱95							
Meals	65	Rides	3	Presents	75	Marienda	20
Cigarettes	24	Coke	7	Ice Cream	15	Seeds	15
						TOTAL	₱224

I got up at 6:10 AM, showered, got ready for the day and went downstairs for breakfast. After eating I went to the dentist and he put the cap on my tooth today. I finished at the dentist at about 9:30 AM or so and returned to Malate Pension. Jennifer and I went to a handicrafts place and looked around there for a while and then we went to BPI and Greenworld for some seeds. After that we went to Baclaran and I got short pants for George. We returned to Malate and I took a 20 minute siesta. I got up and went to Pistang Filipino and found a place to buy some wooden nuangs before I go home. I bought one six-inch nuang for ₱50. The people who run the shop are Ilokano and they're really agreeable to giving me good prices – great! After that I went back to Malate Pension and after a while I ate a late supper and came up to the room again. Now it's 10:43 PM and I'm tired. Goodnight. AWANEN!

Tuesday, February 17, 1987
Host Family, Bonfal East, Bayombong, Nueva Vizcaya

₱95 + 300 – 271 = ₱124							
Meals	23	Presents	15	Rides	51	Marienda	15
Lodging	150	Laundry	17			TOTAL	₱271

I got up at 6:00 AM, showered, got ready for the day and went over to the Peace Corps Office. I gave them three MIF Kits [stool samples collected over a few days] and another fresh stool sample but they couldn't find my worms so they gave me an all-purpose worm killer – some kind of iron pill – and sent me on my way. I went back to the pension and decided to go home, so I checked out at about 11:00 AM, walked to Mabini street and got a jeepney to the Pantranco Bus Terminal. I got a 1:00 PM bus headed north and arrived in Bayombong at 7:00 PM. I walked to the Bonfal East house and the family was happy to see me. Mother had her baby on January 29th and named him Regan. We ate supper and talked for a while and now it's 8:58 PM and I'm ready to sleep. [I can't recall, but I assume that Ronald requested and received his usual blow job from me.] AWANEN!

Wednesday, February 18, 1987
My House, Gomez, Cabarroguis, Quirino

Letters from Bob S. (a new watch too), Steve A. (and a package), JB & Katie F., Jerry J., Ronald, Mike Mc., more books from BOSTID.

₱124 + 200 – 157 = ₱167							
Food	78	Rides	16	Meals	12	Postage	5
Kerosene	7	Marienda	35	Ice Cream	4	TOTAL	₱157

We got up at 6:10 AM, ate breakfast pretty quickly, got ready for the day and at 8:00 AM Ronald and I left for the bus waiting shed. I took a tricycle to Solano and then the Vizcaya Liner to Santiago, where I arrived at about 10:20 AM. I did my marketing, ate a small lunch at Letty's and headed for home. I got out of Santiago at about 12:20 PM, stopped at Gundaway and went to the post office, where I got the above mail. Bob S. sent me a watch and some batteries. Steve A. sent me some ball pens and a calendar. I've been getting lots of packages lately. After the post office stop I continued on to Burgos. I got out of the jeepney at the high road junction and George was there! He came down and sold charcoal today. So we sat and talked for a while and he carried my big box of books that I received from ICE last Wednesday, but didn't pick up from the post office until today. Thank heavens I happened to run into him with the cart. We left at 2:40 PM, went up the mountain and arrived home at 3:30 PM. Alfredo and everybody came immediately and then at about 4:50 PM Alfredo left. I fetched water, cooked, ate, washed dishes, took them there remembrances from the big city and asked George to come early. Now it's 6:21 PM and of course, I'm waiting for George. I'll read my mail until he comes. It's damn good to be home. Amazingly, there's been no rain since I left. AWANEN!

Thursday, February 19, 1987
My House, Gomez, Cabarroguis, Quirino

Letter to Bob S.

We got up at 5:50 AM and George left; he came at about 7:10 PM last night. I started cooking breakfast, drank coffee and went to George's to get my nuang and take her to pasture but Alfredo told me that they'll take her to the farm; okay. I talked with Alfredo for a while and then returned home, finished cooking breakfast, ate, did the dishes and got ready for the day. I did laundry first thing this morning, finished that at about 10:00 AM and laid down for a while, but I couldn't sleep. I got back up at 11:15 AM or so and swept all of the yard. Everything is dry and the soil is cracked open, so it was easy to sweep. That took until nearly 1:30 PM and then I laid down for a little while again. I got up and weeded the southeast garden area and when I finished up, at about 4:00 PM I bathed and then went to fetch water. I wasn't very hungry tonight so I didn't cook. Seeing as I didn't eat lunch, I ate breakfast leftovers for supper. After eating supper and doing dishes I went to George's for a while to talk and ask him to come early; it seems like they're having a late supper tonight so I'll be lucky if he's here before 7:30 PM. Now it's 6:31 PM so I'll write a letter to Bob while I'm waiting for George. The temperature was 62°F this morning but after a while it was up to 80°F, it was a hot sunny day. AWANEN!

Friday, February 20, 1987
My House, Gomez, Cabarroguis, Quirino

We got up at 5:40 AM and George left; he came at 7:30 PM last night because of their late supper. I started cooking breakfast, drank coffee and went to George's to pasture my nuang, but Alfredo told me it wasn't necessary as they're going to the farm today. So, I returned home, finished cooking, ate, got ready for the day and the ISF technician – Rody's replacement – showed up. Alfredo was already waiting for me and George had gone to *agtabas* at Junior's farm so I told Rody's replacement I had to go. We decided to have the March meeting on the 2nd and I left. Alfredo and I went to the farm and weeded until 12:00 noon and then we had lunch and rested until nearly 2:00 PM. After that we returned to work and did some more weeding. We worked until 4:00 PM and headed home. I got home, fetched water, bathed and then at 5:30 PM I started cooking supper. Now it's 6:04 PM and my rice is still cooking. It was hot and partly cloudy today. My nuang snapped (broke) the rope around her horns today. I asked George to come early tonight when I was just there and he said yes, but we'll have to wait and see what really happens. I've become enough of a *baga-oong* lover now so that I even borrowed some from Alfredo tonight. I have a bad cold in my head and chest and I feel like half-baked shit. AWANEN!

Saturday, February 21, 1987
My House, Gomez, Cabarroguis, Quirino

We got up at 5:45 AM and George left; he came at 7:15 PM last night. I started cooking breakfast, drank coffee and went to pasture my nuang. I returned home, finished cooking, ate, did the dishes, got ready for the day and headed for the farm. I got there at about 8:30 AM and several people were cutting grass on George's farm today so his mother also went so that she could cook lunch for everybody. George helped me with my farm until 10:30 AM and then he went to cut grass on his farm. My plow handle broke today. I weeded until 11:15 AM and then we all ate together. At 12:20 PM I started weeding again. I weeded until 4:00 PM and then got my nuang, picked some of my *utong* beans and headed home. I bathed my nuang and myself, fetched water and started cooking supper at about 5:30 PM. When everything was cooked I went to George's to ask him to come early, but undoubtedly they'll be having a late supper tonight. Now it's 7:11 PM and I'll be lucky to see George before 7:30 PM. I nearly finished weeding my farm today – thank God! There are a few winged beans that are three to four inches long. The weather today was a little cloudy but generally sunny and hot. It was only 60°F this morning. AWANEN!

Sunday, February 22, 1987
My House, Gomez, Cabarroguis, Quirino

Postcard to Sue T.

₱167 + 300 – 56 = ₱411							
Plow Repair	30	Cigarettes	7	Food	6	Rides	6

Marienda	7					TOTAL	₱56

We got up at 5:50 AM and George left, he came at 7:30 PM last night. I gave him my *wayway* before he left. I cooked breakfast, ate, did dishes, got ready for the day and went to George's. Alfredo and I are going to get my plow welded today, but we didn't finally leave for Burgos until 8:30 or 9:00 AM and then when we arrived at Burgos we had to wait another hour before we could catch a jeepney to Gundaway, but then the jeepney overheated while we were at market and we had to wait another half hour for it to cool off. We finally got to the welding shop at 11:00 AM or so. We hung around there until my plow was fixed, which was 3:00 PM and then we finally caught a ride back to Burgos. We arrived at 3:40 PM and came home via the high road. I was first and I arrived home at 4:25 PM. I fetched water, prepared things for supper, cooked, ate and went to George's to ask him to come early. I returned home, did the dishes, wrote the postcard to Sue and now it's 7:00 PM and I'm waiting for George to come. The weather today was hot, but now it's mostly cloudy. Now I'm reading my *Newsweek* and waiting for George. AWANEN!

Monday, February 23, 1987
My House, Gomez, Cabarroguis, Quirino

Letter to Steve A.

₱411 + 35 – 30 = ₱416							
Charcoal	28	Cigarettes	2			TOTAL	₱30

I got up at 5:50 AM; George got up at about 4:15 AM and left for the farm so that the nuang could eat and so that he could start plowing early. I started cooking breakfast, drank coffee, pastured my nuang, returned and talked with Alfredo for a few minutes and then came back home. I ate, did the dishes and got ready for the day. The first thing I did was laundry. I finished that and relaxed for a bit and then went to Bebot's charcoal pit and bagged and carried home four sacks of charcoal. I got my nuang, bathed her, returned home and it was nearly noon, so I drank a cup of coffee and napped from 12:20 to 1:15 PM. I got up and drank another cup of coffee and then at 2:00 PM I took my nuang back to pasture. I returned home and pick axed in the tree nursery where the third flat of seedlings would have been and I planted one of each species in a row and then I watered them all. I washed my bucket out and then fetched water, returned, bathed and started preparing things for supper. At 5:00 PM I started cooking and went and got my nuang and bathed her. I returned home, finished cooking, ate, did dishes and went to Alfredo's. George was at Bubot's house trading roosters again. Now it's 6:51 PM so I know that George will be late tonight. The weather today was mostly cloudy, but no rain and it was hot. George has slept here 255 nights now. AWANEN!

Tuesday, February 24, 1987
My House, Gomez, Cabarroguis, Quirino

We got up at 5:45 AM and George left; he came at 7:45 PM last night. I started cooking breakfast, drank coffee and took my nuang to pasture. I stopped at George's on the way home and he showed me his new rooster. I returned home and finished cooking breakfast, ate, did dishes, got ready for the day and then Alfredo, Sip and I went to the farm. George left first. We got there at about 8:15 AM and I started weeding nearly immediately. I weeded until 10:00 AM, then put my nuang in the shade and continued weeding until noon. Then we ate lunch. We ate my cooked turnips and *parya* and it was quite tasty. Then we rested until 2:00 PM and I decided to come home early – no good reason really – I just wanted to come home. So I pastured my nuang on the way home and got here at about 3:00 PM. My nuang yoke broke today – George was plowing with it at the time. I also had a flip-flop strap break today. At 3:30 PM I watered the seedlings that I planted yesterday. At 4:00 PM I fetched water, bathed and then prepared the vegetables for supper at 4:30 PM. At 5:00 PM I went to George's to ask him to come early and then I went and got and bathed my nuang. At 5:30 PM I started cooking supper. Now it's 6:02 PM and my rice is still cooking so it'll be a late supper for me tonight. The weather today was hot and clear, but then it clouded up at 4:00 PM and there were a few sprinkles at 5:45 PM. AWANEN!

Wednesday, February 25, 1987
My House, Gomez, Cabarroguis, Quirino

Letter to Barb W.

₱416 – 186 = ₱230							
Food	72	Rides	4	Marienda	35	Cigarettes	10
Candy	8	Coffee	27	Kerosene	7	Notebook	3
Misc.	20					TOTAL	₱186

We got up at 5:45 AM, I gave George my *wayway* and he left; he came at 7:10 PM last night. I cooked breakfast, drank coffee, ate, did dishes, got ready for the day and at about 7:30 AM Bebot and I left for Burgos. We arrived there and were able to get a jeepney to Gundaway fairly quickly. I stopped at the post office and it was closed, I forgot that today is a National Holiday – the People Power Revolution was one year ago today. I continued on to market, did my shopping and at about 10:00 AM I headed back for Burgos, where I arrived at about 10:40 AM and climbed the high road to come home. I arrived home at about 11:40 AM, unpacked my bag, drank coffee and went to George's – he was home – to see if he wanted to harvest my coffee this afternoon, he said "maybe" so I came home and slept for an hour. Then at about 2:00 PM George actually came and we harvested the coffee beans from 1.5 of my three coffee trees. He left at 4:00 PM and I fetched water and bathed. I cooked supper of fresh squid, ate, did dishes and now it's 6:41 PM and I'm waiting for George. The weather today – it rained last night for several hours and then showered lightly this morning. In the afternoon it was sunny for a while, but clouded up again at about 4:00 PM or so. We'll have to wait and see if it rains again tonight. AWANEN!

Thursday, February 26, 1987
My House, Gomez, Cabarroguis, Quirino

We got up at 5:45 AM and George left; he came at 7:40 PM last night. I started cooking breakfast, drank coffee and pastured my nuang. I returned and talked with George for a few minutes and then returned home. I finished cooking breakfast, ate, did dishes, got ready for the day, and went to the farm, arriving there at about 8:15 AM. George was already plowing. I finished weeding the pallang at about 11:00 AM, put my nuang in the shade, talked with George for a few minutes and started weeding my farm back at the starting point again! George returned home for lunch but I didn't stop for lunch until 12:20 PM. Then at 1:00 PM I started weeding again and I worked until 4:00 PM. I finished weeding the cranberry pole beans and the *parya* again. I asked George if he was ready to come home, but he said not yet, so I came home first, bathed my nuang and tied her for the night. Then I fetched water, bathed, prepared things for supper and started cooking at 5:20 PM. Pedring and Alfredo both came to talk for a while but they left when my supper was cooked. Alfredo "borrowed" my sandpaper and they left. Now it's 7:06 PM and I'm waiting for George. The weather – it rained again last night and it was partly cloudy today, but hot anyway, there's been no rain yet tonight. AWANEN!

Friday, February 27, 1987
My House, Gomez, Cabarroguis, Quirino

Letter to JB & Katie F.

We got up at 5:45 AM and George left; he came at 7:10 PM last night. I started cooking breakfast, drank coffee and took my nuang to pasture. I returned home, finished cooking, ate, did dishes and got ready for the day. Then I went to the farm and continued weeding. At 10:00 AM George, Sip and I returned home. We arrived at about 11:00 AM. I ate lunch, drank coffee and finished the letter to Barb that I started on Wednesday. I napped from 12:20 to 1:00 PM and then went and got George and we sprayed my one coffee tree that is full of red ants. That took until 2:15 PM and then he went home and I took my nuang to pasture again. I returned home and wrote the above letter to JB and Katie until 4:00 PM and then I bathed, fetched water and prepared vegetables for supper. At 5:00 PM I went to get and bathe my nuang, returned home and started cooking the rice at about 5:20 PM. Now it's 6:04 PM and it's nearly cooked. I hope George comes relatively early tonight. Alfredo came and borrowed some batteries for the radio so I hope George doesn't decide to listen to the radio drama at their house, if he does I'll never give them batteries again! The weather was hot and sunny all day today and we had no rain last night. AWANEN!

Saturday, February 28, 1987
My House, Gomez, Cabarroguis, Quirino

Letters to Mike Mc., Tim C. and Bill N.

We got up at 6:05 AM and George left; he came at 7:10 PM last night. I started cooking breakfast, drank coffee and took my nuang to pasture. I returned home and finished cooking, ate, did dishes, got ready for the day and went to Alfredo's to talk for a while. George is plowing Bebot's farm today for ₱50. I returned home and cleaned house. I used the *lampaso* on all the floors and shelves and gave everything a thorough cleaning. By the time I finished with that it was 11:00 AM so I went to move my nuang and then returned home and wrote the letter to Tim C. Then I ate lunch and napped from 1:30 to 2:15 PM. I got up and killed time for a while and Alfredo came and borrowed my orange pack to go to the hospital in Diffun about his ulcer. I went and fetched water at 3:00 PM, returned and worked on the letter to Mike Mc. At 4:00 PM I prepared the vegetables for supper and at 4:30 PM I lit my fire and went and got my nuang, bathed her, bathed myself, finished cooking, ate and did dishes. I just went to George's and they were already eating so he could be here by 7:00 PM tonight. Now it's 6:13 PM and I'm going to start working on a letter to Bill N. now while waiting for George. Today's weather – it rained all night and didn't stop until nearly noon. It remained cloudy the rest of the day. There was no sun today. AWANEN!

[End of handwritten notebook #3 of 5]

Sunday, March 1, 1987
My House, Gomez, Cabarroguis, Quirino

Letter to Bill N.

We got up at 5:50 AM and George left; he came at 6:30 PM last night. I started cooking breakfast, drank coffee, went and pastured my nuang, returned and talked with George for a few minutes and then came home. I finished cooking, ate, did the dishes and got ready for the day. It was cloudy today so I didn't do laundry. I calculated February's expenses, finishing with that at 10:00 AM, and went and moved my nuang. I returned home and wrote the letter to Bill N. and finished that at about noon. I ate lunch and napped for nearly an hour and then I got up and repaired by Indiana Jones hat – it had a small hole in it – and I also sewed around the holes that I made for the chinstrap to reinforce them. Then it was 2:15 PM and I went to move my nuang again. I returned home, trimmed my beard and harvested more coffee; I got about another half sack full of coffee beans. I worked on that until 4:00 PM and then bathed, started cooking my rice and went and got my nuang and bathed her too. I returned home and the rice was nearly cooked. I went to George's for a minute to ask him to come early and now the vegetables are cooking and it's 5:53 PM. I'll finish this and eat supper. The weather today was cloudy in the morning, but no rain, and then clear in the afternoon. Now it's clouding up again. It rained late last night. Oh, one of my pineapple plants is getting a tiny fruit on the top. AWANEN!

Monday, March 2, 1987
My House, Gomez, Cabarroguis, Quirino

Letters to Tony & Janet S. and Yip Chee H.

We got up at 5:40 AM and George left; he came at 6:40 PM last night. I started cooking breakfast, drank coffee, went and pastured my nuang and then talked with George for a couple minutes on the way home. I returned home, finished cooking, ate, did dishes and got ready for the day. I did laundry the first thing this morning, despite the fact that it was cloudy and showering lightly every now and then. I finished that, basically killed time for a while and then I wrote the letter to Tony and Janet. After that I ate lunch and drank coffee and then I attempted to harvest more coffee, but the red ants had returned, so I sprayed some more insecticide. After that I killed time for a while, looked up more words from my little red dictionary and transferred them to the new one. I worked on that until 2:00 PM and then I went to move my nuang. Upon returning home I looked up more words in the little dictionary until 3:30 PM and then fetched water and bathed. It was cool, but after spraying with the insecticide I felt that bathing was necessary. After that I prepared things for supper and at 4:30 PM I started cooking. I went and got and bathed my nuang and then returned home. I finished cooking, ate, did dishes and now it's 6:18 PM. There are bunch of people at Alfredo's house so I haven't gone to ask George to come early. The weather today was light showers until noon, then sunny until 4:00 PM and then it clouded up again. Shall I write another letter? AWANEN!

Tuesday, March 3, 1987
My House, Gomez, Cabarroguis, Quirino

We got up at 5:50 AM and George left; he came at 7:10 PM last night. I started cooking breakfast, drank coffee, took my nuang to pasture, returned home and finished cooking, ate, did dishes and got ready for the day. Then I went to Alfredo's to wait and see if the forestry meeting for March would happen as scheduled for 8:00 AM. I waited at Alfredo's until 10:20 AM and there were 12 of us there, but the technician didn't show up so I returned home and looked up some more words from the red dictionary. Then Sip brought me some cooked balatong beans, so shortly after

11:00 AM I ate lunch. Just before noon I went to George's to see if he was ready to return to the farm, but not yet, so after a while I moved my nuang and then George and I met at the school and we went to the farm. He plowed and I harvested pallang and *utong* on my farm. I also harvested a bunch of *utong* beans that I had left to dry for the seeds and then I weeded some more. I stopped at 4:00 PM and so did George, so we came home together. I got and bathed my nuang and started cooking. I bathed myself and then prepared my vegetables and started cooking those. I finished cooking, ate, did dishes and now it's 6:45 PM and I'm waiting for George. The weather today – it rained last night and it was cloudy most of the day today, but it didn't rain at all during the day. AWANEN!

Wednesday, March 4, 1987
My House, Gomez, Cabarroguis, Quirino

Letters from Bob S., Vicki S., Liz & Randy, Dan T., Steve A., Sue T., San & Jack G. and Mark G.

₱230 + 300 – 501 = ₱29							
Nuang Yoke	57	Rides	16	Cigarettes	10	Kerosene	7
Haircut	5	Soap	20	Coffee	50	Household	28
Lunch	28	Ice Cream	19	Marienda	37	Flip-Flops	14
Food	191	Misc.	19			TOTAL	₱501

We got up at 5:40 AM, I gave George my *wayway* and he left; he didn't come until after 7:30 PM last night. I drank coffee, went to Alfredo's for a few minutes to get George's short pants again (for tailoring) and I left at 6:45 AM. I arrived in Burgos at 7:30 AM and got to Gundaway a little after 8:00 AM. I stopped at the post office, got the above mail and continued on to Santiago, getting there at about 9:15 AM. I took the short pants to the tailor and then I went to the bank and did my marketing, which I finished at about 11:45 AM. I went to the 456 Restaurant for lunch and killed time there until 1:00 PM and then I returned to the tailor and had to wait until they finished resizing George's short pants – at about 1:30 PM. I caught a jeepney from Santiago at 2:05 PM, arrived in Burgos at 3:40 PM and climbed the mountain via the high road, getting home at about 4:25 PM. I bathed and prepared vegetables for supper, cooked, ate, did the dishes and now it's 6:42 PM. I hope George comes early tonight, I have lots of stories to tell and I'm going to give him my old watch – I think. Well it wasn't a very exciting day I guess. At least I got lots of mail. The weather today – it was 66°F this morning, sunny and quite hot in midday. I guess I'll study a bit and enter letter received dates in the HP-71. AWANEN!

Thursday, March 5, 1987
My House, Gomez, Cabarroguis, Quirino

We got up at 5:40 AM and George left; he came at 7:15 PM last night and his twice tailored short pants were finally small enough for him! I started cooking breakfast, drank coffee and took my nuang to pasture. I returned and talked with George for a few minutes and then came home. I finished cooking, ate, did dishes and got ready for the day. I started the day by spending two hours sanding my new *pako* or nuang yoke and then I shelled the *utong* beans that I harvested for seed the other day and when I finished with that it was 11:00 AM. I killed time for a while and then ate lunch. After that I oiled my *pako* and put it in the sun to dry. Oh, I forgot, this morning Alfredo and I spread out the coffee beans to dry in my yard at 10:15 AM and I also went and got and bathed my nuang. I napped from 12:40 to 1:40 PM, got up, drank coffee and by then it was 2:00 PM so I took my nuang back to pasture. Then I returned home and started harvesting more coffee beans. Alfredo came and helped me, we finished the second tree and then he made the notches in my new *pako* and it was 3:30 PM. I fetched water, Alfredo finished making the notches for the rope in my new *pako* and I prepared vegetables for supper. At 4:30 PM I went and got my nuang and bathed her, returned home, started supper, bathed myself and then I ate and did dishes. Now it's 6:50 PM. George plowed today at Bebot's farm. The weather today was clear, sunny and hot all day. I managed to stay busy all day. I hope George comes any minute now. AWANEN!

Friday, March 6, 1987
My House, Gomez, Cabarroguis, Quirino

We get up at 5:45 AM and George left, he came at 6:55 PM last night. I started cooking breakfast, drank coffee and took my nuang to pasture. I stopped at George's to talk for a couple minutes and he left for the farm while I was there. I returned home and finished cooking, ate, did dishes and got ready for the day. I took my bag of valuables to Alfredo's house, got my nuang and went to the farm. I talked with George for a few minutes and then went to my farm to cut grass above the planted area. George finished plowing and he cut grass in the area to the south of my farm. At 10:00 AM I put my nuang in the shade and then I worked until 11:00 AM. I stopped and went and fetched water, ate lunch and then started cutting grass again at 12:20 PM. At 2:00 PM I stopped and pastured my nuang once again and when I got back to the farm George had returned. We finished cutting grass on my farm at about 3:00 PM and I helped George on his farm until 4:00 PM. Then I got my nuang and headed for home. I bathed my nuang, picked up the coffee that Alfredo had spread out in my yard to dry and noticed that he also swept my yard for me – thank you. I bathed, fetched water, prepared vegetables for supper and started cooking at about 5:30 PM. Now at 6:23 PM and everything is cooked and ready to eat as soon as I'm done writing this. I hope George comes early tonight. The weather today – it was 64°F this morning, clear, sunny and hot by 9:00 AM. There were no clouds, no rain and it's now 78°F. Yikes, I got a sunburned back today. AWANEN!

Saturday, March 7, 1987
My House, Gomez, Cabarroguis, Quirino

Letters to Chris & Mary M. and Steve A.

We got up at 5:30 AM and George left; he came at 7:30 PM last night. I started cooking breakfast, drank coffee and took my nuang to pasture. I returned home and finished cooking, ate, did dishes and Alfredo came to give me the new *saud* (like a screen or net) for drying coffee on. He left and I got ready for the day, spread out the coffee beans to dry and cut the weeds on the hill west of the house. After that I killed time for a bit and then I prepared my USA income taxes. My income last year was a mere $2,900!! Then I did the letter to Chris and Mary and by then it was past 10:00 AM so I went to get and bathe my nuang. After I returned I continued the letter to Chris and Mary until noon and then I napped from 12:15 to 1:00 PM. I got up and ate a late lunch and looked up words from the red dictionary and copied them in the other one; I only have ten pages left to do now. By the time I finished that it was 4:00 PM so I went and got George to help me pick up the drying coffee beans and he left as soon as we were done. At 4:30 PM I went to Alfredo's to talk and then at 4:45 PM I went and got my nuang. I returned home, fetched water, bathed and started cooking the rice at 5:30 PM. I prepared the vegetables and then went to George's to ask him to come early, but he said he doesn't know if that will be possible. Now it's 6:23 PM and the vegetables are cooking. After supper I'll work on a letter to Steve until George comes. The weather today was hot and there was no rain. George harvested bananas today. AWANEN!

Sunday, March 8, 1987
My House, Gomez, Cabarroguis, Quirino

Letters to Vicki S. and ordered some stuff from Patagonia Gear.

I got up at 5:45 AM. George got up quietly and left without waking me up at I don't know what time. He came last night at 7:30 PM. I started cooking breakfast, drank coffee and took my nuang to pasture. I returned and stopped at George's to talk for a couple of minutes and then came home, finished cooking, ate, did dishes and got ready for the day. I went to Alfredo's to talk for a few minutes and George had already left for Burgos to sell the bananas that he harvested yesterday. I returned home and did laundry until 10:00 AM and when finished with that I went and got and bathed my nuang. Then I wrote the letter to Vicki about coming here sometime during the first two weeks of August. After that I put the Sunrise/Sunset program in the HP-41 again and did some calculations to find sunrise/sunset times for March 21st, June 21st, September 21st and December 21st, 1987. After that I ate lunch and then napped for 45 minutes. I got up and drank coffee and then at 2:00 PM I took my nuang back to pasture. I returned home and reentered the address file into the HP-71 again – I had a total memory loss again today. That took me until 4:00 PM and then I went and got Alfredo to help me pick up the drying coffee beans. We then drank coffee and I prepared stuff for supper. At 5:00 PM I went and got and bathed my nuang and then returned home, cooked, ate and did dishes. Now it's 6:49 PM and George is listening to the radio contest at their house so he will be late. What should I do to kill time until he arrives? The weather was hot and sunny all day. AWANEN!

Monday, March 9, 1987
My House, Gomez, Cabarroguis, Quirino

We got up at 5:45 AM and George left; he came at 7:30 PM last night. I started cooking breakfast, drank coffee and took my nuang to pasture. I returned and talked with George for a couple minutes and then came home and finished cooking, ate, did the dishes and got ready for the day. I took my bag of valuables to Alfredo's, went and got my nuang and went to the farm. George was cutting grass again today. I took a couple of pictures (see page 229) and asked him where to get some *runo* to use for the climbing poles for the *pallang* and then I went and got about 100 runo poles, which took until 10:00 AM. I put my nuang in the shade and George went home for lunch with his grass cutting to the south of my farm finished. I continued getting *runo* and then I dug up weeds for a while and stopped at noon. I ate my lunch and continued working at 12:30 PM. At 2:00 PM I stopped and re-pastured my nuang and then continued digging weeds. At 3:00 PM George returned and we burned the area they cur grass in a couple of weeks ago. By then it was nearly 4:00 PM and we roasted some corn for a snack. I left at 4:30 PM, came home, bathed my nuang, fetched water, picked up the coffee beans which Alfredo had spread to dry, bathed and started cooking supper. Now it's 6:46 PM and my vegetables are cooking or maybe done. I hope George comes around 7:30 PM again tonight. The weather today was hot and sunny, there wasn't a cloud all day. AWANEN!

Tuesday, March 10, 1987
My House, Gomez, Cabarroguis, Quirino

We got up at 5:15 AM and George left; I went to get him at 7:45 PM last night and Alfredo was very angry about something. I started cooking breakfast, drank coffee and at first light I took my nuang to pasture. I stopped and talked with George for a minute upon returning and then came home and finished cooking, ate, did dishes and got ready for the day. I went to Alfredo's for a couple minutes and he said that he's angry because George acts like he thinks Alfredo is faking his sore stomach – I must admit, I have wondered myself. I went and got my nuang, went to the farm and helped George pick up and move unburned material from yesterday's fire so that he could plow. When we finished that, he plowed and I continued picking up the unburned material and re-piling it. At 10:00 AM I took my nuang to the shade and at

10:30 AM George went home. At 11:00 AM I ate my lunch, rested until 12:10 PM and then continued working on weeding my farm some more. At 2:00 PM George returned and continued plowing and I continued weeding my farm, after pasturing my nuang. I worked until 4:00 PM, got my nuang and headed for home. I bathed my nuang and then picked up the coffee that Alfredo had spread to dry. I fetched water, bathed and started cooking supper. Now it's 6:24 PM and I'm cooking *sabunganay*. I hope George comes early tonight. I got more sunburn on my back today, two hours with no shirt was too long. The weather was hot and dry with a few scattered clouds and it was windy today. AWANEN!

Wednesday, March 11, 1987
My House, Gomez, Cabarroguis, Quirino

Letter from Fred & Cynthia B. Postcard from Ardis B.

₱29 + 300 – 258 = ₱71							
Rides	4	Household	43	Food	51	Cigarettes	10
Marienda	52	Postage	28	Kerosene	7	Coffee	27
Candy	13	Misc.	23			TOTAL	₱258

We got up at 5:00 AM, I gave George my *wayway* and my new nuang yoke and he left. He came last night at 7:35 AM. I cooked a quick breakfast of rice and left-over *sabunganay* from last night, ate, did dishes, got ready for the day and Pedring and I headed down the mountain for Burgos. We arrived in Burgos at 8:05 AM and we caught a jeepney to Gundaway. I got the above mail, did marketing and finished at about 10:00 AM. I caught a jeepney headed back to Burgos and arrived at the bottom of the high road at 10:45 AM. I climbed the mountain and arrived home at 11:30 AM. I read my mail, ate a couple of *bibingka* [a type of fancy rice cake] for lunch and then napped from 12:50 to 1:45 PM. I got up, drank coffee and then at 2:15 PM I took my nuang to pasture. I returned home and looked up the last of the words from my red dictionary and transferred them to the other one. At 4:00 PM I fetched water, at 4:30 PM I bathed, at 5:00 PM I got and bathed my nuang and then I lit my charcoal fire and went to George's for a while. He said he'll come earlier tonight, we'll see. Now it's 6:24 PM and vegetables and Miki noodles are cooking and nearly done. George plowed again today. The weather today was hot and dry and even now it's 84°F in the house. AWANEN!

Thursday, March 12, 1987
My House, Gomez, Cabarroguis, Quirino

I got up at 5:45 AM, but George got up at 4:00 AM and left to pasture his nuang. He came last night at 7:05 PM. I started cooking breakfast, drank coffee and took my nuang to pasture. I returned and talked with Alfredo for a few minutes; George had already gone to the farm to plow. Alfredo went to Steven Natividad's house to see the quack doctor about his stomach. I returned home, finished cooking, ate, did dishes and got ready for the day. Then I did laundry until nearly 10:00 AM. At 10:10 AM I went and got my nuang, bathed her and put her in the shade. Then I cut weeds on the little hill northeast of the house. Oh, I forgot, I spread out the coffee beans to dry before I did laundry. I ate lunch and then napped from 12:30 to 1:30 PM. I got up, drank coffee and at 2:15 PM I went to pasture my nuang again. I returned home and swept the dirt on the north and west sides of the house. By the time I finished that it was 4:30 PM so I bathed and prepared things for supper – I'm having squash. At 5:00 PM I went and got and bathed my nuang and then I started cooking and went to George's to ask him to come early. The quack doctor told Alfredo that he doesn't have an ulcer – that God slapped him and he has to pray and go to church. All I can say about that is – bullshit! Now it's 6:35 PM and the squash is nearly cooked. The weather today was hot and dry, not a cloud in the sky. I hope George comes early tonight. AWANEN!

Friday, March 13, 1987
My House, Gomez, Cabarroguis, Quirino

We got up at 5:45 AM and George left; he came at 7:15 PM last night. He got up at 1:00 AM and released his nuang and then returned and slept some more. I started cooking breakfast, drank coffee and took my nuang to pasture. I stopped at George's for a few minutes on my return and he was already leaving for the farm to plow. I returned home and finished cooking, ate, did dishes and got ready for the day. I spread the coffee beans to dry again and then I did laundry again. I finished laundry at 9:30 AM and killed time for a while. Just before 10:00 AM I went and got and bathed my nuang and returned home. I pulled weeds in the east and southeast yard until lunchtime, ate and then napped for 20 minutes. Then I got up and continued pulling weeds until 2:00 PM. I went and pastured my nuang again, returned home and took the dry clothes off the clothesline, packed and went to fetch water. Then I swept the part of the yard that I weeded and then it was looking like rain, so I bathed at 4:00 PM and prepared things for supper. I went and got and bathed my nuang, started the fire, put on the rice to cook and went to Alfredo's for a few minutes. George's mother said that it will be a late supper for them tonight, shit, I'll be lucky if George comes before 7:30 PM. Now it's 6:43 PM. The weather today was hot and dry, it was 88°F this afternoon and thunderheads started building but then fell apart before anything happened. AWANEN!

Saturday, March 14, 1987
Malate Pension, Manila

₱71 + 300 – 249 = ₱122							
Rides	83	Food	32	Meals	60	Cigarettes	28
Marienda	19	Ice Cream	20	Misc.	7	TOTAL	₱249

We got up at 5:30 AM, I gave George my *wayway* and leftover food and he left. He came last night at 7:30 PM. I drink coffee, got ready for the day took my bag of valuables to George's house. At 6:15 AM I left for Burgos, arrived there at 7:00 AM and took a jeepney to Cordon. From there I took a Dalin Liner Bus to Manila at 8:30 AM. There were lots of stops – morning marienda, lunch and afternoon marienda. We finally got to Manila at about 3:30 PM and I got to Malate pension at 4:15 PM. There was a note from Sue telling me that she had arrived so I went and knocked on her room door and we talked for a few minutes. Then I showered and after that we went downstairs and drank Coke, ate ice cream and talked. Then we went to Robinson's Department store for a few things and then we went to supper at Al-Shams Indian food restaurant, it was pretty good, but nothing special. Sue and I did a lot of good talking and we left there at 10:00 PM. Now it's 10:31 PM and I'm ready to sleep. AWANEN!

Sunday, March 15, 1987
Malate Pension, Manila

₱122 + 300 – 220 = ₱202							
Meals	177	Rides	6	Coke	17	Ice Cream	10
Coffee	10					TOTAL	₱220

I got up at 6:00 AM, showered and went downstairs. I killed time until 9:45 AM and then a bunch of us went to the Seafront Restaurant for breakfast and stayed there until noon. I returned to Malate, changed my clothes and then Sue and I went to Pistang Filipino and wandered around there for a while. Then we went to the Mabuhay Hotel and made reservations for the trip to Puerto Galera tomorrow. Then we went to Divisoria, strolled there for a while and then stopped for a Coke. I spilled the whole damn thing in my lap, so we stayed there for quite a while until I got dried out. Then we returned to Malate Pension and after a while I did laundry and bathed to get rid of the Coke on my clothes and lap area. After killing some time we finally went to supper at 8:00 PM or so to the Steak Town Restaurant, where a measly bowl of soup and a salad was ₱80! We returned to Malate Pension and now it's 9:52 PM and time to sleep. I wish I was home in Gomez. AWANEN!

Monday, March 16, 1987
Big La Laguna Beach, Puerto Galera, Mindoro

₱202 – 172 = ₱30							
Lodging	50	Meals	69	Cigarettes	12	Marienda	24
Coke	5	Coffee	12			TOTAL	₱172

I got up at 6:00 AM, showered, and went downstairs for coffee. Sue and I drank coffee until 8:15 AM and then we headed over to the Mabuhay Hotel to get the bus and ultimately the ferry to Puerto Galera. We spent 2.5 hours on the bus to

Batangas and then a couple hours on the ferry and we arrived in Puerto Galera at about 1:45 PM or so. We strolled around there for a while and ultimately found a place to eat lunch. After lunch we caught a jeepney to Sabang and then we walked from Sabang to Big La Laguna beach and we found a place to stay for ₱40 each per night – okay – we took it. We got settled into a small cabin and after a while we took a beach walk until practically dark. We returned and ate supper and sat in the restaurant for a long time talking. Then we returned to the cabin and talked some more. Now it's 10:00 PM and I'm ready to sleep. AWANEN!

[I need to say some things right here at the start of this adventure. Sue knew that I was gay before we ever planned this trip together. She had known it since we were in training back in Bayombong, she said that it was obvious from the way I looked at some of the guys. I don't know what she was trying to do here, convince me that my life style was not the real me, "cure me" of my homosexuality, so to speak or just what. She needed love and loving, she wanted sex and I was not ready or willing to give it to her. We slept together and she said that cuddling was enough to make her happy, but the way she had her hands all over me, it was obviously not enough. I did not get an erection and did not even offer to satisfy her needs in any way, shape or manner beyond cuddling. She accepted it the first night, the second night she barely accepted it The third night she refused to accept it and told me that if I was not willing to give her what she wanted then I needed to sleep on the floor. Other things also happened on the third day – keep reading to find out – and try not to laugh too hard about it, or maybe I should say try not to cry too hard!]

Tuesday, March 17, 1987
Big La Laguna Beach, Puerto Galera, Mindoro

₱30 + 200 – 144 = ₱89							
Meals	123	Coke	11	Mask/Snorkel	10	TOTAL	₱144

We got up at 6:20 AM, rather late, and went to over to the main house for coffee and then ended up ordering breakfast too. After a while we returned to the cabin and got ready for the day. After that we walked down the beach in search of the best price on a mask/snorkel/flippers rental place. We ultimately found a good price place, rented the stuff and went snorkeling for a while. After we got tired of that we soaked up some sun on the beach for a while and I got my belly sunburned. Then we went to Rosita's Cafe for lunch for 1.5 hours or so. We returned to the cabin and talked for a while longer and then I took a nap from 3:00 to 4:00 PM while Sue went snorkeling again. When she returned we tried to get a *buko*, but nobody wanted to climb the coconut tree for a coconut, oh well, such is life. Then Carrie [another PCV] and Libby [Carries sister, visiting from the USA] happened to show up and we talked with them until suppertime.

Then we all went to eat together and after eating supper we returned to the cabin, just Sue and I, and talked more. Now it's 10:42 PM and time to sleep. AWANEN!

Wednesday, March 18, 1987
Big La Laguna Beach, Puerto Galera, Mindoro

Postcards to Ardis B. and George.

₱89 + 400 – 259 = ₱230							
Meals	120	Cigarettes	12	Ferry	100	Marienda	27
						TOTAL	₱259

We went to sleep late last night [because of you can surmise what] and then we were woken up at 5:30 AM by a rat chewing somewhere in the cabin. Oh my, not much sleep, tired upon waking up! We got ready for the day and went over to the main house for coffee and, after a couple cups of coffee, we ordered breakfast too. After breakfast we killed time for a while and then Sue went snorkeling some more and I sat and read my new *Reader's Digest* until lunchtime. We ate lunch here too, I bought a ₱16 pineapple, Sue made some no-bake cookies and we sat around eating those for a while. By and by Carrie and Libby came here to talk They left after a while – when Sue told Libby not to come to her site to visit!! Then Sue and I went over to the main building for a Coke and upon returning to the cabin she lit into me too, so I got pissed off and went to sit on the porch and read some more of my *Reader's Digest.* After a while I returned to the cabin and we managed to talk about it. It seems that Sue misunderstands what I am saying a good deal of the time, plus – I don't think she really listens to anything that I'm saying, at least one-half of the time. Anyway, she also told me that I shouldn't come to her site to visit. It was a bad day for Sue I guess; she had to tell two of us that we shouldn't come to her site to visit. She's a pretty strange person. I think she has feelings of inadequacy about herself – I mean really big time! Oftentimes when I'm telling her about something I've done or even complimenting her on something she has done, she thinks I'm making fun of her or criticizing her. Even this afternoon, when I asked her what was wrong, trying to be considerate and feeling empathetic, she took it all wrong and thought I was, in a sense, laughing at her. She even said that she transfers her mother's problems to herself. She told me that her mother is insane – she thinks she sees too many of her mother's traits in herself and she also thinks she's on the verge of a nervous breakdown or something. Anyway, after another hour or so we went down to the beach to talk and we took a walk and then returned and ate supper. We're now getting along okay, but it's the first time in my life that I've ever been un-invited to come to somebody's house. Now it's 9:36 PM, what a hell of a day. I can't let this bother me too much, I just don't need anything else to worry about and boggle my mind with. AWANEN!

Thursday, March 19, 1987
Malate Pension, Manila

₱230 + 300 – 420 = ₱110							
Lodging	120	Meals	44	Rides	20	Short Pants	70
Cigarettes	23	Coke	11	Seeds	8	Postage	100
Ice Cream	10	Misc.	14			TOTAL	₱420

We got up at 1:30 AM because the La Laguna Beach Front was burning down! We stayed up and helped fight the fire until 3:30 AM and then we went to sleep. Then we got up for good at 5:30 AM, settled our bill and left. We caught a jeepney at Sabang, took it to Puerto Galera and caught a 7:30 AM ferry to Batangas. The return trip was ₱48, compared to ₱115 pesos for the trip down here via the "tourist route". We arrived in Batangas at about 9:30 AM and caught a bus to Manila. We arrived in Manila at about noon and then went to Malate Pension, checked in, drank a coke and went over to the Peace Corps Office. I gave them some blood and feces for their regular health check and then I talked with Cery and Ed Comstock about Sue. I told them that I think she is on the edge of a nervous breakdown and asked them to please keep an eye on her. I ran into Linda S. there and we went to the post office together. Then I went to Baclaran to get some remembrances for George. I returned to Malate Pension and after a while Sue, Linda and I went to the Seafront Restaurant for supper. I returned alone to Malate and they went to a movie, where I am sure Sue told Linda all about what an asshole I am! The Peace Corps Trainer who will be assigned to San Gabriela was waiting to talk with me when I got back to Malate Pension so we talked for two hours. [I have no recollection as to what this was about.] Now it's 10:40 PM and I'm ready to sleep. AWANEN!

Friday, March 20, 1987
Host Family, Bonfal East, Bayombong, Nueva Vizcaya

₱110 + 100 – 123 = ₱87							
Lodging	25	Meals	6	Rides	48	Presents	26
Marienda	4	Food	14			TOTAL	₱123

I got up at 5:30 AM and there was no water in the pension, so I had to wait a while to bathe, but finally it returned and I bathed and went downstairs for my last cup of coffee with Sue. We parted saying "see you at COS" [Close-of-Service conference] – bummer! I caught a jeepney for the Pantranco Bus Terminal and got a 7:30 AM bus headed north. It was a pretty uneventful trip; I was even able to sleep for about half of it. I arrived in Bayombong at about 1:15 PM, fairly early! I went to the house and told mother and father about my experiences with Sue and they laughed about it. That really surprised me, as I thought they would be more understanding. [Mother and Father did not know that I was gay, although they may have suspected it.] I thought about the last few days happenings all the way north and I'm beginning to believe Sue when she says that she is schizoid. Ronald got home at about 5:00 PM, kind of late, and we talked until supper, which wasn't until 7:00 PM. Now it's 7:54 PM and for some reason we have a house full of kids being noisy so I have escaped to the upstairs. AWANEN!

Saturday, March 21, 1987
Host Family, Bonfal East, Bayombong, Nueva Vizcaya

₱87 – 20 = ₱67							
Coffee	20					TOTAL	₱20

We got up at 6:00 AM and Ronald went to the river to get some fish from their traps. When he returned, mother cooked, we ate breakfast, got ready for the day and I watched Ronald tie bundles of rice seedlings for a while. After tying a bunch of them he threw them in the canal and I went downstream to pick them out at the place where they will be planted. There were 85 bundles in all. Then a while after 10:00 AM Ronald and I went to the river and we cooked and ate lunch there. Then we rested for a while and at 3:00 PM we went to the farm, where Ronald picked some coconuts for us to drink and eat. Then he picked a bunch of *salamagi* [tamarind]. After that we returned home, I rested for a short while and then I started shelling *salamagi* and Ronald returned to the river to get some more fish. I shelled about 85% of the *salamagi* and finished shortly after 6:00 PM. Now it's 6:59 PM and we haven't eaten supper yet. Herbert and father are drinking with the people who planted the rice today and mother and Rebecca are cooking. There was a small thunder storm a while ago, I wonder if there was one in Gomez too? AWANEN!

Sunday, March 22, 1987
My House, Gomez, Cabarroguis, Quirino

Letters from JB & Katie F., Roselynn and San & Jack G.

₱67 + 400 – 102 = ₱365							
Rides	18	Batteries	24	Food	28	Marienda	20
Household	1	Cigarettes	11			TOTAL	₱102

We got up at 6:20 AM, ate breakfast, got ready for the day and Herbert and I headed for the bus waiting shed at about 8:00 AM. I took a jeepney to Solano and then a bus to Cordon, a jeepney to Gundaway, did my shopping and finished about 10:30 AM. Then I went to the post office. Nobody was there so I let myself in with my house key and got the above mail. Then I caught a jeepney to Burgos and arrived at the bottom of the high road at about 11:40 AM. I headed up the mountain at 11:48 AM. It was a very hot and sweaty walk up the mountain to Gomez. I arrived home at around 12:35 PM and immediately went to Alfredo's and gave them one sack of tamarinds, talked for a while and returned home. Junior came here, he has a new cut above his eye and wanted some medicine. Then he slept here for two hours while I unpacked and read mail. At 4:00 PM I bathed and prepared vegetables for supper. At about 5:00 PM I started cooking and went to Alfredo's to talk until 5:45 PM. Now it's 6:08 PM and supper is done cooking, I hope George comes early tonight. The weather today was hot and dry again; there's been no rain since I left. All four of my pineapple plants now have tiny fruits on them. AWANEN!

Monday, March 23, 1987
My House, Gomez, Cabarroguis, Quirino

We got up at 5:30 AM and George left; he came at 7:10 PM last night and we both had lots of stories to tell. I started cooking breakfast, drank coffee, took my nuang to pasture, returned home, ate, did dishes and got ready for the day. I was ready at 7:00 AM and headed for the farm and looked it over. After that I helped George haul wood to make charcoal. We did that until 10:00 AM and then we returned home. Alfredo came and told me that old lady Espinoza was going to pick my remaining coffee tree this afternoon, so I got pissed and said "okay, I'll pick it right now" and therefore Alfredo and I harvested my third and last coffee tree. That took us until 12:30 PM, we ate a quick lunch and then Alfredo's whole family came to help pick up the coffee off the ground. I swept the north and west yards and then fetched water. At 2:00 PM George and I returned to the farm to get more slab wood for making charcoal. We worked until 4:30 PM, came home and bathed our nuangs. Then I bathed myself and started cooking supper. Now it's 6:16 PM and my vegetables are cooking. I hope George comes early tonight. The weather was hot and dry; there were no clouds all day today. Maybe I'll start a letter to San and Jack after supper, see what happens. AWANEN!

Tuesday, March 24, 1987
My House, Gomez, Cabarroguis, Quirino

Letter to San & Jack G.

We got up at 5:25 AM and George left; he came at 7:25 PM last night. I started cooking breakfast, drank a cup of coffee, took my nuang to pasture, returned and talked with George for a couple of minutes and came home. I finished cooking, ate, did dishes and got ready for the day. I was ready at 7:00 AM and got my nuang and headed for the farm. George and I hauled wood to the place where he's going to make charcoal until 10:00 AM and then we came home. We spread the coffee beans out in the sun to dry, I wrote the letter to San and Jack and took a half hour siesta. I cleaned the *utong* bean seeds that George harvested for me while I was gone to Puerto Galera and by then it was 2:00 PM. We returned to the farm and hauled more wood until there was no more wood to haul. Then at 4:20 PM or so we headed home. We got here at 5:00 PM, picked up the coffee beans, I bathed and went to Alfredo's for a while to talk. Then I returned home and started my hot water cooking. I'm not eating supper tonight, I'm just too tired and/or too lazy to cook. Now it's 6:30 PM and I hope George comes earlier than 7:30. Maybe I'll write another letter. The weather today was hot and dry. Even now it's 84°F, although it was only 66°F this morning. AWANEN!

Wednesday, March 25, 1987
My House, Gomez, Cabarroguis, Quirino

Books from Cynthia B.

₱365 – 163 = ₱202							
Rice	50	Coffee	27	Marienda	25	Rides	4
Household	12	Food	18	Cigarettes	10	Candy	5
Misc.	12					TOTAL	₱163

We got up at 5:30 AM, I gave George my *wayway* and he left; he came at 6:50 PM last night. I cooked breakfast, ate, did dishes, got ready for the day and headed down the mountain for Burgos at 7:10 AM. I got there at about 7:50 AM and I immediately caught a jeepney to Gundaway. I stopped at the post office and got the above mail and then continued on to market. I did shopping and returned to the post office, but there was no more mail. I walked to the junction and got a jeepney to Burgos. I climbed the mountain via the high road, arriving home at about 11:45 AM or so. I unpacked and put things away and then went to George's to talk for a few minutes. I returned home, fetched water, rested for a half hour and then I cleaned and packaged the *utong* bean seeds that George picked for me while I was gone. At 2:00 PM I went to George's and we went to the mountain and dug the hole to make charcoal in. We started filling it with wood. We worked on that until 4:20 PM and then we came home. I bathed my nuang, started cooking supper, bathed myself and now it's 6:01 PM and my vegetables are cooking. I hope George comes early tonight. The weather today was hot and dry. It was 70°F this morning and now it's 86°F. AWANEN!

Thursday, March 26, 1987
My House, Gomez, Cabarroguis, Quirino

Letter to Bob S.

We got up at 5:30 AM and George left; he came at 7:10 PM last night. I started cooking breakfast, drank coffee and took my nuang to pasture. I returned home and finished cooking, ate, did dishes and got ready for the day. I was ready at 7:00 AM and George and I went to the farm to harvest bananas. I was able to be of more help than I've ever been in the harvesting of the bananas. We harvested three kinds today – *depig*, *lakaton* and *canton* and we got a full cart of bananas. We finished that at about 11:40 AM or so and we came home, arriving at about 12:20 PM. I ate lunch and old man Andre A. came and asked for *parya* seed, but I don't have any. He also asked what souvenirs I plan to give him when I go home – SHIT! He left at 1:00 PM and I napped until 1:40 PM, got up and went and asked George if we were going to return to the farm this afternoon. He said no, so I came home and pastured my nuang and wrote the above letter to Bob. I finished that at 4:00 PM, prepared vegetables for supper and at 4:40 PM I went and got my nuang and bathed her. I returned home, started cooking, ate, did dishes and now at 6:39 PM and I'm waiting for George. The weather today was hot and dry in the late afternoon; there were a few sprinkles and some thunder but no real rain. It's still windy right now so it might still rain. I hope George comes before the rain starts. AWANEN!

[Notes on harvesting bananas. You may or may not know it, but the banana is not a true tree. It is actually the largest herbaceous flowering plant. When bananas are harvested one starts by cutting the "tree" down with a machete. This is done carefully to avoid injuring the fruit bearing "bunch" (*bulig*). Once the tree is on the ground the "bunch" is carefully cut off with the machete. The bunches are then put on one's shoulder and carried out to the road or trail. Each tree only bears fruit one time, so that is why the entire tree is cut down for the harvest.

The banana sap is very sticky and it stains anything which it comes in contact with. It cannot be removed from clothes and is difficult to even remove from one's hands after spending several hours harvesting and carrying bananas. So, if you ever get involved with harvesting bananas you should wear the oldest clothes you have. I had a special set of old clothes which I used every time I helped harvest bananas.

The photo on the next page shows George as we were loading a water buffalo cart after one harvest. What he is holding in his left hand is what is referred to as a bunch or *bulig*. He is carefully cutting off the individual "hands" from the *bulig*. The "hands" will be carefully loaded into the cart and transported to market. After the "hands" are removed from the *bulig* the *bulig* is tossed into the plantation and stays behind for fertilizer.

Behind George in the photo on the following page is a part of their banana plantation. Each banana tree produces an abundance of suckers from the original stem and one of those suckers is selected to remain as the next banana tree – the one which replaces the one that was cut down. A banana tree bears mature fruit in about one year, so the banana trees that I planted in my yard in Gomez bore fruits before I left to return home.]

Friday, March 27, 1987
My House, Gomez, Cabarroguis, Quirino

Letters to Fred & Cynthia B. and Jim & Roselynn.

We got up at 5:40 AM and George left; he came at about 7:45 PM last night, after his father left. His father wanted to commit suicide last night because he fell off a bicycle! OH MY GOD!! I had to talk him down for a half hour. Anyway, I started cooking breakfast, drank coffee and took my nuang to pasture. I returned to Georges and drank coffee there and then came home and finished cooking, ate, did dishes and got ready for the day. I went to Alfredo's for a while and George and his mother had gone down the mountain to sell the bananas that we harvested yesterday. I returned home and did laundry until 10:00 AM and then went and got and bathed my nuang. I returned home and Boy visited for a while. When he left I ate lunch and then took a siesta from 12:00 to 1:00 PM. I got up, drank coffee, killed time for a while and then at 2:15 PM I took my nuang back to pasture. I returned home and swept the whole lawn and then I went to fetch water. By then it was 4:00 PM so I bathed and prepared vegetables for supper. At 4:30 PM George passed by on the way to bathe his nuang and I asked him to come early tonight – he said yes. Then I started cooking and went and got and bathed my nuang. I returned home, finished cooking and now it's 5:44 PM – supper is cooked but not yet eaten. I'll eat as soon as I finish this. The weather today – there were a few drops of rain last night and this morning but by noon it was hot and dry again. It's 85°F now. AWANEN!

Saturday, March 28, 1987
My House, Gomez, Cabarroguis, Quirino

We got up at 5:30 AM and George left; he came at 7:30 PM last night. I started cooking breakfast, drank coffee and took my nuang to pasture. I returned home and finished cooking, ate, did dishes, got ready for the day and then I left immediately for the farm. George and I continued making the pile of wood for charcoal. At 9:30 AM I put my nuang in the shade and at 10:30 AM George and I came home. I relaxed for a while and then ate lunch and napped from 12:00 to 1:00 PM. I got up, drank coffee and prepared the vegetables for supper. At 1:45 PM I returned to Georges and we returned to the farm, where we continued piling wood until about 4:10 PM. Then I got my nuang and headed for home. George walked today, so he came home first. I asked him to come early tonight and he said yes, but we'll see what happens. I got home at about 4:45 PM, bathed my nuang, started cooking supper, fetched water, bathed myself, went and bought cigarettes and returned home. Now it's 6:07 PM, my rice is cooked and the vegetables are cooking. The weather today was cloudy for a little while this morning and then it was hot and clear in the late afternoon. It clouded up and showered a tiny bit but not even enough to wet the ground. I hope George truly comes early tonight. He has slept here 280 nights now. AWANEN!

Sunday, March 29, 1987
My House, Gomez, Cabarroguis, Quirino

Letter to Liz & Randy, prepare Peace Corps quarterly report.

We got up at 5:25 AM and George left; he came at 6:55 PM last night. I started cooking breakfast, drank coffee and took my nuang to pasture. I returned and stopped at George's to talk for a couple of minutes and then came home, finished cooking, ate, did dishes and got ready for the day. I went to talk with George for a few more minutes and then returned home and did my little bit of laundry that had accumulated since Friday. Then I killed time for a while. After that I cleaned the entire house; I used the *lampaso* on all the floors, the table, the shelves and so on. After that I went and got my nuang and bathed her and then I asked George to take my picture on my nuang. Then I worked on my Peace Corps quarterly report until lunchtime. I ate and then took a siesta from 12:30 to 1:30 PM. I got up, drank coffee and took my nuang to pasture again. I returned home and finished my Peace Corps quarterly report and then went to fetch water, bathed and so on. I prepared vegetables for supper and then went and got and bathed my nuang. I returned home and wrote the letter to Liz and Randy while supper was cooking. I'm having *utong* bean seeds for supper so it took a long time to cook. They are now cooked (I think) but I haven't yet eaten supper now at 6:34 PM. The weather today was cloudy until 10:00 AM and then hot and dry. There wasn't a drop of rain today. I hope George comes relatively early tonight. AWANEN!

Monday, March 30, 1987
My House, Gomez, Cabarroguis, Quirino

Letters from Chris & Mary M. (and photos from last April), Mike Mc., San & Jack G., Bob S., two from Teresa L., Peace Corps – Washington, D.C. Package from Patagonia Gear. *Salaysayan* Magazine. Postcard for George arrived (mailed 3/18).

₱202 + 200 – 175 = ₱227							
Rides	12	Food	61	Cigarettes	12	Marienda	36
Coffee	18	Household	6	Postage	3	Kerosene	7
Contribution	20					TOTAL	₱175

We got up at 5:10 AM, I gave George my *wayway* and he left; he came at 7:00 PM last night. I cooked a quick breakfast, ate, did dishes and got ready for the day. I took my valuables to George's and left for Burgos at 6:54 AM. I got there and went straight to Cordon and did the above shopping. Then I backtracked to Diffun and went to the office. I thought there was a meeting today, but again there wasn't, so it was a waste of time. I hung out there talking with Francisco until lunchtime. We ate and then returned to the office. I left at about 1:00 PM or so, stopped at the post office in Gundaway and got the above mail – lots of it – and then I caught a jeepney for Burgos. I headed up the mountain via the high road at 2:54 PM and it took me 37:39 (37 minutes and 39 seconds) to climb up and get to my house. I read my mail, put away the food and at 4:00 PM I bathed. Alfredo came to talk and I cut up vegetables for supper while we were talking. My main course tonight will be squash blossoms – yummy! I started cooking and after a while Alfredo left. Now it's 6:02 PM and supper is cooked but not yet eaten. The weather today was hot and dry. I hope George comes right about 7:00 PM again tonight. AWANEN!

Tuesday, March 31, 1987
My House, Gomez, Cabarroguis, Quirino
Harvest Corn

We got up at 5:10 AM and George left; he came at 7:00 PM last night. I started breakfast, drank coffee and took my nuang to pasture. I returned home, finished cooking, ate, did dishes and got ready for the day; I was ready a few minutes before 7:00 AM. I went to George's and he was ready too, so I went and got my nuang and we met at the school. George, Sip and I went to the farm and began the corn harvest! We stopped and loaded the cart at about 9:30 AM, finished at about 10:30 AM and came home, arriving at about 11:20 AM. I came home, ate lunch and took a siesta from 12:15 to 1:00 PM. I got up, drank coffee, fetched water, shelled the little bit of corn (10 ears) from my farm, returned to Georges at 1:45 PM and went back to the farm. I carried three sacks of corn to the trail before George arrived. I pastured my nuang and then we finished harvesting, carrying and loading the corn at about 3:45 PM. We got our nuangs and came home, arriving a few minutes before 5:00 PM. I bathed and tied my nuang for the night. I prepared the vegetables for supper and started cooking. I went to George's to talk for a few minutes – we might shell corn tonight – I don't know yet. We harvested all of the corn, not much for the spring crop! – there were only two carts full. Now it's 6:06 PM and I haven't eaten yet, I'll do that as soon as I finish this. The weather today was hot and dry. I hope we don't shell corn tonight, but I think we probably will. AWANEN!

Wednesday, April 1, 1987
My House, Gomez, Cabarroguis, Quirino

We got up at 5:10 AM and George left. We shelled one cart of corn last night and we came here at 8:45 PM; we talked for only a short while and then slept. I started cooking breakfast, drank coffee and took my nuang to pasture. I returned, finished cooking, ate, did dishes and got ready for the day. George went to Burgos today to help load a culvert on a truck. I reentered my USA address file into the HP-71 – there was a total memory lost error again. I also reentered the "Time" and "Search" programs. After that I started weeding in the south yard and it started showering, so I quickly picked up the coffee that was drying and ran to Alfredo's to help pick up the drying corn. They husked the second cart full this morning. I returned home and finished weeding and by then it was noon so I ate lunch and then took a siesta from 12:40 to 1:40 PM. I got up, drank coffee and took my nuang back to pasture. I returned home and swept the south yard and then I weeded the southeast garden. By then it was 4:00 PM so I bathed and prepared my vegetables for supper. At 4:30 PM I went and got and bathed my nuang, returned home, lit my charcoal and started cooking. Now it's 5:39 PM and my vegetables are cooking and nearly done. I went to George's a while ago, he was playing basketball, and his mother said there will be corn shelling tonight – shit! The weather today was hot and clear until 11:00 AM and then it clouded up and showered a bit. After that it was cloudy the rest of the day. AWANEN!

Thursday, April 2, 1987
My House, Gomez, Cabarroguis, Quirino

Letter to *Salaysayan* Magazine.

We got up at 5:25 AM. We shelled corn last night until 9:00 PM and then George and I came here, talked for just a short while and then slept. George left, I started cooking, drank coffee and took my nuang to pasture. I returned home and finished cooking, ate, did dishes and got ready for the day. I was ready before 7:00 AM and I went to George's, but they were still eating so I got my nuang and headed for the farm. George somehow arrived first and we continued to pile wood to make charcoal until about 10:30 AM. Then I came home and wrote the above letter to *Salaysayan* Magazine, ate lunch and took a siesta from 12:15 to 1:15 PM. I got up, fetched water, prepared my vegetables for supper and then at 1:50 PM I went to George's, but he had already left for the farm. So I headed there too and somehow, this time, I got there before him and pastured my nuang. After George arrived we continued to pile wood and we stopped at about 4:20 PM. We headed home and arrived a bit after 5:00 PM. I bathed my nuang and myself and started cooking supper. Now it's 6:04 PM and my vegetables are cooking. I hope George comes early tonight; within the hour if God permits. The weather today was hot and dry until 11:00 AM and then there was a short shower. After that it was partly cloudy the rest of the day. The spring corn crop is all harvested, husked and shelled – two nights only to do it all. Quite different than the autumn harvest. AWANEN!

Friday, April 3, 1987
My House, Gomez, Cabarroguis, Quirino

We got up at 5:10 AM and George left; he came at 6:45 PM last night. I started cooking, drank coffee and took my nuang to pasture. I returned home and finished cooking, ate, did dishes and got ready for the day. I was ready to go at 6:45 AM so I went and got my nuang and headed for the farm. George walked today so I was first to leave. He caught up with me about halfway there. We got some stems of banana trees, split them in half or smaller and put them around the wood for making charcoal. Then we made the walls of the charcoal making place, put the banana *oklaps* [the split banana tree stems] between the walls of the charcoal making pit and the wood that will be turned into charcoal and filled some space between the walls and the *oklaps* with dirt [does that make sense to you?]. We worked at that until 10:30 AM or so and then came home for lunch. I ate lunch, took a siesta from 12:00 to 1:00 PM and then at 2:00 PM I went back to George's and we returned to the farm. We continued walling, covering and filling the charcoal pit with dirt. We worked pretty late at that and we didn't head for home until about 4:40 PM. We arrived shortly after 5:00 PM, I bathed my nuang, started my rice, bathed myself and now it's 6:10 PM, my rice is cooked and my vegetables are nearly ready. I hope George comes at about 7:00 PM again tonight. The weather today was hot and dry until 5:00 PM and then there was a little bit of rain and a little bit of thunder and lightning, but not even enough to wet the soil. I feel like I did a good days work today. AWANEN!

Saturday, April 4, 1987
Charcoal Pit, Gomez, Cabarroguis, Quirino

We got up at 5:25 AM and George left; he came at 7:30 PM last night. It rained most of the night and for a little while this morning. I started cooking breakfast, drank coffee and took my nuang to pasture. I returned, finished cooking, ate, did dishes and got ready for the day. I headed for the farm at about 7:00 AM, arrived and we finished covering the pile of wood with dirt at about 10:30 AM. We lit the fire and after that we came home for lunch. Now it's 11:55 AM and we'll return to the charcoal pit after lunch and we'll be sleeping there tonight – okay? Okay! We returned to the *paguggingan* [charcoal making place] at 1:00 PM and it was still burning – of course, George knows what he's doing. We removed some banana blossoms in the afternoon and did lots of sitting around. George left at about 3:00 PM to go and get his nuang because he's pulling a cart of corn to Burgos tomorrow. At 4:45 PM Sip and I bathed our nuangs and when we finished George had returned. I gave myself a hernia above my navel [an inguinal hernia] today trying to carry too much weight of banana tree stems. It hurts! We took burlap sacks to sleep on, blankets, flashlights, leftover food and coffee to the mountain with us. We ate early and slept early. The weather today – as mentioned above, it rained last night and stopped at about 7:00 AM this morning. Then it was sunny until noon and then it rained for a half hour or so again. It was sunny most of the afternoon. It's nice to sleep on the mountain with George. I'll always remember our "campout". AWANEN!

Sunday, April 5, 1987
Charcoal Pit, Gomez, Cabarroguis, Quirino

Letter to Sue T.

We got up at 5:15 AM on the mountain and we put more dirt on the charcoal. It's burning nicely now. After that, George, Sip and I came home. We got home shortly after 6:00 AM and I started cooking breakfast immediately, but I didn't finish eating, doing dishes and getting ready for the day until after 8:00 AM. I did some laundry, finished that at about 10:00 AM and then I went and got and bathed my nuang. I returned home and cleared the wood that the bulldozer had put on my path to the water place and then I went and fetched water. I finished that and went to talk with Alfredo for a while and then I returned home, ate lunch and slept for an hour. I got up, drank coffee and then wrote the letter to Sue. I told her how sorry I am that things didn't work out at Puerto Galera for us, but such is life. I took my nuang to pasture again, returned home and finished the letter. I took my clothes off the clothesline and started preparing stuff for supper at 3:30 PM. As we're going to stand guard over the charcoal pit again tonight I have to finish everything early and get there before dark. Now it's 4:39 PM, my supper is cooked and I'll eat as soon as I'm done writing this, wash dishes and head for the mountain. The weather today was hot and dry. AWANEN!

Monday, April 6, 1987
Charcoal Pit, Gomez, Cabarroguis, Quirino

Letters from Dad, Yip Chee H., Chad D. and a *Reader's Digest.*

₱227 + 400 – 412 = ₱215							
Food	90	Rides	16	Coffee	81	Clothes	10
Lunch	12	Soap	20	Marienda	13	Household	31
Seeds	50	Cigarettes	10	Postage	10	Candy	49
Misc.	20					TOTAL	₱412

We got up at 5:20 AM at the charcoal pit. We had to get up five times during the night to cover holes in the charcoal pit as it burned. I moved my nuang and came home but George and Sip stayed there. I drank coffee and headed for Burgos at 6:40 AM. I got there at about 7:15 AM and caught a ride to Santiago. I got to Santiago at about 8:40 AM and managed to finish all of my business by 11:15 AM. I went to Letty's Restaurant for lunch, hoping to catch JB and Katie, but they weren't there. I caught a jeepney back to Gundaway at about 12:10 PM, arrived at 1:00 PM, went to the post office and got the above mail and then continued on to Burgos. I came home via the high road – 39 minutes and 30 seconds – and arrived home at about 2:40 PM or so. I read my mail, prepared my vegetables for supper and started cooking at 3:30 PM. George and Sip are eating on the mountain and I'll go there as soon as I finish eating and washing dishes. Now it's 4:21 PM. The weather today was hot and dry and for some reason there was lots of smoke in the air today. Oh, I saw Abe (Diling Mendoza's husband) in Santiago today and he's still an asshole. AWANEN!

Tuesday, April 7, 1987
Charcoal Pit, Gomez, Cabarroguis, Quirino

We got up at 5:15 AM on the mountain and George and Sip started cooking breakfast. I moved my nuang and came home. I cooked breakfast, ate, did dishes, got ready for the day and at about 8:15 AM people started coming to my house for the monthly forestry association meeting. Efren, Rody's replacement as the new technician, arrived at 9:00 AM and after a while we went to the meeting place – the MAF technician's place. There was a grand total of only eight of us for the meeting, so it turned into just a talk and gripe session. We stopped at about 10:30 AM and Efren asked me to cook for them, so there were four of us for lunch at my house. We ate nearly an entire squash. They left at about 1:30 PM and I immediately returned to the farm. George, Sip and their mother were digging up the charcoal, so I helped do that. Mother went home at about 4:30 PM and we started cooking supper. After supper George discovered that Sip had forgotten to feed the chickens, so George sent him home to do that, which meant that it was just George and I on the mountain. This is the last night to guard the charcoal, good deal. It's been nice to be able to talk so much without having to worry about whether I am using precisely the right grammar and vocabulary for the past few days, unlike when I am in a group of people and too shy to make conversation due to those concerns. The weather today was hot and dry. AWANEN!

Wednesday, April 8, 1987
Charcoal Pit, Gomez, Cabarroguis, Quirino

₱215 – 5 = ₱210					
Cigarettes	5			TOTAL	₱5

We get up at 5:00 AM on the mountain, only George and I. We cooked breakfast, ate, did dishes and I pastured my nuang. Then Sip, mother and Alfredo came and we dug charcoal some more. Alfredo mostly sat and watched; I don't know what to think of him these days. Mother left at about 9:00 AM but George and I continued work until 10:00 AM and then came home to bathe and eat. Digging charcoal, killing the last of the fire and bagging it is hot and dirty work. Now it's 12:01 PM and George and I are going back to the charcoal pit at about 1:00 PM. We'll cook and eat there again tonight; this will be the fifth night there. Okay, we went back to the charcoal pit at about 1:00 PM and dug charcoal again all afternoon. It's really hot and dirty work; it's like mop-up on a forest fire. George, Sip, their mother and I worked all afternoon and when mother left, at about 4:45 PM, we started cooking supper. I went to bathe my nuang and when I returned we ate, did dishes, drank coffee and talked until we went to sleep. The weather was hot and dry all day. AWANEN!

[Notes on charcoal making.

From what has been said above, it is probably not clear to you exactly what the process was that we used. So, okay, the first thing is obviously to get enough wood so that you can make charcoal and bring it to the place where the charcoal will be made. Then you dig a charcoal making pit. At this point the use of the split banana tree stems kind of eludes me, but I seem to remember that they were used for the walls of the charcoal pit. After the pit is dug and the walls of it are lined with the banana *oklaps* then the wood is put into the pit, trying to keep it away from the walls of the pit. Then dirt is shoveled into the space between the pit walls (*oklaps*) and the wood. Then banana leaves and more *oklaps* are put on top of the wood and a bunch of dirt is spread on top of it all, leaving one place open so that a person can get in and light the fire.

The fire is lit and then banana leaves and *oklaps* are used to cover that area and one hopes and prays that everything will be okay. Of course charcoal is created by burning wood in an oxygen starved environment. If there is too much oxygen then the wood will just be burned up and you'll end with a pile of ash. This is the reason that the burning charcoal must be watched all night and basically 24 hours day while the fire is going. Sometimes, as the wood is reduced in volume, the banana leaves, *oklaps* and dirt collapse into the pit, opening up a hole where oxygen can enter. These holes must be discovered as quickly as possible and covered over with more banana leaves, *oklaps* and dirt again, cutting off the oxygen supply. I don't know how George knew exactly when the wood had been adequately burned so that it had become charcoal, but he did, probably due to having done this many times before. At that point it was time to start digging up the charcoal, extinguishing any embers which were still "live" and then bagging the charcoal.]

Thursday, April 9, 1987
My House, Gomez, Cabarroguis, Quirino

We got up at 5:00 AM on the mountain and started cooking immediately. I went to move my nuang, but George had already moved her, so I returned and we ate breakfast, drank coffee and started digging and picking up charcoal again. Mother and Sip didn't come until nearly 9:00 AM but they stayed and worked until noon and they started cooking George's and my lunch for us – thank you. George and I ate on the mountain and then rested until about 2:00 PM. I went and pastured my nuang and George searched for his nuang, but the sucker had wandered off – again! Mother and Sip showed up at about 2:40 PM and said that George had gone to search for his nuang. Some other old lady immediately came and mother and her talked ALL AFTERNOON!! I picked up and bagged charcoal some more and finally Sip started helping. I was a bit frustrated by mother and Sip's lack of help. George returned at about 4:00 PM and we removed the rest of the wood and charcoal from the pit. We didn't leave until about 4:50 PM and we didn't, of course, get home until well after 5:00 PM. I was too tired to cook. Now it's 6:16 PM and my coffee water is heating; that will be my supper tonight. The weather today was hot and dry again. I hope George comes early. AWANEN!

Friday, April 10, 1987
My House, Gomez, Cabarroguis, Quirino

Letter to Chad D.

We got up at 5:15 AM and George left; he came at 6:55 PM last night. I started cooking, drank coffee and took my nuang to pasture. I returned, finished cooking, ate, did dishes and got ready for the day. At 7:00 AM I headed for the farm and helped George cut grass until 10:30 AM. Then we went to the charcoal pit and George's mother and father were bagging the last of the charcoal. We finally headed home at about 11:00 AM, got home, ate lunch and then I rested from 1:00 to 1:30 PM. At 2:00 PM I took my nuang to pasture again. I stayed home this afternoon. George and Alfredo went to the farm to haul the charcoal. At around 3:00 PM I fetched water, trimmed my beard and after a while I bathed. At 4:40 PM I started cooking supper and went and got my nuang. At about 5:00 PM Sip came to tell me that my charcoal is waiting for me to pick it up at the junction near the Barangay Hall. I went there and Alfredo brought it to my house in the cart. [They gave me three or four bags of charcoal in return for my help in making it.] Now it's 5:51 PM and George will haul some of the charcoal to Burgos tonight so he'll be very late, probably around 8:00 or 8:30 PM. My supper is done but not yet eaten. The weather today was hot and dry, but mostly cloudy. AWANEN!

Saturday, April 11, 1987
My House, Gomez, Cabarroguis, Quirino

We got up the 5:30 AM and George left; he came at about 9:50 PM last night. I started cooking my rice, took my nuang to pasture, returned home, drank coffee, finished cooking, ate, did dishes and got ready for the day. I went and got my nuang and headed for the farm at 7:00 AM. George and I harvested bananas today. We harvested two kinds today – *lakaton* and *depig*. We finished at about 10:15 AM and went to the charcoal pit, where his mother and father were bagging the last of the charcoal, and then we returned home. We arrived at about 11:15 AM and I immediately ate lunch. After that I did laundry and finished with that at about 1:50 PM. I took a short break to take my nuang to pasture, returned and rested from 3:00 to 3:15 PM. It clouded up and thundered but there was no rain, so after a while I bathed and then at 4:00 PM I prepared my vegetables for supper. I went and got and bathed my nuang and took her back to pasture because George and I are pulling carts to Burgos tomorrow filled with charcoal and bananas. I returned home, fetched water and started supper. Now it's 5:52 PM and supper is nearly cooked. I'll eat when I finish this and hope that George comes early tonight. The weather today was hot and dry until 3:00 PM and then it clouded up and thundered for a while, but there was no rain. My clothes that are hanging on the clothesline are not yet dry – shit! AWANEN!

Sunday, April 12, 1987
My House, Gomez, Cabarroguis, Quirino

Letters to Dad, Peace Corps Health Unit and Bob S.

₱210 + 400 – 453 = ₱157							
Cigarettes	10	Rice	260	Food	40	Kerosene	7
Marienda	51	Batteries	9	Rides	6	Medicine	3
Coffee	27	Clothes	13	Household	5	Misc.	22
						TOTAL	₱453

I got up at 5:00 AM. George got up at 4:00 AM and left to pasture his nuang; he came at 7:05 PM last night. I started the rice cooking and went and moved my nuang. I returned and told George where she was, returned home, finished cooking, ate, did dishes, got ready for the day and headed for Burgos walking at 6:35 AM. There was a change of plans since last night, and Alfredo and George pulled the carts down the mountain. I arrived in Burgos and got a ride to Gundaway, did the above shopping and finished by 9:00 AM. I drank a Coke, ate marienda and headed back for Burgos, arriving at about 10:30 AM. I put my rice in the cart, talked with Alfredo for a few minutes and headed home via the high road, arriving 38 minutes later, at 10:53 AM. I did laundry, slept for a while, got up and wrote a letter to Dad and a letter to the Health Unit telling them about my hernia and asked them to please send me some GG serum so that I can get my Hepatitis shot. At 3:45 PM I bathed and then I prepared stuff for supper. At 4:30 PM I started cooking and at about 5:00 PM George arrived home and I went there, got my *kaban* of rice and came back home. Now it's 5:50 PM and my supper is nearly cooked. The weather today was hot and dry. There was a hard rain during the night. Now it's cloudy. I hope George comes early tonight. We made 13 sacks of charcoal in total. AWANEN!

Monday, April 13, 1987
My House, Gomez, Cabarroguis, Quirino

Ralph P. come and spend the night.

₱157 – 5 = ₱152							
Cigarettes	5	Rice	260	Food	40	TOTAL	₱5

We got up at 5:15 AM and George left; he came at 7:05 PM last night. I started the rice cooking and went to move my nuang. I returned home, finished cooking, ate, did the dishes and got ready for the day. I went to George's, we went to get our nuangs and headed for the farm. We got there and cut grass until 10:30 AM or so and then came home for lunch. I ate and then took a siesta from 12 to 12:20 PM. At 1:00 PM I went to George's and we returned to the farm at 1:30 PM or so. We pastured our nuangs, continued to cut grass until 4:30 PM and then headed home. I got home with my nuang and – surprise – Ralph P. and his companion, Danny were here. I did greetings with Alfredo and those guys, started cooking and then I bathed. Alfredo came to talk for a while and then he went home to eat at about 5:30 PM or so. After a while we ate supper, did dishes and sat around talking. Now it's 8:50 PM, kind of late for me. Of course George won't be coming tonight. The weather today, well, it rained all night last night again but today it was hot, humid and dry. AWANEN!

Tuesday, April 14, 1987
My House, Gomez, Cabarroguis, Quirino

Ralph P. leave.

I got up at 5:00 AM and started the rice cooking, went and pastured my nuang, returned and Ralph and Danny were up. I drank coffee, finished cooking, we ate, did the dishes and got ready for the day. After a while Ralph and Danny also got ready and we went to the farm, where George, Sip and Lito were cutting grass. I showed Ralph all of the farm and we sat and admired the view for a while. At around 9:30 AM we headed back down the mountain. I got my nuang and Ralph rode her home, I bathed her and started cooking lunch. Lunch wasn't done and ready to eat until 12:30 PM or so. We ate, did dishes again, rested, talked until 2:15 PM and then Ralph and I went to pasture my nuang again. We returned home and talked for a little while longer and kind of ran out of things to talk about, so we kind of sat around and looked at each other until they left at around 4:00 PM. At around 4:40 PM I went and got and bathed my nuang, bathed myself, fetched water and started cooking supper. Now it's 5:40 PM and my rice is nearly cooked. I hope George comes early, even before 7:00 PM tonight. The weather today was hot and dry. There was no rain last night but there was a pretty strong earthquake. AWANEN!

Wednesday, April 15, 1987
My House, Gomez, Cabarroguis, Quirino

Letters to Chris & Mary M., Teresa L. and Peace Corps, Washington.

We got up at 5:10 AM and George left; he came at 7:20 PM last night. I started my rice, drank coffee, took my nuang to pasture, returned home, finished cooking, ate, did dishes and got ready for the day. I went to George's for a while to talk. There's no work today because it's a Holy Day – Ash Wednesday. I came home after a while and sorted through all of my notebooks full of papers. I sorted out a stack of paper four inches thick to give to George for toilet paper. I cleaned my bookshelves, cleaned the house and then I worked on the long questionnaire that I received from Peace Corps Washington about work, culture, experiences and etc. I worked on that until 10:15 AM and then George and I went and got are nuangs, bathed them and returned home. I worked on the questionnaire some more until lunch and then I ate, took a siesta from 12:00 to 1:00 PM, got up, finished the questionnaire and then at 2:20 PM George and I went and pastured our nuangs again. I returned home and did the above letter to Chris and Mary. I worked on that until 3:40 PM and then prepared my vegetables for supper. I fetched water and bathed at 4:45 PM, went and got and bathed my nuang and then started cooking. I started a letter to Teresa L., cooked, ate, did dishes and now at 6:50 PM. I hope George comes before 7:30 PM. The weather today was hot and dry with a few clouds until noon or so. There was no rain last night. It was 88°F in midday today. This morning it was 76°F. I'll continue working on the letter to Teresa until George comes. AWANEN!

Thursday, April 16, 1987
My House, Gomez, Cabarroguis, Quirino

We got up at 5:10 AM and George left; he didn't come until 7:40 PM last night. I started my rice cooking and took my nuang to pasture, returned and talked with George for a few minutes and then came home, finished cooking, ate, did dishes and got ready for the day. I took the dry coffee beans to Alfredo's and returned home and didn't do much of anything. After a while I finished the letter to Teresa and then I rested for a while. Alfredo came to talk for a while from around 9:30 to 10:30 AM and then he went home. I pulled some weeds in the tree nursery, it's been a long time since I did any work in it. After a while I went to bathe and move my nuang, returned and talked with George some more. Then I returned home and ate lunch. After lunch I pretty much did more of nothing. I took a siesta from 1:30 to 2:30 PM, got up and did more of nothing. At 3:50 PM I prepared my vegetables for supper and at 4:15 PM I went to talk with George some more. Then at 4:30 PM I asked him to come early, left and went and got my nuang and bathed her. I returned home, started cooking, bathed myself and now it's 5:33 PM. My vegetables are cooking. Please George, come early tonight. The weather today was hot but mostly cloudy all day; it sprinkled for around five minutes this morning. AWANEN!

Friday, April 17, 1987
My House, Gomez, Cabarroguis, Quirino

Letters to JB & Katie F. and Dan & Chris T. Postcards to San & Jack G. and Mike Mc.

We got up at 5:10 AM and George left; he didn't come until 6:35 PM again last night. I started my rice cooking, took my nuang to pasture, returned, talked with

George for a few minutes and then returned home. I finished cooking, ate, did dishes and got ready for the day. I went and talked with George for a few more minutes and then returned home and wrote the letter to JB and Katie. Then I pulled weeds in the tree nursery again. I went to talk with George for a few more minutes and returned home again. By then it was lunchtime so, I ate lunch and went and moved my nuang, fetched water, returned home and took a siesta for an hour. Then I got up and wrote a letter to Dan and Chris T. and postcards to Mike Mc. and San and Jack G. After that I relaxed for a while and read my *Newsweek* Magazine. At 4:00 PM I prepared vegetables for supper and at 4:40 PM I went and got and bathed my nuang. I returned home and started the charcoal, put the rice on and bathed myself. Now it's 5:33 PM and my rice is still cooking. If I'm lucky George will come earlier tonight, but who knows, have to wait and see. George and the other bachelors played volleyball all afternoon, so maybe George will be tired and arrive early. The weather today was cloudy and there was a very light shower this morning. AWANEN!

Saturday, April 18, 1987
My House, Gomez, Cabarroguis, Quirino

Letters to Ronald & family

I got up at 5:00 AM. George got up and left at 4:00 AM for the farm. He came at 7:20 PM last night. I started cooking breakfast and took my nuang to pasture, returned home, finished cooking, ate, did dishes, got ready for the day and headed for the farm. I walked today. George was plowing today. I took some pictures and shook the dirt off clumps of roots; I wasn't really much help, but I tried. I returned home at 10:00 AM, arriving here at about 10:30 after getting and bathing my nuang. I killed time for a while and then slept from 12 to 12:30 PM. Alfredo came to tell me that Junior's sister's son died [*natay*] this morning at about 7:00 AM. I totally misunderstood what he was saying and kept saying "good" and "that's nice" and "wonderful" as he kept repeating himself over and over and looking at me strangely. My brain finally clicked in and realized that he was not saying *kasar* [got married], but *natay* [die] and I felt so incredibly stupid and spent the next 20 minutes apologizing and explaining what I thought he had said. He understood, no hard feelings. After a while he left, I ate lunch and wrote a letter to Ronald's entire family. In the middle of it I stopped and took my nuang to pasture again. After that I finished reading my February *Reader's Digest* and then I went and talked with George for a bit and asked him if he's going to Junior's house tonight. Of course he is. At 4:00 PM I prepared things for supper (*sabunganay*) [banana blossom] and then at 4:40 PM I went and got and bathed my nuang. I met George at the nuang bathing place in the creek and asked him to please come, even if he doesn't return home until 2:00 or 3:00 AM. He said okay. Now it's 6:48 PM and I'm still cooking. The weather today was cloudy until 10:00 AM and then it cleared up and was hot and dry the rest of the day. AWANEN!

Chapter 18
Culture Notes #7

Death

Death is treated very differently than in America. The traditional Ilokano wake always seemed extremely rude to me. I saw entirely too many deaths and wakes in my two year stay. People died regularly, more children than older people. This was the reason the wake seemed extremely insensitive me. A child would die of something like measles or chicken pox because the parents did not have the money to go to a doctor. Then they would have to beg, borrow, or steal enough money to be able to feed all the people who would come to their house for the next nine nights for the wake. And, actually it ended up being more than nine nights because the nine night wake officially began on the day of the funeral.

The first thing that happened after a death was that all the men who had either hand tools or skills would go to the house of the dead and build a coffin. This would generally be early morning as the child would die during the night, and word would spread very rapidly through the grapevine. This would be a time of solemnity and sadness. There would be very little talking among the coffin builders. People would come and go during the day, friends offering condolences, helping in whatever ways they could. That night, anybody who wanted to, was welcome to come over for the first night of the wake. Those who could afford to do so would bring a chicken. Before the night was over there would be a feed for all the people who were present. It would have been considered rude however, to bring fruits, vegetables, or other farm crops. This would have implied that the family wasn't good enough farmers to have enough of those foods. This first night was quite solemn, the body was still in the house, and one should not be rude or noisy. There were certain nights when bachelors could come and certain other nights when the single girls could come. A wake was not considered a time when a boy and girl should meet or court. The single people would go home between about 10:00 PM and midnight and the adults that remained would play cards and converse until dawn. That day the burial would take place. Pallbearers would have been selected during the night, and they would carry the coffin on their shoulders to the cemetery, which was about five miles from Gomez. They would perform the burial, generally marking the grave with a simple wooden cross, and then go home.

The second night the wake would be more joyful. There would be no music for a wake but there would be games and other diversions to keep people awake. The ghost of the dead person was now roaming about the village trying to figure out where to go, what to do, what had happened. If the person had not been ready to die, and was not given a happy send off into the next world, it could make problems for another person by entering their body and causing bad luck or medical problems. Unexplainable stomach problems were often blamed on ghosts.

For nine nights this would continue. Every night the family of the dead would have to feed all the people who came. Because of the fact that the ghost was now roaming around, certain precautions also had to be taken at night while sleeping. People slept as far away as possible from any openings in the house, and on these nights of the wake, they also took particular care to make sure that they were in tight body contact with each other all night. If the ghost entered the house at all, it was a sightless thing and hopefully couldn't find anybody. If it did bump into the sleeping mass of people, it couldn't differentiate one person from the other and therefore couldn't enter into any single one of them. I, when told by George that this was the reason he wanted to sleep legs and arms all intertwined, again showed cultural sensitivity by agreeing to it. This would go on all nine nights of the wake, and then George would once again be happy to sleep with just shoulders or hips touching.

The ninth night of the wake was the grand finale, so to speak. This was the night that the ghost would be given its final send-off. It was a night of special activities. There would be games for even the smallest children. There was supposed to be ample joy and laughter this night. The family of the deceased would also prepare special foods this night, and more people would come than any other night. The younger people would stay until about midnight, and the remainder of the night the older men and women would talk, party, play cards, eat, drink, and generally attempt to be merry. At dawn everybody would again go home, and that was the official end of the wake.

An American visitor to my village of Gomez once said to me that "they don't grieve like we do, they have so many children that death is no problem and they don't truly grieve". I want to emphasize strongly that this is absolutely not true. They grieve as much as any American person who loses a son or daughter, mother or father, grandmother or grandfather. I considered this an extremely ridiculous thing to say.

Chapter 19
April 19, 1987 through June 6, 1987

Sunday, April 19, 1987
My House, Gomez, Cabarroguis, Quirino
Easter Sunday

Letters to Jerry J. and Yip Chee H. Postcards to Ardis B. and Mark G.

We got up at 5:40 AM and George left; he came at 12:20 AM this morning. I started rice cooking and took my nuang to pasture. On the way home I stopped at George's to talk for a bit and then returned home, finished cooking, ate, did dishes and got ready for the day [you have seen this expression "got ready for the day" how many times now? I have no idea. What does it mean? It means to brush my teeth and move my bowels.] I did laundry from about 8:00 AM to 9:00 AM and I just got it hung up on the line and it started to rain – SHIT! I started the letter to Yip and the rain stopped, but then a thunder and lightning storm moved in, so I quickly went to fetch water before it started raining too hard. I returned home and there was a downpour that lasted for an hour or so. Oh well, at least it gave us some badly needed moisture for the cracked earth. I finished the letter to Yip, ate lunch, laid down, but couldn't sleep, so I got up and wrote the letter to Jerry. Then I read my *Urshurak* book for an hour or so. After that I prepared my vegetables for supper and by then it was 4:15 PM so I went and talked with George for a while and asked him if he'll be late again tonight, he said he doesn't know yet. I can only hope that he comes early tonight. Junior was drunk this afternoon so maybe by now he's sick. The funeral was today and George was a pallbearer. At 4:30 PM I went and got and bathed my nuang, bathed myself and started cooking supper. I'm having squash cooked in store bought coconut milk for my Easter supper. The weather this morning was mentioned above and in the afternoon there was no more rain. Now it's 6:06 PM and my squash is nearly cooked. I wrote the postcards to Mark G. and Ardis while the rice was cooking. I told Ardis that I'll mail some film to her tomorrow. AWANEN!

Monday, April 20, 1987
My House, Gomez, Cabarroguis, Quirino

Letters from Vicki S., San & Jack G., Dave W., Vicki K., Bob S., Tony S., Sue T., Cynthia B. and Chris & Mary M. (and package with pants).

₱152 + 300 – 355 = ₱197							
Rides	11	Cigarettes	15	Postage	120	Kerosene	7
Marienda	56	Food	78	Lunch	14	Household	5
Candy	8	Coffee	18	Misc.	23	TOTAL	₱355

We got up at 5:20 AM, I gave George my *wayway* and he left. He came at 11:40 PM last night. I drank coffee, got ready for the day and headed for Burgos at 6:00 AM. I arrived before 7:00 AM and caught a jeepney to Cordon. I did my marketing for the above, finished by 9:30 AM and then went to Diffun and to the office. There was supposed to be a meeting today, but again there was no meeting. I really gave the District Forester hell about my having to spend the time to come to the office every month only to find that the monthly meeting has again been canceled. By and by we went to lunch for nearly two hours and then I said goodbye and caught a jeepney for Gundaway, where I stopped at the post office and mailed everything that I've written from the last ten days and picked up the above mail. Then I continued on to Burgos and started climbing the mountain via the high road at 2:30 PM. I got home at about 3:15 PM and read my mail. Then at about 4:20 PM I bathed. I have a headache and I'm tired; I've been short on sleep the last two nights and therefore I'm not cooking supper tonight. I hope to hell George will come early tonight, but he probably won't – oh well, such is life. The weather today was hot and dry and there was no rain, but now at 6:00 PM it's cloudy, but doesn't feel like it will rain. AWANEN!

Tuesday, April 21, 1987
My House, Gomez, Cabarroguis, Quirino

Letter to Vicki S.

We got up at 4:45 AM and George left; he came at 7:30 PM last night. I started cooking breakfast, drank coffee and took my nuang to pasture. I returned home and finished cooking, ate, did dishes, got ready for the day and read the *"Urshurak"* book for an hour or so and then killed time for an hour or so and then at 9:45 AM I went and got and bathed my nuang. I returned home and weeded the small fenced area north of the house where the *kamote* used to be and by then it was lunchtime so I ate and went and told George that I will come to the farm this afternoon. I returned home, laid down for a while, but I couldn't sleep, so I got up and wrote the letter to Vicki. By then it was 2:00 PM so I went to George's but he had already left for the farm to plow. I took my nuang to pasture and walked to the farm. I mostly just ended up watching George plow but I did pile a few weeds and strolled around all of the farm looking at everything. We stayed there until 5:00 PM and then we came home. I got and bathed my nuang, bathed myself, fetched water and started cooking. Now it's 6:30 PM and my vegetables are cooking. I don't know if George will be early or late tonight, but I hope that he'll be early. Tonight is the fourth night of the wake. The weather today was hot and dry all day. AWANEN!

Wednesday, April 22, 1987
My House, Gomez, Cabarroguis, Quirino

Letter to Sue T.

We got up at 4:50 AM and George left; he came at 7:20 PM last night. I started the rice cooking, drank coffee and took my nuang to pasture. I returned and talked with George for a while and then came home, finished cooking, ate, did dishes, got ready for the day and a bit before 7:00 AM I went and got my nuang and headed for the farm. George was plowing today so all I could do to help was pile up roots, so that's what I did. We headed for home at around 10:00 AM and I stopped at George's house for a while to talk before coming home. When I got home I wrote the letter to Sue and then ate lunch and slept for about 15 minutes. At 1:00 PM I went back to George's and at 1:30 PM we returned to the farm. I burned a few piles of dry banana leaves and pastured my nuang and then piled up roots some more. We worked until about 4:40 PM and then headed home, arriving at about 5:00 PM. I bathed my nuang and myself, fetched water and started cooking. Now my vegetables are cooking and nearly done. I don't know if George will be early or late tonight, it's the fifth night of the Celebration of the Dead – four more nights to go after tonight. Now it's 6:26 PM and if George is late maybe I'll do another letter. The weather today was hot and dry all day. AWANEN!

Thursday, April 23, 1987
My House, Gomez, Cabarroguis, Quirino

Letters to Chris & Mary M. and Tony & Janet S. Postcard to Dave W.

We got up at 5:10 AM and George left; he came at 8:00 PM last night. I started the rice cooking, drank coffee and took my nuang to pasture. I returned and talked with George for a minute or two, came home, finished cooking, ate, did dishes and got ready for the day. George is pulling cants to the Barangay Hall so I did a little bit of laundry and then read the *"Urshurak"* book until 9:45 AM and then I went and got and bathed my nuang. I returned home and wrote the letter to Chris and Mary and after that I ate lunch and laid down for a half hour, but I couldn't sleep because it was too hot. I got up and read *"Urshurak"* until 2:15 PM and then took my nuang to pasture again. Upon returning I asked George if he can help me repair the fence for the squash place and he said maybe, so I started weeding the lower garden and at about 3:00 PM George came and we replaced the squash fence. That took until 4:15 PM and then he went home. I prepared things for supper and then went and got and bathed my nuang, started cooking and bathed myself. I cooked supper, ate, did dishes and went to George's. He said that he's going to Junior's house tonight. This is night number six for the Celebration of the Dead, three more nights to go. Now it's 6:54 PM. The weather today was cloudy until 9:00 AM or so and then very hot and dry. I hope George comes before midnight. AWANEN!

Friday, April 24, 1987
My House, Gomez, Cabarroguis, Quirino

I got up at 5:20 AM. George got up and left at 4:00 AM to pasture his nuang. He came at 10:55 PM last night. I started cooking my rice, took my nuang to pasture, returned home, finished cooking, ate, did the dishes and got ready for the day. I read *Urshurak* for a while and then played with my HP-71, writing another time program, but using the "IMAGE" statement. I worked on that until 10:00 AM and then I went and got and bathed my nuang and returned home. I weeded in the lower garden area for a while and when I stopped it was time for lunch, but I went to talk with George for a few minutes first. I returned home, ate my lunch and then took a siesta from 12:00 to 1:00 PM. When I got up, I prepared my vegetables for supper, drank coffee and then at 2:15 PM I returned my nuang to pasture and headed for the farm. I cleaned up some of the brush along the middle trail going to the farm, so I didn't get there until 3:00 PM. George was plowing so I picked up roots and piled them. We worked until 4:30 PM and then headed for home, arriving about 5:00 PM. I got and bathed my nuang, started the rice cooking, bathed myself and finished cooking. Then I ate and did dishes and now it's 6:46 PM. Again, I don't know if George will be early or late and I also found out just last night that the wake continues for nine nights after the burial, not nine days after the death, so the last night will be Monday. Such is life I guess. The weather today was hot and dry. If George comes late maybe I'll work on a letter. AWANEN!

Saturday, April 25, 1987
My House, Gomez, Cabarroguis, Quirino

Letter to Bob S.

We got up at 5:00 AM and George left; he came at 8:10 PM last night. I started the rice cooking, drank coffee, took my nuang to pasture, returned and talked with George a couple minutes and then I came home, finished cooking, ate, did dishes and got ready for the day. I started weeding in the lower garden spot immediately. After a while Alfredo came to get some Tylenol; I gave it to him and continued weeding until 9:45 AM and then I went and got and bathed my nuang. I returned home and continued weeding until 11:15 AM. I stopped, cleaned up and ate lunch. I took a siesta from noon to 1:00 PM and then got up and read *Urshurak* until 2:15 PM and took my nuang to pasture again. I returned home, fetched water and continued weeding again until finished, at about 3:30 PM. I even weeded the squash place and removed the dead *pallang* vines. At 4:00 PM I prepared things for supper and at 4:45 PM I went and got and bathed my nuang and then I bathed myself and started cooking. I went and talked with George for a couple minutes and he said he'll be coming early tonight. I hope he doesn't change his plan. He plowed today. Now it's 6:03 PM and supper is nearly cooked. Oh, I pounded my dry red peppers into a fine powder this afternoon at Alfredo's house. The weather today was hot and dry. It was only 70°F this morning, but it got up well above 90°F in midday and even now it's 91°F. AWANEN!

Sunday, April 26, 1987
My House, Gomez, Cabarroguis, Quirino

Letter to Vicki K.

We got up at 5:00 AM and George left; he came at 7:10 PM last night. I started my rice cooking, drank coffee and took my nuang to pasture. I returned and talked with George for a couple minutes and then came home. I finished cooking, ate, did dishes, got ready for the day and went to talk with George for a few more minutes. He went to Pinaripad today for a concert and picnic by Mr. Dela Cruz, a congressional candidate. I returned home and did laundry, finishing at about 9:30 AM. I read *Urshurak* for a while and then went and got and bathed my nuang. I returned home and read some more and Alfredo came to talk for a while. He asked me for my dead batteries, I guess he's going to try and recharge them in the sun or something. He left at about 11:15 AM and I ate lunch and took a siesta from noon to 1:00 PM. When I got up I read some more and at 2:15 PM I went and pastured my nuang again and returned home. I weeded and swept the south lawn area, finished at about 4:00 PM and prepared my vegetables for supper. At 4:45 PM I went and got and bathed my nuang and myself. At 5:30 PM I started cooking and now it's 5:56 PM. I don't think George has even returned from Pinaripad yet, so I don't know if he'll be late or early tonight. The Celebration of the Dead is continuing for two more nights too. I hope he comes early. There was a pretty strong and long lasting earthquake last night at about 8:30 PM. The weather today was hot and dry, it was more than 90°F again. AWANEN!

Monday, April 27, 1987
My House, Gomez, Cabarroguis, Quirino

Letters to San & Jack G and Fred & Cynthia B.

I got up at 5:00 AM with no companion. I started cooking, drank coffee and took my nuang to pasture. I returned and stopped at Alfredo's and a few minutes later George arrived, he said that the concert lasted all night. I returned home, finished cooking, ate, did dishes and got ready for the day. I went and got my nuang and headed for the farm. We all piled brush at the extreme north of the farm and below the road. We worked on that until 9:00 AM or so and then I went to where George was harrowing and helped remove roots for him. We headed home at about 10:00 AM and arrived at about 10:30 AM. I came home and after a while I ate lunch and then I took a siesta from 11:45 AM to 12:45 PM. I got up, fetched water and at 1:30 PM I went to George's. At 2:05 PM he still wasn't ready to return to the farm so I left first, pastured my nuang and weeded a small piece of my farm. When George, Alfredo and Sip finally arrived I went and helped George. We worked until 4:45 PM and then we headed home, arriving about 5:00 PM. I bathed my nuang, started the rice. bathed myself, cooked, ate and did dishes. Now it's 7:04 PM and it's the final night of the Celebration of the Dead and George told me he is going, so he'll be late for sure. The weather today was hot and dry again, but I don't think it hit 90°F today. AWANEN!

Tuesday, April 28, 1987
My House, Gomez, Cabarroguis, Quirino

Letter to Tom & Barb H.

We got up at 5:15 AM and George left; he came at 1:30 AM this morning. I didn't sleep until after he arrived. I started my rice cooking, drank coffee and took my nuang to pasture. I returned, talked with George for a few minutes and then came home. I finished cooking, ate, did dishes and got ready for the day. I got my nuang and headed for the farm, where we harvested bananas today. Today we harvested five kinds – *lakaton, dato, depig, guyod* and *canton.* We finished, loaded the cart and headed for home at about 10:30 AM or so. I'm getting to know enough about harvesting bananas now so that I can actually be a genuine help. I ate lunch, laundered one pair of short pants and then took a siesta from noon until 2:00 PM. At 2:15 PM I went and took my nuang to pasture again. I returned home and weeded the north lawn and then I wrote the letter to Tom and Barbara. I finished that at 4:00 PM and prepared vegetables for supper. At 4:30 PM I went to George's to ask him to come early tonight – he said yes, I hope he really does. I got and bathed my nuang, bathed myself and started the rice cooking. Now it's 5:39 PM and I'm tired already, I wonder why, maybe only three hours of sleep last night plus two more hours this afternoon is the reason. The weather today was cloudy until 11:00 AM and then it cleared up and it was hot and dry. Right now it's 90°F. George has slept here 309 nights now. AWANEN!

Wednesday, April 29, 1987
My House, Gomez, Cabarroguis, Quirino

Letters from Sue T., Steve A. and Chris & Mary M.
Keith come and spend the night.

₱197 + 400 – 246 = ₱351							
Food	57	Rides	4	Cigarettes	15	Marienda	64
Postage	24	Coffee	29	Kerosene	7	Candy	8
Household	14	Misc.	24			TOTAL	₱246

[By now you must have wondered how I can possibly eat such an expensive marienda when I go to town – ₱64 today. Well, when I make an entry for marienda and come back home the same day you should assume that it means things for stock at home which can and will be eaten for marienda type snacks.]

We got up at 5:00 AM and George left; he came at 7:20 PM last night. I started cooking, drank coffee and took my *wayway* to George. I finished cooking, ate, did dishes, got ready for the day and headed for Burgos at 6:30 AM. I arrived at Rogel's and the new volunteer was there, so I got trapped talking there for about a half hour. Then I continued on to Gundaway, stopped at the post office, mailed letters and got the above mail and then went to do my marketing. When I finished I drank a Coke and returned to the post office, but there was no truck today so no more mail. I walked to the junction and got a jeepney back to Burgos. I climbed the mountain and came home via the high road in 34 minutes 53 seconds – a new record. I got home before 11:15 AM. I read my mail, ate lunch, took a short siesta and then Rogel, Dominador, Efren, Honorario, Keith and Richard showed up. They spent the day here until around 4:00 PM and then everybody except Keith left. I prepared the vegetables for supper at 5:00 PM, went and got and bathed my nuang and then Keith and I bathed ourselves. Then we cooked, ate and did dishes. After that we drank coffee and talked until 9:00 PM and then we slept. Keith can't ride a nuang without falling off, but at least Richard did not fall off. The weather today was hot and dry. AWANEN!

[It seems strange to me now, but I cannot remember where these two guys were either assigned to or going to be assigned to. The only thing I can remember about Keith is that he tried to get on the nuang several times and every time he did, he would be sliding off when the animal took the first step.]

Thursday, April 30, 1987
My House, Gomez, Cabarroguis, Quirino

Keith leave.

We got up at 5:00 AM, Keith too. I started breakfast, drank coffee and took my nuang to pasture. I returned, finished cooking, we ate and did the dishes and then we both got ready for the day. We sat around talking and not doing anything at all until 9:45 AM and then I went and got and bathed my nuang and returned home. We talked some more until around noon and then I escorted Keith on the shortcut up to the road and I returned home. George and several people were plowing at the farm today so there was nobody to go and talk with for a while, not even at lunchtime. I figured out April's expenses, strolls and visitors and then I ate lunch and took a siesta from 1:00 to 2:00 PM. I got up and at 2:20 PM I went and pastured my nuang again. I returned home, read my new *Reader's Digest* for a while, killed time, fetched water, swept the whole lawn, cleaned house a little bit and at 4:00 PM I prepared the vegetables for supper. At 4:40 PM I went and got and bathed my nuang and then bathed myself and lit the fire to start cooking. I went to George's to ask him to come early and he said yes, I hope he really does. Now it's 6:07 PM and my vegetables are cooking and nearly done. Keith didn't bring a single thing with him, not a cup of rice, not a snack, nothing – what a cheapskate, and rather rude too. The weather today was hot and dry it got up to 92°F in midday, but now it's cloudy and cooler. AWANEN!

Friday, May 1, 1987
My House, Gomez, Cabarroguis, Quirino

We got up at 5:00 AM and George left; he came at 7:35 PM last night. They ate supper last night. I started cooking breakfast, drank coffee and took my nuang to pasture. I returned and talked with George for a few minutes and then came home. I finished cooking, ate, did dishes, got ready for the day and then at about 6:30 AM I went and got my nuang and headed for the farm. We ALL cleaned more of the area to the extreme north and below the road until about 9:40 AM and then came home. I killed time for a while and then ate lunch fairly early. I took a siesta from noon to 1:00 PM, got up and drank coffee. Then at about 1:40 PM I went back to George's. At about 2:00 PM we went back to the farm and continued cleaning, just the two of us this afternoon. Alfredo and Sip planted banana suckers. So, considering it was just two of us, we cleaned a pretty big area. We continued working until 4:40 PM or so and then I went and got my nuang and we all came home. I bathed my nuang, started the rice cooking, prepared the vegetables, bathed myself and went to the store and bought cigarettes. Now it's 6:18 PM and George said that he'll come early tonight; I hope so. The weather today was hot and dry, it was up to 92°F in the house. It clouded up at about 4:00 PM but it doesn't look like there will be any rain. AWANEN!

On the following two pages are photos of my actual Journal for April 30 and May 1, 1987 so that you can see just exactly how crudely it was written. Note the degree of work that was done to make it into a clean and semi-professional sounding manuscript.

GOMEZ - Keith leave

THURSDAY APRIL 30, 1987

351 - 0 = 351 OK
Up at 0500, Keith too, start bkfst, drink coffee, go pasture nuong. Return, finish cooking, eat, do dishes & get ready for the day. We sit & B.S. & not do anything at all till 9:45a, then go get & bathe nuong & return home. B.S. more till noon then escort Keith on the shortcut up to the road & return home. George & several people are plowing the bonhog today - so nobody to go B.S with for a while at noon even! Figure April expenses, strolls & visitors then eat lunch & siesta from 1-2:00p. Get up & at 2:30p go pasture my nuong, return home, read Readers Digest a while, goof off, go fetch water, sweep the whole lawn, clean house a little bit and at 4:00p prepare veggies for supper. At 4:40p go get & bathe my nuong, then bathe myself and then light the fire & start cooking. Go to Georges & ask him to come early - he says yes - hope he does! Now 6:07p, veggies are cooking, nearly done. Keith didn't bring a thing with him, not a thing! Cheapskate! Kind of rude. Wx: HOT & DRY, up to 92° today, now cloudy. Awanen!

GOMEZ

FRIDAY MAY 1, 1987

351 - 0 = 351 OK
Up at 0500, George Leone - he come at 7:35p last nite - late supper for them. Start cooking, drink coffee & go pasture my nuong. Return & B.S. with George a few minutes & come home. Finish cooking, eat, do dishes & get ready for the day & about 6:30a go get my nuong & head for the bonhog. We ALL clean more of the area to the extreme north & below the road - only till about 9:40a & come home. Goof off a while & eat lunch fairly early & then siesta from 12:00 - 1:00p. Get up & drink coffee then about 1:40p go back to Georges & about 2:00p we go back to the bonhog & continue cleaning - just the 2 of us this p.m. Alfredo & Sip plant bananas. So - we clean a pretty big area for 2 of us. Continue working till 4:40p or so, go get my nuong & we all come home, bathe my nuong, start the rice cooking - prepared veggies at 1:00p. Bathe myself then run & buy cigarettes. Now 6:18p - George says he'll be early tonite - hope so!! Wx: Hot & Dry - up to 92° in the house. ~~Cou~~ Cloud up about 4:00p - but looks like no rain. Awonon!

Saturday, May 2, 1987
My House, Gomez, Cabarroguis, Quirino

Letters to Steve A. and Chris & Mary M.

We got up at 5:00 AM and George left, he came at 7:30 PM last night. I started the rice cooking, drank coffee and took my nuang to pasture. I returned and talked with George for a couple of minutes and came home. I finished cooking, ate, did dishes and got ready for the day. Then I used the *lampaso* on the porch, the table, the benches, the house floor, the shelves and everything. I gave the house a real thorough cleaning. At about 9:45 AM I went and got and bathed my nuang. I returned home and put nails to hang the mosquito net on in case there is a *simut-simut* hatch (see page 135) – it's getting to be that time of the year again. When I finished that it was about 11:00 AM so I ate an early lunch and took a siesta from 11:45 AM to 12:30 PM. I got up, drank coffee, read my *Newsweek* Magazine and then prepared vegetables for supper and fetched water. At about 2:00 PM I took my nuang back to pasture and went to the farm. George was plowing and I removed roots for him. He was really angry at his nuang today and it was kind of a bummer to be around him, anyway, we worked until 4:30 PM and came home. I asked him to come early, before 7:00 PM if possible. I got and bathed my nuang, started cooking the rice, bathed myself and now it's 6:01 PM and my vegetables are still cooking. The weather today was hot and dry it was 70°F this morning and 92°F this afternoon. It got cloudy at about 4:00 PM but there was no rain. Maybe I'll write another letter after supper. AWANEN!

Sunday, May 3, 1987
My House, Gomez, Cabarroguis, Quirino

Letter to Sue T.

We got up at 5:00 AM and George left; he didn't come until 8:10 PM last night because they had a late supper due to some political rally on the radio. I started cooking breakfast, drank coffee and took my nuang to pasture. I returned and talked with George for a couple of minutes and came home, finished cooking, ate, did dishes and got ready for the day. I started off the day by doing laundry and finished that shortly after 9:00 AM. Then Alfredo came and talked until it was time to go and get my nuang at 9:40 AM. I got and bathed my nuang and then killed time for a while. I highlighted words I know in the English-Ilokano dictionary, in the "A's", then I ate lunch and laid down from 12:00 to 12:45 PM, but it was too hot and I was too sweaty to be able to sleep. I got up and read my *Reader's Digest* for a while and then at 2:15 PM it was partly cloudy so I took my nuang back to pasture. I returned, talked with George for a minute and then came home and wrote the above letter to Sue. By then it was 3:30 PM so I prepared my vegetables for supper. At 4:30 PM I went and asked George to come early and then I went and got and bathed my nuang. I returned home and shaved my beard and mustache off and then I bathed and cooked supper. Now it's 6:11 PM; please George come early tonight. The weather today was hot and dry, but cloudy after 2:00 PM. There was a little bit of thunder, but no rain. Maybe it will rain tomorrow. AWANEN!

Monday, May 4, 1987
My House, Gomez, Cabarroguis, Quirino

Letter from Ronald. Postcard from San & Jack G.

₱351 + 362 – 571 = ₱142							
Food	106	Rides	16	Cigarettes	13	Marienda	54
Household	114	Postage	56	Coffee	86	Candy	15
Soap	32	Lunch	36	Ice Cream	20	Haircut	5
Misc.	18					TOTAL	₱571

We got up at 5:00 AM, I gave George my *wayway* and he left; he came at 7:35 PM last night, he's been late every night recently. I drank coffee, got ready for the day and left Gomez at about 5:50 AM. I arrived in Burgos at about 6:30 AM, but I had to wait until 7:10 AM for a ride. I arrived in Santiago at about 8:40 AM, did all my shopping, banking and got a haircut by 11:30 AM. I went to Letty's Restaurant in search of JB and Katie, but they weren't there so I went to the 456 Restaurant for lunch. I ate lunch and caught a jeepney back for Burgos. I left Santiago at about 1:00 PM, stopped at Gundaway and got the above mail and then continued on to Burgos, arriving at the bottom of the high road at about 2:30 PM. It took me 41 minutes to climb the mountain today, so I arrived home at about 3:15 PM. I unpacked, put stuff away, read my mail, prepared vegetables for supper and started cooking at about 5:00 PM. I bathed and now it's 5:37 PM and my vegetables are cooking. I'm hoping that George will come early tonight but he probably won't show up until 7:30 PM or later again. The weather today – we had the first rain last night! It was partly cloudy today although there was no rain and no buildup of thunderheads this afternoon, it was just cloudy. Will it rain again tonight, who knows? AWANEN!

Tuesday, May 5, 1987
My House, Gomez, Cabarroguis, Quirino

We got up at 5:00 AM and George left; he didn't come until 9:00 PM last night because of some political bullshitting with the neighbors. I started the rice, drank coffee and took my nuang to pasture. I returned home and finished cooking, ate, did the dishes and got ready for the day. I went through the "B's" in the English-Ilocano dictionary highlighting the words that I know and then I sat around and waited. At about 9:00 AM Efren and a half dozen other people showed up for the non-meeting, which quickly degenerated into a political discussion. Most of them finally left at about 11:30

AM and Efren asked me to cook him lunch. I told him "I don't cook lunch", but I invited him to cook and then I ate my breakfast leftovers! From 12:00 to 12:45 PM I took a siesta and then got up and Efren and Andres Augustine were sleeping. I went to Alfredo's and pounded my peanuts into a kind of "peanut butter" or "peanut powder". I returned home at 2:15 PM, took my nuang to pasture and returned home, got my pickaxe and went to the farm. George is plowing today and I helped him by removing the small tree roots and piling them for him. We worked until nearly 5:30 PM and then came home. Now it's 6:45 PM and my vegetables are cooking, George will probably be late again tonight. The weather today was hot and dry, but at least it was cloudy in the late afternoon. So far there's been no rain today. AWANEN!

Wednesday, May 6, 1987
My House, Gomez, Cabarroguis, Quirino

Letter to JB & Katie F.

I got up at 5:15 AM, but George got up at 3:50 AM and left to pasture his nuang; he came at 7:20 PM last night. I started the rice cooking, drank coffee and took my nuang to pasture. I returned home, finished cooking, ate, did dishes and got ready for the day. Then I went and got my nuang and went to the farm, where George was plowing. I removed small trees, banana trunks and the like. We worked until about 9:30 AM and rode our nuangs home, arriving at about 10:00 AM or so. I killed time for a while and then at about 11:15 AM or so I ate lunch, laid down and tried to sleep from noon until 12:30 PM. I couldn't sleep because it was too damn hot, so I got up and at 1:30 PM I went to ask George if he's going to return to the farm today; he said no. At 2:15 I took my nuang to pasture and returned home. I searched for more words in the English-Ilokano dictionary that I know and highlighted them; I did most of the "C's" today. I worked on that until 4:00 PM and then prepared my vegetables for supper. At 4:30 PM I went to George's again and learned that there's a wedding tonight at old man Espinoza's, so George is going and probably won't come tonight. I got and bathed my nuang, bathed myself and started cooking supper. Now it's 7:08 PM and I've eaten supper and washed dishes. The fucking loud music has already started at the Espinoza's. The weather today was hot and dry all day, there was no rain again. I wish there would be a downpour and drown out the wedding. AWANEN!

Thursday, May 7, 1987
My House, Gomez, Cabarroguis, Quirino

Make Supply Order to the Health Unit.

I got up at 5:15 AM with no companion. I only had a little bit of sleep last night. At 1:00 AM I searched for and used my ear plugs to drown out the noise of the music. I started my rice and took my nuang to pasture. I returned and a big volleyball game was underway at George's so I couldn't talk with him. I came home, finished cooking, ate, did dishes and got ready for the day. I tried to sleep but it was too noisy at George's house. I finished searching the "C's" and highlighting words in the English-Ilokano dictionary and then I spent some time reading the book *"The Clowns of God"*. At 9:45 AM I went and got and bathed my nuang, came home and slept until 11:00 AM. I got up and ate lunch, read some more and tried to sleep some more until 1:00 PM and then I gave up, got up again and read until 2:15 PM. Then I took my nuang to pasture again. When I returned George was bathing his nuang in the creek so I talked with him for a few minutes and then he left to pasture his nuang. I spent until 4:00 PM reading *"The Clowns..."* book and then I went and fetched water, prepared vegetables for supper and went to Alfredo's to talk for a few minutes. At 4:40 PM I went and got and bathed my nuang and then I bathed myself and started cooking. I went and asked George to come right after supper tonight and he said yes, will he really do so? I returned home and now it's 5:44 PM and my vegetables are cooking. The weather today was cloudy until 10:00 AM and then hot. At about 3:00 PM it clouded up again and there was some thunder, but no rain. AWANEN!

Friday, May 8, 1987
My House, Gomez, Cabarroguis, Quirino

I got up at 5:15 AM, George got up and left at 4:00 AM to pasture his nuang. He came at 7:30 PM last night, after I hollered for him. I started the rice cooking, took my nuang to pasture, returned home, drank coffee, finished cooking, ate, did dishes and got ready for the day. Then I went and got my nuang and headed for the farm. George was harrowing today so this morning I removed *bangbangsit* [a type of noxious stick-tight type of weed] for him. We worked until about 10:00 AM and then I put my nuang in the shade and came home. George gave me some mangoes and some bananas and I came home and slept from 11:00 AM until noon. Then I got up, ate lunch and read *"The Clowns of God"* book some more. At 1:15 PM I prepared my vegetables for supper and then at 1:45 PM I went to Georges. At 2:00 PM we returned to the farm, I pastured my nuang, George continued harrowing and I dug up and removed *lidda* roots [a type of tall grass that takes over fields if given a chance]. I did that until 5:15 PM and George still wasn't ready to come home, so I came home first. I bathed my nuang, started the rice cooking and bathed myself. Now my vegetables are cooking. I hope George comes early tonight, please! Now it's 6:39 PM so maybe in less than an hour he'll be here. The weather – it rained a little bit last night and stayed cloudy until 9:30 AM or so and then it was hot and dry again. The daily thunderstorms have still not started, but they should start coming again soon. AWANEN!

Saturday, May 9, 1987
My House, Gomez, Cabarroguis, Quirino

I got up at 5:00 AM; George got up at 4:00 AM and left to pasture his nuang, he came at 8:30 PM last night. I started cooking, took my nuang to pasture, returned and talked with George for a minute and then returned home, drank coffee, finished cooking, ate, did dishes and got ready for the day. The first thing I did today was laundry and I finished that at about 9:00 AM. Then I read *"The Clowns of God"* book until 9:40 AM and went and got my nuang and bathed her. I returned home and laid down from 10:00 to 11:00 AM, got up and read a while longer and finished the book. I ate lunch, drank coffee and went to talk with George for a while. I told him that if Ronald doesn't come that I'll come to the farm in the afternoon. By 2:15 PM Ronald hadn't showed up so I took my nuang to pasture and went to the farm. For a while I piled up roots and then I dug up two big clumps of *runo* grass, which took me until 4:30 PM and then I headed home first. I got my nuang and bathed her, started my rice cooking and bathed myself. Now it's 5:52 PM and everything is cooked. I'll eat when I get done with this. I hope George comes early tonight. The weather today was hot and dry all day, there's still been no rain. I guess maybe it's a drought or something. I started using my new *kaban* of rice today. AWANEN!

Sunday, May 10, 1987
My House, Gomez, Cabarroguis, Quirino

Letter to Dave G.

We got up at 5:00 AM and George left; he came at 7:05 PM last night. I started the rice cooking, drank coffee, took my nuang to pasture, returned and talked with George for a few minutes and then returned home. I finished cooking, ate, did dishes and got ready for the day. First, I did laundry, although there were only two articles to do today. Next, I worked on highlighting words in the English-Ilokano dictionary until 10:40 AM when the sun came out really strong. George and I quickly went and got and bathed our nuangs and then I came home and looked up more words in the dictionary. George came to get some nails, he left and then at about 11:00 AM I started the letter to Dave G. Mateo stopped by for about a half hour or so and after he left I ate lunch and then took a siesta from noon to 1:30 PM. I had a long, restful sleep and when I got up I drank coffee. At 3:00 PM it was partly cloudy so I took my nuang back to pasture, returned home and finished the letter to Dave G. Then I worked on the dictionary some more until 4:00 PM. I prepared my vegetables for supper and at 4:40 PM I went and got and bathed my nuang. I started cooking, bathed myself and now it's 5:57 PM and my supper is cooked and cooling. I hope that George comes early again tonight. The weather today was partly cloudy on and off all day but there's still been no rain other than a dozen drops at about 4:00 PM. AWANEN!

Monday, May 11, 1987
My House, Gomez, Cabarroguis, Quirino

Election Day.

We got up at 5:00 AM and George left; he came at 8:00 PM last night. I started cooking the rice, drank coffee and took my nuang to pasture. I returned and talked with George for a couple of minutes and then came home, finished cooking, ate, did dishes, got ready for the day and then I went and got my nuang and headed for the farm. George was harrowing, so Sip and I piled up roots and after a while Sip burned the piles. At 9:30 AM I got my nuang and moved her into the shade and at about 10:00 AM we headed home. I really pulled a back muscle quite badly today so my lower right back is very sore. I ate lunch at about 11:00 AM, slept from 11:40 AM to 12:40 PM and then got up, drank coffee and prepared vegetables for supper; today will be my third day of squash for supper. At 1:50 PM I returned to George's and at 2:05 PM we returned to the farm. This afternoon he plowed, so I pulled weeds on my own farm. We quit and came home at about 4:30 PM. I bathed my nuang, started cooking supper, bathed myself and then went and bought cigarettes. I returned home and Alfredo came to talk for a few minutes. When my supper was finished cooking he left and I ate, did dishes and now it's 6:45 PM. I hope George comes early tonight – about 7:00 PM. The weather today was again hot and dry; it was up to 92°F again. It seems like it's a drought. I wonder what will happen if it is a drought and if there is no rain this month? AWANEN!

Tuesday, May 12, 1987
My House, Gomez, Cabarroguis, Quirino

I got up at 5:00 AM; George got up and left at 4:10 AM to pasture his nuang. He came last night at 7:25 PM. I started cooking the rice, drank coffee took my nuang to pasture, returned home, finished cooking, ate, did dishes and got ready for the day. I went and talked with Alfredo for a half hour or so and returned home. I highlighted more words that I know in the English-Ilokano dictionary again and I'm now done through "H". After that I laid down for a while – my back is still very sore – and today George is plowing Junior's farm. At 9:40 AM I went and got and bathed my nuang and I got nicked on my right temple by the low-hanging bamboo next to Bebot's canteen, so I went and cut it down. After a while I ate lunch and laid down again. It's hotter than hell today, but at 2:15 PM I took my nuang to pasture and returned home. Alfredo came and got two dead batteries from me. I browsed through the HP-71 owner's manual for an hour or so and at 4:00 PM I prepared my vegetables for supper. At 4:50 PM I went and got and bathed my nuang and then fetched water and bathed myself. I started cooking at about 5:20 PM and now it's 5:46 PM and my rice is still cooking. I hope George comes early tonight, but he still hasn't returned home from plowing at Junior's farm so I don't know. Today the weather was cloudy for a while this morning and then hot and dry. It got up to 96°F today, the hottest temperature that I've yet experienced here. AWANEN!

Wednesday, May 13, 1987
My House, Gomez, Cabarroguis, Quirino

Letters from Dad, Dave G., Bob S. Postcard from Ardis B. *Reader's Digest.*

₱142 + 300 – 295 = ₱147							
Cigarettes	19	Rides	4	Food	71	Household	38
Marienda	66	Stamps	24	Kerosene	7	Candy	9
Coffee	27	Misc.	30			TOTAL	₱295

We got up at 4:50 AM and George left; he came at 7:30 PM last night. I cooked breakfast, ate, did dishes, took my bag of valuables and my *wayway* to Alfredo's, talked with George for a couple minutes and got his watch that I gave him to take for repair – the pin for the buckle broke. At 6:42 AM I headed down the mountain for Burgos and caught a jeepney for Gundaway. I arrived at the post office at about 7:30 AM and I had to wait for it to open. Then I did my marketing, returned to the post office, got the above mail and walked to the junction, where I caught a jeepney back to Burgos. I arrived at the junction of the high road at 10:42 AM, climbed the mountain and got home at 11:20 AM – 38 minutes exactly today. I read my mail, unpacked and put stuff away, ate lunch and then laid down for a short while, but it was too damn hot to sleep so I got up and read my new *Reader's Digest.* It clouded up at about 3:00 PM and looked like rain so I went and fetched water and swept most of the yard. At 4:00 PM I prepared the vegetables for supper and then I bathed. At 4:30 PM I started cooking and at 5:00 PM I went to George's and he arrived home at 5:10 PM, so I asked him to come early, got my nuang and my bag of valuables and came home. Now it's 5:29 PM. The weather today was hot and dry and it was 96°F again this afternoon. At 3:00 PM it clouded up and now there's some thunder, but no rain. AWANEN!

Thursday, May 14, 1987
My House, Gomez, Cabarroguis, Quirino

Letter to Dad.

I got up at 5:00 AM. George got up and left at 3:45 AM to pasture his nuang; he came last night at 7:00 PM. I started cooking the rice, drank coffee and took my nuang to pasture. I returned and talked with George for a couple minutes and then returned home, finished cooking, ate, did dishes and got ready for the day. I went and got my nuang and headed for the farm, arriving there at about 7:00 AM. George was plowing so I removed *lidda* roots. We worked on that until I had to take my nuang to the shade at about 9:00 AM. Then at about 9:30 AM we went and harvested some mangoes and we ate them and we checked to see if there are any bananas that we can harvest on Saturday – there are. We headed home at about 10:00 AM and got here at about 10:20 AM. I drank coffee and took a siesta from 10:50 AM to 12:15 PM – before it got too hot. I got up, ate lunch, finished the letter to Dad and prepared my vegetables for supper. At 2:00 PM George and I went back to the farm. I pastured my nuang and George plowed some more while I removed roots some more. We worked until about 4:40 PM and headed for home. I bathed my nuang and then myself, fetched water and started cooking supper. Now it's 6:18 PM and I hope George comes at about 7:00 PM again tonight – he said that he'll come early. George is a very, very good friend to me. The weather today was hot and dry and it was 96°F again. It clouded up at about 3:30 PM, but so far there's been no rain and there was none last night either. Now it's mid-May and there's been no rain to speak of yet. AWANEN!

Friday, May 15, 1987
My House, Gomez, Cabarroguis, Quirino

I got up at 5:00 AM but George got up at 3:00 AM and took his nuang to pasture. He came at 7:20 PM last night. I started the rice cooking, drank coffee, took my nuang to pasture, returned and talked with George for a few minutes and then came home. I finished cooking, ate, did dishes, got ready for the day and headed for the farm at about 6:30 AM. I arrived at about 7:00 AM. George was plowing and harrowing. I started digging a clump of *runo* and took my nuang to the shade at about 9:30 AM. Shortly after that we headed for home. I ate marienda and took a siesta and then got up and ate lunch. At about 1:00 PM I prepared my vegetables for supper and at 1:50 PM I returned to George's and there was a change of plans; we're going to harvest bananas this afternoon, so I came home and changed into my banana harvesting clothes and then I left first to pasture my nuang, went to the farm and helped George harvest bananas until 4:45 PM. Then we got our nuangs and came home. I bathed my nuang and myself, started cooking and fetched water. My big banana tree fell over this afternoon and I went to George's and asked him to help me with it and he said "we're playing ball" – little fucker, can't help me for five minutes! Now it's 6:18 PM and my supper is nearly cooked. The weather today was hot and dry. It was cloudy this morning and it's cloudy again now but there's been no rain. Damn, I'm pissed at George right now; even though I help every day he can't help me for five minutes. AWANEN!

Saturday, May 16, 1987
My House, Gomez, Cabarroguis, Quirino

Letter to Bob S.

I got up at 5:10 AM, but George got up at 4:25 AM and went to pasture his nuang. He came at 7:40 PM last night. I started the rice cooking, drank coffee and took my nuang to pasture. I returned and talked with George for a couple minutes and then came home, finished cooking, ate, did dishes and got ready for the day. I harvested the bananas from my tree that fell over yesterday, there were 117 bananas on the *bulig.* After that I cleaned and sharpened both of my machetes and also my kitchen knife. Then I did the week's laundry and then killed time for a while. I went and got and bathed my nuang at 9:45 AM and returned home. I killed more time and then slept from 11:00 AM until noon. I got up, ate lunch and then began the letter to Bob – it was a long letter – two sheets of paper. I pastured my nuang again at 2:15 PM, returned home, finished the letter to Bob and then I sacked my bananas and hung them. At 4:00 PM I prepared the vegetables for supper. I saw a big snake at the creek. At 4:30 PM I went to George's and asked him to come early, he said yes, but we'll see. Then I went and got and bathed my nuang, returned home, started cooking supper and bathed myself. George took the cart of bananas to Burgos today. Now it's 5:44 PM and my rice is still cooking. The weather today was cloudy until 9:00 AM and then it was hot and dry. It got cloudy again at 3:00 PM and there was some thunder, but no rain. AWANEN!

Sunday, May 17, 1987
My House, Gomez, Cabarroguis, Quirino

Letter to Dave G.

We got up at 5:00 AM and George left; he came at 7:30 PM last night. I started my rice cooking, drank coffee and took my nuang to pasture. I returned and talked with George for a few minutes and then returned home. I finished cooking, ate, did dishes and got ready for the day. I went and talked with George a few more minutes and then came home and used the *lampaso* on the whole house. That worked up a good sweat! Then I swept all of the lawn and by then it was 9:15 AM so I went and talked with George some more and also went and got and bathed my nuang. Then I killed time for a while and cut off the dead leaves from my banana trees. At about 11:30 AM or so I took a siesta and then at about noon the two guys who are developing the water system came to ask some ridiculous questions until 2:15 PM when I left to go and pasture my nuang again. I returned home, ate lunch and then read my *Reader's Digest* and played with my HP-71. At 4:00 PM I prepared the vegetables for supper and then at about 4:30 PM I went to talk with George for a few minutes and asked him to come early – he said yes. The rain started, I started the rice cooking and the rain stopped so I went and got and bathed my nuang and then bathed myself. By then my rice was done cooking. Now it's 5:36 PM and my vegetables are nearly ready. The weather today was hot and dry, but then at about 3:00 PM it clouded up and at about 4:30 PM the rain started. It didn't rain very hard though, maybe it will rain more later on tonight. AWANEN!

Monday, May 18, 1987
My House, Gomez, Cabarroguis, Quirino

Letters from JB & Katie F., Tom & Barb H. (photos too), Fred & Cynthia B., Mark W., Mike Mc. (package too).

Cery come and spend the night.

₱147 + 300 – 178 = ₱269							
Food	68	Cigarettes	14	Rides	8	Marienda	30
Coffee	27	Kerosene	7	Household	5	Misc.	19
						TOTAL	₱178

I got up at 5:00 AM. George got up at 4:00 AM, I gave him my *wayway* and he left to pasture his nuang. He came at 7:20 PM last night. I cooked breakfast, drank coffee, ate, did dishes, got ready for the day and after a little bit I headed down the mountain to Burgos. I went directly to Cordon, did my marketing and finished that at about 9:45 AM or so. After a while I caught a ride back to Diffun and went to the office. At about 10:40 AM Cery [the Peace Corps Assistant Director for my area] showed up at the office. We talked with Francisco until about 11:30 AM and then we went out to lunch. After lunch, at about 12:40 PM, Cery and I headed out the road in his rig. We stopped at the Gundaway Post Office, I got the above mail and then we continued on to Burgos, arriving at about 2:00 PM. This made the third time I've been able to come up the mountain in a Peace Corps vehicle! We talked with Alfredo for a while and then came home, Cery napped until after 3:00 PM and I read my mail. He woke up and we talked until 4:15 PM and then I prepared the vegetables for supper. At 4:45 PM I started cooking and bathed. Finally we ate, did dishes and Cery and I talked until 8:15 PM and then went to bed. The weather today was hot and dry, there was no more rain last night. What's going to happen if the rain's don't start soon? I don't know. AWANEN!

Tuesday, May 19, 1987
My House, Gomez, Cabarroguis, Quirino

Cery leave.

First May rains began.

We got up at 5:00 AM, both Cery and I, and of course George was not here. I started the rice cooking, drank coffee and took my nuang to pasture. I returned home and finished cooking and then we ate, did dishes and got ready for the day. Cery left even before 7:00 AM. George is hauling gravel to the site of the water system construction this morning so after Cery left I mostly just killed time. I rewrote the address search program for the HP-71 to preserve ALL letters written and received dates and then at 9:40 AM I went and got and bathed my nuang and returned home. George had returned from the gravel hauling so I went and asked him what his plan was for the afternoon. I returned home and took a siesta from 10:30 to 11:30 AM and then got up and ate. After lunch I napped again from 12:30 to 1:15 PM. My back is sore again, or maybe still sore, so I took two 222's [Canadian Aspirin with codeine] and then it was very easy to sleep. When I woke up I prepared the vegetables for supper and at 2:15 PM I took my nuang to pasture and went to the farm. George was harrowing so I piled up roots and so on. At about 4:30 PM rain was threatening so we burned the piles of dead leaves and brush and headed home. I asked George to come early and he said yes. I got my nuang and bathed her and the first rain started, so I got soaked coming home. Now it's 5:53 PM and still raining hard. My rice is only cooking now. I hope the rain stops before dark. The weather was hot and dry and then at 4:00 PM it clouded up and at 5:00 PM the first May thunderstorm happened – very late this year. AWANEN!

Wednesday, May 20, 1987
My House, Gomez, Cabarroguis, Quirino

We got up at 5:00 AM and George left; he came at 6:35 PM last night. I started the rice cooking, drank coffee and took my nuang to pasture. I returned and talked with George for a few minutes and then came home. I finished cooking, ate, did dishes and got ready for the day. Then I went and got my nuang and headed for the farm – everybody is planting today because of the first rain yesterday. I asked George what I could do to help and he said nothing so I went and weeded my farm until 9:30 AM when it was time to take my nuang to the shade. Then I asked George again what I could do to help and he said nothing again so I got my nuang and headed for home. Somehow, I fell off and hit my head on a rock! OUCH! I arrived home at about 10:00 AM, bathed my nuang, tied her and took a siesta until 11:30 AM. Then I got up, ate lunch and repaired my outhouse – two walls fell down last night. After that I fetched water and it clouded up, so I bathed at about 3:30 PM. At 4:00 PM I prepared my vegetables for supper and at 4:30 PM I went and got and bathed my nuang. I started cooking and went to ask George to come early, he said yes, but we'll see. Now it's 5:42 PM and everything is cooked. There's been no rain yet so I put up the mosquito netting in anticipation of a big hatch of *simut-simut* tonight. The weather today was hot and dry and it clouded up at about 3:00 PM, but I fear there will be no rain tonight. I hope George comes early. AWANEN!

Thursday, May 21, 1987
My House, Gomez, Cabarroguis, Quirino

Letters to Tom & Barb H. and Health Unit.

I got up at 5:00 AM. George got up at 4:00 AM and left to pasture his nuang. He didn't come last night until 7:50 PM. I started my rice cooking, drank coffee, took my nuang to pasture, returned and talked with George for a couple of minutes and then came home. I finished cooking, ate, did my dishes and took my time getting ready for the day. George was harrowing today so I stayed home this morning and played with my HP-71 for a while. I laid down for a while because my back was still sore from the fall yesterday. I got up after a while and did the letter to Tom and Barb, telling them that I'll be there on June 10th and by then it was time to get my nuang and George returned home too. I got and bathed my nuang and went to George's to talk for a while and then came home and ate an early lunch. After lunch I wrote to the health unit and sent them three different recipes which I've used for preserving meat for seven to ten days without refrigeration. I also told them about yesterday's fall from my nuang. At 2:15 PM I went and pastured my nuang and went to the farm. George was harrowing so I pulled up roots again. At 4:15 PM rain was threatening so I headed home. I got and bathed my nuang and came home. I bathed myself and started cooking. Oh, I prepared the vegetables at 1:00 PM. Now it's 5:49 PM and the vegetables are nearly done cooking. Surprisingly there was no *simut-simut* hatch last night. The weather today was hot and dry, it clouded up at about 3:00 PM and there was lots of thunder and lightning, but so far no rain. It could still rain though. AWANEN!

Friday, May 22, 1987
My House, Gomez, Cabarroguis, Quirino

Letter to Fred & Cynthia B.

I got up at 5:00 AM, but George got up at 3:30 and left to pasture his and my nuangs because he wanted to borrow mine today. He came at 7:20 PM last night. I cooked breakfast, ate, did dishes and got ready for the day. There were lots of people planting at George's farm today so I stayed home and dug up the small fenced in garden in the southeast corner of the yard until 10:00 AM. Then I stopped because it was too hot to work. I took a kind of a half bath to cool off and after a while I ate lunch and then napped from 11:30 AM to 12:30 PM. I got up and highlighted more words in the English-Ilokano dictionary for a while and then at 2:00 PM I continued digging up the southeast garden and worked at that until 3:00 PM when rain was already looking quite near. I went and fetched water, bathed and relaxed until 4:00 PM and then prepared vegetables for supper. I due up some winged bean tubers – they are about eight inches long and three-quarters to one inch in diameter. I'll have those and *tabungaw* for supper tonight. Now it's 5:03 PM and my rice is cooking. I haven't seen George yet but I hope he comes early tonight, he probably won't though. If it would rain maybe he'd be early, but there's been no rain yet, despite lots of thunder and a heavy cloud cover. The weather today was hot and dry and then it clouded up at about 2:00 PM and there was thunder and black clouds, but so far no rain. AWANEN!

Saturday, May 23, 1987
My House, Gomez, Cabarroguis, Quirino

We got up at 5:00 AM and George left; he came at 7:30 PM last night. He offered to pasture my nuang for me this morning, so, okay. I cooked breakfast, drank coffee, ate, did dishes and got ready for the day. I went and got my nuang and headed for the farm, arriving a bit after 7:00 AM. George was making planting lines and the family was planting, so I weeded my farm. We all worked until shortly after 10:00 AM and then we stopped until the heat of the day passed. We all had lunch, by coincidence, at 12:00 N. At 1:00 PM I went back and removed *bangbangsit* on the new part of my farm; holy cow, there was a lot of it. At about 2:00 PM George continued to make planting lines on his farm and the family planted. They finished at 3:40 PM and we all headed for home. We ate a lot of mangoes today. I think I forgot to mention that this is the month for mangoes; at market they are eight fruits for ₱10 this year. I pastured my nuang beside the school on the way home. George said that he'll come early tonight. I bathed, prepared my vegetables for supper and at 4:30 PM I went and got and bathed my nuang. I returned home and started cooking. Now it's 5:37 PM and my vegetables are nearly cooked. The weather today was hot and dry and then at about 3:00 PM it clouded up. At 5:10 PM there was a light rain, but so far not enough to do much good. I hope George truly comes early. AWANEN!

Sunday, May 24, 1987
My House, Gomez, Cabarroguis, Quirino

We got up at 5:00 AM and George left; he came at 7:10 PM last night. I started cooking, drank coffee and took my nuang to pasture. I returned and talked with George for a few minutes and then I came home. I finished cooking, ate, did dishes and got ready for the day. The first thing I did today was laundry and that took from 7:00 to 9:00 AM. Then I relaxed until 9:30 AM and after that I went and got my nuang and bathed her. I stopped on the way home to talk with George for a few minutes and came home. I started reading the book *"Kane and Abel"* by Jeffrey Archer, took a siesta from 10:00 to 10:45 AM and then got up and read until 11:30 AM. I ate lunch and after that I read until 1:30 PM. It clouded up, so I took my nuang to pasture early this afternoon. I returned home and Alfredo came to talk from 2:00 to 4:00 PM and then he went home and I prepared vegetables for supper. At 4:30 PM I went and got and bathed my nuang and at about 5:00 PM I started cooking and also trimmed my beard; I shaved it off only three weeks ago. I also bathed. Now it's 5:36 PM and my vegetables arc cooking. After supper I'll either read more or write a letter while waiting for George; I hope he comes early tonight. I harvested a single papaya fruit today. The weather was hot and dry, but it clouded up at about 1:00 PM and there were a few drops of rain at about 1:40 PM. After that it stayed cloudy but there was no additional rain. AWANEN!

Monday, May 25, 1987
My House, Gomez, Cabarroguis, Quirino

We got up at 4:45 AM, George took my *wayway* and left. He came at 7:15 PM last night. George is using my nuang today because he is harrowing my farm, so I cooked breakfast, ate, did dishes, got ready for the day and I was ready by 6:30 AM. Then George, Alfredo, Sip, mother and I went to the farm. George started harrowing and the rest of us removed *bangbangsit* and other small trees and so on. We worked until about 10:30 AM and then headed home. We arrived at about 11:00 AM and I reentered the address file in my HP-71; it had a total memory loss again. Then I ate lunch and took a siesta from noon to 1:15 PM. I got up and started to prepare vegetables for supper and George hollered for me, so I put my shirt on and we all went back to the farm at 1:30 PM. We piled up the harrowed up roots and burned them and then George started the second plowing of my farm. I picked up heavy old wood on his new farm, to the south of my farm, I made a big pile of old rotten wood and we lit a fire. We headed home at about 4:20 AM. I bathed and prepared my vegetables for supper. George took care of bathing my nuang for me. Now it's 5:54 PM and my squash is nearly cooked. I hope George comes early tonight. The weather today was hot and dry. It clouded up at 1:00 PM and then at 1:30 PM it sprinkled for ten minutes, but that was all. After that it was cloudy the rest of the day and it's very cloudy now, so maybe it will rain some more. AWANEN!

Tuesday, May 26, 1987
My House, Gomez, Cabarroguis, Quirino

We got up at 4:45 AM and George left to pasture both of our nuangs. He came at 6:50 PM last night. I cooked breakfast, ate, did dishes, got ready for the day and headed for the farm at 6:30 AM. I caught up with George about halfway there and rode my nuang the rest of the way. He plowed my farm again this morning; finished the second plowing. I removed *bangbangsit* on his farm to the south of mine and burned more old wood; the fire was still going from yesterday so I just added more wood to it. We quit and came home at about 10:30 AM. Oh, George used my nuang to plow. We got home at about 11:00 AM, I ate lunch and then took a siesta from 11:30 AM to 12:30 PM. I prepared vegetables for supper; I harvested a jackfruit, cleaned it and sliced it up. At about 2:00 PM George and I went back to the farm. I finished removing *bangbangsit* and George began to harrow my farm. I piled up roots and there were a LOT of them. We quit at about 4:15 PM and headed for home. I left my nuang at the creek and George will pasture her after a little while. Now it's 5:39 PM and my jackfruit is cooking. I hope George comes early again tonight. The weather last night – there was a fairly heavy hatch of *simut-simut* but then there was a strong wind, followed by light rain for an hour. Today it was cloudy most of the day but there's been no rain yet. There's lots of thunder so maybe after a while it will rain again. AWANEN!

[I've been talking about *bangbangsit* for the past few days, so I researched it for you. The Latin name is *Lantana camara.* It is a species of flowering plant within the verbena family, *Verbenaceae,* that is native to the American tropics.

A beautiful plant, often planted in gardens, it has spread from it's native Central and South America to around 50 different countries, where it has become an invasive species. It spread from the Americas into the rest of the world when it was brought back to Europe by Dutch explorers and cultivated widely, soon spreading into Asia and Oceania, where it established itself as a notorious weed.

Lantana camara will often out-compete other more desirable species, leading to a reduction in biodiversity. It can also cause problems if it invades agricultural areas as a result of it's toxicity to livestock as well as it's ability to form dense thickets, which if left unchecked can greatly reduce the productivity of farm land.]

Wednesday, May 27, 1987
My House, Gomez, Cabarroguis, Quirino

Letters from Barb W., Jerry J., Sue T., San & Jack G., *Salaysayan* Magazine and Health Unit.

₱269 + 200 – 297 = ₱172							
Food	82	Cigarettes	14	Rides	4	Household	20
Marienda	59	Coffee	54	Kerosene	7	Soap	10
Postage	3	Batteries	9	Candy	9	Misc.	26
						TOTAL	₱297

I got up at 5:00 AM. George got up at 4:20 AM and left to pasture our nuangs. He came last night at 7:30 PM. I cooked breakfast, drank coffee, ate, did dishes, got ready for the day and left for Burgos at 6:25 AM. I arrived at the bottom of the mountain at about 7:00 AM and caught a ride to Gundaway at about 7:40 AM. I waited until 8:00 AM for the post office people to show up, got my mail and continued on to market. I shopped for the above, finished at about 9:30 AM and then went back to the post office and got more mail. Then I caught a jeepney to Burgos and started walking up the high road at 10:50 AM, arriving home 36 minutes and 59 seconds later. I ate lunch, read my mail read more of the *"Kane and Abel"* book and basically killed time the rest of the afternoon. At about 3:00 PM I went and fetched water and then at about 3:45 PM I saw George at their house so I went and helped him repair the box on their cart until 4:10 PM. Then I came home and prepared my vegetables for supper, bathed and at 5:00 PM I started cooking supper. I hope George comes early tonight, I'm tired and I have a headache. The weather today was hot and dry all day, although partly cloudy. Now it's 5:40 PM and there are thick clouds and thunder. There was no rain last night or yet today though. AWANEN!

Thursday, May 28, 1987
My House, Gomez, Cabarroguis, Quirino

Letters to *Salaysayan* Magazine, Tom & Barb H. and Sue T.

₱172 – 60 = ₱112					
Photos	60			TOTAL	₱60

We got up at 4:50 AM and George left; he came at 6:50 PM last night. I started the rice cooking, drank coffee and took my nuang to pasture. I returned and talked with George for a few minutes and came home. I finished cooking, ate, did dishes and got ready for the day. At 6:30 AM I went to George's and he was ready to leave, so I went and got my nuang and we met at the school. Today was banana harvesting day again. We filled the big cart, Alfredo filled the small cart and we were done at about 10:00 AM and came home. I bathed and tied my nuang and read more in the *"Kane and Abel"* book for a while and then I laid down to sleep, but I couldn't, so I got up and ate lunch and wrote the letter to Tom and Barb, telling them I won't be there on the 10th because I have to go to Manila. Then I wrote to *Salaysayan* Magazine giving approval to Joanne's rewrite of the George story. After that I wrote to Sue T. and then at 4:00 PM I prepared my vegetables for supper. At 4:20 PM Alfredo came to talk for a while and at 4:45 PM I went and got and bathed my nuang and then bathed myself and started cooking. Now it's 5:33 PM and my rice is cooking. I hope George comes early again tonight. The weather today was hot and dry. It clouded up at about 5:00 PM and right now there's lots of lightning, but no rain yet. I'd sure like to hear some news about whether this is a drought or not, what's going on anyway? Is this the longest dry spell for several years, or what? AWANEN!

Friday, May 29, 1987
My House, Gomez, Cabarroguis, Quirino

Letter to Mike Mc.

We got up at 4:50 AM and George left; he came at 7:10 PM last night despite very heavy rain! I started my rice cooking, drank coffee and took my nuang to pasture. I returned and talked with George for a few minutes and then came home. I finished cooking, ate, did dishes and got ready for the day and then I walked up the high road to the big *balate* [a species of *Ficus*] tree to take some photos of the farm because it's easy to see it from there. After that I returned home and read more of the *"Kane and Abel"* book until 9:30 AM. Then I went and got and bathed my nuang. George took bananas to Burgos today so there was no work at the farm. I returned home and finished reading the *"Kane and Abel"* book by 11:30 AM and then I took a siesta from 11:30 AM to 12:30 PM. I got up, ate lunch and didn't do much of anything after that. At 1:45 PM it was cloudy so I took my nuang to pasture again, came back home and did more of nothing. I finished the letter to Sue T. and then did a letter to Mike Mc. and at about 4:00 PM I prepared vegetables for supper. At around 4:30 PM I went and talked with George for a couple minutes and asked him to come early – he said yes. After that I went and got and bathed my nuang and then bathed myself. I started cooking at 5:00 PM and now it's 5:34 PM and my rice is still cooking. There was a very heavy hatch of *simut-simut* last night, but then at 7:00 PM there was a bad thunderstorm and the hatch stopped. Today the weather was hot and dry and it clouded up about 1:45 PM, but there's been no rain yet. I hope it rains so there's no hatch of *simut-simut* tonight. AWANEN!

Saturday, May 30, 1987
My House, Gomez, Cabarroguis, Quirino

We got up at 4:45 AM and George left; he strolled last night and didn't come until nearly midnight. He pastured my nuang for me this morning because he's going to be plowing my farm again today, so I cooked breakfast, drank coffee, ate, did dishes and then I got ready for the day and was ready at 6:15 AM. I got my nuang and went to the farm. Alfredo, Sip, mother and I planted my farm while George made planting rows. We finished at 10:00 AM and came home for lunch. I took a siesta from 10:30 to 11:30 AM and then got up, ate lunch and slept some more because I didn't have much sleep last night. At 1:55 PM I went to George's and we went directly to the farm. He plowed the area south of my farm and I cleaned up roots and broke up clumps of dirt. George also seemed to be tired today and we quit and came home shortly after 4:00 PM. I bathed my nuang and took her to pasture, returned home, bathed myself and started cooking my rice and preparing my vegetables for supper. I started cooking at about 5:10 PM and now it's 5:37 PM and my rice is nearly done. Please, George, come early tonight. Last night it rained lightly for a few minutes. The weather today was sunny but then it clouded up at about 3:00 PM or so and thundered a lot, but there was no rain. At least the soil is now somewhat wet and in pretty good shape. AWANEN!

Sunday, May 31, 1987
My House, Gomez, Cabarroguis, Quirino

Letters to Ronald and Mark W.

I got up at 5:15 AM. George got up and left at 4:15 AM to pasture his nuang; he came at 7:45 PM last night. I started the rice cooking, drank coffee and took my nuang to pasture. I returned home and finished cooking, ate, did dishes and got ready for the day. George and Alfredo both went to Burgos today; George hauled charcoal and Alfredo hauled bananas, so I started the day by doing laundry. I finished that at about 9:00 AM and then relaxed for a while. At 9:40 AM I went and got and bathed my nuang and then I did the letter to Mark W. After that I laid down for 20 minutes and then I ate lunch and drank coffee. After lunch I took a siesta for around a half hour, got up, cleaned my bookshelf and killed time until 2:15 PM and then took my nuang to pasture again. I returned and figured out May's expenses and visitors and then wrote the letter to Ronald telling him that I'll be there on June 18th or 19th. I finished that and then at about 3:45 AM I prepared my vegetables for supper. At 4:30 PM the rain started, so I started cooking and I'll get my nuang after supper. Now it's 5:16 PM, the vegetables are cooking and the rain is continuing. I hope George comes early tonight – please! It rained last night very heavy and there was lightning and thunder at around 2:00 AM this morning. Today it was cloudy for a while but then it got hot and dry. It clouded up again at about 3:30 PM. A thunderstorm started at about 4:30 PM but not a very intense or violent one. George has slept here 339 nights now. AWANEN!

Monday, June 1, 1987
My House, Gomez, Cabarroguis, Quirino

Letter to JB & Katie F.

I got up at 5:15 AM. George got up and left at 4:20 AM to pasture his nuang. He came at 7:05 PM last night. I started cooking my rice, drank coffee and took my nuang to pasture. I returned home, finished cooking, ate, did dishes and got ready for the day. I got my nuang and was off to the farm. George was plowing the area south of my farm today so I removed *kadkadina*, *maramais*, *lidda* [more noxious weeds with huge root wads] and other weeds. We worked until 9:30 AM and then we took a stroll around the farm, looked things over and headed home. When we arrived home I wrote the letter to JB and Katie and then I ate lunch. After lunch I took a very short siesta, only about 20 minutes – it was too hot to sleep. I got up and ate a couple of mangoes and killed time until 1:50 PM and also prepared vegetables for supper. After that I went to George's and at 2:00 PM we returned to the farm. George continued plowing and I continued helping in my own small ways. We quit at 4:00 PM and headed for home. I bathed my nuang, asked George to come early, bathed myself and then at 5:00 PM I started cooking. I took a bunch of my bananas to George's house and returned home. Now it's 5:46 PM and my supper is cooked; I'll eat as soon as I'm done with this. The weather today was hot and dry. It clouded up at about 4:30 PM but so far there's been no rain. Actually, the soil is kind of sticky for plowing right now, so we probably don't need any more rain for a few days. AWANEN!

Tuesday, June 2, 1987
My House, Gomez, Cabarroguis, Quirino

Letter to Barb W.

I got up at 5:25 AM. George got up and left at 4:30 AM to pasture his nuang. He came at 1:30 this morning because they strolled in the light of the full moon last night. I started my rice cooking and took my nuang to pasture. I returned home, drank coffee, finished cooking, ate, did dishes and got ready for the day. I tried to sleep some more after that but I couldn't. At 9:00 AM I went and got my nuang and then went to the forestry meeting, which actually happened today – unbelievable! They decided to keep the same officers for another year and that was all that was done. The meeting finished at about 11:00 AM and Efren and I came to my house. By and by we ate lunch and after that I laid down immediately and slept for about an hour. I got up and by 1:30 PM it was cloudy so I took my nuang to pasture, returned home and at about 2:20 PM Efren left. After that I trimmed some branches off the wild cassava in the north lawn and then went and fetched water. When I returned home I wrote the letter to Barb. At 4:00 PM I prepared my vegetables for supper and at 4:30 I went and got and bathed my nuang. Alfredo came and talked for a while and then at about 5:15 PM I started my rice and bathed. After that Alfredo left and I went and asked George if he's going to stroll tonight. He said no. Now it's 6:12 PM and everything is cooked and ready to eat; I'll eat as soon as I'm done with this. The weather today was cloudy for a while this morning and then hot and dry. It clouded up again at about 1:30 PM but there was no rain. AWANEN!

Wednesday, June 3, 1987
My House, Gomez, Cabarroguis, Quirino

Letter from Vicki S. Postcards from Ardis B. and San & Jack G.

₱112 + 445 – 465 = ₱92							
Food	125	Kerosene	7	Sack	10	Postage	10
Marienda	65	Lunch	31	Ice Cream	23	Toothbrush	17
Household	26	Cigarettes	20	Clothes	14	Coffee	80
Rides	16	Misc.	21			TOTAL	₱465

I got up at 5:00 AM. George got up at 4:00 AM, took my *wayway* and left. He came at 7:50 PM last night. I ate some bananas for breakfast, drank coffee and headed for Burgos at about 5:55 AM. I had to wait quite a while for a jeepney, but I managed to arrive in Santiago at about 8:10 AM. I did my shopping, finished up at about 11:00 AM and went to the 456 Restaurant for lunch. I finished eating lunch a bit after noon and caught a jeepney for Gundaway. I stopped at the post office, arriving there at about 1:20 PM, but they hadn't returned from lunch yet. I waited until after 2:00 PM and they finally returned. I got the above mail and caught a ride to Burgos. I came home via the high road and arrived at about 4:00 PM. I unpacked and put things away, read my mail, bathed and at 5:15 PM I started cooking supper. Now it's 6:01 PM and my rice is nearly done. George doesn't know if he's going to stroll tonight or not, but there are bunch of single girls at his house, so he might. The weather today was hot and dry with no rain again. Please come early George. AWANEN!

Thursday, June 4, 1987
My House, Gomez, Cabarroguis, Quirino

Letter to Ardis B. Postcards to Bill N. & Bill J.

I got up at 5:00 AM. George got up and left at 4:20 AM to pasture his nuang. He came at 7:45 PM last night. I started my rice cooking, took my nuang to pasture, returned home, finished cooking, ate, did dishes and got ready for the day. I dug up the little area directly above the house and screened a bunch of dried nuang manure, mixed it into the soil and then planted sunflower and marigold seeds there, I hope they grow. I went and got and bathed my nuang at 9:30 AM and I noticed that George was home so I went and talked with him for a while. All of the plowing and planting is now finished, I wonder what his next project will be? I came home and slept for about half an hour and then I got up, ate lunch and did the postcards to the two Bills asking why it has been so long with no letters from either of them. At 2:15 PM I took my nuang to pasture again and George returned to the farm to replant an area of corn where nothing came up. I didn't do much of anything this afternoon. Some fucking pigs came and ate two of my pineapple plants, so now I only have two left. At 4:00 PM I prepared my vegetables for supper and then at 4:30 PM I started cooking and went and got my nuang and bathed her. When I got back home I ate supper and bathed myself. Now it's 6:23 PM and I don't know if George will stroll tonight. The weather today was hot and dry and then it clouded up at about 4:00 PM and rained lightly for only about five minutes, not enough to do much good. Please come early George. AWANEN!

Friday, June 5, 1987
My House, Gomez, Cabarroguis, Quirino

We got up at 5:15 AM and George left; he came at 11:40 PM last night, after their stroll to the canteen. He left his blanket this morning, but I don't know why. I started the rice cooking, took my nuang to pasture, returned and talked with George for a few minutes and then came home, drank coffee, ate, did dishes and got ready for the day. I went to the farm and planted *utong* beans where my popcorn didn't come up and then I pulled weeds for George, he's still replanting the area where no corn came up. He also planted ten banana trees. We came home at 10:00 AM and I napped from 11:00 AM to noon, got up, ate lunch, relaxed a while and fetched water. At 2:15 PM I went and pastured my nuang again, returned home and planted *parya*, *kangkong*, squash and *utong* beans in the little southeast garden. I harvested my two remaining pineapples because the pigs got the other two yesterday; I hope they ripen before I go to Manila on the 14th. At 4:00 PM I prepared my vegetables for supper and at 4:30 I went and got my nuang and bathed her. At 5:00 PM I started cooking and bathed myself. Now it's 5:58 PM and my supper is nearly ready to eat. George said that he's not going to stroll tonight and that he will come early, I hope so, but I'll have to wait and see. The weather today was hot and dry and it clouded up again at about 5:00 PM, but there's been no rain yet. There hasn't been very much rain at all since May 1st. AWANEN!

Saturday, June 6, 1987
My House, Gomez, Cabarroguis, Quirino

We got up at 4:50 AM and George left; he came at 7:25 PM last night. I started my rice, drank coffee and took my nuang to pasture. I returned and talked with George for a few minutes, came home, finished cooking, ate, did dishes and got ready for the day. I threw away a bunch of plastic bags from the tree nursery that had nothing growing in them and sifted some of that soil, sifted some dried nuang manure, mixed it all together and planted the 38 Vietnam Guava seeds that I bought the last time I was in Manila; I hope they aren't already too old to germinate. At 9:30 AM I went and got and bathed my nuang, went and talked with George for a while and returned home. I made a frame for the sifter screen, ate lunch and slept from noon until 1:00 PM. I woke up to hear Alfredo and George fighting about something. I went to where George was hiding and tried to talk to him and he said that he's leaving again, but that Alfredo [his father] was guarding the house so he couldn't get his clothes. I followed George around for a half hour or so trying to talk some sense into him but he said he is leaving if Remi [his older sister] will get his clothes for him. At 2:20 PM I took my nuang to pasture again and returned home. I worried for the rest of the day about whether George will leave again or not. At about 4:00 PM I started preparing vegetables for supper and George came here to talk – he still insists that he is leaving. I asked him "what am I to do if you leave?" and he said he doesn't know. I reminded him that I will be very sad if he leaves. At 4:30 PM he left, but he said he'll sleep here tonight and leave in the morning. He also said that he will come early. I went and got and bathed my nuang, bathed myself and at 5:15 PM I started cooking. I went to Alfredo's and he didn't seem too angry anymore. George's mother told me that they used to be richer than they are now and that George is therefore somewhat spoiled. She asked me to tell George that it is bad to holler at his father. I told her that I'd try my best! At 6:00 pm I came home and my rice was a little burned. Now it's 6:21 PM and my vegetables are nearly burned too! Please George, come early tonight and please God, let me be able to talk him into not leaving. The weather today was hot and dry and again it clouded up at about 5:00 PM, but there was no rain. AWANEN!

Chapter 20
Culture Notes #8

Time References

It was somewhere about this time that I finally noted very distinct differences in time references between Filipinos and Americans. Americans are generally taught to be prompt, if a meeting is to start at 9:00 AM we generally arrive at around 8:45 – 8:55 AM. Of course I had noticed that the Filipino was generally at least an hour late to any meeting that I might call. After I gave George my old watch that still worked well I couldn't help but notice that one day when I asked George what time it was, he looked at his watch – a digital readout – and although it said 10:59 AM, George responded that "It is still only ten o'clock." "Ah-ha," I thought, "that must be why everybody is always an hour late for meetings." This happened one day just as we were heading home from the farm for lunch and George and I discussed it for several moments as we walked home. I pointed out to him "But, it's 10:59, in one minute it will be 11:00 AM". George came back with "Yes, but now it's only 10:00 AM" and I gave up arguing. It was too bad that it took me so very long to figure this out.

I'd also noticed a cultural difference in respect to longer time periods. Most people thought no further ahead than to the next harvest. There was no thought about how to get ahead, or make life easier for oneself in the long run. It was for this reason that I had a difficult time convincing people to plant trees, such as citrus trees. Those trees wouldn't, after all, bear fruit for four – seven years! That's longer than forever to a farmer who only has concerns and worries for a time period no longer than four months into the future, a 10th to a 20th of the time that it will take an orange or mandarin tree to bear fruit.

People didn't, however, seem to have the habit of putting off until tomorrow, what could be done today. The farmers of Gomez were (generally) probably the hardest working, most industrious people that I have ever had the experience to work around and with. They usually worked on their farms six days a week, and then used Sunday to relax and plan for the upcoming week.

Chapter 21
June 7, 1987 through November 16, 1987

Sunday, June 7, 1987
My House, Gomez, Cabarroguis, Quirino

Letters to San & Jack G. and Vicki S.

I got up at 5:05 AM. George got up at 4:20 AM and left to pasture his nuang. He came at 7:25 PM last night. I started my rice cooking, took my nuang to pasture, returned and talked with George for a while and then came home. I finished cooking, ate, did dishes and got ready for the day. George is pulling a cart of charcoal to Burgos, will he return? I did my laundry from 7:30 to 9:15 AM and then I drank a cup of coffee and at 9:45 AM I went and got and bathed my nuang. I returned home and killed time for a while and then slept from 11:00 AM until noon. I got up, ate lunch and then wrote the letter to San and Jack. I finished the last of my bananas that I harvested on May 16th. At 2:15 PM I took my nuang to pasture again, returned and talked with Alfredo for a while. Then I came home and swept the north yard and cleaned my rock path. I didn't do much of anything else today. At about 3:30 PM I prepared my vegetables for supper and I saw George return home so I went and talked with him for a while and a thunderstorm began! At 4:30 PM I went and got and bathed my nuang. Then I started my fire and bathed myself. Now it's 5:38 PM and my vegetables are cooking. George told me that he'll come early, but we'll have to wait and see. The weather was mostly hot and dry and then there was a thunderstorm from about 4:00 – 5:00 PM, a nice soaking rain, not extremely hard, not a downpour. Maybe the newly planted things will grow now. Right now it's fairly chilly, it's down to 78°F. AWANEN!

[I cannot recall any details of this "anger episode" of George and Alfredo, but apparently I was able to defuse it before it had gone too far. I expect that if Alfredo had not guarded their house so that George could not get his clothes that George would have run away again. I cannot recall any additional details about it, in fact, there is no further mention of it at all in my Journal.]

Monday, June 8, 1987
My House, Gomez, Cabarroguis, Quirino

Letter to Chris & Mary M.

We got up at 4:50 AM and George left; he came at 7:10 PM last night. I started my rice cooking, drank coffee and took my nuang to pasture. I returned and stopped at George's long enough to tell him I won't be going to the farm today, and then I came home. I finished cooking, ate, did dishes and got ready for the day. This morning I spent a lot of time "practice packing". I sorted all the things I want to take home with me, studied the pile for a while and then put everything back on the shelves, into the corners and etc. By then it was 9:45 AM so I went and got and bathed my nuang. I returned home and killed time for a while. At 11:00 AM I ate lunch and then slept from 11:30 AM to 12:30 PM. I got up, drank coffee, sorted out all the expired medicines from my medical kit then washed the case out and hung it up to dry. At 2:00 PM I went and pastured my nuang again then I returned home, swept the south lawn and started the letter to Chris and Mary. At 4:00 PM I prepared my vegetables for supper and at 4:30 PM it was raining, so I started cooking. At 5:00 PM I saw George at his house so I went and asked him to come early and he said yes. I returned home, ate, did dishes, went and got and bathed my nuang and then bathed myself. Now it's 6:48 PM. The weather today was foggy in the early morning but then hot and dry. It clouded up at about 4:00 PM and there was a nice rain storm from 4:30 to 5:15 PM or so. Now it's nice and cool – nice coffee whether. AWANEN!

Tuesday, June 9, 1987
My House, Gomez, Cabarroguis, Quirino

I got up at 5:10 AM. George got up and left at 4:20 AM to pasture his nuang; he came at 7:15 PM last night, he's pulling another cart of charcoal to Burgos today. I started my rice cooking, took my nuang to pasture, returned home, finished cooking, ate, did dishes and got ready for the day. Then I used the *lampaso* on the porch floor and made it look nice again. After I finished that I started reading the book *"God Emperor of Dune"* by Frank Herbert for a while. Then I spent about two hours sanding an odd shaped piece of wood that I brought home from the farm a week or so ago. It was cloudy all morning so I went and got my nuang and bathed her at 10:45 AM, returned home and ate lunch. I took a siesta from 11:30 AM to 12:30 PM, got up and drank coffee and then at 1:15 PM I took my nuang back to pasture again. I returned home and read some more until about 3:00 PM or so and then I highlighted words I know in the English-Ilokano dictionary until 4:00 PM. I prepared vegetables for supper and at 4:30 PM I saw George at his house so I went and asked him to come early and he said yes, we'll see. I went and got and bathed my nuang, started my fire and bathed myself. Now it's 6:44 PM and I'm waiting for George; supper and dishes are done. I guess I'll read for a while. The weather today was mostly cloudy all day but there was no rain, have to wait and see what happens later tonight. AWANEN!

Wednesday, June 10, 1987
My House, Gomez, Cabarroguis, Quirino

We got up at 4:55 AM and George left; he came at 8:05 PM last night, when I went to get him. I started my rice, took my nuang to pasture and returned home. I finished cooking, ate, did dishes and got ready for the day. I went and got my nuang and headed for the farm at about 6:30 AM. George and I harvested bananas this morning, finishing at about 10:00 AM or so and then we went to where Alfredo, mother and three other women wear weeding and we helped them weed the corn until 11:00 AM. We ate lunch there and then we came home at around noon I guess. I read the book *"God Emperor of Dune"* for a while and then I took a siesta from 1:40 to 2:30 PM. It was cloudy today so I pastured my nuang after we got home and bathed her and therefore I didn't have to take her to pasture this afternoon. I got up at 2:30 PM, drank coffee, read some more and killed time until 4:00 PM. Then I prepared the vegetables for supper. At 4:30 PM I went and got and bathed my nuang and returned home. At 5:00 PM I started cooking and bathed myself. I ate at 6:00 PM, did dishes and went and asked George to come early. He took the cart of bananas to Burgos this afternoon so he said he will come soon, we'll see. I'll go and get him at 8:00 PM if he's not here by then. The weather today was mostly cloudy all day, but no rain – it's very strange weather. AWANEN!

Thursday, June 11, 1987
My House, Gomez, Cabarroguis, Quirino

Letters from Katie F., Tim C., Bill N. and Chad D. (two books too).

₱92 + 300 – 297 = ₱95							
Food	55	Rides	16	Cigarettes	13	Marienda	40
Coffee	53	Household	42	Lunch	23	Ice Cream	20
Candy	23	Soap	12			TOTAL	₱297

We got up at 4:50 AM, I gave George my *wayway* and he left. He didn't come until 8:35 PM last night. I cooked my breakfast, ate, did dishes, got ready for the day and left for Burgos at 6:30 AM. My plan was to get mail, because tomorrow is a National Holiday, and then do my marketing in Diffun, so I went to Gundaway and I suddenly got a craving for ice cream so I decided to go all the way to Santiago, so I got my mail and continued on to Santiago, arriving there at about 9:10 AM or so. I didn't have to get too much today because I'm going to Manila on Saturday. I just mostly bought things to have for stock, so I finished up shopping at about 10:00 AM or so and went to the Ice Cream House for a sandwich and ice cream. That took care of my craving and I got a jeepney for Burgos. I left Santiago at 11:00 AM and finally got home in Gomez at about 12:45 PM. I unpacked, put things away and read my mail. After a while I fetched water and at 4:00 PM I prepared my vegetables for supper. George said he'll come early tonight, we'll see. At 4:30 PM I bathed and started cooking. Now it's 6:23 PM and I'm done with everything and waiting for George. The weather today was mostly cloudy until 2:30 PM or so and then there was a nice rain storm until 4:30 PM or so. Now it's only cloudy, not raining. AWANEN!

Friday, June 12, 1987
My House, Gomez, Cabarroguis, Quirino

We got up at 4:50 AM and George left; he came at 7:10 PM last night. I started my rice, drank coffee and took my nuang to pasture. I returned and talked with George for a few minutes and then came home. I finished cooking, ate, did dishes and got ready for the day. I did laundry and worked on that until 9:00 AM and then I read until 10:15 AM or so. Then I went and got and bathed my nuang. I returned home and read for a while longer and then I took a siesta from 11:00 AM until noon. I got up, ate lunch, drank coffee and read some more. Then at about 1:00 PM I went to George's and talked with them until about 1:45 PM or so and he went to the farm. I returned home, took my nuang to pasture and didn't do much of anything this afternoon. I'm trying to finish the *"God Emperor of Dune"* book before I go to Manila, but I still have about 40 pages to go, so I might not be able to, we'll see. At 4:00 PM I prepared my vegetables for supper and at 4:30 PM I went and got and bathed my nuang. I returned home and lit my fire and bathed myself. I ate, did dishes and went to ask George to come early, but he is out strolling somewhere. Please come early George! Now it's 6:23 PM and I'm already waiting for him. The weather today was cloudy until 10:15 AM or so and then sunny. Then at about 1:00 PM it clouded up again. It rained lightly from about 2:15 to 6:00 PM and now it has stopped, but it's still cloudy. AWANEN!

Saturday, June 13, 1987
Malate Pension, Manila

₱95 + 300 – 143 = ₱252							
Rides	67	Lunch	51	Cigarettes	10	Marienda	15
						TOTAL	₱143

We got up at 5:00 AM and George left; he came at 6:50 PM last night, we slept close last night. I drank coffee, prepared last minute things, took my bag of valuables to Alfredo's and at 6:00 AM I left Gomez barefoot. There was a hard rain last night so barefoot was the easiest way to walk and also allowed me to get to the main road with clean flip-flops. I took a jeepney from Gomez to Cordon, arriving there at about 7:50 AM. I ran into Katie F. and Keith and we talked for a while and then I went to the bus waiting place. A bus finally came at 9:00 AM. It was a long and slow trip to Manila and I arrived there at about 4:30 PM or so. I took a jeepney to Malate Pension and finally got here at 6:30 PM or so, with the usual headache. I checked in, ate supper and retired to the room. After a while Barb W. called and we talked on the phone for an hour. Then I went downstairs, ate a slice of pineapple and talked with a couple of other Peace Corps Volunteers whom I didn't know. Now it's 10:35 PM, way past my bedtime. The weather today – I don't know what it was in Gomez, but there was a hard rain last night and it was cloudy this morning. AWANEN!

Sunday, June 14, 1987
Malate Pension, Manila

₱252 + 200 – 295 = ₱157							
Meals	162	Cigarettes	10	Rides	1	Food	78
Postage	6	Marienda	38			TOTAL	₱295

I got up at 5:20 AM, showered, got ready for the day and went downstairs. I drank coffee and killed time until 10:00 AM when a bunch of us went to the Seafront Restaurant for brunch. We ate brunch from 10:00 AM until 2:00 PM and then I left and went to Harrison Plaza to search for a new journal type notebook, but they didn't have any there so I returned to Malate Pension got out of my shoes and into my flip-flops and went to Robinson's Department store. They didn't have any notebooks there either, but I bought some peanut butter, bread and so on and returned to Malate Pension again. After a while, five of us went to Shakey's Pizza for supper. They had a live band, which was loud, so we ate fast and got out of there and went to Dunkin' Donuts and drank coffee until 8:30 PM or so and then we returned to Malate Pension. I came to the room and there was a party happening – what the hell!? Now it's 9:15 PM and I'm ready to crash. The weather today was rainy on and off all day. AWANEN!

Monday, June 15, 1987
Malate Pension, Manila

₱157 + 300 – 280 = ₱177							
Meals	223	Cigarettes	32	Rides	15	Food	3
Postage	7					TOTAL	₱295

I got up late, at 5:20 AM, showered, got ready for the day and went downstairs for breakfast of banana pancakes. At 8:00 AM I headed over to the Peace Corps Office and the first thing I did was see the nurse. I found out that I have two kinds of worms and got an appointment for the eye doctor, the hernia doctor and the dentist. I had a totally unproductive talk with Cery about reporting nothing but "numbers" and then I talked with Joanne T. about the George story for *Salaysayan* Magazine. After that, four of us went to lunch at the Seafront Restaurant and we ate nothing but the salad bar. Then I went to the eye doctor and got a really shitty eye exam and he told me I need bifocals, I'll wait until I get back to the USA. Then I went to Makati Medical for them to check my hernia and they told me it's up to me whether I should repair it or not. I returned to Malate Pension and off we went to the Seafront Restaurant again for the Mongolian Barbeque. It was very good food but it was a lousy and loud band. We returned to Malate Pension, talked for a while and now it's 10:11 PM. The weather today was rainy off and on all day. AWANEN!

Tuesday, June 16, 1987
Malate Pension, Manila

Postcard to George.

₱177 + 400 – 468 = ₱109							
Meals	97	Rides	2	Postage	238	Marienda	46
Notebook	28	Candy	40	Misc.	17	TOTAL	₱468

I got up at 5:00 AM, showered, got ready for the day and went downstairs for coffee and breakfast. At 7:45 AM or so I headed over to the dentist office for my 8:30 AM appointment. As I suspected, one of my root canals has an infection. I went back over to the Peace Corps Office at about 11:00 AM and told Ann about everything – that I need new glasses, but I'll wait until I get to America; I need teeth work, but I'll wait until I get to America; I need to have surgery on my hernia, which I want now – but she told me I have to wait until I get back to America. Then I filled out a CA-2 form about my hernia, ate lunch and finally got out of the Peace Corps Office at about 1:30 PM. I went back to Malate Pension and ate peanut butter and bread for lunch and then I went to the post office and the National Bookstore on Rizal Avenue. I returned to Malate Pension and talked with Mike P., Kevin and Patty E. for a while and then we went out to eat Italian food for supper. After eating we returned to Malate Pension again and talked until 10:00 PM. Now it's 10:35 PM and I'm ready to sleep. The weather today was once again rainy off and on all day. AWANEN!

Wednesday, June 17, 1987
Malate Pension, Manila

Received ₱931 per diem payment.

₱109 + 350 – 367 = ₱92							
Meals	60	Rides	10	Laundry	40	Lodging	125
Ice Cream	19	Marienda	43	Clothes	66	Seeds	4
						TOTAL	₱367

I got up at 5:05 AM, showered, got ready for the day, went downstairs, ate and then after breakfast Mike P. and I went to Baclaran so that I could buy short pants for George. Then we went to the Peace Corps Office to meet Kevin and Patty and we all went to Chinatown. Patty did some shopping and I bought two T-shirts. Then we ate lunch and after that we returned to Malate Pension and ate ice cream. After that I went and picked up laundry and then we went to the Seafront [not the restaurant] and swam for a while and relaxed. At 5:00 PM we went inside for happy hour [at the restaurant] and then at about 8:00 PM we left. We stopped at Dunkin' Donuts for coffee and donuts and then returned to Malate Pension. Now it's 9:52 PM and I'm tired. The weather today was just a little bit rainy. AWANEN!

Thursday, June 18, 1987
Host Family, Bonfal East, Bayombong, Nueva Vizcaya

₱92 + 100 – 127 = ₱65							
Rides	71	Toilet Paper	7	Cigarettes	12	Marienda	37
						TOTAL	₱127

I got up at 5:20 AM, bathed, got ready for the day and left Malate Pension without even drinking coffee. I went to the Pantranco Bus Terminal and waited one and a half hours so that I could take an air conditioned bus headed north at 8:00 AM. I guess I've been pretty short on sleep lately because I was able to sleep for almost the whole ride. We had a flat tire and stopped for one and a half hours in San Jose to fix it and we also had a couple of marienda stops. We got to Bayombong at about 3:30 PM. I walked from the bus stop and arrived at the house at about 4:00 PM. The family was happy to see me and it's pretty nice to be here again too. They're harvesting sugar cane now so everybody's walking around chewing on sugar cane. Ronald and I went to the farm, harvested a few coconuts and ate them and then after a while we returned home. Ronald now has a calf, a small cow, that he is raising! We ate supper at about 7:30 PM and now it's 8:55 PM and we're ready to sleep right after I finish this and give Ronald what he wants [a blow job]. The weather today was cloudy most of the day and right now it's raining lightly. AWANEN!

Friday, June 19, 1987
Host Family, Bonfal East, Bayombong, Nueva Vizcaya

₱65 + 50 – 95 = ₱20							
Haircut	10	Ice Cream	22	Coffee	27	Marienda	4
Food	11	Cigarettes	9	Soap	12	TOTAL	₱127

We got up late, at 5:40 AM, drank coffee and even bathed before breakfast. We ate at about 7:15 AM or so. We changed clothes to go into town and Ronald I and one of his companions went to a gay barber shop for a haircut. After that, Ronald continued on to school and I went to market and managed to find mother, but she didn't want me to walk around with her while she was marketing or the vendors would quote her higher prices than if she was not with an Americano. Okay, I stayed out of sight and let her shop and we finally headed for home at about 10:15 AM or so. We got home and Ronald was already here. We prepared food for lunch and after a while we ate. I retired upstairs to rest, but it was too hot to sleep. After a while Ronald returned to school and I just killed time all afternoon. Ronald got home at about 5:30 PM and after a while I prepared food for supper and at about 8:00 PM we ate. Now it's 8:47 PM and we're ready to sleep. I'm bored out of my mind here and I still have two days to go – GROAN! The weather today was hot, dry and windy all day. AWANEN!

Saturday, June 20, 1987
Host Family, Bonfal East, Bayombong, Nueva Vizcaya

₱20 – 15 = ₱5							
Cigarettes	9	Beer	6			TOTAL	₱15

We got up at 5:40 AM and killed time until breakfast, ate breakfast at about 7:00 AM and killed time until Ronald's friends came at about 8:00 AM. Then we killed time until we left for the river at about 9:00 AM. Ronald, his three friends, Herbert and I went to the river and used the net and electricity to catch fish and then we found a nice place to eat and we cooked the fish for lunch. We ate at about 11:30 AM and then relaxed and talked until 1:30 PM or so. Then we used the net to try and catch more fish, but we didn't get any, so we went swimming for a while. It clouded up and threatened to rain, so we headed home at about 3:00 PM. We got home and after a while Ronald's friends left. Then we killed time until supper and ate that at about 7:30 PM. Dang this is an extremely noisy place, it doesn't seem like it used to be this noisy here. There are always visitors here it seems. Now it's 8:30 PM and I'm about ready to sleep. The weather today was hot and dry with about a dozen drops of rain at around 3:00 PM. AWANEN!

Sunday, June 21, 1987
Host Family, Bonfal East, Bayombong, Nueva Vizcaya

We got up at 5:50 AM and killed time until breakfast, which was not until 7:30 AM or so. After breakfast I bathed and got ready for the day. A whole bunch of visitors came today, but first Ronald and I went and harvested mangoes. After we returned home they all went fishing with dynamite, but I stayed home, I did not need to experience that type of destruction of fish and fish habitat. We ate lunch at about 1:00 PM and after a while Rebecca and I made rice cake – that took nearly three hours. Ronald and everybody returned home at about 2:15 PM with lots of fish. I killed time while everybody was getting drunk and finally we ate supper at about 8:00 PM. Now it's 8:40 PM and I'm ready to sleep. The weather today was hot and dry and it clouded up at about 3:30 PM. There was a hard rain at about 4:00 PM and then it tapered off and finally stopped raining at about 7:30 PM. AWANEN!

Monday, June 22, 1987
My House, Gomez, Cabarroguis, Quirino

Letters from Chad D. and Barb W. My last letter to Teresa L. was returned as undeliverable. Postcard for George arrived (mailed June 16 from Manila).

₱5 + 245 – 80 = ₱170							
Cigarettes	9	Rides	11	Food	39	Marienda	9
Misc.	12					TOTAL	₱80

We got up late, at about 5:50 AM. I got ready for the day while breakfast was cooking, we ate breakfast at about 7:00 AM and I said my goodbyes. Ronald and I left at about 7:40 AM and walked to the road. I caught a jeepney for Solano and then took a Vizcaya Liner for Cordon. I left Solano at about 8:25 AM and arrived in Cordon at about 10:00 AM. I did my shopping there and then continued on to Gundaway and got the above mail. After that, I got a jeepney for Burgos, got off at the junction of the high road and climbed the mountain starting at about 11:50 AM. I arrived home at about 12:30 PM and went straight to George's with the sugarcane from Bayombong and Coco Jam from Manila. We talked for a while and I came home at 3:00 PM. I took my nuang to pasture and at 4:00 PM I prepared my vegetables for supper. At 4:30 PM I started cooking and at 5:00 PM I went and got and bathed my nuang. Now it's 5:35 PM and I'll bathe myself after supper. I hope George comes early tonight, he said that he will. The weather today was hot and dry, but it clouded up at about 5:00 PM. Right now there is distant thunder. George and Alfredo told me that it rained here while I was gone. One of the pineapples that I harvested on June 5th is beautifully ripe. AWANEN!

Tuesday, June 23, 1987
My House, Gomez, Cabarroguis, Quirino

We got up at 4:50 AM and George left; he came at 7:10 PM last night. It was so good to talk with him again! I started breakfast cooking, drank coffee and took my nuang to pasture. I returned, talked with George for a couple of minutes, came home finished cooking, ate and got ready for the day. At about 6:40 AM I headed for the farm walking. I found George at his farm and we talked for a few minutes and then I weeded four rows of beans on my farm. At 9:00 AM I went and found George again and at 9:15 AM we came home. I got and bathed my nuang, slept for 20 minutes and Alfredo came to talk until 11:45 AM, he left and I ate lunch and slept another 20 minutes. I got up at 1:00 PM, fetched water and prepared my vegetables for supper. At 2:00 PM I went to George's and asked if he was going to return to the farm and he said yes, so we went together to pasture our nuangs and then we continued to the farm on foot. I weeded 11 rows of *utong* beans and at 4:30 PM I went and found George, he was weeding his corn today, and we headed home. We got and bathed our nuangs and continued on home. I started cooking at 5:15 PM, bathed and went to buy cigarettes and then went to talk with George for a couple of minutes. I returned home and now it's 6:05 PM and everything is cooked. I'll eat as soon as I finish this. The weather today – there was a little rain last night, but today it was hot and dry all day with no clouds at all. AWANEN!

Wednesday, June 24, 1987
My House, Gomez, Cabarroguis, Quirino

I got up at 5:00 AM. George got up at 4:00 AM and left to pasture his nuang. He came at 7:55 PM last night. He pulled a cart of avocados to Burgos today. I started cooking, drank coffee and took my nuang to pasture. I returned and talked with George for couple of minutes and he was ready to leave already, so I came home. I finished cooking, ate, did dishes, got ready for the day and first thing I did was laundry – lots of it – from Manila! That took me from 7:00 to 9:00 AM and then I relaxed until 9:45 AM or so and went and got and bathed my nuang. At about 10:20 AM I saw George at their house so I went and talked with him for a while and then came home and took a siesta from 11:30 AM until noon. I ate lunch, swept the north yard and at 2:00 PM I went to George's and he had already left for the farm. I pastured my nuang and cut grass on the hill to the northeast of the house then I fetched water and read my *Reader's Digest.* At 4:00 PM I prepared vegetables for supper and at 4:40 PM I went and got and bathed my nuang. At 5:00 PM I started cooking supper and now it's 5:53 PM and everything is cooked and cooling. I'll bathe after supper. I hope George comes earlier tonight. The weather today was hot and dry, it was up to 95°F in the afternoon. Now it's only partly cloudy so there probably won't be any rain tonight. Oh, I planted six pineapple tops today. AWANEN!

Thursday, June 25, 1987
My House, Gomez, Cabarroguis, Quirino

Letters to Chad D. and Dave & Vicki M.

We got up at 4:50 AM and George left; he didn't come until 8:05 PM last night. I started the rice cooking, drank coffee and took my nuang to pasture. I returned home, finished cooking, ate, did dishes and got ready for the day. I went and got my nuang and headed for the farm, arriving there at about 7:00 AM and George and I harvested bananas. We finished at about 10:00 AM and headed home, arriving at about 11:00 AM. I cleaned up a bit and got off most of the sticky banana sap and then slept from 11:30 AM until noon. I ate lunch and read my *Reader's Digest* until 2:15 PM and then I took my nuang to pasture again. I returned and talked with George for a few minutes and then returned home, where I finished reading my *Reader's Digest.* Then I did the above letter to Chad and then the letter to Dave and Vicki. At 4:00 PM I prepared my vegetables for supper and at 4:35 PM I went and got and bathed my nuang and then started cooking supper. Now it's 5:50 PM and my vegetables are nearly cooked. I hope George comes earlier tonight – he says he will, but we'll have to wait and see. We harvested 46 *buligs* of bananas this morning – the cart is really, really full. I guess I really didn't do much today other than that. Oh, I forgot, I bathed before supper. The weather today was hot and dry, it was 76°F this morning and 92°F at 2:00 PM. There was a little rain between 2:00 and 3:00 PM and now it's thundering and there's a light wind, so maybe there will be more rain later. AWANEN!

Friday, June 26, 1987
My House, Gomez, Cabarroguis, Quirino

Letter to Bill N.

I got up at 4:50 AM. George got up at 4:00 AM and left to pasture his nuang. He came at 7:40 PM last night. I started the rice cooking drink coffee, took my nuang to pasture and then returned home. I finished cooking, ate, did dishes and got ready for the day. I used the *lampaso* on all the floors, the tabletop, the benches and so on and cleaned house really good. Then I rested for a while and then weeded and swept the south yard. I finished that at 10:00 AM and went and got and bathed my nuang. I killed time for a while and then took a siesta from 11:45 AM to 12:15 PM. I got up, ate lunch, drank coffee and then relaxed and read my *Newsweek* Magazine until 2:15 PM. I fetched water, took my nuang to pasture again, returned home and did the letter to Bill until 4:00 PM. Then I prepared my few remaining vegetables for supper – a few Baguio beans. I'll fry some bananas for the rest of my supper. George and all of them went to Burgos today to sell bananas and to buy rice. The price of rice is up to ₱300 per kaban now! At 4:30 PM I went and got my nuang and bathed her, bathed myself and started cooking at 5:10 PM. Now it's 5:40 PM and my rice is nearly cooked. I hope George comes early tonight. The weather today was hot and dry and then it clouded up at about 4:00 PM. Now there are very dark clouds and it's thundering. Will it rain later? I don't know. AWANEN!

Saturday, June 27, 1987
My House, Gomez, Cabarroguis, Quirino

We got up at 5:20 AM and George left; he came at 7:25 PM last night. I started cooking my rice, took my nuang to pasture, returned and talked with George for a few minutes and then came home. I finished cooking, ate, did dishes and got ready for the day and then Alfredo and I headed for the farm; George had already left. We got there and I talked with George for a few minutes and then went to weed my farm. I finished weeding the *utong*, the pepino and two rows of corn. We headed home at around 10:00 AM, I got and bathed my nuang, came home and relaxed for a little while. I took a siesta from 11:45 AM until 12:30 PM, got up, ate lunch and prepared my vegetables for supper. At 1:40 PM I went to George's and at about 2:20 PM we returned to the farm. George weeded his corn and I weeded mine. I weeded five more rows this afternoon. We quit at 4:30 PM and at 4:40 PM we headed home. I got and bathed my nuang, started the rice cooking and bathed myself. Now it's 6:05 PM and everything is cooked and cooling a bit before I eat. I hope George comes early tonight. I started a letter to Tim C. last night, maybe I'll finish it tonight before George comes. The weather today was hot and dry but the humidity was really high. It was mostly cloudy all day, but so far there hasn't been a drop of rain. AWANEN!

Sunday, June 28, 1987
My House, Gomez, Cabarroguis, Quirino

I got up at 5:05 AM. George got up and left at 4:20 AM to pasture his nuang so that he could pull a cart of charcoal to Burgos today. He came at 7:50 PM last night. Alfredo borrowed my nuang to pull a cart of bananas to Burgos today, so I started cooking breakfast, drank coffee, did dishes, got ready for the day and then I did laundry. After that I weeded the lower garden and repaired the fence in the southeast garden. I out-planted the one remaining Damortis tree (*Pithecellobium dulce*) and then I killed time until 11:30 AM and took a siesta until 12:15 PM. I got up and ate lunch, calculated my June expenses, to and including yesterday, and tallied my strolls and visitors for June. Then I worked on and finished my quarterly report for this quarter. I fetched water, filled out a leave request for my planned August vacation and didn't do much else all day. At 4:30 PM I went to the canteen, bought cigarettes and asked George's mother to tell him to come early tonight; he hadn't returned from Burgos yet. Then I bathed and prepared my vegetables for supper. At 5:00 PM I started cooking and now it's 5:41 PM. Please, please George, come early tonight – it's been a long boring day. The weather today was partly cloudy and then at about 5:00 PM there was a thunderstorm. Even now it's still raining, although it's tapering off somewhat. I'll eat my supper as soon as I finish this and then wash dishes. AWANEN!

Monday, June 29, 1987
My House, Gomez, Cabarroguis, Quirino

We got up at 4:55 AM and George left; he came early last night – at 6:55 PM – and we had a nice story telling session. He pastured my nuang this morning so I cooked breakfast, ate, did dishes, got ready for the day and Alfredo came and gave me a pack of cigarettes in return for using my nuang yesterday. I headed for the farm at about 6:30 AM. George cut *panaw* [a type of grass] for the roof of the rest hut at the farm and I continued to weed my corn. I finished four rows this morning and then helped George gather grass for an hour. We headed home a while after 10:00 AM, got and bathed our nuangs and continued on home. I killed time for a while, ate lunch at about 11:30 AM and then slept from 11:45 AM to 12:30 PM. I got up and prepared my vegetables for supper and at 2:00 PM I went to Georges and he was ready to leave for the farm again, so we pastured our nuangs and went to the farm. He gathered more *panaw* for the roof of the rest hut and I continued weeding. I accomplished two rows this afternoon. I headed home first – at 4:50 PM, got and bathed my nuang, came home and lit my fire. I bathed myself and now it's 6:10 PM and my rice is cooked and the vegetables are cooking. I hope George comes early again tonight, but he probably won't. The weather today was dry but mostly cloudy so it was not too hot. It was only about 86°F this afternoon! So far there's been no rain, although there's been lots of thunder this afternoon. AWANEN!

Tuesday, June 30, 1987
My House, Gomez, Cabarroguis, Quirino

Letter to Tim C.

I got up at 5:00 AM with no companion; George came last night to tell me they were going to go to a wedding. So, being alone I didn't sleep very well, I think I slept from around 10:00 PM to midnight and then again from around 2:30 to 5:00 AM or so. I'll surely sleep well tonight. I started my rice cooking, drank coffee and took my nuang to pasture. I stopped at George's on the way home but he hadn't returned yet. I came home, finished cooking, ate, did dishes and got ready for the day. I went to George's again but he still hadn't arrived. Alfredo went to the farm and I came home and cleaned house and tried to sleep, but I couldn't because I was worried too much about why George wasn't home yet. I read *"The P.R. Girls"* book, by Bernard Glemser until 10:45 AM and then I got and bathed my nuang. George returned about then so I went and talked with him for a while and then came home. I ate lunch and slept for a half hour and then I got up because I heard George's mother crying very loudly *"Annak-ko, Annak-ko"* [my child, my child], so I went running, as did everybody else in the neighborhood, and Rosie the youngest daughter [less than one year old] had a high fever and was convulsing and dying. George had run to get the quack doctor and by and by the quack doctor came and managed to revive Rosie. All I did was pray and pray – maybe God heard my prayers, I don't know. I stayed there until 2:30 PM and George and I went and pastured our nuangs and returned. I stayed at their house some more and Rosie got stronger and stronger and was moving around. Her temperature was 39.6°C (103.3°F) – dangerously high. They were getting ready to go to the hospital and then at about 3:00 PM it started raining so I ran to fetch water before it started raining too hard. I returned to my house and spent some time reading about fevers of children in my *"Where There is no Doctor"* book and I took them a half of an aspirin in the downpour and asked them to give her that with some water. I returned home and read more until 3:45 PM and then I prepared my vegetables for supper. I started cooking early, about 4:10 PM or so. I ate supper, did dishes and George and I went to get our nuangs and I returned home. George told me that he'll come as soon as they're done with supper, I hope so. Then I bathed myself and now it's 6:27 PM. The weather today was mostly cloudy until noon and then there was bright sun until 2:30 PM or so. At about 3:00 PM there was a heavy rain, which continued until 4:30 PM or so and then let up and nearly stopped, but then started raining pretty hard again at about 6:15 PM and it's still continuing now. AWANEN!

Wednesday, July 1, 1987
My House, Gomez, Cabarroguis, Quirino

Letters from Fred & Cynthia B., San & Jack G. and Ardis B. (photos too).

₱170 + 400 – 179 = ₱391							
Food	66	Rides	8	Kerosene	7	Cigarettes	13
Marienda	40	Coffee	27	Misc.	18	TOTAL	₱179

We got up at 5:00 AM and George left; he came at 7:05 PM last night. I drank coffee, took my bag of valuables and *wayway* to Alfredo's and left for Burgos at 5:55 AM. I went directly to the Diffun Office and arrived there at 7:30 AM. I waited for Francisco until after 8:45 AM and then asked the District Forester to sign my quarterly report and my leave request. I met Francisco just as I was leaving; he arrived at about 9:00 AM. I went back to Gundaway, did my marketing, got my mail and caught a jeepney headed back to Burgos, arriving there at about 11:50 AM. I climbed the mountain via the high road and got home at about 12:25 PM. My time today was 35 minutes and 28 seconds. I read my mail and then at 1:50 PM I went to George's. At about 2:20 PM we took our nuangs to pasture and then I came home and watched the rain. At 3:45 PM I prepared my vegetables for supper and at 4:10 PM I started cooking. After eating supper and doing dishes I went and got my nuang and now it's 6:11 PM and I'm waiting for George. I hope he comes soon. The weather today was hot and dry and then at 2:00 PM it clouded up and started raining at about 2:20 PM. It continued until about 4:00 PM and now it's partly cloudy. AWANEN!

Thursday, July 2, 1987
My House, Gomez, Cabarroguis, Quirino

Postcard to Bob S.

We got up at 4:55 AM and George left, he came at 7:10 PM last night. I started the rice cooking, drank coffee, took my nuang to pasture and when I returned George was already leaving for the farm. I talked with Alfredo for a couple of minutes and then came home, finished cooking, ate, did dishes and got ready for the day. I left for the farm even before 6:30 AM, got there and started weeding immediately. I finished four rows of corn by 9:30 AM and went to find George. I showed him my cranberry pole beans, which are already blooming and one squash plant, which is also already blooming. I planted those beans and squash that are blooming on May 30th, they have been very fast to grow, I would say. At 10:10 AM we headed for home. We got and bathed our nuangs and continued on home. I slept for a half-hour, ate lunch at 1:00 PM, fetched water and prepared my vegetables for supper. At 2:00 PM I went to George's and at 2:05 PM we companioned to pasture our nuangs and then went to the farm. I weeded three more rows of corn by 4:30 PM and George cut *panaw* grass for the roof of the rest hut. At 4:45 PM I headed home, first again. I got and bathed my nuang, came home, bathed myself and started cooking supper. Now it's 6:12 PM and supper is cooling; I'll eat as soon as I finish this. I hope George comes early again tonight. The weather today was hot, dry and partly cloudy but there was no rain. AWANEN!

Friday, July 3, 1987
My House, Gomez, Cabarroguis, Quirino

We got up at 5:00 AM and George left. I went and got him at 7:30 PM last night and we came here at 7:55 PM. I started my rice cooking, drank coffee, took my nuang to pasture and George was already heading for the farm when I returned. I came home, finished cooking, ate, did dishes and got ready for the day. I left for the farm a little bit before 6:30 AM and managed to weed five rows of corn by 9:30 AM. Then I went and found George, who was carrying *panaw* to the location of the rest hut, and we headed home. We got and bathed are nuangs and arrived home at about 10:30 AM. I took a siesta immediately and slept until 11:15 AM when Junior came to get some Zephiran spray for a small cut! After he left I ate lunch and killed time. At about 1:00 PM the ADF [Assistant District Forester] and Efren came. The ADF wanted to go to the farm, so we left, after asking Alfredo to pasture my nuang. The ADF looked at my farm took some pictures and left, what he came for I'm not sure. I stayed there and weeded four rows of corn this afternoon so the total today was nine rows of corn weeded. I searched for George at 4:30 PM, but he didn't come to the farm this afternoon, so I headed home, got and bathed my nuang, started my rice cooking and bathed myself. Now it's 5:39 PM and my rice is still cooking. I hope George comes early tonight. The weather today was hot and dry all day. There were a few scattered clouds only. AWANEN!

Saturday, July 4, 1987
My House, Gomez, Cabarroguis, Quirino

Letter to Fred & Cynthia B.

We got up at 4:55 AM and George left; he came at 7:45 PM last night. I started my rice, drank coffee and took my nuang to pasture. I returned and talked with George for a minute and then came home, finished cooking, ate, did dishes and got ready for the day. I went and got my nuang and headed for the farm a little before 6:30 AM. George and I harvested bananas today and his folks harvested avocados. We finished shortly after 10:00 AM and headed home, arriving shortly after 11:00 AM. I washed up to get most of the banana "blood" [sap] off my body and then I ate lunch. I took a siesta from 11:45 AM to 12:30 PM, got up and killed time for a while and then at 1:30 PM I took my nuang back to pasture, returned and talked with George for a while and then came home. I fetched water and then wrote the above letter to Fred and Cynthia. I finished that at about 3:40 PM and prepared vegetables for supper. At 4:30 PM I went and got and bathed my nuang, bathed myself and started cooking supper. Now it's 5:56 PM, supper is cooked and I'll eat as soon as I'm done with this. I really, really hope George comes early tonight; I'm feeling lonely but I don't really know why. The weather today was hot and dry this morning and then it clouded up at about 12:30 PM and stayed cloudy. There's been no rain yet but it looks very threatening right now. It was 73°F this morning and now it's a comfortable 82°F. AWANEN!

Sunday, July 5, 1987
My House, Gomez, Cabarroguis, Quirino

Letters to Cery and Chris & Mary M.

₱391 + 400 – 5 = ₱786							
Cigarettes	5					TOTAL	₱5

I got up at 5:00 AM. George got up and left at 4:00 AM to pasture his nuang. I went and got him last night at 7:55 PM again. I started my rice cooking, drank coffee and took my nuang to pasture. I returned and talked with George for a couple of minutes and then came home, finished cooking, ate, did dishes and got ready for the day. The first thing I did today was laundry – from 7:00 to 9:00 AM. After that I highlighted some words in the English-Ilokano dictionary that I know until 10:00 AM and then I went and got and bathed my nuang. I returned home and Junior's wife was here and wanted some medicine for athlete's foot! I told her I have none, showed her my own feet and she left. Shortly after that I took a siesta from 11:45 AM to 12:30 PM. Then I ate lunch and at 1:00 PM I took my nuang back to pasture. I returned and it sprinkled rain a little bit so I pulled my clothes off the clothesline. At 2:00 PM George returned from Burgos so I went and talked with him and his family for about half an hour or so. Then I came home and trimmed my beard. By then it was 3:45 PM so I prepared my vegetables for supper and at 4:30 PM I went and got and bathed my nuang, bathed myself and started cooking supper. Now I'm done eating and dishes are also done. It's 6:33 PM and I hope George comes early tonight, please. The weather today was cloudy most of the day with a few very light showers, but nothing significant. There was no rain last night either. AWANEN!

Monday, July 6, 1987
My House, Gomez, Cabarroguis, Quirino

Letter from Bill J.
Barbara W. come to visit.

₱786 – 499 = ₱287							
Food	159	Rides	16	Cigarettes	13	Batteries	56
Souvenir	50	Marienda	63	Soap	9	Coffee	53
Kerosene	7	Ice Cream	24	Lunch	20	Household	9
Candy	7	Misc.	13			TOTAL	₱499

We got up at 4:45 AM and George left; he came at 7:25 PM last night. I gave him my *wayway* before he left. I drank coffee, got ready for the day and headed for Burgos at 5:40 AM. I caught a jeepney to Santiago and arrived there at 7:30 AM. I did all of my shopping and finished at about 10:00 AM; I even did my banking by then. I went to Letty's Restaurant and waited for JB and Katie. JB came at about 11:00 AM and Barb W. also arrived about then. After a short time Katy arrived and we went to the 456 Restaurant for lunch and hung out there talking until 1:30 PM or so. Then Barb and I caught a jeepney to Gundaway, where I stopped at the post office and got the above mail. Then we caught a jeepney for Burgos and arrived at the bottom of the high road at about 3:30 PM. We climbed the mountain and got to my house at about 4:30 PM. George's mother, Beth and the children came soon after that and talked for a while. When they left I prepared the vegetables for supper and started cooking. Barbara bathed and then I bathed. We finished cooking and now it's 7:18 PM and I hope George comes, but I'm sure he will be reluctant to do so. The weather today was hot and dry all day. AWANEN!

[Late in the evening I got sick and had a terrible bout of diarrhea. I could not make it to the outhouse, but when I got there I purged myself and then continued from the outhouse to the creek and bathed myself. I hollered at Barbara to bring me a clean pair of short pants. I blamed this on a jar of mayonnaise that was sitting on the table at the 456 Restaurant, and which I used on my sandwich when we ate lunch there. Don't ever use restaurant mayonnaise that has been left out on the table for God alone knows how many days.]

Tuesday, July 7, 1987
My House, Gomez, Cabarroguis, Quirino

Barbara W. here.

We got up at 4:50 AM and George left; I went and got him at 8:00 PM last night. I had to get up twice in the night with diarrhea and I had a fever of 101.6°F. I was sick all day! I started cooking rice, drank coffee and took my nuang to pasture – Barbara rode her. We returned to George's and talked for a few minutes then came home. We finished cooking, ate, did dishes and got ready for the day. We were finally ready at about 8:30 AM or so and we headed for the farm. I showed Barb the farm and we went and watched George make bundles of *panaw* grass for the roof of the rest hut. George, Barbara and I headed home at 10:00 AM, got and bathed the nuangs and then we all talked until 12:30 PM. Then Barbara ate lunch, but I didn't feel well enough to be able to eat so I took a siesta until 2:30 PM. I got up, took my nuang to pasture, returned home and relaxed. I went and fetched water at 4:00 PM, prepared the vegetables for supper and then at 5:00 PM I went and got and bathed my nuang. I started cooking and bathed myself. When supper was cooked we ate, did dishes and now it's 7:21 PM. I hope George comes soon, if he doesn't then I'll go to get him in a little while. The weather was hot and dry all day and partly cloudy on and off. Now there's thunder and lightning but it's not yet raining, we'll see what happens in a while. Maybe I'll go ask George to come as soon as I finish this. AWANEN!

Wednesday, July 8, 1987
My House, Gomez, Cabarroguis, Quirino

Barbara W. here.

We got up at 5:00 AM and George left; he came at 8:00 PM last night. I started the rice cooking, drank coffee and took my nuang to pasture. I returned and talked with George for a couple of minutes and then came home. After a while Barbara got up, we finished cooking, ate, did dishes and got ready for the day. This morning we didn't really do anything other than talk. At 9:30 AM we went to Alfredo's and found that George had gone to the farm to harvest avocados and had already returned. We talked until 10:00 AM and then we went and got and bathed my nuang. I reentered my USA address file into the HP-71 again – another total memory loss error. At 12:20 PM I was done with that and we ate lunch. After lunch we tried to take a siesta but it was too hot so we talked some more until 2:20 PM. Then I returned my nuang to pasture. At 3:30 PM Alfredo, George and everybody came to harvest avocados from my tree. WOW, there were lots of them! We finished that at 4:40 PM, prepared the vegetables for supper and then I went and got and bathed my nuang. At 5:00 PM I started cooking and then bathed myself. We ate supper, Barbara did the dishes and now it's 7:24 PM and we're waiting for George. I hope he's a little earlier tonight. The weather today was cloudy until 10:00 AM and then hot and dry the rest of the day. Now there are a few scattered clouds. AWANEN!

Thursday, July 9, 1987
My House, Gomez, Cabarroguis, Quirino

Barbara W. leave.

We got up at 5:00 AM and George left; he didn't come until 9:40 PM last night, but at least he came. We started the rice cooking, drank coffee and I took my nuang to pasture. I returned and talked with George and Alfredo for a few minutes and then came home and finished cooking. We ate, did dishes and got ready for the day and we were ready at about 6:40 AM. We took Barbara's stuff to Alfredo's – he was waiting. We put her stuff in the cart and they left. I then went to the farm and weeded three rows of corn. At 9:30 AM I went and found George and at 10:00 AM we went and got and bathed our nuangs and came home. I slept for 20 minutes, got up, ate lunch and then slept again until 1:00 PM. I got up, prepared my vegetables for supper and at 2:05 PM I returned to George's. At about 2:20 PM we took our nuangs to pasture and returned to the farm. I weeded two more rows of corn this afternoon, for a total of only five rows weeded today. I quit at 4:40 PM and went and found George. We went and got and bathed our nuangs at 5:10 PM and came home. I started cooking and bathed, finished cooking and now it's 6:27 PM. My supper is cooked and cooling. I hope George comes earlier tonight; he said he'll be here between 7:30 and 7:40 PM – we'll see what happens. The weather today was hot and dry again with no rain. Well it was really nice to have Barbara here for a while but it's nice to be rid of her too, you know the expression "after three days fish and visitors begin to smell bad." AWANEN!

Friday, July 10, 1987
My House, Gomez, Cabarroguis, Quirino

We got up at 4:50 AM and George left; he came at 7:45 PM last night. I started the rice, drank coffee and took my nuang to pasture. I returned and talked with George for a couple of minutes and then came home. I finished cooking, ate, did dishes and got ready for the day. I went and got my nuang and headed for the farm. George's whole family went today and they took lunch with them, so I did the same. George cut and cleaned *panaw* this morning and I weeded my farm. They all stopped for lunch at 10:30 AM, so I did the same. After eating, we rested until noon and then went back to work. This afternoon they weeded their farm and I weeded my farm; everybody was weeding except Alfredo and he was roofing the rest hut. The family left at about 3:45 PM except for George and Alfredo, who kept working on the rest hut, so I also stayed and kept weeding until about 4:15 PM. I weeded six rows of corn today and have five more rows to go. George and I got our nuangs and headed home at about 4:45 PM. I bathed my nuang, started my rice cooking and then bathed myself. Now it's 6:21 PM and supper is nearly cooked but not quite. Please George, come early tonight; I'm tired and have a bad cold. The weather today was only moderately hot and continued dry, but it was cloudy all day. There's been no rain in ten days now. AWANEN!

Saturday, July 11, 1987
My House, Gomez, Cabarroguis, Quirino

We got up at 5:10 AM and George left; he came at 8:00 PM last night. I started the rice cooking, drank coffee and took my nuang to pasture. I returned and talked with George for a couple of minutes and came home. I finished cooking, ate, did dishes and got ready for the day. I headed for the farm at about 6:40 AM, walking. I found George, he was weeding his corn. We talked for a few minutes and then I went to work weeding on my farm. I worked until 9:30 AM and then went and found George and at about 10:00 AM we headed home. We parted ways at the school, I got and bathed my nuang, returned home and ate lunch. I took a siesta from 11:40 AM to 12:30 PM and when I got up I prepared the vegetables for supper. At 1:30 PM I went to George's but he wasn't ready yet and it was cloudy, so I took my nuang to pasture and waited for him at the school. He pastured his nuang and we continued on to the farm, where I weeded my farm and he weeded his farm. I worked until 4:30 PM and I finished weeding all of the new part of my farm and started on the old part today. At about 4:45 PM we headed home, we got and bathed our nuangs and continued on home; he said he'll come early tonight. I bathed and cooked and now it's 6:16 PM and my vegetables are cooking. The weather today was 100% cloudy all day; there's a typhoon somewhere, but I don't know where. There was no rain or wind here. We need some rain soon. AWANEN!

Sunday, July 12, 1987
My House, Gomez, Cabarroguis, Quirino

Letters from Steve A. and Ardis B. Postcard from San & Jack G.

₱287 + 300 – 412 = ₱175							
Rice	300	Rides	6	Soap	9	Cigarettes	14
Marienda	18	Coffee	28	Food	21	Household	6
Misc.	10					TOTAL	₱412

I got up at 5:10 AM. George got up at 4:10 AM and left to pasture his nuang. He came at 7:30 PM last night. Alfredo is using my nuang today to pull a cart of avocados to Burgos so I cooked breakfast, drank coffee, ate, did dishes and got ready for the day. At 6:40 AM I headed for Burgos. I stopped at Rogel's, and Richard was there, so I was trapped for a half hour or so. After that I continued on to Gundaway and the post office. I let myself in and got the above mail and then went to market. I actually bought very little today but I needed a kaban of rice so I bought that. I finished my marketing at 9:30 AM, caught a jeepney to Burgos, arrived there at 10:00 AM, put my rice in Alfredo's cart, talked with him for a while and headed up the mountain via the high road. I made it home in a new record time – 32 minutes and 24 seconds. I got home, wrung the sweat out my T-shirt, unpacked, put things away and did laundry until 1:00 PM. I took a siesta for a bit and then swept the whole lawn. I fetched water and then, just as I returned, Alfredo was arriving at his house with my rice so I went and got it, asked George to come early and he said yes. Alfredo brought my nuang home, I cooked supper, ate, did dishes and now it's 6:50 PM. I had a good workout today. The weather today was hot and humid and 100% overcast – that typhoon must still be hanging around. AWANEN!

The photo just below (same as cover photo) was taken by Barb W. when she came and stayed with me from July 6th through July 9th. The grass roofed hut in the background is my house and the banana trees to the right of my house are the ones which I planted around a year ago. Of course the nuang which I am riding is my own. At this moment I am taking the nuang to the creek which is just below my house. This afternoon I will bathe her here, although it is not as nice of a spot for bathing her as the place shown in the photo way back on page 285 it is adequate when one is in a hurry.

Monday, July 13, 1987
My House, Gomez, Cabarroguis, Quirino

Letter to San & Jack G. Postcards to Dad, Tom & Barb H. and Sue T.

We got we got up at 5:00 AM and George left; he came at 7:10 PM last night – fairly early. I started the rice cooking, drank coffee and took my nuang to pasture. I returned and talked with George for a while and then came home, finished cooking, ate, did dishes, got ready for the day and the first thing I did was a postcard to Sue T. Then I wrote the letter to San and Jack G., a postcard to Tom and Barb H. and then one to Dad too. I put up *runo* for the utong beans in the lower garden and cleaned around the edges of the southeast garden. By then it was 10:30 AM and I was ready to siesta, but Richard showed up! We talked until noon, ate lunch and shortly after 1:00 PM we went and talked with Alfredo for a while. Then I moved my nuang and Richard and I headed for the farm. We walked up through George's farm and then went over to my farm, where we looked around. Lots of corn was blown over today due to the moderately strong winds. The typhoon is signal #1 now – SHIT! We weeded on my farm until 4:00 PM and then headed home. I got and bathed my nuang, gave Richard a bunch of books and he left. I started cooking, bathed and went and asked George to come early, but he said that they'll be eating late tonight. I came home, finished cooking, ate, did dishes and now it's 6:37 PM. George pulled a cart of charcoal to Burgos this morning and he rested in the afternoon. He's got a bad sore throat and I've got a bad cold. The weather today was cool, cloudy and windy. There was a light rain last night but not even enough to wet the ground. AWANEN!

Tuesday, July 14, 1987
My House, Gomez, Cabarroguis, Quirino

Letter to JB & Katie F.

We got up at 4:50 AM and George left; he came at 7:20 PM last night. I started the rice cooking, drank coffee and took my nuang to pasture. I returned and stopped to talk with George for a while and then came home, finished cooking, ate, did dishes and got ready for the day. At 6:40 AM I started walking to the farm, I found George there, talked with him for a few minutes and then I continued weeding on my farm. Today I worked on the winged bean area and at 9:30 AM George came to my farm. I showed him everything the new beans, the zucchini, the pepino, the blown down sweet corn and so on and then we went and got our nuangs, bathed them and continued home. I took a siesta from 10:30 to 11:30 AM, got up, ate lunch and then worked on highlighting words in the English-Ilokano dictionary for a while. At 1:00 PM I prepared vegetables for supper and at 2:00 PM I went to George's. At 2:20 PM we pastured our nuangs, but didn't return to the farm; I thought we were going to return, but we didn't, so I came back home and wrote a letter to JB and Katie and then highlighted more words in the dictionary. At 4:30 PM I went and asked George to come early tonight and he said that when they're done with supper he'll come. I went and got and bathed my nuang, bathed myself, cooked supper, ate and did dishes. Now it's 6:54 PM and I have a feeling that George will be late tonight, maybe 8:00 PM. The weather today was hot and dry with hot winds. The typhoon weather still hasn't left the area. It was cloudy from 3:00 PM until now, but there's been no rain yet. It was up to 92°F or more today. AWANEN!

Wednesday, July 15, 1987
My House, Gomez, Cabarroguis, Quirino

Letter to Bill & Andi J.

We got up at 5:05 AM and George left; he came at 7:40 PM last night. I started cooking breakfast, drank coffee and took my nuang to pasture. I happened to meet George on the trail as I was returning home and he was on his way to the farm at 5:30 AM. I returned home, finished cooking, ate, washed dishes, got ready for the day and headed for the farm at 6:35 AM. I got there and found George, we talked for a few minutes and then I went to work on weeding my winged beans again. George came and got me at 9:30 AM and we headed for home. We got our nuangs, bathed them and continued on home. I took a siesta from 10:30 to 10:50 AM only, got up, ate and tried to sleep again, but couldn't, so I did the letter to Bill and Andi J. At 1:00 PM I prepared vegetables for supper and highlighted more words in the dictionary. At 2:00 PM I went to George's and at 2:20 PM I asked him if he was going to return to the farm this afternoon. He said no, so I took my nuang to pasture and went to the farm by myself. I continued weeding the *pallang* until 4:45 PM and nearly finished it all. I headed for home, got my nuang and bathed her, came home, started cooking, bathed myself and then went and asked George to come early and he said yes. I finished cooking, ate, did dishes and now it's 6:49 PM and I'm waiting for George. The weather today – the hot and dry winds continued, the typhoon still hasn't left the area. The corn is really badly wilted, what's left standing. It clouded up at about 4:00 PM but there was no rain. AWANEN!

Thursday, July 16, 1987
My House, Gomez, Cabarroguis, Quirino

Letter to Steve A.

We got up at 5:05 AM and George left; he came at 7:35 PM last night. I started the rice cooking, drank coffee and took my nuang to pasture. I returned and talked with George for a little while and then came home. I finished cooking, ate, did dishes and got ready for the day. I headed for the farm at about 6:40 AM, found George and talked with him for a few minutes and then continued on to my farm and finished weeding the *pallang*. Then I started weeding the whole north and west edges of my farm. After that I helped George – he was cleaning around the Mandarin orange trees to the north of my farm. We quit at about 9:30 AM, George harvested vegetables for his family and we headed home. We got and bathed are nuangs and then continued on home. I bought a Coke to celebrate the finishing of weeding my farm. I took a siesta from 10:30 to 11:15 AM, got up, ate lunch and highlighted more words in the dictionary for a while. At 1:00 PM I prepared my vegetables for supper. At 1:45 PM I went to George's and a bunch of people were getting drunk there. At 2:00 PM I took my nuang to pasture and at 2:15 PM I returned to George's. At 2:25 PM we returned to the farm and George continued working around the Mandarin orange trees and I cut dead leaves off the banana trees. It feels like I did a good days work today. At 4:30 PM we headed home. We got our nuangs, bathed them and came home. At 5:10 PM I started cooking and now it's 6:46 PM, everything is done and I'm waiting for George. I hope he comes early tonight. The weather today was hot and dry. It was cloudy off and on and at 4:45 PM it showered lightly for about 45 minutes or so, but not enough to help out very much. AWANEN!

Friday, July 17, 1987
My House, Gomez, Cabarroguis, Quirino

Letters from Dad, Yip Chee H. and Vicki S. Postcard from San & Jack G.

₱287 + 300 – 155 = ₱320							
Cigarettes	20	Food	59	Rides	6	Marienda	32
Coffee	27	Kerosene	7	Misc.	4	TOTAL	₱155

We got up at 5:00 AM, I gave George my *wayway* and he left. He didn't come until 11:10 PM last night – there was another death in Gomez – Lakey Espinoza died. I cooked breakfast, drank coffee, ate, did dishes, got ready for the day and headed for Burgos at 6:40 AM. I got there and talked with Richard for a while and talked him into coming to Gundaway with me, so we headed off together for Gundaway. We stopped at the post office and I mailed the letters that I wrote over the last several days and got the above mail. Then we continued on to market and I bought the above items. We finished up at about 10:00 AM and returned to the post office; there was no more mail. Then we caught a jeepney for Burgos, arrived at the bottom of the high road at about 10:30 AM and I started climbing. I climbed up and arrived at home today in 33 minutes and 52 seconds; I think that's my second fastest time so far. I wrung the sweat out of my T-shirt, unpacked, put things away and slept from 11:45 AM to 1:00 PM. Then I got up and read mail and at 1:45 PM I went to George's. At about 2:20 PM we took our nuangs to pasture and I went to the farm, where George was cutting paths to plant banana trees. We worked until about 4:00 PM and headed home. We got our nuangs, let them drink, bathed them and continued on home. I cooked supper, bathed myself, ate, did dishes and now it's 6:47 PM and I'm waiting for George. I hope that he comes early tonight. The weather today was hot and dry and then it clouded up at about 3:30 PM and rained from about 4:30 to 5:30 PM, it wasn't a hard rain, just nice. AWANEN!

Saturday, July 18, 1987
My House, Gomez, Cabarroguis, Quirino

We got up at 5:00 AM and George left; he came at 7:15 PM last night. I started my rice cooking, drank coffee, took my nuang to pasture, returned and talked with George for a minute, came home, cooked quickly, ate, did dishes and got ready for the day. Before 6:30 AM I went and got my nuang and headed for the farm, where George and I harvested bananas. Today we got 22 *buligs* from the north banana plantation and 18 from the one above the bamboo area. Alfredo was there too, so we filled two carts with bananas and headed home at about 10:45 AM. We got home at about 11:25 AM, I bathed my nuang and took a siesta from 11:40 AM to 12:20 PM. I got up, ate lunch and then relaxed for a while. At 2:00 PM I went back to George's, but he said he's not going back to the farm today, so at about 2:20 PM I took my nuang to pasture, returned and worked on my Close-of-Service skills assessment questionnaire that the Peace Corps requested. I worked on it until it was completed and then I went and fetched water. At 4:00 PM I prepared my vegetables for supper, at 4:30 PM I went and got and bathed my nuang, lit my cooking fire, bathed myself and then I finished cooking, ate, did dishes and went to ask George to come early tonight. He said yes, but we'll have to wait and see. The weather today was cloudy off and on all day, but it was hot and there was no rain. It rained lately during the night last night but by the time we left for the farm the corn was wilted again. There's been really insufficient rain lately. AWANEN!

Sunday, July 19, 1987
My House, Gomez, Cabarroguis, Quirino

Letters to Ardis B. and Dave G.

I got up at 5:15 AM. George got up at 4:40 AM and left to pasture his nuang. He came at 7:35 PM last night. I started the rice, drank coffee and took my nuang to pasture. I returned and talked with George for a half hour or so and then came back home. George and Alfredo took the two carts of bananas to Burgos today to sell them. I finished cooking, ate, did dishes and got ready for the day. I started out by doing laundry from 7:30 to 9:30 AM or so and then I sprayed the bees nest in my eaves with Folidol and after a while I removed it. At 10:30 AM or so I went and got and bathed my nuang and then returned home and slept from about 11:00 AM until noon. I got up, ate lunch and then highlighted words in the dictionary until 1:30 PM, when I took my nuang back to pasture. By then George had returned from Burgos, so I talked with him for another half hour and then returned home. I highlighted more words in the dictionary until 4:00 PM and then prepared my vegetables for supper. At 4:30 PM I went and got and bathed my nuang and then I started cooking supper. I bathed myself, finished cooking, ate, washed dishes and went to George's to ask him to come early. He told me that they are going to the Celebration of the Dead at Lakey Espinoza's again tonight and that maybe he'll be here at around 11:00 PM or so. Now it's 7:17 PM. The weather today – it rained lightly during the night and then it was cloudy until noon. It rained lightly again from noon until about 2:00 PM and then it was cloudy the rest of the day. AWANEN!

Monday, July 20, 1987
My House, Gomez, Cabarroguis, Quirino

We got up at 5:30 AM and George left; he came at 2:15 this morning, which is why we slept in today. I couldn't sleep until George got here last night. I started cooking, drank coffee, took my nuang to pasture, returned and talked with George for a few minutes and then came home. I finished cooking, ate, did dishes and got ready for the day. George was repairing their cart today so I went through my #1 Journal and highlighted some important things. At about 9:30 AM I went back to George's and at 10:00 AM we went and got and bathed our nuangs. We returned home and I read the book *"Dune"* by Frank Herbert for a while and then slept from 11:00 AM to 1:00 PM. I got up and ate lunch, drank coffee and then at 2:00 PM I took my nuang back to pasture. I returned home and read the *"Dune"* book until 4:00 PM and then prepared my vegetables for supper. At 4:30 PM I went and asked George if he will be early tonight and he said yes. At 4:45 PM I went and got and bathed my nuang, bathed myself, cooked supper, ate and did dishes. Now it's 6:53 PM and I'm waiting for George. I hope he truly comes early. He told me this morning that he may stroll to Escoting tomorrow, but I hope not. Four of the Vietnamese guava seeds that I planted on June 6th are finally sprouting, it took them a long time to germinate it seems like. The weather today – it rained last night, but not very much. It was cloudy for a while this morning and then hot and dry until about 3:30 PM, when it clouded up again. Now there's some thunder and lightning so it will probably rain again tonight. AWANEN!

Tuesday, July 21, 1987
My House, Gomez, Cabarroguis, Quirino

₱320 + 60 – 5 = ₱375				
Alfredo repaid ₱60 of the ₱110 that he owed		+60	Cigarettes	5
			TOTAL	₱5

We got up at 5:00 AM and George left; he came at 7:40 PM last night and told me there are a bunch of Satanists with 666 tattooed on their foreheads here in Quirino, so we slept with our machetes within easy reach. I started the rice cooking, drank coffee and took my nuang to pasture. I returned and finished cooking, ate, did dishes and got ready for the day. I went to ask George if he's going to stroll to Escoting but he said that he's too lazy to go, so he continued working on the repairs to their nuang cart today. I cleaned in the tree nursery again, removed some dead banana leaves and at 10:15 AM I went and talked with George and we went and got and bathed our nuangs. I returned home and slept from 11:00 to 11:40 AM and then ate lunch, drank coffee and read the *"Dune"* book until 2:00 PM. Then I took my nuang to pasture and went to the farm. I harvested some winged beans and utong beans for supper plus a nice bunch of hot chili peppers. George stayed home this afternoon so I did some minor work around the farm until 4:00 PM and then headed for home. I got and bathed my nuang, came home, prepared the vegetables for supper, started cooking and bathed myself. I ate supper, did dishes, went and bought cigarettes and asked George to come early. He told me that the Satanists got three children in Zamora last night, really, what did they do with them? The weather today was mostly cloudy and windy all day – even the winds were hot again. The farm really looks bad. Now it's 7:00 PM and I'm waiting for George with my machete on the table beside me. AWANEN!

Wednesday, July 22, 1987
My House, Gomez, Cabarroguis, Quirino

We got up at 5:00 AM and George left; I went to get him last night at 8:00 PM and we came here at 8:25 PM. I started my rice cooking, drank coffee and took my nuang to pasture. I returned and talked with George for just a moment and then came home. I finished cooking, ate, did dishes, got ready for the day and headed for the farm before 6:30 AM. George planted *depig* bananas downhill from the corn, so I helped him plant 13 bananas and then we headed home at about 9:00 AM, kind of early. We got and bathed are nuangs and continued home. I took my dried hot chili peppers that I bought in Santiago on the 6th and crushed them at Alfredo's house and then I came back home and put the chili powder in the sun to dry even more. I took a siesta from 11:30 AM until noon, got up, ate lunch, drank coffee and read the *"Dune"* book until 2:00 PM. I went to George's to see if he was going back to the farm and he said no, so I went and pastured my nuang, returned to Alfredo's and pounded my dried chili pepper again. Then I came home and highlighted words in the dictionary until 4:00 PM. I prepared my vegetables for supper and at 4:40 PM I went and got and bathed my nuang and started cooking supper. I bathed myself, finished cooking, ate, did dishes and now it's 6:51 PM. I hope George comes early tonight. The weather today was hot, up to at least 94°F and dry all day, again it clouded up at about 5:00 PM and there was some thunder, but no rain so far and there probably won't be any. It's still 92°F. It was an uncomfortable day. AWANEN!

Thursday, July 23, 1987
My House, Gomez, Cabarroguis, Quirino

Letter to Dad.

₱375 – 5 = ₱370							
Cigarettes	5					TOTAL	₱5

We got up at 5:00 AM and George left; he came at 7:50 PM last night. I started my rice, drank coffee and took my nuang to pasture. George had already left for the farm so I returned home, finished cooking, ate, did dishes and got ready for the day. I headed for the farm at about 6:40 AM. George was cutting grass in the banana plantation so I cleaned dead leaves from banana trunks today. We did that only until 8:45 AM and then we both harvested some vegetables and headed for home. We got and bathed our nuangs and arrived home at about 9:30 AM. I read the *"Dune"* book until 10:30 AM and then took a siesta until noon. I got up, ate lunch, drank coffee and read the *"Dune"* book some more. At about 1:00 PM Alfredo came, wanting to borrow ₱300 because a blankets and pots and pans seller was at their house and they wanted to buy some stuff. SHIT! I gave it to him, so now he's in debt to me for ₱350. At 2:00 PM I went and asked George if he was going to return to the farm and he said no, so I took my nuang to pasture, returned home and read some more. I wrote the above letter to Dad and at 3:30 PM I prepared my vegetables for supper. At 4:15 PM I went and got my nuang and it started to rain at 4:30 PM. I started cooking, ate, did dishes and then bathed myself. Now it's 6:36 PM and I'm hoping that George will come early tonight. The weather today was cloudy off and on mostly all day, but hot. It clouded up totally at about 3:30 PM and there was a thunderstorm from 4:20 to 5:00 PM. It rained hard and the creek is flowing full, in fact very high. AWANEN!

Friday, July 24, 1987
My House, Gomez, Cabarroguis, Quirino

Letters from Barb W. and Cery A.

₱370 + 100 – 410 = ₱60							
Cigarettes	14	Food	153	Coffee	53	Rides	24
Marienda	29	Kerosene	7	Soap	38	Household	17
Ice Cream	20	Candy	7	Lunch	42	Misc.	6
						TOTAL	₱410

We got up at 5:00 AM, I gave George my *wayway* and he left; he came last night at 7:40 PM, after I hollered for him. I cooked breakfast, ate, did dishes and got ready for the day. I headed down the mountain for Burgos at 6:30 AM and talked Richard into going to Santiago with me, so off we went, not arriving there until after 9:00 AM.

We did marketing and ran into Bill S. at Marilen's and Bill talked Richard into going to Banaue with him, so after that I was alone. I went to the 456 Restaurant for lunch and finished with everything at about noon. I went to Santiago specifically to cash my July subsistence check. I got a jeepney for Gundaway shortly after noon, stopped at the post office and got the above mail. I had to wait at the post office until 1:30 PM for them to return from lunch. After that I continued on to Burgos and arrived at about 2:00 PM. I began climbing the mountain at 2:08 PM and arrived home at 2:52 PM. It took me 44 minutes today because I had a heavy pack. I didn't even really try to hurry. I wrung out my T-shirt, unpacked, put things away, read my mail, fetched water and at 4:00 PM I prepared my vegetables for supper. At 4:30 PM I went and asked George to please come early and he said yes, we'll see. Now it's 6:36 PM, I'm done eating and dishes are washed. Oh, I bathed too. The weather today was hot and dry all day. Again there was no rain. AWANEN!

Saturday, July 25, 1987
My House, Gomez, Cabarroguis, Quirino

Letter to Barb W.

We got up at 5:15 AM and George left; he came at 7:20 PM last night. I started my rice cooking, drank coffee and took my nuang to pasture. I returned and talked with George for a few minutes and then came home. I finished cooking, ate, did dishes got ready for the day and headed for the farm at about 6:45 AM. I helped George weed his corn today and we got some corn stalks to use for nuang food until about 9:45 AM and then we headed for home. I got and bathed my nuang and then played with the HP-71 calculating average monthly expenditures. I worked on that until about 12:30 PM for the annual expenditure survey and then I ate lunch. After that I took a siesta from 1:15 to 1:50 PM, drank coffee and took my nuang back to pasture. Alfredo stopped me to tell me to let my nuang eat some corn stalks too, so I hung out there until about 3:00 PM and then returned home. I played around with the expenditures survey some more until 4:00 PM and then prepared my vegetables for supper. I went and got my nuang from Alfredo's house, bathed her and returned home. I started my fire and bathed myself, finished cooking, ate, did dishes quickly and used the *lampaso* on the floor of the house. Now it's 6:38 PM and I'm waiting for George; he said he'll be early tonight but will he? I hope so. The weather today – there was light rain during the night and it was cloudy and relatively cool all day today. Not bad weather. It sprinkled a bit about 4:00 PM. AWANEN!

Sunday, July 26, 1987
My House, Gomez, Cabarroguis, Quirino

Postcard to San & Jack G.

₱60 + 300 – 0 = ₱360			
Alfredo repaid ₱300 that he owed me	+300	TOTAL	₱0

We got up at 5:10 AM and George left; he came at 8:05 PM last night. I started the rice cooking, drank coffee and took my nuang to pasture. I stopped and talked with George for a couple of minutes and then came home. I finished cooking, ate, did dishes and got ready for the day. I started out the day by doing laundry, and worked on that until 9:30 AM or so. After that I killed time for a while and at 10:00 AM I went and got and bathed my nuang. I returned home and killed some time and then I recalculated ALL averages of monthly expenditures for the last 19 months. Everything matches now. There was one small error back in December which threw everything off. After that I ate lunch, drank coffee and took a siesta from 12:15 to 1:00 PM. Alfredo came to return the ₱300 pesos that he borrowed on July 23rd and to talk for a while. After that I sprayed my utong beans for aphids; holy cow they were thick! By then it was 1:15 PM so Alfredo left and I took my nuang back to pasture. I returned and talked with George for a few minutes then came home and highlighted more words in the dictionary until 3:45 PM. Then I prepared my vegetables for supper and at 4:15 PM I went and got and bathed my nuang. I returned home, started supper and bathed myself. Now it's 6:41 PM, everything is done and I'm waiting for George. I hope he comes early tonight. The weather today was partly cloudy all day. It wasn't too hot and it wasn't too cold. There was no rain, although it was very threatening at around 4:00 PM. AWANEN!

Monday, July 27, 1987
My House, Gomez, Cabarroguis, Quirino

₱360 – 5 = ₱355					
Cigarettes	5			TOTAL	₱5

We got up at 5:10 AM and George left; he didn't come until 9:50 PM last night because they had a card game. I started cooking my rice, drank coffee and took my nuang to pasture. I returned, talked with George for a minute and then came home. I finished cooking, ate, did dishes and got ready for the day. Supposedly there was to be a forestry meeting today, but Efren didn't show up. I waited until 9:45 AM and then went and got and bathed my nuang. I met George at the creek and we came home together. I took a siesta from 10:30 until 11:45 AM; I didn't sleep last night until after 11:00 PM for some unknown reason. I got up, ate lunch, drank coffee and read the book *"Amaranth – Modern Prospects for an Ancient Crop"* and then highlighted words in the dictionary. At 2:00 PM I went to George's, asked him if he was going to return to the farm and he said no, so I took my nuang to pasture, returned home and highlighted more words in the dictionary. After that I sharpened both of my machetes and went and pounded more hot chili peppers at Alfredo's house. Then I returned home and at 4:00 PM I prepared my vegetables for supper. At 4:45 PM I went and got my nuang and the rain started. I returned home, cooked, ate, did dishes and then bathed. Now it's 6:47 PM and I hope George comes early tonight. The weather today was partly cloudy and hot and then at 3:30 PM it clouded up. At 4:45 PM there was a nice rain for about 45 minutes. Now it's cool and pleasant. AWANEN!

Tuesday, July 28, 1987
My House, Gomez, Cabarroguis, Quirino

We got up at 5:00 AM and George left; he came at 7:30 PM last night. I started my rice cooking, drank coffee and took my nuang to pasture. I returned and talked with George for just a moment and then came home. I finished cooking, ate, did dishes, got ready for the day and at 6:40 AM I headed for the farm. George was still cutting grass in the south banana plantation so I cleaned dead leaves from the stems of the banana trees. We worked on that until 9:00 AM or so and then we got more corn stalks for nuang food and headed home at about 9:30 AM. I got my nuang, we bathed our two nuangs together and then we continued home. I arrived at my house at about 10:30 AM, killed time for a while and then ate lunch at about 11:30 AM. I took a siesta from noon until 1:00 PM, got up, prepared my vegetables for supper, fetched water and at 2:00 PM I went to George's and found out that he was not returning to the farm after all because it was threatening rain. I pastured my nuang and came home. I read my *Newsweek* for a while, finished reading the *"Amaranth...."* book and killed time. I started cooking at 4:10 PM, ate, did dishes and then went and moved my nuang. I returned and asked George to come early and he said yes, but we'll have to wait and see. I bathed myself and now it's 6:26 PM, everything is done and I'm waiting for George already. The weather today was mostly cloudy all day and it wasn't too hot. Rain started at 3:00 PM and it's still continuing, a nice steady gentle rain. Okay George, you can come anytime now. AWANEN!

Wednesday, July 29, 1987
My House, Gomez, Cabarroguis, Quirino

₱355 – 20 = ₱335						
Marienda	12	Cigarettes	8		TOTAL	₱20

We got up at 5:15 AM and George left; he came at 6:58 PM last night. I started my rice, drank coffee, took my nuang to pasture, returned and George was eating, so I just came home. I finished cooking, ate, did dishes and got ready for the day. I went to Alfredo's and he and I went to Burgos in search of the document for my nuang. We found the people that have it, but the bank is still holding it for collateral. The original owners still owe ₱1,500 pesos on it, SHIT! We went to Rogel's canteen, ate marienda, talked for a while and headed up the mountain again. We got home at about 10:45 AM and I went to see if George had got my nuang for me; he had, so I came home, ate lunch at 11:30 AM and then took a siesta from 12:15 to 1:45 PM. When I got up at 2:00 PM, I went to George's to see if he was going to return to the farm and he said yes so we pastured our nuangs and went to the farm. He cut grass in the banana plantations some more and I cleaned more dead banana leaves from the banana stems and also from around them. We worked until about 4:15 PM and then headed home. We got and bathed our nuangs and came home. I bathed myself and then started cooking at 5:15 PM. I ate, did dishes and now it's 6:46 PM and I'm hoping George will be here soon. The weather today was mostly cloudy all day, but hot. Thunder started at about 4:15 PM and rain started at about 5:30 PM and is still continuing now, a nice gentle rain. AWANEN!

Thursday, July 30, 1987
My House, Gomez, Cabarroguis, Quirino

Letter to Chris & Mary M.

₱335 – 3 = ₱332			
Cigarettes 3			TOTAL ₱3

We got up at 5:10 AM and George left; he came at 7:30 PM last night. I started my rice, drank coffee and took my nuang to pasture. I returned and talked with George for just a moment and then came home. I finished cooking, ate, did dishes and got ready for the day. I did laundry from 7:00 to 9:00 AM, even my blanket and doormat rags and then I killed time until 9:45 AM. I went and got and bathed my nuang and by then George had returned from the farm, so I went and talked with him for a few minutes and then returned home. I took a siesta from 11:00 to 11:30 AM and then got up, ate lunch and drank coffee. I killed time for a while and then went and fetched water. At 1:00 PM I prepared my vegetables for supper. At 2:00 PM I took my nuang back to pasture. I thought George had gone to the farm so I headed there, but I met him coming back from pasturing his nuang, so we didn't go to the farm. I crushed some more dried chili peppers at his house, came home, did the letter to Chris and Mary and asked Chris to send some winter clothes to Oregon for me [keep reading to December to discover why]. Then I highlighted words in the dictionary some more. At 4:30 PM I went and got and bathed my nuang and asked George to come early; he said yes, but we'll see what happens. Then I bathed myself, cooked, ate and did dishes. Now it's 6:50 PM and I'm waiting for George; I fear he'll be late tonight. The weather was partly cloudy and then bright sun until 4:00 PM, at which point it clouded up and threatened rain. Fortunately or unfortunately there has, so far, been none yet though. AWANEN!

Friday, July 31, 1987
My House, Gomez, Cabarroguis, Quirino

Letter from Katie F. Postcards from San & Jack G. and Liz & Randy.

₱332 – 147 = ₱185							
Rides	4	Coffee	27	Cigarettes	15	Marienda	41
Food	38	Kerosene	7	Misc.	15	TOTAL	₱147

We got up at 5:00 AM, I gave George my *wayway* and he left; he came at 7:30 PM last night. I cooked breakfast, ate, did dishes got ready for the day and headed for Burgos at 6:40 AM. I talked with Richard until nearly 8:30 AM and then caught a jeepney to Gundaway. I stopped at the post office and got the above mail and then continued on to market. Today I bought primarily for stocks and when finished I went back to the post office and got the mail that had arrived today. After that I caught a ride to Burgos and headed up the high road. I climbed the mountain in the fastest time yet – 32 minutes and 18 seconds. After wringing out my T-shirt and drying out for a few minutes I went to talk with George for a few minutes and then came home, put things away and did laundry. After that I took a siesta from 1:30 to 2:00 PM and then I took my nuang to pasture and came home. I calculated July's expenses, visitors and strolls and then washed my water jug and fetched water. By then it was 4:15 PM so I prepared my vegetables for supper. At 4:45 PM I went and got and bathed my nuang and then bathed myself and cooked supper. Now it's 6:07 PM and my vegetables are nearly cooked. I hope George comes very early tonight, I'm tired and want to sleep early. The weather today was hot and dry all day. There was no rain last night and although it's now threatening rain, it looks like maybe there will be none again. AWANEN!

Saturday, August 1, 1987
Malate Pension, Manila

₱185 + 300 – 285 = ₱200							
Rides	127	Cigarettes	20	Ice Cream	3	Candy	7
Food	56	Marienda	35	Meals	30	Misc.	7
						TOTAL	₱285

We got up at 5:00 AM, I gave George my *wayway*, leftover food, said goodbye and he left. He came last night at 7:20 PM. I drank coffee, got ready for the day, took my bag of valuables to Alfredo's house and headed down the mountain at 5:45 AM. I caught a jeepney to Santiago and arrived there at 8:00 AM. I finished the Peace Corps cost questionnaire at Marilen's and then I went to the Pantranco Bus Terminal and caught a 9:20 AM bus to Manila. I arrived in Manila at 4:30 PM and I got off at Balintawak, took a jeepney to Monumento and then the LRT to Quirino Avenue. I got to Malate Pension, bathed, drank a Coke, talked with people for a while and then went to the airport. Dave and Vicki did not arrive on the 8:30 PM flight and according to the flight manifests which the airport people were kind enough to search for me, they were not on the flight which would arrive at 11:30 PM flight or the 12:30 AM flight, so I headed back to Malate Pension at 11:00 PM. SHIT! What the hell's going on with them? Oh well, now it's 11:22 PM, way past my bedtime. Oh, including last night, George has slept at my house 391 nights now. AWANEN!

Sunday, August 2, 1987
Malate Pension, Manila

₱200 + 300 – 388 = ₱112							
Meals	165	Rides	62	Cigarettes	23	Phone	47
Clothes	15	Food	53	Marienda	23	TOTAL	₱388

I got up a little late, at 5:30 AM, showered, got ready for the day and went downstairs for pre-breakfast. I talked with people until 9:30 AM and then went to the Seafront Restaurant for brunch with four other people. We hung out at the Seafront until 1:30 PM eating and talking and then we returned to Malate Pension. For some unknown reason they took away my flip-flops when they cleaned the room and they can't find them either, so I had to go to Robinson's and get a new pair. After that I returned to the pension and relaxed for an hour, showered again and Willie and I went to supper. From there I continued on to the airport at 7:00 PM. I checked the incoming flight manifests and finally found Dave and Vicki's name on the flight arriving from Seoul at 11:45 PM, so I waited around until their plane arrived and met them, finally. Oh, I forgot to say that I called Vicki's house when I went to Robinson's Department Store to get a new pair of flip-flops and found out they were for sure still coming. Anyway, after I met them we came to Malate, talked until 1:40 AM and then slept. It seems that they had misunderstood their tickets coming from Fairbanks. Their flight was scheduled to leave at exactly 12:00 AM and they got the date wrong. Stupid airlines, scheduling flights at 12:00 AM, how many people come on the wrong day I wonder, probably a lot of them. AWANEN!

Monday, August 3, 1987
Malate Pension, Manila

Traveling with Dave & Vicki M.

₱112 + 300 – 327 = ₱85							
Meals	230	Rides	33	Clothes	10	Postage	54
						TOTAL	₱327

I got up very late, at 6:00 AM, showered, got ready for the day and went downstairs. Much to my surprise Dave and Vicki were already down there waiting for me.

We ate breakfast and then walked down Mabini Street so that they could change some money. Then we continued on to United Nations Avenue to find an American Express office so I could get my new American Express card. It couldn't be done at that office and they told me that I had to go to the Makati office tomorrow. We took the LRT to Quirino Avenue and went to the Peace Corps Office. I did my business there and then we took the LRT downtown and continued on to Chinatown. We ate lunch in Chinatown and then we went to Quiapo to search for new Dragon brand flip-flops. After that we caught a jeepney to Mabini, but we ended up in Cubao. So we got the correct jeepney and got to Malate Pension at about 5:00 PM. We relaxed until 6:00 PM and got ready to go to the Seafront Restaurant for supper, but on the way we stopped at Robinson's Department Store to buy Vicki some new shoes and a nice blouse to go to the Seafront in. Then we went to the Seafront Restaurant, drank some beer during happy hour and ate Mongolian Barbeque. After that we came back to Malate Pension at 9:00 PM. Now it's 9:35 PM and Dave and I are having a final beer for him and a Coke for me before sleeping. AWANEN!

Tuesday, August 4, 1987
Malate Pension, Manila

Traveling with Dave & Vicki M.

₱85 + 1,546 – 1,407 = ₱225							
Airplane	1,247	Rides	25	Marienda	35	Postcards	10
Laundry	40	Supper	50			TOTAL	₱1,407

I got up at 5:30 AM, got ready for the day and went downstairs. I was first today. Dave and Vicki arrived a few minutes later, we drank coffee and after a little bit we ordered breakfast. After breakfast Dave and I went to get tickets to go to Palawan tomorrow. Then I changed a hundred-dollar traveler's check and we cruised through Pistang Filipino and then after that we returned to Malate Pension. We got Vicki and then we went to Makati to get my new American Express card; the office wasn't too hard to find and the process was not very difficult. After that we went to lunch at the Jade Garden, finished eating at about 1:25 PM or so and then we went to Malacanang Palace and took the tour. We saw Imelda Marcos' legendary 3,000 plus shoe collection, as well as everything else and we finished that at about 4:00 PM or so. Then we took a jeepney to Quiapo and then to Mabini. We cruised through Pistang Filipino again with Vicky and then returned to Malate Pension. After a while we ate supper and talked and now it's 10:11 PM and we're tired, burned out and going to sleep. AWANEN!

Wednesday, August 5, 1987
Duchess Pension, Puerto Princesa, Palawan

Postcard to George.
Traveling with Dave & Vicki M.

₱225 + 745 – 265 = ₱705							
Rides	31	Cigarettes	22	Lodging	100	Marienda	10
Food	65	Rice	32	Household	5	TOTAL	₱265

I got up at 5:30 AM, showered, got ready for the day, went downstairs, met Dave and Vicki and we had breakfast. I did a postcard to George and mailed it and then we packed and went to change money for Dave and Vicki. We went to the Peace Corps Office for Band-Aids and some other first-aid equipment and then we bought some fruit at the San Andreas fruit market. We returned to Malate Pension, got our stuff and checked out. We went to the airport and our flight left for Puerto Princesa at noon. We arrived a little bit after 1:00 PM and took a tricycle to the Duchess Pension, drank some Coke and talked with Joe P. and Scotty O. and decided to go to the underground river, sounds like a cool place. Vicki and I went to market and got some food. We left Dave behind at the pension, he's got the shits. Then we returned to the pension and the park ranger offered to take us in his boat for ₱50 pesos each, so we said yes. After a while we went to the refugee camp for supper; they had good food. We returned to the Duchess Pension and talked until a few minutes ago. Now it's 9:57 PM – past bedtime again. AWANEN!

Thursday, August 6, 1987
Cabin in Puerto Princesa Subterranean River National Park, Puerto Princesa, Palawan

Postcard to George.
Traveling with Dave & Vicki M.

₱705 – 113 = ₱592							
Lodging	30	Meals	32	Rides	47	Soap	3
Cigarettes	1					TOTAL	₱113

We got up at 5:30 AM, got ready for the day and then we went downstairs at the Duchess Pension and ate breakfast. Then we waited for the park ranger until 8:45 AM or so. He came by to pick us up in his jeepney then we went back to the jeepney terminal, got more passengers and headed for Bakeli at 9:15 AM. We arrived at Bakeli at 10:45 AM or so and by the time they were done loading the boat it was noon. The park rangers suggested that we eat, but the restaurant was out of food, so we left. We were out on the boat until about 3:00 PM and then walked two kilometers to the Puerto Princesa Subterranean River National Park headquarters. We got checked in to a cabin and after a while we took a walk to the swimming beach. Dave bought six lobsters for supper and the park staff cooked them for us, so at about 7:00 PM we had supper and talked and then filtered some water with Dave's Katadyn water filter. Now it's 9:16 PM and bedtime. The weather today was hot and dry until 2:00 PM and then there was light rain for part of the boat ride. It was so cold I had goose bumps! AWANEN!

[If you go back to the map on page 284 and look to the southwest you can easily find Palawan Island and Puerto Princesa. The national park is a ways north of Puerto Princesa and on that bump of land just to the south of the "n" in the word Palawan.]

Friday, August 7, 1987
Cabin in Puerto Princesa Subterranean River National Park, Puerto Princesa, Palawan

Traveling with Dave & Vicki M.

We got up at 5:00 AM, the earliest in a week. We went and bathed and got ready for the day, but then we sat around and waited until nearly 9:00 AM for breakfast to be ready. We finally ate breakfast, just rice and pineapple, and then we headed off on the two kilometer trail to the underground river. It was a beautiful trail, what they call a monkey trail, a trail built of boards, catwalks and ladders – and it was STEEP! We got to the underground river and then they took us for a two kilometer boat ride up the river. It was really incredible, very cool, some kind of bats and some kind of swallows flying all around us. Then we returned back to the mouth of the river and after a swim and some relaxation on the beach we headed back to our hut. We arrived at about 1:30 PM or so and Vicki did some laundry, Dave filtered some water and I helped and watched. I didn't tell them that the water in Manila was undoubtedly more dangerous to drink than it is here. I took a siesta for an hour, got up at 4:00 PM and it rained. We watched the sunset from the beach and then ate supper. Now it's 8:41 PM and Dave and Vicki have already crashed; I'm going to as soon as I finish this. The weather today was hot and dry until 3:00 PM and then cloudy. At 4:00 PM a thunderstorm came through but then it cleared up again. There's nearly a full moon tonight. AWANEN!

Saturday, August 8, 1987
Nancy's House, Tagnipa, Puerto Princesa, Palawan

Traveling with Dave & Vicki M.

₱592 – 133 = ₱459							
Lodging	85	Rice	16	Food	17	Beer	15
						TOTAL	₱133

We got up at 5:00 AM, got ready for the day, bathed and then at about 7:00 AM we settled our bill, ate and checked out. We started walking the 17 kilometer trail to Tagnipa at about 7:55 AM. It was a long hard walk in the hot sun. I noticed that there were lots of nuangs here with torn out nose holes. We saw a couple of monkeys, stopped and patched up Vicki's blistered foot, crossed a nostril deep lagoon, after searching for a place that was ONLY nostril deep, but Vicki had to swim for it because she's shorter than Dave and I. We hit Cabayugan at 11 kilometers and it was about lunch time, so we took a break and then continued on for the remaining six kilometers. We got caught in a light rain and finally managed to get to Tagnipa at about 1:30 PM. We sat out a rainstorm and rested and then we asked the canteen lady where to stay and she said "here", so we went and searched for some rice, a squash and some drinks and returned to her home. After a while we played Frisbee and got the local kids to play with us, finally, although they were too shy to take part for quite a while. You should have heard the laughter and seen the smiles! The lady cooked spaghetti for us and really put on the hospitality. Now it's 7:19 PM and the weather today was sunny and warm until 12:50 PM, and then there was light rain until 2:30 PM. After that it was nice weather again. AWANEN!

Sunday, August 9, 1987
Malate Pension, Manila

Traveling with Dave & Vicki M.

₱459 – 159 = ₱300							
Rides	75	Meals	77	Cigarettes	7	TOTAL	₱159

I got up at 5:15 AM, went outdoors at Nancy's house and played with the dog until Dave and Vicki got up, then we talked until breakfast was ready, ate and got ready for the day. At about 7:30 AM we went to the boat place but the boat didn't come, so ultimately we had to hire a boat for ₱300 to get from Tagnipa to Bakeli. There were lots of problems with the boat – they had to pull the prop shaft and fix something with that and then they had to play with the carburetor, but finally the guy got it running and we got into by Bakeli at about noon or so. It was only supposed to be a one-hour trip, HA! Then we waited until 3:00 PM for the jeepney to go to Puerto Princesa. We finally got into Puerto Princesa at about 5:00 PM and we went to the Duchess Pension to bathe and repack. After that we went to the airport to try and get on a plane. We lucked out and got on a flight that got us into Manila at about 9:15 PM. We went straight to Malate Pension, ate supper and now it's 11:02 PM and we are going to crash immediately. AWANEN!

Monday, August 10, 1987
St. Mary's Pension, Baguio City, Benguet

Traveling with Dave & Vicki M.

₱300 + 185 – 220 = ₱265							
Lodging	25	Rides	142	Souvenir	5	Cigarettes	30
Meals	18					TOTAL	₱159

I got up at 5:10 AM, bathed, went downstairs and waited for coffee until Dave and Vicki came down. We ate breakfast and checked out then we went to the PAL Office [Philippine Airlines] to get a ₱185 refund on each of our tickets from Puerto Princesa last night [I can't recall why we were entitled to this refund, but they gave it to us, so I guess we were]. After that we went to the bank and I bought some 1 centavo coins and Vicki bought some of the new money. Then we took a taxi to the Pantranco Bus Terminal and took a 10:25 AM ordinary bus to Baguio City. It was a pretty uneventful ride to Baguio City and we arrived there at about 2:30 PM. We took a taxi to St. Mary's Pension, got checked in and then shortly after that Vicki and I went to Camp John Hay to try and do some laundry, but they wouldn't let us do it, so we returned to the pension and after a while we went to Shakey's Pizza for supper. When we finished we returned to St. Mary's Pension and talked until a few minutes ago. Now it's 9:29 PM and bedtime. The weather today was rainy in Baguio City from the time we arrived until now. AWANEN!

Tuesday, August 11, 1987
St. Mary's Pension, Baguio City, Benguet

Postcard to George.
Traveling with Dave & Vicki M.

₱265 + 200 – 140 = ₱325							
Meals	50	Marienda	24	Rides	6	Clothes	30
Cigarettes	25	Misc.	5			TOTAL	₱140

I got up at 5:30 AM and there was no water to bathe, so I just brushed my teeth and waited for Dave and Vicki to wake up. They were up and ready at 7:30 AM or so and we went to Session Road and ate breakfast at the 456 Restaurant. Then we went to the Maharlika Livelihood Center for looking around and we ran into Kevin, Patty and Michael and went for marienda with them. After that we went to the public market and did some shopping. Dave and Vicki bought a bunch of blankets and so on and then at noon we returned to St. Mary's Pension. We all napped from about 1:00 to 2:00 PM and then at about 3:00 PM we went to the Easter School Weaving Room and Dave and Vicki bought a bunch of stuff. After that we returned to St. Mary's again and then we took a taxi to The Attic, where Dave proceeded to get pretty plastered, so we ate supper there too; we were there from 5:00 to 9:00 PM. Oh, I forgot, we went to Burnham Park this morning too. All in all, today was pretty long and dull for me; I'm tired, burned out, tired of hearing stories about firefighting, their dog, Alaska bullshit and so on. I'm really wondering how long I can make it when I return to Alaska. The weather today was cool in the morning and then hot; by 6:00 PM it was raining again. Now it's 9:36 PM and time to sleep. AWANEN!

Wednesday, August 12, 1987
St. Mary's Pension, Baguio City, Benguet

Traveling with Dave & Vicki M.

₱325 + 500 – 505 = ₱320							
Soap	5	Presents	20	Meals	90	Marienda	52
Lodging	105	Laundry	95	Candy	10	Rides	3
Food	10	Ice Cream	15	Blankets	100	TOTAL	₱505

I got up at 5:20 AM and got ready for the day. I woke up Dave and Vicki at 6:00 AM, the taxi came and got us at 6:30 AM and took us to breakfast. After breakfast we went to a wood carving shop and I special ordered a carved wooden nuang with a calf so that I can have a nice nuang souvenir to take back to Alaska with me. Dave and Vicki bought a few things and then we went to a silversmith shop and Dave and Vicki bought a bunch of stuff there. After that we went to the Banaue Handicrafts store to look around and then we went to the bank to change some dollars for Dave and Vicki. We returned to the public market and bought more blankets and I got a blanket too. Then we returned to the Banaue Handicrafts store because Dave and Vicki wanted to buy more stuff, so they bought a bunch more there and then we returned to St. Mary's Pension, took a siesta and then we went out to supper. After supper we walked home. We saw lots of things I'd like to own today, but which I can't afford – I'm a bit jealous of Dave and Vicki, they bought some really nice things today. Now it's 9:29 PM and I'm tired, but have to pack yet. Tomorrow we're leaving here. The weather today was cold and then hot, but no rain until about 7:00 PM and then it rained a little bit and stopped. AWANEN!

Thursday, August 13, 1987
Happy Home Inn – Bontoc, Mountain

Traveling with Dave & Vicki M.

₱320 – 155 = ₱165							
Rides	70	Food	6	Coke	18	Lodging	20
Meals	20	Misc.	21			TOTAL	₱155

I got up at 5:40 AM, quickly woke up Dave and Vicki, brushed my teeth and went and found a taxi. We used that to go to the Dangwa Tranco Bus Terminal for breakfast and then we got our tickets to Bontoc and boarded the bus. We left Baguio

City at 7:00 AM and we had a long and slow bus ride to Bontoc. It was rainy, windy and cloudy most of the day so not too great as far as being able to see the amazing scenery which I knew there was! Vicki got about half motion sick so she didn't have too good of a time at all. We got to Bontoc at about 3:30 PM, checked in at the Happy Home Inn and Dave got a good start on two or three bottles of San Miguel. After that we went to the museum and to the market. We got a squash for supper and then returned to the Happy Home Inn. At 6:30 PM we went down to eat and now it's 8:13 PM. I'm going to go and talk with Dave for a few minutes before I crash and then I'll sleep. Dave wants to come back to the Philippines and bring a three-wheeler with him, I can't believe this guy – he's really something else. Anyway, we're all having a good time, at least I hope so. AWANEN!

Friday, August 14, 1987
Stairway Lodge – Banaue, Ifugao

Traveling with Dave & Vicki M.

₱165 + 300 – 189 = ₱276							
Lodging	20	Meals	89	Rides	50	Cigarettes	15
Presents	15					TOTAL	₱189

I got up at 5:00 AM, got ready for the day and went downstairs at 5:40 AM. Dave and Vicki came down shortly after, we ate breakfast, got ready for the day and went to the Banaue bus stop. We left Bontoc at 7:40 AM and got into Banaue at 10:05 AM. We went directly to the Stairway Lodge and they didn't have any rooms cleaned yet so we drank coffee and waited until they finished cleaning and then we checked in and went and looked around for a while. We then went to change some dollars for Dave and Vicki again and they looked around in several shops and bought some stuff. After a while we ate lunch, they bought some more things and then we returned to the Stairway Lodge. We took a siesta from 2:15 to 3:00 PM then Dave and Vicki packed their new purchases. By-and-by Frederick came home and came upstairs to talk with us for a while and then we went downstairs for supper. Now it's 8:54 AM and Frederick and I are going to bed together soon. [Frederick was a real sex hound, so use your imagination to visualize what we did together.] AWANEN!

Saturday, August 15, 1987
Host Family, Bonfal East, Bayombong, Nueva Vizcaya

Traveling with Dave & Vicki M.

₱276 + 300 – 224 = ₱352							
Machete for George	150	Meals	25	Rides	44	Cigarettes	5
						TOTAL	₱224

I got up at 5:00 AM, got ready for the day, packed up again and then went downstairs at the Stairway Lodge. We ate breakfast and after breakfast we went to the Banaue public market and searched for machetes, but there were none, so we returned to one of the shops and I bought a new machete for George – a really nice one. Then we went back to the Stairway Lodge, got our stuff and found a jeepney headed for Solano. We left Banaue at 8:00 AM, got to Solano and took a tricycle from there to Bonfal East, arriving there just before noon. After lunch Dave, Vicki, Ronald and I went to Solano to get some food and then we returned home and went to the farm to get some sugar cane and eat some coconuts. After that we returned home, Ronald went and bought some beer and we drank beer until suppertime. We ate supper and then it rained really hard. Now it's 8:06 PM and I'm going to sleep soon. Dave and Vicki are both badly affected by food or water or maybe both, they've had diarrhea for days and Dave vomited several times last night. I fear that it's a bummer of a trip for them, but I hope that at least some parts of it are fun and enjoyable. AWANEN!

Sunday, August 16, 1987
Host Family, Bonfal East, Bayombong, Nueva Vizcaya

Traveling with Dave & Vicki M.

₱352 – 15 = ₱337							
Cigarettes	15					TOTAL	₱15

We got up late, at 6:00 AM, and after a while we ate breakfast and got ready for the day. Then we began to make a rice cake and we worked on that until 11:00 AM. After we finished that I went upstairs and took a siesta for a while. I got up and killed more time, ate lunch, killed more time, took a siesta again from 3:00 to 4:00 PM, got up and the whole house was full of people! They all wanted their pictures taken with all of the Americanos, that plus the fact that today was Ronald's 18th birthday brought people from the entire neighborhood. After all of the picture-taking we ate again. It seems like we ate all day long today, one thing after another. Now it's 9:08 PM and I'm tired and going to crash. AWANEN!

Monday, August 17, 1987
My House, Gomez, Cabarroguis, Quirino

Letters from Vicki K. (2), Chris & Mary M., Steve A., Tom & Barb H., Keith H., Dave G. and State of Alaska Dept. of Revenue. Postcards from San & Jack G. (4) and Katie F.

Dave & Vicki M. staying here.

₱337 + 500 – 295 = ₱542							
Cigarettes	13	Food	113	Rides	44	Coffee	102
Household	19	Postage	4			TOTAL	₱295

We got up at 6:00 AM again, drank coffee, bathed and then after a while we ate breakfast. We got ready, said our good-byes and took a tricycle to Solano. We arrived there at about 8:40 AM and had to wait until 10:00 AM for a bus to Santiago. We got to Santiago at about 11:00 AM, went to the bank, did marketing and then we went to Letty's Restaurant for a snack. We left Letty's at about 1:00 PM and caught a jeepney to Gundaway. We had to wait until 2:30 PM for the workers to return to the post office from lunch. I got the above mail and then we got another jeepney bound for Burgos. We got to Burgos and started walking up the mountain at 3:35 PM. We arrived at my house at about 5:15 PM and I went directly to George's for a few minutes to say hello and talk while Dave and Vicki relaxed. I returned home and unpacked and after a little while I started cooking. We ate, did dishes in the dark and now it's 9:15 PM and we're all tired and ready to sleep. The weather today – well, Dave & Vicki are experiencing their first typhoon; it rained all day and the wind is getting stronger and stronger as time passes, bummer. AWANEN!

Tuesday, August 18, 1987
My House, Gomez, Cabarroguis, Quirino

Dave & Vicki M. staying here.

₱542 + 50 – 0 = ₱592			
Alfredo return ₱50 – debt fully repaid	+50	TOTAL	₱0

Typhoon Ising!

We got up at 6:00 AM, late because of the typhoon. I started the rice cooking, drank coffee and went to George's to move my nuang but he was already gone so I returned home and finished cooking. We ate breakfast, told stories and got ready for the day. After a while we did dishes and watched the typhoon. I went to George's, took them there remembrances and asked when we should go and move our nuangs. George said around noon so we went at noon and it was raining really hard, so I just came home and laid down for a while, but I couldn't sleep. We ate some bananas, drank coffee, talked and at 1:40 PM the rain stopped for a while so George and I went and moved our nuangs. When we returned it was raining again so I hung out at George's for an hour, told stories about our adventures and then came home at 3:00 PM. I went and fetched water and at 4:15 PM started cooking mungo beans for supper. At 5:00 PM I went to move my nuang, in the rain. Supper was cooked at 7:30 PM, we ate, did dishes and now it's 8:58 PM and we're all tired and burned out, ready to sleep again. The weather today – Typhoon Ising continued all day. There were strong winds all night. All of my banana trees were blown over, the farm was destroyed and we're all poor again this year, damn typhoon. AWANEN!

Wednesday, August 19, 1987
My House, Gomez, Cabarroguis, Quirino

Dave & Vicki M. staying here.

₱592 – 2 = ₱590				
Cigarettes	2			TOTAL ₱2

We got up at 5:30 AM, started the rice cooking, drank coffee and I went to move my nuang. I stopped and talked with George for a few minutes and then came home. We finished cooking, ate, did dishes and then we did laundry. After that we removed the broken coffee tree from beside the porch. We put the clothesline prop back up and then drank coffee again. At 10:30 AM we all went and got and bathed my nuang and returned home. I swept the north yard and then took a siesta from noon to 1:00 PM. I cleaned up the blown down banana trees below the house and then took my nuang to pasture again. I returned and talked with George for a few minutes and then came home. Dave swept part of the south yard and I pulled weeds behind him, then we removed the uprooted papaya tree and gave Alfredo all the unripe papayas. At about 3:20 PM or so, a bunch of people started coming until there were 16 people here staring at poor Dave and Vicki! They all finally left at about 4:50 PM, I went and got and bathed my nuang, we cooked supper, ate and did dishes. Now it's 7:32 PM; we're done pretty early tonight. The weather today – it showered lightly on and off most of the day. Needless to say, our laundry is not dry. We did quite a bit of cleanup today, it feels good. AWANEN!

Thursday, August 20, 1987
My House, Gomez, Cabarroguis, Quirino

Dave & Vicki M. staying here.

We got up at 5:30 AM, started the rice cooking, drank coffee and I took my nuang to pasture. I returned and talked with George for a few minutes and then came home. I finished cooking, Vicki and I ate breakfast, but Dave kept sleeping. We did the dishes, got ready for the day and then after a while Vicki and I went to the farm and looked at the typhoon damage – it was BAD! We harvested a bunch of sweet corn and a few utong beans, talked with George for a while – he was planting a few banana trees today – already getting a start on replacing the ones that were destroyed by the typhoon. LIFE GOES ON! At 9:00 AM we all started for home. We got to George's house a bit before 10:00 AM and I gave them a bunch of sweet corn and gave them instructions on how to cook it. Then we came home. Dave was finally awake and he got up when we returned. We went and got and bathed my nuang, returned home and sat around talking. We ate lunch at 12:30 PM, took my nuang back to pasture at 2:00 PM – Vicki rode the nuang to pasture and did pretty good. Dave stayed at the house. We returned home, killed time until 3:45 PM or so and then I prepared supper stuff. Dave wanted fried potatoes, okay. We cooked everything, ate, did dishes and now it's 7:49 PM and we're done with everything. Dave didn't gone farther from the house today than the creek. He's constipated and he hasn't bathed since he's been here either. The weather today was partly cloudy but mostly hot and sunny. The ground is drying out pretty good. AWANEN!

Friday, August 21, 1987
My House, Gomez, Cabarroguis, Quirino

Dave & Vicki M. leave.

Letter from Barb W. Postcard from Sue T.

₱592 – 270 = ₱322							
Cigarettes	13	Batteries	39	Food	44	Rides	35
Postage	4	Ice Cream	24	Coke	6	Breakfast	19
Candy	7	Household	6	Marienda	14	Haircut	5
Counting error correction			54			TOTAL	₱270

We got up at 5:00 AM, drank coffee, ate leftover corn, went and gave George my *wayway* and we headed down the mountain for Burgos at 5:45 AM. We got a jeepney bound for Santiago at 7:00 AM and we got to Santiago at about 8:05 AM. We ate breakfast at the 456 Restaurant and then went to the Pantranco Bus Terminal. Dave and Vicki managed to get a 9:00 AM bus bound for Manila. I mailed my Myers-Briggs indicator thing that the Peace Corps asked for, I got a haircut, did some minor shopping and ran into Keith. We ate ice cream together and then I got out of Santiago at 10:30 AM. I got to Gundaway at noon, got the above my eye and continued on to Burgos. I climbed the mountain via the high road and got home at 1:00 PM. I unpacked, put things away and then took a siesta until 2:00 PM. I went to George's, got my nuang, pastured her and returned home. I used the *lampaso* on the porch, table and so on and then I read my mail. At 4:00 PM I prepared my vegetables for supper, went and got my nuang and bathed her, came home, started cooking, bathed myself and now it's 5:54 PM and supper is nearly cooked. George said that he'll be real early tonight, I hope so. The weather today was mostly cloudy and not too hot. AWANEN!

Saturday, August 22, 1987
My House, Gomez, Cabarroguis, Quirino

Letter to Vicki K.

We got up at 5:15 AM and George left; he came at 7:00 PM last night. I started the rice cooking, drank coffee and took my nuang to pasture. I returned and talked with George for a couple minutes – he's hauling a cart of bananas from Bikibik to

Gomez today – and then I returned home. I ate, did dishes, got ready for the day and the first thing I did was swept and weeded the entire yard – north and south of the house. Then I cleaned the shelves in the house, there was lots of fallen *panaw* due to the typhoon; everything was really dirty. By then it was 11:00 AM so I went and got and bathed my nuang and returned home. I fetched new drinking water from George's new spring, the typhoon destroyed the old one. I ate and took a siesta from 12:20 to 1:20 PM and when I got up Alfredo came. We talked until 2:10 PM when I took my nuang back to pasture. I returned home and cut the grass on the little hill northeast of the house and then highlighted some words in the English-Ilokano dictionary until 4:00 PM. I prepared the vegetables for supper – tonight's supper will be *utong* and winged beans. At 4:30 PM I went and got and bathed my nuang and then I bathed myself and cooked supper. I ate, did dishes and now it's 6:46 PM and George has not yet returned from Bikibik, so I guess that he will be late tonight. Last night he was very, very happy with his new machete that I got for him. The weather today was cloudy and relatively cool all day; there was no wind and no rain. AWANEN!

Sunday, August 23, 1987
My House, Gomez, Cabarroguis, Quirino

Letters to Chris & Mary M. and San & Jack G.

I got up at 5:30 AM. George got up and left at 3:00 AM to pasture his nuang; he came last night at 8:50 PM. I started the rice cooking, took my nuang to pasture, returned, talked with George for a few minutes and then came home. I finished cooking, drank coffee, ate, did dishes and got ready for the day. Today George pulled the cart of bananas from yesterday to Burgos. I started out the day by doing laundry from 7:30 to 9:15 AM and then I relaxed and read my *Newsweek* until 10:00 AM, when I went and got and bathed my nuang. I returned home and did the letter to San and Jack, ate lunch and then took a siesta from 12:10 to 1:30 PM, a nice long siesta. I got up, drank coffee and at 2:00 PM I took my nuang back to pasture. I returned and did the letter to Chris and Mary. I worked on that until 3:30 PM and then I prepared my vegetables for supper, took my clothes off the line, folded them and put them away. At 4:00 PM I went and talked with George until 4:25 PM, when I went and got and bathed my nuang. George said he'll come early tonight, I really hope so. I started cooking supper, bathed myself, finished cooking, ate, did dishes and now it's 6:28 PM and I'm waiting for George already. Today was actually a pretty lazy day. The weather today was mostly cloudy until 10:00 AM and then it was bright sun until 3:30 PM or so. That's when it clouded up and then it rained lightly from 4:30 to 5:15 PM or so. Now it's a nice comfortable temperature. AWANEN!

Monday, August 24, 1987
My House, Gomez, Cabarroguis, Quirino

Letter to Steve A. Change of address to *Reader's Digest.*

₱332 – 10 = ₱312					
Charcoal	10			TOTAL	₱10

We got up at 5:00 AM and George left; he came at 6:50 PM last night. I started the rice cooking, drank coffee, took my nuang to pasture, returned and talked with George for a few minutes and then came home. I finished cooking, ate, did dishes and got ready for the day. Then I went to Kudog's and bought a sack of charcoal. I carried it home and at 9:30 AM I saw George at their house, so I went and officially gave him my plow. I officially gave Alfredo my hammer yesterday. At 10:00 AM I went and got and bathed my nuang and came home. I made a new "last wrote" and "last received" sheet and then took a siesta from 11:10 to 11:45 AM. I got up and ate lunch, read *Newsweek* and at 1:00 PM I prepared my vegetables for supper and fetched water. At 2:00 PM I went to George's and we went and bundled up some *panaw* grass that he recently cut for repairing their roof. We loaded the cart with six bundles and we headed home at 4:00 PM. We bathed our nuangs and came home. George said he'll be early tonight, I hope so. I started cooking supper at 4:40 PM, bathed myself, went and bought cigarettes and talked with George for a couple minutes. I returned home, finished cooking, ate, did dishes and now it's 6:36 PM. The weather today was hot, dry and clear. There was some thunder at about 3:00 PM, but no rain. Now it's mostly clear again and it's cooler than it was before. Maybe I'll work on a letter until George comes. AWANEN!

Tuesday, August 25, 1987
My House, Gomez, Cabarroguis, Quirino

We got up at 5:10 AM and George left; he didn't come until 10:50 PM last night because they played cards. I started my rice cooking, drank coffee, took my nuang to pasture, returned and talked with George for a couple of minutes and then came home. I finished cooking, ate, did dishes and got ready for the day. I went and got my nuang and went to the farm, where we harvested a few bananas – a lot less than a full cart due to everything being destroyed the other day by Typhoon Ising. I picked some sweet corn and we headed home at about 9:30 AM. We bathed our nuangs and came home. I killed a bit of time and then took a siesta from 11:30 AM to 12:30 PM because it was late to bed last night. I got up and ate lunch, read my *Newsweek* and at 2:00 PM I went to George's. We took our nuangs to pasture and returned home. I packed for the Banaue trip tomorrow and then at 3:00 PM I went back to George's and helped him make the belt for his new machete that I gave him the other day. I returned home and at 4:00 PM I trimmed my beard and then prepared my vegetables for supper, which will be squash tonight. At 4:35 PM I went and got and bathed my nuang, started the rice cooking, bathed myself, fetched water, finished cooking, ate and did dishes. My corn is still cooking now, I guess it will be dessert. Now it's 6:43 PM and I'm waiting for George – he said he will be early tonight, but we'll see. The weather today was hot and dry all day, there were no clouds, no thunder. AWANEN!

Wednesday, August 26, 1987
Halfway Lodge – Banaue, Ifugao

Letters from Cynthia B. and Dad. Postcard from San & Jack G.

₱312 + 300 – 78 = ₱534							
Rides	27	Cigarettes	23	Marienda	9	Notebook	8
Coke	6	Candy	5			TOTAL	₱78

We got up at 5:15 AM and George left; he came at 7:40 PM last night. I drank coffee, took my *wayway* to George, returned home, ate leftover corn and got ready for the day. At 6:00 AM I took my bag of valuables to George's and shortly after that we headed down the mountain. He carried the bananas that we harvested yesterday and I walked with him. We got to Burgos and I caught a ride to Gundaway, got the above mail, bought the above and then caught a ride to Cordon. From Cordon I took a jeepney to Bagabag and then from there I used Immanuel Transportation to go to Banaue. I arrived at the Halfway Lodge at 1:00 PM, ate lunch and after a while Ralph P., Dave F. and I went to a waterfall and then to a bronzesmith. At 4:30 PM or so we returned to the Halfway Lodge and after a while JB and Katie F., Chester and I went uptown and did some shopping around. We didn't buy anything, but we looked at machetes. We returned at 6:00 PM and we just beat the rain. We ate supper, talked a lot and now it's 9:31 PM and I'm in the room with Ralph and Dave. Hopefully we'll sleep soon. AWANEN!

Thursday, August 27, 1987
Halfway Lodge – Banaue, Ifugao

Received ₱187 per diem payment.

₱534 + 187 – 78 = ₱643							
Bread	18	Knife	40	Cigarettes	20	TOTAL	₱78

I got up at 5:20 AM, bathed and got ready for the day. I went down for coffee and they actually started serving breakfast immediately. We ate breakfast, talked for a while and then we went to the morning classes at around 10:00 AM. We stopped for marienda and then we continued classes until lunch. After lunch, Katie, Chester, Shannon and I got a ride up to the Banaue Viewpoint looking for machetes. So far this trip I haven't found a machete that I want to own. The best one was the one I got for George two weeks ago; there seem to be more no more like that one, unfortunately. We continued classes at 3:00 PM and they were pretty worthless. [At this point in my life I have absolutely no recollection of what this particular training session was intended to give us, maybe it was an introduction to what would be expected before our COS (Close-of-Service).] We finished at 6:00 PM and came to supper, which was good food. Cery presented me with a birthday cake! I was totally surprised. After supper we sat around and talked for too long and now it's 9:22 PM and time for bed. AWANEN!

Thursday, August 28, 1987 – My 40th Birthday
Halfway Lodge – Banaue, Ifugao

₱643 + 300 – 853 = ₱90							
Marienda	20	Room	25	Baskets	125	Trinkets	40
Meals	93	Machete	550			TOTAL	₱853

I got up at 5:20 AM, showered, got ready for the day, went downstairs for breakfast, ate and after breakfast I paid the bill up to date and changed rooms. JB, Katie and I went uptown for a while and then we went across the valley and up to the bronzesmith again. Today the guy sold me two of the bronze nuang heads and put *alipuspus* on them for me. [An *alipuspus* is like the crown of your head, where the hair grows in a circular pattern. According to folklore, the more *alipuspus* that a nuang has, the better for being healthy and long-lived – my nuang had several of them]. Then we returned and ate lunch. After a while we went back uptown again and I still couldn't find a machete that I really wanted so I bought two others and a small knife, plus a couple of baskets. We returned to the lodge, drank a Coke and a cup of coffee and then we went back uptown again. The one place I've been to several times called me in when they saw me passing by to tell me that they got more machetes in today. One of them was really fine, so I just had to get it. So, I bought three machetes today!! In the last two days I've bought five edged tools; a small knife was ₱40, one machete was ₱140, another machete was ₱130 the finest machete for ₱240 and the small knife was ₱40, a total of ₱590. In addition, I bought a large basket for ₱65, a small basket for ₱30, fruit bowls were ₱20, cups were ₱10, for a total of ₱125. Now it's 8:10 PM, we're done with supper and sitting around killing time. Right now it's raining lightly. We leave and head for home tomorrow. AWANEN!

[Keep in mind that the end is in sight for us now. At this point I am attempting to purchase items that I want to take home to Alaska with me. You may recall that on August 12 when Dave, Vicki and I were in Baguio City that I special ordered a carved wooden nuang with a calf to take home with me. Eventually you will read about the day I returned to pick it up. And, that also explains why on this, probably final trip to Banaue, I purchased some nice machetes and some nice rattan baskets – to take to Alaska with me and have for souvenirs of my 2+ year stay here.]

Saturday, August 29, 1987
My House, Gomez, Cabarroguis, Quirino

₱90 + 200 – 213 = ₱77							
Rides	30	Food	57	Kerosene	8	Meals	47
Household	13	Cigarettes	5	Presents	22	Marienda	10
Misc.	21					TOTAL	₱213

I got up at 5:20 AM, got ready for the day and went downstairs to eat. After a while JB and Katie showed up and we all ate breakfast together. Shortly after 8:00 AM we got it together to leave. We caught a ride to Bagabag, drank a Coke and ate a biscuit there and then we caught a ride to Santiago. We arrived in Santiago at just about noon and we went to Letty's Restaurant for lunch. We said our good-byes until our Close-of-Service conference, I did a quick trip through the market and Marilen's and then caught a jeepney for Burgos. I got to Burgos at about 2:40 PM and climbed the high road, getting home before 3:30 PM. After unpacking and relaxing for a few minutes I went to George's, gave the family the presents that I bought for them and talked until 4:20 PM. Then I came home and bathed. George said that they may stroll tonight and if so he'll be late – SHIT! Now it's 5:33 PM and I'm too tired and lazy to cook supper so I'm just boiling coffee water and that's what I'll have for supper. I really hope they don't stroll and that George comes early. The weather today was hot, dry and windy. There's another typhoon on its way so that means hot winds, but no rain, not yet anyway. George has slept here 396 nights now. AWANEN!

[By now, you are probably thinking about, or at least wondering about the sexual relation that George and I had, no? Well, to be perfectly honest, George was not very much interested at all in having sex with another male. In all of the nights we slept together, shoulder to shoulder, hip to hip, he permitted me to give him a blow job just exactly one time. He knew my desires and he knew how horny he made me, he knew that very well. Therefore he was always willing to help me reach an orgasm when I needed to do so. He would rub my stomach, play with my balls, give me a few strokes with his hand when I wanted it. He had no problem at all with that. Interesting, eh!]

Sunday, August 30, 1987
My House, Gomez, Cabarroguis, Quirino

₱77 + 10 – 0 = ₱87 [I gave no indication in my Journal as to why.]

I got up at 5:15 AM. George got up and left at 4:00 AM to pasture his nuang. He came last night at 7:25 PM. I started the rice cooking, drank coffee, took my nuang to pasture, returned and talked with George for a few minutes; he's pulling a cart of bananas to Burgos today and then he's going to continue on to Santiago and go to a movie. I returned home, finished cooking, ate, did dishes and got ready for the day. I started out by doing laundry, I even washed my blanket. I finished with laundry at about 10:00 AM and then I went and got and bathed my nuang. I returned home and killed time until lunch. I read my *Reader's Digest* and then took a siesta from 11:30 AM to 12:30 PM. I got up, drank coffee and went to talk with Alfredo for a while. At 2:20 PM I returned my nuang to pasture, came back home and cleaned and oiled all of my machetes that I bought at Banaue. Then I wrapped them up to take to America with me. At 4:00 PM I prepared my vegetables for supper; I'm having *utong* and *tarong* for supper. Then I watered the guapple [guava/apple] seedlings and at 4:30 PM I went and got my nuang, bathed her, returned home and started cooking supper. I bathed myself and went and asked George to come early – he said yes, but we'll have to wait and see. Now it's 6:00 PM and my supper is nearly cooked. The weather today was hot and dry but mostly cloudy. There's been no rain in so long now that the ground is cracked again. It was up to 90°F today and it's still 87°F. AWANEN!

Monday, August 31, 1987
My House, Gomez, Cabarroguis, Quirino

₱87 – 37 = ₱50						
Cigarettes	3	Charcoal	34		TOTAL	₱37

We got up at 5:05 AM and George left; he didn't come until 9:35 PM last night. I started the rice cooking, took my nuang to pasture, returned home, drank coffee, finished cooking, ate, did dishes and got ready for the day. I went and talked with George for a while and he's cutting the bamboo for their new roof today. I returned home again and went through all of my remaining books and papers to see what I have. At 10:00 AM George and I went and got our nuangs, bathed them and we both returned to our homes. I started reading the book *"Hotel"* by Arthur Hailey and then at 11:15 AM I ate lunch. I laid down from 11:30 AM until noon but couldn't sleep. I got up and read more until 1:40 PM and then it was cloudy so I took my nuang back to pasture. I returned and helped George with cutting the bamboo to the correct lengths that he wants until 3:00 PM. I fetched water and then read until 4:00 PM and prepared my vegetables for supper – *utong* and *tarong* again – and then at 4:25 PM I went and asked George to come early and he said yes, but as always, we'll have to wait and see. I went and got and bathed my nuang and then started cooking. I bathed myself and now it's 5:32 PM and my vegetables are nearly cooked. The weather today was hot and dry and then it clouded up at about 1:30 PM and there was some thunder and lightning. It rained lightly from about 3:00 to 4:00 PM, but now it's nice again. Please come early George. AWANEN!

[End of handwritten notebook #4 of 5]

Tuesday, September 1, 1987
My House, Gomez, Cabarroguis, Quirino

Letter to Fred & Cynthia B. Postcards to Ardis B., Liz & Randy and Bob S.

We got up at 5:15 AM and George left; he came at 7:05 PM last night. We sorted lots of my things and I gave him three full bags of stuff that I don't want to take home with me. I started cooking, went and pastured my nuang, returned and George had already gone to cut *panaw* at the farm, so I talked with Alfredo for a while and came home. I drank coffee, finished cooking, ate, did dishes and got ready for the day. There wasn't much of anything to do this morning except continue reading the *"Hotel"* book. At 10:00 AM I went and got and bathed my nuang, returned home and wrote the letter to Fred and Cynthia. I took a siesta from 11:30 AM until noon and then ate lunch and read some more. I killed time until 1:40 PM and it was cloudy so I took my nuang back to pasture, returned, talked with George for a half hour and then came home. I wrote a postcard to Ardis telling her the film is on the way. I read some more and then at 4:00 PM I prepared my vegetables for supper; tonight I'll be eating *utong* and *tarong* again. At 4:30 PM I started the rice cooking and went and got my nuang and bathed her. Then I asked George to come right after supper and he said yes, but we'll have to wait and see. I bathed myself, finished cooking, ate and did dishes. Now it's 6:16 PM and I'm waiting for George. I'll read *"Hotel"* some more until he comes. Tonight we'll sort through my duffle bag if George comes early. The weather today was partly cloudy all day and then from 4:30 until 5:15 PM there was a nice rain, but now it has stopped. AWANEN!

Wednesday, September 2, 1987
My House, Gomez, Cabarroguis, Quirino

We got up at 5:35 AM and George left; he came at 7:35 PM last night and we sorted through more of my stuff. I gave him three more full bags of stuff, mostly clothes, extra blankets, a sweatshirt and so on – he seemed quite happy. I started my rice cooking, took my nuang to pasture, returned, talked with George for a few minutes and then came home. I drank coffee, finished cooking, ate, did dishes and got ready for the day. I read the *"Hotel"* book until I was finished with it. At about 10:30 AM Alfredo came and found me repacking and consolidating the stuff that I want to take home with me. He stayed until 11:40 AM and then went home. He was asking me if I'm going to take this and that and the other thing home; is he being greedy, does he want more than I am giving him and his family? I ate lunch and then took a siesta from noon until 1:30 PM. I got up and went to talk with George for a few minutes and then I went and bathed and moved my nuang. I returned home and read *Newsweek* and then highlighted more words in the dictionary for an hour. At 3:30 PM I prepared my vegetables for supper – tonight I'll be eating squash. At 4:15 PM I went and asked George to come early and he said "right after supper". At 4:30 PM I started cooking and then I bathed. My nuang is staying at pasture tonight. Now it's 5:35 PM and my supper is nearly cooked. The weather today – it rained lightly all night long last night and continued for most of the day. Right now it has quit for a few minutes again. I hope George is truly early tonight. AWANEN!

Thursday, September 3, 1987
My House, Gomez, Cabarroguis, Quirino

Letters to Tom & Barb H., JB & Katie F. and Munsayac Handicrafts. Postcards to Vicki S. and Jim W.

₱50 + 410 – 5 = ₱455							
Cigarettes	5					TOTAL	₱5

We got up at 5:10 AM and George left; he came at 7:05 PM last night and I gave him four more bags of my things, that's the last of it until I'm nearly ready to go home. I started my rice cooking, drank coffee, went to move my nuang, returned, talked with George for a couple minutes and then came home. I finished cooking, ate, did dishes and got ready for the day. I wrote the letter to Tom and Barbara first and then the letter to Munsayac Handicrafts, enclosing some photos of my nuang so that they can make it accurately [Munsayac is the place in Baguio City that is carving my wooden nuang with calf which I plan to take back to Alaska with me]. At 9:40 AM I went and talked with George until it was time to go and get our nuangs and bathe them. After we did that I came home and after a while I ate lunch and then took a siesta from noon until 1:20 PM. I drank coffee and then at 2:00 PM George and I took our nuangs back to pasture and I came back home. I did the postcard to my brother Jim, wishing him a happy birthday and then I did the one to Vicki. After that I highlighted more words in the dictionary until 4:00 PM and then I prepared my vegetables for supper – squash again. At 4:30 PM I went and got and bathed my nuang and started cooking. I bathed myself, finished cooking, ate, did dishes and then went to George's to talk until 7:05 PM and they still hadn't eaten, but he told me that he will be here soon. Now it's 7:12 PM and I hope George really does come soon. The weather today was rainy on and off this morning and then fairly hot and no rain at all in the afternoon. AWANEN!

Friday, September 4, 1987
My House, Gomez, Cabarroguis, Quirino

Letters from San & Jack G. (2), Mary M., Mike Mc., Nestor and Jerry J.

₱455 – 190 = ₱265							
Cigarettes	21	Batteries	9	Rides	4	Food	58
Coffee	29	Household	5	Kerosene	7	Marienda	33
Soap	10	Misc.	14			TOTAL	₱190

We got up at 5:20 AM, I gave George my *wayway* and he left; he didn't come until 10:40 PM last night because of a card game. I cooked breakfast, ate, drank coffee, did dishes, got ready for the day and at 7:00 AM I took my bag of valuables to

George's and headed for Burgos. When I got there I talked with Richard for a while and then continued on to Gundaway. I got my mail, went to market, returned to the post office and got more mail and then I got a jeepney for Burgos. I arrived at the bottom of the high road at 10:45 AM and came home via the high road in a new record time of 31 minutes and 46 seconds. After wringing out my T-shirt out and relaxing for a few minutes I went to George's and talked for a while. Then I returned home and took a siesta from noon until 1:00 PM. I got up and at 1:30 PM George and I went to pasture our nuangs. We returned and talked for a while and then I came home. I read my mail and then at 2:30 PM I went back to George's and we talked until 3:15 PM when he and Bubot left for Bikibik to haul bananas. That means that George will not be coming tonight because they won't return until tomorrow. At 4:00 PM I prepared my vegetables for supper – tonight I'll be eating squash blossoms. At 4:30 PM I went and got and bathed my nuang and started cooking. Then I bathed myself, ate, did dishes and now it's 6:37 PM. What to do tonight with no George? It will be a long evening, for sure. The weather today was mostly cloudy this morning and then sunny and hot, no rain at all. The trail is quite dry now. AWANEN!

Saturday, September 5, 1987
My House, Gomez, Cabarroguis, Quirino

I got up at 5:20 AM with no companion. I started my rice cooking, drank coffee, took my nuang to pasture, returned and talked with Alfredo for a few minutes and then came home. I finished cooking, ate, did dishes, got ready for the day and then I sorted through my duffle bag and washed what was easy to wash. I hung the rest of it on the line to just air out and by the time I finished with that George was home so I went and talked with him for a while and then I came back home. At 9:30 AM I went to talk with George again, until 10:00 AM, and then I went and got and bathed my nuang. I returned home and killed time for a while and then took a siesta from 11:00 to 11:45 AM. I got up and ate lunch and then I saw George heading off for Burgos with the bananas at 1:30 PM. It was cloudy so I took my nuang back to pasture, returned home and highlighted words in the dictionary until 3:30 PM. Then I took the clothes off the clothesline, put them away and prepared vegetables for supper – tonight I'll be having squash and *tarong*. At 4:30 PM I started the rice cooking and went and got and bathed my nuang. I returned home, bathed myself, finished cooking, ate, did dishes and now it's 5:52 PM. I don't think George has returned from Burgos yet, I wonder why – it's been about five hours since they left. I'll go and check in a little while. I hope he comes early tonight. The weather today – there was a hard rain during the night and then it was sunny and hot today. It clouded up at about 1:30 PM and then at 4:00 PM the rain started lightly and continued on and off until now. AWANEN!

Sunday, September 6, 1987
My House, Gomez, Cabarroguis, Quirino

Letter to Dave G.

We got up at 5:20 AM and George left; he came at 10:20 PM last night because he and Florenti took a stroll together. I started my rice cooking, drank coffee and took my nuang to pasture. I returned and talked with George for a few minutes and then came home. I finished cooking, ate, did dishes and got ready for the day. I did laundry and then killed time until 10:00 AM and then I went and got and bathed my nuang. I returned home, went to George's, we talked for a few minutes and then I came home and took a siesta from 11:00 AM until noon. I got up, ate lunch and went and talked with George for another half hour then returned home. I killed more time until 2:00 PM and then took my nuang back to pasture. I met George on the way home as he was going to pasture his nuang so I went with him to talk for a few more minutes. Then I returned home, took my clothes off the line, put them away and then at 3:00 PM I went to George's again and asked him to please, please, please come early tonight. He said yes, but we'll have to wait and see if he really does. At 4:00 PM I prepared my vegetables for supper – *utong* beans and corn-on-the-cob. At 4:30 PM I started cooking, went and got and bathed my nuang and then bathed myself. I returned home, finished cooking, ate, did dishes and now it's 6:11 PM. The weather today was partly cloudy on and off all day, but there was no rain. AWANEN!

Monday, September 7, 1987
My House, Gomez, Cabarroguis, Quirino

We got up at 5:30 AM and George left; he came at 11:25 PM last night because there was another card game. I started my rice cooking, drank coffee and took my nuang to pasture. I returned and talked with George for just a moment because he's angry about something. I came home, finished cooking, ate, did dishes and got ready for the day. I didn't do much of anything this morning except clean the kitchen of everything and spray for ants – they were everywhere, even living between my plates. It was cloudy so I waited until 10:30 AM to go get and bathe my nuang. I came home and then went to talk with George for another half hour or so. Everybody is building Junior's new house today, northwest and uphill from mine. I came home, ate lunch and took a siesta from noon until 1:00 PM. I got up and prepared vegetables for supper and at 2:00 PM I took my nuang back to pasture and returned. George and I went to the farm, it was nice to be with him for a few hours. We came home at 4:10 PM. He got vegetables for their supper. At 4:30 PM I went and got and bathed my nuang, started my rice cooking and bathed myself. Now it's 5:21 PM and George told me that he'll be real early tonight; I'll believe it when he gets here. My rice is now cooking. I started using my new kaban of rice today. The weather today was cloudy all day with just a few minutes of rain at 2:00 PM. Now it's threatening rain again, have to wait and see what happens. AWANEN!

Tuesday, September 8, 1987
My House, Gomez, Cabarroguis, Quirino

Letters to Chris & Mary M., make a Patagonia Gear order. Postcard to Sue T.

We got up at 5:20 AM and George left; he came at 9:40 PM last night because they played cards again. I started my rice cooking, drank coffee and took my nuang to pasture. I returned and talked with George for a few minutes and then came home. I finished cooking, ate, did dishes and got ready for the day. I read my *Newsweek* for a while and then trimmed the weeds under the clothesline. I read some more, swept the north yard, killed time and then at 10:00 AM I went and got and bathed my nuang. I returned home then I went off in search of George, he was supposedly hauling *panaw* today, but after an unsuccessful search I finally found out that they started harvesting corn today. They harvested one cart full. I ate lunch and took a siesta from noon to 1:00 PM, got up, drank coffee and then went and talked with George for a few minutes and came home. At 1:45 PM I took my nuang back to pasture, returned and talked with George some more. I came home and highlighted words in the dictionary for a while and then went and talked with George yet again. I fetched water and at 4:00 PM I prepared my vegetables for supper, I'm having *tarong* tonight. At 4:30 PM I went and got and bathed my nuang, started cooking, bathed myself, finished cooking, ate and did dishes. Now it's 6:26 PM and I hope George comes early tonight. The weather today was partly cloudy all day. Now it's really dark and there are very thick clouds, but no rain yet. AWANEN!

Wednesday, September 9, 1987
My House, Gomez, Cabarroguis, Quirino

Postcard from San & Jack G.

₱265 + 200 – 155 = ₱310							
Food	27	Cigarettes	19	Rides	4	Kerosene	7
Marienda	33	Coffee	27	Candy	12	Household	8
Misc.	18					TOTAL	₱155

We got up at 5:10 AM, I gave George my *wayway* and he left; he actually came at 6:55 PM last night. I cooked breakfast, ate, did dishes and got ready for the day. At 6:45 AM I left for Burgos. I got there and talked with Richard until 8:30 AM and then continued on to Gundaway. I got my mail and went to market. I finished my marketing and returned to the post office to get the rest of my mail and then I caught a ride back to Burgos, arriving at 11:15 AM. I climbed the mountain via the high road in a new record time of 30 minutes 36.5 seconds. I got home at about 11:45 AM and after wringing out my T-shirt and relaxing for a few minutes, George arrived with two carts of corn. I went and talked with him for a couple minutes and returned home. I took a siesta from 12:15 to 1:00 PM and prepared my vegetables for supper. Tonight I'll be having *utong* beans only. At 2:00 PM I took my nuang to pasture and returned. We husked corn, did both carts by 4:15 PM and I came home. At 4:30 PM I went and got and bathed my nuang, bathed myself and started cooking. Now it's 5:33 PM and my rice is nearly cooked. I think there will be corn shelling tonight, so I'll go help with that and George and I will probably come here late, oh well, it is September, this is what is to be expected. The weather today was partly cloudy all day. It rained a little during the night last night, but very little. There probably won't be any rain this evening. AWANEN!

Thursday, September 10, 1987
My House, Gomez, Cabarroguis, Quirino

We got up at 5:10 AM and George left; we came here at 10:50 PM last night after shelling corn until 9:00 PM and then talking for quite a while. I started my rice cooking, drank coffee and took my nuang to pasture. I returned and talked with George for just a moment and then came home. I finished cooking, ate, did dishes, got ready for the day and then I went and talked with George until he left for the Quirino Days Festival at about 8:45 AM. I came home and separated out and packed everything I'm taking home with me; there are six parcels. I went and got and bathed my nuang at 10:00 AM, returned home and began unpacking. Alfredo came and watched me until 11:45 AM and then he went home. I ate my lunch and took a siesta from 12:15 to 1:45 PM. I got up and took my nuang to pasture again. I returned and George was already home he was sad and came home early because his watch that I gave him was stolen! We talked for a few minutes and I came home. I highlighted more words in the dictionary until finished and then I fetched water. At 4:00 PM I prepared my vegetables for supper. Tonight I'll be having beans, eggplant and banana. At 4:30 PM I started my rice cooking, went and got and bathed my nuang, bathed myself and now it's 5:34 PM and my supper is ready and cooling. We'll be shelling corn again tonight, so after supper I'll go to George's and help with that. The weather was hot and dry all day, no rain again. AWANEN!

Friday, September 11, 1987
My House, Gomez, Cabarroguis, Quirino

Letter to Ronald.

We got up at 5:10 AM and George left. We shelled corn last night until 10:30 PM and then we came here at 11:00 PM and slept. I started my rice cooking, drank coffee and took my nuang to pasture. I returned and talked with George for a few minutes and then came home. I finished cooking, ate, did dishes and got ready for the day. I repacked the stuff in the round basket this morning and sorted out a few more things that I'm going to give to George. That took until 9:50 AM so, then I went and got and bathed my nuang. When I returned George was helping put the new roof on their house. I came home and highlighted words in the dictionary until 11:30 AM and then ate lunch. After that I took a siesta from noon until 1:30 PM. I got up and highlighted more words and then at 2:00 PM I went and pastured my nuang, returned and talked with George for a few minutes. I returned home and highlighted words until 4:00 PM and then prepared vegetables for supper – tonight will be *utong* and *tarong*. At 4:20 PM I went and got and bathed my nuang and then bathed myself. I started cooking and went and asked George to come early. Now it's 5:30 PM and my supper is nearly cooked. I hope George comes early tonight. The weather today – it rained last night from 6:30 to 7:40 PM and it was hot and dry today. It clouded up at about 3:30 PM and a hard rain started at about 5:15 PM and is still continuing. AWANEN!

Saturday, September 12, 1987
My House, Gomez, Cabarroguis, Quirino

Letter to Yip Chee H.

We got up at 5:10 AM and George left; he came at 7:20 PM last night. I started my rice, drank coffee and took my nuang to pasture. I returned and talked with George for a while and then came home and my fire had gone out, so I had to start it again and then I cooked, ate, did dishes and got ready for the day. I removed everything from the east wall of shelves and used the *lampaso* to clean real good; the whole wall, and by then it was 9:45 AM so I went and got and bathed my nuang. Upon returning I went and talked with George for a few minutes and came home. I did the letter to Yip and by then it was 11:30 AM so I ate my lunch and took a siesta from noon until 12:45 PM. I got up and drank coffee and Vergilio Mendoza and three friends of his stopped by to tell me they're going to cook their lunch here! At 1:45 PM I went to pasture my nuang and stopped at Alfredo's and asked him to come here while I'm gone because Vergilio and his friends were still here. He did, I pastured my nuang, returned and talked with George a few minutes and then came home. Vergilio and his friends left at 3:15 PM and then I sewed up my old pants that had a bad tear. At 4:00 PM I prepared my vegetables for supper *utong* and *tarong* again. At 4:30 PM I went and got and bathed my nuang, started cooking and bathed myself. Now it's 5:22 PM and my rice is cooking. I hope George is early tonight, but I have a feeling he'll be late. The weather today was rainy early this morning and then partly cloudy all day. It rained again from 4:30 to 5:00 PM, but it has stopped now. AWANEN!

Sunday, September 13, 1987
My House, Gomez, Cabarroguis, Quirino

I got up at 5:20 AM. George got up and left at 4:20 AM to pasture his nuang. He came last night at 7:05 PM. I started my rice cooking, took my nuang to pasture, returned and talked with George for a few minutes and then came home. I finished cooking, ate, did dishes and got ready for the day. George and Alfredo both went to Burgos today to sell the corn and a few bananas, which they harvested yesterday. I started my day by doing laundry and I was finished with that at about 9:30 AM. I relaxed for a while, went and got and bathed my nuang and returned home. I highlighted more words in the dictionary until 11:30 AM and then I ate lunch and took a siesta from noon to 1:00 PM. I killed time until 2:00 PM and then I took my nuang back to pasture. I returned home and removed everything from the west wall and shelves and cleaned that wall really good. I didn't hang the postcards back up on the wall; I'll give them all to George tonight. At 4:00 PM I prepared my vegetables for supper – *tabungaw* is what I'll be eating tonight. At 4:30 PM I went and got and bathed my nuang, started the rice cooking and then bathed myself. George and Alfredo had then returned from Burgos so I went and talked with them and asked George to come early, but he said he doesn't know yet. Now it's 5:31 PM and my rice is cooking. The weather – it rained again last night and then it was cloudy today until 9:30 AM. After 9:30 AM it was hot and dry the rest of the day. AWANEN!

Monday, September 14, 1987
My House, Gomez, Cabarroguis, Quirino

Letter to Barb W.

We got up at 5:10 AM and George left; he came at 7:45 PM last night. I started my rice cooking, drank coffee and took my nuang to pasture. I returned and talked with George for a few minutes and then came home. I finished cooking, ate, did dishes and got ready for the day. I separated the medicines in my medical kit that I plan to take home with me, laundered a couple of items, spread out charcoal to dry, swept the north lawn and by then it was 10:00 AM so I went and got and bathed my nuang. I returned home, highlighted more words in the dictionary for a while and then did the letter to Barb. By then it was 11:30 AM so I ate lunch and went and talked with George for a while. I came home and took a siesta from noon to 1:00 PM and then read my *Newsweek* for a while. I saw George at their house at 1:30 PM so I went and asked him what he's doing this afternoon and he said that he was cutting corn stalks and piling them and that tomorrow a bunch of people will come and harvest the corn from them, so I went and helped cut corn stalks. At 4:45 PM we headed home. We got and bathed our nuangs, I came home, started cooking, bathed myself and now it's 6:13 PM and my squash and *tabungaw* are cooking. I hope George comes early tonight – he said he will, but we'll see what happens. The weather today was hot and dry all day. It rained really hard last night from 8:00 to 9:00 PM. AWANEN!

Tuesday, September 15, 1987
My House, Gomez, Cabarroguis, Quirino

Letter to San & Jack G.

We got up at 5:10 AM and George left. We shelled Boy's corn last night until 9:30 AM and then we came here at 9:45 PM and slept. I started my rice cooking, drank coffee and took my nuang to pasture. I returned and George was eating breakfast so I came straight home. I finished cooking, ate, did dishes and got ready for the day. I highlighted more words in the dictionary for quite a while – until 10:00 AM – and then went and got and bathed my nuang. I returned home and wrote the letter to San and Jack and then ate lunch. After that I took a siesta from noon until 1:00 PM and then I got up and drank coffee. At 1:30 PM I went to George's – they brought back two carts of corn, arriving at noon. At 2:00 PM I took my nuang back to pasture, returned and George was just leaving for the afternoon corn run so, I said "we'll see each other soon" and he left. After a while I came home and highlighted more words in the dictionary. At about 3:00 PM Francisco and Efren came and stayed until 4:00 PM; I have no idea what they came for, just to be friendly? I prepared my vegetables for supper – tonight will be squash. At 4:20 PM I went and got my nuang and bathed her, then I bathed myself and went to buy some cigarettes. George wasn't home yet so I came straight home and started cooking. Now it's 5:06 PM and my rice is cooking. I hope George comes early tonight. The weather today was cloudy until 10:00 AM and then hot and dry. It clouded up at about 3:00 PM and then it started raining at about 5:00 PM and it's still raining now. AWANEN!

Wednesday, September 16, 1987
My House, Gomez, Cabarroguis, Quirino

Letters to Nestor and Mike Mc.

We got up at 5:10 AM and George left; he came at 7:40 PM last night. I started my rice cooking, drank coffee and took my nuang to pasture. I returned and talked with George for a few minutes and then came home. I finished cooking, ate, did dishes and got ready for the day. What did I do this morning? Well, I finished highlighting words in the dictionary and I have now completed both the Ilokano-English and the English-Ilokano dictionaries. After that I killed time until 10:00 AM and went and got and bathed my nuang. I returned home and read *Newsweek* and then took a siesta from 11:30 AM until noon. I got up and ate lunch and then did the letter to Nestor, enclosing some photos. After that I started reading *"The Hobbit"* book. George returned home at 1:00 PM, kind of late. At 2:00 PM I took my nuang back to pasture, returned and helped George unload the two carts of corn he brought in today. He's not returning to the farm to get more this afternoon, so I stayed and talked with him until 3:00 PM. I came home and prepared my vegetables for supper – squash again – and fetched water. I read more of *"The Hobbit"* until 4:25 PM and then I went and got and bathed my nuang. I returned home, started cooking, went and asked George to come early, he said yes and I came home and bathed myself. Now it's 5:30 PM and my squash is cooking. The weather today –

there was rain early this morning, it was sunny and dry after that and now it's relatively cloudy and rain is threatening again. AWANEN!

Thursday, September 17, 1987
My House, Gomez, Cabarroguis, Quirino

Letters to Tony & Janet S. and Hewlett-Packard.

₱310 + 180 – 5 = ₱485							
Cigarettes	5					TOTAL	₱5

We got up at 5:10 AM and George left; he came at 7:55 PM last night. I started my rice cooking, drank coffee and took my nuang to pasture. I returned and talked with George until he left for the farm to harvest corn and then I came home. I finished cooking breakfast, ate, did dishes and got ready for the day. I read *"The Hobbit"* until 9:50 AM and then went and got and bathed my nuang and returned home. I wrote the letter to Tony and Janet about my coming home party and then I ate lunch and took a siesta from noon to 1:00 PM. I got up, drank coffee and read more of *"The Hobbit"* until 2:00 PM and then I took my nuang to pasture again. I returned and talked with Alfredo until nearly 3:00 PM. George took his lunch with him to the farm today. I came home and mostly did nothing; oh, I wrote a letter to Hewlett-Packard and asked for an HP-41 family, product catalog. At 3:30 PM I prepared my vegetables for supper – squash again. Junior came to ask me what he's going to get when I leave and I told him I'm taking it all home with me and that Alfredo is going to get my nuang and kitchen stuff. At 4:30 PM I went and got and bathed my nuang, bathed myself and went and talked with George for a few minutes, he only got one cart full of corn today; I'm not sure why. Now it's 5:41 PM and my supper is cooking. We'll shell corn tonight. The weather today was partly cloudy in the morning and then hot and clear. It clouded up at 3:30 PM, started raining at 4:50 PM and it's continuing now. AWANEN!

Friday, September 18, 1987
My House, Gomez, Cabarroguis, Quirino

Letters from nobody. *Readers Digest* and *Newsweek* only.

₱485 – 415 = ₱70							
Coffee	65	Food	132	Rides	13	Kerosene	7
Household	20	Cigarettes	27	Marienda	30	Postage	3
Tools	26	Ice Cream	23	Candy	7	Meals	31
Misc.	31					TOTAL	₱415

We got up at 5:10 AM, I gave George my *wayway* and he left. We shelled corn last night until 9:40 PM and then we came here, talked just a few minutes and went to sleep. I cooked breakfast, ate, did dishes, got ready for the day and at 6:45 AM I headed for Burgos. I talked with Richard for a while and then continued on to Gundaway and got my mail – only a *Reader's Digest.* After that I continued on to Santiago and did the little bit of marketing that I needed to do. I mostly bought stocks, as I have to go to Manila on Monday. I went to the bank and cashed my September checks and then ate ice cream at the 456 Restaurant. After that I caught a jeepney for Burgos and stopped at the Gundaway Post Office again, but all I got was a *Newsweek*, I got no letters at all this time. I continued on to Burgos and I started climbing via the high road at 2:00 PM exactly, but due to my heavy pack I didn't even try for a new record time. It took me 41 minutes to come up the mountain. I wrung out my T-shirt, unpacked my bag and put things away, cooled off for a while and then I prepared my vegetables for supper – squash again. At 4:30 PM I started cooking supper and now it's 6:11 PM, I'm done eating and dishes are washed. We'll shell corn again tonight. The weather today was partly cloudy and hot, but then it clouded up at about 4:00 PM, began raining at about 5:10 PM and it's still continuing to rain very hard. AWANEN!

Saturday, September 19, 1987
My House, Gomez, Cabarroguis, Quirino

We got up at 5:10 AM and George left. We shelled corn last night until 10:00 PM and then came here and slept immediately. I started my rice cooking, drank coffee and took my nuang to pasture. I returned and talked with George for a while, helped empty the cart of corn and then came home. I finished cooking, ate, did dishes and got ready for the day. I started out by doing laundry and by the time I finished it was 9:15 AM so I read my *Readers Digest* until 9:50 AM and then went and got and bathed my nuang. I returned home and counted the number of highlighted words in the Ilokano-English dictionary. At this point it seems that I know about 1541 words. Then I ate lunch and took a siesta from noon to 1:00 PM. I got up and read my *Reader's Digest* again until 1:50 PM and then I took my nuang back to pasture. I returned and helped empty the cart of corn that George brought this morning. George returned to the farm for another cart. I helped pick up all the drying corn in Alfredo's yard and when we finished that I came home, took my clothes off the line, folded them and put them away. At 4:00 PM I prepared my vegetables for supper – *utong* and *tarong*. At 4:30 PM I went and got and bathed my nuang. Then I started my rice cooking and bathed myself. Now it's 5:32 PM and my vegetables are cooking. We're going to shell corn again tonight. The weather today was clear and quite hot all day and then it clouded up at 3:00 PM, started raining at 4:00 PM and continued until 5:30 PM or so. Now it's just sprinkling. AWANEN!

Sunday, September 20, 1987
My House, Gomez, Cabarroguis, Quirino

₱70 + 300 – 50 = ₱320							
Chili Peppers	50					TOTAL	₱50

I got up at 5:20 AM. George got up and left at 3:40 AM to pasture his nuang because he went to Burgos today to sell corn. We shelled corn last night until 9:30 PM and then came here, talked for a little bit and then slept. I started my rice cooking, drank coffee and took my nuang to pasture. I returned and talked with George for a few minutes and then came home. I finished cooking, ate and Alfredo came to tell me there was a lady with some hot chili peppers [*sili*] to sell, so I went and bought all that she had – lucky for her, she didn't have to go to market with it! [I bought this to dry and then crush into a fine powder to take back to America with me. You will see several more references to this as the process of drying and crushing to a powder continues.] Alfredo and I spread it all out to dry and then I returned home and did dishes. I also did a few items of laundry and then at 10:00 AM I went and got and bathed my nuang, came home and cleaned all of my Philippine coins that I plan to take to America with me. At 11:30 AM I ate lunch and then took a siesta from noon to 1:15 PM. I got up and read *Reader's Digest* until 2:00 PM and then took my nuang back to pasture and returned home. I did several small things – fetched water, removed clothes from the line, packed for the trip to Manila and then went and picked up the hot chili – but Alfredo had already picked it up, so I went and talked with him for a little while and then came home. I prepared my vegetables for supper – *utong* and *tarong* – and then at 4:15 PM I went and talked with George for a minute and then went and got and bathed my nuang. At 4:45 PM I started cooking and now it's 5:13 PM and my rice is nearly done. We'll shell corn again tonight. The weather today was partly cloudy on and off all day and then it clouded up at 3:00 PM and started raining at 4:45 PM. Now it's still raining. AWANEN!

Monday, September 21, 1987
Malate Pension, Manila

₱320 + 100 – 323 = ₱97							
Rides	72	Meals	156	Cigarettes	20	Marienda	27
Ice Cream	7	Food	34	Candy	7	TOTAL	₱323

We got up at 5:05 AM, I gave George my *wayway* and leftover food and he left. We shelled corn last night until 8:55 PM and then we went to my house, talked for a short while and slept. I drank coffee, got ready for the day, took my bag of valuables to George's and said goodbye. I left Gomez at 5:45 AM, got to Burgos, talked with Richard for a few minutes and then continued on to Santiago. I took the 9:00 AM bus to Manila and it was a pretty uneventful ride. I got off at Balintawak again, took the LRT to Quirino Avenue and then walked to Malate Pension from there. After taking a shower, JB and Katie F., Linda S., Teresa L. and I went to the Seafront Restaurant for Mongolian Barbeque. We stayed there until after 9:00 PM eating and talking and then we returned to Malate Pension. Now it's 9:37 PM and I'm ready to call it a day and sleep. AWANEN!

Tuesday, September 22, 1987
Malate Pension, Manila

₱97 + 500 – 450 = ₱147							
Meals	213	Postage	126	Coke	8	Food	80
Soap	7	Rides	5	Marienda	11	TOTAL	₱450

I got up at 5:35 AM, showered and went downstairs for coffee. Several of us talked, ate breakfast and killed time until 7:30 AM and then went to BPI and asked about and got a hand-held corn sheller. Then I went to the Peace Corps Office, left a MIF Kit [stool sample to check for parasites] and got some medical supplies. After that I went to the bank and got 25 one centavo coins for souvenirs. Then I went to the drug store and got some Tinactin and to a coin dealer to ask if there's silver in the Rizal ₱1 coin – there isn't. Then I went to the dentist office to meet Sue T. and we went to Chinatown for lunch. After lunch she returned to the dentist and I went to the post office. After that I walked all the way back to Malate Pension and found that Tom and Barb H. had just arrived, so we talked until 4:00 PM and then I went back over to the Peace Corps Office, got a Career Resource Manual and returned to Malate Pension. After a while Tom and Barb, Sue and I and two other people went to the Seafront Restaurant for supper. We stayed there until 9:00 PM and then came back to Malate Pension. Now it's 9:46 PM and I'm ready to sleep. AWANEN!

Wednesday, September 23, 1987
Admiral Hotel, Manila

Postcard to George.
Received ₱471 per diem payment.

₱147 + 400 – 307 = ₱240							
Meals	64	Lodging	50	Presents	70	Cigarettes	33
Misc.	18	Candy	7	Coke	22	Rides	4
Food	9	Souvenir	30			TOTAL	₱307

I got up at 4:55 AM, showered, got ready for the day, went downstairs for coffee and after a while, also ate breakfast. I wrote the postcard to George and filled out my per diem form while waiting for breakfast. After breakfast I went over to the Peace Corps Office and got my per diem and then Sue T. and I went to Baclaran and I got two pairs of short pants for George. We took the LRT to United Nations Avenue, went to the American Express office, I cashed some traveler's checks and then we went to Harrison Plaza for lunch. After that Sue went to a movie and I went to the Central Bank of the Philippines to get a ₱500 banknote [this was a new series, with the face of Benigno Aquino, Jr. on the front]. I returned to Malate Pension, checked out and came over to the Admiral Hotel. After a while I went over to Harrison Plaza, bought some Coke and bread and then returned to the Admiral Hotel. At 5:00 PM our first Close-of-Service Conference session started. After a while we ate supper, talked until 9:00 PM and then I came to the room. Oh, I forgot, I converted $50 to ₱1,030 pesos this afternoon too. Now it's 9:21 PM and I'm about ready to crash. I'm in a shared room with Ralph P. and Willie S. Ralph has already crashed. AWANEN!

Thursday, September 24, 1987
Admiral Hotel, Manila

₱240 – 15 = ₱225							
Taxi	12	Beer	3			TOTAL	₱15

We got up at 4:55 AM, showered and killed time until 6:00 AM and then we went downstairs for breakfast at 6:30 AM. After breakfast we talked for a bit and then our sessions began at 8:00 AM. We took a break for lunch from noon to 1:30 PM and then continued again until 5:00 PM. When we finished we went to Ed Slevin's house [Peace Corps Director for the Philippines at the time] for dinner at 5:15 PM. Supper was not served until 7:30 PM. It was pretty fine food. After that we just hung out and talked at Ed's house until about 9:00 PM and then headed back to the Admiral Hotel. Now it's 9:21 PM and I want to do some more paperwork before I crash in a few minutes. AWANEN!

Friday, September 25, 1987
Admiral Hotel, Manila

₱225 + 12 – 45 = ₱192							
Cigarettes	25	Household	5	Misc.	15	TOTAL	₱45

We got up at 5:30 AM and went downstairs for breakfast at 6:30 AM. Sessions began at 8:00 AM, we stopped for marienda at 10:00 AM and then our next stop was noon, and lunch. We had another marienda break at 3:00 PM and the sessions ended at about 5:15 PM. At 6:00 PM we had supper and then at 8:00 PM there was a slide-show. Oh, I forgot, I also did some laundry during lunch hour. Now it's 9:19 PM and it's nice that the conference is finished, I'm tired of sitting around and listening to people talk and talk and talk and talk. Tonight I seem, at least to myself, to be in a really hostile and pissed off mood, but I'm not exactly sure why. Could it be because our service is coming to a close? Tomorrow night I'll be in Bayombong. AWANEN!

Saturday, September 26, 1987
Host Family, Bonfal East, Bayombong, Nueva Vizcaya

₱192 – 147 = ₱45							
Rides	67	Marienda	25	Coke	6	Presents	15
Ice Cream	24	Household	6	Misc.	4	TOTAL	₱147

We got up at 5:30 AM, got ready for the day and went downstairs for breakfast at 6:10 AM. We drank coffee and then we had to wait until 6:30 AM for breakfast. We ate breakfast and after that I packed and Chester and I went to the Pantranco Bus Terminal and got a 9:00 AM bus headed north. There were bus problems at Cabanatuan City and again at San Jose, so it took us until 4:00 PM to get to Bayombong. I went to the house in Bonfal East and this time Herbert and Rebecca are not here. It's kind of nice because it's more quiet. At 6:30 PM we ate supper and now it's only 8:04 PM and Ronald and I are ready to crawl under the mosquito net, play around for a while and I'll give him what he wants. Wonder if he has anybody else doing this for him? If he doesn't, I wonder if he'll find a new guy to give him blow jobs when I leave? AWANEN!

Sunday, September 27, 1987
Host Family, Bonfal East, Bayombong, Nueva Vizcaya

₱45 + 100 – 45 = ₱100							
Beer	22	Rides	7	Movie	15	Household	1
						TOTAL	₱45

We got up late, at 6:00 AM, drank coffee, ate breakfast and got ready for the day. After a while Ronald and I went to the farm and we looked at the cattle for a while. Then we picked some guava, returned to the farm, ate some sugar cane and then came home at about 11:30 AM. We ate lunch and then I took a siesta from 12:30 to 1:30 PM. I got up and after a while we went to Solano and went to a movie. The movie got out at 7:20 PM and we stopped for a couple of beers, came home at 8:00 PM, ate supper, watched TV for a while and now it's 9:18 PM and I'm ready to crash. AWANEN!

Monday, September 28, 1987
My House, Gomez, Cabarroguis, Quirino

Letters from Tony & Janet S., Vicki S. and Sandy F.

₱100 + 300 – 207 = ₱193							
Cigarettes	24	Lunch	34	Candy	7	Food	61
Rides	16	Presents	10	Marienda	25	Ice Cream	27
Coke	3					TOTAL	₱207

We got up at 6:00 AM, I bathed before breakfast and then we ate and got ready for the day. Ronald and I walked to the bus waiting shed at about 7:45 and I took a jeepney to Solano, another jeepney to Santiago, arrived in Santiago at about 10:00 AM, did my marketing, ate lunch at the Ice Cream House and then I went to catch a jeepney bound for home. I waited quite a while and the jeepney finally left Santiago at about 12:45 PM. I stopped at the post office in Gundaway and the workers had not yet returned from lunch, lazy bastards. They came back at 2:30 PM, I got the above mail and then got a jeepney for Burgos. I started climbing the high road at 3:01 PM and arrived home at about 3:45 PM. I unpacked my bags, put stuff away and then I went to Alfredo's to discover that the corn harvest has finished – there were 24 carts of corn total. George was busy cutting down the dead corn stalks this afternoon. After a while he arrived home, we talked for a few minutes and then I came home. I bathed and started my charcoal fire. I'm not cooking supper tonight because I'm too tired. Now it's 5:51 PM and I'm drinking coffee, that's my supper. There's corn shelling tonight so I'll go to George's in a while and help with that. AWANEN!

Tuesday, September 29, 1987
My House, Gomez, Cabarroguis, Quirino

We got up at 5:15 AM and George left. I went to shell corn last night, but we didn't end up shelling any, so we came here at 7:20 PM and we told stories for a while and then slept. It was so nice to be with George again! I started my rice cooking, took my nuang to pasture, returned and talked with George for a few minutes and then came home. I finished cooking, ate, did dishes and got ready for the day. I went and got my nuang and went to the farm. Today George and I harvested my corn. We finished that at about 10:30 AM and then we went and got our nuangs and came home. My corn amounts to less than one full cart, maybe one kaban of shelled corn. We got home at about 11:15 AM, I ate lunch and then I took a siesta from 11:45 AM to 1:00 PM. I got up and drank coffee, prepared my vegetables for supper and Efren came. He said there was a forestry meeting today, but nobody came – including me! At 1:30 PM I went to George's and at 2:00 PM we took our nuangs to pasture and returned to the farm. George cut more dead corn stalks and I did some weed pulling and that was all. We stopped work at 4:15 PM and headed home. We got and bathed our nuangs and got home at about 4:50 PM. I started cooking, bathed myself and now it's 5:37 PM and my supper is cooking – beans and *tarong*. There will be corn shelling tonight, so I'll go to George's at about 7:00 PM. The weather today was partly cloudy all day and now it looks like it might rain. It rained last night from 6:20 to 8:30 PM or so. George has slept here 419 nights now. AWANEN!

Wednesday, September 30, 1987
My House, Gomez, Cabarroguis, Quirino

Do Peace Corps Quarterly Report – the final one!

We got up at 5:25 AM and George left. We shelled corn last night until 9:30 PM and then came here and slept pretty quickly. I started my rice cooking, took my nuang to pasture, returned and talked with George for a few minutes and then came home. George pulled a cart of corn to Burgos for Junior today. I finished cooking, ate, did dishes and got ready for the day. I worked on my Peace Corps quarterly report, sorted all of my papers from the Close-of-Service conference and filed the ones I need to keep. At 10:00 AM I went and got and bathed my nuang, returned home and finished the quarterly report, the sorting of papers and then ate lunch at 11:30 AM. I took a siesta from noon until 1:00 PM, drank coffee and then at 1:40 PM I took my nuang to pasture and Alfredo and I made the handle for my *kumpay* [rice cutting knife]. After we finished that I came home, sanded and oiled it and then returned to Alfredo's and pounded the hot chili peppers that I bought before the COS conference. Then I came back home and at 4:00 PM I prepared my vegetables for supper – *utong* and *tarong*. Then I went and talked with George for a few minutes; he returned home at 3:30 PM. I went and got and bathed my nuang, came home, started cooking and bathed myself. Now I've finished eating and doing dishes. There will be corn shelling tonight. The weather today was partly cloudy most of the day, but no rain. AWANEN!

Thursday, October 1, 1987
My House, Gomez, Cabarroguis, Quirino

Letter to Chris & Mary M.

We got up at 5:15 AM and George left. We shelled corn last night until 9:15 PM and then George came at 10:15 PM because people hung around at their house for a while after we finished. I started my rice cooking, drank coffee and took my nuang to pasture. I returned and George had already left for the farm to cut grass so I talked with Alfredo for a few minutes and then came home. I finished cooking, ate, did dishes and got ready for the day. I did some laundry, but not all of it, and then I did the letter to Chris and Mary. At 10:45 AM I went to get my nuang and George was already home so, I talked with him for few minutes and then went and got and bathed my nuang. I returned home, ate my lunch and after a while I took a siesta from 1:00 to 2:00 PM. Oh, I forgot, I put the crushed and powdered chili peppers out to dry more at 11:00 AM. At 2:00 PM I took my nuang back to pasture, returned home and worked until 3:30 PM on my Close-of-Service package. I went to George's and pounded the hot chili pepper powder again and then came home and prepared my vegetables for supper – *utong* and *tarong* again. At 4:30 PM I went and got and bathed my nuang and then at 5:00 PM I started cooking. I ate, did dishes and now it's 6:33 PM and we're going to be shelling corn again tonight, so after a little while I'll go help at George's house. The weather today was cloudy until 10:45 AM, then bright sun until 5:00 PM and then it clouded up again. There's been no rain though. AWANEN!

Friday, October 2, 1987
My House, Gomez, Cabarroguis, Quirino

We got up at 5:20 AM and George left. We shelled corn until 9:30 PM last night and then came here immediately, talked for a few minutes and slept. I started my rice cooking, drank coffee and took my nuang to pasture. I returned and talked with George only a minute and then came home. I finished cooking, ate, did dishes and got ready for the day. At 7:00 AM I went to George's and we shelled corn straight through until 10:30 AM. We went and got and bathed our nuangs and I came home. After a little while I ate lunch, read *Newsweek* and then I took a siesta from noon to 1:00 PM. I got up, drank coffee and then went back to George's and worked at shelling corn until 2:00 PM. We took our nuangs back to pasture and then I helped shell corn until we finished with it at 3:00 PM. I came home, fetched water, bottled my dried chili pepper powder, which I sun dried again today, and prepared my vegetables for supper – squash tonight. At 4:20 PM I went and got and bathed my nuang and then started cooking. I bathed myself, went to buy some cigarettes and returned home. We'll be shelling corn tonight too – maybe several people, but have to wait and see how many people show up. Now it's 5:15 PM and my rice is nearly cooked. I've already worked at shelling corn today for five to six hours and will be doing so for maybe four more hours tonight! The weather today was partly cloudy off and on all day, but no rain. The soil is dry again. AWANEN!

Saturday, October 3, 1987
My House, Gomez, Cabarroguis, Quirino

Letter to Tony & Janet S.

We got up at 5:30 AM and George left. We shelled corn, about ten of us I guess, until 11:45 PM last night, came here and slept nearly immediately. I started my rice cooking, drank coffee and took my nuang to pasture. I returned and talked with George for a few minutes and came home. I finished cooking, ate, did dishes and got ready for the day. The first thing I did was write the letter to Tony and Janet. Then I worked more on my Clothes-of-Service final report until 10:30 AM. I went and got and bathed my nuang, returned home, ate lunch and then took a siesta from 11:40 AM until 1:00 PM. I got up and after a while I took my nuang back to pasture, returned and prepared my vegetables for supper – squash again – early because I thought we'd shell corn again this afternoon, but we didn't so I returned home and read *Reader's Digest* and after a while I went back to George's and helped pick up the corn that was spread out to dry. We finished doing that at 4:30 PM and then I went and got and bathed my nuang, bathed myself and started cooking supper. I asked George to please come early tonight because there is no corn shelling, but he said he doesn't know because they may stroll. Now it's 5:28 PM and my rice is nearly cooked. The weather today was cloudy until 10:30 AM and then sunny and hot. It clouded up again at about 5:00 PM but there's been no rain yet. AWANEN!

Sunday, October 4, 1987
My House, Gomez, Cabarroguis, Quirino
Nuang Calving Day!!

Postcards to Sue T., Tom & Barb H., JB & Katie F. and Health Unit.

We got up at 5:20 AM and George left; he came at 8:20 PM last night. I started the rice cooking, drank coffee and took my nuang to pasture. I returned and talked with George for a few minutes and came home. I finished cooking, ate, did dishes and got ready for the day. The first thing I did was laundry and after that I worked on my Close-of-Service final report until 10:00 AM. Then I went and got and bathed my nuang. I returned home and after a little while I ate lunch and then took a siesta from noon to 1:10 PM. I woke up and my nuang had just finished calving, and I missed it! George and several kids were watching the mother lick the calf clean. I grabbed my camera and took several pictures and then George and I continued to watch the process until about 3:00 PM. It took about one-and-a-half hours for the calf to stand up. At that point I fetched water and bathed. At 4:30 PM the afterbirth was finally expelled and the mother ate it. The calf finally found the teats at about 5:00 PM. At 4:45 PM Alfredo and his wife returned from Burgos – they sold corn today. Alfredo got a truck to come and get the corn. The weight of mine was 91 kilograms and I was paid ₱260.90. We all watched the calf for a while and at 5:00 PM I came inside and started cooking. I'm eating Armour Beef Stew that Brooke brought one-and-a-half years ago.

It was quite an exciting day, really. It was the first time I've ever seen a nuang have a calf. It was good that George was here so he could see it too; it was real nice to be with my best friend while my nuang was calving. So, let's see, I bought her on October 22, 1986, George's nuang mated her on November 23, 1986 and she calved on October 4, 1987, that's a 315 day gestation period. At approximately 1:00 PM she calved. The calf found its feet one-and-a-half hours later and then finally began suckling at about 5:00 PM. The silly calf kept searching for the teats under the front legs and possibly it would have suckled earlier if it would have searched in the proper place. Beth told me that I am very *nalaing* [expert, efficient or capable] as I've only been here a short time and already my nuang has calved [like I planned this or something]. Anyway, I feel good today and I hope George comes early tonight to share in my happiness. In addition, Alfredo said that the people at the corn buying place were amazed that I was farming and actually selling corn! So, today was really a "feather in my cap" sort of day. I'm happy and feeling good about it. Now it's 5:38 PM and my rice is nearly cooked. The weather today was partly cloudy this morning and then sunny and hot. it clouded up again at about 5:00 PM but looks like it probably won't rain tonight. AWANEN!

(There are some photos on the following two pages.)

The photo just below shows the nuang mother licking the calf clean shortly after she gave birth.

This photo shows the nuang mother and calf at about three hours after birth. The calf had not yet started to suckle and is not yet very sure on its feet.

The photo below shows the nuang calf suckling. This photo was taken on the day following birth.

Monday, October 5, 1987
My House, Gomez, Cabarroguis, Quirino

Postcard to Tony Sachet.

₱193 + 300 – 2 = ₱491							
Cigarettes	2					TOTAL	₱2

We got up at 5:20 AM and George left; he came at 8:00 PM last night. I started the rice cooking, drank coffee and took my nuang to pasture on the other side of the creek. I returned home, finished cooking and then went and talked with George for a few minutes. I came home, ate, did dishes and got ready for the day. I trimmed the grass in the west lawn and cleaned dead leaves from all of the close-by banana trees. I swept the north lawn and started sweeping the south lawn and then went and checked on my nuang. I returned and read *"The Drastic Dragon of Draco, Texas"* by Elizabeth Scarborough. At 9:45 AM I went and got my nuang, put her in the shade and read some more. At 11:20 AM I ate lunch and then took a siesta from noon to 1:00 PM. I got up and went to George's but he took his lunch to the farm today, so at 2:00 PM I took my nuang to pasture again and finished sweeping the south lawn. After that I went and checked on my nuang again, came home and read some and at 4:20 PM I started cooking my mungo beans. At 4:30 PM I went and got my nuang and then went and talked with George for a few minutes and we watched the calf together. I asked him to come early tonight and he said yes. I came home and bathed and now it's 5:36 PM and my mungo beans are nearly done, but I haven't started cooking the rice yet. The weather today was partly cloudy off and on all day. It rained for about ten minutes at noon and then again from 3:45 to 4:00 PM, but only lightly. AWANEN!

Tuesday, October 6, 1987
My House, Gomez, Cabarroguis, Quirino

Letters from Roselynn S., Tim C. and Chad D. Postcard for George arrived (mailed September 23 from Manila).

₱491 – 469 = ₱22							
Food	89	Rides	16	Kerosene	8	Meals	25
Cigarettes	48	Film	120	Soap	16	Coffee	53
Household	8	Marienda	31	Postage	22	Haircut	5
Ice Cream	16	Candy	12			TOTAL	₱469

We got up at 5:10 AM, I gave George my *wayway* and he left. He came at 8:20 PM last night when I went to get him. I cooked breakfast, ate, did dishes, got ready for the day and headed for Burgos at 6:45 AM. I arrived there at 7:20 AM and caught a ride to Gundaway. I got the above mail and continued on to Santiago, where I mailed all the letters I'd written over the past week. I did my shopping, went to the bank and pulled most of my money out of my savings account and also cashed my checks. Then I ate lunch, got a haircut and after that I caught a jeepney back to Burgos. I arrived at the bottom of the high road at 1:55 PM and started climbing the mountain at 2:00 PM. I got home at about 2:40 PM or so, unpacked, put things away, read my mail and then fetched water. At 4:30 PM I bathed and then I went to talk with George until 5:20 PM. I came home and made hot water for coffee; I'm not eating supper tonight because I'm really tired. The weather today was clear, very sunny and hot all day long. It clouded up and sprinkled a tiny bit at 3:30 PM and then cleared up again. It seems like it has been quite a long time with no rain. I hope George comes earlier tonight. AWANEN!

Wednesday, October 7, 1987
My House, Gomez, Cabarroguis, Quirino

Letter to Vicki S. Postcard to Sandy F.

I got up at 5:10 AM, but George got up at 3:40 AM and left to take his nuang to pasture as he's plowing at the farm today. He came at 7:45 PM last night. I started my rice cooking, drank coffee and took my nuang to pasture. I returned and finished cooking, ate, did dishes and got ready for the day. I worked on my Close-of-Service final report until 8:00 AM and then went and looked at my nuang. When I returned I continued working on the COS report and at 9:30 AM I went and got my nuang. I managed to finish the report before lunch; it's 15 pages in all. I ate lunch and took a siesta from 11:30 AM to 1:15 PM, got up, drank coffee and at 2:00 PM I took my nuang to pasture again and returned home. At 3:00 PM I went to George's house and crushed the hot chili peppers that I dried today and talked with George's mother until 3:35 PM or so. I came home, washed up and prepared the vegetables for supper – I'll be having *utong* and *tarong* again. At 4:30 PM I went and got and bathed my nuang, it was her first bath since she calved and she was happy. I started cooking, bathed myself and now it's 5:44 PM and my vegetables are nearly cooked. We'll be shelling corn tonight, so at about 7:00 PM I'll go to George's to help with that. The weather today was very hot and dry, it's weather more like April than October. At about 5:00 PM it clouded up and at 5:30 PM it sprinkled a little bit, but that's all. Oh, I finished *"The Drastic Dragon…"* book in my spare time today. AWANEN!

Thursday, October 8, 1987
My House, Gomez, Cabarroguis, Quirino

I got up at 5:30 AM. George got up and left at 4:40 AM to pasture his nuang. We shelled corn last night until 10:30 PM, Junior came to help just as we were finishing, a typical Junior stunt! I came home and George followed at 11:55 PM, after Junior finished running off at the mouth. I started my rice cooking and took my nuang to pasture. I returned home and finished cooking, ate, did dishes, got ready for the day and then I sorted papers for a while. When the sun got strong I put out another batch of chili pepper powder to dry prior to the second crushing. At 10:00 AM I went and got my nuang and had to search for the calf for one hour – the little fucker is very good at hiding. I returned home, ate lunch and took a siesta from noon to 2:00 PM. I got up, took my nuang to pasture again and George was home when I returned so I talked with him for a while – he's got a bad headache. After a while I came home, fetched water and prepared my vegetables for supper – *utong* and *tarong*. Then I went to George's to crush the hot chili powder again and returned home at 4:00 PM. At 4:30 PM I went and got my nuang and again had to search for the calf, but this time only for a half hour. I returned home and started the rice cooking, bathed myself and now it's 5:59 PM and my vegetables are nearly cooked. There will be corn shelling tonight, I hope we stop earlier than last night. The weather today was hot and dry all day – the weather of April continues. AWANEN!

Friday, October 9, 1987
My House, Gomez, Cabarroguis, Quirino

Letter to Jim & Roselynn S.

I got up at 5:10 AM with no companion. We shelled corn last night until 9:30 PM and George had such a bad headache that he didn't even shell corn, he just wanted to sleep. I started my rice cooking, drank coffee and took my nuang to pasture. George was feeling okay this morning so he went to plow today. I returned home, finished cooking, ate, did dishes and got ready for the day. I swept and pulled weeds in the north yard and one half of the south yard and then sorted out some things to give to Ronald; he was supposed to come today, but didn't. At 9:40 AM I went and got and bathed my nuang and returned home. I wrote the letter to Jim and Roselynn, ate lunch and took a siesta from 12:20 to 1:00 PM. I got up and drank coffee and then at 2:00 PM I took my nuang back to pasture and returned home. At 3:00 PM I crushed another jar of hot chili peppers; I have now finished four of them and there are still two to do. Then I came home and prepared my vegetables for supper and at 4:20 PM I went to get my nuangs and bathe them. I did that, came home, started supper and then I bathed myself. I went to George's and he's got a bad headache again; I hope it goes away so he'll come to sleep here tonight, please God. Now it's 5:47 PM and my vegetables are nearly cooked. Of course there will be corn shelling tonight. The weather today was hot and dry again, there's been no rain in well over a week now. AWANEN!

Saturday, October 10, 1987
My House, Gomez, Cabarroguis, Quirino

Ronald come and spend the night.

I got up at 5:10 AM with no companion again. George is still not feeling well. We shelled corn last night until 9:45 PM. I started my rice cooking, drank coffee and took my nuang to pasture. I returned and talked with George for just a bit because he is still sick and he went to Diffun to go to the doctor today. I came home, finished cooking, ate, did dishes and got ready for the day. I started the day by doing laundry and that took from 7:30 until 9:15 AM. At 9:30 AM I went and got and bathed my nuangs, returned home and started reading the book *"Moreta: Dragonlady of Pern"* by Anne McCaffrey. I slept from 11:00 AM until noon and then got up and ate lunch. Ronald arrived at about 1:00 PM and we talked and looked at/watched the nuang calf until 2:00 PM and then we went and pastured them once again. We returned and talked some more and then at about 3:00 PM we went to Alfredo's, talked for a while and I crushed the fifth jar of hot chili peppers; now I only have one more jar left. I got some sweet corn seed for Ronald. George was home, but he was still feeling really bad; the doctor told him he has he's having a malaria recurrence. After a bit we came home, took the clothes off the line, prepared vegetables for supper – we'll be eating beans and pepino. At 4:30 PM we went and got and bathed the nuangs once again, returned home and started cooking. I bathed myself and now it's 5:47 PM and the rice is cooking. The weather today was hot and dry all day. There were thick clouds for a little while this morning but it was clear by 7:30 AM. There's no rain in sight AWANEN!

Sunday, October 11, 1987
My House, Gomez, Cabarroguis, Quirino

Ronald leave.

We got up at 5:10 AM, started the rice cooking, drank coffee and went and pastured the nuangs. We returned and talked with George for a couple of minutes and then came home. We finished cooking, I did dishes and got ready for the day and then Ronald and I talked for a while. I put out the last bottle of hot chili pepper powder to dry and also a bag of charcoal. At 9:30 AM we went and got and bathed the nuangs and returned home. Ronald and I talked until 11:10 AM and then we ate lunch. He is extremely jealous of George as he accused me of loving him too much and having him as a sex partner. Of course Ronald would not believe that George doesn't enjoy what he does, nor even want it. Anyway, after that we took a siesta from 11:30 AM to 12:30 PM and at about 1:15 PM he packed up and left. Okay, I was getting bored and frustrated by his "problem" with George and I anyway. At 2:00 PM I took my nuangs back to pasture. The calf is one-week old today; it's fat and healthy and I feel good about that. I returned home and read the *"Moreta"* book until 3:00 PM and then I prepared my vegetables for supper – beans. I picked up the charcoal that was drying and went to George's to crush the hot chili pepper powder for the second time. After a while I came home, fetched water and at 4:30 I went and got and bathed my nuangs. After that I bathed myself and started cooking supper. I went to ask George if he was coming tonight and he said yes, I hope so. Now it's 5:37 PM and my beans are cooking. I hope George really does come early tonight; if he isn't here by 7:30 PM I'll go and get him. The weather today was hot and dry all day again, still no rain in sight. AWANEN!

Monday, October 12, 1987
My House, Gomez, Cabarroguis, Quirino

Letter to Chad D.

₱22 + 135 – 7 = ₱150							
Cigarettes	3	Soap	4			TOTAL	₱7

I got up at 5:20 AM with no companion again. I went to George's at 7:30 PM last night and he said he was still too sick. I started my rice cooking and took my nuangs to pasture, returned and talked with George for a couple of minutes and came home. I finished cooking, ate, did dishes, got ready for the day and then I washed both pairs of my shoes and read the *"Moreta"* book until 9:30 AM. I went and talked with George for a few more minutes and then went and got and bathed my nuangs. I returned home and sifted all of the dried chili pepper powder to remove the seeds and then I put the seeds out to dry some more. By then it was 11:30 AM so I ate lunch and then I laid down from noon until 12:30 PM, but I wasn't able tó sleep. I got up and read the *"Moreta"* book some more until 2:00 PM, then took my nuangs back to pasture and returned home. I did the letter to Chad and then prepared my vegetables for supper; I'll be having beans again. At 4:00 PM I went and crushed the dried chili pepper seeds and then came home and sifted them again. About half of them are still remaining; I'll dry them more tomorrow and crush them again. At 4:30 PM I went and got and bathed my nuangs and went and asked George to please come tonight. He said that he's not sure, so he probably won't – shit! Now it's 5:49 PM and my vegetables are nearly cooked. Please George, come tonight. The weather today was hot and dry all day. There's been no rain in two weeks now. AWANEN!

Tuesday, October 13, 1987
My House, Gomez, Cabarroguis, Quirino

Letters to Tim C. and Adelle S.

₱150 + 300 – 60 = ₱390							
Ulcer Med.	50	Cigarettes	10			TOTAL	₱60

We got up at 5:10 AM and George left; he not only came last night, but he came at 6:30 PM. WOW! Was I happy! I started my rice cooking, drank coffee and took my nuangs to pasture. I returned and talked with George for a minute and then came home, finished cooking, ate, did dishes and got ready for the day. The first thing I did was write two duplicate letters to Adelle, one with ₱50 [for Alfredo's ulcer medicine, which she gave me] enclosed and one without to be sure that she gets at least one of them. At 9:30 PM I went and got and bathed my nuangs – the calf can now climb out of the deep bathing place. When I returned I talked with George for a while and then came home and ate lunch. I took a siesta from noon to 1:10 PM and then got up, drank coffee and did the letter to Tim. At 2:00 PM I took my nuangs back to pasture again; George and I went together. I returned home and after a while I went to George's to crush the very last of the dried chili pepper powder. We talked for a while and then I came home, fetched water, bottled the hot chili pepper powder, washed the chili dishes and prepared my vegetables for supper – beans again. At 4:30 PM I went and got and bathed the nuangs, returned home, started my rice cooking, bathed myself and went and asked George to come early tonight. He said maybe there will be corn shelling tonight; if there is I'll go and help with that. Now it's 5:45 PM and my vegetables are nearly cooked. The weather today was rainy for about one-half hour very early this morning, but it was hot and dry again all day after that. AWANEN!

Wednesday, October 14, 1987
My House, Gomez, Cabarroguis, Quirino

GG injection receipt mailed to Peace Corps.

Letters from Barb W., San & Jack G., Barb H., Steve A., Bob S. and Ardis B. (photos too).

₱390 – 202 = ₱188							
Food	41	Rides	5	Kerosene	8	Cigarettes	47
Coffee	32	Marienda	42	Household	9	Postage	4
Candy	6	Misc.	8			TOTAL	₱202

I got up at 5:15 AM. George got up and left at 4:00 AM to pasture his nuang because he plowed some of the farm today. We shelled corn last night until 9:45 PM and then came here and slept very quickly. I started my rice cooking, drank coffee and took my *wayway* to George. We talked for a minute and then I came home, finished cooking, ate, did dishes, got ready for the day and headed for Burgos at 6:50 AM. From there I went to Gundaway, stopped at the post office and got the above mail, did marketing and then went to San Marcos Hospital for my GG shot. After that I returned to the post office and then continued on to Burgos. I went to see if the guy had the document for my nuang yet, but he wasn't home so I talked to his neighbor and told him I'll return on October 27th and then I headed back to the high road and started climbing the mountain at noon. I made it home in a new record time of 29 minutes 32.51 seconds, getting here at 12:30 PM. I wrung the sweat out of my T-shirt, unpacked and put things away and then took a siesta from 1:00 to 2:00 PM. I got up, read my mail and relaxed until 3:15 PM and then I went to Alfredo's and helped pick up the corn that we shelled last night that was drying in the sun. I came home at 4:00 PM and prepared my vegetables for supper – *tarong*. At 4:30 PM I started cooking and now it's 6:27 PM and everything is done, so I'll eat as soon as I finish this. There will be corn shelling tonight. The weather today was cloudy until 9:00 AM and then hot and dry all day. AWANEN!

Thursday, October 15, 1987
My House, Gomez, Cabarroguis, Quirino

Letters to Tom & Barb H., Bob S. Postcards to Tony S. and Ardis B.

I got up at 5:10 AM. George got up and left at 4:45 AM to pasture his nuang. We shelled corn until 9:45 PM last night, came here, I showed and gave George some new photos that Ardis had sent and then we slept. I started my rice cooking, drank coffee and took my nuangs to pasture. I returned and talked with George for a minute and then came home. I did laundry and then I wrote the postcard to Ardis. I made a list of everything that I have in the big round basket and after that I read the *"Moreta"* book until 10:30 AM. Then I went and got and bathed my nuangs and took some photos of them at the bathing hole. I went to George's and helped shell corn until 11:30 AM and then came home. I ate lunch and then took a siesta from noon to 1:10 PM. I got up and did the letter to Bob S. and then at 1:45 PM I took my nuangs back to pasture. I returned home and prepared my film for mailing, did the postcard to Tony and then the letter to Tom and Barbara. By then it was 3:30 PM so I prepared my vegetables for supper, tonight will be squash. I fetched water and then killed time until 4:25 PM. I went and got and bathed my nuangs, talked with George for a couple of minutes and he told me there will be corn shelling tonight. I returned home and started cooking, bathed myself and now it's 5:33 PM and my rice is nearly cooked. Maybe there will be two more nights of corn shelling and we'll be done for the season. The weather today was cloudy until 11:00 AM and then it cleared up, but it didn't get too hot. It clouded up again at 4:30 PM, but there's been no rain yet. AWANEN!

Friday, October 16, 1987
My House, Gomez, Cabarroguis, Quirino

Letters to Barb W., Steve A. and John D.

We got up at 5:15 AM and George left. We shelled corn last night until 10:20 PM and finished the last of it. We then came here and slept immediately. I started my rice cooking, drank coffee and took my nuangs to pasture. I returned and talked with George for a minute and then came home. I finished cooking, ate, did dishes and got ready for the day. I made a list of everything that is in my big black notebook and then sorted out all of the Peace Corps medicines to give to George tonight and loaded the medical kit with books. At 10:45 AM I went and got and bathed my nuangs, returned and talked with George for a couple of minutes and then came home. George is searching for more corn at the farm today – corn that was somehow overlooked during the rush of the harvest. I ate lunch and then took a siesta from noon to 1:10 PM. I got up and did the letter to Steve and then took my nuangs back to pasture at 2:00 PM. I came home and did the letter to Barb W. and killed time until 3:15 PM and then I prepared my vegetables for supper – I'll be having squash and a potato. I killed more time until 4:30 PM and then went and got and bathed my nuangs and talked with George for a while longer. He found about another half cart of corn so, we'll shell corn tonight, but probably only for about an hour or so; I may not bother to go, but I don't really expect George until 8:30 or 9:00 PM anyway. I came home started supper, bathed myself, ate, did dishes and now it's 6:37 PM. I hope George isn't too late to come. The weather today was cloudy until 10:30 AM, then sunny until 4:00 PM and then it clouded up again, there was no rain though. AWANEN!

Saturday, October 17, 1987
My House, Gomez, Cabarroguis, Quirino

Letter to San & Jack G.

We got up at 5:30 AM and George left; he came at 7:45 PM last night. The corn shelling is now totally done and there were 59 kabans in all. I started my rice cooking, took my nuangs to pasture, returned and talked with George for a couple of minutes and then came home. I finished cooking, ate, did dishes and got ready for the day. I did my laundry and finished that before 9:00 AM. I packed another backpack and made a list of what's in it and then killed time until 10:00 AM. I went and got and bathed my nuangs and then I returned home. George was plowing and harvesting bananas today and I'm not helping, it feels strange. I ate lunch at 11:00 AM and then took a siesta from 11:45 AM to 1:15 PM – a long siesta. I got up, trimmed my beard, drank coffee and at 2:00 PM I took my nuangs back to pasture. George had already returned to the farm so there was nobody to talk with and I came home. I did the letter to San and Jack and then fetched water, removed the clothes from the clothesline and killed time. I dug some of the ginger from Batanes and prepared my vegetables for supper – squash and winged beans. I packed to go to Baler tomorrow and at 4:30 PM I went and got and bathed my nuangs. I went and talked with George for a couple of minutes and asked him to come early, but he said he didn't know. I came home, started cooking, bathed and then went and gave George some pepino, eggs and *pusit.* Now it's 5:50 PM and my supper is cooked. I'll eat as soon as I finish this. The weather today was cloudy until 10:00 AM and then clear and hot the rest of the day. AWANEN!

Sunday, October 18, 1987
Amihan's Guest House, Baler, Aurora

₱188 + 200 – 249 = ₱139							
Rides	85	Meals	28	Cigarettes	46	Household	7
Souvenir	50	Coke	3	Marienda	30	TOTAL	₱249

We got up at 5:20 AM, I gave George my wayway and nuang medicine and he left; he came at 6:45 PM last night. I drank coffee, got ready for the day, took my bag of valuables to Alfredo's, said goodbye and left Gomez at about 6:05 AM. I got to Burgos and caught a ride to Gundaway and stopped at the post office, but there was no mail. I continued on to Cordon and got a ride on a Dalin Liner Bus at 8:50 AM. I had to sit on top of the engine compartment all the way to Cabanatuan. We arrived there at 1:45 PM and I searched for the station where I could get a ride to Baler, but there were no more buses today. A jeepney was leaving at 3:00 PM so I took that and it was a long and dusty trip to Baler. I didn't arrive until 7:30 PM or so. Two other Ilokano people got off here at Amihan's, so the three of us are sharing a room. We went and found a cheaper place to eat supper. Tomorrow I'll search for a cheaper place to stay too, this place is ₱40 per head per night and the local disco is here too so, it's noisy. Now it's 8:47 PM and I'm tired and ready to crash. AWANEN!

[If you go back to the map on page 284 you can find Baler not too far south of Gomez. I wanted one final fling at traveling to a new place before I left the Philippines and made the decision to come here as my travel guide indicated that this was a good place to visit.]

Monday, October 19, 1987
Beach View Lodge, Baler, Aurora

₱139 + 100 – 152 = ₱87							
Meals	106	Room	40	Cigarettes	6	TOTAL	₱152

I got up at 5:10 AM, bathed and got ready for the day. I went to Mely's Restaurant for breakfast and then I returned and checked out of Amihan's and went to the Beach View Lodge and checked in there. I drank another cup of coffee and then walked down south to Cemento. I sat there and talked with Don, a fellow from California, until about noon and then headed back to the Beach View Lodge for lunch. I ate and started working on my Farming Practices Report and then Don returned and came and sat with me. We talked until 2:30 PM, I went to the post office and mailed the letters which I brought with me and then returned to the Beach View. I tried to work on the report for a while longer but Don wanted to talk with me again so I couldn't. I ordered supper at about 6:00 PM or so and finally got served at about 7:30 PM. I ate and sat killing time for a while and now it's 9:05 PM and I'm ready to sleep.

There was disco last night at Amihan's and tonight there is some kind of sing-along here – another noisy place and therefore I'll probably move again tomorrow. So far I fail to be impressed by Baler. AWANEN!

Tuesday, October 20, 1987
Beach View Lodge, Baler, Aurora

₱87 + 100 – 87 = ₱100							
Food	28	Meals	59			TOTAL	₱87

I got up at 5:30 AM, bathed and ordered breakfast, which was finally served to me about one hour later. In the meantime I worked on my farming report. At about 10:00 AM or so I went strolling around the town, got some peanut butter and bread and then walked through the market. I saw some squash so I decided that's what I wanted for supper. I came back to the Beach View and worked on my farming report more and then at noon I ate lunch of peanut butter sandwiches. I took a siesta from 12:20 to 1:15 PM and then got up and basically killed time all afternoon. I talked with Don, the surfer from California some more. At about noon I told the lodge that I wanted to order squash for supper, cooked in coconut milk at 6:00 to 6:30 PM. At 6:00 PM the guy told me there were no squash at the market, so I had to end up eating beans, carrots and fish for supper. Then I found an *"Outside"* Magazine and read it cover-to-cover until about 9:00 PM. Now it's 9:15 PM and the fucking sing-along is going on tonight too so I can sleep. AWANEN!

Wednesday, October 21, 1987
Beach View Lodge, Baler, Aurora

₱100 + 100 – 93 = ₱107							
Meals	50	Food	40	Soap	3	TOTAL	₱93

I got up at 5:00 AM, drank coffee and ordered breakfast and finally ate it. Then I went and bathed and after I finished that, I continued working on my farming reports more. At about 8:00 AM I went to market and got more peanut butter, bread, squash and coconut, the latter two things for supper. Then I found out when buses leave, returned back to the lodge and worked on my report until noon. I ate my peanut butter and bread for lunch and then took a siesta from 1:00 to 2:00 PM. I got up, drank coffee and worked on my report again, until it was finished, and then I took a walk north on the beach from 4:00 to 5:30 PM and returned to the lodge. I had already asked for supper for 6:00 to 6:30 PM, but I didn't finally get served until about 7:15 PM. All during my supper Madonna was asking what I'm going to give her for a remembrance when I leave. I told her "nothing". The shitty music has been going on at this place since noon. I'll probably move tomorrow; I'm getting angrier and angrier every day now. It's 8:45 PM, good night. AWANEN!

Thursday, October 22, 1987
Beach View Lodge, Baler, Aurora

₱107 + 400 – 325 = ₱182							
Meals	74	Room	240	Cigarettes	11	TOTAL	₱325

I got up at 5:30 AM, drank coffee, bathed and was served breakfast at 7:50 AM. I read over my whole farming report, crossed out a few words and added a few words and then I read some book that I started last night, oh yes, the book was *"The Tenth Man"*. I took a siesta from 9:00 to 10:00 AM, got up, drank more coffee and started reading *"The Book of Lists"*. At noon I ate peanut butter and bread and took another siesta from 1:00 to 2:00 PM. I got up and continued reading *"The Book of Lists"* again until finally suppertime came around at 7:00 PM. The ocean has really high waves today and this afternoon's high tide brought water practically to the doorstep. After supper I paid my bill and bathed. I'm leaving tomorrow morning as early as I can get out of here. I don't know if I'll eat breakfast here or not, I'll just see what happens – maybe I'll have coffee only. Now it's 9:03 PM and I hope that I can sleep tonight after all of the sleeping I did during the day. AWANEN!

Friday, October 23, 1987
Golden Rose Lodge and Restaurant, Santa Fe, Nueva Vizcaya

₱182 + 100 – 272 = ₱10							
Rides	48	Room	40	Cigarettes	12	Meals	96
Presents	28	Souvenirs	35	Candy	13	TOTAL	₱272

I got up at 5:15 AM, got ready for the day and left, without even drinking coffee – nobody was even awake. An ocean wave came up to the door of my room during the night; it's a pretty angry ocean! I went to the bus terminal and got a Pantranco Bus from Baler to Cabanatuan. I left Baler at 6:00 AM and got to Cabanatuan shortly after 10:00 AM and then I waited there for a northbound Pantranco Bus until 11:00 AM and was finally able to continue north. I stopped in Santa Fe, arriving at 2:00 PM. My purpose in getting off here was to search for a small basket, but I couldn't find exactly what I was looking for so I ended up buying a different one. I ended up walking six miles in my search, but there were just none of the small ones like I was really wanting to find. I finally returned to the Golden Rose Lodge and Restaurant, where I'm staying, ate supper and relaxed. Now it's 7:14 PM and I'm sitting here in my room thinking about George, I miss him. I'm thinking about the fact that two weeks from tomorrow I leave Gomez for the last time; it will be a happy and sad day, for sure. There's a weak typhoon going on now, Typhoon P something. They're already up to "P" so it's the 16th typhoon of the season. WOW! AWANEN!

Saturday, October 24, 1987
Host Family, Bonfal East, Bayombong, Nueva Vizcaya

₱10 + 100 – 80 = ₱30							
Rides	11	Cigarettes	9	Presents	25	Meals	35
						TOTAL	₱80

Typhoon Pepong!

I got up at 5:20 AM and it was still dark, windy and rainy; the typhoon really came in strong during the night. I ate breakfast, got ready for the day and caught a ride to Bayombong at 7:00 AM, arriving at the house in Bonfal East even before 9:00 AM. The family was surprised to see me so early. After a little while Ronald and I went to the farm and he got some coconuts – the last time that I get to eat fresh *buko* right from the tree. We dug, ate and cooked some *kahoy* and after a while we came back to the house. We ate lunch and then I took a siesta from 1:00 to 1:40 PM. We got up and ate a second lunch and after a while we made an easy type of rice cake. The wind has been blowing very strong all day, and on and off there's been heavy rain, but only for five minutes at a time. Now it's only 5:16 PM so we haven't eaten supper yet. (Later) Now it's 8:01 PM, supper is finished and I'm ready for bed, but supper is just now cooked – chicken and *kahoy*, so I guess we'll eat that and then I'll crash. Wonder if Ronald will request a final blow job? AWANEN!

Sunday, October 25, 1987
Host Family, Bonfal East, Bayombong, Nueva Vizcaya
Final Night to Stay Here

₱30 + 100 – 18 = ₱112							
Rides	9	Cigarettes	9			TOTAL	₱18

We got up at 5:20 AM, drank coffee, I bathed and got ready for the day and then after a while we ate breakfast. At about 8:00 AM Ronald and I went to Santo Domingo to get Herbert and Rebecca. We arrived there at about 8:45 AM and they hadn't even eaten breakfast yet, so finally they were ready at about 11:00 AM and we all came to Bonfal East. After a while we ate lunch and then I took a siesta from 12:45 to 1:30 PM. I got up and they were butchering a goat for my *despedida*, so of course that means there were TOO many people here and too much alcohol. After a while everybody was drunk, father was quite drunk and telling me stories about how he doesn't want to run for Barangay Captain for 45 minutes or an hour. Finally, I escaped to the upstairs. Now it's 6:03 PM and Rebecca is downstairs crying; I have no idea why, I don't know what happened, I heard something about a quarrel. I hope it was nothing too serious. I've never yet heard Herbert and Rebecca quarrel, but Herbert is very, very drunk so who knows what happened. AWANEN!

Monday, October 26, 1987
My House, Gomez, Cabarroguis, Quirino

Letters from San & Jack G. (2), Tony S., Cynthia B. and my Patagonia Gear order arrived (see September 8).

₱112 + 300 – 307 = ₱105							
Food	124	Meals	39	Rides	14	Presents	13
Candy	7	Marienda	18	Cigarettes	53	Postage	3
Coke	3	Ice Cream	18	Clothes	15	TOTAL	₱307

We got up at 5:50 AM, I drank coffee and bathed and then after a while we ate breakfast and I left. Ronald walked me to the road for the last time and we said our sad goodbyes. I caught a jeepney to Solano and finally from there, I got a ride to Santiago, but I had to take a Vizcaya Liner, so I didn't arrive in Santiago until 11:30 AM. I went to the bank and withdrew all but ₱10 and then I did my shopping and went to the Ice Cream House for lunch. Paul B. stopped in and said that JB and Katie would be at Letty's Restaurant at 1:00 PM, so we went to Marilen's and ate ice cream. We then went to Letty's and I waited until 1:40 PM for JB and Katie, but they didn't show up, so I left. I caught a jeepney to the Gundaway Post Office, picked up the above mail and then continued on to Burgos. I started climbing via the high road at about 3:45 PM and got home at about 4:30 PM. I unpacked, put things away and went to George's to talk with them for a while. I came home, bathed and started making coffee water – my supper, as I'm too tired to cook. Now it's 6:08 PM and I hope George comes early tonight. The weather today was hot, dry and partly cloudy, they told me there's been no rain since I left! AWANEN!

Tuesday, October 27, 1987
My House, Gomez, Cabarroguis, Quirino

Letter to Tony S.

I got up at 5:10 AM. George got up and left at 4:30 AM to pasture his nuang. He came last night at 6:55 PM. I cooked my rice, drank coffee, ate, did the dishes, got ready for the day and headed for Burgos at 7:00 AM. I got there and talked with Richard until nearly 8:00 AM and then I went to the guy's place who has my nuang papers. He wasn't there again. The neighbor said he told him I'd come today, so we talked for awhile. Alfredo and I will go together on Thursday and the guy said that we'll go to the bank and try to trade documents – SHIT – no luck again. I drank a Coke at Rogel's Canteen and headed back up the mountain. I arrived home at about 10:00 AM and after a while I went to Alfredo's and told him what had happened and what I had learned. I came home, ate lunch and then took a siesta from 11:30 AM to noon. I read *Newsweek* and at 2:00 PM I took my nuangs to pasture. I returned and talked with Alfredo until 2:40 PM and then I came home and swept the north yard and prepared beans for supper; I'm also having corned beef hash. At 4:30 PM I went and got and bathed my nuangs, bathed myself, started cooking and went to talk with George for a few minutes and ask him to please come early. Now it's 5:35 PM and my rice is nearly cooked. The weather today was cloudy until 8:00 AM and then it cleared up and got very hot. It clouded up again at about 3:30 PM, but it probably won't rain. There's been no rain here in a month now. AWANEN!

Wednesday, October 28, 1987
My House, Gomez, Cabarroguis, Quirino

Letter to Cynthia B.

I got up at 5:10 AM. George got up and left at 4:30 AM to pasture his nuang; he came last night at 7:35 PM. I started my rice cooking, drank coffee and took my nuangs to pasture. I returned and talked with George for a minute and then came home. I finished cooking, ate, did dishes and got ready for the day. I did laundry, finishing that at about 8:45 AM and then I calculated my expenses for October up through today. At 10:00 AM I went and got and bathed my nuangs and then went and talked with Alfredo until 11:00 AM. I came home, ate lunch and took a siesta from 11:45 AM to 12:45 PM. I got up and started reading the book *"Lonesome Dove"* by Larry McMurtry. At 1:30 PM I took my nuangs back to pasture and then George was home because the plow broke, so I talked with him for a while. Then I came home and read for a while and Efren came and stayed here from 2:30 – 3:30 PM. He climbed the mountain merely to remind me about the forestry meeting next Tuesday. He left and I prepared my vegetables for supper – beans. At 4:15 PM I went and talked with George and asked him to come early. At 4:30 PM I went and got and bathed my nuangs, returned home, started the rice cooking and bathed myself. Now it's 5:45 PM and my vegetables are cooking and nearly done. The weather today was cloudy until 10:00 AM, then sunny, then clouded back up and rained from 11:30 AM to 1:00 PM and then cleared up again. Now it's partly cloudy. AWANEN!

Thursday, October 29, 1987
My House, Gomez, Cabarroguis, Quirino

₱105 + 200 – 30 = ₱275							
Rides	24	Cigarettes	3	Marienda	3	TOTAL	₱30

We got up at 5:15 AM and George left; he came at 7:00 PM last night. I gave him my *wayway* before he left. I cooked breakfast, ate, did dishes, got ready for the day and then Alfredo and I headed down the mountain for Burgos to try and get the document for my nuang again. We went to the guy's house and he came home at about 9:15 AM. He immediately broke out a bottle of Ginebra [a bad sign], but Alfredo and

I refused to drink any. We had to eat lunch there and by the time we finally left for Diffun to go to the bank it was already 1:00 PM and by the time we got to bank it was practically 2:00 PM and we went to the guy's mother-in-laws house. Apparently they are the ones who are paying off the debt for the guy. The mother-in-law said they still don't have the money to pay off the debt and won't have it until Monday – SHIT ONCE AGAIN! Alfredo and I left and arrived back in Burgos at about 3:00 PM. We talked at Rogel's Canteen for a while and then climbed the mountain via the low road, arriving about 4:15 PM. I prepared my beans for supper, started cooking and Alfredo left. I went and asked George to come early and I hope he does – he said maybe. The weather today was rainy on and off during the night and off and on most of the day, maybe rainy season has started. Now it's 5:36 PM and my rice is cooking, it's going to be a while before everything is ready to eat. AWANEN!

Friday, October 30, 1987
My House, Gomez, Cabarroguis, Quirino

We got up at 5:15 AM and I officially gave George my nuangs. We sat on the porch for a couple of minutes and talked about it and then he left. He came at 6:55 PM last night. I have no more nuangs to pasture! I cooked breakfast, ate, did dishes and got ready for the day. I cleaned my machetes really good, oiled them and wrapped them up in preparation for packing them. Then I went through the entire house and sorted everything except clothing. I have to repack my small pack because of the two baskets I got in Santa Fe last week. I packed my big green duffel bag and at 10:45 AM I went and talked with George until 11:30 AM. Then I came home, ate lunch and took a siesta from 12:15 to 1:00 PM. I got up and emptied my duffle bag and then repacked it very tightly, making a list of everything that it contains. Then I fetched water and prepared beans and squash for supper. I went and talked with George for a few minutes and he was half sick again with a headache. I came home at 4:30 PM and started cooking, bathed, finished cooking, ate, did the dishes and now it's 6:13 PM and I'm waiting for George. I hope he comes early tonight, if he even comes – if he's sick again, he might not make it. The weather today was rainy on and off all night last night and all day again today. It seems like rainy season has begun. AWANEN!

Saturday, October 31, 1987
My House, Gomez, Cabarroguis, Quirino

Letter from JB & Katie F.

₱275 – 120 = ₱155							
Cigarettes	42	Rides	8	Food	31	Household	10
Clothes	14	Marienda	8	Kerosene	7	TOTAL	₱120

We got up at 5:20 AM and George left; he came at 6:50 PM last night. I'm giving him more things every night now. I cooked breakfast, ate, did dishes and got ready for the day. I headed down the mountain at 7:15 AM, got to Burgos, talked with Richard and looked at his house and then finally headed for Diffun at 8:45 AM or so. I did my marketing, mostly just the ingredients for rice cake tomorrow, and then headed back to Gundaway and stopped at the post office, where I got the above letter and then I headed home. I started climbing via the high road at 11:32 AM and got home at about 12:15 PM. I unpacked and laundered my pack and hat, ate lunch and then took a siesta from 1:15 to 2:00 PM. I got up and did the final calculation of October's expenses. At 3:40 PM I prepared squash for supper and then went to George's, talked for a few minutes and asked him to please come early – he said maybe. I fear he'll be late tonight. I came home, started cooking at 4:40 PM and then bathed. Now it's 5:29 PM and my squash is cooking. George has now slept here 439 nights. The weather today was partly cloudy all day, but no rain last night or today. Somebody is now building a house up above mine on the hill. At this point I have six more days to go and I'll be leaving Gomez. AWANEN!

Sunday, November 1, 1987
My House, Gomez, Cabarroguis, Quirino

Letters to San & Jack G. and JB & Katie F. Postcard to Dad.

We got up at 5:15 AM and George left; he came at 6:25 PM last night and I gave him another bag of stuff. I cooked breakfast, ate, did dishes, got ready for the day and then I swept the south yard. When finished with that I did a little bit of laundry, including my blanket. I rewrote all of my lists of stuff that is in my various bags and packs and then sorted out the last of my stuff. I did the letter to San and Jack and the postcard to Dad and by then it was 11:30 AM, so I ate lunch. I took a siesta from noon until 12:45 PM, got up, drank coffee and Sip brought me some *tambotambong*, a kind of thing something like a big *bibingka*. I ate that and got very full, but then they even brought some rice cake. I read the *"Lonesome Dove"* book for a while and then I even packed my clothes and nearly everything into my blue pack – I'm packed! I still have to make a list of what's in the blue pack is all that remains to be done. At 3:30 PM I went and talked with George until 4:00 PM, asked him to come early and he said yes. I fetched water and then at 4:30 PM I bathed. I got the guapple seedlings from the nursery and also the red *kamote* to give to George tonight. I took a sack of charcoal there today too. Now it's 5:11 PM and I'm not cooking tonight; I'm full of rice cake and the other things that George's mother gave me today. The weather today was partly cloudy off and on all day, but there was no rain. AWANEN!

Monday, November 2, 1987
My House, Gomez, Cabarroguis, Quirino

I got up at 5:15 AM. George got up and left at 4:45 AM to pasture his nuangs. He didn't come until 9:20 PM last night because they strolled. I cooked breakfast, ate, did dishes and got ready for the day. I pulled four of the fireball trees and went to George's house and he was still there, so we left for the farm at about 7:30 AM. It was probably the last time for us to companion to the farm. He harrowed until 9:30 AM, we planted the fireball trees, burned what he had harrowed and came home, arriving at about 11:00 AM. I came home and after a while I ate lunch and then took a siesta from 11:45 AM to 12:45 PM. I got up and Junior came to talk, and then Alfredo too. They left at about 2:00 PM and I sorted more stuff to give to George tonight. This will be about the last until Thursday night. At about 3:00 PM I went to Alfredo's and talked with them until 3:40 PM, came home and prepared my squash for supper. At 4:30 PM I started cooking and bathed. I finished cooking, ate, did dishes and now it's 6:03 PM and I'm waiting for George. Please come early tonight George! It was nice to go to the farm with him for the last time probably. The weather today was cloudy in the morning with a light shower and then it cleared up and was sunny. It clouded up again and then it started raining at about 4:15 PM and is continuing now, but only lightly. AWANEN!

Tuesday, November 3, 1987
My House, Gomez, Cabarroguis, Quirino

We got up at 5:00 AM and George left with another bag of stuff. He came last night at 6:50 PM. I cooked breakfast, ate, did dishes, got ready for the day and then did laundry – only five articles. Then I managed to stuff my green duffel bag into a burlap sack, it was extremely tight and it was like putting on a condom. After that I finished packing my old blue pack, my blue attaché case and I put my nuang yoke into another sack. I looked at all of my COS stuff once again and reread and did a tiny bit of editing of my COS report. I addressed some aerogrammes to myself and will give them to George tonight. By then it was 11:15 AM, so I ate lunch and then took a siesta from noon to 12:30 PM. I got up and read the *"Lonesome Dove"* book for a while. At 1:00 PM or so I went to George's, but he had taken his lunch to the farm, so he wasn't home. I came home and sorted out more stuff to give him tonight, actually quite a bit again, but not much remains in the house now. At 4:30 PM I started cooking, it's my second last can of Armour Beef Stew that Brooke brought me a year-and-a-half ago. I bathed, fetched water, ate and did dishes. Now it's 6:04 PM and I'm hoping that George will be here within the hour. The weather today was cool and partly cloudy and it sprinkled a couple of times during the day but only for about ten minutes each. The cooking oil has been sleeping [changed to a solid] the last five mornings now, fall has most definitely arrived. AWANEN!

Wednesday, November 4, 1987
My House, Gomez, Cabarroguis, Quirino

₱155 + 200 – 223 = ₱132							
Food	80	Rides	15	Cigarettes	20	Marienda	12
Nuang Meds	78	Contribution	10	Haircut	5	Household	3
						TOTAL	₱223

I got up at 5:10 AM. George got up and left at 3:10 AM to pasture his nuangs. He came at 7:40 PM last night because they had a late supper. I cooked breakfast, ate, did dishes and got ready for the day. I went to Alfredo's and he and I went to Burgos once again to see if we can get the nuang document today, but unfortunately we could not – SHIT! So Alfredo came home and I continued on to Gundaway but there was no mail today. I gave them my forwarding address and continued on to Santiago. I got the above, cashed my final two paychecks and headed back for Burgos. I arrived at the bottom of the high road at about 2:10 PM or so and **set another new record climbing the mountain home – 28 minutes 14.3 seconds**!! I wrung out my T-shirt, unpacked and put things away and went directly to Alfredo's house for the forestry meeting and my *despedida*. Of course I ate lunch there – there were lots of people. Then we went to the Barangay Hall and everybody gave a short speech for me. Of course I also spoke, thanking everybody for everything they've done for me over the last two years. Francisco, Efren and one other person from the forestry office came for the meeting, which broke up at about 2:30 PM. The forestry people left immediately and several people came and got tree seedlings and left. I took the one-and-a-half kilograms of pork and one kilogram of *pancit* to George's house, but of course George wasn't there because he's plowing today and took his lunch with him to the farm. I just stayed there for a few minutes and then came home. I drank coffee, figured the day's expenses and I was in a very thoughtful mood again. Now it's only 3:27 PM and I'll bathe after a while. Tonight we're having a family dinner at George's house and I hope we can come here by 7:30 PM or so because I'm very tired – I practically jogged up the high road today. I'll only be here in Gomez two more full days now – tomorrow and Friday. George's and my plan is to get up at 3:30 AM on Saturday morning, drink coffee and leave at 4:00 AM, with my belongings in the nuang cart. We'll see how close to that thing's actually happen. As long as George and I can companion for my good-bye trip I'll be happy. Maybe I'll go to the farm tomorrow, just to be with George for the last time there. Saturday morning is going to be difficult, leaving here, saying goodbye to George and his family, probably forever and so on. [I specifically told Alfredo and all of George's family not to tell other people precisely when we are leaving so that there does not have to be a huge early morning farewell sendoff.] I might someday make it back and I might not, who knows? The weather today was partly cloudy off and on all day. There's been no rain yet to speak of. The little rain we've had so far hasn't even been enough to wet the ground. Oh, my cooking oil was sleeping again this morning. AWANEN!

Thursday, November 5, 1987
My House, Gomez, Cabarroguis, Quirino

Letter to Steve A.

We got up at 5:20 AM and George left; we came here last night at 7:40 PM, after our mini-*despedida* at their house. I sent him home this morning with another bag of stuff. I drank coffee, cooked, ate breakfast, did dishes, got ready for the day and then I did laundry again – only six articles. I went to Alfredo's to talk for just a couple of minutes and then came home and packed my blue "carry-on" bag neatly and it seems like my one kerosene lamp will fit into it too. I wrote the letter to Steve and about then the MAF technician came and injected my ex-nuangs with some medicines, give them worm killers and then he opened up the swelling on the belly button of the calf and removed a bunch of pus and filled the hole with Negasunt and he left. George stayed at the farm for lunch today so I came home and took a siesta from 12:30 to 12:55 PM and then read the *"Lonesome Dove"* book. After a while I cleaned my faucet jar so that I can give it to George tonight. I got my clothes off the line, folded them, put them away and then I took down the clothesline wire. Then I found even more stuff to give to George tonight. At 3:30 PM I prepared my squash for supper, at 4:10 PM I bathed and at 4:30 PM I started cooking. George was home by then so I went and asked him to come immediately after supper tonight and he said yes, I hope so. Now it's 4:57 PM and my rice is nearly cooked. There are two nights and one day to go here in Burgos. The weather today was cool and partly cloudy all day, but no rain. My oil was sleeping again this morning. AWANEN!

Friday, November 6, 1987
My House, Gomez, Cabarroguis, Quirino
The last day, the last night!

I got up at 5:15 AM. George got up and left at 4:15 AM to pasture his nuangs. He didn't come until 8:00 PM last night because Junior was there and running off at the mouth. George woke up at 11:30 PM last night and thought it was time to go to pasture the nuangs because for some reason the rooster crowed. That gave us something to laugh about all day today! I cooked breakfast, ate, did dishes, got ready for the day and took my lunch to the farm. George was plowing so I picked up roots behind him. We quit that at 10:00 AM, made a bunch of piles and burned them. We stopped for lunch at about 11:30 AM. We ate and then took a siesta from 12:15 to 12:45 PM. George went and got his nuang and then we went to the banana plantation and cut a bunch of *marakawayan* to feed the nuang before we leave tomorrow morning. We finished that at about 2:45 PM and headed home. No sooner did we get home than Sip came to tell me not to cook supper, to eat at their house tonight – okay, great. So I boiled water for coffee, filled my thermos and boxed up the last of my stuff. I carried the bag of charcoal to

George's and then the last two boxes of stuff, mostly kitchen stuff. At 4:20 PM I bathed and now it's 5:01 PM. There's very little left in the house. I'll go to George's at about 6:00 PM and I hope we can escape and come here by 7:00 PM. The weather today was hot and dry, not a cloud in the sky all day. AWANEN!

Saturday, November 7, 1987
Malate Pension, Manila
Bye-Bye Gomez, George and everybody else.

₱132 + 158 – 290 = ₱0							
Rides	114	Meals	148	Cigarettes	5	Coke	11
Ice Cream	6	Misc.	6			TOTAL	₱290

We got up at 2:55 AM; Alfredo and Boy came and woke George and I. After supper last night George and I went to my house at 6:50 PM. Everybody was crying and it was a very sad time; George even cried. Then we cried more at my house. We pulled the remaining nails out of the walls and slept. This morning we put everything on my porch that was left, George and I drank coffee, I changed clothes and we all carried my stuff to George's house. George and I ate breakfast, just the two of us. I said goodbye to all of his family and we all cried some more. George and I headed for Burgos at 4:00 AM. We got there at 5:00 AM and George sat with me until it got light, at about 5:30 AM. We said goodbye and he wished me a happy trip. I wished him a happy life and he headed back up the mountain. The first jeepney didn't come until 6:30 AM, so I got to Santiago at 8:00 AM and took the 9:00 AM Pantranco Bus. I paid the jeepney from Burgos a little extra and he took me right to the Pantranco Bus Terminal with all of my bags so that I didn't have to transfer everything to a tricycle. I got into Manila at 5:00 PM and due to having lots of stuff, I took a taxi to Malate Pension, arriving here at 5:30 PM. I bathed and then a bunch of us went to supper and then we returned here to Malate. I talked with JB, Katie and Ralph until now – 10:00 PM, but now it's time to sleep. All total George slept at my house 446 nights. AWANEN!

Sunday, November 8, 1987
Malate Pension, Manila

₱0 + 230 – 228 = ₱2							
Meals	203	Coke	8	Cigarettes	11	Ride	1
Misc.	5					TOTAL	₱228

I got up at 5:00 AM, showered and went to Dunkin' Donuts for coffee and donuts. After that I returned to Malate Pension and read some more of the *"Lonesome Dove"* book until other people came down to talk with. At 9:45 AM we headed over to the Seafront Restaurant for brunch and we sat there pigging out until 12:40 PM or so. Then we returned to Malate Pension and went over to the Peace Corps Office to type our Close-of-Service final reports. I managed to complete my entire report and I photocopied it too – it was nine pages. We all left the Peace Corps Office at 6:00 PM, went back to Malate Pension and after a while we went to the Steak House Restaurant for a salad bar supper. We left there at 9:00 PM or so and returned to Malate Pension. We talked for a while longer and now it's 10:15 PM and time to sleep. AWANEN!

Monday, November 9, 1987
Malate Pension, Manila

Letters from Tony & Janet S. (2) and Chris & Mary.

₱2 + 230 – 280 = ₱22							
Meals	227	Rides	11	Cigarettes	8	Coke	24
Misc.	10					TOTAL	₱280

I got up at 5:00 AM, showered, went downstairs and waited until the coffee was ready. I drank coffee, ate breakfast and talked with people until about 7:30 AM and then I headed over to the Peace Corps Office. I checked in at the medical unit and gave them some MIF kits, blood and urine samples and had an interview with the nurse. After that I went and got one-third of my readjustment allowance in the form of a US Treasury check. I turned in my checkbook, had to get a bunch of signatures on the signature form and in general had to do a lot of running around. I managed to get a copy of the *Salaysayan* Magazine with my George article in it. I fixed up a few typos in my Close-of-Service final report and turned it in. Michael P. and I returned to Malate Pension at 1:00 PM for lunch and then we went to the dentist for a check-up and cleaning. After that I went to the American Express office on United Nations Avenue and they wouldn't cash my readjustment allowance US Treasury check. Then I went to the Manila Medical Center for an EKG and chest x-ray. I returned to the Peace Corps Office and then back to Malate Pension. A bunch of us went to the Sea-front Restaurant for Mongolian Barbeque for supper. Now it's 9:11 PM and we're back at Malate Pension and ready to crash. AWANEN!

Tuesday, November 10, 1987
Malate Pension, Manila

₱22 + 300 – 248 = ₱74							
Food	55	Rides	14	Meals	142	Cigarettes	12
Marienda	20	Postage	5			TOTAL	₱280

I got up at 5:20 AM, showered, got ready for the day and went downstairs for coffee and eventually breakfast. I went over to the Peace Corps Office to get some medical forms and then over to Makati, where Michael P. and I went to the American Express office and they won't catch US Treasury checks either. After that we went to

Thomas Cook and they wouldn't give us our airplane tickets. Then I went to the doctor's office for my 11:20 AM appointment, but didn't finally get to into the doctor until 12:45 PM. I finished with that and returned to the Peace Corps Office again. I turned in the medical forms, had an exit interview with Barbara and had to do more bullshit paperwork. I finally headed back to Malate Pension at 4:40 PM or so. Several of us talked for a while downstairs and then Chester, Katie and I went to a Thai food restaurant for supper. After supper we came back to Malate Pension and now it's 8:06 PM and I'm going to crash in a little while. AWANEN!

Wednesday, November 11, 1987
Malate Pension, Manila

₱74 + 514 – 523 = ₱65							
Meals	108	Cigarettes	13	Books	29	Clothes	318
Ice Cream	19	Marienda	32	Coke	4	TOTAL	₱523

I got up at 5:20 AM, showered, went downstairs for coffee and eventually breakfast. I ended up at the Peace Corps Office at 7:50 AM and typed my farming report, finishing up at about 12:40 PM. I made some photocopies of it too and then Chester and I went to Chinatown for lunch. After lunch we went to the Crispa T-shirt store and I bought six T-shirts to take home with me. After that I took Chester to the Pistang Filipino place, where he bought a few things. I didn't buy anything. After that we returned to Malate Pension, talked for a while and then Chester and I went to the Aristocrat Restaurant for supper. After eating supper we returned to Malate Pension again, talked again for a while longer and then I came up the room. Now it's 9:36 PM and I'm ready to crash. AWANEN!

Thursday, November 12, 1987
Malate Pension, Manila

Postcard to George.

₱65 + 400 – 435 = ₱30							
Meals	183	Souvenirs	18	Coke	33	Laundry	40
Cigarettes	8	Food	10	T.C.	143	TOTAL	₱523

I got up at 5:40 AM, went downstairs for coffee and then breakfast. I took some laundry to the Laundromat and then I went to the Peace Corps Office. I got the last of my paperwork completed there by noon, got the last money, an airplane ticket, got my ID card voided and **everything** else. I returned to Malate Pension and a couple of us went out for lunch. After lunch I went and bought the pre-1967 coin set for ₱18 pesos and then I went to the bank to purchase some Traveler's Checks. After that I returned to Malate Pension and some of us went to Pistang Filipino again, but, again,

I didn't buy a thing. We returned to Malate Pension, talked some more until 6:00 PM and then a bunch of us went back to the Thai restaurant for supper. After supper we returned to the pension and we had a small party out back. I didn't hang out there very long. Now it's 9:58 PM and I'm ready to sleep. AWANEN!

Friday, November 13, 1987
On Bus to Baguio City, Benguet

₱30 + 200 – 110 = ₱120							
Meals	26	Cigarettes	12	Clothes	40	Rides	24
Food	8					TOTAL	₱110

I got up at 5:00 AM, showered and went to Dunkin' Donuts for coffee. After that I returned to Malate Pension and after a while I ate breakfast. Then after another while I went to the Peace Corps Office and just sat around in the air conditioning until about 10:30 AM. Then I took the LRT to Baclaran and bought a pair of short pants to take home. After that I returned to the Peace Corps Office to find some other people to lunch with. Tom and Barb, Chester and I went to the Seafront Restaurant and after that then we returned to Malate Pension and then back to the Peace Corps Office for a bit, and then back to Malate again. I waited for Ralph P. until 6:00 PM so that I could get into our shared lockbox because he had the only key, but he didn't return, so Chester and I went to the Seafront Restaurant and met Tom and Barbara there. They were so slow to take our order that we got up and left without ordering. We went back to Malate Pension for supper. Now it's 9:39 PM and after my shower Siobhan, Andy and I are going to head to Baguio City on an 11:30 PM bus, so I guess that I won't get much sleep tonight. AWANEN!

Saturday, November 14, 1987
Malate Pension, Manila

₱120 + 6,000 – 5,978 = ₱142							
Rides	226	Meals	27	Silver	3,600	Tips	15
Cigarettes	15	Coke	16	Munsayac	310	Blankets	410
Easter Sch.	659	Handicrafts	700			TOTAL	₱5,978

As I said yesterday, Siobhan, Andy and I headed to Baguio City last night on an 11:30 PM bus. We got there at 4:00 AM and we went to the Dangwa Tranco Bus Terminal canteen for coffee and breakfast. Andy left for Sagada and Siobhan and I strolled to Burnham Park to kill time until 8:00 AM. Then we went to the Banaue Handicrafts store and I bought ₱700 pesos worth of souvenirs. Then we went to Munsayac Handicrafts to look at my custom carved nuang with calf that I ordered back August 12th. It came out great! I bought ₱310 worth of more stuff and asked them to box the nuang for transport to America. We continued on to return in a few hours. We then went to IBAY's and I spent ₱3,600 on silver items. Then we went to the Easter School Weaving Room and I spent ₱659 on things there. After that we went to the public market and Siobhan bought sweaters and I bought ₱410 worth of blankets. Then we ate lunch and went back to Munsayac and picked up my hand carved nuang and then went to the Victory Liner Bus Terminal. We got a 2:00 PM bus headed back to Manila and got into Manila at 7:30 PM. We took a taxi to Malate Pension and ate peanut butter sandwiches. I talked with Linda S. for a while and now it's 9:15 PM and I'm really, really tired. It was an extremely long day. AWANEN!

Sunday, November 15, 1987
Malate Pension, Manila

₱142 + 400 – 462 = ₱80							
Meals	130	Lodging	225	Cigarettes	15	Rides	13
Laundry	27	Lockbox	20	Coke	14	Misc.	18
						TOTAL	₱462

I got up at 5:00 AM, showered, went downstairs and went to Dunkin' Donuts for coffee and donuts. I returned to Malate Pension and sat around talking with people, repacking my stuff and making additions to my "Philippine purchases" list until about 10:00 AM. Then Kris I. and I went to the Seafront Restaurant for breakfast/brunch. We ate until shortly after noon and then returned to Malate Pension. I added up the final total value of my Philippine purchases and it came to about $415. Then we all sat around saying goodbye to people as they left for wherever they're going. I went to Robinson's Department Store for a new toothbrush and then returned to Malate Pension and read the *"Lonesome Dove"* book until 6:30 PM. Then we went to the Thai restaurant again and Siobhan was there so we ate with her and her friends. At about 9:00 PM we returned to Malate Pension and my laundry that I left with them and told them that I needed to be ready tonight was not done yet, washed, but far from totally dry – damn it! Now it's 9:30 PM and I'm ready to crash. AWANEN!

Monday, November 16, 1987
On Airplane

₱80 – 80 = ₱0							
Meals	20	Rides	35	Porter	25	TOTAL	₱80

$152 – 111 = $41							
Baggage	107	Coffee	4			TOTAL	$111

I got up at 5:20 AM, bathed and went downstairs at Malate Pension for coffee and breakfast. I finished eating breakfast, got my wet laundry, packed up and left Malate for the last time at about 7:30 AM or so. The Golden Taxi was full with my four bags plus nuang yoke and myself. I got to the airport, went to the United Airlines check-in counter and they informed me it would cost $107 for my big box with the hand carved nuang in it, so I paid it and checked everything through to Portland. I proceeded through customs and left Manila at 10:10 AM. The plane arrived in Tokyo at 3:00 PM, Tokyo time, or 2:00 PM, Manila time. It was about a three hour and forty minute flight. I waited in Tokyo until 7:00 PM, Tokyo time, for the next flight. Now it's 9:12 PM, Manila time, so I've been airborne for three hours and twelve minutes, there's only about five hours to go and I'll be in San Francisco. It's going to be an extremely short night tonight I guess. We're racing towards the sun. I think I'll try and sleep a bit. AWANEN!

Chapter 22
November 16, 1987 through December 10, 1987
HOME AGAIN!

Monday, November 16, 1987 (#2)
Tony & Janet's House – Durham, Oregon

Postcard to George.

$41.00 – 12.74 = $28.26							
Book	3.14	Postage	2.63	Lunch	5.97	Porter	1.00
						TOTAL	$12.74

I went to sleep at about 9:30 PM, Manila time, last night and woke up at about 1:00 AM, Manila time. They gave us only coffee for starters and then after a little while they served breakfast. We landed in San Francisco at about 4:00 AM on November 17th, Manila time or about 12:00 N on November 16th, San Francisco time. So, due to crossing the International Date Line I get to live November 16th all over again! I ate lunch and wrote a postcard to George. Then I bought a book and went and checked in and read the book. Oh, I forgot to say that Customs was no problem at all, the guy just passed me right through. I showed him my list of Philippine Purchases and he just told me "keep going". The plane was supposed to leave San Francisco at 1:20 PM but didn't leave until 2:20 PM and when I arrived in Portland Tony was at the airport waiting for me. He brought me home and we all talked. I re-did the laundry that was wet when I left Manila this morning (or was it yesterday morning) and then dried it in the dryer. We ate supper and watched TV and now it's 10:00 PM November 16, 1987 here and 2:00 PM November 17, 1987 in Gomez. The Philippines is 16 hours ahead of West Coast Time. Goodnight. AWANEN!

Tuesday, November 17, 1987
Tony & Janet's House – Durham, Oregon

Letter from Chris & Mary M.

$28.26 – 21.54 = $6.72							
Supper	5.00	Food	2.35	Batteries	3.59	Coke	0.60
Loan to J.	10.00					TOTAL	$21.54

We got up at 6:40 AM. My body is still confused about what time it is! We drank coffee, ate breakfast and got ready for the day. I looked at all the slide photos that I have here and spent a lot of time trying to figure out what order to put them in. That took until about noon. Tony stayed home from work this morning and helped.

We ate lunch and then we headed out towards the coast in his rig because he had to go check out some logging operation. We completed that, walked around the woods for a while and after that we headed home. On the way home we stopped at the Camp 18 Restaurant, got some coffee-to-go and continued on home. In the evening some carpet cleaning people came, did their job and left. Then we went to a place called RAX for supper – they had a salad bar and a pasta bar and it was pretty good for only $3.79. Then we came back home and I unpacked a bit more tonight. I unpacked the big hand carved nuang last night. I called Bob S. Oh, I forgot, I called Chris M. this morning at 6:00 AM their time and Bob S. tonight at midnight his time, oh well. Now it's 10:48 PM and way, way past my bedtime. AWANEN!

Wednesday, November 18, 1987
Tony & Janet's House – Durham, Oregon

$6.72 + 10.00 – 0 = $16.72 (Janet repaid $10 loan)

I slept in really late, until 7:30 AM. I got up, drank coffee and talked with Tony for a bit and then I started labeling slides. By and by I called the Alaska Marine Highway System and made reservations for December 4th from Seattle to Haines. Then I called Truman Bell and told him we'll be there to pick up my truck tomorrow afternoon [see August 29th, back on page 4]. After a while Bob S. called and offered to pay my way to come and visit him in Michigan, but I asked him to come here with the money that he would have spent for my airplane ticket. I continued labeling slides, stopped for lunch and after a while I called Teresa L. about coming and staying with her from November 30th to December 4th and she said it was okay with her, so I will. I labeled slides some more until 4:00 PM and then stopped and washed and dried all the dishes that were on the counter. After a while Janet dropped Kevin off and she went to aerobics. Then Tony came home and we went out and got supplies for supper, came home, cooked and ate. Then Steve A. called; he'll be here Wednesday the 25th in the afternoon. Then I called Ardis B. and she can be down here this Saturday she said. So, we pretty much know that I'll have a chance to see nearly everybody before I head north. I have lots of things to do between now and December 4th when I head to Alaska on the Marine Highway. Now it's 10:47 PM and I'm tired and going to sleep. AWANEN!

Thursday, November 19, 1987
Tony & Janet's House – Durham, Oregon

$16.72 – 0.65 = $16.07					
Coke	0.65			TOTAL	$0.65

We got up at 6:05 AM, drank coffee, ate breakfast and after a while Tony left for work and I worked on labeling slides. A little later Bob S. called and said he can't afford to come to either Portland or Seattle. We talked for about 35 minutes or so and then I finished up labeling slides – there are 475 of them in total, plus a few more still in the camera. Then I bathed and got ready for the day. I cleaned my small pack and also my blue pack because a jar of the hot chili pepper powder came open and spilled. By the time I finished that Tony had come home, so we ate lunch and then we went to Truman Bell's shop to pick up my rig. It looks real nice but the total price was $6,133.47, a bit high it seem to me. We talked and storied for quite a long time and finally Tony and I left. We took the long way home and got here at about 5:30 PM. Later on we ate some really tasty spaghetti for supper. Oh, I read my Close-of Service report to Tony at noon and I broke down crying. Chris M. called tonight and we decided that we might be able to get together for supper tomorrow night. Now it's 10:23 PM, goodnight. AWANEN!

Friday, November 20, 1987
Tony & Janet's House – Durham, Oregon

Letters from Barb W. and Dad.

$16.07 + 100 – 68.42 = $47.65							
Rig	39.10	Tip	1.00	Food	19.35	Tools	8.97
						TOTAL	$68.42

We got up at 6:10 AM, drank coffee, ate breakfast and talked with Tony and Janet for a while. We got ready for the day and I walked over to G.I. Joe's for some car parts I needed, a new positive battery cable for starters. I also got some antifreeze, some windshield washer antifreeze and a bunch of tools like screwdrivers, pliers and so on to replace what I gave away to George. I finished there and walked around in the Safeway store for a while looking at things and having a good time. I came back to Tony and Janet's house at about noon and started working on my rig right away and finally got totally done with repairing and putting everything back in it – the stuff under the seat, into the glove box and so on, by about 4:30 PM. Then I showered and cleaned up the mess I had made. In the evening Tony, Janet, Kevin and I went out to supper with Chris M. and a friend of his. We stayed out until after 10:00 PM and then came home and talked some more. We didn't sleep until after midnight. Oh, I called Alexander & Alexander today and they'll send new insurance forms. AWANEN!

Saturday, November 21, 1987
Tony & Janet's House – Durham, Oregon

$47.65 + 100 – 80.47 = $67.18							
Gasoline	52.05	Rice	8.49	Knife Set	7.49	Caulk	11.89
Coffee	0.55					TOTAL	$80.47

We got up at 6:40 AM or so, very late. We drank coffee, got ready for the day and then Tony and I went out to Truman Bell's and spent until practically noon requesting him to fix up some minor things. Then we got gas and came home. We sat down to lunch and Chris and his friend Jed came. They looked at my truck while we ate lunch. After that Ardis B. came and we all talked for a while. After a while Jed left and the rest of us went to Costco to try and blow some money. What I bought, shown above, shows that I did find some stuff that I wanted to buy. After that we returned home and divided up the Costco booty and talked for a while. By and by we looked at one tray of slides and then we went out to eat at Capone's Pizza. After we finished we came home and looked at two more trays of slides. Now it's 10:39 PM and Ardis and Chris are staying here for the night. It's time to crash. AWANEN!

Sunday, November 22, 1987
Tony & Janet's House – Durham, Oregon

$67.18 – 21.97 = $45.21							
Marienda	2.35	Coffee	3.90	Vitamins	7.60	Food	8.12
						TOTAL	$21.97

I got up at 6:40 AM, made instant coffee and sat around killing time until Chris woke up. Then he and I made real coffee and sat and talked while drinking coffee. After a while everybody got up, but it took until 10:30 AM or so before we finally finished with breakfast. Then I escaped outdoors and did stuff with my truck and cleaned some minor things on the inside of the cab. Ardis and Chris left at about 11:30 AM or so and then Tony, Jim and I went bicycling from about 1:30 to 4:30 PM – mostly in the rain – it was good exercise. When we returned, Ardis called and reported that their car had been broken into while they were at the bookstore. Chris's pack and Ardis's briefcase were stolen. We ate supper after a while and then went to Tony's office and the grocery store for some shopping. We returned home, watched TV and now it's 11:12 PM. I'm tired and going to sleep. AWANEN!

Monday, November 23, 1987
Tony & Janet's House – Durham, Oregon

$45.21 + 800 – 744.75 = $100.46							
Muffler	210.00	Cigarettes	1.65	Coke	0.60	Blank Tapes	12.90
Car Audio	180.70	Warranty	39.00	Home Tape	299.90	TOTAL	$744.75

We got up at 6:40 AM, drank coffee and Tony and I talked until he left for work. Then I went to the Midas Muffler Shop and I was the first one there at 8:00 AM. I got my new exhaust system installed and left at 10:00 AM and went over to Washington Square, where I ended up getting a new home tape deck plus a complete sound system for my pickup. That took until nearly 1:00 PM and then I went back to Tony's house for a sandwich. After that I started installing the truck sound system. I worked on that until about 4:30 PM, when it got too dark to work. I came in the house and started filling out all the paperwork, guarantees, extended warranties and so on for the stuff that I bought today. Tony came home and after a while I made squash with coconut milk for supper. It was really good and even Janet liked it – and she doesn't like squash. Now it's 9:21 PM and I'm nearly ready to sleep. AWANEN!

Tuesday, November 24, 1987
Tony & Janet's House – Durham, Oregon

$100.46 – 25.01 = $75.45							
Cigarettes	1.55	Lunch	1.99	Wire	2.49	Ammeter	8.99
Gas Cap	9.99					TOTAL	$25.01

We got up at 7:00 AM, drank coffee and Tony left for work. I started pretty much right away on finishing up the installation of the radio and tape player in my truck. I finished that at about noon and went out to Truman Bell's to try and get my ammeter replaced, it doesn't work any more. He told me that it can't be replaced without replacing the entire instrument panel cluster, okay. So I headed back towards Tony's house and stopped at G.I. Joe's to get a new ammeter and a new locking gas cap. Then the brake warning light came on in my rig. I came home and there was no brake fluid in the master cylinder – SHIT! What did Truman Bell do to me anyway? I looked for a leak, but there was nothing obvious so I gave up, showered and then read my book until Tony came home. After a while Janet came home and after a while we ate supper. After that I sorted out some papers, 3-hole punched them and put them in a notebook. Then we watched TV for a while and now it's 10:22 PM and I'm ready to sleep. AWANEN!

Wednesday, November 25, 1987
Tony & Janet's House – Durham, Oregon

$75.45 – 13.48 = $61.97							
Wire	4.98	Screw	0.10	Fuses	5.67	Wire Clips	1.18
Cigarettes	1.55					TOTAL	$13.48

We got up at 7:00 AM, drank coffee and Tony and I talked until he left for work. Then I went outdoors to work on my rig. I filled the brake fluid reservoir and went to buy cigarettes, just to check out the brake system and the brake failure light only came on now and then. Then I started to install the new ammeter and found that I needed more wire and parts than I thought, to be able to do the job. So, I went over to G.I. Joe's for more stuff. I returned home and Tony was already back from work, so we made lunch, ate and went out to the woods for the afternoon. We got home at around 5:30 PM and after a while we ate supper. Then Steve and Deb A. and Tim S. came. We talked for a long time and now it's 11:09 PM and I'm ready to sleep. AWANEN!

Thursday, November 26, 1987
Tony & Janet's House – Durham, Oregon
Thanksgiving Day

$61.97 – 15.00 = $46.97							
Dinner	15.00					TOTAL	$15.00

I got up at 6:45 AM, started drinking a cup of instant coffee and went out to Steve's rig to wake him up. After a while he got up, we made real coffee and by then pretty much everybody was up. After breakfast, Steve, Tim and I worked on hooking up the new ammeter in my rig. By noon we were done and soon after that San and Jack G. arrived. It was good to see them! Then after a while longer Bob D. showed up. Then I took a shower and did some laundry and at about 3:15 PM or so Tim C. and his wife, Kathryn came. At 4:00 PM we went out for supper. We returned home at about 6:30 PM or so and then I sorted out 270 slides and we had a slideshow. We all talked together for the evening and Tim C. and Kathryn left at about 11:00 PM. Everybody else is staying here tonight. Peg S. did not come to this party, she stayed home. Everybody looks pretty much the same as they did two years ago, and ten years ago too, for that mater. Now it's 11:30 PM and people are watching a movie on the VCR called *"Rock & Roll of the Last 20 Years"* or something like that. Goodnight. AWANEN!

Friday, November 27, 1987
Tony & Janet's House – Durham, Oregon

$46.97 – 14.54 = $32.43							
Food	10.00	Cigarettes	1.55	Lunch	2.99	TOTAL	$14.54

I got up at 7:00 AM, made some instant coffee and went out to wake up Steve. San and Jack cooked breakfast of perogies and we ate those. We didn't really finish with breakfast until around 10:30 AM. At about 8:00 AM or so Steve and I snuck off to get cigarettes and go look at skis at G.I. Joe's. After breakfast we all just basically talked and killed time for a while. At around noon we went for a walk and had a Frisbee game in the park. We ate lunch at McDonald's. Oh, I forgot – Bob D. left at about 11:30 AM or so. After lunch at McDonald's we walked in the park a bit more and then returned to Tony's house. We got here at about 3:15 PM and I took a siesta until 5:00 PM. San and Jack left and Deb cooked a really great supper for us. After supper, Steve, Janet and I went to get some VCR movies and came back to watch them. Tim and Tony were making chocolate chip cookies when we got home. When those were finished we watched the VCR *"The Gods Must Be Crazy"* and also *"Crocodile Dundee"*. Now it's 12:22 AM Saturday, I'm tired and going to sleep. AWANEN!

Saturday, November 28, 1987
Tony & Janet's House – Durham, Oregon

$32.43 + 100 – 68.10 = $64.33							
Lunch	3.00	Food	8.00	Rope	4.95	Socks	9.00
Flashlight	29.90	Shaker	1.30	Batteries	9.45	Bottles	2.50
						TOTAL	$68.10

I got up at 7:00 AM, drank coffee and killed time until other people got up. After a while we got around to eating breakfast and then at about 9:45 AM we all went to REI at Jantzen Beach. Now Steve, Deb, their two kids, Tim, Tony, Janet and Kevin are here – nine of us. We had lunch at Jantzen Beach and then after a while we came back to Tony and Janet's house. We didn't really do a lot this afternoon. After a while Tim, Deb and I went to the store to get groceries for supper – we made chili-con-carne and when it was cooked we ate supper and then talked some more. Now it's 9:23 PM and everybody's about ready to crash very soon. I miss George a lot and find myself out on the porch talking to him, asking him what he's doing and telling him what's going through my mind. AWANEN!

Sunday, November 29, 1987
Tony & Janet's House – Durham, Oregon

$64.33 + 100 – 89.52 = $74.81							
Tupperware	49.37	Cooler	9.99	Antifreeze	9.98	Tape	3.49
Scissors	14.25	Hose	0.89	Cigarettes	1.55	TOTAL	$89.52

I got up at 7:00 AM, drank coffee and read my book until other people got up. Then we all ate breakfast and at 11:00 AM or so Steve, Deb and Tim left for home. Now it's just Tony, Janet, Kevin and myself here, I'll bet Tony and Janet are happy that everybody is gone. Tony and I changed the location of my engine block heater and then we bled the brakes and now hopefully everything is set to go. After that I started packing a bit, I got three boxes loaded full. Janet's mother and father came to visit, it's her father's birthday today and we went out for Mexican food for dinner. Tony and Janet paid for everybody, that was nice of them. After that we came home and after a while Bob S. called and wished me a good trip north and so on. Now it's 9:11 PM and I'm tired and ready to crash. AWANEN!

Monday, November 30, 1987
Teresa's House, Vashon Island, Washington

$74.81 – 20.77 = $54.04							
Gasoline	13.55	Cigarettes	3.30	Coffee	1.45	Lunch	2.47
						TOTAL	$20.77

We got up at 6:45 AM, drank coffee and Tony and I had breakfast. I said goodbye to Janet and she left for work, and then after a bit I said goodbye to Tony and he left for work. Then I kind of went crazy throwing things into boxes, putting the tarp on my rig and then getting everything into it. I finished packing at 9:30 AM or so and called Teresa L. to be sure it's still okay to go there and stay for a couple of days and also to get directions. [This is the same Teresa L. whom you first met way back on page 13.] Tony came home at 10:00 AM to say goodbye and I left after getting gas and checking my tires. I got out of town at 11:15 AM. It was a pretty uneventful trip to Seattle and I arrived at about 3:50 PM. I got my ticket for the Alaska Marine Highway System and waited there for Teresa until 5:00 PM when she finished work. We went to the Vashon Island Ferry Dock and took the ferry to Teresa's house on Vashon Island. She cooked a nice supper and we ate and told stories. WOW! Now it's 8:53 PM and I'm about ready to crash. It's nice and peaceful and quiet here. AWANEN!

Tuesday, December 1, 1987
Teresa's House, Vashon Island, Washington

$54.04 + 200 – 150.81 = $103.23							
Money Order	121.00	Lunch	4.11	Coke	2.49	Food	11.14
Cigarettes	2.98	Toiletries	1.19	Books	7.90	TOTAL	$150.81

We got up at 5:40 AM, drank coffee and Teresa left for work. I sat around and drank coffee some more and read *"The Rolling Stones"*, a Heinlein book, until I finished it. Then I went outdoors and checked to see why my brake warning light was coming on again and discovered that my brake fluid was low again. I made an appointment with the mechanic here on Vashon Island for tomorrow morning at 8:30 AM to get it checked. At about 11:00 AM I went into town and looked around, ate lunch at Dairy Queen, did some grocery shopping and then came back to Teresa's house. By and by I split some wood and carried it to the house. Then I had to get under the tarp of my truck to get a copy of my Close-of-Service report and my farming report to show to Teresa. I built a fire in the wood stove at about 3:15 PM or so and killed time until Teresa got home from work at about 7:00 PM. I prepared supper of leftovers and we ate and talked for a while. Now it's 9:30 PM and I'm ready for bed. AWANEN!

Wednesday, December 2, 1987
Teresa's House, Vashon Island, Washington

$103.23 – 22.58 = $80.65							
Cigarettes	1.39	Beer	1.98	Breakfast	6.00	Food	9.18
Toiletries	4.03					TOTAL	$22.58

I got up at 6:30 AM, drank coffee, got ready for the day and then took a shower. I went uptown to get my truck's brakes checked out. While they were doing that I went to the Bishop's Cafe and ate breakfast. I returned to Island Automotive and they figured out that I need a new master cylinder plus I have some leaks in some of the brake lines. They ordered the parts and I came home. They said they'll have it all ready to go sometime tomorrow. I read my book *"Deep Six"* by Clive Cussler most of the afternoon. I split some more firewood and not much else. At 3:00 PM I started the fire in the wood stove and at 5:30 PM Teresa called and asked me to come and pick her up at the ferry terminal as she's getting her rig repaired too, so I went and picked her up and we came home. After a while we ate supper and talked until bedtime. Now it's 9:31 PM and time to sleep. AWANEN!

Thursday, December 3, 1987
Teresa's House, Vashon Island, Washington

Postcards to Ronald and Dad.

$80.65 + 200 – 239.42 = $41.23							
Rides	2.00	Food	42.22	Postage	0.65	Clothes	119.96
Cigarettes	1.39	Household	32.82	Meals	7.85	Marienda	3.17
Silver	29.36					TOTAL	$239.42

We got up at 5:20 AM, drank coffee, I took Teresa to the ferry dock and returned home. I drank more coffee, got ready for the day and then at about 7:30 AM I took my rig and left it at Island Automotive for the repairs on the brakes. Then I caught a bus, went to the ferry terminal and went into Seattle. The first thing I did was eat breakfast at Woolworth's and then I went to Eddie Bauer for some chamois shirts. I went to the Pike Street Market and got a few things and then I went to the Peace Corps Office and met Teresa for lunch [she was working for the Peace Corps]. After lunch I went over to Chinatown and bought a few more things and then I went and waited for the bus to the ferry terminal. I took the ferry to Vashon and then I went to Island Automotive, but my rig wasn't done yet. Luckily Teresa's rig was in town getting fixed too, so I called her at work to get a ride home. When she arrived on the ferry she picked me up and we came home, getting here at about 7:00 PM. I cooked supper, we ate and now it's 9:32 PM. I'm really beat tonight after spending the whole day in Seattle. AWANEN!

Friday, December 4, 1987
On Board Ferry, Headed for Alaska

$41.23 + 300 – 215.61 = $125.62							
Meals	11.73	Cigarettes	1.50	Truck	176.72	Toiletries	5.16
Gasoline	18.60	Candy	0.55	Misc.	0.50	Coke	0.85
						TOTAL	$215.61

We got up at 5:15 AM, talked for a while, drank coffee for our last time and Teresa left for work. I got ready for the day, bathed and then packed my stuff one last time. At 9:50 AM I started walking uptown to see about my rig. I got to town at 10:40 AM and the parts still hadn't arrived, so I read Ken Kesey's, *"Sometimes A Great Notion"* for a couple of hours and then went to lunch. When I returned to Island Automotive the parts were just being unloaded at 12:30 PM. My rig was finally repaired and ready to go at 2:10 PM. I returned to Teresa's house and rushed to get my rig packed. I left her house at 2:45 PM and I got a ferry to Seattle pretty quickly. I arrived at the Alaska Ferry dock at 3:50 PM for a 4:00 PM check in – close! The ferry loaded at 6:30 PM and left at 7:00 PM. I changed my watch to Alaska time, back one hour, so the Philippines is now 17 hours ahead of me. It's 9:00 PM, December 4th here and 2:00 PM, December 5th there; good afternoon George. I just added up what I've spent on my rig since I picked it up at Truman Bell's, supposedly restored to "good as new" condition. The total, not including gas, is $650.79, which includes today's repairs, the tape deck, speakers, wire, ammeter and so on.

It was nice staying with Teresa for four nights, much more relaxing than being around Tony and Janet. Teresa and I had some good talks about life after Peace Corps – is there one? I haven't figured that out yet. There sure are a lot of things that I miss about the Philippines. I wouldn't be surprised to find myself back there one day. Well, shit, there's no good reason to depress myself by continuing with this train of thought. I'm tired, so goodnight. AWANEN!

Saturday, December 5, 1987
On Board Ferry, Headed for Alaska

Postcards to George and Sue T.

$125.62 – 17.65 = $107.97							
Meals	16.15	Candy	0.50	Postage	1.00	TOTAL	$17.65

I got up at 6:00 AM, ate breakfast, drank coffee and wandered around on the deck of the ferry outdoors. Then I got ready for the day. I didn't do much of anything today except eat, read the *"Sometimes A Great Notion"* book and do the above two postcards. It was rainy and windy off and on all day, mostly on. Now it's only 8:44 PM, but I think that maybe I can sleep. AWANEN!

Sunday, December 6, 1987
On Board Ferry, Headed for Alaska

Postcard to Tony & Janet S.

$107.97 – 25.20 = $82.77							
Meals	11.19	Cigarettes	3.59	Coke	2.82	Food	6.51
Candy	1.09					TOTAL	$25.20

I got up at 5:00 AM, went and drank coffee and read until they started serving breakfast and then I ate breakfast, came back to the room and got ready for the day. I read some more and at 10:00 AM we docked in Ketchikan and I got off the ferry to buy some Coke, apples and etc. I came back to the ferry in the, rain arriving at about noon. After that I read and took a siesta from 12:15 to 1:00 PM or so. I got up, went and drank coffee and then we left Ketchikan at about 2:00 PM. This afternoon I did a lot of thinking about George and how much I miss him. At 7:00 PM or so I went and ate supper and read while I was eating. At 7:30 PM we docked at Wrangell and left there at 8:30 PM. Now it's 9:15 PM and I'm about ready to crash after a bit more reading. AWANEN!

Monday, December 7, 1987
Dan & Chris T's House, Haines, Alaska

$82.77 – 9.30 = $73.47							
Meals	8.50	Postage	0.80			TOTAL	$9.30

I got up at 5:00 AM, went and drank coffee and then when the kitchen opened for breakfast, I ordered and ate. At 8:00 AM we stopped in Juneau and we left there at 10:00 AM. I finished reading the *"Sometimes A Great Notion"* book and then sat around in the observation lounge looking at the scenery. At about 12:30 PM I ate lunch and then I went and got packed to be ready to get off the ferry. At about 2:15 PM we docked in Haines and I got off, stopped at the gas station to check the antifreeze and it's good to minus 35°F so no problem. Then I went to the post office to mail my postcards and I asked where Dan and Chris are living now [I used to live in Haines, so the post office personnel knew me]. They told me that Chris works at the Highways Department so I went and found her and together we went and found Dan. We went to their place, arriving at about 4:30 PM or so. We talked until supper, ate and then watched the VCR movie *"Lethal Weapon"* and then we talked some more. Now it's 9:46 PM and I'm ready to crash. Tonight was my first experience driving on snow since the spring of 1985. It's been 2.5 years since I last drove on snow. AWANEN!

Tuesday, December 8, 1987
Kelly's Motel, Delta Junction, Alaska

$73.47 + 100 – 75.20 = $98.27							
Cigarettes	4.70	Gasoline	23.00	Meals	12.50	Lodging	35.00
						TOTAL	$75.20

We got up at 5:00 AM, drank coffee and Dan and Chris and I talked. We ate breakfast, got ready for the day and I left at 6:45 AM. I crossed the Canadian border at about 7:15 AM and they didn't even do a cursory check of the glove box. I stopped in Haines Junction to look for 222's [Canadian Aspirin, with codeine] and there were none. I made another stop for a thermos full of coffee and then continued on. A few miles beyond Haines Junction my gas line froze up, but I thought it was actually a clogged fuel filter so I stopped, put on a new filter and continued, but it happened again and again so I had to put some "Heet" in the gas tank and then everything was okay after that. I entered back into Alaska at about 3:00 PM and again customs didn't even check the glove box. I passed through Tok Junction at about 4:30 PM, continued on to Delta Junction and checked in at Kelly's Motel at about 7:00 PM and I also got one tank of gas. I called Mary M. to confirm that I'll be arrive in Fairbanks tomorrow morning and she said that she thinks maybe Dave G. is staying at my house because the renters moved out on Saturday. After that I went out to eat supper, but I already forgot the restaurants name. I talked with the lady who was working there for a while and then I returned to the motel. Now it's 9:58 PM, pretty late. My mileage driven today was 562 miles. It was a long day, goodnight. AWANEN!

Wednesday, December 9, 1987
My House, Fairbanks, Alaska

$98.27 – 29.88 = $68.39							
Cigarettes	2.38	Meals	9.10	Household	12.41	Coke	5.99
						TOTAL	$29.88

I got up at 5:30 AM, bathed and tried to start my truck, but it was too cold. I had to plug it in for a couple hours. In the meantime I went and ate breakfast at the Evergreen Restaurant and then I went back to Kelly's Motel, my rig started and I left Delta Junction at 7:30 AM. I got into Fairbanks at 9:30 AM, stopped at the store for cleaning supplies and came home. It was 40°F inside the house and -10°F outside. I looked at the house, unpacked the rig and started cleaning up. At about 12:30 PM Dave G. called up and then he came out to the house at about 3:30 PM or so and I was cleaning the kitchen. After a while Armond D. stopped by to talk for a while, he left and Mary M. came out and she brought me supper. Then Dave and Vicki M. came out and after a while I unpacked everything that I brought home with me. Now it's 10:28 PM and Dave G. is staying here tonight. It's nice to be home again. I left here 838 days ago, August 23, 1985 to December 9, 1987 – WOW! Now I'm tired and Dave G. and I are going to sleep. Goodnight. AWANEN!

Thursday, December 10, 1987
My House, Fairbanks, Alaska

I got up at 6:30 AM, drank coffee and worked on putting things away until Dave finally got up at about 10:00 AM or so. Then he and I continued with cleaning the house. We finished that up and started bringing boxes in from the storage shed at about 2:00 PM and we finished bringing everything in at about 3:15 PM. Then I started unpacking things and putting some boxes upstairs. After all the kitchen stuff was found I cleaned up the mess as much as possible for tonight and then cooked supper of macaroni and cheese. We also had rice with supper. We did the dishes and then the electricity went out for about 25 minutes, wonder why? Now it's 9:40 PM, late again. I'm about to go to bed. The weather was -3°F this morning and there was light snow on and off all day. It only got up to about 0°F during the day and now it's 0°F. Dave G. left tonight, thank you for all of your help over the last couple of days. AWANEN!

[End of handwritten notebook #5 of 5]

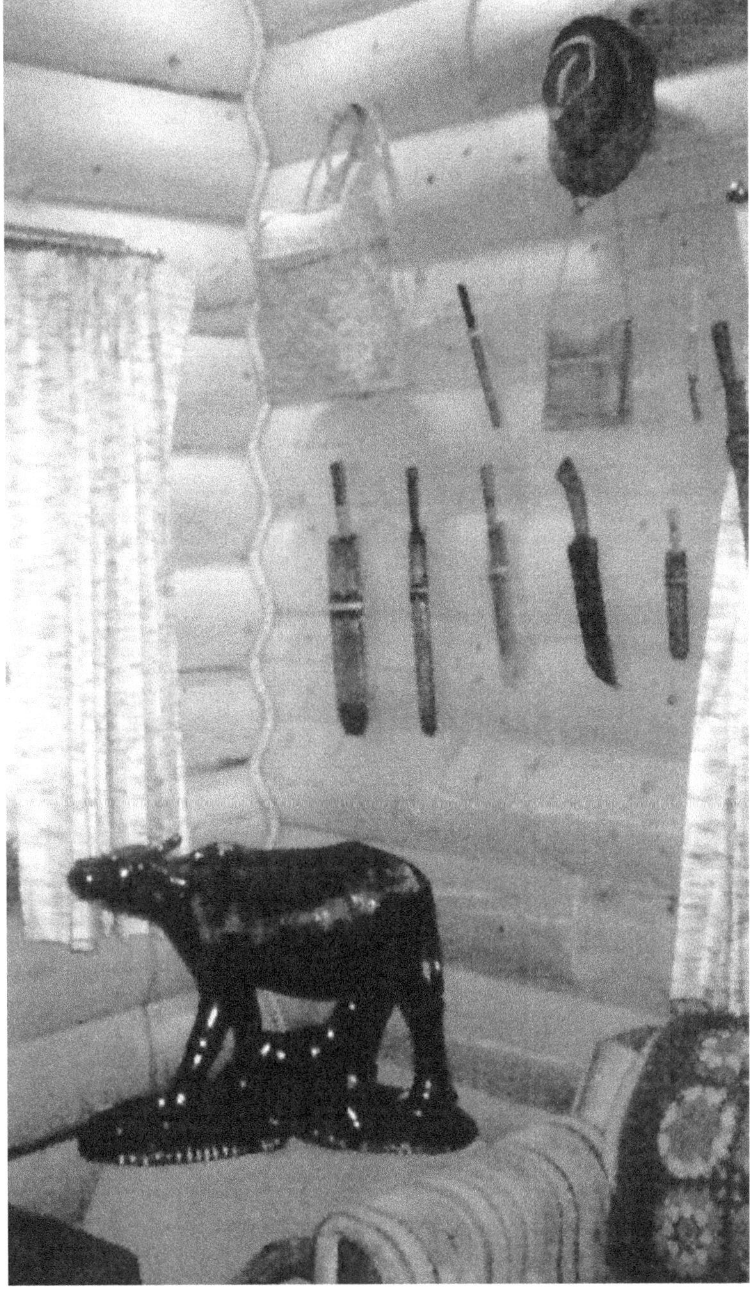

Here is a photo which I took in my house after I was unpacked. You can see the hand-carved nuang with calf which has been referred to several times and you can also see some of the machetes that I purchased and a couple of the rattan backpacks. Near the upper right you can also see my Indiana Jones hat which I used when I traveled around to different places.

THE END

I found these nice little summaries in the back of the final notebook.

Visitors, some to my house, some to the Philippines to visit me.

November 1985		**June 1986**		**March 1987**	
Ronald	1 day	Rody	2 days	None	
December 1985		Ronald	3 days	**April 1987**	
Nestor	2 days	Nestor	2 days	Ralph P.	2 days
January 1986		**July 1986**		Keith	2 days
Ronald	1 day	Nestor	3 days	**May 1987**	
February 1986		**August 1986**		Cery	1 day
Rody	1 day	Rody	3 days	**June 1987**	
Ardis B.	13 days	**September 1986**		None	
Rody	4 days	P.C. Nurse	2 days	**July 1987**	
Nestor	3 days	**October 1986**		Barb W.	4 days
March 1986		None		Richard	1 day
JB & Katie	2 days	**November 1986**		**August 1987**	
Ronald	1 day	None		Dave & Vicki	5 days
Rody	2 days	**December 1986**		**September 1987**	
Nestor	2 days	Tom & Barb	3 days	None	
April 1986		Ronald	1 day	**October 1987**	
Nestor	1 day	**January 1987**		Ronald	2 days
Rody	1 day	None			
Brooke F.	2 days	**February 1987**			
May 1986		Nestor	2 days		
John D.	15 days				

Places I traveled to during my 2-years in the Philippines.

December 1985		**May 1986**		**March 1987**	
Villa Miemban	10 days	Manila[5]	5 days	Manila[12]	3 days
Bayombong	5 day	Cebu City[6]	5 days	Puerto Galera[12]	3 days
Cordon	1 day	Guba	1 day	Bayombong	2 days
January 1986		Villa Miemban	1 day	**April 1987**	
Villa Miemban	3 days	**June 1986**		None	
Sinsayon	1 day	None		**May 1987**	
Gomez	3 days	**July 1986**		None	
Bayombong	2 days	Bayombong	3 days	**June 1987**	
February 1986		Villa Miemban	2 days	Manila[13]	5 days
Bayombong[1]	2 days	**August 1986**		Bayombong	4 days
Villa Miemban[1]	1 day	Manila[7]	3 days	**July 1987**	
Lagawe[1]	1 day	Tuguegarao[8]	1 day	None	
Banaue[1]	3 days	Ivana[8]	5 days	**August 1987**	
Bontoc[1]	1 day	**September 1986**		Manila[14]	5 days
Baguio City[1]	2 days	Ivana[8]	2 days	Puerto Princesa[14]	1 day
March 1986		**October 1986**		St. Paul's Pk.[14]	2 days
Villa Miemban	3 days	Baguio City[9]	3 days	Tagnipa[14]	1 day
Banaue[2]	2 days	Vulcan	1 day	Baguio City[14]	3 days
Cababuyan[2]	1 day	Villa Miemban	1 day	Bontoc[14]	1 day
April 1986		**November 1986**		Banaue[14]	4 days
Banaue[3]	1 day	Manila[10]	4 days	Bayombong[14]	2 days
Tadian[3]	3 days	Tagaytay City[10]	2 days	**September 1987**	
Gayang[3]	1 day	Bayombong	2 days	Manila[15]	5 days
Sagada[3]	1 day	**December 1986**		Bayombong	2 days
Bontoc[3]	1 day	Bayombong	2 days	**October 1987**	
Lawig[3]	1 day	**January 1987**		Baler	5 days
Caba[4]	7 days	Diffun	1 day	Santa Fe	1 day
Villa Miemban	1 day	Maddela	2 days	Bayombong	2 days
Cababuyan	1 day	**February 1987**			
		Manila[11]	6 days		
		Bayombong	1 day		

[1] With Ardis B.
[2] Supervisor's Conference.
[3] With Nestor.
[4] First Language Follow-up Training.
[5] In Service Training.
[6] Resource Days.
[7] Foot Problem.
[8] Nestor and I.
[9] Nestor and I.
[10] Mid-Service Conference.
[11] Medical reasons.
[12] Sue T. and I.
[13] Medical reasons.
[14] With Dave and Vicki M.
[15] Close-of-Service Conference.

NOTES

About the Author

Daniel Wieczorek was born in 1947 in Ionia, Michigan. He graduated from the University of Michigan with a B.S. in Forestry in 1969. He moved to Oregon to work in the field of forestry in 1971. That was followed by a move to Alaska in 1975, where he continued his career in forestry. After about a 14 year career in forestry, Daniel decided to do something different and he served as a Peace Corps Volunteer in The Philippines from 1985 – 1987. Upon completion of his Peace Corps service he returned to Alaska, where he attended the University of Alaska – Fairbanks and received an M.B.A. in 1991. This was followed by a move to South Korea in 1992, where Daniel taught English to Korean people wishing to improve their English Language skills. Daniel's next stop was in New York City, where he worked as temporary staff at Deutsche Bank from 1998 – 2001. He left NYC in March 2001 and moved on to his present home in Mitaka City, Tokyo, Japan. He is teaching English in Japan and at this time he's been teaching as a career for about 17 years. He has been hiking, climbing and doing photography since he was about 12 years old.

At the present time he's been in Japan for 15 years. He and his same-sex life partner were married in Ashland, Oregon on August 10, 2015 and at this time he and his partner are in the middle of the long process of getting a green card so that they can go to and live in Alaska. It will, of course, be a return for Daniel, but for his partner it will be his first experiences of Alaska, his first opportunity to see the Aurora Borealis in the winter, the midnight sun in the summer and much, much more.

By the way, if you're curious, he never did make a return trip to the Philippines. Eventually he lost contact with George, Ronald, Nestor and everybody else in the Philippines. At the present time the only fellow PCV's that he still has contact with are JB and Katie F.

www.ingramcontent.com/pod-product-compliance
Lightning Source LLC
Chambersburg PA
CBHW062011090426
42811CB00005B/822